Popular Dance and Music
in Modern Egypt

Popular Dance and Music in Modern Egypt

SHERIFA ZUHUR

McFarland & Company, Inc., Publishers
Jefferson, North Carolina

This book has undergone peer review.

Library of Congress Cataloguing-in-Publication Data

Names: Zuhur, Sherifa, author.
Title: Popular dance and music in modern Egypt / Sherifa Zuhur.
Description: Jefferson, North Carolina : McFarland & Company, Inc., Publishers, 2022 | Includes bibliographical references and index.
Identifiers: LCCN 2021032305 | ISBN 9781476681993 (paperback : acid free paper) ∞
ISBN 9781476643113 (ebook)
Subjects: LCSH: Dance—Egypt—History. | Dance—Social aspects—Egypt. | Music and dance—Egypt. | Dance music—Egypt—History and criticism. | BISAC: PERFORMING ARTS / Dance / Regional & Ethnic | MUSIC / Genres & Styles / International
Classification: LCC GV1709 .Z84 2022 | DDC 792.80962—dc23
LC record available at https://lccn.loc.gov/2021032305

British Library cataloguing data are available

ISBN (print) 978-1-4766-8199-3
ISBN (ebook) 978-1-4766-4311-3

© 2022 Sherifa Zuhur. All rights reserved

No part of this book may be reproduced or transmitted in any form or by any means, electronic or mechanical, including photocopying or recording, or by any information storage and retrieval system, without permission in writing from the publisher.

Front cover image: Dancer Samrah, photograph by Ayşe Gürsöz, costume by Madame Noussa.

Printed in the United States of America

*McFarland & Company, Inc., Publishers
Box 611, Jefferson, North Carolina 28640
www.mcfarlandpub.com*

To Egyptians
who have shared their joy
in music, dance, and conversation with me,
Amina who shared many ideas,
and *sammi'ah* everywhere

Acknowledgments

Many individuals have helped me on the journey of this book. Amina Goodyear encouraged me and collaborated with me in presenting workshops on these dances and musical forms, and then insisted that I write this book and encouraged me as I did so.

I thank my anonymous reviewers for their suggestions and criticisms, and my editor and the press for all their diligence and hard work. I want to thank Tonia Rifaey who graciously hosted me during several visits in Cairo, and all those who have taught me, or performed with me, or shared information with me, concerning music and dance in Egypt. I owe a great deal to Afaf Lutfi al-Sayyid Marsot in terms of training and her intellectual example.

I am grateful to the Center for Middle Eastern Studies at the University of California, Berkeley, and Dr. Emily Gottreich who hosted me there in 2015 and 2016 when I began working on this project. I thank the Association for the Study of the Middle East and Africa for a travel grant in 2018. As well, I want to thank Marlyn Tadros, Yasmin Amin, Andrea Rugh, Nezar AlSayyad, Hussein Ahmad Khan, Ali Paris, Georges Lammam, and Mina Girgis for permissions, communications, or certain insights. Suad Joseph and the curators at l'Institut du Monde Arabe convinced me to contribute to their ongoing projects as I was preparing this book. This was beneficial as it forced me to crystallize and condense the history of women performers' experiences in Egypt and the Arab world.

I thank Susu Pampanin, Amina Goodyear's and my mutual students and supporters, and the Aswan Dancers, as well as Sausan Molthen for the opportunity to stage several extravaganzas which explored this dance history, including twice recreating a *mulid*.

I am thankful for the support of my Aswat Music Ensemble family, Nabila Mango, Salah Bedouis, Salwa Ghamrawi, Loay Dahbour, Jalal Takesh, and all the rest of you; my musical trio partners, Kristina Ben Arab and Amina; and my vocal group. Also, my dear family members and friends, who put up with long periods of limited communication.

Table of Contents

Acknowledgments vi

Introduction and Notes on Music and Transliteration 1

One. The *'Awalim*'s Path to the *Sala* 11

Two. From the *Sala* to the Silver Screen and Beyond 32

Three. *Ya Dall'a, Ya Dall'a*: Demeanor and Flirtation 63

Four. *Mulid*: Reinvigorating Spiritual and Popular Legitimacy in Egyptian Music and Dance 85

Five. From *Sha'bi* Music and Culture to *Mahragan* Dance Music 103

Six. *Al-Raqs al-Sha'bi wa al-Musiqa Sha'biyya*: Egypt's Regional Particularist Dances and Music in Transition 125

Seven. Bad, Bad *Baladi*: Sama al-Masry and Dance as Sarcasm 147

Eight. Globalization of Egyptian Dance 166

Glossary 195

Chapter Notes 227

Bibliography 251

Index 265

Introduction and Notes on Music and Transliteration

This book was written to share my exploration of Egyptian dance and dance music, an interest of mine for five decades. It is only a portion of my experience with Arabic music and dance; certainly, Egyptian dance and dance music is a sufficiently large field of its own. I have also written about specific Arab singers, actors, and musicians dating back to two collections on performing and visual arts that I edited in 1999 and 2001,[1] and most recently for an exhibit on the pioneers of Arabic song and cinema in France. I have, along the way, written extensively about Egypt's politics, Islamist movements, women's issues and legal reform pertaining to these issues, and the counterterrorism campaign in the Sinai.

I spent a lengthy part of my life and scholarly career following Egypt and am perennially amazed by Cairo as a multi-layered urban environment. Since my first visits in the early 1970s, Egypt has undergone myriad changes. Likewise, the scholarly literature on Egypt has transformed over time, impacting the canon of knowledge on development, transformation, revolution, stagnation, and transcultural interaction. Though I was very fortunate to have had research opportunities in multiple countries, Egypt has remained central to my research agenda.

Mark Twain is credited with telling us, "Write what you know." Yet, novelist Rabih Allameddine retorted, "The whole notion of 'write what you know' is not just wrong, but boring."[2] Fiction, naturally, differs from academic research. Researchers are granted greater authority and recognition the further and more detached they are from their topics. Practitioner/experts, especially virtuosos, are granted authority to teach but not as often in research. While the latter may be nationals or internationals, the former are expected to have a professional and external position towards their subject. This situation has been especially problematic in the formerly colonized world, due to the prestige accorded to publications in foreign languages and foreign academic institutions. Familiarity with sources is key, and over time, one may develop more important insights and strong views deriving from these. I certainly did not "know" the full depth of Islamist movements when I began studying them, but I was familiar with Egypt and Cairo prior to plunging into that controversial area which formed the basis of my first book, *Revealing Reveiling: Gender Ideology in Contemporary Egypt*.[3]

I was an aficionado of Arabic music and dance in that period. I had performed since childhood, attended music conservatory, and switched over to Arabic music after Ali Jihad Racy, the Lebanese-American ethnomusicologist, arrived at UCLA. It was serendipitous that I met Simon Shaheen through A.J. Racy, just a year after he arrived in New York, and also Yusuf Kassab and Adel Sirhan, both fans of older Arabic music, and worked with literally hundreds of performers who each have amazing, but often undocumented insights, memories, and expertise. I had further good fortune in pursuing graduate studies UCLA just when Farida (Melda) Fahmy was there. And, I witnessed a limited but growing respect for dance and music ethnology. However, as a "practitioner," I had grown very weary of the performing scene, limited to nightclubs, festivals, restaurants, parties, and occasional concerts. I wanted to expand my intellectual abilities beyond music into understandings of power and politics, and my very compelling mentor, Afaf Lutfi al-Sayyid, encouraged me.

After that first book about Islamism and gender in Egypt was published, I wanted to write a film for television. I then received a Fulbright fellowship to research the life of the singer, Asmahan, whose personal history had been situated in the Levant, Egypt, and Palestine. My new topic was frowned on by some—whether due to the expansion of the *sahwa islamiyya*, the Islamic revival movement and the privileging of religiosity in the academic world, or that writing about the arts was considered trivial. Nonetheless, one learns more about a society by examining its multiple dimensions. It is not only the religious or political dimensions of life that elucidate. Part of that research extended far beyond my biography of Asmahan and has been helpful to the preparation of this book. For instance, there were the interviews with musicians who had some connection with her or her brother, Farid al-Atrash, and often with dancers of their period, people who had lived in and been politically active in that era, and who knew details about the working relationships between musicians, singers and dancers.

Then, in the politically turbulent 1990s, I was hired to teach history and the Islamic studies current in the Arabic Studies department at the American University in Cairo, and thereafter, in its newly formed history department. Once again living in Egypt as I had earlier in three different time periods and during my fieldwork, I could not help being struck by the lack of respect, juxtaposed to sentimental and context-linked appreciation, for dancing, dancers, and musicians (except for the most famous of superstars). At that time, Arabic music was not yet taught in that university, although this situation began to change by 1997. I was able to travel to many different governorates and towns in Egypt, and naturally benefited from the expertise of other scholars at the AUC, and as well from fellow lovers of classical and Arabic music. When I left the AUC, I had hoped to resituate myself in Beirut, and while that did not happen, I was very fortunate in being able to continue traveling and researching in the region almost every year and visiting Egypt every few years up to the present.

Earlier, as an impoverished graduate student in Egypt (prior to returning to UCLA), I was able to explore the worlds of dance and music, and yet, all my requirements toward professional development were in an entirely separate world guarded by elite and middle class values. The only allowable cross-over between these two lives was as a soloist with the folkloric troupe at the American University in Cairo, learning versions of the folkloric dances performed by the Reda and Firqat

Qawmiyya groups, or playing Arabic classical music, but only in certain venues, or singing Western classical music. Still, I was able to either be part of or closely observe the entertainment scene over quite a long time, from the early 1970s to 2000, and then in the twenty years after that, to witness the increasing impact of globalization on that scene.

Dance is among the most ancient of the expressive arts and yet the least respectable art form in the broader Arab world. Vocal music of certain genres is deeply appreciated, as is instrumental music, though the social position of the entertainers is problematic as was shown by A.J. Racy in his study of proverbs and sayings about musicians.[4] Many of these ideas and similar proverbs are found in Egypt.

It might seem counterintuitive to insist that dance, dance music, and populist music are an essential aspect of Egyptian culture. Yet, scholars have been primarily interested in (a) a classical tradition in Egyptian music deriving from the Arabo-Ottoman repertoire as part of a preservationist and educational effort, or (b) the oldest forms of rural music (and not dance), or (c) pan-Arab classical or pop music. For this book, I chose to write less about these three genres, as scholarship about them is available by A.J. Racy, Dwight Reynolds, Frédéric Lagrange, Salwa al-Shawan Castelo-Branco, Akram Rayyes, and the various contributors to AMAR (Foundation for Arabic Music Archiving and Research), Virginia Danielson, in Johnny Farraj and Sami Abu Shumays' work on *maqam*, although not restricted to Egyptian composers/performers, and many others.[5] Pan-Arab pop music is less explicitly Egyptian in nature, at least for many artists and audiences, and has been explored by Daniel Gilman, who comments with insight on Egyptian musicians' preference for classical Arabic music, or varieties including it, rather than the genre he was studying.[6]

Meanwhile *sha'bi* (popular, lower-class) music and dance and *musiqa sha'biyya* has provided much of the vitality of Egyptian entertainment. It is related to music played for *raqs sharqi* (Oriental dance, belly dance) because many of the Egyptian dancers and musicians come from *sha'bi* backgrounds, or perform there, or explicitly or implicitly acknowledge a *sha'bi* lineage and spirit in stage work. Others began their dance training and performance in folklore, and carried that into their solo performances or teaching. Think of *sha'bi* music as a parallel to crime fiction in Egypt: never in the same category as higher literature and poetry, yet deeply expressive of society and extremely popular since the 1940s.

As Egypt has exported its dance and dance music, the world is now able to see both more of it and less of it, live and in recordings, given technological advances. The framing of *mahragan* (a new form of *sha'bi* based on electronic music influenced by hip-hop and reggae and described in Chapter Five) as protest music occurred in Europe, and Hakim, a pop-*sha'bi* star, appeared in the U.S. alongside leading American performers. Conversely, the outside world is exposed to much less of Egyptian dance styles, given the selectivity of such samples, particularly from the pre-video era, and also because of intense interest in *raqs sharqi* within a niche market of instructors and hobbyist performers, as compared to global interest in Egyptian folkloric dance.

Unfortunately, the teaching of Arabic music outside of Egypt often excludes its connection to dance. Thus, music and dance technique and appreciation are taught separately, but also formats not traditionally performed with dance are often privileged over dance music, except for compositions by certain composers such as Muhammad 'abd al-Wahhab. A distaste for dancers and dancing or a lack of familiarity with the larger repertoire for dance has permeated the sensibilities of those presenting Arabic music on the concert stage, where audience interaction is expected to be limited to applause. This is paradoxical because most working musicians needed income and at one time or another played for dancers, and inside Egypt, they continue doing so. The situation inside Egypt was further impacted by the Islamic revival and its insistence on removing dance as a spectacle, even from many weddings. That egress was incomplete though, as many *sha'bi* weddings and parties continued to feature dancers until fairly recently. And now they feature a different type of male dancing as explained in Chapter Five.

Due to the influence of foreign dancers, new aesthetics, and globalized influences, *raqs sharqi* may be on the verge of such a significant transformation that we will not recognize it in the future. Considering its expression from the turn of the century until the 1950s, it is nearly unrecognizable today. Yet, other dance genres, folkloric and regional dances, are seemingly frozen back in the period from the 1960s to the 1980s. Therefore, just as it was important that folklorists, travelers, and anthropologists described the oral poetry of folk-poets prior to its disappearance, we should thoroughly review Egyptian dance's history, current status, and future directions.

The dance's history is controversial and plagued with Orientalist, colonialist, and other problematic frameworks. Perhaps no one has been as interested in the history of dance in Egypt as Western dancers of *raqs sharqi*. Some of them claim it as a cosmopolitan fusion emerging in the 1920s and 1930s, and therefore not uniquely Egyptian. Simultaneously, there has been an effort to declare the dance an ancient art form dating back to birth rituals and cementing it, like Egypt itself, in the dusty past, rather than the living present. Certain points of historical emphasis have been challenged and aptly demonstrated by Heather Ward in her book, *Egyptian Belly Dance in Transition: The Raqs Sharqi Revolution*.[7] *Raqs sharqi* has been de-historicized and decontextualized when it is explained as developing in the 1920s primarily by Badia Masabni, as shown in Wendy Buonaventura's writing: "The first Egyptian cabaret, the Casino Opera was opened in 1926 by Syrian actress-dancer Badia Masabni … with an eye on Western entertainment, she decided to broaden the scope of *baladi*."[8] As if she alone, out of hundreds of other *sala* owners and entertainers had stumbled on a unique cross-fertilization or fusion instead of actually reflecting a broader tendency in her milieu and generation. Countless others have replicated not only the error in this statement, but went on to assume that entertainment was primarily "for tourists" or implied that *raqs sharqi* sprung up *sui generis* in the "1920s" as a "hybrid" form,[9] thus overstating its hybridity and distinctiveness from mere *raqs baladi*.

The dance's history in public venues predates Masabni. She was *shami* (Eastern, Levantine), Lebanese, legally per her father's nationality, not Syrian according to her mother's nationality, although in that era, "Syrian" was used as a descriptor in Egypt for both nationalities. There were a large number of Levantines in Egypt at that time as it continued to served as a mecca for the arts, literature, and politics. But also, Syria had undergone severe turmoil and starvation in the latter part of the nineteenth century and then again in the latter years of World War I. Casino Opera was not Masabni's first establishment, and she did not present dance in her then current location until 1927. Ward and Omar Foda, on the beer industry[10] (see Chapter Two), indicate there were numerous other clubs and dancehalls; these were popular with Egyptians, i.e., their audiences were not primarily Westerners. Coffee houses and *buza* (a locally-made alcoholic drink) halls were present in Cairo and even towns like Mahalla al-Kubra, where women were landladies and becoming vendors and owning coffee shops.[11]

The interactions of state authorities and women arrested for prostitution showed the overlap of this profession and that of entertainment even before the Napoleonic invasion (See Chapter One). The gradual movement of women into the public sphere was not without tension. So, although, Ziad Fahmy's purpose[12] in his book *Ordinary Egyptians: Creating the Nation through Popular Culture* was not primarily to describe the role of women or dancers in vaudeville, we learn from him that theatrical troupes were presenting women onstage who acted, danced, and sang nationalist lyrics, and the Egyptian public loved it. That their honor might be questioned or that the public found the presence of women dancing and singing onstage to be controversial went without saying.

Moreover, as Frédéric Lagrange explains, women in this era were singing songs about their own condition, such as the conventions of marriage in Egyptian society.[13] A revolution in entertainment was accompanying a social and political one (in 1919), but it had been taking place gradually as women began to write under their own names, established journals, and started to acquire formal educations.

Dance scholars, whether practitioners or not, and certain scholars interested in post colonialism and Orientalism have also emphasized an interactive creation of the dance, finding equal or more importance in Western influences and thus removing the Arab identity, or Middle Eastern identity, from dance.[14]

This book consists of eight essays on Egyptian dance, its history, genres and sub-genres, and evolution, the demeanor of dancers, trends old and new, and social and political criticism using the imagery of dance or a dancer. It covers *raqs sharqi*, *raqs sha'bi* (folkloric dance whether staged or spontaneously performed and genres of popular dance music or dance such as *sha'bi*, *mulid*, and *mahragan*). What is sometimes called *maqam* music, or Arabic classical music, is referenced, but is not the main focus of this book, because as mentioned above, there are many works focusing on it, but the only dance performed to it is under a nebulous category, "classic *tarab*" (which actually may utilize earlier "pop" music), and that is described in Chapter Eight.

In Chapters One and Two, the history of Egyptian dance will be reviewed, including its important artists, and musicians, and relationship to vaudeville theater and music, and in the context of state efforts to control public dancing, new sites for entertainment, and the entry of many foreign dancers into the profession. Chapter One moves to approximately the 1880s, while Chapter Two describes the situation from the building of Shari'a Muhammad 'Ali in Cairo to the present.

Chapter Three presents and analyzes a quality particular to Egyptian dance, which is in danger of being lost at the present time, described as *dall'a* or flirtatiousness. The role of flirtatiousness and its operation within the ethos of social class is explored. Then discussion follows regarded the nature and basis of this quality in the work of specific dancers and singers.

Chapter Four explains the origins of a new dance music trend, *aghani mulid*, which references the traditional culture of the *mawalid*, or saint's day festivals in Egypt, and the true purposes of morality and spirituality. Although this draws on the Sufi tradition, young people who enjoy or dance to the new *mulid* music are drawn to it primarily for its spirit of *farah* (partying, i.e., its wildly festive mood) and connections with the *sha'bi* or populist spirit.

Sha'bi music and its use in dance is explored in Chapter Five and the development of *mahragan* by youth from poorer urban areas of self-crafted and produced music, disseminated initially and mostly outside of radio, television, and state sponsorship. *Mahragan* has its own dance styles and is all the rage at weddings and parties, having spread more widely after Egypt's 2011 revolution despite a recent banning in 2020. While the style has been described as protest music, I believe that notion was more attractive to outsiders than the reality of the *sha'b*'s plaintive lyrics of distress as an individual form of expression, which allowed performers and poet/lyricists an outlet despite political and economic oppression. I would suggest that it is dangerous for the *sha'b* to counter the political system with its fearsome security apparatus unless in a depoliticized manner. The parallel would be artists and writers who cannot overtly address certain problems in today's Egypt but have turned instead to such genres such as *noir*, mystery, or personal and intimate stories of individuals' relationships in drama, novels, and poetry.

In Chapter Six, Egypt's traditional and staged regional and particularist dance genres are described. Some of these stagings and choreographies are, for now, preserved by national ensembles and smaller regional groups which are to some degree subsidized by the state. Other forms of dance, such as that in rituals connecting persons to the spirit world, the *zar*, may or may not be preserved in the future. The *zar* has been banned from *mawalid* (saint's day festivals, the mulids) and from convening in public for decades, and the *salafi* (purist Muslims who are numerous in Cairo, Alexandria, and elsewhere deplore the *zar* as a practice giving agency to beings other than Allah). Nubian dances and music and those of the Siwa oasis and the North Coast and Sinai Bedouin are also discussed because Egypt's minorities are extremely important to the tapestry of the country's culture. Whereas these dance are regarded, for the most part, as part of *turath* (authentic heritage), *raqs sharqi* is far more controversial. *Raqs sharqi* dancers used to include *raqs sha'bi* into their performances either by choice, the reputation of the performer (if she had previously performed them or ethnic connection), or a director's idea in film segments. Today, *raqs sha'bi* is presented in a rather wooden manner as a "special category" in international festivals, which is a sad situation when it could be more holistically integrated into dance performance.

The controversial and comic image of the *raqs sharqi* dancer is explored in a cameo of actress/dancer Sama al-Masry in Chapter Seven. Sarcasm and comedic political comment have long been part of life in Egypt and range from early political cartoons to jokes on comedian Bassam Youssef's program "Barnamag." Sama al-Masry's film and video efforts are definitely a part of contemporary sarcasm, in which she consistently plays a dancer (or dances), constantly invoking Egypt and Egyptian customs and customary forms of mockery.

Chapter Eight considers the globalization of Egyptian dance which has occurred through migration away from and to Egypt, and the replication or fantasies of the dance outside of Egypt, as well as the adoption of *raqs sharqi* as a hobby, competitive dance form, and focus of international dance festivals. That situation has meant that the teaching of dance has become, in some instances, very significant to the dance's maintenance and transformation. An Islamizing trend decimated the numbers of Egyptian female entertainers, while foreigners took their places. The Egyptian state continues to try to control the licensing and appearance of dancers and the rules in their performing venues.

While the coverage of *raqs sharqi* was lengthier than some other dance forms in the book, I hope readers will understand that I believe it is vital to review information about the various dance and musical forms emerging in Egypt and how they relate to each other. This information reveals who is performing and consuming these genres. Ultimately, I am most interested in performance (and this includes paid *raqs sharqi* and unpaid *raqs baladi*, the term used in Egypt for the local dance style). Although dance may have once been part of ritual, the aesthetics of performed dance, and music inspiring the dance, have changed. To those who prefer a book solely about *raqs sharqi*, there are many available, but I hope this one re-contextualizes that genre and the others mentioned as an event of meaning occurring especially in Egypt. That is true for economic, historical, and cultural reasons, despite impulses to attack, ignore, or deride dancing and music. It is a complement to the overall privileging of *farah* (a party or celebration) or a culture of celebration as will be seen in the discussion of *mulid* music, but is as true for other genres.

As the teaching of *raqs sharqi* and to some degree folkloric dance is mediated through the expertise, knowledge, and personalities of various individuals, there are some misunderstandings of "rules" or norms to be found in the dance. These may have been pronounced to make a point, but though less than correct, have been transmitted onwards, thus creating something of a mythology about certain dance forms. It is helpful to think of the difference between the charismatic imparting of some wisdom about the dance and the academic setting, where we aim for rigor, and how difficult that is to achieve in layer over layer of adaptations.

A few examples of Egyptian dance and music's impact on artists in Lebanon are given, inasmuch as artists traveled frequently between the two countries in the past, and family relationships in music and dance shaped the profession inside Egypt and elsewhere. Nevertheless, this book is centered on Egypt. Because many other dance scholars (more than my scope permits me to review) now treat the dance as an intercultural or hybrid phenomenon, I insisted on focusing here on its Egyptian nature and origins and development within Egypt's theatrical, musical, and dance history.

Beyond the question of whether *raqs sharqi* is being miscast as an international, rather than an originally Egyptian, or Middle Eastern phenomenon, are important and unresolved questions about the dance's future direction. It is by no means clear where Egypt is going—being a country made up of multiple lifestyles, environments, and cultural outlooks, it is best understood as many Egypts. Overall, though, there is less political freedom as a result of the suppression of the Muslim Brotherhood and the enactors of the 2011 revolution. While "less Islamism" may appear at face value to be a boon to the arts, it was not long ago that Egypt's government under Mubarak practiced quite extensive censorship. That situation, now revisited, may not translate to an environment in which dance can continue without the extreme commodification we now see. I am heartened, though, by interest in the arts that exceeds that which I experienced in the past.

A Note About Arabic Music with Dance in Mind

Comments about Egyptian music and its features appear throughout the text, as my aim is to expand on music's relationship to dance. Although many aficionados of Egyptian and Arabic dance are quite knowledgeable about dance, dance personalities, and the commercial aspects of Egyptian dance and dance music, not all are from the MENA (Middle East and North Africa) region, and they may not understand the close relationship of Arabic or Egyptian Arabic music to dance aesthetics. Many foreign performers are perfectly content with performing Egyptian or other Middle Eastern inspired dance to Western music, or perhaps to some other regional music which radically eviscerates its own beating heart and all appropriate motivations and inspirations of the dance. Unfortunately, dance fusion trends and lack of emphasis on studying Arabic, and other problems such as prejudice against the Middle East, have meant that some neglect musical studies, whereas some others who study Arabic music are not the least bit interested in dancing.

Al-musiqa is the word in Arabic for music, derived from Greek.[15] *Al-musiqa al-'arabiyya* (Arabic music) developed on the Arabian peninsula and the territories conquered by the Arab tribes after the establishment of Islam as a religion and political force, as briefly described in the beginning of this book. It is very important to note the relationship between the Arabic language and poetry and music and certain key features distinguishing it from other musical traditions.

The unique sounds of Arabic and Egyptian music are due to the aural character, or "voices" of the musical instruments, and their use of modal structures that include microtones and multiple and distinct meters. The key elements of Arabic music are described in Chapter One. Nonetheless, non-musicians may not understand that the microtones included in the *maqamat* (the modal system on which Arabic music is built) cannot be properly replicated on non-adapted Western instruments. So, with certain exceptions (like the use of specially adapted scores, or a soloist on an acoustic Arabic instrument), it is not possible to imagine the playing of Arabic music by a large Western orchestra because it cannot replicate the tones of particular *maqamat*. Moreover, the aesthetics of the music, with its lack (usually) of polyphony, usage of call and response and ornamentation, are not well understood or replicated by Western musicians until they are educated in these forms and their conventions. Also, typically, creative chaos, in which instrumentalists ornament, emphasize, and bow (in the case of the string sections) as they please, is the preferred aesthetic, in comparison to the precise or grand and blended sound of Western ensembles.

Vocal aesthetics and the popular love of poetic and lyrical expression require knowledge of Arabic. In other words, the words to dance songs, or music played for dancing, are not incidental at all, but at the core of the performer's purpose. This is so whether one is discussing the *'awalim* style singing of the singer, Munira al-Mahdiyya, or the use of the accordion, the *org* (electronic keyboard and thereafter, the Oriental Keyboard in *sha'bi* music or the role of the lyrics in *mahragan*).

Musicians who have studied in national music conservatories learn at least some of a common repertoire from the Arabo-Ottoman tradition, which might otherwise have become obsolete. Study of the musical forms of *qudud, qasa'id, muwashshahat, longat, sama'iat* (see Glossary), and others were considered very helpful to increasing musicians' expertise in the *maqamat*. Additionally, they learned to improvise, either by copying others or by becoming more proficient in the possibilities of the *maqamat*. Musicians/singers who did not study formally were expected to excel in *taqasim* (instrumental improvisations) and *'ataba* and *mawawil* (vocal improvisational forms).

Without improvisation, though, Arabic music, singing, and dance loses its soul and languishes in the dry territory of replicated composed scores and strict choreography. That some dancers in the twenty-first century inside and outside of Egypt do not necessarily know how to interpret the *taqasim* except with greater and greater athleticism and hand gestures intended to signal words whilst over-emoting is quite a sorry comment on the art form's evolution.

Dance is furthermore represented by or may explore the color of the music according to overall philosophy about Arabic music. So, we may hear *lun baladi* (literally the color of the country, or the common people), *lun tarab*, (Arab classical musical color—the color of enchantment), *lun gharbi* (Western color), *lun sha'biyya* (color of the rural countryside), or *lun Sa'idi* (color of Upper Egypt). Thus, one of my aims in writing this book with the particular selections I made is to encourage Egyptian dance and dance music's retention of many colors, adding on those of the new(er) joyous *aghani mulid* and strutting *mahragan,* and neither freezing, constricting, nor forgetting its rich repertoire.

A Note About Transliteration

This book contains certain words in classical Arabic and many in Egyptian colloquial Arabic. These are quite distinct, and also, Egyptian dialect varies in different areas of the country. I have used the transliteration system usually employed by the American University in Cairo Press. It is modified from the IJMES (*International Journal of Middle East Studies*) system but differs in that diacritics are omitted. In addition, I have dropped the "h" of the *ta marbuta*, when not in construct (*idhafa*). Egyptian colloquial Arabic changes the vowel sounds, for instance from "u" to "o"—thus in lyrics and speech; hence, *moza*, not *muza*. It changes the letter *jim* to a hard "g" and the letter *qaf* is eliminated in Cairene and Alexandrian dialect, but not necessarily in others (Sa'idi or in Nubian words, or Nubian Arabic). *'Ammiyya* features elision of articles and sometimes prepositions, and this is shown in comparison to the rules for *fusha*. Specifically, the article *alif lam* elides with sun letters. i.e., *ish-shams*, whereas in the transliteration of *fusha*, that would be rendered *al-shams*. Other words may be shortened in colloquial. The ' indicates the letter *'ain*, while the glottal stop or hamza is shown as ' (which may not be pronounced in *'ammiyya*). The vowels, *fatha*, and *kasra* are rendered when possible as "a" or "i" (and not "e" as may be seen in some other sources) and the "u" for the *damma* is used here instead of "ou." If a source is quoted from a language other than Arabic, then I replicate its use of transliteration is as it is printed. For individuals or terms well known or published in English or sometimes other languages, the common transliteration is used, thus 'abd al-Nasser and Nasserism, rather than 'abd al-Nasir and Nasirism; the Reda Troupe, rather than the Ridha troupe; Nelly Mazloum, rather than Nelly Mazlum.

ONE

The *'Awalim*'s Path to the *Sala*

Egyptians have long created and enjoyed dance and music both in public and private settings. The difference between these two spheres, the legal apparatuses governing them, and anxiety over women's behavior and changing lifestyles has impacted the reception of these art forms. I will first consider this change in development of *raqs sharqi* in the nineteenth and twentieth century, as it emerged from the harem and the street into outdoor casinos, theaters, and *salat* (clubs or music halls), a transition eventually portrayed in cinema. Then, I will briefly backtrack in history to explain some of the enduring characteristics of dance and music, the introduction of other influences, and cover some of the aesthetics of this form and other genres of Egyptian dance and dance music.

Elite women were confined in different degrees to the private sphere in the pre-modern period, but entertainers crossed these boundaries, becoming quite important in vocal music in public settings in the early twentieth century, far more so than their male co-singers. The public enjoyed the novelty of women performers, who transgressed various rules that pertained to and constrained other women. The advent of recordings in Egypt, beginning in 1904,[1] meant that other more restricted women, as well as the rest of society, could hear women's voices.

In nineteenth century Egypt, singer/dancers entertained in private homes, and others, female and male, danced in the streets. These included the *'awalim* singers and instrumentalists, many of whom also danced and managed other dancer/singers, the *ghawazi* (dancers reputedly of tribal origin), rope dancers and acrobats, male impersonators of women (*khawalat*), and men dancing as males (a *gink* in the Egyptian dialect, from the word *jank*). There were also jesters/comedians, puppeteers, storytellers, musicians, and by the early nineteenth century, actors, although dramatic genres differed from European forms.

Ghawazi dancers were descended from particular clans and performed in public as an entertainer caste. Although the tribal names differ from the Levant, these are thought to be Dom or Domari people, who migrated from the eastern Arab countries and were said to have originally migrated from India. It is more likely that they picked up their dancing style in Egypt rather than importing it, although some dance teachers prefer to emphasize aspects they view as being similar to other nomadic groups, now no longer insultingly labeled "gypsy." Their dance style, as it has been handed down, is unique, resembling Egypt's *raqs baladi*, native folkloric dance, distinct from the solo modern performances of staged Oriental dance, *raqs sharqi*.[2] The *ghawazi* typically traveled less in their stage space, but the style was intricate in terms of steps and hip-work; they moved their torsos and played *sagat* (metal finger cymbals attached to the thumbs and middle fingers, and sometimes described as castanets by European travelers). Two styles of dance are discussed—the Upper Egyptian *ghawazi* and the Sunbati *ghawazi*, from the Delta area (who are said to have come from Upper Egypt, or were banished to there and returned). Dance historians differentiate these performers' styles from that of the *'awalim*, even though travelers writing about dance and music may have confused them.[3] The *ghawazi* styles were not preferred by Mahmoud Reda, a founder of a famous Egyptian folkloric ensemble that debuted in 1959.[4] Although he included steps that may be attributed to them, he altered both the dance styling and staging and simplified certain movements. This was also true of the other large national ensemble, the Firqat Qawmiyya (est. 1960) (see Chapter Seven).

The personages, status, and art of the *'awalim* in Egypt is itself a disputed topic. There is a linguistic debate about the word's origins—whether it derives from Arabic, "a learned woman" from the trilateral root, *'ain, lam, mim,* or from the Hebrew or Aramaic *alamoth*[5]; both connote women learned in singing and dance, but the latter may have alluded to the sacred performance of music and dance by women who specialized in these areas as priestesses. Were foreigners who were intent on meeting *'awalim* in Egypt simply giving prostitutes who were "locally called *ghawazi*" the wrong name ("*almeh*") as John Rodenbeck asserts? Rodenbeck accepts Edward Lane's distinctions and faults Gustave Flaubert, the traveler who so romanticized his dancer acquaintances. He points to these distinction between types of dancers to question Edward Said's appellation of *'alima* to dancer Tahia Kariuka in Said's elegant obituary to her.[6]

Edward Lane distinguished some of the *'awalim* as being accomplished, while stating that many were inferior performers wrongly termed *'almé* (his transliteration; both *'alima* and *'alma* are used in Egyptian Arabic).

> There are among the 'Awálim in Cairo, a few who are not altogether unworthy of the appellation of "learned females"; having some literary accomplishments. There are also many of an inferior class, who also dance in the hareem: hence travelers have often misapplied the term *almé* meaning 'á'lmeh to the common dancing-girls of whom an account will be given in another chapter of this work; or they may have done so because the girls themselves occasionally assume this appellation and generally do so when (as has been often the case) the exercise of their art is prohibited by the government.[7]

Lane drew a sharp line between singers and dancers when it is clear that no such sharp distinction existed in his time. The other classifications that he emphasized concern the social class of the performer, the hosts, and the venue in which they perform. Lane arrived in Egypt at the age of twenty-four in 1825 to seek new opportunities and because of his poor health in England. The information in *Manners and Customs of the Modern Egyptians* came from this two and a half year period of residence,[8] and from his readings of other sources, like those of the Swiss Orientalist and traveler, Johann Ludwig Burckhardt. At that time, European travelers could gain a following in their home countries by relating the exotic customs and sights of the Orient. As a man, Lane lacked access to "the hareem" (the female areas of the elite household which was divided into the *haremlek* [private area restricted to the family] and the *salamlek* [an area where unrelated men might visit, and the women of the family were restricted from their view by *mashrabiyya*, turned-wood screens]). In retrospect, his pronouncements on dance, dancers, and music are curiously authoritative given that they were drawn from the statements of Egyptian men. Lane sent for his sister Sophia Lane Poole, who could visit "hareems," but this was more than twenty years after his original information gathering. The resulting work—*The Englishwoman in Egypt: Letters from Cairo Written During a Residence There in 1842/3/4 with E.W. Lane Esq., Author of "The Modern Egyptians" By His Sister (1844)*—has a greater amount of and more accurate information about women's lives than his own (although his own material also reappears here).[9]

In his own book, Lane also provides a chapter on the other sort of dancing girls—the most famous of whom he identifies as *ghaziya* (and the word continues to be translated as "gypsy"):

> The error into which most travelers in Egypt have fallen, of confounding the common dancing girls with the 'A'lmehs [sic], who are female singers has already been exposed. The Ghawa'zee perform unveiled, in the public streets, even to amuse the rabble. Their dance has little of elegance.

Lane distinguished between *'awalim* who sang, and those who danced, and *ghawazi* who danced; and a fourth type of performer, "some other dancing girls and courtesans who call themselves Ghawazee, but they do not really belong to that tribe."[10]

Lane considered the *ghawazi* to be part of a family or tribe, because the daughters were raised in the profession[11] and their menfolk played instruments for them. Hence, he added to Burckhardt's idea that they are "Gypsies" or connected to them.[12]

Lane traveled to Egypt more than two decades after the conquest of Napoléon Bonaparte and the reaction and response to that invasion that followed under the rule of Muhammad 'Ali Pasha which had encountered several crises over the role of women in public, and "public women" including the *ghawazi* and *'awalim*. Karin van Nieuwkerk clarified that by the early nineteenth century, *'alma* had come to mean a singer/dancer who could play musical instruments and that *'awalim* were known for their *mawawil* (vocal improvisations).[13] Sarah Graham-Brown further explained that *'awalim* began their career in elite households, but later "discarded by their master," they sang in public and could be paid well if they had "a good reputation."[14] If not, they had to perform in cafés and live more insecurely on payments from their audiences.[15] It appears there were actually many women performing in Cairo even during the ban, although not outdoors. As new public spaces for performance were created from the 1870s onwards, female singers, singer/dancers, and club owners invented their professions anew in the late nineteenth and early twentieth centuries.

Karin van Nieuwkerk surmised that the *'awalim* coming from the lower classes, and who entertained the lower classes, were the most prevalent background of those who grew up and learned to dance and sing. This was reasonable as these were the backgrounds of those she interviewed under the guidance of musician, Sayyid Henkish. However, the time frame of her initial live research was in the late 1980s and early

1990s, relying on interlocutors who may have known about circumstances reaching back into the 1950s but not much earlier, although she also deftly employs relevant written sources.[16] In the late nineteenth century, we find other sources describing musicians and their performances with or marriages to women who are still given the appellation *'awalim*. The distinction of *ghawazi* as "public dancers" and *'awalim* as a better or differently-trained entertainer still operated,[17] but was blurred. Dancers tend to associate the former with the style of Upper Egyptian *ghawazi* and the latter with specializing in the *raqs al-sham'adan*, (dancing with a chandelier balanced on the head or molded into a helmet) but there was overlap, and the style of the Lower Egyptian (Sunbati) *ghawazi* needed to be accounted for. In the mid–1970s, Edwina Nearing asked Egyptians to define it.

> "What kind of dancing did the ghawazi do?" "Bad" everyone agreed. "But what kind?" I insisted. "Just *hazn al-batn* and *hazn al-sidr*" (shaking of the stomach and shaking of the chest) answered a woman, who then demonstrated a particular tossing of her belly[18] (that some dance teachers call the "pony," not the Western belly dancers' isolated belly roll).

Nearing described the nature of the Luxor *ghawazi*'s hip and shoulder shimmies, their costuming, and the way they played *sagat* in detail.

Popular music for dance and public consumption and modern public presentations of dance were deeply affected by their previous history in a gendered and class context. Women singers captured public imagination in the first half of the twentieth century and sang *taqatiq*, a more modern song form which contained texts deliberately commenting on social issues experienced by women or concerning women[19] as will be explained below.

Since Egyptian sources did not give too many details about women performers, and researchers and historians often read no Arabic, they more frequently used sources written by travelers in Western languages. These are problematic due to the travelers' cultural baggage and tendency to eroticize. Certain traveling artists created artistic renderings of dancers, sometimes using European models. Beyond travelers' literature and artwork, historians trained in Arabic sources have examined court records, theater, musical history, and accounts of prostitution. Records of entertainment such as advertisements may also be used. One difficulty is the amount of anecdotal information in magazines and journals describing artists and an absence of sourcing.

Most music specialists acknowledge that women performers were *'awalim* or called "*'alma*" but provide few details about those who actually played or composed music (until the advent of recording, when such details could be aurally captured and appeared in labeling). These female vocalists were accompanied by female instrumentalists in a *takht* (made up of *'ud* [lute] and percussion at least, and sometimes other instruments such as the *qanun*, a zither). The women either lived with a patron or resided with each other in their own households. Their particular vocal style was distinct, and commentators on AMAR's series on early recordings remarked on "'*alima*/*'awalim* style" of singers recording after the turn of the century, and also how the *taqatiq* changed. For example, Frédéric Lagrange remarks of Munira al-Mahdiyya:

LAGRANGE: Note that Munīra al-Mahdiyya's vocal technique is an *'ālima*'s, more so than Asma al-Kumthariyya's or Bamba al-'Awwāda's, or later Fatḥiyya Aḥmad's and Umm Kulthūm's.
MUSTAFA SAID (INTERVIEWER): True. Munīra is the closest to a *'ālima* and much simpler.
LAGRANGE: Her performance was simpler and included more ornaments, such as the repeated *'afq*—a technique also characterizing Bahiyya al-Maḥallawiyya's performance.
SAID: True. And the "neigh" of Munīra al-Mahdiyya that is rarely performed by another....[20]

In the nineteenth century, the *'awalim* commanded a certain degree of respect and income from their musical knowledge (comprised of singing, composition, and playing of musical instruments), dance, and conversation, and they taught and organized younger performers into groups. But this was mostly tolerated only because they performed in private space where they were part of the households of patrons, or they traveled there to entertain the womenfolk of these households.

The singer Sakina, known as Almaz (1860–1896, born in Alexandria), was identified as being an *'ālima*. Like many other artists, she was trained by another *'ālima*, in this case, the most famous or best known at the time, Sakna. However, her performances in public venues were the exception, not the norm.[21] When she married singer 'Abduh al-Hamuli, he forced her to quit singing. She had been his main rival in terms of popularity. With some pressure from the Khedive Isma'il (ruling from 1863 to 1879) who favored her, al-Hamuli and she performed together on some occasions before she again ceased singing.

Musical and dance performances moved from private, sex-segregated homes and palaces or special public occasions like weddings and *mawalid* (saint's day festivals) and also ordinary coffeehouses to outdoor public entertainment spaces and what we may call a "nightclub"—a *sala*, where mostly male or mixed audiences watched theater, music, dance, and other performers. Let us take a minute to reflect on the certain common themes to be found in the history of dance and music in Egypt going back in time—these are the social position of entertainers as a sub-caste requiring special education, the uses of music and dance in ritual, and the state's efforts to tax and regulate entertainers.

Origins of Dance in Egypt

It is commonly believed and asserted by Egyptians that their own music and dance date back to Pharaonic times. The actual sound of ancient Egyptian music is a mystery other than some surviving elements in musical instruments, although modern composers have dabbled in fantasy Pharaonic compositions. Nor is it very certain what ancient Egyptian dance consisted of other than its depictions in drawings and murals. Gymnastic postures were shown, backbends, leg lifts, and what may be hops or leaps, but we do not know which traveling or stationary movements connected these poses. We can read about the costume of dancers, sometimes in open robes, or in very little clothing by the time of the New Kingdom, and that they wore short aprons (similar to men's) or beaded girdles decorated with rattling cowry shells.[22]

Men and women were not depicted as dancing together; rather, women danced

Detail from lower left of the top two registers of a banquet scene, showing dancers, musicians, and clappers, 18th Dynasty, from the tomb of Nebamun, c. 1350 BCE–1370 BCE (© The Trustees of the British Museum. All rights reserved).

with other women, and men with men. Slaves and the lower classes danced in public settings, and those attached to upper class or royal households entertained in these more private spaces. Professional groups of musicians, singers, and dancers performed at festive and religious occasions and funerals.[23] Musicians could be female or male, and attached to a patron or freelancers. For example, the female duo of Hekeni and Iti were shown in the Old Kingdom tomb of the accountant Nikaure.[24] A female dinner band is playing a large harp, a smaller *tanbura*-like lyre, and a stringed, long-necked instrument. (Instruments imported from Asia and a flute are shown in a Theban tomb, and we know that other bands featured many percussion instruments—tambourines, drums, and clappers.)[25]

Dancers and musicians, including choral singers, also served temples of the deities like Hathor,[26] the goddess of music, love, and drunkenness. These musical performers called *khener* were led by women until later in the Old Kingdom.[27] The ancient Egyptians held festivals (known as *heb*); their purpose was to allow people to thank the god or goddess for their gifts and to see the gods—images of them—with their own eyes. (Here we see a philosophical connection across time to the medieval festivals, the *mawalid*, saint's day festivals which honor the *awliya'*, holy men and women.) The followers of the gods could ask them questions through an oracle. The Tekh festival centered on the goddess Hathor and was a feast commemorating drunkenness. The god Ra had sent Sekhmet to destroy humanity, but he had a large quantity of beer dyed red to resemble blood sent to her. She drank it, slept, and awoke as Hathor, who had a peaceful nature. The festival celebrating this history was held at the Temple of Mut at Karnak. People drank, slept, and woke to drumming, danced, and apparently had sexual experiences with Mut (or her representatives) who was connected to Hathor, according to Egyptologist Carolyn Graves-Brown.[28] The festival of Hathor was held at Dendera and was similar to the Tekh festival featuring dancing, drumming, and possibly sex. At the festival of the cat-goddess, Bast, women danced, drank, and displayed their genitals in a fertility rite described by the Greek traveler, Herodotus, at which he claimed an attendance of more than seven hundred thousand.[29]

Female dancers plaited their own hair or wore wigs in a plaited style. Some continuities with modern folkloric Egyptian dance should be noted: the use of *kohl* to darken the eyes and henna to decorate the hands; wearing ribbons or garlands on their heads and bracelets; dancing with a cane (ornamented with little gazelle heads)[30] or sticks in solo or paired dancing. The association of alcohol and entertainment in ancient Egypt persisted in the drinking of *buza* (a low-proof alcoholic beverage) and was reinvigorated with the beer industry founded in 1897 and later on, in *fath* (opening bottles with customers or consumption) in nightclubs by female entertainers.

Women musicians, circa 1422–1411 BCE.

During the New Kingdom, female costumes evolved into transparent cloaks, or nothing but a belt, and the performers accompanied themselves with castanets or tambourines, according to Lexova.[31] This would seem to be the earliest usages of the *sagat*, or finger cymbals, in Egyptian dance and music.

In Hellenistic Egypt, girls received primary education similar to boys, including the study of musical instruments. Also, girls learned dancing, whereas boys were taught gymnastics.[32] Certain women became accomplished artists, philosophers, and musicians. However, certain slaves or *hetairai* (a prostitute, slave or free, of a higher or more educated status) were also musicians, for instance, Satyra, a *cithara* player (harp or lyre) in the household of Appolonius. Sarah Pomeroy writes that Satyra would have expected to entertain Appolonius and his guests musically and sexually.[33]

With the conquest of Egypt by the Muslims in 641 AD, what little remains of ancient Egyptian music is found in certain instruments, types of horns, flutes, percussion instruments, and the *tanbura*, and to some degree in aspects of the Coptic liturgy, in which certain ancient percussion instruments accompany that liturgy.

The Muslims brought a musical tradition with them. *Al-musiqa* is the word in Arabic for music, derived from Greek. *Al-musiqa al-'arabiyya* (Arabic music) developed on the Arabian peninsula and the territories conquered by the Arab tribes after the establishment of Islam as a religious and political force. The Arabic language and the customs of Arabian peninsula were not monolithic, and may be roughly divided between the cultures of the Bedouin (nomads) and people of the settled towns and agricultural settlements. Poetry and music counted for more than entertainment; the poet was an intellectual and a representative of a tribe. He was sent to declare war, ask for a truce, or praise a new ruler. It was believed that the *jinn* (supernatural creatures who are neither innately good nor evil) revealed a poem to the poet, and they also inspired musicians. The early Arabian poets did not sing, but hired composers and women with beautiful voices to perform their poems once they were set to music. In addition to the *jinn*, the ancient Arabs in the *jahiliyya* (the period before Islam) believed in a pantheon of gods and goddesses.

Ancient Arabic poetry documented the hardships of life, success and tragedy in love, and bravery in warfare, and certain music used in ritual worship before Islam. This poetry was considered to attain and convey *tarab*, enchantment or ecstasy, if it was excellent and compelling. The Arabs so admired poetry that they hung seven long poems, the Mu'allaqat, from the Ka'ba, the sacred building in Mecca. These were the poems of Imru' al-Qais, Zuhair, Tarafa, Labid, 'Antara ibn Shaddad, 'Amr ibn Kulthum, and Harith ibn Hilliza al-Yashkuri—poems which are studied to this day.

In the towns of the Hijaz in western Arabia, a tradition of women musician courtesans, *qiyan*, either free or slaves, had developed. A *qayna* raised a flag to advertise her house and offered song and verse in excellent Arabic, wine, and pleasure to her guests. The song genres she sang were *sinad* (serious and in longer meters) or *hazaj* (short meters and simpler). Some *qiyan* were well known: Jarada of 'Ad, Mulayka, Bint 'Afzar, and Hurayra.[34] Music of the Bedouin, in the categories of *huda*, the camel-driver's song and *nasb* (travel songs and dirges which became *ghina*), were distinct from those of the *qiyan*.[35] In the Ummayad period, the *qiyan* tradition continued with singers of the Hijaz dominating. 'Azza al-Mayla was a famous *qayna* as was Jamila (d. 720). As well, there were singers of Persian, Ethiopian, and African origins.[36] In the Abbasid period, *al-ghina' al-mutqan*, the "perfect singing" style held its own against other influences until the middle of the ninth century. The caliphs patronized music, as did rulers in Egypt.

There gradually developed differing attitudes towards the use of music in religious ceremonies. Some rejected the use of music in any relation to religion other than the chanting of the *adhan* (call to prayer which is heard five times a day) and *tajwid* (reciting of the Qur'an). However, music was integral to the Sufi practices of the *dhikr* (Sufi ceremonies for the remembrance of Allah), the *mawalid* (saint's day festivals), in songs sung as religious praise or hymns, and for mourning.

Basic features of Arabic music that set it apart from other traditions and which have influenced Egyptian music are as follows:

- melodic construction on *maqamat*, seven tone modes, further divided into three to five note units called *ajnas* which include microtones,[37] and were believed to lend particular tones and emotions (this point is disputed with reference to more modern compositions). Certain *ajnas*, *maqamat* (and *iqa'at*) have been or become popular particularly in Egypt, but it shares many with other regions.
- lack of polyphony
- driving and complex meters, *iqa'at*

- use of improvisation and ornamentation, and call and response
- instruments which provide special texture and tonality to the music, some of which date back to the Islamic conquest along with others pre-existing in Egypt, or adapted from Western instruments.

By the fourteenth century, Ibn al-Hajj attacked Cairene women's impropriety and wanted them to be confined to their homes.[38] He railed against "those who are called sheikhas" who performed the Sufi *dhikr* (the ceremony of remembrance of Allah) because he held that women's voices were *'awra* (pudendal, or meaning the part of the body which must be covered) and must not be heard. He criticized the sheikhas for influencing their followers to adopt practices that were—according to him—like that of Christian women in convents who lived outside of patriarchal rules, and for visiting cemeteries, even staying the night and attending mixed gender festivities for the departure of the *mahmal al-sharif* (the processional palanquin, or carriage bearing the covering for the Ka'ba which was sent yearly from Egypt for the *hajj,* the annual pilgrimage to Mecca from the thirteenth century until 1926).[39] From his tone, we may infer that Egyptian women had some freedom from strict gender segregation.

In the medieval period, dancers and musicians were organized into guilds, which regulated and protected various occupations and crafts. The *damina maghani*, a woman, was responsible for collecting taxes from those performers who were paid and who were not slaves attached to the court or wealthy owners. She also purchased, trained, and sold entertainers.[40] These singers performed at weddings, funerals, *dhikr*s, and the parties held seven days after a baby's birth (called the *sabu'a*). Funeral singers were periodically banned in Egypt. Certain religious opinion held that hired female mourners' wailing, crying, and singing had been disliked by the Prophet (probably as these had signified political opposition to his conquests and had been part of pre–Islamic tradition). The bans were typically rescinded, at least once upon the intervention of the *damina maghani* who argued that the government would lose the tax revenues she collected from these singers.[41]

Another important influence in Egyptian dance and music was that of the Turkic peoples. The literary culture of the Mamluks (enslaved soldiery obtained from Circassia, Macedonia, the Caucasus, and other areas) who successively controlled Egypt was in Turkish as well as Arabic (and some Persian). The singers and dancers known as the *'awalim* date back to that earlier tradition of *qiyan*, women, whose role was to entertain. They might have been concubines of a ruler or a well-to-do man, or they served elite and well-to-do women. If they were attached to a private household, they performed separately for men and women. Besides their owners, they had fans who attended their concerts, their *marbutin* (those "tied to them" in attraction).[42] In the nineteenth century, these were often women of the Caucasus who were enslaved, as the male Mamluks were, or they might be black slaves, as slavery was not forbidden until 1877.[43] Some of these *'awalim*, who composed poetry and music, played music, sang and danced, were also Egyptian women, but of the lower classes. Unlike *ghawazi*, they performed in private settings, some only for women and others for women and men. Some lived in harems with the segregated females of a wealthy or elite man; others lived elsewhere and came to their patronesses' homes. They also might perform for the men of the family and their guests in the *mandara*.[44] This was a sitting room used for entertaining visitors in the harem; and as these included males unrelated to the family, the women of the family did not enter.

In the eighteenth century, a large portion of Egypt's elite was either non-Egyptian in origin or of mixed ethnicity—usually of Turkic or Circassian background (or Bosnian, or Albanian, who are also Turkic). From the 13th to the 16th centuries, the Mamluks had ruled—slave soldiers who formed their own dynasties and came from the Caucasus, Armenia, and Albania. The ruling class of the Ottoman empire was formed the same way as the Mamluks, by attachment to their owners' household. The armies of the Ottoman sultan, Selim I conquered the Mamluks in 1517, but ruled indirectly. The Mamluks retained some power until 1798 when Napoléon Bonaparte conquered Egypt.

Dancing and music survived throughout. In seventeenth century Egypt, the guilds were divided by gender into one for female dancers, another for male dancers, one for female singers, another for male singers, or male jesters and so on. By 1670, one hundred and seventy different kinds of entertainers were listed and taxed by the official known as the *amin al-khurda*,[45] including different types of musicians, singers, dancers, storytellers, and performers with monkeys.

By the mid-nineteenth century, despite the ban on female dancers from performing in public, 'awalim continued to perform for the elites, and to possess musical skills, and some had returned from exile. At the royal wedding of Muhammad 'Ali's daughter Zaynab to Kamil Pasha in 1845, female entertainment was offered for all females in Cairo who wished to attend during the eight days of festivities at the harem building of Muhammad 'Ali's Citadel palace. A hired orchestra of 'awalim performed and danced in Arab and other Middle Eastern genres as described by Sophie Lane Poole, who provided many details although she detested dancing "in the manner of the 'almeh." (Apparently, she found it too suggestive.) Kathleen Fraser quotes her as saying, "The first Arab singers of Egypt ... they ... danced in the Arab manner, for which performance they are also celebrated as the first of their day."[46] Fraser points out that Lane Poole's account indicates there was a known ranking of performers; that there were slave dance troupes from Turkey, the Caucasus, and Georgia, and that the 'awalim could play their requisite music, and also that these foreign dancers might also imitate Egyptian-style dancing.[47] We also deduce that it would unthinkable to have a royal wedding without music and dancing.

After the end of the "ban" period and when taxation of performers resumed, 'awalim performed for the lower classes and elites, at weddings (to which they traveled in carts and were veiled), and even in front of coffeehouses. Dancers were either *ghawazi*, or lower-class 'awalim, and thus dancer/historian Heather Ward employs the term *'awalim/ghawazi*.[48] The link we are establishing here is also the fact that the original families of Muhammad 'Ali street (see below) referred to their female performers as 'awalim.

Travelers frequently requested the "love dance," performed by two *'almas*. Fraser shows that this "Love Dance" was of great interest to Napoléon's learned information-gatherers (the *savants*) Du-Bois Aymé and Jollois, at a wedding in Mahalla al-Kubra (in the Delta) at some point between 1798 and 1801.[49] This dance concerns the pursuit of the beloved by the lover, and its culmination was a simulation of lovemaking. Villoteau also attended and wrote about what he thought a progressively staged struggle between "modesty and love," which ended with very immodest postures.[50] Gilbert Joseph Gaspard de Chabrol and Edmé François Jomard also described this dance and that it could be a solo, during which the dancer loosened her belt.[51] The dance continued to be performed for some years. Prisse d'Avennes described it in 1830, and James St. John in 1834.

Another dance known to tourists and Egyptians was the "Bee," in which the performer tears off her clothes to get at an insect. An Egyptian source holds that the "Bee" is a "native dance," the relic of a Coptic dance.[52] Or, it might have been imported and adapted from an Iranian dance about ants.[53] Travelers at the time thought it not dissimilar to a "fly dance" performed by Spanish *gitanas*. It is referred to with great distaste in a different Arabic source, which suggests it was the reason for the ban on dancers.[54] (It is not my opinion that this was the reason for the ban, but it is interesting that the local historian attributes this cause to the ban rather than dancers' association with prostitution.) Although the "Bee" is a mimetic dance, and both above-mentioned dances incorporated eroticism, Ward cites an anthropologist of dance and tribalism, Najwa Adra, who thinks non-natives overemphasized eroticism (and semantic intent) in the dance.[55] Yet, Ward reminds us that the eroticism carried into the modern period.

Other dances extent in the early nineteenth century encompassed ones centered on an egg or a cup (of coffee or wine) or holding an *asaya*, a bamboo stick or a sword, or tambourine. Flaubert, who expressed great ambivalence about the dancer, Hassan al-Balbaissi (he was sexually attracted to him, but managed to convey disgust), described Kuchuk Hanim after he and his companions had given her and the musicians *raki* to drink at her house in Thebes (Luxor):

> Another dance: a cup of coffee is placed on the ground; she falls before it, then falls on her knees and continues to move her torso, always clacking the castanets, and describing in the air a gesture as if she were swimming. That continues, gradually the head is lowered, she reaches the cup, takes the edge of it between her teeth, and then leaps up quickly with a single bound.[56]

He also describes her posture as she plays the *darabukah* (*tabla*) earlier in the evening,[57] though he detests the music of the *rabab*. Flaubert's eroticization of his subject is evident. He writes that when she dances with Bamba, her servant, he finds Kuchuk's dance to be "brutal," and that he "has seen this dance on old Greek vases." He also mentions having sex with her before her dance, as did his friend Max, and twice later.[58]

The overt eroticization of this dance by Westerners continued, as did dancing with a prop in particular, dancing with the '*asaya*, or cane, which as already noted dates back to ancient Egypt.

France's Invasion of Egypt

When Napoléon Bonaparte's troops invaded Egypt in 1798, the guild system was weaker than in the seventeenth century, nonetheless, there were three guilds for female and male singers and dancers. There were also three guilds for prostitutes. Officials might catch a woman, and then list her as a prostitute to collect taxes. Tax farms (*iltizam*) were established to make more money; for example, a brothel could serve as a tax farm for an official called a *multazim*.[59]

Napoléon had intended to turn Egypt into a permanent colony of France, and on July 1, 1798, he landed in Egypt with 400 ships and 54,000 men. He brought a vast number of troops aiming to advance from Egypt to conquer British-controlled India. Napoléon issued a proclamation, identifying the French as true Muslims who had traveled to save the Egyptians from the tyranny of the Mamluks. It exhorted the "Qadis," "Shaykhs," and "Imams" to "tell your nation that the French are also faithful Muslims, and in confirmation of this they invaded Rome and destroyed there the Papal See, which was always exhorting the Christians to make war with Islam."[60] All villages were ordered to send emissaries to submit to the French and raise the French flag, and any villages that rose against the French were to be burned to the ground.[61]

Napoléon placed some *'ulama*, religious scholars, on his *diwan*, ruling council. This strategy was unsuccessful. Unsurprisingly, the Egyptians did not regard the wine-swilling French as Muslims, and they rebelled. Al-Jabarti critiqued the facts and intent in Napoléon's announcement, including its poor Arabic, and described the French in great detail, noting their ranks indicated in dress, shaving styles, vulgarity, lack of cleanliness, and that "their women do not veil themselves and have no modesty; they do not care whether they uncover their private parts."[62] (Covering was enjoined on Muslim women and modesty practiced by Egyptian Muslims and Christians.)

Napoléon, also fortuitously for us, brought a large team of *savants* (academics) who wrote *Descriptions de l'Égypte*, an illustrated history about Egypt at time, including information on costume, dance, music, and architecture in huge folios.[63]

The invasion was violent and extremely shocking to the Egyptians, some of whom, like al-Jabarti, wrote unfavorably about the French. Egyptians first raised their rebellion in Cairo in October of 1798.[64] They rebelled as a response to the cruelty of the invasion, French tax collection, and innovations contrary to Egyptian customs: the permitting of the sale and consumption of alcohol, forcing women and girls to go out without covering their faces, and the destruction of mosques and minarets.[65] Napoléon's troops looted from Egyptians and tore down Sufi shrines as they widened roads in al-Azbakiyya. During a second rebellion, the Ottoman military had arrived and encouraged the Egyptians, but a massacre took place, and Niqula El-Turk wrote, "General [Belliard] ordered that the massacre should stop, but the soldiers continued to rob and to rape women."[66] Muslims attacked Christians as well.

Those in charge of Napoléon's troops were said to have beheaded four hundred women and thrown their bodies in sacks into the Nile in 1799. Some sources identify these as *ghawazi*, Egypt's dancing girls; others claim they were prostitutes. Modern Egyptian and European sources take it for granted that many of the *ghawazi* were, in fact, prostitutes.

Al-Jabarti, an *'alim* (learned scholar—the word does not imply a male musician and dancer) and graduate of al-Azhar, regarded the French invasion, which he described in detail, as a calamity and blamed it on the Mamluks' sins. He was

"Almés," in *Descriptions de l'Égypte, ou Recueil des observations et des recherches qui ont été faites en Égypte pendant l'expédition de l'armée française. Publié par les ordres de Sa Majesté l'empereur Napoléon le Grand*, Paris: Imprimerie impériale, 1809–1828. Drawing circa 1800.

indignant when Egyptians, particularly women, adopted behavior like that of the French. He wrote, "Another aspect was the licentiousness of the women; most of them abandoned modesty and decency."[67] And:

> When the Nile water was high and had entered the Canal upon which boats were plying, the women's dissolution and their mingling with the French was in full view on the boats where they sang and danced and drank during the day, as well as at night by the light of candles and lanterns.[68]

Napoléon banned prostitutes, "*al-nisa' al-mashhurat*," from Cairo in this tumultuous year in an effort to control their relations with soldiers garrisoned there and threatened them with death.[69] Later in colonial history, the French allowed prostitution and subsequently registered, regulated, and medically examined prostitutes during their twentieth century campaign in Syria and Lebanon, as well as in Vietnam and Morocco, where they confined them to the quarter of Bousbir, in Casablanca.

Officials put in charge by Napoléon are said to have killed dancers/prostitutes (four hundred of them, or many) to prevent fraternization, venereal disease, or the plague.[70] A few dancer-historians questioned the account, or if these women were in fact, dancers (*ghawazi*).[71] More than 2,000 French soldiers died of venereal disease, and historian Juan Cole emphasized the French fear of the plague. Various other sources claim that the French killed four hundred (or many) women, sewed their bodies into sacks, and threw them into the Nile and imprisoned many others.[72] The use of sacks and drowning was a "Turkish method" of criminal execution at the time, and beheading was also employed by the French. They had beheaded men and women, some thirty every night following the rebellion, and an entire Arab tribe. Moreover, some accounts claimed that Napoléon arranged for his doctors to poison those of his own troops afflicted with the plague. The overall import of this incident is that (a) gender relations in sex-segregated, predominantly Muslim Egypt impacted by French "ways" necessitated punishment, or at least, regulation of prostitutes, and (b) most historians saw dancers as prostitutes or at least working in an environment that included prostitution.

Upper-class women did not escape consequences of encounters with the French. After the French departed, women were punished for having fraternized with them, including the daughter of Shaikh al-Bakri, Zainab who had dressed in European clothes (unveiled) and allegedly had an affair and was put to death.[73] No men were similarly punished upon the French exodus.

Change Under Muhammad ʿAli Pasha and Khedive Ismaʿil

According to my dissertation supervisor and mentor, Afaf Lutfi al-Sayyid Marsot, although the French shocked the Egyptians, they did not greatly transform Egypt, as their occupation was too brief. After Napoléon's withdrawal, Muhammad ʿAli Pasha, of Albanian descent, battled for a few years (1801–5) with the Mamluks, and then ruled Egypt from 1805 as the Ottoman viceroy, or governor. Nevertheless, the French established two journals, *Décade égyptienne* and *Courrier égyptien*. They had also introduced modern theater, acting in their own plays, and importing a theatrical troupe from France, and then building a theater across from Azbakiyya Pond. After it was destroyed in the 1799 rebellion, General Menou rebuilt it, calling it the Masrah al-Jumhuriyya, and some of the *savants* acted in its dramas.[74]

Egypt did not possess a theatrical tradition like France's, with written scripts and political messages enacted on a proscenium stage, but it had a dramatic tradition in sung epic poetry, shadow plays, and predecessors to comedic monologues (from the jester tradition). Singer/reciters (*rawi*, or known as *shuʿara* [poets]) of the *sira*, (epic poems) which spread into Egypt at the time of the Crusades, would recite and improvise on verses about Abu Zayd al-Hilali.[75] Lane wrote that there were about fifty *shuʿara* in Cairo during his stay there who had memorized that long text and sang it while playing a *rabab*.[76]

In addition to narrative and epic poems, acting troupes made up entirely of men called *muhabbazin* (the term *muhabbiz* was used for a live actor in Egypt as opposed to one performing with shadow puppets) in what Lane called "low farces." In the nineteenth century, traveling *commedia dell'arte* troupes performed in Egypt as well. The gradual development of a modern theater with didactic moral or political messages in Arabic translation was patronized by the elites under the family of Muhammad ʿAli Pasha, who took over Egypt following the defeat and withdrawal of the French. Muhammad ʿAli's descendants took the title Khedive of Egypt as he

The Ban and Its Aftermath

Muhammad 'Ali Pasha banned prostitutes from cities and female dancers from performing in public in 1834[77]—both *ghawazi* and certain *'awalim*—and forced many of these dancers to move from Cairo to Upper Egypt. The reason for the ban appears to have been Muhammad 'Ali's concerns about the health and discipline of his troops, as it operated only at major cities including Cairo.[78] Khaled Fahmy describes the efforts of Antoine Barthelemey Clot, known as Clot Bey, who directed the Qasr al-'Aini school of medicine. He worked to control, cure, and prevent syphilis and other diseases, give vaccinations, impose quarantines and regulations,[79] construct better housing, and also, elsewhere, train female doctors.[80] Fahmy discounts Judith Tucker's earlier statement that the *'ulama* had convinced Muhammad 'Ali Pasha to ban prostitution to make himself look like more of a reformer.[81] Some suggest that the sexualized nature of performances was the reason for the ban, yet this is not really borne out in the surviving dance styles of the *ghawazi*. There is a claim that the Sunbati *ghawazi* were exiled to Upper Egypt, as well.[82]

This key event impacted entertainers' livelihoods, though foreign tourists, even the Prince and Princess of Wales, traveled to see them in Upper Egypt, and it also influenced ideas about the acceptability of women dancing in public. The ban's precise date is disputed, as it was not immediately put into effect, and certain dancer/singers remained in Cairo.

Zenah, Dancing girl of Kenah (Qena). From Sir William Howard Russell, *A Diary in the East: During the Tour of the Prince and Princess of Wales* (London: Routledge, 1869), p. 112. Russell was a British war correspondent who accompanied the prince and princess to Egypt, Constantinople, the Crimea, and Greece.

Also, some dancers were able to resort to their patrons' intervention and temporarily resisted deportation, at least a few who were allegedly involved with 'Abbas, the grandson of Muhammad 'Ali Pasha.

In the absence of female street dancers, males dressed as females and affecting female mannerisms danced at weddings, coffeehouses, public festivals, and even in private homes. Fraser observes that because they performed the same dances as women, they indirectly show the key significance of female identity to this dance.[83] These transvestite dancers were termed *khawalat*. Flaubert wrote about seeing Hassan al-Balbaissi and another *khawal* dance with isolated shimmies, and he seems troubled by his own appreciation of their dancing.[84] Also, Gérard de Nerval described the *kohl*-ed *khawalat* and claims it reflects on "peculiar Egyptian morality"—that women would be banned from dancing, but that people considered the *khawalat* "more respectable."[85] A different sort of male dancer was a *gink*, often performing folkloric dances of the minorities of the Ottoman world.[86]

In this period, European travelers wrote of their experiences, using their published memoirs as a ladder to sophistication and notoriety. Gustave Flaubert wrote about Kuchuk Hanim, a *ghaziya*, at great length, eroticizing her. Another was Safiya (or Sophia), a *ghaziya* who danced from 1830 to 1850. She was supposedly discovered by 'Abbas, and became his mistress, but she was exiled to Isna, continued performing there, and retired by 1851.

Combes wrote of Safiyya:

> Everything the most supple and wavelike body can produce of wanton and provoking contortions ... all that Asiatic abandon has of voluptuous and inebriating poses ... captivating and irresistible seductions. All that Safia had, the dancer of Egypt, and something else more one could not know how to describe or imagine.[87]

Europeans described the *ghaziya* Badawiyya, who performed her sword dance for them (and on whom, along with Orientalist paintings, the American dancer, Jamila Salimpour may have modeled her sword-balancing dance a century later). These Europeans had attended the opening of the Suez Canal in 1869, and then went on a Nile cruise, on which they hoped to see *ghawazi* dancing. In addition to entertainers displaced to Upper Egypt, or the Sudan, some remained in the Delta area where they entertained. There were also areas for prostitutes at that time in certain Delta towns, further confusing the connection between dance and the world's oldest profession.

The ban of 1834 somewhat dislocated the geography of entertainment and made women's appearances in public more suspect, but did not terminate women's (often skillful) musical, vocal, and dance performances. Liat Kozma explains that illicit behavior such as prostitution or loss of virginity was punishable, and managing women and men in public space became the concern of the police. Peasants were required to have a *tadhkira* to leave their village and travel to other areas or to Cairo.[88] Within Cairo, neighborhood leaders were expected to monitor illicit activities in their own areas.

As the conditions of the ban relaxed, it was said that Khedive Isma'il allowed more entertainers to return; it was rumored that he was eager to tax prostitutes and became known for this reason as Pimp Pasha. This rather vicious claim may also be related to the Khedive's role in opening up public entertainment venues.

Elite women were still "safe" in private space where their segregation was practiced. One of Khedive Isma'il's consort princesses, Jeshm Affat Hanim (d. 1907), had her own female *takht*, showing us that an *'alima* was able to marry the ruler of the Egypt. She was photographed with her female orchestra in 1872.[89]

Meanwhile, the format of performances changed over the nineteenth century from duets and group dances to include longer solos and dance "choruses" or back-up dancers, interspersed with comedians and singers. And their venues changed from private to public settings. Khedive Isma'il spent a great deal of effort and money on a redesign of Cairo, and additionally, in the construction of the Suez Canal. Indeed, he was said to have bankrupted Egypt with these improvements and a war with Ethiopia, and had to sell Egypt's shares of the Suez Canal Company to the British government. The European Caisse de la Dette took over control of the country's finances, resulting in an Egyptian rebellion.

A specific area of Cairo was designed to accommodate public entertainment at Azbakiyya Gardens, built on the area of the drained Birqat Azbakiyya. It was an octagonal park, adjacent to four large squares, or *sahat*: Ataba al-Khadra, Opera, Khazindar, and Kantarat al-Dakka. Here *salat* (music halls) and kiosks opened and offered entertainment, including variety shows, such as the El Dorado in 1886 and Sala Santi. Entertainment also was provided in Rod al-Farag district. Khedive Isma'il built an opera house, designed by Italian architects, between Azbakiyya and Isma'iliyya which was inaugurated November 1, 1869, with a performance of *Rigoletto*, and remained until it was burned in 1971.

In Azbakiyya, the Clot-Bey area was most known for its "promiscuity," meaning brothels and taverns and coffee shops. The concerns expressed were for the normal residents (*al-ahrar*) because prostitutes were not relegated to some other area and might disturb these residents.[90] In other words, their activities were problematic because they were visible.

Close to Azbakiyya was a red-light district divided into two areas: the Wagh al-Birqa, which had foreign, licensed prostitutes and the Wasa'a, where native—meaning Egyptian, Nubian and Sudanese—prostitutes worked, near the fish-market, coffee houses, and more *salat* and bars. Pimps and procurers become a problem after about 1850.[91] Judith Tucker notes that when the state interfered less in prostitution, this had not been the case, but once the state heightened regulations, then pimps/procurers were resorted to as a means of eluding the state's control over prostitution and the income it brought.[92]

Kozma explains that in 1880, legislation referred to as the Dabtiyya Law (Legal Procedures and Jurisdictions of Quarter Police Stations Commissioners) was passed to control vagrancy, and specifically, lower class women's movements, although not their regular employment. In these regulations, she notes that singers were mentioned as well as street performers, and that the rules aimed to control women's sexual behavior.[93] It is clear that the police associated entertainers with bars, brothels, and threats to family control over women. Cairo, in that era, became markedly more crowded, and hence, the authorities were increasingly interested in controlling immigrants and others in the streets.[94]

The British invaded Egypt in 1882, ostensibly to put down the nationalist 'Urabi revolt (1879–1882)[95] and established a de facto, or "veiled" protectorate. The Khedives of the house of Muhammad 'Ali were forced to acquiesce to British control and European management of Egypt's finances. Public sentiment grew against the British and the harshness of rule under Lord Cromer (Evelyn Baring, Consul-General from 1883 to 1907), Sir John Eldon Gorst (1907–1911), and Lord Kitchener (1911–1914).

Publications, essays, journals, and theater came to reflect nationalist ideas, and these were presented in colloquial Egyptian Arabic. This occurred as more and more Egyptians acquired education and became part of the *affandiya* (the Effendi, or white-collar class). They began producing ideas, writing plays and songs for ordinary Egyptians in colloquial Arabic and in a counter-hegemonic manner. Ziad Fahmy describes this process as one of constructing a new mass culture which contrasted with the elite culture previously imposed on or self-imposed by Egyptians.

The work of *zajjalun*—composers of street poetry, which could be humorous or full of insults and jokes—were included in Abdullah Nadim's weekly journal *Tankit wa al-Tabkit* which also contained nationalist essays (in classical Arabic).[96] This along with other journals and newspapers became popular and were read by the literate to their illiterate compatriots. Hassan al-Allati, a musician, was a famous *zajjal* poet in Alexandria and Cairo who published *Tarwih al-nufus, wa mudhik al-'ubus* (Promenade of the souls and laughter of the melancholic) in 1889. He organized special evenings of entertainment.[97]

Meanwhile, with the growth of Azbakiyya and the proliferation of other public venues, like coffee houses, bars, and *salat* (nightclubs and dance halls), were gaining patrons. Women played a role in managing coffee houses, bars, and nightclubs. Clubs serving alcohol were managed or owned by women, both foreign and Egyptian. Omar Foda mentions Caterina Bakesova (Austrian-Hungarian), owner of the Anglo-American Bar in 'Abbasiyya, Ann Fielder (Austrian) who managed the Steinfield Bar in Abdin, and owners Jawhara bint Haslan, Sayyida bint Muhammad al-Zakiyya, and Marie Bittar.[98] By 1899, there were more than 4,000 establishments serving alcohol. Greeks and Italians were important in this business, "receiving 75% of licenses" in the year 1893.[99] Egyptians were also important in such commerce. For instance, Yusuf Qattawi Bey, a member of the leading Jewish family at that time, owned eight places that sold alcohol, mostly in Muski and Azbakiyya.[100] Muslims owned alcohol-serving establishments ranging from clubs to restaurants, taverns, and dance halls. Muhammad al-Muwayhili[101] described a dance hall (*marqas*) as a dirty site of dancing and prostitution, and noted that he saw a *shaykh* drinking beer there. We know by the turn of the century that women also managed and owned clubs and bars (see below).

Personages in Entertainment

Biographical information on performers frequently shows that they fled their families to pursue music or dance as these were not "respected" professions. 'Abduh al-Hamuli (c. 1841–1901) was born in Tanta and fled his father who disapproved of his going into music. He went to Munia al-Qamh, where he was trained by Professor Sha'ban, who also taught the great Jewish musician, Dawud Husni (1870–1937). Sha'ban brought al-Hamuli to Cairo where he performed *muwashshahat* (a song genre) at the 'Uthman Agha café in the Azbakiyya area in his youth (the 1850s).[102] He left Sha'ban and joined his competitor Muhammad al-Muqaddam, then formed his own band which included Muhammad al-'Aqqad (*qanun*) and Ahmad al-Laythi (*'ud*). Khedive Isma'il liked him and brought him to Istanbul to perform. His beautiful voice, the combining of Egyptian and Turkish elements, night concerts, and Opera appearance led to fame and he married the *alma* Almaz, as mentioned earlier.

Adam Mesyar points out that by the 1860s, there were some 1,200 coffeehouses in Cairo, and these were full of musicians. Rather than Azbakiyya representing a fully-European quarter, its musical (Egyptian, Italian, French) and theatrical offerings and their patrons were a mélange.[103]

Almaz was born in Alexandria to a Lebanese family and had become famous for her singing, attracting the attention of Khedive Isma'il. After she married al-Hamuli, he forced her to stop singing but wrote an elegy for her as a *dawr*[104] that begins "*Shribt al-sabr min ba'd al-tasafi, wa al-'amr al-hal ma'riftish asafi* (I had to be patient after the recovery/Time passed, I did not know the extent)." Their story was the subject of the film *Almaz wa 'Abduh al-Hamuli* (1962), directed by Helmy Rafla and starring Warda al-Jaza'iriyya (1939–2012), Nadia al-Gindi (b. 1946), and Tawfiq al-Deken (1924–1988). Many entertainment venues and restaurants (as well as dancers) are named for Almaz. Other important *'awalim* named by Esmat al-Nimr, a folk music enthusiast who established MisrFone, an internet channel devoted to older Egyptian music, were Amina al-Sarfiyya, Bamba Kashar, Shafiqa al-Qibtiyya, and al-Hagga Hoda. He described the *'awalim* groups as consisting of as many as eight women who did not dress in revealing fashions. Their *usta*, or leader, would cover her face, presumably since as the arranger and coordinator, she might need to speak with men.[105]

Shuq is sometimes mentioned as the "first Oriental dancer" by Egyptian and Western dance sources. It is a little unclear why she was so called, perhaps because her career predated that of her famous student, Shafiqa al-Qibtiyya. She was an important *'alima* who was reportedly invited to the opening of the Suez Canal (where she danced socially, not onstage). Her career was at its peak in 1871.

Shuq reportedly discovered the young Shafiqa al-Qibtiyya (d. 1926) at a Coptic wedding. Shafiqa trained with Shuq at her home on Muhammad 'Ali street, and her family disowned Shafiqa when she began dancing at the *mawalid*. Shuq died and Shafiqa performed widely, including later at the Alf Laila club. She is said to be the first to dance while balancing the *venyara* (candelabra or *sham'adan*) on her head. (This claim is also made of Zuba al-Klubtiyya, who was much younger.) It is also claimed that she was among the last of the *'awalim*. This assertion is also confusing as the *'awalim* recorded and persisted past the turn of the century. Rather, the basis of class origin of the singer/dancers was changing. She traveled to Paris and performed at an exhibition there. There were many tales of her; one of her admirers bought champagne for the horses that pulled her carriage, and she was showered with gold when she danced.[106] She was abandoned by fans as she aged, was cheated by men, and forced to return to dancing in her old age (by the mid-1920s). Heather Ward cites a 1908 *Odéon* recording of the *'alma* Bahiyya al-Mahallawiyya who imitates Shafiqa. In a little skit, it is clear that Shafiqa is very drunk. She giggles as she speaks with a "Mohammad," orders more beer, and is then unable to dance.[107]

Famous dancers earned a fee, and also *ba'shish* (from *baqshish*; tips in this case, rather than its other meaning of a bribe) or gifts. Dancers might forcefully demand remuneration during the ban[108] or at other times. The host of a party paid a fee, but the guests also tipped. Men licked coins and placed them on the face of a "Ghazeeya" wrote Edward Lane.[109] That style of tipping persisted. Huda Sha'rawi (1879–1947), the founder of the Egyptian Feminist Union, who was famous for removing her face veil in 1922, grew up in a harem, and wrote that guests licked coins and pasted them on the dancer's face at her 1892 wedding when she was 13 years old.[110] Earlier, Dauzats (1846) and Clot Bey (1840) had written of the great expense of a wedding, and Minutoli wrote (in 1827: 199) that a cashmere shawl was sent to the singer Nafisa[111] (who performed behind a screen) before she would agree to perform, and that she announced its value after she sang.[112]

The *mutayyib(a)* was an intermediary who arranged events for musicians and singers, collected money for entertainers so as not to render the relations between patrons and entertainers crass or impolite, and also communicated the wishes of the audience to the entertainers. The *mutayyib* (who was often, but not always male) would very loudly praise the singers and dancers. This person might also be called the *nabatchi*. Today, his/her role has been replaced by artistic managers, and the singer may announce or praise other artists and thank audience members.

Less famous dancers would engage in *barrada* (a term in the secret slang of entertainers, *sim al-fannanin*[113]), acting both to encourage tips or attract an audience. Entertainers might tip each other if the audience wasn't generous. Also, dancers stood in front of dance halls or coffee houses in costumes playing *sagat* and danced to attract attention and encourage customers to enter.

After the turn-of-the-century, the *'awalim* had a double repertoire; they sang the light songs called *taqatiq*, which were more modern, but could require a singer with a good voice who had command of the *maqamat*. They also sang the older *adwar*, depending on their audience, and some could sing *qasa'id* and *muwashshahat*. (These were either in *fusha* [classical Arabic] or later, an intermediate language mixing *fusha* and *'ammiyya*.) Recordings of Asma al-Kumsariyya, and Bamba al-Awwada exist and there are accounts of other *'awalim* in literature, as that of playwright Tawfiq al-Hakim's (1898–1987) fiction.[114] The *'alima* Sayyida al-Lawandiyya became a favorite of singer Munira al-Mahdiyya[115] (see below).

Salama al-Higazi (1852–1917) was raised in Alexandria. He was a trained *munshid* (singer of *anashid*, Sufi religious songs) who formed a *takht* for secular music in the 1880s and became known as a *mutrib* (singer who possesses *tarab*). *Tarab* is enchantment achieved through the mastery of text, *maqam*, emotion and innovation, or an "aesthetic quality that causes enjoyment, reciprocation of emotion, and communication between performers and their audiences."[116] The term is also understood as part of the construct of "*tarab* music" or *lawn tarab* (*tarab* color), and a traditional style of music, either that actually from "the pre World War I musical practice of

Egypt and the East-Mediterranean Arab world and is directly associated with emotional evocation,"[117] or music similar to it, but composed later.

In 1885, al-Higazi joined the al-Qurdahi-Husain troupe as an actor; he then formed his own troupe in 1888, teaming up with actress Labiba Manoli and singers Milya Dayan, Mariam Sumat, and the 'Ukasha brothers and toured outside of Egypt.

A great deal of novelty in music and in theater came from such troupes as al-Higazi's and their productions. A parallel to their development was that of *kanto* (*kantolar*, plural) in the 1870s in Istanbul.[118] *Kanto* referred both to singing on stage in an improvisational theatrical performance which included *çifteteli* and the songs written for this purpose from the 1870s in Istanbul. Most of the *kantocular* (kanto performers) were non–Muslims (Greek or Armenian).

It is important to realize the continuity of dance in Egypt from the nineteenth into the twentieth century, even as political and social realities were rapidly changing. The old guild system and the traditions of women who played, sang, and danced to music as well as the growth of nationalist feeling in Egypt wielded influences on the performance spaces, practices, and ethos which developed from them.

Two

From the *Sala* to the Silver Screen and Beyond

Between 1872 and 1874, Shari'a (street) Muhammad 'Ali was built. It extends from 'Ataba Square up to the Rifa'i Mosque, the Mosque of Sultan Hassan and the Citadel. Below, it was a part of the theater district. This street became famous at the beginning of the twentieth century, housing musicians, dancers, circus performers, and actors who passed on their trade to their children, and for that reason, it was known as *shari'a al-fann* (the street of art). People went to the *suq al-musiqiyin* (musicians' marketplace) on Muhammad 'Ali street to hire a quartet, a marching band, music for a wedding or a *mulid*. It held sway in the musicians' milieu until the 1970s, by which time many performing venues had relocated out to the Shari'a Haram (Pyramids Street) in Giza, and some of the performers had also moved out there. A much smaller proportion of Shari'a Muhammad 'Ali's musical life remained in contemporary Cairo, with workshops for musical instruments and some musicians' cafés, but others have been replaced with furniture stores. This neighborhood and the problematic reputation of working class entertainers, despite their decency, was shown in films like *Ahibbak ya Hassan* (1988) which starred Na'ima 'Akif, *Shari'a al-Hubb* (1958) starring 'Abd al-Halim Hafiz, and *Khalli Ballak min Zuzu*, starring Su'ad Husni, Husain Fahmy and Tahia Kariuka (1972). The temporality of Cairo's performers and their location is visible now with the city's further expansion, and the dissolution of guild-based guardianship over entertainment occurred. Though the best paid performers in Azbakiyya or more humble residents on *shari'a al-fann* could survive with luck for years in their professions, they might also end their lives in poverty. That class, income, and entertainment were in a constant state of interplay could be seen as the *salat*, then recordings, cinema, and other new technologies impacted dancers, singers, and musicians over the next one hundred and forty-five years.

The performers of the Shari'a Muhammad 'Ali and its alleys included Bamba Kashar (c. 1860–c. 1930). One source claimed that her father was a famous Qur'an reader and her mother, the granddaughter of a Mamluk Sultan (the Mamluks ruled prior to the French invasion).[1] In 1874, Bamba's mother remarried, so she and her siblings left home and settled next door to the Turkish *'alima*, Salem, who helped train her. Bamba Kashar sang *muwashhahat* and became well known as a singer and dancer until the end of 1920s. After leaving Salem's troupe, she started her own troupe and created an annual festival called the Zar Concerts. These outdoor events opened with a *hasabullah* band. Muhammad Hasabullah was a clarinetist in the military band of Khedive Abbas Hilmy (ruling from 1892 to 1914) who were taught by Italians. His band, established on Muhammad 'Ali Street, merged Western and Turkish band music with Egyptian music and beautiful singing girls. Two famous singers, Salah 'abd al-Hayy and 'Abd al-Latif al-Banna, sang in a *zaffa* (procession) in which Bamba Kashar was carried in seated in a Zar chair, and then she danced. Bamba Kashar married eight times, and several films were made about her. Her niece was the singer Fathiyya Ahmad (1898–1975). Shafiqa al-Qibtiyya was her contemporary and competitor, and Munira al-Mahdiyya was also a competitor.[2]

Apparently, a ban on dancers in public cafes was imposed in about 1894, yet paradoxically, dancers became ubiquitous in public *salat* in this decade. Heather Ward suggests that the 1894 regulation may have been due to residents' concerns about numerous dance venues in Rod al-Farag (expressed for the reasons explained in Chapter One). She shows that the government began using licensing requirements to control and police establishments presenting entertainment and serving alcohol and that such laws stiffened by 1912, according to a journalist, Sydney Moseley,[3] who lived in Egypt in that decade and was an editor for the Egyptian *Daily Mail*.

The 1894 regulation applied to Egyptians, not foreigners. The division of licensed foreign prostitutes and unlicensed Egyptian (and Sudanese) prostitutes and entertainers made for a complicated relationship between non–Egyptian or "foreign" men and women in the overlapping portions of entertainment and prostitution. Although the leading personalities described in this book did not have to resort to prostitution, other dancers and singers might have. A foreign, female brothel owner was known as a *badrona*, and they apparently proliferated. Some, referred to as "foreigners," were non–Egyptians but had lived in Egypt for most or all of their careers, but others were Westerners. There were Greeks, Levantines, and Maltese referred to as *mutamasirin* (would-be Egyptians).

Ward suggests, "Foreign-owned entertainment halls may have had a particular attraction for Egyptian dancers, because they provided a means to evade contemporary restrictions on public dance."[4] This is part of a discussion of an article in the journal *al-Zuhur* noting that Greek café and theater owners whose establishments had been closed (between 1887 and 1897) went to court and won re-instatement.[5] Restrictions were inconsistently applied. Disguised prostitution with little police restraint was possible in part because of distinctions dating back to the Capitulations, which were treaties made between the Ottoman sultans and Christian nations exempting traders from local prosecution, searches, and taxation. It meant that those holding a foreign passport (but who might be Egyptian or born in Egypt) could engage in illicit activities, yet were protected from severe prosecution due to the separated nature of the judicial system with Egyptian, consular, and mixed courts. Francesca Biancani describes the situation stemming from these different standards, which carried over for some decades. The lawlessness of Azbakiyya had grown due to the presence of foreign troops during World War I. Biancani depicts bar girls' (*fatihat*) work as simply a prelude to sex, that they made much more money drinking than dancing, and that often they were too drunk to dance.[6]

Entertainment was never solely for the lower classes or foreigners. Venues for the Egyptian elite also continued to proliferate, for example in the suburb of Helwan which was developed in the 1890s. Here, outdoor garden venues hosted musical entertainment and also theatrical troupes like Salama al-Higazi's which presented foreign language plays adapted into Arabic.[7]

Tensions had mounted in the pre–World War I years, especially when the British-controlled Egyptian government meted out extremely harsh punishments to villagers of Dinshaway in 1906 after a British soldier died of heat stroke, and a villager was assumed to have killed him. That incident galvanized public opinion and strengthened the cause of Egypt's nationalists like Mustafa Kamil. These nationalists would eventually prevail under other political leadership.

From 1910 to 1920, and particularly after restrictions on European theatrical groups from traveling to wartime Egypt, indigenous theater and theatrical troupes became increasingly popular, playing an important role in nationalist sentiment and featuring songs enshrining it. Dancers benefited, both because many were multi-talented—acting, dancing, and singing—and also because the practice of watching dance shows with musical and theatrical interludes became more widely acceptable and not only restricted to lower-class venues. The appearance of unveiled women onstage fascinated audiences. The performers were also beneficiaries of a transition in entertainment and communication in vernacular Egyptian Arabic and the notion of "Egypt for the Egyptians." This idea was powerfully conveyed in theater and song, and probably to understand this fully, we must backtrack somewhat to the inclusion of colloquial Egyptian speech into discourse. As well, I think this is a most important advent linking the dancers and singers of the new vaudeville theaters to popular Egyptian culture and which mitigates against certain claims that *raqs sharqi* was mostly created later by ideas drawn from Hollywood.

Ya'qub (James) Sanu'a (1839–1912), a satirical journalist and playwright, has been called the father of Egyptian theatre. He was an Egyptian nationalist and polyglot born in Cairo to a Jewish family. His father worked for Prince Yakan, grandson of Muhammad 'Ali Pasha. At the age of thirteen, he recited a poem for the prince, who sent him to Italy to be educated. On his return, he tutored the prince's children. He headed a theatrical troupe from 1869, wrote plays, presented the first opera in Egyptian Arabic, and established a national theater in 1870, first presenting in French and Italian, then writing his plays in Arabic.[8]

In 1877, he started *Abu Naddara Zarqa*, a satirical journal, the first to feature cartoons and using Egyptian Arabic. His journal mocked the sale of Egypt to foreign bidders, the rulers, censorship, and lionized the rebellion of Ahmad al-'Urabi. As Sanu'a encouraged local nationalism over the next decades, musical theater would eventually become a vehicle for its sentiments and symbols.

Other pioneers in musical theater were the above-mentioned Higazi and Shaikh Hassan al-Azhari, the 'Atallah brothers, George al-Abiad, Nagib (Najib) al-Rihani, and 'Ali al-Kassar. Although men are mentioned more often, women are important in this story as well, since they acclimated the public into seeing women in theater. Salama al-Higazi had founded a theatrical company with Iskander Farah in 1891. Mariam Sumat claimed to be the first female acting on stage in Egypt (Muslim women followed, although debates about whether to include women or not continued well into the teens), and seemed to be the first to engineer an actors' strike.[9]

The plays performed were sometimes Arabized versions of English or French works.

It was not overnight, but rather a gradual and lengthy process of change whereby upper-class Egyptian women began to speak in public, attend schools and colleges, enter professions, and work with, and even supervise, men. The course of the Egyptian nationalist cause from 1919 onwards legitimized women's public activity and visibility. Such elite women protested from March 16 to March 19 or 20 of 1919 for the first time in Egypt, marching on foot to the home of the Sa'd al-Zaghlul Pasha (1859–1927, leader of the Wafd party, and later Prime Minister), waving banners.[10] Nationalist and also philanthropic and charitable activities of women, who saw such endeavors as a social duty, helped quash resistance to those objecting to their public presence.[11] Women had already moved into publishing and theater. However, entertainment was still thought of as dishonorable. Exceptions were made, as when as the previously-mentioned Bamba Kashar ran away with her sisters and took up the lifestyle of an 'alima as a means of needed income. As with other women working for a wage, employment was not considered as dishonorable if it was a necessity. Women performers were subject to rather strict behavioral controls and supervision of family members.

Sami al-Shawwa (1889–1965) was born in Cairo, where his father, Antoine, a violinist, had performed with 'Abduh al-Hamuli. His great grandfather was also a violinist, heading the Nubat Shawwa *takht* in the eighteenth century, and his grandfather was a *qanun* player. Sami's family moved to Aleppo in Syria where he became known as a child prodigy on the violin. He returned to Egypt when he was fourteen. There he played for leading singers and taught music using European notation with Mansour Awad. He acquired a contract with Baidaphon Records (established in Beirut), and his recordings of dance music are well known; there were constant references to (covers of) his "Raqs al-Hawanim" (also referred to as Raqs al-'Awalim) in film and music until now.

The earlier 'awalim tradition had rewarded performers who were *shamla*, that is "complete"—they could sing as well as dance, play an instrument, and even compose verse or songs. Munira al-Mahdiyya (1885 [possibly 1884]–1965, born as Zakiyya Husayn Mansur) was an example of that tradition. She was born probably in Zagazig, or in the village of Mahdiyya in Sharqiyya, and grew up in Alexandria.[12] She attended a convent school but was attracted to entertainment and secretly snuck out at night to hear the singer Sayyida al-Lawandiyya (an 'alima). Muhamad Faraj "discovered" her voice in 1905 at her school and invited her to sing in his café. Then Kamil al-Khula'i heard her sing and hired her at his café in the Birhamas neighborhood. She sang in clubs and was among the earliest to make recordings with Baidaphon, also Zonophone and Odeon. She recorded under the name Sitt Munira, and her earlier songs were in the 'awalim style, whereas after the 1920s she made the transition to a *mutriba* style, singing "a high standard repertoire" for elite audiences.[13] Some of her less well-known recordings refer plainly to alcohol, drugs, and love affairs.[14]

Munira opened a *sala* in Azbakiyya, calling it Nuzhat al-Nufus, and sang there by 1913, and then at the Alhambra and the El Dorado clubs, by which time she had married Mahmud Jabr. At the Alhambra, she earned 124 LE a month for singing a forty-minute show, and this was in addition to her income from Baidaphon.[15] Encouraged by her example, the nieces of the *'alima* Bamba Kashar, Fathiyya and Ratiba Ahmad, also performed in local operettas.[16] Fathiyya, Ratiba, and their sister, Mufida, all singers, opened a *sala* as well.

Munira sang in the *'alima* style[17] (not the *mutriba* style which followed), the forms of music known as *qasa'id*, *taqatiq* and *adwar* and also wonderful *mawawil* (vocal improvisations). As a general observation—it is only through recordings that we gain a sense of what was performed for dancers, or by singers when there was no dancing—purely instrumental compositions intended for dancing provided an opportunity for composers and musicians to showcase their talents prior to a singer's appearance or in between performers. The recording format (of 6-minute songs) lent itself to much briefer performances than would normally have occurred at a party, wedding, or possibly within a performed play, since when encouraged by a live audience, singers might add improvisation, an extra verse, or repeat an entire section.

Despite Munira's command of neoclassical forms, as well as *taqatiq*, she mostly became famous through theater, and notorious for her nationalist *salon,* and was called *sultana al-tarab*. The British caused Nuzhat al-Nufus' closure. Munira joined Salama al-Higazi's theater as the first Muslim Egyptian *mutriba* to perform on stage without a veil in 1916. When Higazi was ill, she got her big break and sang the role written for him while dressed as a man. Apparently, she had already recorded the *qasida* "Inn kuntu fi al-gaish" in 1914 and 'Aziz 'Id decided she should sing it onstage.[18]

Munira al-Mahdiyya, the Sultana al-Tarab. Included in "Munira al-Mahdiyya 4" on "Min Al Tarikh," Frédéric Lagrange, hosted by Mustafa Said (courtesy AMAR, Foundation for Arab Music Archiving and Research, August 27, 2015).

She became a leading singer and established her own theatrical/dance/musical company in 1917. It lasted for a decade, and her company often performed nationalistic songs, as she did in her private gatherings, and supported the nationalist efforts, leading to the saying "*hawa al-hurriya fi masrah Munira Mahdiya*" (the breeze of freedom is in Munira al-Mahdiyya's theater [group]). Sa'd al-Zaghlul and Husain Rushdi Pasha (who served as Prime Minister between 1914 and 1919) admired her.[19] Her fame was eventually eclipsed by that of Umm Kulthum. Her life was the subject of the film *Sultana al-Tarab* (1978) in which Sharifa Fadil played the role of Munira al-Mahdiyya.

This film is a very revealing example of Egyptians'

perceptions of social class barriers and the role of the entertainment industry both in nationalism and in women's lives—women, dancers and singers, who are portrayed as only marginally honorable, yet true Egyptians. The film also depicts the guild-like process of recruitment and training of women entertainers by older, experienced women.

Munira al-Mahdiyya also composed many of her own songs, as did Na'ima al-Masriyya (1894–1976) who performed at the Alf Laila wa Laila music hall and purchased the Alhambra Casino in 1927, where she sang as well as running the establishment. Sayyid Darwish, the composer, thought very highly of Na'ima al-Masriyya's musical knowledge and consulted her on his own songs.[20] Unfortunately, after her daughter's marriage in 1937, her son-in-law forced her to stop performing and destroyed or got rid of almost everything related to her musical career.[21]

'Aziz 'Id (1884–1942) playwright, actor, and director (who gave Munira al-Mahdiyya her opportunity) established a theater dedicated to vaudeville comedy in 1907, the al-Juq al-Kumidi al-'Arabi (the Arabic comedy troupe). He encouraged many dancers, actors, and composers who often went on to join the theatrical companies of Munira al-Mahdiyya, 'Ali al-Kassar, Higazi, and Rihani. He wrote very controversial plays after World War I began, but the censors were less harsh on theater than on print publications. He mentored various actors including Fatima Rushdi (the Sarah Bernhardt of Egypt) and then converted to Islam to marry her, and they formed their own theatrical troupe. The troupe dissolved, but he reorganized it, and it became

Munira al-Mahdiyya. Possibly from 1927, as she was photographed on *Ruz al-Yusuf*'s January 1927 issue cover in a man's suit and tie. This alludes to her occasional playing of men's roles onstage a decade earlier. In "Munira al-Mahdiyya 3" on "Min Al Tarikh," Frédéric Lagrange, hosted by Mustafa Said (courtesy AMAR, Foundation for Arab Music Archiving and Research, August 27, 2015).

popular when the European theatrical companies were blocked from travel to Egypt once World War I began. His plays were popular and daring; one starred the actress Ruz al-Yusuf, who wore only a bathing suit onstage, and was entitled *Ya Sitti Ma Timshish Kida 'Iryana* (O Lady, Don't Walk [Around] Naked Like This). Another play criticized the *shari'a* courts, *Dukhul al-Hammam Mish Zayy Khuruguh*[22] (Entering the Public Bath Is Not Like Getting Out of It). The lyrics in these plays were composed in the above-discussed *azjal*; their melodies were shorter and catchy, and everyone could understand them and hum the lyrics.

Ruz al-Yusuf (1898–1958), born Fatima in Lebanon, had moved to Egypt and became a vaudeville actress. She was in 'Aziz 'Id's and 'Ukasha's troupes, and she played music. She had not attended school, and 'Id hired a *shaykh* to teach her to read and write. She became quite famous in the above-mentioned play and in other roles. Ruz al-Yusuf moved into journalism and established her own magazine, *Ruz al-Yusuf* in 1925, followed by *Ruz al-Taba'i* covering entertainment and politics. This publication capitalized on the public's interest in entertainers.

Poster for the film *Sultana al-Tarab,* about the life of Munira al-Mahdiyya, starring Sherifa Fadil and Farid Shawqi (1978) (author's collection).

Vaudeville expanded a combination of acting, dancing, comedy, spectacles and music to attract a greater audience. Fahmy quotes an advertisement for a February 23, 1917, performance which included gymnastics, dancing, magic acts, a clown, the Munira al-Mahdiyya troupe's performance of *'Aida* (with all songs sung by Munira), and then al-Rihani's play *Khala'at al-Nisa'* (the loose behavior of women) followed by Muhammad al-Nagi's play *al-'Umda al-'Abit* (the stupid village chieftain). The cost was only 5 piasters.[23]

While popular and nationalistic theater coupled with affordable entertainment appeared a boon for the public, we should remember that both Egypt's nationalists and the lower elements in entertainment were still regarded very unfavorably by the British. The British police commandant Harvey Pasha banned *raqs sharqi*, "*la danse du ventre*," in 1916 from coffee houses, music halls, and all public places, arrested and detained transvestites, and prohibited the selling of alcohol in Azbakiyya all night.[24] Certified "artistes" could continue with *fath*, (drinking with customers) however.

The 'Atallah brothers, Salim and Amin, had a theatrical troupe, which traveled to Syria in 1912, incubating within it the great, though short-lived, composer Sayyid Darwish (1892–1923), who learned various forms of music composition while in Syria. Amin 'Atallah, born in Alexandria, then joined 'Id's troupe in 1915. Sayyid Darwish was born in Kom al-Dikkah, Alexandria, where he trained in religion and as a *munshid* (singer of religious songs). After his travels to Syria, he began singing in *salat* (nightclubs) and cafes, but he was not as popular as certain singers. He began composing for Nagib al-Rihani and 'Ali al-Kassar's troupes and Munira Mahdiyya's, often teaming with Badi'a Khairi, who wrote lyrics in colloquial Arabic. Many of his songs were wildly popular and became musical standards. Some associated with nationalism were even revived after the 2011 revolution. He deleted a good deal of improvisation in his songs. He wrote a series of songs about different humble professions (waiters, pot-makers, stonecutters) and while composing them, he would immerse himself in the subject—what the stonecutters said and sang, or what the Sudanese who lived in Cairo said and sang—which he learned by spending time with them in a *buza* (a lower-class bar) when he was writing the song "Dingi, dingi."[25] Many plays featured revolutionary songs, expressing national unity against the British,[26] and any play featuring Darwish's songs was a guaranteed success.

Nagib al-Rihani (1889–1949) was an Egyptian actor, born in Bab al-Sha'riyya in Cairo to an Assyrian Iraqi father from Mosul and a Coptic mother. He attended the French school "Les Frères" (this usually refers in Egypt to Collège des Frères, a La Sallian school, also attended by Farid al-Atrash and his brother). He earned the moniker of the "father of comedy." He formed his own theatrical group, adapted several French plays for the stage and film, as well as many Arabic plays. He invented the character of Kish Kish Bey, a rich village headman, an *'umda*, squandering his fortune on women in Cairo. He married Badi'a al-Masabni, who became well-known as a singer. Their marriage suffered as, according to her, he paid little attention to her, preferring to go out with his male friends, but they remained married for eighteen years (since divorce was not allowed in his sect). She wasn't afraid to let the public know that she broke a chair over his head, insulted him, and threw him out.[27] However, they made up and saw each other until his death, according to Badi'a.[28]

Just as al-Rihani was identified with Kish Kish Bey, 'Ali al-Kassar (1887–1957), born 'Ali Khalil Salim, became known for the character he played in blackface makeup, 'Usman 'abd al-Basit, al-Barbari al-Wahid fi Misr (the Only Nubian of Egypt).[29] His theatrical troupe rivaled Rihani's. His deep connection to the Egyptian nationalist movement surfaced in his dramas. Many were written by Amin Sidqi who, when attacked by a critic, defended his use of exaggeration in vaudeville as it counters immorality even while sparking laughter.[30] The comedic tradition in vaudeville continued on in film, and also with comedically talented actors like Isma'il Yasin (1912–1972), who at first joined al-Rihani's troupe, then Badi'a Masabni's and later, 'Ali al-Kassar's troupe, starring in eighty-one movies. Yasin imitated Samia Gamal in a skit while wearing a *badla*. Gender-bending, or men playing women's roles for comedic effect, was not uncommon, especially with dancers. Mahmud al-Maligi, who later played villains, posed in a two-piece costume with a little vest while he worked in Yusuf Wahbi's theatrical troupe in the 1920s.

Zinat Sidqi (1913 [or possibly 1912]–1978) was a dancer/singer and became mainly known as a comedic actor. She migrated in an opposite direction away from Egypt to Lebanon, and joined al-Rihani's troupe, working often with Yasin and later in Yasin's theatrical troupe. She suffered from poverty later in her life, being without work.

Badi'a al-Masabni (1894–1974), who acted in al-Rihani's troupe and married him, was born in Damascus. She endured poverty and rape as a child, and had some terrible relationships with certain family members. She traveled to Buenos Aires as a child, where she attended boarding school, then back to Syria, to Lebanon, and then to Egypt where she joined George al-Abiad's theater group and eventually married al-Rihani. She was central to the development of *raqs al-sharqi* and its glamorization in the nightclub setting. When asked about her own dance style, she shared that she considered herself a master of the *sagat*. She characterized herself as elegant, saying she preferred to wear long gowns (often backless, and without a brassiere—this being a feature of ladies' fashions in the "Roaring Twenties") rather than the more revealing *badla* (the *raqs sharqi* costume of a decorated bra, belt and skirt) or Moroccan, Tunisian, or Levantine robes (long dresses) when she performed.[31] Badi'a could speak Spanish, Arabic, French, Greek (the language of her church), and Turkish and said she had added Latin, Turkish, and Persian influences into her dance spectacles so the audience wouldn't get bored.[32]

She first opened Sala Badi'a Masabni (formerly the Sendex) on 'Imad al-Din Street in 1926, and dance was first offered at this location in 1927-28. She opened a club in Alexandria for just one summer in 1928, and then a summer nightclub/garden casino in Giza City in 1930, and expanded it with a theater and cinema in 1931.

Beba (Biba) 'Izz al-Din (1910–1951), who began her career in Beirut, was a dancer/owner and rival of Badi'a Masabni. She bought Badi'a's club on 'Imad al-Din street from Badi'a's nephew Antoine (who was also Beba's lover) in 1936 and then refused entry to Badi'a. In 1939, Beba owned Teatro Beba and was just next door to Badi'a's Casino Opera. She bought Badi'a's Casino in 1950 but was killed in an automobile accident just a few months later.

Because of Antoine's betrayal, Badi'a had to rent the Bretania in 1937, and then in 1938, she renovated the Majestic theater and opened it as Casino and Cabaret Badi'a. In 1940 she moved to Ibrahim Pasha Square, which was also known as Opera Square (Midan Obera) so that her club was known as Casino Opera. This was torched during Black Saturday (26 January 1952) when following the killing of fifty Egyptian policemen by British troops, hundreds of establishments connected with Western influence—hotels, banks, nightclubs—were burned or ransacked. Casino Opera was replaced by the Opera Cinema.

Badi'a maintained her interest in theater and film acting, but her efforts to quit her clubs and star in a film was a failure. Her clubs transformed certain singers and dancers into stars and expanded their appeal with new formats, and as these were among many other clubs, such a pattern occurred more broadly. She herself taught dance but was careful to hire talented dancers and employed choreographers, making *raqs sharqi* more spectacular with the accompaniment of large orchestras combining Western and Eastern instruments, dramatic sets, use of the veil, sequined costumes, and staging. After touring Europe, she sold her club as explained above because her nephew stopped running it properly and had run up debts. The Egyptian tax authorities were pursuing her, so she relocated to Lebanon, where she subsisted on income from a dairy farm and a store in Shtura, although her relatives tried to bilk her.[33] The bitterness of her forced exodus is similar in tone to that of other "foreigners" forced out of Egypt.

Many other clubs were important but some remained in popular memory like the Kit-Kat Club, a cabaret which features in a novel, a film, and songs. It gave its name to KitKat Square, a Metro stop, and to an area of the Nile river where nightclubs and bars aboard *dahabiyyat* (houseboats) were once plentiful.

Badi'a and other *sala* owners created a nightclub atmosphere, which like vaudeville, offered a wide variety of entertainment and opportunities to many singers, actors and dancers. For example, Afranza Hanim was already an established Turkish and *raqs sharqi* dancer when she performed at Badi'a's club. (That the two styles were differentiated is pointed out by Ward, as part of her argument that the public now understood *raqs sharqi* as a form separate from other dances of the Eastern Arab countries, and also distinct from dancing European style, male with female.[34]) Similarly, Hikmat Fahmy (1907–1974) who had worked in 'Ali al-Kassar's theater, was a featured dancer at al-Sala al-Masriyya (Salat Mary Mansur), then Badi'a's sala and later at the Kit-Kat club. Fahmy was later charged and imprisoned for spying on British officers for the Germans through her involvement with John (Johann) Eppler, a half–German, half–Egyptian spy. She supposedly danced for Hitler and Mussolini. When she was released from prison, she was forty, and younger, new dancers had taken her place. She appeared in six films, including *al-'Azima* and *Rabab*. She not only appeared but invested in al-*Mutasharida* (1947), but it was a failure. At the end of her life, she found refuge in the church. Nadia al-Gindi starred in a film about her: *al-Jasusa Hikmat Fahmy* (1994).

Huda Shams al-Din danced at Badi'a's *sala*, as did Na'ima 'Akif (1929–1966), a very talented dancer, who additionally sang and was a featured performer, although she worked only briefly due to jealousy from other performers. Then she went to the Kit-Kat. Na'ima and her sister Fatma were acrobats as children in their family's circus and subsequently, dancers. They knew some repertoire of the Sunbati *ghawazi*.[35] Na'ima was very beautiful and married Husain Fawzi, director and screenwriter, and made fourteen musicals with her husband. She portrayed the *ghaziya* Tamr Hinna in the 1957 film of that name. Fatma left Egypt in 1946 for Europe and South America, and then San Francisco.

In the early 1930s, Badi'a's dance troupe posed for a photograph wearing *badlat* and holding their arms in a vaguely Oriental pose. Included were Imtithal Fawzy,

Gina (probably Markissian), Fathia Sharif, Layla 'Amiriyya (who was Badi'a's adopted daughter, Juliet), Bahiya 'Amr, Hikmat Fahmy, Biancha, Salma, Fardus Shalaby, Khairia, Kiki, Nina and Zinat.[36]

Huriyya Muhammad (1917 or 1918–1970) was also a feature dancer at Badi'a's club by 1933 and a leading dancer in the early 1930s. She had learned to dance from Na'ima 'Abdu. She quit in 1936 because she was jealous of Tahia Kariuka and toured Egypt with her own troupe.

Badi'a hired the choreographer Isaac Dickson to train and spark up her ensemble dancers, and he was also hired as a coach by individual dancers, like Samia Gamal, having quite an impact on choreography for dancers in films. Dickson has been described as being English (by Mohamed Shahin), Lebanese (by Priscilla Adum), and Lebanese Armenian. Anwar Wagdy, the actor, brought Dickson in to train the child star Fairuz so that she could imitate Badi'a Masabni's, Tahia Kariuka's and Samia Gamal's dancing in a routine in the film *Yasmin*.[37]

Muhammad 'abd al-Wahhab (1902–1991) was born in Bab al-Sha'riyya, Cairo. He was an *'ud*ist, and prolific composer of 1,820 songs; he also sang and appeared in seven films and was very important to careers of certain singers, for example, Asmahan. He had run away from home, as his father disapproved of music, and Ahmad Shawqi, called the Prince of Poets, promoted him and instructed him in manners and culture, so that he gained entrance to world of the elite.[38] He first wrote traditional melodies but became famous as a modernist who incorporated certain Western or other non–Arabic elements into his songs. After years of rivalry with Umm Kulthum, she sang his composition "Inta 'Umri" in 1964, which was a huge hit. He later sang some more serious songs, which remain a standard for performers of music with a *tarab* feeling. His instrumental pieces which are used by dancers are worthy of their own scrutiny. Take for example, "'Aziza" which was a hit that he composed in 1943 and was so popular that it was played in every musical circumstance. It is still used and is suitable as a separate dance piece or as part of a longer show. "'Aziza" opens with the accordion, popular in the period prior to the electronic keyboard, and it transitions through several rhythms.

Muhammad 'abd al-Wahhab joined Baidaphon as an Egyptian partner in the 1930s, and the company became known as Cairophone in the 1940s. Up to the 1940s, another Egyptian recording company was owned by Setrak Mechian, an Egyptian Armenian. After World War II, Muhammad Fawzi founded Misrophone, and by the late 1940s, the Egyptian government took it over under the name of Sawt al-Qahira. On these labels one may find dance and vocal music. Muhammad 'abd al-Wahhab composed many pieces not only suitable for, but which complemented, *raqs sharqi* over his career. Nabil Azzam who wrote a dissertation on 'abd al-Wahhab described him as a great musical leader because he used "his antennae to go beyond the instruments or his voice. It became a reaching out to give—to give melody, to give answers to different questions. Social questions. Human questions."[39]

Tahia Kariuka (1915–1999) became a dance star at Badi'a's *sala*. She was born Badawiyya Muhammad Karim al-Nirani in Isma'iliyya to an older father who died; she then lived with her brother who "tortured her" and shaved her head (to prevent her from running away). She moved to Cairo, and worked with Su'ad Mahasan at her club, then Badi'a Masabni hired her in 1933. She began performing as a solo dancer and learned a version of the samba called the "*kariuka*" from Dickson. Since the audience would ask for her by this name, she acquired the appellation Tahia Kariuka instead of Muhammad. Sulaiman Nagib, the head of the Opera, convinced her to learn foreign languages, read books, and acquire good manners, and she was featured as a dancer in films from the early 1940s.

Although her dancing in film segments and stage shows may have included choreography, she danced as if she was improvising. Her rival as a dancer was Samia Gamal, although Samia described herself as unequal initially to Tahia.

She married fourteen times, including an American army officer and to Mustafa Kami Sidqi, an Egyptian army officer who was part of the so-called Ring of Iron. (The two of them were jailed in 1954 for a plot to overthrow the government.) She once beat a U.S. congressman with her shoe because she felt he had insulted a performer, according to actor Samir Sabry. In 1962, she formed a theater troupe with her husband of that time, Fayiz Halawa. The Kariuka-Halawa troupe was very important to the continuity of theater because of the extremely heavy censorship was wielded in the 1970s. When threatened with censorship of the play *Yahia al-Wafd*, Tahia went to court, won the case, and mounted the play. Tahia's film appearances were not usually depictions of the nightclub scene in which she performed, but glamorizations of performances in hotel or wedding venues, and sometimes in more intimate settings.

Badi'a also featured great singers at her establishments, for example, Fathiyya

Tahia Kariuka as Nanousha in *Bint al-Hawa*, 1956. She claimed to have only appeared as an actress (although often in dancing roles) after the age of thirty-two.

Ahmad (1898–1975), Farid al-Atrash (1910–1974), and Asmahan (1917–1944). Fathiyya Ahmad began singing in 1910 and appeared in Nagib al-Rihani and Amin Sidqi's theater companies. She was known as Toha by her fans and was said to sing "in the tradition of the *'awalim*" including the *wasla* (a cycle of musical pieces more commonly performed early in the century). She was popular in Syria and Palestine, as well as Egypt. Fathiyya went on tour to Syria, but she returned with a recording contract to Odeon, and then sang for six years at Sala Badi'a, often advertised as a "Turkish-style" singer. Her classical style and mastery of the *mawwal* made her special,[40] but this also resulted in other singers with a more modern style surpassing her.

Asmahan, whose mother sang and recorded under the

Tahia Kariuka kissing Zainab Sidqi after she was released from jail and returned to her apartment. She was very emotional about having been imprisoned and had support from fellow artists. *Al-Kawakib* (no. 133, 16 February 1954).

name Amira 'Alia (Princess 'Alia), had traveled from Syria to Egypt. She sang as a soloist in Badi'a's *sala* as a teenager and embarked on a promising musical career, but was convinced by her family to return to Syria and marry her cousin, Hassan, who became minister of defense. She returned to Egypt after splitting with him and resumed a vocal and film career, cut off by her death in a car accident in 1944.[41] Her brother Farid al-Atrash played in the *takht*, accompanying his sister Asmahan at Sala Mary Mansur as early as 1931 and was recommended by Riyadh al-Sunbati to the radio where he was hired as an *'ud* player and singer. He starred with his sister in *Intisar al-Shabab* (1941), composed more than five hundred songs, and starred in thirty-one films, nine of them with Samia Gamal (1924–1994). He was called Prince of the 'Ud for his instrumental virtuosity, especially in his *taqasim* (improvised solos). After Asmahan's death, Farid teamed up with different singers and dancers in films, among them Nur al-Huda (1924–1998).[42]

Many of his compositions (or adaptations) are part of the dance repertoire of the mid–twentieth century and beyond, and provide a very good sense of how dance music was constructed, and how impressive it could sound with a large and elaborate ensemble (though many establishments had much smaller bands). Farid created

Tahia Kariuka and Farid al-Atrash. Still from *Ma'darsh*, directed by Ahmad Badrkhan, 1946 (courtesy Sherif Boraie, ed., *The Golden Years of Egyptian Film: Cinema Cairo, 1936–1967*, Cairo: Zeitouna; Cairo: American University in Cairo Press, 2008, 72).

dance songs with singing as well as purely instrumental numbers, and those with vocals were more popular because audiences were emotionally attracted to lyrics if sung well. The linearity of Farid's pieces, with their many varied sections and recurring refrains, was helpful to a dancer who could highlight different movements or ideas in each section. In those pieces showcasing dancer Samia Gamal, one sees a great deal of choreography and direction, guided by the cinema format. Farid produced and co-starred in *Habib al-'Umr* in 1947 with Samia Gamal, directed by Henri Barakat, which became a huge hit and made him wealthy for a time.

Badi'a also trained many dancers who debuted in group performances and graduated to solo status such as Samia Gamal, who will be discussed again in Chapter Three. She claimed to have employed forty or fifty dancers at a time, including male dancers who performed in group choreographies.[43] Certain special dances were described such as the Village Dance, the Peacock Dance, the Charleston, and dancing using props or veils. Badi'a paid her dancers a small salary at first, seven to ten LE a month, increasing it to fifteen to thirty LE. She gave them costumes and invited them to perform at private parties and weddings, supplying the band. She estimated that she performed at 3,000 to 4,000 weddings with Arabic musicians; she also employed Western musicians at her *sala*, which could function in her absence.[44]

The most elegant *salat* invited women as well as men, but typically also featured a weekly matinée for women (Badi'a's *sala* offered one on Tuesdays) as did venues that screened films. This allowed women to attend in a segregated atmosphere, or as couples, making entertainment more palatable to a conservative public which was

Asmahan and Farid al-Atrash on the poster for the opening of the film *Intisar al-Shabab* (*The Triumph of Youth*), March 24, 1941. Mirroring reality, the brother and sister play two singers, brother and sister, in the film.

still obsessed with preserving female honor. Some women were still heavily covered. For example, Asmahan, when she first began performing, did so in a black *izar*.

Whereas elite men could visit a club, or dance hall, or coffee house, respectable women could only visit elite establishments which served alcohol, so we surmise that no "respectable women" entertained in any, nor visited any others.[45] Nonetheless, elite women were shown in films to drink or have alcohol, as in Salah Abu Seif's 1952 film *Usta Hasan* where Kawthar's (played by Zuzu Madi) refrigerator is stocked with beer.[46]

Male customers employed *fath* (buying drinks for entertainers or bar-girls) "as a ritual of displaying their masculinity and wealth." They enjoyed buying a dozen beers and having many waiters serve them.[47] In one film, Farid al-Atrash plays a musician who wants to escape the shameful atmosphere of such clubs, but Samia Gamal, his co-star, accepts working in such a place, for which he reproaches her and slaps her. Musicians tried hard to escape the club atmosphere for a concert stage, as was achieved only by the most successful, like Umm Kulthum.

Club ownership was a natural expansion of activities for entertainers Shafiqa al-Qibtiyya, Su'ad Mahasan, Badi'a al-Masabni, Na'ima al-Masriyya, Beba 'Izz al-Din, Mary Mansur, Imtithal Fawzy, the Ahmad sisters, and Safiya Hilmy. Safiya Hilmy was an actor and dancer who performed for Badi'a and later bought the Arcadia nightclub. Women entertainers continued to manage establishments on into the next generation of performers as, for example, the dancer Lucy with Parisiana, dancer Mona al-Saʿid (a part owner) at Omar Khayyam in London, and singer Sharifa Fadil with her club, al-Lail.

Salat Masriya was owned by Mary Mansur and was the club where the singer Asmahan first performed in the early 1930s. Mansur then opened a *sala* with Imtithal Fawzy, a dancer and actor, renting a space for this purpose on the roof of the al-Bosfur club. By this time, crime had increased, perhaps due to the impact of the world-wide Depression, and thugs demanded protection money from club owners. A thug (*baltagi*) and crook, Fuʾad al-Shami demanded that Imtithal pay him protection money. She refused, saying she would when it was possible and refused entry to his thugs when she saw they were at the club. One of them, a Kamal al-Hariri, stabbed and hit her. Though wounded, she continued working. Then, another of the thugs killed her some days later. Her story was memorialized in a 1972 film, *Imtithal*, directed by Hassan al-Imam.

Egypt's criminal groups were both Egyptian and foreign, as were prostitutes who might double as *fatihat* (bar girls who are bought drinks by the customers) or dancers. That does not mean that all dancers were *fatihat*, or that all owners were criminals, but that entertainers were surrounded by ambiguity.

The more fortunate singers and singer/actresses/dancers of this era elevated their status to middle-class and became "neo-*ʿawalim*" (Lagrange's term) with "an intricate image of sophistication and gentle debauchery." They no longer used the appellation *ʿalma* (*ʿalima*)[48] but rather *mutriba*.[49] Lagrange also points out that in certain *taqatiq* lyrics, both male and female singers presented debates on the lifestyles of women and girls. This was an era when the idealized New Woman was threatening society with her *sufur* (unveiling). The songs addressed many topics about prospective brides, and their outrageous tastes, and marriage itself, polygamy, and the often-ridiculed notion of working women.[50]

For dancers there was more of a two-tier path, with some attaining a more polished image in the *salat*, and others continuing in the Muhammad ʿAli street *ʿawalim* tradition. Some performed at weddings, at *mawalid*, and also in clubs. Zuba al-Klubtiyya was a Muhammad ʿAli street dancer who danced with the *shamʿadan* (candelabra). She was part of an *ʿawalim* group who found the dancer's Lucy's mother when she got lost as a child, and adopted her, keeping her at home until she married at the age of fifteen. Zuba married three times, and each husband was a musician. She danced in the 1945 film *al-Khamsa Gnai* and with an extremely heavy *shamʿadan*. She claimed to make thirty LE per performance—quite a high fee compared to other dancers.[51] For the sake of comparison, Badiʿa Masabni said that she only made a profit of about 10, 20 or 25 LE per night in her clubs in the late 1930s due to all the expenses and salaries she had to pay, and that later, before she left Egypt (in the early to mid–1940s), her profits were about 50 LE per night.[52]

Egypt's recording industry and changes in musical taste were beneficial to certain performers, and increasingly the radio was important. That Arabic music could be regarded as high art and performed in tasteful public settings was very important to its longevity. Although Badiʿa aspired to and achieved an atmosphere that was comfortable for the elites to attend, as compared to more dangerous or compromised settings, that was unfortunately not how dance was envisioned in comparison to sung music. As the "*sala* scene" hit its height, dance became a less preferred profession than singing or acting, but not automatically so, nor for every performer.

Egyptian radio became a crucial element in musical success, and it promoted both Arabic and Western music. The Arabic music listeners and those organizing radio programs did not agree with each other. Some supported the old repertoire, the Turkish influenced music, or Arabo-Turkic style (*al-qadim*) like Mustafa Reda, director of the Arab Music Institute, and some like composer Midhat Assim preferred (and composed) *al-jadid*, new music. Umm Kulthum, Farid al-Atrash, Asmahan, Fathiyya Ahmad, Laila Murad, and many others sang on the radio.[53]

Decades later, Umm Kulthum and Muhammad 'abd al-Wahhab were remembered as sponsoring "art" and high culture. Yet the dancers of the same period were portrayed in Nasserist-era film often as unfortunate social victims of their milieu.

Umm Kulthum (1904 [est.]–1975), who outshone 'abd al-Wahhab during her lifetime, was born Fatima Ibrahim al-Baltagy. Referred to as "Kawkab al-Sharq" (Planet of the East) "al-Sitt" (the lady), and "Souma" (a short version of her name), she came from the village of Tummay al-Zuhayra. Her father was an *imam* who sang at weddings and *mawalid*; she began to sing with him as a child, dressed as a boy. She moved to Cairo in 1923 where she studied music, poetry, French manners of the wealthy, and improved her image. She was in demand as a singer by the late 1920s, when she competed mainly with Munira al-Mahdiyya and Fathiyya Ahmad (1898–1975) with her Turkish style of singing. Fathiyya appeared in Nagib al-Rihani and Amin Sidki's theater companies, and for many years at Badi'a's sala.

Umm Kulthum starred in the first of six films in 1936 (*Widad*). From 1937 she regularly offered a concert on the first Thursday night of the month, from June to October, and these performances were broadcasted. She began with a *takht* led by composer Muhammad al-Qasabji (who quit her group later for Asmahan) and collaborated with poets and lyricists Ahmad Shawqi, Ahmad Rami, and Bayram al-Tunsi with composer Zakariyya Ahmad, and with composer Riyadh al-Sunbati. She also collaborated on ten songs with 'abd al-Wahhab. She eventually became the head of the musicians' syndicate and sang many patriotic songs as well as romantic and poetic ones and raised money for Egypt after the country's defeat in the June '67 (Six Day) war.

The popularity of music and dance were amplified by the growth of Egypt's film industry, which gave entertainment context and human interest within the country's history and national struggles, and glamorized, professionalized, or criticized the role of entertainers. From 1939 to 1944, one hundred and four films were made; then, from 1945 to 1951, three hundred and sixty-four were produced. Story lines were typically punctuated by music and romantic songs, providing spectacles with dance or theater. Musicians, singers, and dancers often starred in films which featured their talents, and these relied often on some historic and social elements or fictionalized biographies of past entertainers and might show the social class struggles of entertainers.

The silent film *Laila* (1927), directed by 'Aziza Amir, featured a dance sequence by the *'alima*, Bamba Kashar. Amina Mohammed, who danced at Casino Badi'a, acted in nine films, and wrote, directed, and produced *Tita Wong* in 1937. Few other women would have opportunities to direct, but quite a few produced films in which they wished to appear. A star system developed from existing actors, musicians, singers, and dancers. Stars remained very important to cinema's financial viability, even past the Golden Age.

The public was intrigued by characters who selected their own love interests instead of agreeing to arranged marriages. The stars appeared onscreen to value love and freedom, although the requisite happy endings required certain compromises between tradition and the characters' modernist appeal. Another theme in cinema was the contrast between the simple life in the villages, and the temptations and corruptions of the big cities to which many Egyptians were migrating.

Su'ad Husni (1943–2001), half Syrian and half Egyptian, began acting in 1959, playing romantic or socially critical roles as in *Cairo 30* or *Khalli balak min Zuzu*, which showed the difference between elites' and the *awlad al-kar*'s (entertainers) view of dancing. Nadia Lutfi (b. 1937), half Egyptian and half Polish, first appeared in *Sultan* (1958) then in a small role in *Bab al-Hadid*. She also danced in several films including *Abi Foqq al-Shagara* where she mesmerizes 'Abd al-Halim Hafiz. As mentioned, Umm Kulthum, Asmahan, Farid al-Atrash, Tahia Kariuka, Na'ima 'Akif, and Samia Gamal were in many films. Among Farid's co-stars was the previously mentioned Nur al-Huda, a talented singer who was recruited in Lebanon by Yusuf Wahbi and starred in thirty films; she sang over a hundred songs. Laila Murad (1918–1995) made many successful films, as did Shadia (1931 [or 1929]–2017), who eventually "repented" from acting and singing and put on the *hijab*.

Every wedding and party scene in cinema included a solo dance performance or dance numbers with female and sometimes male troupe dancers and music. Onscreen, a dancer might be a repudiated wife, or poor woman who needed to earn an income, as dance was considered less than respectable.[54]

Singing and music were to some degree less suspect than dance. Singer Umm Kulthum and singer/composer 'abd al-Wahhab obtained a neo-classical image, whether through acceptance by the elite or their intricacies of their craft. Dancers also were recognizable as a mediated image of Egyptian culture, yet they retained the suspicious taint of impropriety or direct references to immorality.

For instance, *Khamsa Bab* (Five Doors Bar), starring Nadia al-Gindi as Taragi and 'Adil Imam, concerns singing, dancing, and prostitution in the 1940s in a *hara* (alley, traditional small neighborhood) in Azbakiyya where Kullu Mashi (played by comedian Fu'ad Muhandis) owns a bar. The plot was supposedly based on *Irma La Douce* (by Billy Wilder). Imam plays Mansur, an honest policeman who can't be bribed, but Taragi's pimp 'Abbas (Yusif 'Id) plants drugs on him and gets him fired. Mansur tries to get Taragi to leave her life of prostitution (repent) by disguising himself as a customer, spoofing the accent of a *khawaga* (a non–Egyptian).

Films were made based on the lives of Bamba Kashar and Shafiqa al-Masriyya starring Nadia al-Gindy, Magda al-Khatib, and Safia al-'Amary (also Dalal al-Misriyya from the Cairo Trilogy of Mahfouz). Hind Rustum (called Egypt's Marilyn Monroe for her glamorous appearance) also played in *Shafiqa al-Qibtiyya*, directed by Hassan

Samia Gamal in *Night Train* (Qitar al-Layl), directed by Ezz al-Din Zulfiqar, 1953 (courtesy Sherif Boraie, ed., *The Golden Years of Egyptian Film: Cinema Cairo, 1936–1967*, Cairo: Zeitouna; Cairo and New York: American University in Cairo Press, 2008, 72).

al-Imam (1963). In Farid and Asmahan's debut film, *Intisar al-Shabab* (1941), the two play entertainers who are rejected as marriage partners to the elite, and yet they succeed through their art. Although the seedier image of the *sala* persisted through film, some artists, like Farid al-Atrash, continuously endeavored to professionalize the image of musicians—and dance in his collaborations with Samia Gamal—by presenting them on stage and in formal or beautiful settings, the orchestra in tuxedos or suits with ties.

After Farid al-Atrash halted his partnership with Samia Gamal in 1951, he teamed up with Laila al-Jaza'iriyya (born as Nadia Bougettaya in Oran, Algeria, in 1927 or 1930) whom he met in Paris in several films including *Lahn Hubbi* (1953). He had also appeared with Tahia Kariuka. Additionally, al-Atrash played for Nadia Gamal, whose career was primarily in Lebanon, and Nagwa Fu'ad, who became a big dancing star in the Golden Era of the 1970s. Susi Khairi was another "in-between" era dancer who appeared in films in the late '50s to 1974.

In the 1940s, Western dances and dancers appeared in nightclubs, and couple dancing was popular, even as *raqs sharqi* held its own. Levon Boyodjian, known as Van Leo, was a truly gifted portrait photographer who teamed up with his brother Angelo in 1941 and then separated with him in 1947 and took over Metro Photo Studio. (Angelo hand-signed their photos as Van Leo.) There he took photo portraits

Line of dancers in a Cairo nightclub in the 1940s, photograph by Van Leo (courtesy Shira.net, from the collection of Priscilla Adum).

Chorus line of dancers in a Cairo nightclub, 1940s (courtesy Rare Books and Special Collections Library, The American University in Cairo).

of many celebrities without charge.⁵⁵ The photos on the previous page show Western-style reviews in the clubs.

Thanks to films and photographs, one may perceive a record, although incomplete, of movement styles demonstrating links between *raqs sharqi* and the *'awalim* and *ghawazi* styles of movement. This is apparent in the dancing of Nabawiyya Mustafa, who was popular in the late 40s into the '50s appearing in many films including *'Aida* (1942), *Sirr Abi* (1946), *Sahibat al-'Imara* (1948), *Ana [q]Albi Dalili* (1947), and with Muhammad 'abd al-Mutallib in *Wana Mali*. Nabawiyya typically executes some extremely low back bends, *al-milla* (a back-bend dropping the head all the way to the ground, and which could continue into a drop flat into a "frog" position, though Nabawiyya typically sprang back up again), the splits (*al-fashkha*), and extraordinarily flexible hip work as in *Nargis* (1948) in a *zambalak* (springy, energetic) style.⁵⁶ While dance history aficionados have tended to see "*'awalim*-style" as urban, she was also apparently identified by directors as Queen of the "*baladi*" [style] and cast as a *fallaha* (a peasant dancing in a cotton field) in *Khadhra wa Sindibad al-Qibli* and as a Sa'idiyya (a woman of Upper Egypt) in *Ibn al-Fallah* (1948).⁵⁷

Meanwhile dancers like Tahia Kariuka performed in a very personal style framed by an elegant setting, as were the dancers Katy and Nagwa Fu'ad. Their movements still bear the imprint of the *'awalim* tradition with much focus on the torso and a pleasant presentation of arms and upper body. Other movements that had been linked to the *'awalim*, like the use of floor work, including the above-mentioned *fashkha* and *ghawazi*-like shimmies as in the films showing Nazla al-'Adil. It is fair to say that dance has continued to progress away from this repertoire of movements, but with differing individual styles and degrees of incorporating new movement combinations. One reason was the forbidding of floor work (except in films).

The Nasser era also marked ambivalence about dance and state sponsorship of the arts and cinema, including attempts to shape them into a more socially-conscious, nationalist presentation. The Free Officer's Revolution took Egypt by surprise but had been in its planning stages for two years. The revolution endeavored to end, once and for all, the Western domination of Egypt and presence of British troops in the Suez Canal region. On January 25, 1952, British troops killed fifty Egyptian policemen in Isma'iliyya, when they refused to vacate their station and turn over *fida'yyin* (resistance fighters). This ignited Black Saturday, January 26, 1952, when rioting crowds burned and looted seven hundred and fifty buildings including the Opera House, and establishments thought to be owned by Westerners or which catered to them, like Shepheard's Hotel (founded in 1841). The monarchy was thought to be pro–British and corrupt. The revolution on July 26, 1952, actually took place without violence, being more of a military coup, and the Free Officers abolished the monarchy. Gamal 'abd al-Nasser assumed power after two years, and his principles of Arab socialism, Arab nationalism and anti-colonialism influenced the arts by promoting the image of ordinary Egyptians in folkloric arts and in a type of cinematic realism which portrayed the plight of Egyptians, oppressed by poverty or the British or elites under the monarchy. When Nasser nationalized the properties of many Egyptian business-owners of non–Egyptian backgrounds like Levantines, Greeks, Maltese, or Jews, then many others fled the country. The Egyptian government also periodically went after entertainers thought to have made a great deal of money and to be tax delinquent. In consequence, certain entertainers left the country, among them Badiʻa Masabni, Nelly Mazloum, and eventually Farid al-Atrash.

Nelly Mazloum (Nelly-Catherine Mazloum-Calvo 1923–2003), born in Alexandria to an Italian father and Greek mother, performed modern dance and ballet as a child for Badiʻa's casino, acted and danced in other theaters, and appeared in seventeen films. She established her own ballet school and had a stint as the prima ballerina of the Royal Opera House. She also choreographed folkloric dance for her own troupe which also performed *raqs taʻbiri*, (expressionist dance) from 1955, carrying out field work to stage folkloric dances prior to Mahmoud Reda's efforts. She assisted Alexei Jukov of the Bolshoi in founding Egypt's National Ballet Academy in 1959–1960. She then assisted Boris Ramazen in 1961 in forming the National Folkloric Academy, actually teaching him Egyptian movement. She was driven out of Egypt when the government threatened to nationalize her dance company. She then established the Athens International Dance School and taught ballet, modern dance, and Oriental dance in Greece assisted by her daughter, Marianna (Marhaba). Various *raqs sharqi* performers, like Nagwa Fuʼad, studied with her; therefore, she is important to a transition in dance and cross-over between dance styles.

In 1959, Mahmoud Reda (1930–2020) organized his folkloric dance company, and its female star was Farida Fahmy (Melda Reda), born in 1940 to a British mother and an Egyptian father. Reda, like Mazloum, observed dances in their local setting and then re-choreographed and set them for the stage, making use of his gymnastic training and dramatic sense. His Reda troupe performances were considered wholesome family entertainment, and Farida Fahmy appeared in them as the typical *bint al-balad* (urban lower class woman) or peasant girl in a variety of roles. She obtained a masters degree in dance ethnology and has taught Egyptian dance around the world. Following the formation of the Reda Troupe, the National Ensemble of Folkloric Arts was established, also a dance company, and many regional ensembles were set up.

Golden Era

The so-called Golden Era of Egyptian dance (described in the West from the early '70s through 1979, though Egyptians sometimes speak of the Golden Era as predating Nasser's Egypt) came about as oil revenues increased and five-star hotels put on elaborate evenings of musical and dance performances. This period faltered after the Camp David peace accords with Israel, which resulted in Egypt being thrown out of the Arab League. Gulf patrons ceased traveling to Cairo for about a decade. Also, Islamization, which arrived with the *sahwa Islamiyya* (Islamic revival), impacted Egypt and many local female entertainers ceased performing and were replaced by foreign dancers.

Among the stars of the Golden Era was Nagwa Fuʼad (b. 1943), born ʻAwatif Muhammad ʻAjami in Alexandria to a Palestinian mother from Nablus and an Egyptian father. Her mother died, and her father remarried. She began dancing at Sahara

A young Nagwa Fu'ad in rehearsal with the al-Firqa al-Qawmiyya al-Funun al-Sha'biyya, January 15, 1962 (courtesy Hytham M. Hammer).

City (a large nightclub in Giza) after being discovered by a theatrical agent, and then got her first real break at the Auberge des Pyramids nightclub.[58] She trained in Nelly Mazloum's dance school and in the Firqat Qawmiyya. She had already married composer/musician Ahmad Fu'ad Hassan, seventeen years her senior, who helped her career. Thanks to him, she was able to dance in "Adwa' al-Madina," the 1960s stage show.[59] Her use of Fu'ad Hassan's music was quite significant to her success. His Diamond orchestra survived for forty years, and his dance compositions (due to both their reputations) were among the most well-known and influential for dancers both inside and outside of Egypt; certain among them are still played.

Nagwa also became famous through a film, *Shari'a al-Hubb*, with the singer 'Abd al-Halim Hafiz (1929–1977). She then remarried to Sami al-Zughby, an area manager of the Sheraton hotel in 1974. She was coached by choreographer Muhammad Khalil which helped her personalize her dancing style and was a boon to her career.[60]

'Abd al-Halim Hafiz was born as 'Abd al-Halim Shabana in al-Hilwat in Sharqiyya province. When his mother died, he lived in an orphanage and then with relatives in Cairo where he studied voice, the oboe, and other instruments at the Higher Music Institute. He was booed off the stage in his first concert in Alexandria in 1951 as he sang "Safini Marra" (a story has it that he fainted and had to go to the hospital). He got his first big break on the radio in 1953, filling in for singer Karim Mahmud

(1922–1995), and appeared in films as a romantic singing lead from 1955 to 1969. He sang in an emotional and modern style, with lyrics that were closer to popular folk songs than others had been. He was identified with the age of Nasserism and sang compositions by Muhammad Mugi, Muhammad 'abd al-Wahhab, Baligh Hamdi and many others.

In *Shari'a al-Hubb*, Hafiz plays the role of a *hasabullah* band musician who becomes an educated artist. Following this film appearance, Fu'ad danced as an opener to 'Abd al-Halim's concerts. Muhammad 'abd al-Wahhab composed "Qamar al-Arba'tashar" for her in 1976. Her performances were elaborate, artistic experiences including excellent musicians and a male and female dance chorus. Her athletic frame was complemented by a somewhat angular face. By the time I observed her shows, she had the reputation of being a "dancer's dancer"

Dancer Nagwa Fu'ad with singer 'Abd al-Halim Hafez playing the *as-sakit* (a *daff*). From "Daff wa Guitar," *al-Shabaka*, 1971. Taken at the wedding party of guitarist 'Omar Khurshid to Amina al-Subki held at the Cairo Hilton and attended by Umm Kulthum, at which singer Sherifa Fadil sang. The party then moved to the Auberge Nightclub. It was attended by Suhair Zaki, Zizi Mustafa, Muhammad al-'Izabi, Su'ad Husni, Sherihan, and many more luminaries of Egyptian music and cinema (courtesy Hytham M. Hammer).

(more famous for her skill than her beauty).[61] Many other dancers emulated her opening choreographies with choruses and continue to do so today.

The songs composed for 'Abd al-Halim also became standards in dance music for *raqs sharqi*, often in an abbreviated form. This occurred after the novelty of the recordings wore off and because not all dancers had music original to their shows, though that was expected of the more popular performers. Strongly radiating emotions (*ihsas*) were part of his appeal, and that carried through to his songs even without his presence.

Suhair Zaki (b. 1944 or 1945) was another major dancing star. She was born in Mansoura, moving first to Alexandria, then to Cairo. She appeared on television and in over one hundred films. She danced for many heads of state and was reportedly admired by Anwar al-Sadat. Her performances were simpler in format than Nagwa's; she did not rely on choreographers and did not include a dance chorus. Her arm movements were more restrained and her hip movements were very articulated and complex. She occasionally used music written for singer Umm Kulthum in her routines, most notably in a brief interlude in the 1974 film *Layali Lan ta'ud*, where it was probably selected by the film's director. However, most other artists did not use this music at that time. Nagwa Fu'ad disclaimed rumors that they competed. She insisted that they appear together in her program "Maktabat Nagwa."[62] Suhair married Muhammad 'Amara and retired in 1992 after being pursued, as many artists were, for back taxes. An American belly dancer Dahlena (approximately the second generation of dancers there as she started out in 1959) recorded Suhair's band's music from her Versailles show from 1981 in Egypt in 1991, and thereafter it was used in stage performances outside of Egypt, even recently. In particular, the driving percussion section and *tabla* solos were appreciated. Other dancers and musicians have also traveled to Egypt to record during brief visits. Today this Golden Age music when played at festivals accompanies a very different style of dancing than Suhair's.

Nelly Fu'ad, a star of the 1970s, was born in Alexandria and took her Armenian grandmother's name as a stage name. She joined an *'awalim* troupe trained by Sinaya at the age of thirteen. She filled in for Suhair Zaki in a stage production and that led her to Cairo where she danced in five-star hotels and in films. She also performed in Farid al-Atrash's nightclub in Lebanon for a year.

Fifi 'Abdu, was born 'Atiyat 'Abd al-Fattah Ibrahim, April 26, 1953, in Cairo (or possibly outside of Cairo). She danced at the Arizona Club, al-Lail, and major hotels in the 1970s. A dynamic performer, she displayed tremendous energy in her show. She has been identified with *bint al-balad* due to her *shisha* tableau, in which she smokes, flirts, and dances and subsequent film and television roles. She continued acting after semi-retiring from dance, frequently cast as a loud, strong-minded *bint al-balad* and is still performing at private events. She teaches dance and is enjoying a revival of interest in her thanks to her use of social media.

'Azza Sharif (1947–2019) began dancing at the age of eighteen in Cairo, then in Lebanon, England, and Germany, and then returned to the Mena House in Giza and performed frequently in Beirut prior to the Lebanese civil war. She appeared in twenty-one films including *Khalli Balak min Zuzu* and *Nibtidi Mnain al-Hikaya* and married Kat-Kut al-Amir, the drummer who became a *sha'bi* singer.

Hayatim (July 22, 1950–2018), Nahid Sabry and Nadia Hamdi will be discussed in Chapter Three. Zizi Mustafa danced in numerous films from the 1960s into the 1980s and with *sha'bi* star, Ahmad 'Adawiyya. She is not as well known outside of Egypt as the superstars and some dancers mentioned in Chapter Three. Her daughter is the actress Mena Shalabi.

Following the Golden Age, Egypt underwent several political crises that impacted the field of entertainment. To go slightly out of chronology, we must not forget that the Khedivial Opera House was burned completely to the ground on the

October 28, 1971, and that crime was never solved. The National Theater was burned down in 2008, and the Institut d'Égypte containing very important archives was burned in 2011. A great cultural struggle between Egyptians, mostly over the role of religion in political life (though also due to lack of political freedom), has flared up periodically.

In 1974, President Anwar Sadat introduced economic reforms known as the Infitah or open door economic policy, aimed at increasing investments. The World Bank and the IMF urged Egypt to cancel some of its subsidization of foods, which helped the population meet their needs. The bread riots broke out in January 1977 in multiple cities, and in Cairo, Islamists were among those who attacked and burned nightclubs on Haram Street, calling them symbols of corruption. An underground Islamist organization, Gama'at al-Muslimin, more widely known as Takfir wa al-Higra, kidnapped the Minister of Awqaf and then assassinated him when the government would not release their members in captivity. Sadat regained control after mass arrests but earned the enmity of many Islamists. He additionally antagonized them and other Egyptians by signing the Camp David Treaty and traveling to Jerusalem to speak to the Knesset. For these reasons he was assassinated in 1981. The Egyptian government pursued fairly harsh policies against the Islamists, but their numbers grew. Meanwhile other dancers rose to fame but in a markedly different environment.

Mona al-Sa'id was born Mona Ibrahim Wafa' in the Suez Canal Zone (c. 1954) to Bedouin parents from the Sinai oasis of Musa who came to Cairo. She was "discovered" at age 12 by Anwar Amar, the owner of Sahara City, and the singer Laila Murad. She danced for two months at Sahara City and then fled her father's wrath, dancing for five years at Casino Lebanon in Beirut, then the Cairo Meridien for a year, then in London where she bought the Omar Khayyam club. She was known for her composure, graceful arms, and height (5'11"). The musicians who worked with her in London were among the first to introduce the "new" Egyptian style of music for dancers to the United States and Europe, along with compositions first played for Nagwa Fu'ad and others.

Lucy Sa'd is another dancer linked to the Muhammad 'Ali street tradition, although most other dancers are today actually foreigners, and by the time she began dancing, most were not from the traditional entertainment families (the *awlad al-kar*). Born En'am Sa'd Muhammad 'Abd al-Wahhab circa 1960 in Cairo, she grew up in the Old City near Muhammad 'Ali street. Her mother had been rescued by Zuba al-Klubtiyya and married into her family. She is still performing at the time of writing and is the owner of the nightclub Parisiana. Drummer Hossam Ramzy considered her the best dancer of *baladi* style (as contrasted with *raqs sharqi*), although he also praised Nagwa Fu'ad's *baladi* styling in particular performances.

As will be explained in Chapter Five, *sha'bi* (urban lower-class) music is deeply entangled with and vital to Egyptian dance. In addition to the compositions of 'Abd al-Wahhab, Farid, Ahmad Fu'ad Hassan, and those who composed for 'Abd al-Halim were many other *sha'bi* songs, or songs adapted from folklore or traditional melodies. In the 1970s, *sha'bi* music became more popular through the low cost of audio cassette tapes and the great success of the singer Ahmad al-'Adawiyya, despite his being banned from radio and television. Also, the ease of the re-recording process as a cottage industry boosted sales. Most *sha'bi* singers were/are men (Hassan al-Asmar, Kat-Kut, Hakim, Sha'ban 'abd al-Rahim and his son 'Imad, Sa'd al-Soghayar, Ramadan Prince [I and II], and Mahmud al-Laithy).

During the Golden Era, quite a few dancers added a *sha'bi* or other folkloric dance to follow their *raqs sharqi* routine. In such a routine, the dancer typically wore a *galabiyya* or what became known in dancer parlance as a *baladi* dress. The music might feature a brief *mawwal* (vocal improvisation) or jump to a song, and possibly include a *baladi* progression, an improvised interaction between a melody instrument such as the accordion with the *tabla*. The Queen of Baladi is Fatma Sarhan, who sang both rural folk music (*musiqa sha'biyya*) and urban-based *sha'bi* music. She regularly performed with dancers Nagwa Fu'ad and Dina Tal'at in such segments.

During the 1970s, Egypt's sector for classical music, opera, ballet, classical Arabic music, theater, and contemporary visual arts expanded and solidified as institutes and the conservatory trained musicians, singers, artists, and actors. Many worked at the Opera, which later referred to the complex of the Cairo Opera House at the National Culture Center in Gezira. At the same time, many musicians were not formally trained, or only partially formally trained. Some found employment at the Balloon Theater in Agouza, which provided them a steady salary (women musicians as well as men) as was true of the dancers on the rolls of the folkloric ensembles. Such venues, along with radio, television, cinema, other non-state funded theaters, hotels, nightclubs and private events constituted the entertainment sector.

As the Golden Age singers died, Farid al-Atrash in 1974, Umm Kulthum in 1975, and 'Abd al-Halim Hafiz in 1977, the centrality of Egypt's recording industry shifted with the growth of a recording industry in the Gulf. Egyptians' musical preferences changed, and the music video clip came to dominate via satellite television. In the 1980s and beyond, music fans were attracted to *shababiyya*, or youth music, and not the neoclassical sound of earlier in the century. The Egyptian *shababi* singers often signed with the Gulf-based company Rotana, competing with other "pop" music singers from other Arab countries. Most popular in Egypt by the mid–2000s of the female *shababiyya* singers were Ruby, Shirin 'Abd al-Wahhab, Nancy Ajram, Haifa Wahbe, and Angham. Fans of these singers were not always (typically not) fans of *sha'bi* or *raqs sharqi*.

One could actually consider some of the male singers of *shababiyya* to represent popular Egyptian music, and certain *sha'bi* themes are included in their music. However, they have not been analyzed as such in the Western literature on music, but rather, in light of their financial success in the greater Arab world, perceived as "pan-Arab" singers. Here, I have 'Amr Diab in mind, whose songs certainly allude to numerous Egyptian themes, but admittedly within a cleaner and more predictable sound, larger ensemble, and bigger budget than many *sha'bi* singers.

Earlier, the musicians' syndicate and the government tried to punish or censor the sexiness of female singers' video or film appearances, particularly Ruby (Rania Husain Muhammad Tawfiq, b. 1981) and Haifa Wahbe (b. 1976, she is half Egyptian and half Lebanese). Nancy Ajram (b. 1983) was considered the top Middle Eastern artist for the decade ending 2010. Her career took off with a new and sexier image around 2003; she remains extremely popular in Egypt and has recorded certain Egyptian-style hits in Egyptian Arabic, although she is Lebanese. These performers' music videos were in some cases deemed so suggestive when released, that they were banned, and they led overall to an emphasis on sexuality in video or film clips of dancers.

At the same time, the growing religious revival had an impact on the state-supported arts. Live *raqs sharqi* was banned from Egyptian television channels. However older films could be broadcast. As satellite channels proliferated, some included live dance and dance clips and will be discussed in Chapter Eight.

The newest music styles in Egypt are called *mulid* (a type of *sha'bi* music) and *mahragan* (see Chapters Four and Five). Male singers dominate these two genres, but women dance to both.

Egypt's dance scene was severely affected by the retirement of many female performers in the "repentance" movement spurred by increasing Islamization of society which began in the mid–1980s. Singers, actresses, and dancers publicly denounced or repented of their entertainment careers, quit, and adopted the *hijab*. Simultaneously, many dancers' jobs were replaced by non–Egyptian performers from the countries of the former Soviet bloc and elsewhere. Visually, the current scene also has been affected by a global emphasis on physical perfection via cosmetic surgery and a quite athletic style of dancing generally blamed on foreign dancers, but which many Egyptian dancers also perform.

The top Egyptian dancer in the country at the time of writing was Dina. Dina Tal'at Sayed Muhammad (b. 1964 in Rome) has a master's in philosophy from 'Ain al-Shams university. She began dancing in the Mahmoud Reda troupe in the '70s and performed *raqs sharqi* in the 1980s, becoming a major star in the '90s. Early in her career, she worked in Yemen. She has written an autobiography, *Hurriyati fi-al-raqs* (2011, appearing in French as *Ma liberté de danser*). Dina was considered wildly controversial for several reasons. First, and foremost was simply her employment as a very popular *raqs sharqi* artist. Secondly, she wore quite daring, that is, revealing costumes. There is a style of bra cup named after her designed to show maximum cleavage. Thirdly, there was a scandal over a pornographic film made and circulated of her by her vengeful ex-husband, a vicious form of harassment which has become common in Morocco as well as Egypt. Fourthly, she has a unique dance style which looks far simpler than it is to execute, and this will be described in Chapter Three. All of this has simply added to her popularity.

Dandash is one of the last Egyptian dancers to perform in an authentic and individual style, less influenced by the athleticism of the foreign dancers. She is from Alexandria, where her parents were a singing duo, and began dancing at age seven. Her family traveled to perform in Mansura and Sunbat, where she saw Sunbati *ghawazi*, and she was also influenced by the Cairo *'awalim* style. She says she idolized Suhair Zaki and mimics some of her movements in her "Manga" routine, where she demonstrates a few seconds of the signature moves of Tahia Kariuka, Nagwa Fu'ad, Suhair, Dina, Samia Gamal, and Sahar (Hamdi)—these are announced by her singer, in case the audience was in any doubt, and then her own complex style.

Raqia Hassan may currently be the top, or most well-known, teacher of dance of Egypt, and is primarily connected with dancers from outside of Egypt. She was a soloist with the Mahmoud Reda troupe and later began teaching *raqs sharqi*. She has taught or worked with 'Azza Sharif, Mona al-Sa'id, Nani, Nelly Fu'ad, Dina, Amani, Soraya, Dandash, and Randa Kamel and produces an annual international festival, Ahlan wa Sahlan, attended by foreign dancers in Egypt. Randa Kamel (b. 1976) also performed with the Reda Troupe for seven years and began dancing *raqs sharqi* in Alexandria and then in Cairo. She remains a top performer, including in 2016 and 2017 on the *Nile Maxim*, one of the cruising Nile boats which caters to tourists, and she teaches internationally. 'Aida Nur has also taught internationally, although she was more active in the early 2000s.

Safinaz (born in 1983 as Sofinar Grigoryan) is a very popular Armenian dancer in Egypt. She appeared in films since 2013 with video clips on the channel *Dalaa*. She was sentenced in 2015 for wearing a costume made to look like the Egyptian flag, but this sentence was overturned. Her fans admire her for her chest pops (a punctuated lifting and dropping of the rib cage) and cheerful exuberance despite some comments that she includes vulgar movements.

At the time of writing, the Egyptian dancers who perform frequently and are most popular are Dina, Lucy (described above), Shams, Amani, Camelia (al-Eskandaraniya), Bardees, Maya Maghraby, 'Aziza, Shakira El Masri, Sahar Samara, Kawakib, Randa Kamel, Amie Sultan (a former ballet dancer now performing *raqs sharqi*), Kawkab al-Fann, Nany, and others. The most popular foreign dancers are Safinaz (Sofinar Grigoryan), Oxana Bazaeva (Russian), Alla Kushnir (Ukrainian), Shahrzad (American), Soraya (Brazilian), Mercedes Nieto (Hungarian), Magdalena, Johara (Ekaterina Andreeva, Russian), Luna (Diana Esposito, American), Farah Nasri (French Algerian), Brenda, Anna, Magdalena, Maris, Sonya, and Lorna. Quite a few of these dancers have altered their appearances to have a slim body, large breasts, long straight hair (or wearing extensions or hair pieces to achieve this), or they adapted to this expectation after a few years. Some wear tinted contact lenses to change the color of their irises, and owners and managers prefer dancers of lighter skin tones. Not all dancers are on this list. Leila Farid (American) was highly praised by Egyptians. She worked mostly as a wedding dancer and co-ran Camp Negum but is now in America. Khairiyya bint Mazin is the only remaining well-known *ghaziya*, and Farida Fahmy was the best known of folkloric dancers. Egyptians, even those who do not attend dance shows, know of certain dancers, whereas foreign dancers are aware of others, particularly if they travel abroad to teach including male dancers (discussed below) such as Tito Seif, Mohamed Shahin, Karim Nagi, the above-mentioned 'Aida Nur, Randa Kamel, Raqia Hassan and some others.

The pool of performers has greatly decreased. Dina had estimated that only one hundred dancers are now licensed for *raqs sharqi* (perhaps this number is restricted to Egyptians) whereas at one time, there were five thousand.

The numbers of nightclubs/bars, which in addition to five-star establishments had offered *raqs sharqi*, have greatly decreased in downtown Cairo and on Shari'a Haram. Many Egyptians moved out of the downtown area years ago, and the bars and nightclubs that hosted intellectuals or music-lovers closed and crumbled. Speaking of the King Faruq era, novelist 'Alaa al-Aswany (author of *The Yacoubian Building*) observed: "They were part of an Egypt that doesn't exist any more. This Egypt was very liberal, very tolerant. You had the bars. You had the synagogues. You had the mosques. Everyone was absolutely allowed to practice religion, to go and drink or whatever."[63] To placate the growing number of Islamists, the government made it more difficult to renew licenses to sell alcohol. Bar operators are now mostly Christian, whereas in the history of the beer industry as described by Omar Foda, numerous Muslims ran bars and clubs.[64] The lower ranked police made problems for bar owners, harassing their customers. The five-star hotels still offer *raqs sharqi*, as do several Nile boats, such as the Nile Maxim, the Nile Pharaoh, the Crystal Nile boat, and some remaining night clubs on the Haram (Pyramids) Road.

In addition to the attacks on nightclubs and hotels in 1952, and in 1977 mentioned above, the low-grade civil war between Islamists and police which smoldered through the 1980s and 1990s took a toll on entertainment. During Egypt's revolution in 2011, some establishments were also attacked by thugs (*baltagiyya*) including Lucy's club, the Parisiana, just prior to the announcement that Hosni Mubarak would be forced to step down. This was not because sinful dancers perform there but because of the growing tendency to associate clubs with Western influence, though they were fully Egyptian-operated, as well as the propaganda of the *sahwa*, the Islamic revival, against music and dance. It may sound conspiracist, but many Egyptians were hired to attack the revolutionaries in Tahrir, and amongst those hired, rumors spread that Western countries had somehow instigated the 2011 revolution.

Male dancers were and sometimes remain unable to pursue careers in Egypt without harassment or interference because of the stigma toward homosexuality. Men perform folkloric dance but performing *raqs sharqi* whether in female or male costume was frowned on. However, with a demand for male dancers in the West since the 1970s that has transferred to competition venues, establishments with live music are more uncommon. In the early 2000s, former folklore dancer Khalil Khalil danced for tourists and internationally, and Khalid Mahmoud, Tito Seif, and others mostly danced internationally. In 2008, Farid Mesbah was performing as a dancer, and Mahmoud Karim danced, although he pretended to be a customer in case there were objections from the audience.[65] Tito, as was true of many other performers, male and female, began in folkloric dance (see Chapter Six) and then moved to *raqs sharqi* where his dynamic choreographies and masculine appeal earn him admirers.[66] Teaching, coaching, and choreographing *raqs sharqi* provide a secondary career for some dancers who offer international workshops[67] like Muhammad Shahin. In fact, many male teachers who were formerly folkloric dancers have also taught or coached Egypt's female dancers and other dancers, whether foreigners or college folkloric ensembles, such as Ibrahim 'Akif and Mahmoud Reda, also Faruq Mustafa and Mo Geddawi.

The latest advent on the Egyptian scene are dance clubs in which dancers perform in extremely skimpy costumes and suggestive styling to *sha'bi, mulid* or *mahragan* music. Dancers are not observing the official costume regulations, and the dance area may be a pen close to the audience or near or atop a bar. These opened up, either separately or within existing clubs and boats, after the 2011 revolution when many curfews had limited performances. Christine Sahin interviewed dancer Amie Sultan who said that in these clubs:

They'd tell me to stop dancing so much! They said just be sexy and give a wink here and there, twiddle my hair, and stop trying to be so classic. There wasn't even a stage or space for me to move! They paid peanuts, and the crowd was all A-class elites mostly high on ecstasy looking for somewhere to go out.[68]

These are essentially no more shocking than the appearances of dancers at lower-class weddings in past decades wearing *badlat* (the bra and belt of the costume) with short skirts or none at all, or *baladi* dresses, or some of the current costumes and movements in cabarets. One difference results from the release and circulation of videos of such dancers taped on cell-phones. Egyptians patronize these clubs, although there remain five-star venues which offer a more respectable version of *raqs sharqi*. The degree of influence of one type of venue on the other is unclear, but dancers complain of managers and customers who demand an aggressively sexy performance. Dancers also complain about each other if this is how they perform. Have the more salacious tastes of customers and athletic tastes of foreign dancers on the competition circuit indelibly influenced *raqs sharqi* performers?

Far into the Golden Age, one could see a visual connection between the dance styles of the "Sala Age" and the earlier *'awalim* and *ghawazi*, sometimes in specific references or movement vocabulary. With today's dancers, that is not always the case. In a recent, short film on dance, Dina and Nagwa Fu'ad were interviewed. Both defended their lives and creativity in dance but were extremely critical of the overt sexual moves and those derived from striptease in use at the present in other dancers' *raqs sharqi* routines and in "club dancing" and contrasted these with the spirit of the Golden Age.[69] Yet both of these dancers were at one time (or remain, in Dina's case) on the receiving end of criticism about their own sexual appeal. If one gives credence to these kind of comments, or contrasts old with modern performances, it seems that the true emotions and mood or *mazag* of the *sala* ended in the Golden Age, except for the nostalgia of certain radio stations, musical programs, and aficionados of Arabic music who may include references to it in theatrical and musical performances, and film. Yet, even Golden Age performances were rooted in commercialism.

In the next chapter, I will depart from this historical overview of the dance and discuss a key aspect of popular Egyptian dance which may be seen in different decades and settings and which distinguishes it from the heavily athleticized competition, festival circuits, and much of current dancing styles, *dall'a* which uses flirtatiousness and coquettishness.

Three

Ya Dall'a, Ya Dall'a

Demeanor and Flirtation

As this book's purpose is not only to provide an overview of *raqs sharqi*, but also to explicate its popular meaning and variations of popular dance and dance music, I will focus on one special quality or aspect of dancing in this chapter. With the international adoption of *raqs sharqi* as a competitive dance form serving as the draw for commercial festivals, the increase in the numbers of foreign dancers in Egypt, the exodus of some Egyptian dancers from entertainment, and the fact that others make more money teaching outside of Egypt than they do performing there, the changes in nightclubs' practices, song styles, and performance formats, criticisms have mounted of dancers as being "too sexy," "too sleazy," "too suggestive," and "too foreign." One may also observe dancers who perform without soul or emotion or whose facial emoting is suspect. Outside of Egypt, this may be because teachers instruct dancers in the expressions to adopt, as foreign dancers do not initially comprehend the lyrics. In a competition or workshop framework, with brief performances, it may be over-reaching to expect dancers to attend to the emotional aspect of presentation. Most have not had the experience of nightly performance that is still available to dancers in Cairo, Egypt. Yet, just as Arabic music aficionados expect *sidq* (sincerity) from a *mutrib/a*, dance fans would like to sense it in a dancer. Inside of Egypt, it is more often the case that a dancer's show could unevenly express emotion, since as one complained of having to add hundreds of "steps" as the foreign dancers do, and some shows are lengthy variety acts.

The absence or presence of *dall'a* or being or not being *dalal* (coquettish or adorable) is something that Egyptians and Arabs note about women in general, and foreign women in particular, in daily life, and therefore, also in dance, singing, and cinema. The sensuality of dance is admired by women as well as men. Yet there are numerous red lines that must not be crossed in its expression. *Dall'a* is a very complex quality imparted by a dancer, singer, or actress. It involves flirting in a feminine rather than a sexual manner: playing with the music itself, the musicians, and the audience. Rather than a set of movements, it is an attitude, a presence, and a style of oral or danced communication. It requires viewers or an audience or a recipient. The adorable one interacts with her target or object of affections. Interaction in and of itself is a key quality of an excellent performance, between dancer and audience, and dancer and her musicians. The additional element of flirtation is important.

This quality is not possessed by all dancers, even great dancers. It is very significant for at least two related reasons. Flirting is a way of acknowledging the importance of male-female relations, which in Egypt are limited. Sexual relationships are forbidden except for those within legal marriages. Men and women do communicate and have other types of relationships, as urban society is not as strictly segregated by sex as outsiders may think. Secondly, this aspect of performance is a part of dance's invocation of sex in a ritual manner, due to its "embodiment," which has long been among its functions, indeed, since ancient times.

Many Egyptians—including dance ethnologist Magda Saleh, and dance teacher, Mohammed Shahin—attribute their dance to the ancient Egyptians. Egyptians do not usually ascribe the dance to Western inspiration (as have some belly dance and dance historians). The sacred and sexual use of dance before Islam existed in many other ancient cultures, not only Egypt. A few aspects of ancient Egyptian dance, its costuming and context, were described in Chapter One. To reiterate, dancers were a professional group or caste. Some similarities like plaited hair, ribbons, or garlands on their heads, and the use of *kohl* to darken the eyes, carry over to the present day, as does dancing with a cane, a stick, or the use of *sagat* (finger cymbals) and tambourines.

Some ancient holidays survived from ancient Egypt such as Sham al-Nassim ("smell the breeze," but close to the Coptic name), the spring festival, and Lailat al-Nuqta, the night before the annual flooding of the Nile. Sham al-Nassim invoked fertility as well, and in outdoor picnics held then, Egyptians eat *fasikh* (smelly pickled fish), dyed eggs, and green onions, and celebrate the burgeoning of life in the spring with music and dance. Dancers have throughout the centuries been hired for wedding celebrations, where the performance of a dancer was considered good luck, to ensure fertility, and to be necessary for the enjoyment of all. They sometimes performed at the *sabu'a*, a party held the seventh day after a baby's birth when the baby is placed in a *ghurbal*, a sieve (once made of leather, now made and decorated commercially), to drain out any bad spirits, and the celebration announces the baby's gender. A special clay jug of a specific shape, female or male, is decorated for a girl or a boy. Candles are lit and songs are sung to the banging of a mortar and pestle. Dancers were hired for the *mawalid* (saint's day festivals) although not for some decades. Instead today, ordinary people dance, or sometimes the *tannura* (spinning dervishes, see Chapter Six) dancers perform. Dancing may be performed in *zars* (rituals of exorcism, or communication with spirits). All of these celebrations have ritual aspects. Dancing also relates to the performance of gender.

Gender is seen in Egypt and Arab society as being the performance and fulfillment of complementary traits. Men and women are not thought to be equal nor similar (even if women argue for equal rights with men). Naturally, this is not as simplistic, nor as binary, as one might think. As Judith Butler wrote, "Gender is also the discursive/cultural means by which 'sexed nature' or 'a natural sex' is produced and established as 'prediscursive,' prior to culture, a politically neutral surface on which culture acts."[1]

In my earlier research with hundreds of Egyptian women, I found they emphasized biological, physical, emotional, and social differences between the sexes in their discourse, even though women's public roles have been changing rapidly for the last 120 years. This was true across the board for women whether they espoused liberal or Islamist values and despite variations in their class backgrounds.[2]

Femininity is defined in Egypt in terms of qualities of gentleness, sensitivity, caring, sweetness, compassion, tolerance, nurturance, deference, and long-suffering patience. Aggressiveness towards peers or anyone threatening her chastity may be encouraged in a girl. However, a child who wants to copy her brothers' behavior, cross-dress, or act in a masculine manner is a cause of great concern. *Dall'a* expresses the opposite, a teasing appeal through femininity. That quality could apply to a covered woman, not only to the uncovered dancer, or to a toddler or a cute child.

Women are expected to be virgins at marriage and chaste wives, and their male relatives consider women's sexual behavior to reflect their family's honor, *sharaf*. Nonetheless, a man wants his ideal woman to be alluring to him, so the fact that many marriages were arranged could complicate the acquisition of a woman with these aspirational feminine traits. Although the Western Madonna-whore complex is not really very similar to the way that women are idealized in Egypt,[3] the good wife and the very problematic dancer are two contrasting sides of women. A woman who strongly flirts with everyone, rather than being flirted with, is considered to be *la'biyya* (this has a very negative connotation for a woman, that she runs after all men). And, while a woman may not flirt off-stage, she is considered to be encouraging business and her fans by flirting onstage and will be pursued by males and attract tips (of money). As seen in Chapter One, women's "aimless" movement in the Cairene streets was made illegal, but men are permitted to walk about as a leisure activity.

I also mentioned in Chapter One that ever since Egypt's hostile encounter with the West in the Napoleonic invasion, and the chronicler al-Jabarti's writing about the differences between Western women and Egyptian women, serious debate raged over the idealized comportment of women. To al-Jabarti, Western women were immodest, and it appalled him that Westerners' less constrained behavior towards men could be adopted by Egyptians.

In Egypt, the overwhelming social expectation is that a woman must marry. This is borne out in statistics. An unmarried woman has limited social power; though her mobility has increased, she cannot live alone—an unmarried aunt, a widow or a divorced woman usually returns to live with their own family members. Women who live alone are strongly criticized.[4] Indeed, most people believe all men as well as women should marry. A common saying is "*al-zawaj nisf al-din*," marriage is half of religion, meaning Islam (the value pertains as well to Egyptian Christians). Parents are obsessed with getting their daughters and sons married off; however, the male usually proposes. Sometimes the bride's family does, hence the expression "*akhtob l-bintak wa matakhtobsh li-ibnak*" (get your daughter engaged, but don't get your son engaged).

Women are expected to rely on their husbands or other men for economic support. For example, Sayyid Henkish, the subject of Karin van Nieuwkerk's study into masculine ideals, repeatedly expressed his responsibility to provide for his wife and not permit her to work.[5] This ideal is complicated by an economic reality in which increasingly more households are primarily headed by women,[6] or families for whom women's income from work is essential.

To marry, a woman must be a virgin, and she should as swiftly as possible after marriage bear children and be an ideal mother. This is in addition to any career goals she might have. There is (ideally) no substitution of career for marriage. As a woman is defined by her relationship with men and as a parent, she may use the name Umm Khalid, mother of Khalid (the name of her first-born son, or daughter if she has no son) as her name instead of her own first name.

The process of marital engagement in Egypt is lengthy, from an initial meeting and possible flirting—not as overt as is stereotyped in dance or film—perhaps in a "group date" or at a gathering. The families negotiate. Then, in a ceremony with the reading of the first verse of the Qur'an, they are betrothed. A party is held and rings are exchanged.[7] During the earlier stages of engagement, the groom agrees to a specified *mahr* or bride price, and that he may present his fiancée with other gold jewelry, and requirements specified by her family such as the purchase or building of a flat, perhaps a car, and the cost and location of a wedding party. The bride must acquire the *gihaz*—furniture (although sometimes she may demand this of a man nowadays), appliances, jewelry, china, bedding, and her own wardrobe. In a village setting, or a traditional urban neighborhood, her *gihaz* has its own *zaffa*, or procession to the new marital abode, accompanied by music. The *zaffa* used to process with animals, and later in open lorries, so everyone in the neighborhood could see what the bride had acquired and was transporting. A very expensive wedding party may be required, possibly in a hotel, and these might be composed of events in several stages including a *zaffa* of the groom, and finally the consummation of the marriage. The only possible love object is a fiancée; the only legitimate romantic encounter is a marriage or engagement. Anything else carries severe consequences. Hence, anthropologist Samuli Schielke noted that flirting is the most dangerous avenue by which young men may deal with boredom, for it can lead to "unhappy love stories,"[8] and requires concealment; indeed, it must be kept secret.[9] Contrast these restrictions with flirting onstage, a reasonable performance of the forbidden.

Sometimes, a man simply cannot meet the financial promises he has made to his fiancée's family, and the engagement is broken off. This is considered a bad outcome or bad luck, as is divorce. Women and men generally want to avoid divorce, although for different reasons. Men, at least those of lower income, do not wish to divorce in part because of the cost of marriage. Families also worry about the devaluation of a divorced woman as a future bride. It was quite easy for a man to divorce, via *talaq*, but was very difficult for a woman to obtain a divorce until legal reforms agreed on in 2000,[10] and even in the form of divorce then sanctioned, she gave up her rights to the deferred portion of the *mahr* and had to return gifts. Today, many men's popular perception is that women use engagements and then a divorce as a way of obtaining income.

With marriage as the most important and carefully negotiated rite of passage in one's life, flirting is a way of responding to possibly eligible men. Women may or may not otherwise have much influence over the identity of her groom. If her marriage is arranged, she has a veto right, which is not always exercised. At the same time, her reputation can be ruined if anyone flirts overtly, or makes verbal insinuations against her. A woman may ignore the flirting, or even attack the flirter verbally and physically if she believes that his advances could diminish her reputation. A woman can be very strong, a bit domineering, and yet she is expected to interact with men in a feminine manner, meaning she should try to charm them into doing what she wants and uphold society's expectations of her as a female.

Social class enters into this equation of flirting and influencing the choice of a partner, or even how flirting is ritualized. Egypt is strongly divided by social class (as are other Arab countries) into the divisions of *fallahin*, (rural peasants); *awlad al-balad* (urban lower class); and *awlad al-zawat* (elite or former elite). These also reflect the social divisions in Egypt: the former two categories make up the *'amma* (the masses, common people) and the latter, who come from different occupational groups or were hereditary and later elected officials, are the *khassa* (also meaning elite).

The *fallaha*, the country or village girl, wears a modest *galabiyya* (long dress) and covered her hair with a *tarha* before the popularity of the *hijab* increased. The great twentieth century singer Umm Kulthum proudly called herself a *fallaha* years after she moved to Cairo and became an educated and cultured artist. The segregation of men from women in the daytime was never as strict in lower class urban Egypt or rural Egypt as it was for urban elites. But the prevailing code of honor is as strict, perhaps more strict. The *fallaha* is strong and works in the fields but doesn't mix socially with men. She is thought to be naïve about the activities and customs of the larger cities and was commonly illiterate before the nationalization of education. Egypt's minorities—Bedouin, Berbers (Siwis), and Nubians—are also rural people, but who may be partially urbanized or have migrated to Cairo.

Bint al-balad means "daughter of the country" and is a lower-class urban Cairene-born woman. She is reputed to be smart, if not educated, tough; she will insult, slap, or smack with her slipper any men who harasses or speaks improperly to her. She deems herself an authentic Egyptian as compared to Westernized elite women. She wore the *malayya laff* (a large black shawl wrapped around the body and head) before the increasing popularity of the *hijab* since the late '70s and 1980s. She resides in *ahya sha'biyya*, the popular quarters of Cairo, possibly in a *hara* or alley. She would prefer to marry a man with enough income to allow her to be a *sitt al-bayt*, a housewife.

Her male counterpart *ibn al-balad* may work in a traditional craft, own or work in a business, or any job not requiring a college degree. In Cairo, those in the trades were organized into guilds known as *fituwwat*. In the past, he would wear a *galabiyya* but these days, that isn't always the case. He would endeavor to be called *gada'a*—a strong macho guy. He was expected to be generous and not stingy.

Bint al-suq is a *bint al-balad* who works. As her name implies, she may work as a merchant, or in the *suq*, or marketplace, possibly in an occupation associated with men, like a butcher or a hashish merchant. However, like all *banat al-balad*, she is expected to and expects to care for her husband, clean the home, cook for him, prepare his bath, and dress nicely for him.[11]

Bint al-zawat, in contrast to *bint al-balad*, is an elite or aristocratic woman or girl. She is considered by *bint al-balad* to be less friendly, more reserved, and lazy because she doesn't do housework. She uses Western utensils and wears Western style clothing, lives in an *afrangi* (foreign, or upper-class) neighborhood, and is more stingy with others than is *bint al-balad*. She is rumored to (though she may not) mix with men more than *bint al-balad* would. From this perspective, *bint al-zawat* is a somewhat pejorative title. More positively, people say "*hiyya bint al-nas*," or of her male counterpart, *ibn al-zawat* that "*huwwa ibn al-nas*"—s/he is a person of noble stock or good family equivalent to the Spanish term *hidalgo/hidalga*. This could also apply to *ibn al-balad*, and in that case, implies that he is a "decent guy," as Sayyid Henkish explained to Karin van Nieuwkerk.[12] If a woman behaves properly, she is *muhtarama* (respectable). It is important to understand that these are not personal concepts that I am making up, but rather, ideas expressed by Egyptians repeatedly and on many different levels.

As Egypt has urbanized and modernized and certain economic changes took place, these class categories became more layered or confused. For example, when people migrated from rural villages to Cairo, and as their children acquired education, they became urbanized; and more like *awlad al-balad*, but Cairenes still know and distinguish between those who are or are not Cairene born. In the *infitah* (Economic Open Door policy) era, some of the urban migrants became wealthy. Earlier in the Nasser era, the property of non–Egyptians was seized by the state, and some of *awlad al-zawat* were imprisoned or persecuted; they either left Egypt or became much more poor. With reference to these two trends, some began referring to the "baladization" of Egypt's consumer society in the 1970s and 1980s.

Sha'bi music emanates from *awlad al-balad*. It is performed for them or about them. Its lyrics enumerate and glorify or bemoan *sha'bi* traits. In years prior to the 1970s, many songs also acknowledged rural origins or genres.

Social class differences have been stereotyped in film and in dance tableaux, becoming more brittle than they actually are. For example, the famous dancer Dina Tal'at is actually a *bint al-zawat*, as is Sama al-Masry, the satirist/dancer; both attended college yet choose on occasion to project the image of a *bint al-balad*, who is *khiffat al-damm* (or *dammha khafif*), light-blooded, and has a heart of gold. In one of Sama al-Masry's satirical videos mocking ex-president Morsi (who was from Sharqiyya province), she dressed as a *fallaha* and mocked him and his supporters using tropes about the *fallahin*. (See Chapter Seven.)

Other dance stars or singers/actresses are actually *banat al-balad* in origin, and either draw on that background or not. Furthermore, they use flirting and dance or acted commentary about flirting in their performances.

This could be performed in a sweet and innocent manner as by the Egyptian singer Laila Nazmi (b. 1945). She was an Alexandrian who graduated from the High Institute of Music in 1968, and her career spanned the late 1960s and 1970s. She collected popular songs for her dissertation on Egyptian folk music, which she released in a 1970 album.[13] These songs portray the small-town girl, or *bint al-balad* or the *fallaha*, as symbols of Egyptian national identity and sweet wholesomeness. Her deliberate speaking and singing in a little girl's voice, as in "Mashrabsh shay,"[14] is charming, and before and after, countless others have used the interjection of a flirty woman's speaking voice within songs. (The Iraqi dancer, Samia Nasser active from the 1960s and 1970s in California, had a similar speaking voice, using it onstage to great effect.[15]) Laila Nazmi appeared with Nagwa Fu'ad and Sa'id Saleh in the 1974 film *Anisat Sayidat* (also starring Nur al-Sharif and Suhair Ramzi). Fu'ad, the dancing star, in her miniskirt, despite her terpsichorean skills, was really unable to upstage or out-flirt the softer, calm Nazmi.[16]

A Lebanese singer, Marwa (b. 1974) who sings in Egyptian, Lebanese, and *khaliji* styles and recorded CDs in 2004 and 2005, began making films in 2006 and covered Nazmi's songs, and also Warda al-Jaza'iriyya's. Marwa's rendition is unabashedly sexy, exaggerated, and somewhat manic, and the video is set in a New Age bar that resembles an elegant pharmacy. Nazmi threatened Marwa with a lawsuit. Others loved Marwa's interpretation which drew on "Singing in the Rain" and Marilyn Monroe as well as a dancing *dalal* (coquette).[17] The refrain to the original is "I don't drink tea, I drink soda." As if to say, "I, a lady don't drink tea—but men drink tea—I drink soda—I'm kind of a spoiled pampered girl." The lyrics explain how a man who is flirting with her gives her presents, first a hand fan, then an umbrella, then an apricot; the final verse is about a girl's cheeks which are like peaches, causing a boy to faint.

This song and others were part of a long-running Lebanese theatrical production on Egyptian music from earlier in the twentieth century entitled *Hishik Bishik* which opened in 2015. It illustrates that not only Egypt, but the region is emotionally attached to Egyptian music and entertainment of that era, although it is *hishik bishik*—meaning something like the carnival, related to low-class dancing, with a connotation of being trashy.

One may find many other examples of sweet or softer-styled dancing in a flirtatious manner, in both *raqs al-baladi* and *raqs sharqi* styles. An example was Katy (or Kati) (1927–1980) who danced in a number of films from the 1940s to 1965. She was from Alexandria, born to an Egyptian mother and a Greek father. The clips that now remain of her dancing show her as a soloist in the midst of a large audience, or a large group of dancers, and in one instance, a small group of women musicians. The opening music is quite speedy, but the *dall'a* section begins with a more slowly paced violin *taqasim* in *Lailat Hanna* (1951), which starred Shadia, Kamal al-Shinnawi, and Mary Munib. The violinist plays in the Turkish-sounding style popular at that time.[18] In 1965, Katy left for Athens as she was suspected of being involved in a spy plot with Egyptian-Israeli double agent Raf'at al-Gamal (or al-Hagan), who had also acted in minor roles.

Another example is the dancer, Hayatim (1950–2018) born Suhair Hassan in Alexandria and appeared in her first film *Lailat Hubb Akhira* in 1972. She also dances in the 1981 *al-Wahsh dakhil al-Insan* (*The Beast Within*) based on Émile Zola's lugubrious novel *Thérèse Raquin,* which starred Nahid Sharif, Mahmud Yasin, and Sa'id Saleh. She singles out the handsome patron in a dance bar, dressed in what appears to be a Sunbati-style *ghawazi galabiyya*, dancing confidently but lightly.[19]

Hayatim also appeared with Kat-Kut al-Amir, the *sha'bi* singer in the film *al-Darb al-Ahmar* (1980) starring Mahmoud 'Abd al-'Aziz, Suhair Ramzi, and Mahmoud Isma'il.[20] Kat-Kut started out in the music business as a good *tabbal* (drummer), but he aspired to be a singer. He traveled to London and back to Egypt, took voice lessons, and then became known for the song "Ya Ghazal Darb al-Ahmar," which concerns a beautiful girl in this traditional neighborhood in Old Cairo. It was supposed to have been written for the daughter of a drug-dealer. In a scene is celebrating a wedding, Hayatim, playing Basbusa, imbues the party with *sha'bi* feeling and *dall'a*, and Kat-Kut al-Amir as Mahmud is a young, sensitive-looking man, singing quite well, and spiffy in white trousers.

The song experienced a revival of interest in recent years after it was taught by Randa Kamel, who has had quite a successful teaching experience outside of Egypt. Subsequently other dancers used it, including Tatiana Eshta, a Russian dancer who performed in Egypt and was a teacher at Camp Negum, a belly dance camp cruise, in 2013.[21] Lylia Bourbia used this piece in the Eilat Festival in February 2019,[22] and the first place winner of the *sha'bi* category used it at the Cairo Mirage (even if in a far speedier and athletic version than its original).[23] It is encouraging that dancers would resort to older pieces with some history in Egypt's *baladi* (or *sha'bi*) identity and with potential for *dall'a* in their quest for new material.

Costume worn by Suhair Zaki (Cornelia van Aken collection).

Nahid Sabry, born in Tanta in 1925, studied with Nelly Mazloum and became a leading dancer in the 1960s and 1970s. She has a decidedly coquettish presence. In a 1963 song, "Fallahat Baladna," she poses as an artist's model, while the singer Karim Mahmud, playing the artist, declares the virtues of the *fallahat* of Egypt.[24]

A quintessential symbol of ladylike *dall'a* and subtle flirtation was Suhair Zaki. She began her dancing career in Alexandria and then moved to Cairo (see Chapter Two). The existing film clips on the internet do not do justice to this graceful, perennially smiling, and serene dancer who I first saw performing in Cairo in 1973.[25] Her lengthy shows required great stamina, but she did not emphasize the amount of athleticism required as do some contemporary dancers who sometimes jump into positions to create excitement (Alla Kushnir and ʿAziza described in Chapter Eight come to mind). Rather, Suhair transitioned smoothly from one actually arduous movement to another as if it were the easiest action in the world.

Nelly Fuʾad entertained in a very artful *raqs sharqi* manner, yet with flirtatiousness. She was born in Alexandria (interesting that many Golden Age dancers and musicians came from Egypt's second largest city) and took her Armenian grandmother's name as a stage name. She drew on what some dancers and musicians call ʿ*awalim* movements due to her experience dancing as a teen in an actual ʿ*awalim* troupe. She came to Cairo to fill in for Suhair Zaki in a stage production and had a career in the 1970s and 1980s, dancing in five-star hotels and in films. She also performed in Farid al-Atrash's nightclub in Lebanon for a year.[26]

When observing Nelly, it becomes clear that *dallʿa* need not incorporate folklore or be part of a skit concerning a *bint al-balad*, although on the other hand, a dance may do so, or refer to folklore in a section, thereby adding to a cannon about the *bint al-balad* within Egyptian dance. One can find other examples in the dancing of Samia Gamal, Tahia Kariuka, Shu Shu Amin, Fifi ʿAbdu, ʿAzza Sharif, Huwaida al-Hashim, Lucy Saʿd, Mona al-Saʿid, Nadia Hamdi, and Dandash. It is most interesting to note the combinations of ʿ*awalim*-style steps and patterns in their routine, and also some very possibly from the Sunbati *ghawazi* (*ghawazi* dancers from the Delta town of Sunbat), most specifically in movements of Tahia Kariuka, Nadia Hamdi, and Dandash, and which relate to a *dallʿa* charm, not calculated, but unselfconscious.

Tahia Kariuka, whose biographical details were described in Chapter Two, began her life in entertainment as a teenager, first working at Suʿad Mahasan's and then Badiʿa's *sala* by 1933. Tahia was a *bint al-balad* who acquired education and better manners, appearing in films since the early 1940s. As Edward Said wrote, there is no proper biography of her, but with her achievements, marriages and connections, she was a part of Egypt's political as well as its cultural life. When threatened with censorship of the play *Yahia al-Wafd*, she went to court, won the case, and mounted the play. Tahia Kariuka is associated with the transformative process in *raqs sharqi* which made it a solo or tableaux on-stage art form, combining steps traditional to *raqs sharqi* with graceful turns and dance floor patterns. In a surviving film clip used to advertise Badiʿa Masabni's club, Tahia is one of a corps of dancers.[27] They are beautiful and elegant in keeping with the projected image of the club. Her film appearances included the very sensual, soft dancing appreciated at the time. Sometimes, in a film scene, flirting is part of the plot, as when Anwar Wagdy teases her with a flower in *Laila, Bint al-Rif* (1941), eventually handing it to her.[28] I would argue that subtle hip-work of Tahia (and others of the Golden Era) and the *ghawazi* influences on the hip-work of Nadia Hamdi and Dandash relate to one another.

Nadia Hamdi was born ʿAʾisha ʿAli Mohammad Mahmoud to an entertainment family of Muhammad ʿAli street. She was a great-niece of Najia al-Iskandarani. She began dancing in her teens and at weddings and parties since the early 1970s. Perhaps it is her sweet and youthful appearance in the Syrian film *Sah al-Nom*, contrasting with the stiff portrayal of the ruler and the antics of master comic Duraid al-Lahham as the band leader, which adds to its feeling of *dallʿa*.[29]

Hamdi could play *sagat*, do the splits, and touch her back leg up to her head while balancing the *sham'adan* on her head in the same manner as demonstrated by Nazla al-'Adil. The American dancer and dance teacher Morocco (Carolina Varga Dinicu) discovered Hamdi in 1972 dancing in the wedding circuits. Hamdi began dancing in hotels in 1981 after marrying a folkloric dancer. Then, she was pressured, as were many, to wear the *hijab* and stop dancing. However, Morocco convinced her to come to the U.S. and teach in 1995.[30] While on this teaching tour for Morocco and for the American dancer Amina Goodyear in San Francisco, she danced with the *sham'adan*, in what contemporary dancers have been calling an "'*awalim*-style."[31] She also performed with marked flirtatiousness in a rather lengthy *malayya-laff* dance (manipulating the outer wrap once worn by *bint al-balad*). Her version is not Alexandrian in style as is mentioned in Chapter Six but is a bit softer than that of Farida Fahmy (who danced with a *malayya-laff* in the Reda Troupe); she is smaller in stature and uses different movements. She wears heeled shoes and anklets, and the dance aims to give the feeling of a dancer from a truly *baladi* neighborhood. She wraps the *malayya* tightly over her hips and then swings it to loop backwards around her arms, but the latter part of the dance is performed barefoot.[32] Hamdi also choreographed a *malayya-laff* routine for the American dancer Sahra Saeeda (Carolee Kent) who toured in the United States briefly with her Egyptian band in 1996. This dance references the Ghuri neighborhood where fabric is sold. Sahra carries a large straw *shanta* (handbag) with fabric inside of it, which the singer draws out at one point. She reveals her flowered sundress under her *malayya* and flirts with the singer throughout the song. As with the dance Hamdi performed, the movements are charming, playful, and not exaggerated.[33]

Dandash, a contemporary dancer, is from Alexandria where her parents were a singing duo. Her family traveled to perform in Mansoura and Sunbat, where she says she saw Sunbati *ghawazi*. (Could this be true, when Nearing visited in the late 1970s and no-one wanted to own up to knowing *ghawazi*? Perhaps the outsider and insider status of Nearing vs. Dandash are part of the answer.) It seems that *'awalim* of Cairo also influenced her style. After moving to Cairo, she became a dance star. Dandash says she idolized Suhair Zaki. Some of her signature hip drops appear in Dandash's impressive "Manga" routine,[34] in which she also demonstrates some of the best-known movements of Samia Gamal, Tahia Kariuka, Nagwa Fu'ad (and Sahar Hamdi in a different performance), and then her own. (In other performances she has added segments based on other dancers.) Her *dall'a* comes within a high-energy performance centering on many varied hip and shimmy movements and beams out from her towards the audience and sometimes with special and prolonged interactions with her singer or her drummer and/or *sagat* player.

Huwaida al-Hashim danced with vigorous shimmies, shown off by the heavily fringed elaborate beaded costumes of the late 1980s and early 1990s and Lebanese-style *'asaya*, and yet has a shy and sweet demeanor. She presented a dance introduced by her *mizmar* player, moving into a duet with her *tabl* (an extra large drum played with sticks) drummer while using the *'asaya*.[35] She also appeared during her heyday in Lebanese television, and her performances were quite delicate (as compared to Turkish dancers then appearing on television).[36] Egyptian music and dance has strongly influenced Lebanese entertainers; although they retain their own styling and technique, both musicians and dancers referred to their use of "Egyptian style." As certain Egyptian entertainers, like Mona al-Sa'id got their start in Lebanon, these styles are not so distinct as one might think.

Samia Gamal's (1924–1994) dancing is now largely available in film clips that were heavily choreographed and simplified. These contrasted with her own live shows. Many dance teachers model her arabesque-step turns, though she incorporated many other movements. Born Zainab Ibrahim Mahfuz in Wana al-Qiss in Bani Suwaif to a Moroccan mother and an Egyptian father, she moved to Cairo near the Khan al-Khalili. She joined Badi'a Masabni's troupe as a chorus dancer and studied with Lebanese choreographer Isaac Dickson who worked with Casino Opera. She also studied ballet and Western and Latin dance forms. Important to her career were the series of films in which she co-starred with

Samia Gamal by Van Leo. Van Leo was Levon Alexander Boyajian. He and his brother Angelo opened a photography business in 1941 and gained many clients in entertainment and elite circles due to his masterful portraits. However, this portrait is credited to Angelo, who signed the brothers' photographs as Van Leo. Appears in *Nazar* 115, "Van Leo," by Barry Iverson (courtesy Shira.net, from the collection of Priscilla Adum).

Farid al-Atrash. She appeared in fifty movies from the '40s to the '60s. She briefly married a Texas "millionaire" playboy and then in 1958, the actor and her co-star Rushdi Abaza. Then, she did not dance for some years, until the actor Samir Sabry convinced her to return to the stage, despite her being over age 60 at that time, as she had debts and needed income.[37] I had the good fortune to see her perform in Cairo during the period when she had "officially retired" but yet had club appearances. Her photographic portrait by Van Leo draws on a self-Orientalism, popular in Egypt at that time.

As with Tahia Kariuka, Samia's graceful figure and assiduous self-application to her art were partial reasons for her success. Her smile beams out at one, here even in a staged choreography for a film.[38] King Faruq named her the National Dancer of Egypt in 1949. Samia spoke about her desire to meet Badi'a Masabni as a teenager and her efforts to become a good dancer like Tahia Kariuka, instead of *'ageen al-fallah* (peasant bread dough—her description of herself at the time).[39] Despite her many appearances in a formal setting, Samia Gamal said, "I personally prefer dancing in a nightclub because I am closer to the audience and I live with them. The theater places too much distance between the people and me."

Shu Shu Amin, who began dancing in the 1970s in Cairo and traveled with Hassan Siʿud to Japan for a year, continued dancing through the 1980s. She also frequently danced in London. She was famous for a shimmy done all the way to the floor, and a shimmy with abdominal accents. Her demeanor included *dallʿa*, yet she was said to be "nice"; a man could bring his wife to watch her.[40]

Fifi ʿAbdu was born ʿAtiyat ʿAbd al-Fattah Ibrahim, April 26, 1953, in Cairo (however some sources say in a village outside of Cairo). She danced at the Arizona, the al-Lail clubs, and five-star hotels in 1970s. She was one of the top three dancers (with Lucy and Dina) when she retired from dance in 2004, although she continues to dance at private events and in videos on Instagram, to teach dance, and continues acting. A dynamic performer, she has been identified with *bint al-balad* because of her *shisha* tableau (an act in which she puffs on the water pipe and acts like *bint al-balad*) and the *baladi* roles she played in films and on television. She has two daughters and an adopted daughter. This was a child adopted by Tahia Kariuka, and when Tahia died, Fifi agreed to adopt her. Fifi is said to be extremely wealthy and was noted for the Ramadan *iftar*s (a meal that breaks the fast at the end of the day) that she hosted for the poor. Fifi exuded sweet and sassy coquettishness as a young dancer (she was then called the Filly), and also bad or naughty *dallʿa* in her "*Ya Muʿallima*," (this signifies a working woman of *bint al-balad* background) routine with the *malaya laff*.[41] In this particular performance, with a male and a female singer, she mostly walks around the stage using her *malayya laff* as *a bint al-balad* might, in different positions, to show off her body as she dances, as well as in some of her current videos.

ʿAzza Sharif, Lucy Saʿd, and Mona al-Saʿid may not be as well known as other Golden Era dancers, although they are familiar to Egyptian dance aficionados. ʿAzza Sharif (1947–2019) began dancing at eighteen in Cairo, then in Lebanon, England, and Germany, and then returned to the Mena House Hotel and continued back and forth to engagements in Beirut prior to the Lebanese civil war. She appeared in twenty-one films including *Khalli Balak min Zuzu* (with an iconic portrayal of a dancer) and *Nibtidi Mnain al-Hikaya*, was very close to her percussionist, and married Kat-Kut al-Amir.[42] In addition to her attractiveness in *raqs sharqi*, she was very skilled in the folkloric style of *al-hagallah* from northwestern Egypt. She has performed this to a Tunisian song in a charming presentation.[43]

Lucy Saʿd was born Enʿam Saʿd Mohammad ʿAbd al-Wahhab (c. 1960) in Cairo. She grew up in Cairo's Old City, near Muhammad ʿAli street. Following a tradition of entrepreneurship in *raqs sharqi*, she became the owner of the nightclub Parisianna. Her mother lived with Zuba al-Klubtiyya and married into her family. National Geographic made a documentary about Lucy's life. It opens with a younger unknown dancer's observations about dancing and Lucy.[44] The documentary shows Lucy's love for Muhammad ʿAli street and its traditions where her origins lie.[45] Lucy defended the dancers' occupation in that interview and felt their portrayal in film had gradually improved. She is still performing, including Nubian themed shows, as here in this clip.[46] Her nightclub, Parisiana, was attacked and burned after the January 25,

2011, revolution with all her costumes inside, causing her to fall into a temporary depression.[47]

Mona al-Sa'id was born Mona Ibrahim Wafa' in the Suez Canal Zone (c. 1954). Her parents were Bedouin from the Sinai oasis of Musa. When the family was evacuated during the 1967 war from the Canal Zone, she came to Cairo. At age twelve she was seen dancing in a disco, and Anwar Amar, the owner of Sahara City, and the singer Laila Murad told her she should dance professionally. She danced for two months at Sahara City, and then had to flee her father's wrath because he opposed her dancing. She danced for five years at Casino Lebanon in Beirut, then the Cairo Meridien for a year, then in London where she bought the Omar Khayyam club. This clip shows her regal entrance, due to her calm composure, graceful arms and height (5'11").[48] These qualities carry on even during an extended drum solo.[49] As she stated in an interview, "I don't like hands down or ugly stomach or ugly back. I like to be lifted."[50] "Lifted" is a quality that some attribute to ballet, but it certainly is used in other dance genres. Although lifted, she is also relaxed, delicate, and fluid in her extended *baladi taqsim* ("progression") as filmed outside of her nightclub routine.[51]

'Aida Nur (b. 1956) began in an Alexandrian folkloric ensemble and then danced in the Reda Troupe. She performed *raqs sharqi* in the five-star hotels including with a small group of male folkloric dancers as became popular in the 1980s.[52] Her style is very feminine and flowing. She began to teach internationally, and then to choreograph and make costumes. She uses her face and her body to express *dall'a*.

All of these *raqs sharqi* performers have occasionally integrated certain movements from *raqs sha'bi*. That is not, however, precisely what makes *dall'a*, but it enriches their movement repertoire and presents symbols and small narratives with which the audience may identify.

Dall'a *in* Mulid

An example of hilarious, loud *dall'a* by singer Mahmud al-Laithy is in "Suq al-Banat." We could term this *dall'a mulid*, since *mulid* songs (*aghani mulid*, see Chapter Four) is al-Laithy's specialty. The dancer in the scene is actress Aytin 'Amir[53] (b. 1990)—in comparison to al-Laithy, she is very restrained, and sweet.[54] Just as al-Laithy mock-flirts with Aytin, dancers may also utilize *dall'a* to dance directly with a singer or to the musicians, and more controversially, with an audience member to inject a little drama in the performance or (in a club) to encourage tipping. This is typically not true flirting, just acting or subtle flirting.

Provocative Dall'a

The degree of sexiness varies. Some performances go well beyond folklore groups' standard of providing family entertainment. For example, Dina Tal'at and Safinaz (Sofinar Grigoryan) incorporate *dall'a* as well as lock and freeze and extended shimmies movements, and Safinaz' eye-catching chest pops and splits.[55] Dina

Dancer Dina Tal'at from her Facebook page, January 24, 2018.

Dina Tal'at (photograph by Laura Boushnak).

appeared much earlier in her career in a typically *dall'a* song interacting with the singer and with milder versions of her trademark steps.[56] As previously mentioned, she has pushed the envelope on occasion with costumes that were more daring and unusual than some other performers wore (although others outside the five-star hotels now wear less). Both Dina and Safinaz are bona fide entertainers who are playful and almost make fun of their *dall'a*.

Dina is, in fact, a truly great dancer, incorporating many movements with breath catches, or which go in an non-intuitive direction, as might be called in the modern dance techniques of Martha Graham and Twyla Tharp, bound flow movement. Then, she switches to the intuitive direction, then, back again. She sometimes tests her balance, appearing to move forward, then back, or tweaks her giant hip circle in mid-movement. All of this communicates complete control and an effortless presentation of what is actually quite effortful. She also allows herself to really enjoy and appear moved by the music.

Naughty or Bad Dall'a

One might include Fifi 'Abdu's dancing to the song "Ya Mu'allima" with the *malayya laff*,[57] although that was far tamer than in some of her current actress/dancer short videos posted on Instagram and Twitter. Incidentally, this performance, like that of Nadia Hamdi, suggests the use of the *malayya laff* in Old Cairo neighborhoods and not a folklore version framing in Alexandria.

In contrast with Fifi, Nagwa Fu'ad sometimes utilized less *dall'a* in her appearances. Perhaps it is her angular or very slim body, or that she improvised less and performed choreography more. In an above-mentioned scene in *Anisat Sayidat* with Laila Nazmi, it is Nazmi who

Malayya laff, Cairo, c. mid–1970s. In this period, lower-class women still typically wore *malayya laff* in Cairo before the wide-scale adoption of *hijab*. Sketch by Elizabeth Rodenbeck in Andrea Rugh, *Reveal and Conceal: Dress in Contemporary Egypt*, Syracuse: Syracuse University Press, 1986, p. 111. (courtesy Max Rodenbeck).

appears *dall'a* and Nagwa who looks a bit frenetic or tense, whether due to the physical contrast between them, because she was in ordinary street clothes for that era (a miniskirt), or because the vocal evoking of *dall'a* by Nazmi is the center of the scene. Elsewhere, Nagwa Fu'ad shows intense *dall'a*, for example in an appearance with a young Muhammad 'Abduh (the Saudi Arabian singer) not by flirting with him, but in her delight at the song, which was costumed and staged as an Egyptian fantasy of the Bedouin, not particularly distinguishing between the Hagalla of the northeast (the styling of her dress) and the dances of the Sinai.

In 2018 and 2019, some videos were criticized like this one March 2019 Instagram posting, of a dancer in a shorter costume dancing on a bar with an over-the-top *dall'a*—too sexual.[58] In her study of dancers in Cairo on the tour boat the *Nile Maxim*, Christine Sahin distinguishes between those who use a teasing, playful *dall'a* and focus on their own solo show, and others who more overtly and deliberately interacted with customers by leaving the stage to dance near them, and using less subtle, more sexual movements to solicit tips.[59]

The Ukrainian dancer Allah Kushnir has *dall'a* in her performance in "Ya Mna'na." She is on the balcony flirting with the singer who is serenading her below; she isn't in a dance costume, and it is entirely the flirtation and the melodic beauty of the song that is captivating. Although she was invited as a result of this video to various programs including the "Abla Fahita Live from the Duplex" show, she said in an interview that she did not regard this appearance as constituting dancing. In her dance shows, she tends to the hyper-athletic, although she is improving over time in sensing how to selectively emphasize moments in the music.

"Naughty *dall'a*" has crossed over to other Arab countries, like Lebanon, Syria, and Iraq in different vehicles. Dominique Hourani of Lebanon, born Dima Hourani is a *bint zawat*—as the daughter of an archaeologist—a beauty queen/model turned actress/dancer. Yet she very naughtily films herself in zumba classes, or here in an over-the-top rendition of "al-Wad Hado'a."[60] While *raqs sharqi* was popular (and hardly documented in English) in Syria as well as the addition of "*baladi* sets," a large influx of refugees from Iraq post–2003 and the growing popularity of *chobi* (Iraq's version of *sha'bi*) resulted in many dance performances of different genres within this classification, but also rising prostitution and exploitation of young girls. *Dall'a* is also important to these forms.

Over-the-top flirtatiousness to the point of disruption is parodied in the comedic 1977 film, *al-Azwag al-Shayatin* (*The Devilish Husbands*) by the actress Nahid Sharif (1942–1981). In this scene, she dances for the groom and bride, but sits in the groom's (played by 'Adil Imam) lap, and so overtly flirts with him that the ladies at this party are shocked.[61] Sharif had danced in other films; as mentioned earlier it was not uncommon for Egyptian and Arab actresses to dance quite well. She moved to Lebanon in 1973 and appeared there in films as well.

Sahar Hamdi fulfilled an era-specific fantasy dancing in an animal print leotard and tights on the beach in the film *al-Mushaghibun fi-Nuwaiba* (1992). The dancing is overshadowed by the sexy vocal duet and teasing lyrics.[62] Sahar Hamdi acquired a poor reputation for being outrageously *dall'a*, but some years earlier her dancing was considered exciting, and she was not thought to be excessively naughty.

Sama al-Masry is an upper class, educated actress/dancer who employs the image of the *bint al-balad* and her flirtatiousness for satirical purposes in her own videos. The sinful and corrupt environment of dancers was a key part of her first film (which she wrote and starred in), and the hypocrisy of political figures are prominent in her videos, so her use of *dall'a* is rather obvious and extreme.

In the song "Ahmad al-Shibshib Dha'" she lampoons her own extreme version of *dall'a* and an *ibn al-balad* who, due to his narcissism, doesn't even have the energy for her. The song title is a parody of a different song title—"Aha al-Shibshib Dha'" by al-ShibShib (which translates to "Oh fuck, or shit—I lost my slipper"; *aha* is supposed to be the sound of a woman's orgasm).[63]

Whereas al-Masry's distasteful display of *dall'a* is a parody, many skillful Egyptian dancers balance *dall'a* with power and restraint in their movements. A dancer identified as Dareen shows this in a *sharqi* routine,[64] as well as dancing with the *'asaya*, in skintight, torn jeans and bra, what passes now for a *sha'bi* costume.[65] She includes the currently popular isolations, and dropping of the head to the ground, suddenly tossing it back, and swift side-step as an accent, as performed by both foreign and Egyptian dancers. But she manages to retain softness in her arms and expression.

"Ya dall'a, ya dall'a" was composed by Farid al-Atrash (c. 1910–1974) to lyrics by Tawfiq Barakat for the Lebanese singer Sabah (1925–2014) and recorded in 1973 from the musical play *Sitt al-Kull*.[66] Sabah was born Jeanette Gergis al-Feghalli and affectionately called "Sabuha" and "Shahroura" by Lebanese. She recorded fifty albums, releasing more than 3,000 songs, and appeared in ninety-eight films, and while not an Egyptian singer, was highly regarded in Egypt. She continued performing until 2009,[67] appearing in elaborate evening dress into her old age, and married seven times. In an interview, she said she had unhappy relationships; men "called her Mrs. Bank" (this is somewhat similar to Tahia Kariuka's revelations about her husbands). Sabah flirted, dancing lightly in the re-recordings of this song. The lyrics are simple and clear although love as represented in the song isn't necessarily a sweet experience for "all hearts have been broken because of separation from their beloved."

"Ya Dall'a, Ya Dall'a"

Chorus/Taslim
Ya dall'a ya dall'a idall'a, bayn al-hilwin itall'a x2

Verse

Ruhi habbat ruhak, wi-albi fik itwall'a x2
Albi fik itwall'a
Repeat Chorus

Albi ghair albak ma habb, yalli albak atyab alb x2
inti ghanili al-hubb, w-ana ba'ud bitsamma' x2
Repeat Chorus

La tdi wi-la tdayani, da'at albak samm'ani x2
Wi bhibbak la tlawa'ani, albi mil hubb mlaww'a x2
Repeat Chorus

Mawwal:
Kel[68] *al-habayib bil-gharam tdalla'u* x2
W-kel al-ulub mnal-fura' twajja'u x2

Ya ya 'aini
Min yum, min yum ma 'ayunak hakuna bil-wama
W ba'adu[n] 'ayuni fik 'am yittala'u ya layl
Verse

Albi bihusnak maghrum, la tkhalili b-albi hmum x2
Ya tislamli shu mahdum wi shu byilba'alak tidalla' x2
Repeat Chorus

"O Adorable One"

O adorable one, be adorable, let your beauty shine x2 [Chorus]
My soul has loved yours, and my heart has fallen for you x2
My heart has fallen for you
Repeat Chorus

My heart loved no other heart but yours, the kindest heart ever (yours) x2
Sing about love for me and I'd sit and listen to you x2
Repeat Chorus

Don't lose [the] track and don't let me lose it, let me hear your heartbeats x2
I love you, please don't put me in pain, my heart is already fatigued because of love x2
Repeat Chorus

Mawwal
All beloveds have had pleasure in their love x2
And all hearts have been broken because of separation x2
Oh oh dear
From that day, that day when your eyes have spoken to mine
And until now, my eyes are looking at you

My heart is in love with your gorgeousness, don't leave me in sorrow x2
How sweet you are, you only have been created to act with sweetness x2
Repeat Chorus

This song, quite *shami* in style, is nevertheless appreciated by many Arabs, so much so that it featured as an exhibition song for Sherine Bou Saad, Youssef Hassan, and Lynn Hyak on MBC's "The Voice Kids" to the delight of the judges (who may have enjoyed it more than the children).[69] The song is a *taqtuqa*. Its chorus line opens in the *sayr* (direction of the *maqam*) of Kirdan/Sazkar.[70] It modulates numerous times through the *mawwal*, and then resolves in the chorus.

Dall'a is not really a specific genre of music,[71] but also appears in romantic songs, so for example we can contrast its use in the famous song for Umm Kulthum, "Al-Hubb Kulluh," composed by Baligh Hamdi, with lyrics by Ahmad Shafiq Kamil, first performed in 1971, and in various *sha'bi* songs.

All the Love (al-Hubb Kulluh)

All the love I loved was yours
All the love
And all my time I lived for you
All my time
Darling, tell the world with me
And feel every heartbeat
Oh world, my love
This lifetime is only love
Water me and fill me
And water me again

Three. Ya Dall'a, Ya Dall'a

Water me again with your love
From you
From the light of my time
Water me you who I've not seen in a day
I felt as if I fell behind again

Soul of my heart, oh life of my days
Oh soul of my heart
Oh darling angel of my dreams
Oh soul of my heart
What was I before I saw you?
What was I?
And why was I living my days, my darling?
Why?
I walked the road of my life, your heart in the long night
No heart beside me feels for you except a beautiful apparition
And when I saw you for the first time
You found me with all the desire of the world
Tight to you
And in all the love of the world I went to you and experienced you
I called I called on the world herself
And feel every heartbeat
Oh world my love
This lifetime is only love

The thirsty love thirsts in my heart calling for you
Insomnia from a person and most beautiful of the angels
You are my soul and all my years and light of my life
Oh my life what am I compared to you
My love I am created for you solely for you, for you
And my heart lived on the touch of your affection solely your affection
Your affection
Beautiful days
Beautiful dreams
Beauty of my life
Oh so beautiful
Beauty that passes through soft clay
Beauty infiltrate my life
Oh time
Oh long nights with beautiful dreams … with you
Oh time
Oh nights that pass killing my hopes and leaving us ashes
What's in it if you forget two in love?
Melting and living
Living, we tell the world herself
And all my heart beats feeling
Oh world, my love
This lifetime is only love

Oh darling, oh aroma of desire
My destiny from my nights of desire
What is the feeling of this talk in your eye
The openness of the most beautiful words changes
What is the scent of this perfume in your hands
Your hands say let's prepare the perfume
That which is in your lips is from spring
That which is in your eyes is from the nights

> That which is in your cheeks is from flames
> That which is in your hands is from affection
> The journey misled my soul and I got lost in it
> It concealed me for so long
> And far from his eyes it hid me
> About the great joy
> My fear is that he won't take it nor will he leave me
> Let us tell the world
> And feel every heartbeat
> Oh world, and my love and my love and my love
> This lifetime is only love

These lyrics are very direct and accessible. The song would not have been played for a dancer in the Golden Age, but as fashions in music have changed, it may be played today, probably not in the full-length version of the song.

We could compare the above to a *sha'bi* song full of *dall'a*, "al-Zayid fil-Halawa" as sung by Ahmad 'Adawiyya. To driving rhythm, a soloist introduces the melody, and the full *firqa* (ensemble) responds. 'Adawiyya begins singing, then the female and male choruses repeat the refrain.[72] This singer indicates that the object of his affection is simply playing with him, but to the words "*ta'ala 'andina*," (come here to us) she can playfully approach him.

"Al-Zayid fil-Halawa" (The extra sweet and beautiful)

Refrain

Ya zayid fil-halawa, 'an ahl hayena
Matbatal al-sha'[q]awa wi-ta'ala 'andina—wi-ta'ala, ta'ala 'andina
(O you who are extra beautiful, more than the people of our neighborhood
Stop playing games and come to us) Chorus repeats after the singer.

(Ana) *Ashuf husnak, asammi 'alayk min al-hasad*
wi la marra bitigi yammi
Wi la marra bata'[q]asad x2
(When I see your beauty, I say God's name to protect you from envy,
you neither come near me nor cheer me)

(Ana)-*Al-laghi fik w-adadi, w-a'[q]arab mi[n]layla di*
Naditlak w-al-assawa ma'ak mitmakena
Ma-a-tbatal[i] al-sha'[q]awa w-ta'ala 'andina, ta'ala, ta'ala 'andina
(I play with you and spoil you, and I approached on this night
I called you and inclemency is overwhelming you [you are sick as can be]
Stop playing games and come to us, come, come to us.)

Chorus repeats refrain after the singer.

Many *sha'bi* songs reference flirting, in the context of the traditional neighborhoods. (See Chapter Five.) In this context, it would be likely for the love object to "play" with the lover and reject him.

Certain fascinating aspects of Arabic music and dance performance are their self-Orientalism, constant references invoking authenticity (*asala*) (as here, our neighborhood), and great ambivalence about modernity. This should not surprise, as these ideas were prominent in Arabic literature of the mid-century. What is interesting is that by the 1970s, it was already "out of the ordinary" or *avant-garde* for a *sha'bi* singer to overtake and overwhelm elite tastes, as 'Adawiyya did.

In a recent study of the *avant-garde* in Arabic music, one becomes painfully aware that the measure of creativity or being at the forefront is a series of literal comparisons with the West. Heavy metal, hip-hop, and Western modern classical music by Syrian composers are *avant-garde* in the Arab world, yet, certainly not so much outside of it.[73] Unfortunately this tends to exclude the creativity within traditional formats that we see in *sha'bi* and dance music. As will be shown in Chapter Five, *mahraganat* are perceived as innovative precisely because electronic music was hybrid, yet that genre is thoroughly imbued with qualities peculiar to Arabic music.

To a great degree, the study of Arabic classical music (now called *tarab,* or "*maqam* music" by some musicians and dancers) has privileged a formal approach, and showcased instrumental and vocal music while generally ignoring dance. Actual dance music is less well known by younger musicians of classical music, or they substitute classical music for dance music. This is true of music instructors outside of Egypt, who are unaware of much of the dance music repertoire and have only played in only limited performances with dancers but who may indeed have expertise in Arabic music. Ensembles focus on a stage-based concert, and some never feature dance, or possibly have one choreographed dance element or finale. This is also true of certain ensembles in Egypt, but musicians are certainly aware of dance and that many of their own colleagues make a living playing for dancers. For example, in Lebanon, the violinist Nidaa Abou Mrad (a virtuostic performer with a background in early music) focused mainly on music from 1935 or earlier.[74] This is also true of the AMAR project.

Many of the larger orchestras performing Arabic music in the West (in Europe and the United States) also tend to select older repertoire. Overall this signals unease with dance as if it is a competing activity that would disrupt the performance. Or, it is based on the fact that the majority of dancers (except for *dabka* troupes) are non–Arabs. This has provoked some Arab men and women, including those born in America, to identify the dance as a form of cultural appropriation, either performed by someone who "looks wrong," or is in Arab blackface, as explained by Randa Jarrar.[75] This particular critique operates differently in Egypt; indeed most Arab musicians who are not hobbyists in any location don't have the luxury of agreeing with Jarrar, as performance opportunities are limited. But, even if that is not a consideration, the flirtatiousness of the dancer is perceived as a problematic trap and detriment to a "serious art,"—if that is the aim of a musical performance. The avoidance of dance adds to a situation in which music has become a predominantly male sphere while dance is a mostly female area—which was not the case historically in Egypt (and which is discussed in Chapter Eight).

In weddings and parties where dancers do perform, Egyptian audiences and performers allude to actual—not staged, as in demonstrating *dall'a* in the performance—*amruzat* (the *sim* [entertainers' argot] word for romancing someone, or attempting to) by performers or customers and are well aware that festivities and performances offer opportunities for indicating interest.[76] Certainly it is this social situation that has gained the most amount of attention in literature on Egyptian dance. Hopefully, we will not confuse *dall'a* with this more banal aspect of performing.

Conclusion

This was not an exhaustive review of allure and coquettishness, as numerous other dancers and songs could have been described. Yet, this quality is sadly absent sometimes from the globalized versions of *raqs sha'bi* and *raqs baladi* that have proliferated in the last few decades. One hopes it can be retained or recaptured in its special relationship with Arabic dance and music genres.

We will now move away temporarily from *raqs sharqi*, and towards the development of new dance music which has its roots in some of Egypt's most unique, beloved, and celebratory of festivals, the *mawalid*—saint's day festivals. As will be seen, this new music is entering dance formats whether by professional dancers or in parties and weddings where non-professionals nevertheless enjoy dancing.

Four

Mulid

Reinvigorating Spiritual and Popular Legitimacy in Egyptian Music and Dance[1]

The music and entertainment of traditional Egyptian *mawalid* (saint's day festivals, the plural of *mulid*) has inspired a new sub-genre of popular music and dance since 2001. Because readers may not be familiar with the traditional *mawalid* and Sufism (*tasawwuf*, a form or methodology of Islam emphasizing an inward search for God), these will be described prior to a discussion of new dance music simply called *mulid* or *aghani mulid*. The *ghawazi* and *'awalim* described in Chapters One and Two performed regularly at *mawalid* until banned from doing so by the government. These were occasions that mixed spirituality and entertainment. This chapter also examines certain assumptions made about this sub-genre of *sha'bi* or popular music and the dance forms accompanying it as situated in class-constructed themes of deprivation and fatalism and in the music industry's endeavors to profit from their recent popularity.

Mulid music and dance is a venue for music-makers and consumers who differ from the bourgeois idealism and pan-Arab presentation of pop music performers. It alludes to the Egyptian masses, who historically followed Sufism and were devoted attendees of *mawalid*. This is despite the fact that the *aghani mulid*'s fans are often unfamiliar and uncomfortable with the *dhikr* (the Sufi ceremony of remembrance of Allah). Their discomfort may be due to the influence of salafism, a different, more puritanical religious reform movement which counters Sufi traditions and is critical of Egyptians who follow the Sufi path. *Mulid/aghani mulid* has much in common with Egypt's *sha'bi* (urban, lower-class) music in its musical structure and shares certain dance features and similarities in production with *mahragan* (the music genre discussed in Chapter Five). *Mulid* points to the elevation of lower-class philosophy, satire, and self-identification in a period when divisions between "high" and "low," "external" versus "internal," and modernist aspirations versus frustrating material conditions are stronger than ever.

It is estimated that fifteen to twenty percent of Egyptians (and possibly even more, who are now more than at one hundred and one million) are followers of the Sufi orders, or brotherhoods, known as *tariqat*. The purpose of the *tariqat* is to guide the Sufi. Many more Egyptians were Sufis, proportionally, in the past as compared to today. Sufis—usually defined as followers of mystical Islam—have sometimes been apolitical, partly out of the need to survive, and yet in other locations and historical instances, highly politicized, and at the heart of resistance to the colonialist order in the Sudan and Libya for example. The Egyptian government has bureaucratized its control over the *tariqat* via the Supreme Council of Sufi Orders, which was founded in 1903. The Council is composed of *shuyukh* (leaders) of the Sufi *tariqat* and five appointees from al-Azhar University. Many of al-Azhar's senior professors are Sufis. About twenty-five of Egypt's *tariqat* are unregistered, while seventy-seven are registered (and can hold *mawalid*).[2] The largest of them are the Borhamiyya al-Disuqiyya, al-Shadhliyya, al-Rifa'iyya, and al-Badawiyya.

The Council appoints the *shuyukh* (*shaykh*s, or heads of Sufi orders), regulates Sufi practices, and issues the permits needed to hold a *mulid*, a celebration for the Sufi holy men and women, the *awliya'*. Under President Mubarak, the power of his National Democratic Party was uncontested, but after the January 25 revolution (of 2011) the Supreme Council of the Armed Forces permitted the formation of new parties, including those representing Sufis, such as Hizb al-Tahrir al-Masri, Hizb al-Nasr, and Hizb Sawt al-Hurriyya. Parties largely supported by salafis also formed. Candidates campaigned for Sufi votes since the January 25, 2011, revolution.[3] Sufism has been treated as a moderate current in Islam in Egypt, as compared to salafism and the outlawed Muslim Brotherhood.

A *mulid* literally means birth or birthday, as in the celebration of the birthday of the Prophet Muhammad, the Mulid al-Nabi. The hundreds of other *mawalid* actually celebrate the dates of death of the Friends of God, the *awliya'*, holy men and women (similar to saints) of Islam, convened at their tombs, or shrines erected to them. The *awliya'* are thought to possess *baraka* (blessedness and spiritual charisma) and many people believe that they can intercede[4] for ordinary believers, now or on the Day of Judgment, so they and their families may reach paradise, are cured of an illness, or obtain a wish or a need. Shaykh Mazhar of the Borhamiyya order explained that the reason to "highlight" the *awliya'* is to enable Muslims to learn about those who actually practiced Islamic virtues, instead of leaving these as theoretical values as this will strengthen their beliefs.[5] The *awliya'* performed and are identified with supernatural feats known as *karamat*; for instance, their bodies did not disintegrate, they gave predictions of the future, or people saw/see them in dreams.

The *wali* (male holy person) or *waliya* (female holy person) given the honorific of Sidi or Sittna might be a descendent of the Prophet Muhammad. Some were great scholars and leaders of Sufi orders. Many composed poetry, which is sung by a *munshid* (singer of *anashid*, hymns) to music during the *mulid*, connecting the modern celebrations to their inspiring past spiritual leaders.[6] A small musical ensemble might accompany the *munshid* with a *rabab* (stringed fiddle) and *kawala* (a reed flute) and percussion, or a larger one with a full complement of instruments.

The festivals, which previously took up an entire week but are now briefer in length, create a gigantic party (*farah*) for the saint. This aspect of joyous celebration is so crucial to the Egyptian notion of *mawalid* that anthropologist Samuli Schielke entitled his study *Perils of Joy: Contesting Mulid Festivals in Contemporary Egypt*[7] and the meaning(s) of "celebration," or *farah*, is the main focus of his study. It is relevant to my exploration of popular music and dance because there can be no celebration of the *awliya'* without a giant *farah* in Egypt. And no *farah* is joyous without music and dancing.

The *mulid* opens with a *mawkib*, or procession of the Sufi brotherhoods and often ends with a *zaffa* (procession).[8] It is an opportunity to ask for the saint's intercession, or assistance (*madad*), with special requests and to receive transferable blessings (*baraka*). This process offers psychological relief to the uncertainties of life. To the Sufis, or *muhibbin* (those who love), each *mulid* centers on their love of Allah, love of the particular saint therein honored, love of the Prophet Muhammad, love of their fellow members in the *tariqa* (order or brotherhood), and love for all the people who attend the *mulid*.[9] The festivals are also open to ordinary (non–Sufi) Egyptians who relish their carnivalesque atmosphere and spirituality, or benefit financially from commercial activities at the *mulid*, and may travel from one *mulid* to another (*mulidiyyin*). *Mawalid* feature fun activities (children's rides, shooting booths) or sales of various crafts and services such as barbers, circumcisions, and tattoos.[10] They provide occasions for strengthening political, personal, commercial, or religious ties with others at the festival. In Upper (southern) Egypt's *mawalid*, special exhibitions of horses by their riders are held and called the *mirmah*.[11]

Schielke highlights the transgressive nature of the *mawalid*, wherein the abnormal becomes normal. Activities occur at night under bright lights to blaring music, people sleep in the day, gender mixing is permitted, and wealthy attend alongside the very poor. Just as the *mawalid* subvert life to a gigantic rollicking party,[12] the makers and consumers of new *mulid* music resist the salafists' crusade in Egypt (and elsewhere) against "fun, playfulness and diversion."[13] This is true despite the fact of replication and amplification of salafist ideals by ordinary Egyptians, especially if these are similar to the values of the *awlad al-balad*. And true despite Egypt's history of music and dance, which manifests as alternative medicine or magic (in the *zar* and *sabu'a* ceremonies).

Sufism has a legacy of honoring and loving the Prophet and the *awliya'* that can be seen visually throughout Egypt in many shrines and burial sites. Though difficult to accurately estimate the number of Sufis, the participation in the *mawalid* could be at thirty million because not all attendees are Sufis.

Salafists have deplored the Sufi *mawalid* since the burgeoning of salafism in the nineteenth century. They have attacked the Sufis in al-Azhar University and in other prominent positions, although the Egyptian government officially recognizes the Sufi orders. Salafists claim that the *mawalid* assign deity/worship to that other than God; that these and other Sufi practices smack of polytheism (*shirk*). They are no longer held in some other parts of the Muslim world where they were once prevalent precisely because of the influence of salafism. The salafists succeeded in pressuring the Egyptian government to ban the *dhikr* ceremonies in April of 2010 and were pleased with the cancellation the *mulid* of Sayyida Zainab that year over concerns about swine flu.[14]

Schielke, in an ethnography of young Egyptian Muslims in a northern Egyptian village, describes a few who pursued religious commitment through salafism. The level of religiosity without ambivalence demanded by salafism was so difficult for certain of his interlocutors that they eventually gave up on their "commitment."[15]

Ambivalence about religious movements has swung from state-approved Islamism before the January 25, 2011, revolution to the re-outlawing of the Muslim Brotherhood since 2013.[16] Young people and the musicians who began the *mulid* trend are well aware of the *salafi* claim that music is *haram*, and that *mawalid* are a *bidaʿ*[17] (an illicit innovation). However, music's pride of place in *shaʿbi* [read as popular and lower-class] culture is undeniable. Many of these young people paradoxically believe that music and *mawalid* are *haram* and also personally consume *aghani mulid*.

At most *shaʿbi* gatherings, music and dance are a method of celebrating and expressing the *mazag*, the heightened mood of the participants. The word *mazag* literally means blend, or mood of the individual, and in Cairo meant feeling happy or inspired due to companionship, music, coffee, or some other leisure activity done with feeling. Cairenes and other Egyptians now frequently use the word to mean a habit or something one craves, as well as to being high and happy due to drugs which alter one's mental state.[18] Ethnomusicologist A.J. Racy explains that musicians say that someone *biy[q]ul bi-mazag* is singing or playing with inspiration or criticize by saying "*ma fish mazag*," the musician is not inspired.[19]

A *dhikr* in a traditional *mulid* (called *hadhra* or *laila*) encompasses a ritualized set of movements, chants, and *anashid* performed by a singing *munshid* with a band while the *muhibbin*, the devotees or *darawish*, may dance or sway, turn, or use *tahtib* (a stick) to punctuate their movements. They too experience *mazag* and express it in their dancing. The poetry of the great Ibn al-Farid (1181–1284) of Egypt and Ibn ʿArabi (1165–1240) of Spain are famous examples of *anashid* (singular *inshad*) performed in Egyptian *mawalid* to music deriving from the *shaʿbi*, folk (rural) or *tarab*[20] types of music. As Michael Frishkopf has explained, the *inshad* connects the *munshid*, who sings it, to the originating poet's spirit and that of the holy man or woman being celebrated and thus to the origin and purpose of the lyrics.[21]

Other forms of music could appear in the *mawalid*: folk music, such as that played for the dancing horses (*khil*), epic poems (*sirat*) sung with self-accompaniment on the *rabab* (a stringed fiddle), music for Oriental dancers, the *tannura* dancers (who spin in their brightly colored circular skirts), or for the *zar* (exorcism ritual) which in years past were performed in some part of the *mulid*[22] but which are currently convened inside private flats. People gave cash tips to the dancers and the musicians, and dancers with *tahtib* also tipped the bands at the *mulid*.

The government has attempted since the era of British colonialism to rein in the *mawalid*, outlawing certain spectacular feats, *dusat* (*dosat*), which demonstrated the believers' faith in their *murshid* (spiritual leader), such as placing swords on their necks and walking over them or piercing the cheek with a skewer.[23] Prostitutes, Oriental dancers, and *ghawazi* dancers were periodically discouraged from appearing at *mulid*s. In recent decades, renewed governmental efforts at control over *mulid*s involved police blockades of areas previously used in the festivals and some cancellations of events as part of efforts to discourage post-revolutionary protests. Due to the restrictions, *mulid*-goers have complained that the celebrations are not as enjoyable as in the past. The Egyptian government has not yet eviscerated and sanitized the core practices of the *mulid* as in Morocco, where festivals aimed at tourists replace

Tannura dancer of the Mahdi clan in front of a Rifa'i *zaffa* at the Mulid of Sayyida Zainab (courtesy Nicolaas H. Biegman from his *Egypt: Moulids, Saints, Sufis*, London: Kegan Paul International, 1990, p. 19).

the traditional practices of these holidays, and performances are formalized and placed on stage.

Some *mulid*s are extremely large and important to local economies, for instance the enormous annual *mulid* of Sayyid Ahmad al-Badawi in Tanta, the capital of Gharbiyya province. Sayyid al-Badawi was born in Fes in 596 CE, moved to Mecca, then Iraq, and then to Tanta in Egypt where he died. He was called *al-farraj* (he who liberates from sorrow) as he was said to have liberated Muslim captives from their Christian captors. He could fight with two swords simultaneously and had a humble attitude.

Mulid Sayyid al-Badawi is the largest of the *mawalid* in Egypt. In 2017, some three million people were expected from all over Egypt. The al-Badawi mosque can accommodate about 20,000 persons. People are familiar with the slogans of this festival, "*Madad ya Badawi, ya ahl al-baraka*" (Aid us, o Badawi, you man of spiritual charisma) or "*Madad ya Sidi, ya Ahmad, ya Badawi*" (Aid us oh sir, oh Ahmad, oh Badawi), and its tents and banners.

Ever since the 1970s, Muhammad 'Ali street in the old Cairene entertainment quarter of Azbakiyya lost its prior centrality to the music profession. From its coffee-houses, ensembles could be hired for the *mawalid*, *zars*, or *zaffat* for weddings. Some of the families of entertainers moved away in that decade. Newcomers to entertainment, *khashana*,[24] who did not grow up in these traditional families and who do not speak the secret language of entertainers[25] or share their values entered the scene. This occurred as formerly elite areas declined in status, new compounds sprang up, and unregulated slum areas (*ashwayyat*) expanded. Accompanying these spatial and social changes was an increasing prevalence of recorded music, now mounted on private channels and shared by cellular phone. The musicians' marketplace moved into the virtual sphere.

Amidst these changes, the new *mulid* songs developed as a sub-genre coexisting with others, love songs, hard-luck songs, and those with transformative intent in the field of *sha'bi* and electro-*sha'bi* music. They are better appreciated by youth than the traditional *mada'ih* (hymns of praise) and the *anashid* of Sufi ritual. Many non–Sufi Egyptians, especially youth, are actually unfamiliar with the rituals of the *dhikr*, the Sufi ceremony of remembrance of Allah. They were not taught the movements or chants and find it strange to participate if they attempt to do so.

Yet, references to the traditional *mulid* are pervasive in Egypt. The *'arusa al-mulid*, an elaborate sugar doll with a full skirt, is sold at the *mawalid*. The *'arusa al-mulid* was the subject of a dance choreographed by Mahmoud Reda for his troupe. Tahia Kariuka performed a long dance segment in the film *al-'Arusa al-Mulid*. Annually, a film is televised based on the puppet show, *Lailat al-Kabira*, to Salah Jahin's poetry and Sayyid Makawi's music, first performed in 1959 at the Cairo Puppet Theater. The film's characters come from the *aragoz* [Qaragoz] an historic form of shadow puppetry, which used to be performed in public and at the *mawalid* where they delighted children. *Aragoz* puppets were made from animal skin with wooden, and then later on, plastic heads. This form of puppetry dates back to Mamluk times, yet only a few trained performers remain, like Mustafa Othman, who began his career by performing the puppetry for ten years at *mawalid*. The *aragoz* actor uses a kind of whistle in his mouth to speak in a high, tinny voice.

Based on the main parade on the "great night," or climax of the *mulid*, the operetta and film of *al-Lailat al-Kabira* memorialized many familiar characters and references from Egypt's popular culture. Many associate the *mulid* with their childhood when viewing the filmed version of this puppet show, which was broadcast on television. The play/film of *al-Lailat al-Kabira* has been remade as a ballet, a musical, and again in film.[26]

Many novels and poems reference the *mawalid*, the piety of those who honor the saints and the moral challenges in this world, as in Yahya Haqqi's novella, *Qindil Umm Hashim* (*The Lamp of Umm Hashim: The Saint's Lamp*) (1944), with its allusion to the *diwan* (court) of the *awliyya*, who could (but do not) alleviate all the injustices afflicting the community.[27] Salah Enani's painting "al-Hara" (1996) shows an Egyptian neighborhood along an alley with all of its chaos and congestion, featuring a roster of *sha'bi* characters from the bicyclist balancing *'aish baladi* (bread) loaves on his head to a woman carrying her child up on her shoulder and a *shaykh* swinging the incense (*bakhur*) holder and chanting.

When cinema writers or directors wish to illustrate the authenticity of a rural or lower-class urban location and its insecurity, anarchistic, or anti-modern tendencies, they may show a *mulid*. For example, *al-Mouled* (1989), starring 'Adil Imam, an actor who thrived on depicting the plight of the ordinary man, tells the story of a child named (ironically) Barakat who was kidnapped during the *mulid*'s chaos and raised among gangs. The film's opening scene shows the family traveling to the *mulid* on the train. As they arrive, a figure identical to that in Enani's painting swings burning incense and yells "*Madad, madad, hayy, huwwa, hayy*"—a typical Sufi chant.[28]

Mulid *Music*

Current films may include the new *mulid* songs. Or they may simply reference *mulid* dancing within a wedding party scene as in Hamada al-Laithy's hit remix *sha'bi/mulid* song "'Ala Rimsh al-'Ayyun,"[29] in *al-Qashqash* (2013) which features the dancer Safinaz, who was extremely popular at that time, clad in a leopard-printed dress popping her chest (moving her rib-cage forward and back) and using a dizzying "choo choo" shimmy (a hip shimmy which is produced by hitting the feet on the ground, instead of swinging the hips). The singer loves the song, as does the band wearing pink shirts, one man dancing while balancing objects on his head or forehead, another slashing a sword to the left and right of Safinaz in the *mulid* dance style. In the song's second section, the keyboardist accents by alternating the low Si (B) and high Si (B), with a squeaky tone on the higher octave 1 (low B) 2 (high B) 3 (low B) 4 (high B) 5 (low B) 6 (high B), achieving a vampire effect. Here is rocking dance music, recast as a party to show everyone how to party.[30]

Video and film have been very important to the new *mulid* trend by demonstrating the appeal of entertainers and symbols of the festival. The video clips advertise the song and the performers who are available for wedding bookings and contain the agents' phone numbers. The music is meant for dancing, not sitting. This musical style is innovative and therefore "cool,"—not simply *turath* (cultural heritage).

The new songs entitled *mulid* emerged solely in Egypt. They are a sub-genre of *sha'bi* music. Their musical and textual aspects may overlap with *sha'bi*, and are distinct from *mahragan* (sometimes called electro-*sha'bi*, to the chagrin of the musicians who deliberately named it *mahragan*, see Chapter Five). The lyrics express the dynamic tensions between pleasure in this lifetime and the need to care for the Muslim's eternal soul, and the music introduces various references to the earlier "real" *mawalid*. The genre has repeatedly used the setting of a music party, a *farah*, as made popular on television shows and Arabic music contests, to market the music on videos and in films.

Because Sufi orders exist throughout the Islamic world, *mawalid* have been transformed in other urban contexts.[31] In Arab countries, outside of Egypt, and Muslim communities elsewhere, modern forms of *anashid* (religious hymns) are being produced, but their musical content is closer to *tarab* music, or Westernized styles. These are stylistically and atmospherically the antithesis of the new *mulid* music; they are sometimes performed and recorded *a capella* (not accompanied by instruments) in a very sober and serious tone. *Anashid* as war songs have been recorded by various Islamic militias from al-Qa'ida[32] to the Islamic State.

Egypt's government has encouraged some efforts to preserve and stage folkloric (rural) music and also *anashid* and *mada'ih* as in the al-Hadhra Collective.[33] This rather staid *turath* format sharply contrasts with new *mulid*'s self-generated, joyous, and raucous vibe.

Jennifer Peterson makes an important point about the reciprocal process of references to the traditional *mulid* anchoring the new music in a recognizable tradition, while that new music enlivens wedding performances and *mulid*s themselves. In 2007, she noted that DJ stations had been added on the streets, where young people could listen and dance on the way to or from the *mulid*: seven at the *mulid* of Sayyida Fatima al-Nabawiyya and four at Sayyida Sakina's.[34]

Sha'bi music (literally music of the people) is a current of urban popular music as will be described in Chapter Five. Its development coincided with migration to urban centers, the incorporation of villages into urban life, and the changes in musicians' origins, residences, and guild ethic. *Sha'bi* music has been described as counterculture because it is loud, comedic, wild, and may protest corruption or bad circumstances of life. The majority of Egyptians are from the lower classes; thus, they are the mainstream culture—in a country with more than one "culture." They do not fit sociology's definition of "counterculture"—a subculture whose values and norms differ substantially from mainstream society and its cultural mores.

Ahmad 'Adawiyya (b. 1945) was an icon of *sha'bi* music who advanced from singing at *mulid*s and weddings to five-star hotels and clubs in the 1970s. Another was Sha'ban 'Abd al-Rahim (b. 1957), nicknamed Sha'boula. Hakim ('Abd al-Hakim 'Abd al-Samed Kamil, b. 1962) from Minya is another *sha'bi* star who has achieved some recognition beyond the Arab world, in Europe and America.

Not all *sha'bi* singers perform *mulid* songs, but as certain songs have become more popular, singers have an incentive to learn them. *Sha'bi* and *mulid* singers can improvise musically by modulating from one *maqam* (the modes which are the key structure of Arabic music) to another *maqam*, and are "*saltangi*" (they wield *saltana*).[35] *Saltana* is inspired by the feeling of ecstasy while playing (while still being in control of what is played), thus creating or hearing music which has *tarab*. (This might not necessarily be acknowledged today as "*tarab* music"—a situation which speaks to stratification or levels of elite transmission of music and of governmental support for certain, but not other, genres.) The musician/singer concentrates on his improvisation or playing and "gets deeper into it." The listener is swept into *mazag* (see above) and is so intoxicated with feeling that he experiences *saltana*.

Mulid singers come from many of the same lower-income areas as those specializing in *mahragan*. Some are newcomers to entertainment whereas others, such as Mahmud and Hamada al-Laithy's family, were entertainers who once resided in the Muhammad 'Ali street area. This gave them exposure to *anashid* and *mada'ih*. Peterson describes al-Laithy's company as follows:

> Sawt Al-Tarab for Acoustics, the producer of *sha'bi* star Mahmoud Al-Leithy's mulid hits, is a family business located in the central fruit market of the *sha'bi* neighborhood, Imbaba. Its space is split between a studio/office upstairs, where music is produced, and, downstairs, a

baladi lingerie store displaying a full range of apparel in *lamé*, feathers, and sequins. Family members staff both enterprises, and cassette tapes from upstairs are shelved among the bedroom attire showcased on the ground level. As an example of more amateur-sounding homemade productions, some other mulid tracks are recorded at extremely low cost and quality by a singer accompanying a computer-mixing DJ in a makeshift studio or on the street.[36]

The latter type may have a poor sound quality, but nevertheless such recordings were very popular. These smaller or newer outfits and DJs didn't much care if the recordings are bootlegged because that merely functioned as advertising for the agents listing their phone numbers on them to obtain bookings for parties or weddings.

Mulid artists were initially unaccepted, scorned, and ignored by the major purveyors of musical culture, television, radio, and the elites. They produced their own work, from audiotape to MP3 files or YouTube, transmitting it by phone and Internet, and *mulid* was then played on the streets. Its commercial potential was realized following the success of certain songs. Only later did labels and channels sign singers who were invited to perform for elite parties, in top hotels, on music channels and in films. Nevertheless, the majority of performers survive mostly from wedding parties.

Ahmad al-Souissi, Mahmud al-Laithy, and Mahmud al-Husaini—performers who sing certain *mulid* compositions (and also other genres)—have singing styles which are melodious, not based on rap, and each can sing *mawawil* (vocal improvisations). Usually, *mulid* has instrumentals in addition to the electronic tracks and live percussion in *mahragan*. Witty rhyming lyrics are essential to *mulid* as they also are to *mahragan* and are memorized by their fans.

Mulid is dance music. Men and women perform both *mulid* and *sha'bi* forms in contrast to romantic Arabic pop, which is listening music. More men and fewer women perform today,[37] although there is a slight reversal in the fervor of public piety since the governmental shift of 2013–2014. Egyptian society is more socially conservative than it was forty years ago, and dance and singing as female careers are frowned on. Those with familial or professional relations to the earlier *'awalim* tradition are thought of as traditional entertainment families, who intermarried with one another and were chaperoned prior to marriage and conducted themselves in a fairly strict manner, or claimed to do so.[38] Outsiders (to such families) also became entertainers. Those of both origins weigh the social condemnation of entertainers' behavior against their need to earn an income. Even as many women repented and gave up acting, singing and dancing, some had no choice but to work in these fields, and even after adopting *hijab* in the daytime, they would remove it at night to work singing in nightclubs[39] or weddings.[40] Islamization also affected musicians' perceptions of their own honor and status, with the growing "condemnation of Cairo's 'Western'-appearing nightclub scene."[41] Not all women remove *hijab* onstage; for instance, Fatma Sarhan covers her hair but in a more traditional style. However, currently, nearly all others are forbidden from wearing *hijab* so as not antagonize audience members and per managers' and owners' expectations. Also, customers in nightclubs may not wear *hijab*.

Crime, thuggery, and drug use have intermittently plagued Egypt's entertainment scene ever since the 1920s and 1930s, sometimes due to the activities of drug lords or gang leaders, and conflicts among them. As was explained in Chapter Two, in Cairo, women often managed brothels, which were located near music clubs, and club managers were forced to pay protection money to gangs. *Shaʻbi* and *mulid* performers allude in lyrics to the tough masculine images and thuggish behaviors in their environment including the real-life mafia-type figures in nightclubs and entertainment.

The association of prostitution and alcohol with entertainment troubled the reputation of musicians as well as singers and dancers. Musical superstars overcame the resulting social stigmatization through their purchasing power and through promotion of the state and the media. Lower-earning entertainers struggled, however, to convince dubious families to let them marry their daughters. *Mulid* performers remain part of a highly competitive industry with fairly low odds of success sufficient to change their social standing.

Mulid, like *shaʻbi* and *mahragan*, express sentiments that the poor suffer no matter who leads the country, that love is often a painful experience, and that fate is wayward. To this, *mulid* adds a joyful spirituality. The young performers of *mulid* are considered edgy by their elders. Youth culture in Egypt allows for license in dress, hairstyles, drugs, and lyrics, but not in taking advantage of girls or young women. Over the last several decades, many Egyptian men have quit or cut down on drinking alcohol but do not agree that Islam disallows *hashish* or marijuana smoking. The above mention of drugs is not unusual, but very much a part of many young men's lives, and the mood-altering power of music amplifies their expressions of "being into it," "fucked-up," or "stoned."

All three currents—*shaʻbi, mulid,* and *mahragan*—claim to "speak straight" (*dughri*, not compromising and not accepting abuse), in the style of Shaʻbula and that of the *awlad al-balad* (urban lower-class).

Singers and promoters turned to the theme of the *mulid* to signal identification with their own culture and its musical themes. *Mulid*ness signals Egyptianess; the idea is that life in Egypt, like in a *mulid*, is out-of-control insanity. The world (*ad-dinya*) is a bizarre and *mulid*-like experience. This internal image of Egyptian life contrasts to the external world's nearly ubiquitous association of Egypt and Egyptians with Pharaonic life and symbols.

Aghani mulid emerged on recordings for dancing made in the Matariyya district for weddings, in particular those by keyboardist Salah al-Kurdi in 2001. Wedding singer Gamal al-Sobki sang and later recorded his hit "Hanruh al-mulid" in 2002.[42] Others using this style were DJ Moulid, DJ Sufi, DJ Ragab, DJ Karkar (see below for relevance), and DJ ʻAlaʼ. In 2004, singer Saʻd al-Soghayar, already a *shaʻbi* star, came out with a *mulid* hit, followed by the digital cassette *Immortal Records* in 2005. The *shaʻbi* singer Mahmud al-Laithy produced an album in 2005 called *al-ʻAsfurayn* (Two Birds), which included a *mulid* song "Qasadt Babak" (I aimed for your door) in which he sings in the musical style of *inshad* masters Skaykh ʻArabi Farhan al-Balbisi and Shaykh Yasin al-Tuhami.[43] Then al-Soghayar performed the 2006 *mulid* hit song, "Lakhmat Ra's" (Mixed-up Head) in the movie of that name, directed by Ahmad al-Badrawi. In that year, al-Laithy issued his second album, *Ya Rabb* (O, My Lord) which includes a song "Al-Anbiya'" (The Prophets). In 2008, various DJs produced computer mixes on cassettes that included sounds of the *mulid*,[44] and al-Laithy issued his third album, *Kan Fih Walad* (There Was a Boy).

Mahmud al-Husaini sang in the 2009 film *al-Farah* (The Celebration) which also featured 'Abd al-Basit Hamuda's song "Ana Mish 'Arafni" (I Don't Recognize Myself). (In real life, 'Abd al-Basit Hamuda had recorded weddings, producing them on cassette in order to make money, just as in the plot of *al-Farah*.) Mahmud al-Husaini showed the use of *dhikr* themes, as in the song "Inti Dinya Dhikr" (You, the World, are a Dhikr). His occasional screaming adds to the excitement of the song but drew contempt from some online commenters. Not only his screaming was deemed *sha'bi*, but so was the quality of his voice, as the public's ideas about the aesthetic for the male voice have changed. Instead of a preference for a *sha'bi*, gritty, harsh, nasal sound, the melodious, smooth, and non-nasal voices of *shababiya* (pop music) singers are now an ideal.[45]

Comedic actor Muhammad Sa'd, attained fame (or infamy) with his loud, whacky, improvising anti-hero Lembi,[46] and also starred in *Karkar* (2007). He plays three characters in this film, including a cross-dressing potential bride. In the film, he drives a motorcycle blasting *mulid* music, even inside the house. Throughout, he keeps screaming the word "*uluh*" (tell him) in the film and Reda responds with "Allah." The film could have been mocking the *mulid* trend, but the song in the film was worked into some remixes, and therefore illustrates that *mulid* music had become associated with *sha'bi* culture. Thus, *mulid* is not simply a religious reference, but also one signifying crazy, loony, *sha'bi* taste.

Mulid included other features, which instantly conjure up the *dhikr* ceremony, like the chants of "*huh*" from the word "*huwwa*," which sounds like a giant heart beating incorporated into the songs. Costuming and staging in videos continue to suggest *dhikr* performances at a real-life *mulid* where the special banners, headbands, and sashes of some participants indicate allegiance to particular Sufi *tariqat*.

José Sánchez Garcia (a social anthropologist specializing in youth) reprimanded *mulid* music for imitating a "real" *mulid* whilst the musicians and fans were not Sufis.[47] Yet, hybrid genres appear with regularity in the performing arts, and hybridity and ambivalence to tradition, as well as to innovation, are intrinsic to Egypt's popular culture(s). Inside the music industry, new genres are often disparaged; for example, Fahed Ballan, a popular Syrian singer who migrated to Egypt to have a career, told me with some exasperation, that the only important marker of a musical hit is whether or not it is danceable. (He meant that musicianship and musicians' opinions are meaningless in comparison to audience preferences.[48]) Yet, this current trend, *mulid* has had some staying power.

Mahmud al-Laithy sang the song "Flus" (Money) in the film *Kabareh* (Cabaret) directed by Samih 'Abd al-'Aziz in 2008. The plot concerns a terrorist who intends to blow up the nightclub, but he discovers that some of the people there do not deserve to die. This song has a predictable *sha'bi* opening but explodes into the *mazag mulid* with the injection of *tannura* dancers and snippets of scenes from the movie.[49] In the closing credit shots, al-Laithy sings another of his signature *mulid* songs. Al-Laithy can and does sing outside this genre; for instance he sang rap/fusion with Arabian Knightz in "al-Dunia Mulid" (The World is a Mulid) in 2012.[50] He appeared in a traditional style *mulid* setting within the film *al-Laila al-Kabira* (2016) in the song "Sayidna al-Husain."[51] In 2015, he produced a rollicking Sa'idi version of a *mulid* song, complete with a dancing live horse, *tahtib*, a *mizmar* band, and celebrating policemen in "Sa'idi Ya Ra's."[52]

Mulid lyrics draw on historic metaphors in Sufi poetry as in Gamal al-Sobky's first song which instructs the "sick person" (*ya mubtali*) to turn for his cure to the Prophet Muhammad, the doctor (*ya tabib*):

> *Matkhafsh ya mubtali gayt at-tabib garah*
> Don't be afraid, oh sick person, you've come to a surgeon
> *Ma dam dalkhalt al-ayada hat-la'i 'indak rah*
> As long as you enter the clinic, you'll find that what ails you will disappear.
>
> *Ya marid al-(q)alb, yilli ramak al-hawa*
> You who are heartbroken, who love has thrown
> *Ruh al-habib an-Nabi, huwwa at-tabib wa dawa*
> Go to the Beloved, the Prophet (Muhammad) for he is the doctor and the cure
> *Ya tabib, ya tabib, ya tabib, ya tabib, ya tabib, ya tabib*
> O you Doctor (six times).[53]

Mahmud al-Husaini's song, "al-'Abd wa-l-Shaitan" (The Believer and Satan) begins with a *mawwal* (vocal improvisation), powerfully rendered. The lyrics express Satan's voice as he scornfully addresses a good Muslim, advising him to drink and play with his female neighbor, and the good Muslim refuses.[54] Mahmud al-Laithy's song "Qasadt Babak" also contains witty and rough sentiments about the temporality of life wherein people endure corruption, injustice, and bullying.[55] These lyrics are similar to others which illustrate the masses' lack of recourse in Egyptian society.

Another *sha'bi* song, "al-Nar" (with similar musical styling as certain *mulid* songs), sung by 'Isam Sha'ban, the son of Sha'ban 'Abd al-Rahim, names and shames many of Egypt's and Lebanon's most famous actresses, singers, and belly dancers who are known throughout Egypt by their first names alone: Nancy (Ajram), Haifa (Wahbe), Ruby, Nagla, Sara, Marwa, Katya, Nagwa, Nicola (Nicole Saba), Fifi ('Abdu), Lucy, Dina, Rola, Maria, etc. The lyrics begin "*yakhsara! Yakhsara, yakhsara 'ala al-ihtiram wa-l-adab, wa kaman 'ala al-ikhlas*" (Oh loss, loss, loss of respect, and manners and also of ethics) and bemoans the change from the "era of *tarab*" to today's disrespectable artists, who will go to hell (*ti[q]la hatkhosh in-nar*), whereas she who covers her hair (*tilbis hatkhosh il-ganna*) goes to heaven—as the video contrasts the photos of the "naked" women with one of Nancy [Agram] (who would never veil) wearing a *hijab*.[56] Certain Egyptian audiences loved this somewhat misogynistic song and video because *sha'bi* sentiment elides with salafists over the question of female modesty.

Are *mulid* themes simply an elaboration of *sha'bi* themes, or are they more spiritual? Peterson describes the new *mulid* as a grassroots folklorization.[57] In the Egyptian context, "folklorization" is a slightly problematic label because folk music, *musiqa sha'biyya*, is rural in origin and identified with the past, whereas this musical form is urban, youthful, and creative. Drawing on authentic heritage is a very positively associated trope in the production and reproduction of Egyptian culture. We may view it as a revenge of the *'amma*, so "in" that it has now interested the *khassa*, the elites. Egypt's *khassa* (meaning special groups) in its history were composed of the ruling elite, business classes, the upper levels of the military. These might ally with intellectuals, clerics, and professionals.[58] These stand in contrast to the *'amma*, peasants, craftsmen, retailers, some professionals, industrial workers, the rank and file of the police, and the military.[59] The modernizing groups who acquired education and professions in the late nineteenth century became known as the *afandiyya*, and thus part of the *khassa*.

It is not the first time in Egypt's history that vernacular culture overtook and reshaped preceding trends. Ziad Fahmy detailed the processes taking place from 1907 through 1922 whereby theaters, city squares, and streets became revolutionary spaces, spreading *azjal* (colloquial poetry), *ta'ati'* (*taqatiq*), and plays in colloquial Egyptian Arabic in defiance of hapless British censors.[60] The songs promoted nationalism and sometimes anti-elite sentiments.

Also problematic to defining the aim of *mulid* as folklorization is that Peterson's interlocutor, the *mulid* singer al-Laithy, directly states his goal as "chicifying" the *anashid* and *dhikr* tradition. He tells Peterson: "We took this art and made it chic (*shayyaknah*). We made it into 'Amr Diab."[61] Al-Laithy understands his own role as a musician in innovating existing themes in Arabic music.[62] He has glamorized the *mulid* into a dance party and made the songs exciting in a way that often repetitive older rural or *sha'bi* music and *zar* music are not.

Lyrics or Music?

Mulid lyrics often reference the dilemma of the good person trapped in a society filled with perfidy, sin, and bad luck. The only recourse is Allah, but here, also the intercession of the Prophet Muhammad and the *awliyya*. Ahmed Shiba's song "Ah Ya La'bt Ya Zahr" (What If the Dice Has Been Rolled) in the film *Ocean 14* (2016) relates the anguish of a poor man, "who never kept a cent" and "many betrayed" him but "if the dice were rolled and conditions changed, and he were to become a millionaire," he would help the one who denied him and be patient.[63] This success of this song changed Shiba's own fortune. He had, in addition to his musical engagements, needed to work at a second job as a body repairman on automobiles and was finally able to afford to buy an apartment and a car.

> The one who has money, doesn't sleep
> What you think of the one who owes money
> Poverty is cursed—that makes me indebted to the rascals
> It humiliated the honorable for the sake of the poor
> The need is cursed, and humiliation of demand is burdened
> What if the dice has been rolled and conditions change?
> I may take the first step to become millionaire.
>
> I would go to the first one who I asked for a need (to borrow from)
> He disappointed me and made me feel the need
> I'll do the right thing and help him in time of distress
> I'll assist him in ordeals and will be patient.
>
> And will tell him that money will not make him a real man
> and that need is made bitter

and that need is made bitter
But I am getting tired now....

The song's great success—it was the biggest dance song hit since Hakim's in the censored film *Halawat al-Ruh* (2014)[64] with actress Haifa Wahbe—may well have been boosted by the inclusion of Alla Kushnir, an athletic and popular dancer of Ukrainian origin.[65] A beautiful dancer never hurt a *mulid* song. Or, the song's success might primarily be due to its lyrics and musical appeal. The refrain is set to a rhythm following an initially spare *mawwal* to the accompaniment of violin and keyboard. The song has the hypnotic repetition common to *sha'bi* music, yet it is punctuated by interesting vocal, percussive, or melodic occurrences.

Another powerful hit was by singer Ahmad Sa'd in "Bahabbak ya Sahbi." This song was stylistically similar to the above-mentioned Ahmad Shiba song and one (mentioned below) by 'Abd al-Basit Hamuda.

Sha'bi and *mulid* lyrics all reference the plight of the disenfranchised poor, the *ghalaba*.[66] *Mulid* lyrics also explained the need to battle Iblis' (Satan's) influence as in drinking or drugs. They may call for piety, or repentance, or simply explain the salubrious effects of the high. Yet, they are not utopian; many express despair since the individual is powerless against fate. This is the case in 'Abd al-Basit Hamuda's (b. Abu Qir, Alexandria in 1960) "Ana Mish 'Arafni," a very powerful song in the film *al-Farah*,[67] in which he loses recognition of himself. He has aged and is in a bad condition, which is also a metaphor for the Egyptian people at this crucial point in history.

Ana, ana, ana, ana, ana	I, I, I, I, I, I, I
ana mish 'arafni	I couldn't know myself
Ana kunt mani	I was not me
Ana mish ana	I am not myself
La, di malamhi	This is not my face
Wa la wa la da shakli, shakli	And my look doesn't belong to me
Wa la da ana	And it is not me

Lyrics alluding to drugs were obvious in mix titles like 'Abd al-Magid al-Mahdy's 2007 tape *Mulid al-Kharbana al-Gadid* (new *mulid* of the fucked-up one) and others like *Mulid al-Maganin* (*mulid* of the crazy ones). This theme persists in *mulid* and *mahraganat* as in "Sigara Bunni" (2010) (A brown cigarette) sung by Mahmud al-Husaini. The lyrics began with the syllables "*Ku, ka, ku, ka, ku, ka* and *Go go go go go*." But the latter is not simply nonsense; it refers to the "*Go, go, go, go daddy*" lyrics from Gamal al-Sobky's song "Hanruh al-mulid."[68]

Layli, layli ... my bad friends tricked me
They gave me something brown and got me to smoke it.
Then I started to feel weird and didn't know what was wrong with me.
I didn't know my right from my left.
The world began to spin around me
and they asked me what happened to me....

After the singer describes all of his sensations while getting stoned, he asks to "light it up" in the refrain. But then al-Husaini declares emphatically, "*Mush hashrab!*

I won't smoke (Chorus: Aha) I won't smoke (Chorus: Aha) I won't smoke anything brown. I'll know it when I see it again. Oh uncle light it up. O sir, this is too much. Ku ka ku ka ku ka."[69]

In this genre, the lyrics admit to the use of *hashish* or marijuana (the most frequently-used drugs in Egypt followed by Tramadol and heroin). Then, the lyrics express regret. This is in striking contrast to the defiance of female singer Luka Blue in the Westernized style and elite lyrics of "Hashrab Hashish" (I'm Going to Smoke *Hashish*) in the documentary *al-Khit wal-hit*.[70] With or without drugs, this form of music acknowledges the power of music, being moved by music and dance to enhance one's mood.

The new *mulid* music definitely validates faith. Yet, this is not done in a puritanical fashion,[71] and the allusions to Sufi ritual are shown fleetingly, not as in a complete *dhikr*. Listeners' enjoyment of the *tarab* and abandon of their music are a hip form of spiritual intoxication even as the tensions between the temporal and the hereafter are evident in the lyrics.

The *mulid* songs used musical, visual, and emotional elements to their advantage. For example, the complaint about deprivation and pain in this earthly life, or *shakwa* (described in greater detail in Chapter Six), typical of the rural *sira* poets, as well as *sha'bi* singers features in 'Abd al-Basit Hamuda and Dunia Samir Ghanim's duet in "Bab al-Haya." He sings in a *sha'bi* vocal style, rough, intense and high-pitched through the *mawwal* set to rhythm, and his pimp-like outfit and demeanor provide a contrast with Ghanim's sweet voice and the respectability her fans credit her with.

'Abd al-Basit:

Da'ait 'ala bab al-haya, lama angarah kafi. I knocked on the door of life until my hand hurt.
Da'ait 'ala bab al-haya, lama angarah kafi. I knocked on the door of life until my hand hurt.
'Ala 'add hali, 'ala 'add hali, wi-dinyati wi-dinyati, wi-dinyati, ti'ud wala tawafi. Always down to the ground (repeats) and yet this life, this life, this life takes and doesn't give back.
Daaah (he screams here), *ana illi maksur fil-haya, wa mashait fi-milyun itigah, wid-dinya halfa kidah, ahhhh id-dinya halfa kida, matigi fi yum safi,*
I'm the broken one in this life, I took a million different directions, yet this life still promises to be terrible (then the *nai* plays, and the percussion begins)

Ghanim:

Leh illi [q]asi wa muftari id-dinya bitbusuh, wa illi 'ala fidh al-karim, al-khalq bidusuh, Why is that life kisses the one who is rough and scandalous, and steps on the one who is always kind? ('Abd al-Basit repeats the line)
Ya dinya, leh biy'ani? Li-imta ana ha'ani ... wa radhait ana b-hali, wa 'ayza eh tani?
Oh life, why am I on sale? Until when will I suffer ... even though I accepted my situation, what else do you want? (Abd al-Basset repeats the line)
Li-imta ana ha'ani ... wa radhait ana bi-hali, wa 'ayza eh tani?
Oh life, why am I on sale? Until when will I suffer ... even though I accepted my situation, what else do you want?
Leh al-'aseel [q]imatuh ta[q]il, hayatuh tab'a 'adhabu murr,
Why [life] do you disrespect the respectful ones ... why does his life have to be torture or pain?
Amma al-qawwi ma'diha, wa 'ayishha bi-flusuh
But the one who has power, he enjoys and lives on his money
Ya dinya illi mashaylana humum tu'al ... mutashakkirin 'ala kull hall Oh, life that gave us a lot of pain, thank you anyway
Mutashakkirin 'ala khawf 'ala al-'ala' 'ali hama at[q]al min al-gibal
Thank you for fear, for anxiety, for pain heavier than any mountains

Leh illi [q]asi wa muftari id-dinya bitbusuh, wa illi 'ala fidh al-karim, al-khalq bidusuh, Why is that life kisses the one who is rough and scandalous, and steps on the one who is always kind?

As the two sing these tragic verses, the video caricatures the "good life" as viewers see Donia being manicured and fanned by servants and 'Abd al-Basit is massaged. Muscular, handsome, black-clad black bodyguards with leashed dogs stand by. The scene shifts to a *mulid*-inspired performance with psychedelic lighting, *tannura* and a *dhikr* ensemble, explosions, and money being poured as tips onto the stage.[72]

Dance

Mulid fans dance. Dance is the ultimate performance of happiness, and also, of sadness, lovesickness, and tragedy. The rehabilitation of music and dance in *mulid* is partially accomplished by the spiritual themes. The dance movements are *raqs baladi*, but also draw on specializations (*tashkil*) like the use of knives—this may be in an older style, as with the staged sword dance of the single male dancer in "Ana Mish 'Arafni," or in the faster-paced and improvised dancing acrobatic couple dancing of male fans or using *'asaya* or *tahtib* (the men's martial dance originally from Upper Egypt) movements. Very energetic percussion (for which Egyptian musicians are famous) drives the music, encouraging dancing.[73] In many dance settings in real life, most of the participants are male. In film or video versions of *mulid* dancing, women are intentionally included to add to the appeal of the spectacles.

Singer Mahmud al-Laithy is aware of the need to make his music danceable. He says he sings for his own generation which "dances […] so […] it has to make people dance." He claims that when his audience dances, they remember the lyrics and his purpose—a spiritual and rehabilitative one—is achieved.[74]

Neither spinning nor the figure-eight-shaped torso swaying of the *dhikr* are the main movements of new *mulid* dancing, although such movement allusions are often captured on the videos or films used to promote the *mulid* music. The spinning associated with the dervishes has been performed in Egypt by professional male dancers, often from the Mahdi or Abu al-Ghait clans. (See Chapter Six.) Their spinning symbolizes the earth's movement around its axis. The axis of the earth is the Qutb, also a name for the Grand Master or spiritual leader of a Sufi brotherhood. Whereas in Turkey, dervishes in the Mevleviyya Sufi order spin rather slowly and decorously, in Egypt, the *tannura* dance is wild and showy with brightly colored and electrically-lit costumes creating optical illusions. The *tannura* dancers are shown alongside with other types of performers in videos of *mulid* songs.

Musicians are more frequently hired at weddings than within actual *mulid*s. Weddings are occasions for all-night celebrations, sometimes for entire neighborhoods.

Mulid tunes are also played constantly by taxis and *tuktuks*, so adults and children are familiar with the lyrics. When women dance in a social (non-professional) capacity to a *mulid* song, they usually do so in a feminine style distinct from men's movements and style.

Since new *mulid* music grew in popularity, it has appeared in dance videos featuring top female performers, including the popular *raqs sharqi* performer Dina Tal'at. Her dancing is very important to Mahmud al-Laithy's song "Inta Inta" (2013), which also features the *tannura*, and *dhikr* "dancers."[75] Dina is so well known that ordinary women and girls imitate her signature movements (as have other professional dancers)—like her giant, slow hip circle in which she bends her head down near her ankles—when they improvise to *mulid* or *sha'bi* songs.

Other songs contain references to famous songs of *tarab* or romantic genres. Within a 2015 segment by Mahmud al-Laithy with Hassan al-Radad from the film *Zanqat al-Sittat*, the first musical reference is to the song "Ib'ad 'Anni," and the singer cleverly enacts a rivalry with the other singer.[76] At 3:42, the singers riff on the lyrics from the first section of "Lailat Hubb" composed by Muhammad 'abd al-Wahhab and sung by Umm Kulthum ("ta'ala, ta'ala").[77] The song aptly illustrates the jumping, joyous *mulid* style of dancing. The addition of all of these broader musical and dance references evidence the performers' and producers' commercial instincts, which aim to widen *mulid*'s audience.

Possibly those primarily interested in *raqs sharqi* will shrug at the coverage of *aghani mulid* in this volume. They might be aware of a few of the *mulid* hits in recent years but not see any reason to dance differently (with a differing movement vocabulary) to these songs, even as they painstakingly learn certain folkloric choreography or copy the routines shown in films to *sha'bi* hits. At best, they might see this as another *tashkil*, or variation, which may not attract their fans or students. I hope such readers will bear in mind my aim to present a more complete portrait of Egypt's popular dance and music in its entirety and as it has transformed. To understand how a larger number of Egyptians view *raqs sharqi, raqs baladi, mulid, mahrag*an and *fulklur*, and why, is as important as abstracting any given form and more important than decontextualizing them. The aim to draw on images and ideas which are authentically part of Egypt's culture has positive and negative aspects. Like any sign language, or form of partially non-verbal discourse, it is best recognized by those who know the symbols and references. At the same time, lyrics make other aspects of its intent very clear. It runs the risk creating a sort of prison out of nostalgia, yet, the very fact of a younger audience for such music is important.

Conclusion

For *mulid* singers to keep earning higher fees, artists must rapidly record or circulate hit songs, and films and videos showcase famous, as well as lesser-known, performers to that end. Driven commercially, these are not state-promoted art forms. And, those in the music industry who promote certain artists may or may not be of the same class origins as *mulid* performers.

Mulid is an *intifadha* (shaking-off, revolt) against formality and a re-inventing of *turath* (cultural legacy) rather than its replication. Young men who are partially influenced by *salafi* teachings about veiling, modesty, and proscriptions against music and dance joyously celebrate the spirituality and earthiness of *mulid*, whether or not they are versed in or close to Sufism.

It is important to show how new dance and music forms developed from *sha'bi* culture and musical and poetic conventions. I will present this development in the next chapter and then move to the dance music form, *mahragan*, which is also a musical *intifadha* and an expression of identity.

Five

From *Sha'bi* Music and Culture to *Mahragan* Dance Music

Whereas music and dance as part of the traditional *mawalid* developed over centuries, the *aghani mulid* featured in the previous chapter are relatively recent. They were but one sub-development of *sha'bi* music amongst others. In this chapter we will outline *sha'bi*'s history and aesthetics and those of *mahragan*, a genre appealing to youth.

Egypt's *sha'bi* music developed outside of state sponsorship and control. It is the product of the common Egyptian, long downtrodden, and who finally in the era of President Nasser, was considered—at least for certain political purposes—as the true Egyptian. The elites up to that time benefited first from Turkic origins or connections and also from Western affiliations, second passports, and education. They were criticized for Westernization, particularly by Islamist movements like the Muslim Brotherhood (est. 1929), Young Egypt (est. 1933), and the Young Men's Muslim Association (est. 1927), a pan-Islamist regional organization that countered the missionary activities of the Young Men's Christian Association.

In fact, Nasser's government heavily repressed many Egyptians: those associated with elite families, workers, communists, the Muslim Brotherhood, and their political expression. However, under Minister of Culture Tharwat 'Ukasha, the government encouraged and preserved local and "authentic" arts. A huge proportion of Egypt's population remained very poor under Nasser's state socialist policies. Even by the time of President Sadat, they could not survive without government-subsidized foods provided in special stores. The middle class was not huge, as in the West, but rather those living under $2 a day were the majority.

Sha'bi as an adjective means of the people, popular, but was often considered low-brow, lower-class, and that which "ordinary people would like or understand." This general meaning is much like *baladi* (literally, of the country, as opposed to Western-imitating). In the fields of dance and music, the two words were sometimes used synonymously but at other times have particular implications. The *sha'b* are the common people of Egypt, otherwise known the *'amma* or masses, as opposed to the *khassa* or elites. They are not their equals. They were at the mercy of the elites and could not move socially upwards to become elites unless special circumstances took place.

Sha'bi music is more specific in suggesting lower class urban popular music; music and themes of the *awlad al-balad*—people of lower-class neighborhoods who were born there before the massive rural-urban migration that gathered steam in the middle of the twentieth century.

It should not be confused with *musiqa sha'biyya*, which implies folkloric music of the rural areas or which is historic (see Chapter Six), yet there are some strong similarities in its musical structure and lyrics. Since rural-urban migration was a marked feature of Egyptian life in the mid-twentieth century, it should not be surprising that features and hints of one's village of origin should be carried into the cities.

Sha'bi music is characterized by energetic rhythms (*iqa'at*) and vocal and instrumental improvisations (*mawawil* and *taqasim*) which express the modal system, the *maqamat*. The lyrics are in *'ammiyya* (Egyptian colloquial) usually in rhyming *azjal*. There is nothing obscure or elusive in these lyrics—although they might use euphemisms and symbols—as they avoid anachronistic *fusha* (classical) terms, drawing on words and expressions in use in Egypt's *sha'bi* areas. However, they may use symbols or double *entendres* instead of bluntly describing reality. Songs might allude musically or textually to other earlier *sha'bi* songs and challenge ideas about politics, love, culture, religion, or bewail the bad fortune of the ordinary person. Most importantly, these songs are danceable,[1] and they contain numerous references recognizable to Egyptians, or which they know to be part of their parents' legacy.

In 2018, while attending a conference at the University of Seville, I visited one of the respected flamenco schools in that beating heart of Andalusia. On the wall of the studio/performance area was a framed drawing of an imagined flamenco tree with its roots; on the leaves were variations in different cities and genres. We may likewise visualize a vast music and dance tree in Egypt. Its roots are Arab, Mediterranean, Nubian/African, Red Sea, Hellenic, western, Coptic, Turkic or Arabo-Turkic, Saharan (Amazigh, music from the Libyan tribes, and the Maghreb).

The leaves of this tree include:

- Western music composed by Egyptians[2]
- Ottoman-Turkish influenced—tarab/Arabic classical
- "Hasabullah" marching brass band music
- Folk music—*musiqa al-sha'biyya* like the singing of epic poetry to *rabab*, or traditional songs in Siwi, or music of the *tanbura* and *simsimiyya*
- *Anashid* and *mada'ih* as sung at traditional *mawalid*
- Egyptian and Sudanese-style music for the *zar*
- Nubian music
- Sa'idi bands and *al-khil*—dances either by or emulating horses
- Arab pop
- Arabic classical, and *tarab al-gadid*
- Jazz
- *Sha'bi* music
- Music for *raqs sharqi* (with or without lyrics)
- Rap in Arabic
- Westernized protest music drawing on earlier Arabic classical as well as rock-and-roll/Western folk
- *Mulid*—both traditional and the modern *aghani mulid*

Five. From Sha'bi *Music and Culture* to Mahragan *Dance Music*   105

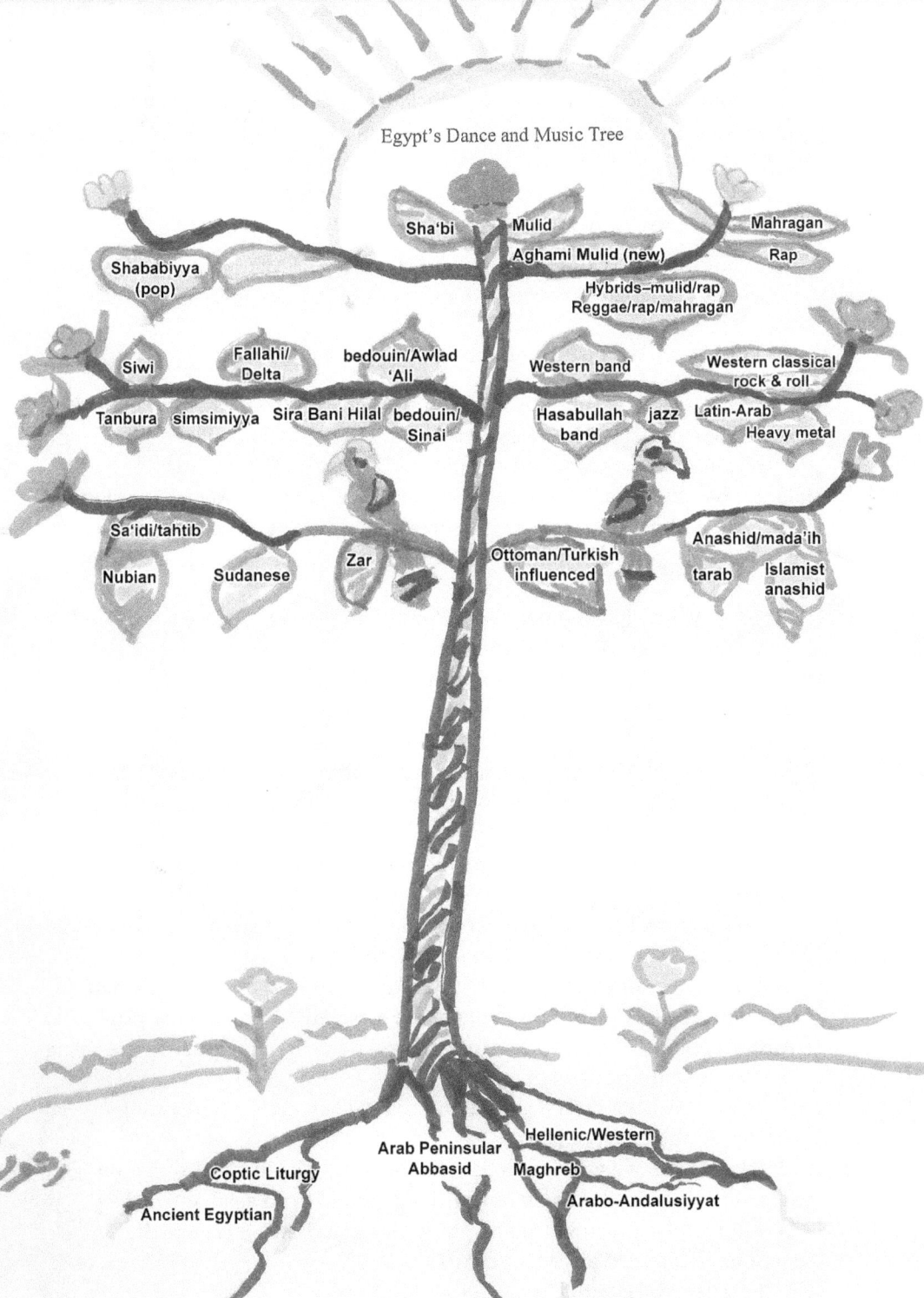

Egypt's Dance and Music Tree (sketch by author).

- *Mahragan*—which shares *sha'bi* and westernized jazz and techno/*sha'bi* influences.
- Children's songs
- New "Islamic" music—*anashid a cappella* and Islamic songs with piano, keyboard, or other Western instruments.
- Roots of the tree include: Ancient Egyptian music; Coptic liturgy, Arab peninsular *badu* (Bedouin), Arabo-Islamic classical; Arabo-Andalusiyyat/Saharan/Maghrebi, Western/Hellenic influences

As another tool to understanding the development of Egyptian vocal and dance music, the events below should be kept in mind while reading this chapter.

Sha'bi to Aghani Mulid and Mahragan Timeline in Egypt

1951–1977 Career of singer 'Abd al-Halim Hafiz.

1952 Military coup (July Revolution) by the Free Officers deposed King Faruq. They rule as regents for baby Ahmad Fu'ad II until 1953.

1953 Muhammad Nagib becomes the first President of the Republic of Egypt.

1956 Gamal 'abd al-Nasser becomes President. Nasser's philosophy involved elevating the common man, Egypt as part of the Arab, African, and Islamic circles, Arab unity, Third Worldism, and state socialism.

1956 Suez War (Tripartite War) with the British, French, and Israelis. 26 July–Suez Canal nationalized.

1958–1961 The United Arab Republic was a political union between Egypt and Syria, was declared. Syria withdrew in 1961. Egypt was thereafter the Arab Republic of Egypt.

1960–1970 Building of the Aswan High Dam with a loan from the USSR following the Czech arms deal. Many Nubians were relocated or moved to Cairo.

1962 Cassette tape is invented (1968 for the durable version used as audio cassette tape).

1967 Six Day War between Israel and Arab states. Israel defeats the Arab forces and occupies the West Bank, Gaza, Sinai, and Golan Heights.

1970 Nasser dies and is succeeded by Anwar Sadat, who opened the country economically to Western investment and gradually adopted more pro-Western policies than Nasser. More than 50 percent of Egyptians were living in poverty or near poverty.

1971 Ahmad 'Adawiyya first gains fame as a *sha'bi* singer with the song "as-Sah ad-Dah Ambu."

1973 Ahmad 'Adawiyya releases the song "Zahma, Ya Dunya, Zahma" on cassette. October War breaks out with Egypt and Syria against Israel.

1974 Kat Kut al-Amir, a *sha'bi* star produces tapes. Badi'a Masabni dies. December 26: Farid al-Atrash dies.

1975 February 3 death of Umm Kulthum.

1977 Death of 'Abd al-Halim Hafiz. Bread riots over cuts in subsidies and strikes. Rioters burned nightclubs on Shari'a Haram, completely destroying

Five. From Sha'bi *Music and Culture to* Mahragan *Dance Music*

the Auberge, the Arizona, and Nadi al-Lail, part of Casino Opera and the Sheraton.

1979 Egypt and Israel sign a peace treaty. In response, the Arab League suspended Egypt's membership until 1989.

1980s Sha'ban 'Abd al-Rahim's cassette tapes circulate.

1980s (early) Juan Atkins, Derrik May and Keven Saunderson begin mixing techno in Detroit.

1981 Atkins and Sauderson release records as Cybotron. President Sadat is assassinated by Islamists and succeeded by Hosni Mubarak

1985 Hasan al-Asmar and 'Abd al-Basit Hamuda's cassettes circulate.

1986 17,000 conscript police of the Central Security Forces, upon hearing their term of service would be extended, rioted and burned hotels, nightclubs, and restaurants on Haram Street in Giza.

1988 Hamdi Batshan cassette, which contains the song "Aih al-Hikaya" (about a lecherous older man), is issued. Batshan is thrown out of the musicians' syndicate. 'Ali Hamida, a singer of Bedouin background performs Hamid al-Sha'iri's "Lolaki," considered the first of *gil* or *shababi (shababiyya)* music.

1990 *Yallah* cassette with Sha'ban 'abd al-Rahim, Sami 'Ali, Hasan al-Asmar (with his song "Kitab Hayati.") Hakim begins to produce songs.

1991 *'Adawiyya 91* (compilation of Ahmad al-'Adawiya's earlier hits including "Habba fo[qq], habbah taht" and "Kulluh 'ala Kulluh") is the top cassette of the year.

1991 Muhammad 'abd al-Wahhab dies.

1999–2000 Broadband internet introduced to Egypt.

1999 Tahia Kariuka dies.

2001 DJ Mulid is circulated; Sha'ban 'abd al-Rahim records "Ana Bakrah Isra'il" (I Hate Israel) which is a huge hit.

2002 Singer Gamal al-Sobky performs, then records the hit, "Hanruh al-Mulid" (Let's Go to the Mulid). It is banned and then re-issued. DJ Moulid, DJ Sufi, DJ Ragab, and DJ 'Ala' play this style.

2004 Sa'd al-Soghayar's hit song in the *mulid* genre.

2005 Sa'd al-Soghayar's hit digital cassette "Immortal Records."

2005 Mahmud al-Laithy's album, *al-'Asfurayn* includes a *mulid* song "Qasadt Babak" in the musical style of Shaykh 'Arabi Farhan al-Balbisi and Shaykh Yasin al-Tuhami.

2006 Sadat, DJ Figo, and others begin mixing *mahragan* music for weddings.

2008 DJs 'Ala', 50 Cent, and Sadat team up with sound guru 'Amr Haha which improves their production. Al-Laithy comes out with his third album, *Kan Fih Walad*.

2008 Cassettes including DJ computerized mixes in mulid styles. The film *Kabareh* includes Mahmud al-Laithy's DJ Mulid-style song.

2009 The film *al-Farah* includes 'Abd al-Basit Hamuda's (b. 1960) song "Ana Mish 'Arafni." Hamuda sings "Ya Basha" about President Hosni Mubarak.

2009 *Mahragan* singers upload music to YouTube.

2010 Mahmud al-Husaini sings "Sigara Bunni" (A brown cigarette).

2010 Oka and Ortega put out their second song, "Mahragan Smoking." https://www.youtube.com/watch?v=egXmFDkJzMc

2011, January 25 Popular demonstrations held on Police Day turn into a revolution. "Egypt Burning" https://www.youtube.com/watch?v=w3FQXYdyHCg

Feb 11 Hosni Mubarak steps down. October 9–10 Police put down Copts' protest at the Maspero building killing twenty-four.

2011 Figo, 50 Cent and Sadat put out "Rap al-Sha'b wal-Hukuma." https://www.youtube.com/watch?v=LuaQklJlbog

2012 Recording of "'Ana Nifsi 'Ayyiz Ra'is," (I Just Want a President) https://www.youtube.com/watch?v=BumLRk_ji2k

2012 Muhammad Morsi of the Muslim Brotherhood organization is elected president of Egypt. He Islamizes the constitution and arrests demonstrators. In 2013 he appoints an Islamist to the Ministry of Culture and holds a "*jihad*" conference with various Islamist groups, declaring *jihad* in Syria.

2012 Oka and Ortega and Shehata Karika sing "Khuda [Hati] Bosa Ya Bit" (Give Me a Kiss, Girl, which contains the line "*yalla al-mulid*").[3]

December 2012–Spring 2013 Tamarrod movement circulates a petition asking President Morsi to step down.

2012 Mahmud al-Laithy sang a rap/fusion song with Arabian Knightz in "al-Dunia Mulid" (The World is a Mulid, 2012).

2013 Minister of Defense 'Abd al-Fattah al-Sisi enacts a *coup d'etat* (or "coup-volution") deposing Morsi on July 3. August 14, security forces break up six-week sit-ins at Nahda and Rab'a al-'Adawiyya squares, killing somewhere from 817–1000 protesters; the others were imprisoned and sentenced to death in 2018.

2013 Anti-protest law is passed.

2013 Cairo Liberation Front (all non–Egyptians who dress up in Arab clothing) by then produced nine "electro-*sha'bi*" mixed tapes and organized tours in Belgium and the Netherlands and issued the Cairo Liberation Front Electro Chaabi Volume 2 Mixtape: https://www.youtube.com/watch?v=XSR4sH8O7Q4

2014 Hakim sings "Halawat al-Ruh," in the film *Halawat al-Ruh* starring actress Haifa Wahbe.

2014 'Abd al-Fattah al-Sisi elected President.

2015 Ahmad Souissi is signed by 100 Copies and tours Europe.

2015 Souissi sings "Hitta Minni" with Hysa and Halabesa. https://www.youtube.com/watch?v=RnhKBJzWBaA&list=PLFJ_U7BpJ4h3fDfc6prmXcff948EzupC&index=9

2015 Mahmud al-Laithy sings "Sa'idi Ya Ra's" and "Mulid Sayidna Husain" in *al-Laila al-Kabira* (dir. Sameh 'Abd al-'Aziz).

2015 Actor/dancer Sama al-Masry is barred from running for election to the parliament on the grounds that she "lacks a good reputation."

2016 Ahmad Shiba sings "Ah, Ya La'bt al-Zahr" (What If the Dice Has Been Rolled) in the film *Ocean 14*.

2016 'Abd al-Basit Hamuda and Dunia Samir Ghanim sing "Bab al-Haya." https://www.youtube.com/watch?v=mhs3y8b2IGk&feature=youtu.be

2017 Mahragan duo of MCs Dok Dok and Funky who sang "La'" December 2017. https://www.youtube.com/watch?v=xf9s_h8S2XM

2017 December. Ahmad Makki raps "Wa'fat Nasyat Zaman." https://www.youtube.com/watch?v=DjLpLaGPANM

2018 President Sisi is re-elected. All other candidates are arrested and jailed (except one who is his adamant supporter). Prices increase as the value of the Egyptian pound drops. New capital city is being constructed.

2018 Oka and Ortega record "El'ab Yalla." https://www.youtube.com/watch?v=7YVydzZHU6U

2018 Mohamed Ramadan's song "al-Mali" takes on a cynical, megalomaniac tone. https://www.youtube.com/watch?v=3440XgqAU04&index=2&list=RD4rvhp9YOnQY

2018 Foreign *raqs sharqi* star Johara is arrested under suspicion of not wearing the regulation length underwear, or any at all. She is released due to the intervention of a Libyan businessman.

2020 January 1, Mohamed Ramadan releases "Bum Bum." **February**, Musicians' syndicate bans *mahraganat*. **March–May**, Numerous social media personalities are arrested or detained for "debauchery." **April 27**, Sama al-Masry detained and charged with libel, slander and posting immoral photos of herself.

Over time, *sha'bi* music and dance has further developed via new phases and into sub-genres. It is represented by dancers in Egypt's national folklore ensemble and by the Mahmoud Reda troupe along with rural-based folkloric dances, and also by a wide variety of Oriental dancers who used it to accompany a specialty act performed in a *baladi* dress, or *galabiyya*, rather than the two-piece *badla*, or with *tahtib*. *Mulid* music is a form of *sha'bi* music, as is *mahragan*, in my opinion, although the latter may be electronically generated. Many other folk genres mentioned in Chapter Six are also related to but not precisely the same as *sha'bi* music.

Sayyid Darwish and other early composers who composed *taqatiq* (light songs for theater) were a starting point for *sha'bi* music from about 1910–1923. These expressed Egyptians' courage and defiance in confronting their British-controlled government. Darwish's songs sometimes represented the *sha'b*, for example, the *harafish*, the lowly professions and the unemployed, and the aspirations of Egyptians to free themselves from British governance and repression.

The development of *sha'bi* music in the middle of the twentieth century coincided with migration to urban centers, changes in musicians' origins, residences, incomes, and the availability and affordability of audio cassettes (*sharayit*) and audio cassette players. The themes of music often invoked the corruption of life in the big city and the helplessness of men (or women) in the trials and tribulations they faced. *Sha'bi* music has controversially been described as counterculture because it is loud, comedic, wild, and may counter attitudes of others in society. It was not until the 1970s that it impinged on the elites and was thus thought of as multiplying out of control by the state, being played when it was forbidden, and disliked by those of refined tastes.

In the 1940s and 1950s, *mawwal* singers like Anwar al-'Askari and Abu Dira sang *sha'bi* songs to acoustic and rural instruments like the *arghul* (a double piped reed instrument). In the 1950s and 1960s, the singers Muhammad Taha (1922–1996, a singer from Upper Egypt, with a very dynamic and engaging style), 'Abd al-'Aziz Mahmud[4] (1914–1991), Shafiq Gallal, Muhammad 'Abd al-Muttalib (1919–1980) who sang such songs as "'Amrak 'Agab" and "La 'Abiltak Wala Kallimtak" "Ya Qalbi Gharam," "Law Kunt Yum 'ala 'Albi," and "Ah min Gamal 'Ayyun,"[5] Muhammad al-'Izabi, and Muhammad Rushdi (1928–2005) especially his *mawwal* prefacing "Ya 'Aziz 'Aini," were all acknowledged by the great *sha'bi* singer Ahmed 'Adawiyya as key inspirations for his own singing."[6] 'Adawiyya: "I consider myself an extension of prominent popular singers such as Shafiq Galal, Mohamed Rushdi and Mohamed 'Abd al-Muttalib, who have preserved a kind of traditional singing that could be assimilated by simple, uneducated people."[7]

These singers usually delivered powerful *mawawil*, but their bands might have a classic sound, and they played acoustic instruments, like the *'ud*, violin, and accordion. They were generally more staid in their performances than 'Adawiyya. By the 1970s, the *org*, or electrified keyboard, had become more and more important to *sha'bi* music, and the electric guitar of 'Omar Khurshid and saxophone of Samir Surur were featured in the music composed for 'Abd al-Halim Hafiz and other top singers.

A key feature of traditional Egyptian oral epic poetry is the *shakwa*. Dwight Reynolds, who spent a year (and more) studying the poets of al-Bakatush in the northern Egyptian Delta, writes about their use of the *shakwa*—literally meaning complaint—to use allegorical language to lament and complain of the cruelty of fate and addressed to the world, fate, time, and so on. The singer does not complain about Allah, though the singer may beseech him for strength, because one is supposed to accept one's fate and be patient. However, the *shakwa* permits the poet/singer to lament in a manner not employed in ordinary speech. This singer/poet of the *sira* Bani Hilal usually sings the *shakwa* as a *mawwal*, and then continues into the epic itself.[8] The *shakwa* dates far back in time to the early *qasa'id* in the *jahiliyya* and has been studied in the Abbasid period.[9] The rural tradition of *shakwa* has carried into *sha'bi* music in Egypt, as was demonstrated in certain examples of lyrics previously in Chapter Four and also in this chapter.

The expansion of *sha'bi* music ensued during the oil boom when Gulf Arabs summered in Cairo, and nightclubs and casinos at five-star hotels became key venues for parties and weddings. It also coincided with the *infitah* era, Egypt's economic opening to the West which began in 1974, and when sudden profits gained by certain individuals called *infitahiyun* were often resented by those of the middle classes or former elites on fixed, and therefore falling, incomes.

Sha'bi was distinct from the classical or *tarab* music preferred by Egypt's Conservatory, established in 1959,[10] and unlike rural folkloric genres, it used adapted Western instruments such as the accordion, and later, electronic instruments. The musician's union often refused to issue permits to *sha'bi* musicians. This meant they were, in essence, working illegally, but they were still very popular and could play in the wedding circuit without permits at that time. Egypt's National Radio (formed in 1931) committee forbade songs by Ahmad 'Adawiyya to be played. Walter Armbrust, who traced the rise of a new mass culture in Egypt, was intrigued by his interlocutors' insistence that 'Adawiyya's music was "vulgar." By this term, "*habit*," they meant low-class, devoid of meaning and sensitivity. Admittedly, not all of his respondents agreed with each other.[11] He uses their explanations as a device to explain the operation of class sentiment on aesthetics.

Ahmad 'Adawiyya (Ahmad Muhammad Mursi al-'Adawi) was born in 1945 in Ma'adi (certain sources claim he was born in Minya and grew up in Ma'adi) and became a superstar of *sha'bi* music. He advanced from working as a waiter who moonlighted by singing at *mawalid* and weddings to being a major entertainer performing in hotels and clubs in the 1970s. In this Golden Age for Egypt's entertainment, his songs became hits without the sponsorship of radio or television, spreading via inexpensive audio cassettes. Despite the ban, by the mid–1980s, they were played on all Egyptian radio channels.

He did not resemble the previous musical icons. Rather than wearing a tuxedo or claiming noble birth like Farid al-Atrash, he dressed in a *galabiyya* or in snappy clothes, tight pants, and an open necked-shirt. He lacked the spectacles and professorial nerdiness of composer/singer/oudist Muhammad 'abd al-Wahhab. 'Adawiyya did not move into music as 'Abd al-Halim Hafiz did through the Higher Music Institute and film credits with well-known actresses and director.[12] Yet, 'Adawiyya's shows were attended by stars like 'Abd al-Halim Hafiz, comedian 'Adil Imam, and anyone who was anyone in the entertainment business. His song "Zahma, Ya Dunya, Zahma" in 1973 expressed the insanity of life in crowded Egypt, turning the Nasserist values upside down. The song was written by Hani Shanuda, a graduate of the *konservatoire* (the Conservatory). The *nai* (reed flute) solos in the song had *tarab,* but the lyrics were "street smart." The song mocked the serious tone of the formal love songs,

> It's crowded on my way to him
> And I'm hemmed in by the crowd
> Have stuff to say, need him to hear me out
> This way none of it will get to him
> Finally he gave me a date
> And I'm going to miss my date....
>
> Crowded, my world, you're crowded
> Crowded, and I've lost my loved ones
> You're crowded and there's no mercy
> No saint at this saint's anniversary *(mulid)*....[13]

With his song "Salamitha Umm Hassan," he referenced a hope that Egypt would recover from the military defeat of 1967. In these lyrics, Umm Hassan represented Egypt who needed a *zar* (a ceremony to communicate with troublesome spirits described in Chapter Six) to cure her. Hassan stood for President Gamal 'Abd al-Nasser, or Egypt's son. From his first song "as-Sah ad-Dah Ambu," (1971) and "Kulluh 'ala Kulluh," on up through "Ya Bint al-Sultan," he produced highly danceable songs that eventually became standards in music played for dancers, so much so, that forty years later, they are used as a *sha'bi* reference by Sama al-Masry in her comedic videos (see Chapter Seven). Western, European, Asian, and South American dancers learned to interpret *raqs sha'bi* through these songs.

'Adawiyya performed in singer Sharifa Fadil's club al-Lail in the early 1970s. His dynamic performance, which caused the customers to applaud wildly, was followed by dancer Fifi 'Abdu performing a *raqs sharqi* set followed by her cheeky *sha'bi* dance act in which she holds and smokes a *shisha* (water pipe) and dances. The audience were almost entirely Egyptians and Gulf Arabs. It was expensive to attend: there was one set price for a table, and another for a better-positioned table with a bottle of Johnny Walker scotch already set onto the table and added onto the bill.¹⁴

Ahmad Adawiyya singing "Ya Bint Sultan."

'Adawiyya's songs were also described as vulgar because not only the elites, but also the leftists, had contempt for Sadat's era, and the political and socioeconomic changes it brought. While his song "Habba Fu[q] Habba Taht" (A Bit Above and A Bit Beneath; referring to the one who lives upstairs and the one downstairs) has been continuously explained as referring to social class differences, nevertheless certain leftists condemned music or art which did not emphatically allude to political action as empty. They described 'Adawiyya as "superficial" and pointed to 'Abd al-Halim Hafiz as "Nasserist" and even today unfavorably compare him with Mohamed Munir.¹⁵ Nevertheless 'Abd al-Halim Hafiz and Nagib Mahfouz supported 'Adawiyya precisely because of the combination of his *sha'bi* ethos and popularity.

Musically, *sha'bi* is full of *tarab*, although at the time, those who loved the older, less raucous, and more classical music denied that fact. Certainly, the *shakwa*, or lament, that either prefaces a song or is inserted into it conveys *tarab*. *Sha'bi* performers understood *saltana*—a condition or state of feeling ecstasy while playing or hearing music deriving from its *tarab*. This is not a trance state, but rather the singer or musician is conscious and is able to deeply delve into his improvisation or delivery. The listener is swept into *mazag* (as described in Chapter Four).

Also, it must be understood that musicians frequently played for different groups and in different genres. One could be a *sha'bi* musician from a *sha'bi* milieu and also play with an upscale orchestra with an invitation from a fellow musician, perhaps for specific weddings, and be employed by a dancer of *raqs sharqi* in a nightclub, and also perhaps, be hired by a national folkloric ensemble, as was Sayyid Henkish. His motivation to perform was economic; he explained that although some disliked "playing behind a dancer" (*bita' al-'awalim* if in a wedding, and *bita' al-ra[qq]asin*, if in clubs), he needed to do so to provide for his family.¹⁶ Having learned scores by ear, he could do this. Music reading skills were required at a certain point in time by Umm Kulthum's own *takht* (but with exceptions made for certain players), for radio orchestra performances, or for state-organized ensembles for Arabic music. Musicians I met often played with two or three different groups; some also had to juggle their army service requirements into the equation.

'Adawiyya's popularity continued; despite being banned from radio and television, he made twenty-seven films. He became wealthy and invested in buildings in Ma'adi, the suburb just south of Cairo where he started out. His success continued until he was found comatose in a hotel in 1990, allegedly the victim of a jealous Kuwaiti husband of a princess.[17] It was rumored that he had been castrated or had overdosed, and it is usually admitted that he had a stroke. He recovered partially and began singing again some years ago. Yet, when he issued a new video clip "Wala 'Aishq Wala Hubb" in 2006, it was by no means as popular as songs of the younger currents of *sha'bi* and pop singers.

Kat-Kut al-Amir was another *sha'bi* star best known for "Ya Ghazal al-Darb al-Ahmar" (You Gazelle [a girl] of Darb al-Ahmar, a *sha'bi* area). He married 'Azza Sharif and also Nelly Fu'ad. Hasan al-Asmar (b. 1959), who came from Qena to the 'Abbasiyya district of Cairo, was considered the second best *sha'bi* singer after 'Adawiyya or achieved this status following 'Adawiyya's health problems. Al-Asmar became well-known for his songs "Kitab Hayati," "Mawwal 'Umri" and others. He was featured in the TV series "Arabesque," and then in "Qamar." Just prior to his death in 2011 at age fifty-two, he was angry with the April 6 movement (a youth movement that had allied with workers) for its protest march through his neighborhood, 'Abbasiyya.

Sha'ban 'Abd al-Rahim (b. 1957) was formerly a *makwagi*, an ironer. He became popular in the 1980s after Sadat's assassination and a household name in Egypt with his 2001 release, "I Hate Israel," which countered the government's official position following the Camp David accords. 'Abd al-Rahim used a predictable musical introduction, with intoned sighs, *ahhh, ahh, ahh*, and then in rhyming and sarcastic lyrics introduces the subject of his song, whether Osama bin Ladin, Iraq, or *bango*. His tapes were extremely popular because of the politics and angry vehemence of the lyrics. His artistry was mocked as was 'Adawiyya's. Sha'bula was reportedly proud of wearing a shirt made from his mother's flowered couch cover and was said to keep chickens, even though he sold millions of cassettes.

Sha'bi lyrics often decry the loss of the *awlad al-balad*'s (Cairene, indigenous, urbanites) customs and values. The lyrics of Sha'bula's "al-Bango" (Marijuana) declare: "In everything, we became Westerners. There is no *malaya laff* (traditional outer wrap of the *bint al-balad*) and no scarf. Every day there is a new fashion. Even language is no longer Arabic, Arabic, Arabic.... We forgot our habits and traditions."[18] Somewhat in this nostalgic vein, Ahmad Makki, a currently popular rapper/actor, included a *sha'bi mawwal* in his song "Wa'fat Nasyat Zaman" (Standing on the Street Corner of Old), which recalls the "hood's" traditions wherein men protected women, and all shared in Ramadan preparations. He introduces the song by asking: "Do you remember at Ramadan, the people would hang decorations and sweep the floor and put colored sawdust in designs ... a plate went between every apartment (people would share cooked dishes and sweets with their neighbors) ... but now a motorcycle with three riders will pinch a girl [in the same neighborhood] for no reason." Scenes depicting his descriptions of the lights, plates, and the harassment of the girl are shown in the video.[19]

Sometimes, *sha'bi* songs were more vague, and yet everyone understood their intent, as in Hamdi Batshan's "Aih al-Hikaya," released in 1988. Batshan, from Alexandria, deals with the behavior of a dirty old man hitting on a young woman. It was understood widely as a reference to vulgarity, which is so common as to be accepted.[20]

The singer Hakim decided to pursue *sha'bi* singing and succeeded to the point that he is a cross-over from *sha'bi* to pop, meaning that his songs are heard by a very wide audience. 'Abd al-Hakim 'Abd al-Samid Kamil (b. 1962), known as Hakim, is from Maghagha, Minya, and not from a traditional *sha'bi* neighborhood in Cairo. His father, the town's mayor, did not want his son to pursue music. He played music as a teen, moved to Cairo to go to college, and then returned to music, against his father's wishes, and claimed to have learned a lot on Muhammad 'Ali street.[21] He respected the traditional musicians who apprenticed and mastered their profession there and was quoted: "I always say that the musician who never worked on Mohamed 'Ali is not a musician, and I cannot trust them to stand behind me.... Mohamed 'Ali is the ultimate academy."[22]

In 1989 he met producer Hamid al-Sha'iri and signed with Sonar Lmtd/Slam. His recordings sold well from his first album *Nazra* (1992) to *Efrad* (1997) and his great success *Essalam 'Alaiku* (2001) and *'Ala Wad'ak* in 2017. He had sold more than eight million records by 2004 and is referred to as the King of Egyptian Sha'bi, appearing internationally and collaborating sometimes with Western artists.

Hamid al-Sha'iri, a Libyan-Egyptian composer, was said to be the leading figure in *al-gil* (pronounced al-geel)—a term referring to the new generation's use of the electronic keyboard music, more polished than *sha'bi* and oriented to the Arab world. Later on, this trend was called Arab pop or *shababiyya* and confusingly includes Hakim as well. Al-Sha'iri's claim to fame came with his arranging the song "Lolaki" sung by 'Ali Hamida in 1988, who was of Bedouin origin, and his production of Hakim's work.

Then, the boom period for entertainment began to dry up. The Gulf Arabs stopped coming to Cairo for at least a decade following Sadat's signing of the Camp David Accords in 1978 and Egypt's ouster from the Arab League. After Sadat's assassination in 1981, the government feared Islamist organizations and their influence on the population. These Islamists opposed music and dance and were known for threatening entertainers.

There were attacks on the night clubs and hotels on Shari'a al-Haram twice (prior to the 2011 revolution): during the bread riots of 1977 and after the Central Security Forces revolted in 1986. Egypt needed tourism, but the violent Islamist groups began to target tourists in the 1990s as well as Egyptian judges as part of their campaign against the government.

Through the 1980s and 1990s, more and more women began wearing the *hijab*, and dancers and actresses repented and gave up entertainment. Also, music videos and music clips from film became far more important and were widely shared. As time went on, those hiring performers for weddings became less generous (refusing to pay tips), and weddings could be rougher in atmosphere. Weddings held in the street were considered *sha'bi* (in a negative way), and these were expensive, as food had to be provided. If they were held in army clubs or sports clubs, the performers had to be registered with their syndicate (union).[23] Couples sometimes preferred to bring a male dancing folkloric troupe, a *firqat zaffa* (and when in a dance show, rather than at a wedding, termed *funun al-sha'biyya* [see Chapters Seven and Eight]) to perform in their wedding *zaffa* (procession).[24] To the detriment of most musicians' incomes, in the 1990s, people began hiring DJs, often in lieu of a band, and in the 20-teens, a *mahragan* artist or group. By the mid–1990s, the wedding circuit, which had been so important to the entertainers of Muhammad 'Ali street, was almost entirely gone, causing them to resort mainly to performances in nightclubs.[25]

Relationship of Raqs Sharqi *and* Sha'bi *Music*

Sha'bi dance is often a segment or a specialization in the shows of *raqs sharqi* performers, but is also more broadly an Egyptian dance style potentially performed by anyone and everyone: young, old, male, or female, and not only solo performers. (It was and remains referred to as *baladi*, and the switch in terminology is not unanimous.) Not all hotel and club dancers performed it; it might be part of the teaching circuits' repertoire while less so of individual dancers. Also, different ways of using *sha'bi* musical themes in particular spots in a *raqs sharqi* show came in and out of vogue.

Suhair Zaki did not initially include such a segment in her show in the early 1970s, but Fifi 'Abdu did and it was wildly popular. However, 'Adawiyya and Kat-Kut al-Amir appeared by Suhair's side, singing in promotional videos. Other dancers experimented with adding a *baladi* or Sa'idi segment or dancing with the *ballas* (clay jug). Suhair can be seen dancing in extended *baladi* segments in the early 1990s. The *sha'bi* sound and feeling, its sense of ownership by ordinary people, meant that anyone (musically talented) could perform it, but the nationalist feeling that *sha'bi* conveys (as well as with *raqs sha'bi*) is also apparent.

In certain of Nagwa Fu'ad's shows, her musical selections begin with a different song and then introduce a new theme of 16 or 32 bars with a Sa'idi sound (*lun* or color) or a *sha'bi* sound, which then revert to a fast-paced *raqs sharqi* song. In numerous dance shows, the accordion or other instruments were used in what performing dancers often termed a "*baladi* progression" consisting of *'awadi baladi* and/or *tet baladi* and then a segue into a drum solo or a new song. An instrumental *taqasim* began this section of the dance, often (but not always) on the accordion (another melody instrument might substitute). The *'awadi baladi* was said to originate with the *'awalim* and is a female version of the dance, meaning that women and men tended to incorporate different movements into this solo or duet between accordion (or later, keyboard) and percussion. It could be played with the songs "Baladi ya wad" or "Habibi, ya 'aini" or a different instrumental riff with the musical formula of question (*su'al*) and response (*gawab*, or a *lazima*). Typically, the accordion, *riqq*, and *tabla* responded to each other, and the dancer to them.

The *tet baladi* was a final section (considered to derive from male dancing and some insist, from the Sa'id). After a *taqsim*, either "Aminti billa" or "Ya Hassan" are played or sometimes both songs. This segues into the percussion (or *tabla/daff/riqq* section) giving staccato accents on the off-beat. The dancer might balance on one leg and then touch her toe down to the ground, as if pawing the ground like a horse. Then, the lead instrument and percussion come together and either a new song is played (*sha'bi* or folkloric) or the percussion section or *tabla* begin to play a solo. Sometimes a *baladi* progression could begin with 'Adawiyya's slower paced "Ya Bint al-Sultan," or a song like "Taht al-shibbak" with rhythmic stops rather than a faster paced *sha'bi* song. Because this particular style of routine was exported by dance students and teachers beyond Egypt, certain songs became *de rigeur* whereas others were forgotten or unknown.

As with *raqs sha'bi* in Chapter Six, it is important to stress that *sha'bi* (or *baladi*) is more than a specific song(s) or a dance. It is a life style, an attitude, a quality, and a style of music and dance.

There are fewer famous women *sha'bi* singers than men. Fatma Sarhan, who was called the Queen of *Baladi*, sang both rural and urban types of music, and when she teamed up with Nagwa Fu'ad and then with Dina, this boosted the popularity of the performance. There are different reasons for the lower visibility of women, first being the Islamic revival; as Kate Zirbel put it, "There was no place for a veiled woman onstage."[26] A singer in the family of her interlocutors had veiled for four years, then got a job in a dancer's band and had no choice but to unveil.[27] In the nightclub, or cabaret circuit, women performers need, beyond being unveiled, to present an appearance, clothing, and makeup that is less *sha'bi*.[28] Many *sha'bi* weddings where work was once plentiful were made up of people who were familiar with each other, and women felt more comfortable performing there than in nightclubs. Another reason is the continuing stigma by the music establishment against *sha'bi* and its newer forms. If women singers were included, they would often sit behind the band, possibly helping to protect them from harassment by customers. Recently, a foreign dancer who knew the rules of her nightclub, but did not understand why these practices exist, related that she is told by her manager or the organizer in nightclubs to perform with male singers, but she had never performed with a female singer,[29] since her role is to entertain and attract the male customers.

Some women singers can sing *sha'bi* but have earned their reputation by performing Arab pop, for instance, Dunia Samir Ghanim (b. 1985) actress/singer, and daughter of actor Samir Yusif Ghanim. She first became well known for being able to imitate other singers of very popular songs.

Egyptian rap and *mahragan* have few women performers, and those who perform speak about the fact that Egyptians find it strange that "a girl raps." One example is Missy Maira, of Alexandria, who has been recording since 2008. She explains the paucity of female rappers, noting that before the January 11, 2011 revolution, one could go to jail just for one song.[30] (Being detained and going to jail might often involve sexual harassment or worse.) Another is Mayam Mahmoud, a rapper who wears *hijab* and who raps about the harassment of women and appeared on "Arabs Got Talent" in 2013.[31] Rules against *hijab*-wearing in nightclubs or some establishments notwithstanding, it became more common to see some performers outside Egypt play instruments, sing, or rap.

DJ Basma Galal said she realized that she hadn't the voice to be a "*mutriba*" (to sing) so she resolved to be a DJ.[32] A clever *sha'bi* song "Ya Bit" juxtaposed her with singer Ahmad Shawqi (who certainly can sing).

It would be wrong to assume that rap is always anti-government; certain performers employ overtly nationalistic images and messages in their songs, like Ahmad Makki's "Naighy al-Mustahil."[33] Overall, the 2011 revolution legitimized protest in lyrics in different genres, yet *sha'bi* has for years allowed the individual's protest to stand in as a metaphor for more pointedly political types of protest.

Other great singers of *sha'bi* perform such as 'Abd al-Basit Hamuda born in Abu Qir, Alexandria, in 1960, and Sa'd al-Soghayar (b. 1970) who also sings *mulid* and was described in Chapter Four. Al-Soghayar began singing in the early to mid-2000s and Hamuda much earlier. Al-Soghayar has frequently teamed up with dancers, for example in the "al-'Inab" song video, singing and dancing with Dina.[34] He is a dynamic, occasionally manic performer, and the percussion section of his band also performs choreography to liven up the show. Also, there was Sami 'Ali who played for many dancers in the 1980s and 1990s including Sahar Hamdi and Hindiyya (who both later adopted the *hijab*). His song "Shokolata," as produced in 2008, got a lot of attention (and one album on which it appears is banned in Egypt).

The Importance of Cinema for Sha'bi

The *sha'bi* environment and neighborhoods became a device within film scenarios to explore contradictions in Egypt's society. The plots of Egyptian films often feature *sha'bi* enjoyment of, or production of music and dance, and the *sha'b* individual as the underdog, or participating in some forbidden or shameful activity due to poverty—even if the actor/actress may be pious. One sees instances of their bad luck or involvement with crime or drugs. The disdain of the elites for the *sha'b* is normally evident in the plot.

Entertainers usually were cast in the roles of singers and dancers. If they were already known to the public, then their casting and songs boosted movie sales. Certain actresses danced well or looked appealing as dancers. They might be typecast as *sha'bi* characters, especially if they previously played such a role.

In the past, the *sha'b* were sometimes portrayed as broken-down characters, resigned to their fate, but the casting of certain dynamic and handsome or beautiful actors, like Ahmad Zaki (1949–2005), tended to change that sort of stereotyping. The films in which he appeared often took up questions of governmental, police, or social corruption. Recently, although censorship is quite strong since 2014, many television shows and films about the police mention such issues.

Beginning in 2001, certain *sha'bi* musicians began playing and recording *mulid* as was explained in Chapter Four. Their bread and butter remained wedding performances at which audiences might expect to hear *sha'bi* songs along with some of the new *aghani mulid*.

Mahragan

Mahragan is a form of electronic dance music home-produced in certain neighborhoods in Cairo since 2006: Madinat al-Salam, Matariya, Amiriyya, Sayyida Zainab, Imbaba, Bulaq, and 'Ataba.[35] These areas of greater Cairo are not elite. *Mahragan* is a Persian cognate meaning a festival, but in *'ammiyya,* it also implies something loud and messy. This type of music has spread all over Egypt since about 2014.

Social Setting

Mahragan represents those from more deprived neighborhoods to the informal *ashwayyat,* slums of illegally built housing—poor to moderately poor. The Egyptian government does little to improve these areas. Many youth are unemployed; there are no fancy malls or restaurants. To understand the elements of protest by and the *Weltanschauung* of *mahragan* artists, consider the following:

1. Egyptians are somewhat poorer than the official statistics published about the economy, especially if one considers the rising prices of food, fuel, and consumer goods. The GDP per capita of Egypt in 2018 was $2,549, a drop from the previous year. That means slightly over $200 per month. The 2020 GDP per capita was $3,587 but prices increased substantially. In 2016, the official rate of youth unemployment was 31.3 percent (and that probably means 40 percent). In 2017, the rate was at 34.3 percent.[36] Most recently, it was shown that Egyptian income has fallen as the poverty level is measured at earning the equivalent of $1.50 a day (the measure was previously $1.80) per day. This was all complicated by measures which allowed the Egyptian pound to float freely in 2016, as thereafter the pound devalued by about 32.3 percent, and then rose again.

2. Unemployment among young men increased from 1998 to 2012. There was a huge drop in tourism following the 2011 revolution, and any recovery from that has been marred in 2020 by the advent of the novel coronavirus. Young men may be employed, but many don't earn enough money to live on, support a family, or save. Only 23 percent of young women were employed. Young men aspire to earn money for marriage, which is far more expensive than in the U.S. They must purchase a flat with appliances and gifts of jewelry, a bride price must be paid, and a large wedding party held. Couples cannot cohabit outside of marriage as in the West, and to remain unmarried is socially unthinkable. Young men often work for years in order to afford to marry and borrow money from relatives.

3. Music is consumed and played in the *sha'bi* neighborhoods on mobile phones by individuals and by *tuk-tuk* drivers, on motorcycles, and on mini-buses. Playing music is part of the *sha'b*'s self-identification. Their identity, appearance, and ideas have changed over years. Previously, they wore *malaya laff* and *galabiyyat.* More recently, many women adopted the *hijab.* Beyond clothing and taste, Egypt's national ID card, the *butaqa,* shows one's profession, and manual professions or those not requiring education are now a marker of social class, as is

one's speech. The provision of university training without charge, first introduced under President Nasser, was intended to break down class barriers, but for the most part, this has not occurred.

4. As the *mahragan* artist Weza put it, "The rest of society doesn't see them" [the *sha'b*]. The dominant and powerful elements of Egyptian society both look down on and ignore the *sha'b*. Governmental development schemes do not always take into account long term effects on them; for instance, different areas of *ashwayyat* were slated for demolition by the end of 2018. Some areas were demolished, as in the Maspero Triangle where residents were offered compensation, relocation, or a rental in another location.[37] Although this is thought to be an ambitious and mostly positive scheme, not much information exists as to how this has materially or psychologically impacted the former residents.

Those of humble social backgrounds usually do not and cannot marry with elites. To save up for marriage, they try to emigrate to the Gulf or the West, or work in perhaps more than one job or in a very boring and unsatisfying job.[38] Therefore, if young men can get hired as musicians, singers, DJs, or rappers for weddings, it is both a social and economic boost for them.

5. Arab pop music (*shababiyya*) was preferred outside of *sha'bi* neighborhoods. It has included Egyptian and non–Egyptian singers who migrated to Cairo, the music Mecca (or to Dubai). The performers had the backing and investment of production companies. Their music was played on radio and television; they have licenses from the musician's union, while the *mahragan* artists (usually) don't.

This background may help us understand why *mahragan* artists see their music as an act of rejecting their elders, and "presenting social issues rather than love."[39] As the *Madfa'giyya* (a band whose name means artillery men) lyrics go: "We turned magic into insolence. We sedated your father."

6. *Mahragan* was much admired in Europe and taken to be revolutionary. Actually, it predated the January 25, 2011 revolution, and the young artists could not afford to go to jail for directly incendiary lyrics. Yet with the revolution, some artists were asked to explain their music. After a few encounters with the media, they are now far less awkward and defensive about the music and its purpose, whereas they might earlier have denied any political connection.

Mahragan *Music*

Sadat (a founder of *mahragan*): "Do you think politics is only about who is president and who is in parliament? It's about what you sing for the people, it's not about what you sell to the people."

Young men began making *mahragan* songs (*mahraganat* refer to the songs themselves and the parties where they are staged) on home computers, mixing tracks with cheap software, creating beats, amplifying/doubling and adding tone to voices. Some were vocalists or rappers; many were or became DJ's and were identified as MC

So and So. They added keyboard or vocals against music tracks or entirely electronic tracks without voice as by EEK with Islam Chipsy, or Mohamed al-Gazawe,[40] with trap drums (or digitized percussion).

Mahragan with lyrics is more popular than purely electronic music because of the social value given to poetry and lyrics. There are generational differences: in earlier *sha'bi* music, lyrics might feature double *entendres* but not obscenities. In *mahragan*, obscenities are audible.[41]

Sadat, 50 Cent, Haha, Figo, and Oka and Ortega began within the DJ scene. The music and lyrics were raw and fresh.[42] They shared the music on MP3 files and by their phones, and then by YouTube.

Sha'bi and *mulid* singers, and some *mahragan* artists, can improvise musically by modulating from one *maqam* (the modes which are the key structure of Arabic music) to another *maqam* and are "*saltangi*" (they wield *saltana*[43]).[44] For example, Ahmad al-Souissi's voice has a beautiful classical quality in his "Aznabto Ya Rabbi" although he sings *mulid* and *mahragan*. But others singing *mahragan* may not be trained or experienced singers.

The pioneering *mahragan* artists were shocked to hear their own music files being played in the street in 2006. Five of them formed a group called 8% and upgraded their electronic skills. Of these originators, Sadat 'Abd al-'Aziz insists that *mahragan* is not *sha'bi*.[45] In fact, the music delivers certain patterns typical to *sha'bi* music while also drawing from hip hop, reggae, or earlier forms of techno and rap (Arabic and Western-style).

These patterns may consist of:

- An *A, B, A, C, A* structure.
- A *mawwal* at the outset or inserted in the middle of the song, which contains elements of *shakwa*.
- Lyrics set up a situation and the difficulties of a character with a catchy refrain of a short string of words.
- Driving percussion. *Mahragan* adopted a slower beat as well as a speedier tempo.

The distinctive musical patterns of *mahragan* set it apart from rap or other types of rap/fusion as a recent hit by rapper Wegz in "21."[46] This song expresses the crisis of the singer's generation, that he cannot prosper in his country, and refers to migration: "Rome isn't far. The friends are drowning and I am deep below."[47] But while the lyrics rhyme, there is no percussion in Egyptian *iqa'at* and no strong *maqam* structure to the melody of the music, as one expects in *mahraganat*.

Scene, Image, Style

Mahragan artists make music and relate to their own audience in commercial and anti-commercial ways. They boast of playing for some events in their neighborhood for no money, and the circulation of their music by MP3 files and on YouTube brought them no money. They also arranged their own parties, and these, along with the circulation of their music, caused them to be in demand at weddings.

They want attention and recognition and yet, they were banned (although not totally) in 2020 and decried by the head of the music syndicate. They want to be stars and are aware of their image as alluded to in the lyrics to the 2015 hit "Hitta Minni": "*Al-nas biykallim 'anni /Biykallim 'ala fanni*" (The people talk about me and my art). They succeeded quite notably in wedding venues; where families might have hired *raqs sharqi* dancers in the past, now they wanted a *mahragan* band. And the bands attracted young men from the entire neighborhood, possibly from other areas altogether, leading to the success of the wedding and the greater notoriety of the musicians.[48] As certain *mahragan* artists succeeded in playing for mainstream venues and on television, they became more commercial. This is true of the duo Oka (Muhammad Salah b. 1991) and Ortega (Ahmed Mustafa). They were discovered and became very successful circa 2013. They had performed together with (Shehata) Karika in 8%, making such hits as "Ana Aslan Gamid" and "El'ab Yalla."

Mahragan has been described as pure *yang,* since the most noticeable aspect of the scene primarily is men performing for (mostly) men who dance with each other. But that is because men are now most visible in street parties or weddings. Women also are dancing to *mahragan,* and their dance style differs from typical *raqs baladi.*[49]

Mahragan performers arose largely from outside entertainment families (the *awlad al-kar*).[50] Crime, thuggery, and drug use were rampant in the neighborhoods in which these artists lived. *Mahragan* and rap singers are aware of gang emulation in reggae, rap, and hip-hop, and inject it into their image. In so doing, they were accused of promoting thuggish behavior.[51] Sometimes performers go shirtless, and let their pants hang, showing their boxer underwear as is common for rap performers and rap fashion.[52]

Fans of *mahragan* are called and call themselves *sarsagi,* or *sarsagiyya* in the plural. The word is close enough to pun off of *sabrsagi,* meaning a person so impoverished that he would pick up cigarette butts from the ground and smoke them. They are mocked for being vain, fashion-forward, or self-centered, unlike the devout, hardworking men of their parents' generation.[53] Those who deride or make fun of *mahragan* call them *wlad al-sis,* meaning that they care a lot about their image and their clothes, (*sis* is a somewhat feminine quality) and are constantly online or on their phones. They never wear the traditional *galabiyya*; they may streak or dye their hair, grow it long, wear it in a ponytail, or gelled and long on the top and shaved on the sides.[54]

Revolution and Counterrevolution

The revolution of January 25, 2011, which caused President Hosni Mubarak to step down, was a watershed for Egypt. The *sha'b* joined in the revolution, though the initial protesting liberals were mostly from the elite or middle class. Some *mahragan* artists issued some revolutionary songs. This interested the international world music scene, and some of the *mahragan* artists were invited to Europe. Not all senior musicians disapprove of the *mahragan* artists. They found an older sponsor in Mahmoud Refaat, who produces, records, and plays with them in 100 Studio, a studio he established to produce small quantities of jazz, experimental, and other music, which he has played all his life. He is appreciative of their innovations.[55]

Mahragan *Lyrics*

Mahragan lyrics could protest, but cynically comment: "The people want something new [to think about].[56] The people want five pounds' phone credit. The people want to topple the regime. But the people are so damn tired."[57] However, a counterrevolution followed the 2011 revolution. Protesters were killed in the initial revolution and also in demonstrations against President Morsi's government, and then again, after the transition from Morsi to a provisional government under 'Adly Mansour. After his election, President Sisi passed a law making it illegal to hold protests or demonstrations without a permit. People have been sentenced to death for protesting and have been in jail for years at the time of writing. DJ Zo'la, a *mahragan* artist, was killed in the Matariyya clashes in 2015. The government claimed those killed were Muslim Brotherhood protesters,[58] but DJ Zo'la was standing away at a distance from the protest. His peers were understandably furious. Thus, despite the revolution of 2011, it is once again too dangerous for people with limited resources to challenge the government. *Mahragan* can and does speak to social and economic rights. So, Sadat implies there is a political aspect to *sha'bi* identity,[59] just as hip-hop singers have expressed that just staying alive in their communities is a political stance.

Prior to Egypt's 2012 elections, 'Amr Haha, Sadat, Figo, and 'Alaa' 50 Cent sang, "I Just Wish for a President," expressing their hope for a president "who would hear me, or even once motivate me. Who he is, isn't important, just his message. Freedom and social justice."[60] Sadat sang "Catcall but Don't Grope" about the pervasive *taharosh* (sexual harassment). The song was criticized in some quarters (since catcalling is an aspect of harassment), but as the problem is very severe, others approved his intent. The refrain is: "If you are a real man protect, don't harass."[61]

There are numerous songs concerning drugs in *sha'bi*, *mulid*, and *mahragan* from "Sigara Bunni" to "Hashish" to Sha'bula's "Bango" to the *mulid kharbana* mixes as discussed in Chapter Four. Oka and Ortega, who ironically became household names to Egypt's wealthy youth, also refer to the *kharbana* (the "fucked-up" [high on drugs] one).[62] Despite the fact that drugs are illegal, such references are common, as the rates of use and addiction have increased, particularly among youth.[63] Also, songs and videos mention and show alcohol, along with drugs and heavy partying in an elite club scene, as in actor/singer Mohamed Ramadan's *mahragan*/rap "Bum Bum."[64] Although Ramadan declares "I don't drink," the video indicates the opposite. Other lyrics on drugs often indicate a mixture of regret and resignation, like al-Husaini's "Sigara Bunni." The musicians' syndicate and the Censorship of Works of Art objected strongly to this tendency in its February 2020 banning of *mahragan* in response to Hassan Shakosh's lyrics "I drink alcohol and smoke hashish," in the song "Bint al-Giran," as performed with Omar Kamal at the Cairo Stadium on February 14, 2020. Hani Shaker, head of the syndicate, was also furious with Ramadan, because Shaker said Ramadan had been warned but appeared in a recent concert in a "sheer chiffon shirt and naked" (if a singer appears shirtless, that would be considered indecent clothing). He indicated the ban applies to all *mahragan* singers including Oka and Ortega, as, "this type of genre does not represent Egypt, which is based on promiscuous and immoral lyrics."[65]

Hysa, Halabeesa, and Ahmad al-Souissi's "Hitta Minni" (Piece of Me) opens with the singers calling "*Yalla bina* (Come on!)" and introducing themselves, then declaring [take] "a piece of me, a piece of you." It names the neighborhoods in which the *mahragan* artists (and the *sha'b*) live. It notes social divisions, quoting from 'Adawiyya's lyrics about "the stuff upstairs" (*habah fo*[*q*]) and downstairs in reference to a girl (*habah taht, gamda taht*, "who is very sexy"). One asks his pals to wait a second. The plaintive solo by al-Souissi ends with "so I can [just] live in a happy world." Then, nihilistically: "There's a lot of talking, there's no interpretation, in our world, the would-be victor is defeated. ... A friend sells ... betrays ... keeps humiliating his friend."[66] Betrayal of friends is a very common theme in *mahragan*.

The duo *al-Sawarikh*'s song "La'" (No) complains of a girl who "leaves you if you have no money ... acting like her father is a doctor, when he's the most famous *hantur* (horse-drawn carriage) driver." To the verse and the refrain "are you okay with it?" (*yinfa' kida*?), the other singer responds, "*la', la', la', la'*!"[67] This song has been a wildly popular dance hit.

Dance

Mahragan's basic dance movements combine an athletic approach to hip hop movement with *raqs baladi* (Egyptian-style folk dance). Social dancers of *mahragan* may show off their specializations (*tashkil*) like dancing with large or small knives, (as filmed in *Electro Chaabi*[68]) or *tahtib*, (the bamboo sticks used in Upper Egyptian men's martial dances) and refer as well to *tet* (a term discussed above with reference to its performance in *raqs sharqi*). Of the often acrobatic hip-hop steps in *mahragan*, one sees rib and arm isolations, moon-walking, kicking and jumping steps, gymnastic stunts, and duet (male and male) dancing, leaps, cartwheels, walk-overs,[69] and coffee-grinder movements[70] as well as some hip-hop standards—a kick, ball-change sequence, or the "Running Man," as performed in the Western hip-hop in the '80s and certain movements from capoeira and reggaeton. "Extreme" dancing—in which the dancer appears to have lost his mind—is admired, but so are movements that might have been practiced.

In "Aywa, Aywa," by 8% with Shehata Karika, Weza, Oka, and Ortega, the choreographed show for television presents a wide range of movements from gymnastic feats to robotic mirroring to a slower *mahragan* meter. This is carefully planned and not spontaneous as at an actual *mahragan* party.[71]

Men typically dance with other men at street parties and weddings while women watch from above from windows or balconies. Or women may dance in other areas with each other (but without being bothered by men). In a wedding party held in a hotel or other indoor space, there could be mixed dancing. Women either dance (1) in a feminine style distinct from the men's movements or (2) athletically, mixing hip-hop movements, and bouncing and kicking footwork. In this sample of street dancing, men and women dance in a fairly similar style.[72] There may be less or more *raqs baladi* movements, and the use of hip and shoulder shimmies.

As *mahragan* artists became so famous that television could no longer ignore the phenomenon, it seemed there was an "American Bandstand" moment where the hosts, who weren't *sha'bi* and who would have complained about the *mahragan* artists a few years previously, now promote them, as if to say, "Hey, look at what all the kids are doing!" *Raqs sharqi* dancers had begun using *mahragan* in shows in dance clubs outside of Egypt's top hotels several years ago, from about 2015–6. These have more of a B atmosphere, and dancers are criticized for scanty clothing and wild movements. Outside of Egypt, this music has also been introduced in *raqs sharqi* venues, and in festivals and competitions, but very few understand the lyrics. An online discussion about Mohamed Ramadan's song "Bum Bum" reveals the difference between Egyptian and Western notions of red lines. One person pointed out a line where Ramadan claims he is so stoned his eyes became Japanese (and he manipulated his eyes to squint with his fingers) as being potentially offensive, but yet, Ramadan's inebriation, drug high, sexist interaction with women, and violence were not being objected to.[73] Another recent dispute concerned Islam Chipsy's remarks on social media after the suicide of Sarah Hegazy, a gay activist, that he might fool around with women, but at least he wasn't gay. Artists of these genres may not express liberal attitudes, and some may even express a "new misogyny" and homophobia alongside the rebelliousness of a new generation. However, the efforts of the music syndicate to oppose the artists' expression of identity outside the red lines of the state and public morality may very well not prevail.

Asef Bayat has observed that the poor try to "better their lives" by encroaching on the "propertied and the powerful." He observes that rural migrants (whether to Cairo or Istanbul) took over space in cities, illegally squatting on properties and using the sidewalk to vend their goods or park cars, assuring themselves a "right to city."[74] The people—the *sha'b*—also invade and take over cultural space. With *mahragan*, as with *sha'bi* earlier, and *aghani mulid*, they enacted an *intifadha* (uprising) against formality. Whether the ban on *mahragan* continues or not, ordinary people will influence aesthetics and the consumption of music.

The *sha'bi* neighborhoods with their *mahragan* music, *tuk-tuk*s, poverty, and messiness operate outside the aegis of the state. They were ignored and not considered a respectable image for modern Egypt. Yet, Egypt's rural heritage as manifested in dance and music received some attention and state sponsorship dating back to the 1960s. We will next turn to these forms of dance and expression and their impact on the construction of popular culture.

Six

Al-Raqs al-Sha'bi wa al-Musiqa al-Sha'biyya

Egypt's Regional and Particularist Dances and Music in Transition

Raqs baladi is essentially *raqs sharqi*—they share movement vocabulary and the emotional sensibility and understanding of Arabic music. It is a solo improvised form danced by amateurs, professionals, or ordinary people who may be very skilled, and thus not "amateur" but who are not paid. As a convenience of terminology, we have begun distinguishing *raqs sharqi* as a dance performed by professionals in costume and usually as a solo, and the dance is referred to as *raqs sharqi* outside of Egypt and by many Egyptians. Another reason for distinguishing them is that this style of dancing is also performed, with certain variations, from Egypt throughout the Levant, to Turkey and Greece and even in areas of Central Asia, yet, the term *raqs baladi* is not used in all of these areas. Furthermore, the professional format of *raqs sharqi* in Egypt most decidedly influenced its counterparts in Lebanon, Syria, Tunisia, Morocco, Algeria, Turkey, Greece, and Iran.

All of these areas also have developed rural and regionally distinctive dances, which are equally not *raqs baladi*. Regionally distinctive dances are found in different areas of Egypt as well—these are *raqs sha'bi*, and the music accompanying them is *musiqa sha'biyya*, although it may have been arranged for modern, urban orchestras.

Some dances have not been studied in depth and have even disappeared over time. Others were altered, formally choreographed for stage by the National Folklore ensemble (al-Firqat al-Qawmiyyat lil-Funun al-Sha'biyya), the Mahmoud Reda Troupe, Al-Nil Folkloric Group, and many other subsequently formed regional folklore ensembles.

Many excellent dancers of *raqs sharqi* began their careers in folkloric dance, among them 'Aida Nur, and Nagwa Fu'ad. It is somewhat futile to discuss which form is more respected. In social terms, dance by females is not respectable; the question was whether performers were considered marriageable (and if they married other entertainers or others). However, the *premiere danseuse* of the Reda Troupe, Farida (Melda) Fahmy, is regarded with love and affection all over Egypt and not with the approbation accorded to many stars of *raqs sharqi*.

One reason for this was the elite status of the founders of the Mahmoud Reda Troupe and the support given to the idea of this project by the Egyptian state via the

Ministry of Culture, the staging and composed music that was more attractive than actual dances and music in the field to their mostly urban audiences. The intent was to produce a show that would make Egyptians proud and happy to view it, in a theatrical setting where women and families could attend. Farida Fahmy explained:

> Mahmoud's goal was creating a new theater dance form rather than transplanting dances from their local setting onto the stage. His works were never direct imitations or accurate reconstructions. They were his own vision of the movement qualities of Egyptians.[1]

It should be admitted then that the dances that could be observed in Luxor or the Sinai or Siwa, or those that could (prior to the growth of Islamism) be seen in other areas, are only part of what has been staged. Simultaneously, they may differ from community-level dancing because the national folklore troupes introduced balletic or gymnastic approaches to movement.[2] And, they simplified or modified certain movements considered vulgar or unclear. This has a circular effect in that dancers in the North Coast area (from Alexandria westward to Sidi 'Abd al-Rahman) performing in festivals in a troupe format tend to recreate similar versions of what has already been staged. This tendency also relates to Arabic music. There is some healthy discussion about this tendency today amongst Egyptians and other Arabs, especially Lebanese.

Magda Saleh, Egypt's former prima ballerina who traveled to the Soviet Union with four other dancers for her training, collected a vast amount of material about *raqs sha'bi* in her two volume dissertation completed in 1979 which deals with the "raw dance" material she observed; there is an accompanying film.[3] She credits Tharwat 'Ukasha, the Egyptian minister of culture, with possessing a grand vision to preserve and educate about Egypt's arts and history. She notes that the movements are not very similar from dance to dance and region to region:

> There are many forms in diverse sub-cultures as well as regional and local variants to the forms. It is a surprisingly rich and varied dance culture, as I discovered while working on "Egypt Dances," the feature-length documentary film complementing my dissertation. It was eye-opening, a voyage of discovery of my own country, and I was amused by the astonishment of many Egyptians who demanded to know "…where I had got the dances?" as if I had made them up![4]

Of the dance forms that Saleh documented, not all are still performed. This is a rather sad aspect of the center/periphery divide in Egypt, wherein many Cairenes are ignorant about the heritage of the Sa'id, its *'aish shamsi* (a kind of sourdough bread), *bamia wika* (okra with coriander and garlic) or other local dishes,[5] or those of the Western desert or the Red Sea area, and do not care to know. Some consider music or dance from the Sa'id as a rather embarrassing and primitive vestige of the past. There have been other field visual and audio recordings made in Egypt, including those by Aisha Ali.[6] But probably much of the rural heritage is already lost or will soon be lost.

As with all forms of folkloric dance that foreigners or native outsiders to regional cultures learn and perform, perhaps the oversimplification of the dances or stress on their special character has helped preserve them. The government has also played a role in determining which forms of dance (and music) are sponsored or not, where they are performed, and in licensing performers.

Ghawazi

The *ghaziya* (singular) bears this name from the verb *ghazw* (to invade) as the performer is said to conquer the hearts of her audience. Another theory about this name is that it might derive from small, thin, gold coins called *ghawazi* which used to be sewn onto dresses and headdresses,[7] though most probably that appellation was built from the earlier term.

Apart from *raqs sharqi*, the dances most identified with Egypt by the outside world were the rural styles danced at the early international world fairs, which were most probably Algerian and *ghawazi*-style dances but performed in some cases by non–Egyptians.

As was related in the historical review of Egypt's dance in Chapter One, dancers were classified as either being *ghawazi* or *'awalim*, the former performing in public, in the streets, and were expelled from Cairo in or around 1834. *Ghawazi* dancers represent two regions. One was from Upper Egypt, and the other were the Sonbati[8] *ghawazi* from the village of Sunbat[9] in Gharbiyya, and the *ghawazi* of Tanta. The Sunbati *ghawazi*'s style has been incorporated into the dance movements of certain *raqs sharqi* performers. Earlier in this text, Lucy, her mother, Dandash, and Fatma 'Akif were mentioned as having been so influenced along with movements of the Alexandrian *'awalim* or Tanta (or possibly Sunbat) or Cairene *ghawazi*. It is possible that the use of the *venyara*, or *sham'adan,* balanced on the head came from the Sunbati or Tantawi *ghawazi*, who have also been filmed performing with chairs in their teeth and tables while performing at the Sahara City club. Khairiyya Mazin, from Luxor, mentioned that her aunts who taught her and her sisters to dance used to go and watch the Sunbati *ghawazi*.[10] Although the dance provided a living for her family, she and her father did not like the term *ghawazi,* as it is pejorative.

Quite a number non-*ghawazi* dancers attempt to dance in this style as a result of commercial efforts inside Egypt and hybridization and emulation by Western dancers. Khairiyya, the youngest of the five Banat Mazin sisters, may be the last of the true *ghawazi* who

Khairiyya Mazen, the last *ghawazi* of Luxor, dances with the Mizmar band led by Migahed Kenawi, October 2019, Luxor, Egypt (courtesy Carolee Kent).

inherited their dancing and musical knowledge from their antecedents. The Banat Mazin are of the Nawwar tribe; however, even their patriarch did not know much about their true origin or language—possibly the *nawwar*[11] of Aleppo. Other *ghawazi* from nearby areas outside of Luxor are of different tribes. Khairiyya's father, Yusuf Mazin, was said to know several hundred words of his language. Their music was recorded in the field by Aisha Ali[12] and is included in Jeremy Marre's 1981/1992 video, *The Romany Trail: Gypsy Music into Africa*, Vol. 1, a further argument for southern Egyptians being gypsy.

Alain Weber arranged a touring group of musicians and himself, the Musiciens du Nil, after meeting these Upper Egyptian musicians in 1975. This was a smaller and more select ensemble derived from an Egyptian government-established national folkloric musical ensemble. First, a claim was made that the *rabab* players had intermarried with gypsies. Within Musiciens du Nil, the *rabab* players were related, and Weber stated they were Bahlawat (a name of one of the gypsy tribes). Also, the *zummarin* (or *mizmar* players) were related, and Weber called them Halab, basing his claim on Canova's work. Others in the group, the *tabbal*, singer and double clarinetist, were not related to each other.[13] They performed at the World of Music Arts and Dance in 1983 billed as "gypsy musicians" and made three recordings. When the 1993 film *Latcho Drom*, directed by Tony Gatlif, which concerns the Romani people's travels from India to Spain, appeared and a CD was made from its music, Europeans were fairly convinced that the Egyptian southern musicians were "gypsies" and promoted them as such in international festivals, including in Switzerland. However, an anthropologist observing them realized they could not communicate with the other groups at the festival, and interpreted it as a "Halab event" and a meeting of those from *bait al-shi'r* (meaning the tents of the Bedouin, i.e., other nomadic groups).[14]

At first this touring group included, but later excluded, *ghawazi* dance. One reason given was that this was due to negative reviews. Another explanation was that the female dancers, who were filmed rehearsing with the musicians, never arrived due to reasons of family honor. Or perhaps the dancers did not receive a visa. It is unfortunate that the true dancing of Upper Egypt was not seen, though the music was a hit in the world music scene. *Ghawazi* dancing has for decades been most often seen as performed by non-*ghawazi* women.

Since Islamization expanded in Upper Egypt, dancing and singing by women became much less popular. Also, two of the Banat Mazin sisters have died of cancer and two got married; therefore, only one performed only infrequently with their younger sister, Khairiyya. In 2012, Raja, though in pain, was able to accompany her sister Khairiyya on demand.

Their dances were partially choreographed and encompass slow and fast sections. When Edwina Nearing first studied with them, they referred to different dance sections or choreographies; the *raqs al-takht* which was performed by three or four dancers as an opening dance at parties to *mizmar* and *tabl baladi*; *al-na'asi*—shimmies performed from side to side in unison while playing *sagat*; the *'asharat al-tabl*, when the drummer plays the *tabl* and the dancer leans across the barrel of the drum, following the drummer as she dances; the *raqs al-jihayni*, a stick dance performed by two dancers which had some aspects of *tahtib* (see below); the *nizzawi*, a dance with

Six. Al-Raqs al-Sha'bi wa al-Musiqa al-Sha'biyya

two staffs which are twirled, and the dancers pivot away from each other, then back together to the audience.[15]

Nearing explained that the *ghawazi* might dance to folklore songs or to well-known compositions, as for example, songs of Muhammad 'Abd al-Wahhab, but also their own songs of the "Nawara." Some of their songs mention the sisters themselves:

> Listen till you see, then you can judge.
> We are at Qena and Mazin's daughters,
> Khairiyya and Raja', and the third is Su'ad.
> Art is beautiful and its lovers are happy.[16]

Nearing learned from the family that the Egyptian government had deliberately closed a folklore ensemble to which Su'ad Mazin and her husband had belonged in order to promote a different government-funded ensemble.

Each *ghawazi* family designed their own costumes. These costumes are not actually traditional, but have evolved, probably from styles worn in the 1940s and 1950s. They are *baladi* dresses with bugle beading and paillettes and padding at the hip to show the movement. The dresses were once longer, and then the Banat Mazin shortened them to below the knee. They ceased wearing a *mandil*, the thin head-scarf decorated with pompoms, and substituted a *taj* (crown), a somewhat turban-like headdress which is beaded and jeweled and keeps their hair back like a headband. In 1967, the three elder sisters performed with bare arms, leotards, a type of Pharaonic collar shoulder necklace and gold hanging necklace, and heavily decorated skirts.[17] The dancers wear low-heeled shoes. In recent years, Khairiyya was filmed wearing a *baladi* dress with spangled fringe and taught in bare feet as she plays the *sagat*.

In the 1980s and 1990s, the Islamic fundamentalists (Islamists) multiplied in Upper Egypt and as a consequence, in the early 1990s dancing was banned in the villages of Qena. Until then, the *ghawazi* typically danced for many hours at *farahat* (wedding parties), but this ban wiped out some of Khairiyya's work opportunities. She could perform for

Khairiyya Mazen dances with the Mizmar band led by Megahed Kinawe, October 2019, Luxor, Egypt. Photograph by Sahra, who brings her Journey to Egypt participants to take a dance class with Khairiyya (courtesy Carolee Kent).

tourists in the winter. However, the hotels and tour agencies preferred to import belly dancers from Cairo instead of hiring Khairiyya, not caring about the authenticity of the dance and her lineage. These dancers would wear folkloric garb but use the wrong hairstyles and makeup, noted Khairiyya. Other *ghawazi* are in Balyana—of a different lineage.[18]

Khariyya reported that a prominent teacher who once hired her to teach at her festival for international dancers had worked out a scheme with a *rabab* player (the *rabab* players had developed some friction with the Banat Mazin—one allegedly ran a prostitution ring) who presented a dancer named Hanan who falsely claimed she was from the Mazin family. Khairiyya wrote a letter to Edwina Nearing in 2011 to complain of this and also that work was very scarce.[19] She was still performing as of the time of writing. The paucity of resources in Upper Egypt affects the dance and dancers, unfortunately pitting them against each other and against musicians, and causes them to commercialize with the hope of pleasing tourist audiences.

Where the *ghawazi* dances or individual movements were adopted by Egyptian folkloric ensembles, the movements and styling were altered, since the idea was to present them in a theater to a family audience. Supposedly, certain movements were too vulgar, as for example when dancers balanced their sticks against each other's stomachs, so this was said to be edited out by the National Ensemble. It is not possible to sort out where this information came from or if it is fully accurate. When I was taught a version of this particular movement by one of the original Reda Troupe members back in 1980, the stick-against-stomach movement was retained, and there was no discussion of its vulgarity.

Western belly dancers adopted their own versions of *ghawazi* movements and particularly costume, with much inspiration taken from Orientalist artworks and movement styling due to the fascination with this genre by an American dancer of Sicilian and Greek heritage, Jamila Salimpour, and others active in the 1970s. Unlike Aisha Ali, Salimpour (1926–2017) did not study in Egypt but melded ideas about the *ghawazi* and *'awalim* with movements she observed and performed in night clubs in the 1950s and 1960s or those from the films for early world expositions and from the Golden Age in Egypt. She hired American musicians to play traditional reed instruments and *tabla* and created a large ensemble entitled Bal Anat. Other dance students traveled to the Banat Mazin and studied and sometimes performed with them, but their legacy seems to be evaporating quickly, to be drawn on by Oriental dancers or dance companies presenting folkloric content who incorporate some of their styling.

It is striking that Mahmoud Reda said he did not use the *ghawazi* for inspiration as he did not meet them when carrying out his research, saying in an interview: "The dances of the fellahin and the Ghawazi have no refinement." Yet that early dance I learned, and which he choreographed, contained both *ghawazi*, and Sa'idi movements.

He was also dismissive of nightclub dancers for a different reason—their nakedness and that "they have nothing to say, no story, no theme, just sexy movements."[20] Is it possible that what is most unique and admired by outsiders about Egyptian culture is considered banal by Egyptians? Here, perhaps the historic image of the *ghawazi*, who like the modern *raqs sharqi* performer, catered to an outside audience, is the problem, or perhaps the narrowness of a form which gradually came to be practiced by just a few dance families. That said, dancers were being hired nine years ago to perform, and even to teach in *ghawazi* style according to Khairiyya Mazin[21] who are "fake *ghawazi*"—not from actual *ghawazi* families but who have some other background in *raqs sharqi* or folkloric dance or both.

Tahtib

The *tahtib* is a martial art from Upper Egypt performed by men accompanied by music. Its original name was *fann al-nazaha wa-l-tahtib* (art of being honest and chivalrous and [with the] stick). It is a format of attack and parrying that first was known in the Middle Kingdom and was depicted in ancient stelae. The aim is to hit the head or a body part but not the arm or shoulder. There is a Nubian version. The stick held is called *'asa, 'asaya,* and *nabut.* It features slow deliberate circles of the stick over the head, as well as hops and skip steps, movements of attack, and twirling of the stick. The Sa'idi music for the *tahtib* includes the *tabl,* the large bass drum played with a stick, and *mizmar,* or several *mizmar* players.

It has also evolved into *raqs al-'asaya* or dance of the stick, performed by women as well as men, not only in the Sa'idi but elsewhere in Egypt. A variation is performed in Lebanon, and there is a similar dance performed in the Hijaz (although these are not based on Egypt's). *Raqs al-'asaya* is danced in a certain manner by Oriental dancers, who may demonstrate "female" and "male" movements, often using a cane instead of a stick and twirling it very rapidly. They may balance the cane on the head, the hip, or the chest. They may also place weight on the cane placed vertically on the ground and deliver a hip pivot in front of the cane or move to the front and the rear. As explained above, the Banat Mazin also had their own style of *raqs al-'asaya*, using it differently than men as they advanced in the dance while holding them, and also putting the *'asaya* between each two women, poking in on their stomachs and as they turned in a circle. Just to be clear, not all *raqs al-'asaya* is *tahtib*.

The *tahtib* is also performed in the Delta, in Mahalla al-Kubra, where it was part of the greeting to a wedding by the *fitiwwa* (tough guys, protectors) of the groom's neighborhood.[22] An international center for preservation of the traditional "*fann al-tahtib*" (art of the *tahtib*) was established by Sabri Mahmoud, and it is occasionally shown on television,[23] but it should be differentiated from the dance form. Young boys are trained in *tahtib* and perform it, not primarily for its value on stage but to preserve traditional movements. It has been performed in France by Hassan al-Geretly of al-Warsha, who directed Mallawi Dancing Troupe and was developed into "modern *tahtib*" by Adel Boulad in France.[24] The *tahtib* is now on UNESCO's list of Intangible Cultural Heritage practices.

When I studied in Egypt, *mizmar* bands with dancing horses and dancers with *tahtib* were hired for special occasions and performed sometimes in the garden of the original building at the American University in Cairo's downtown campus, once the Khairy Pasha palace. They also performed elsewhere outdoors in Cairo. In our college folklore troupe, we also performed a dance from the early days of the national folkloric troupes in which female dancers imitated the horse dance, *al-khil*, with a male dancer as their trainer. He brings one "horse" after another to stage center to dance, guiding them with his *'asaya*.

Dancing by horses to music, usually from the Sa'id or certain Delta areas, is called *al-khil* and is regarded as an art of the trainer and the horse. It is featured at the Mulid Abu al-Qomsan, at other festivities, and at other *mawalid*. The audience tips the horses and the rider,[25] who is usually male, and its fans claim it is "better" than having belly dancers at a *farah*.[26] Female teen-aged equestrian Abir Magdy of Belqas in Daqahliyya, northeast of Cairo, has become well known in her area for the *khil*.[27]

The *khil* is also represented by two human dancers in a horse costume made of fabric, led by a male or female dancer, which used to be presented at the Felfela Village in Giza. Hassan Saber and his folklore troupe performed there for at least thirty years.

For *raqs al-'asaya,* specific poses are typical—leaning on the *'asaya* as if it were a cane, holding it overhead with two hands, dynamic twirling it on one side, or from right to left, or overhead in a circle. Certain performers add a second *'asaya* (double), or besides twirling, may toss and catch the *'asaya*. As was noted in Chapter Four, at the *mawalid*, many attendees may choose to dance with an *'asaya*, showing their *sha'bi* or perhaps originally rural background.

Raqs al-'asaya is included in categories for dancing with props in international dance competitions. These are overwhelmingly attended by non–Egyptian dancers and one may see *raqs al-'asaya* performed from Japan to Spain to Mexico.

Sa'idi *and* Fallahi Dances

Sa'idi dance is also performed without *'asaya*, and has been included in

Farida Fahmy and dancers of the Mahmoud Reda Troupe in front of the Pyramids. She is wearing a Sa'idi style dress made from *assiut* (*tulle talli*) with a *kirdana* necklace. Postcard circa 1974 (courtesy www.faridafahmy.com).

Farida (Melda) Fahmy of the Mahmoud Reda Ensemble early in her dance career. Photographed by Van Leo (courtesy Rare Books and Special Collections Library, The American University in Cairo).

dance segments in cinema and *raqs sharqi* routines (although the use of the *ʿasaya* marks it immediately, and incorrectly sometimes, as being Saʿidi). The Saʿidiyya is represented in net dress with metallic embroidery of *tulle talli* (or its facsimile after it ceased to be made; this fabric is known outside of Egypt as "assiut") and a *kirdan*, a bold necklace of gold hanging inverted crescents. The first group to perform regional dances was actually Nelly Mazloum's (see Chapter Two) who then served as choreographer and assistant for the Qawmiyya ensemble. Like Mahmoud Reda, she took many liberties to create dances, believing that when they were set in an expressive form for soloists and chorus and dramatized, they would interest audiences more than the original, authentic versions.

Fallahi *Dances*

The areas represented in these dances are usually in the Northern Delta or center of Egypt, the provinces of Gharbiyya, Sharqiyya, Minufiyya, and al-Bahaira. The population is very conservative here, but rural women did not cover their faces, only their hair. Their local accent may distinguish them in Cairo; see Chapter Three for the distinction between the *fallaha,* or country woman, and the *bint al-balad*.

Farida Fahmy posing with dancers of the Mahmoud Reda Troupe in *assiut*, or *tulle talli* dress, and a *kirdan* in front of the Sphinx of Giza. The men are dressed as well in Sa'idi style (wider) *galabiyya* and holding *'asayat*. Postcard circa 1974 (courtesy www.faridafahmy.com).

The *fallaha* is also present in the Sa'id—what differs is her special style of dress, accent, and the dress of any male dancers. Andrea Rugh describes different styles of dress and head-covering which were worn in Egypt from the middle to the late '70s prior to the widespread adoption of the *hijab* and *zayy islami* (Islamic dress), which obscured geographic differences. The distinct differences were vague to the bourgeois Cairene residents, who simply thought of rural dress as being long and full with a black scarf. Basically, the northern Delta dress style was *galabiyya bi sufra*, a granny style gown with a yoke, whereas from Beni Suef to Assiut, the *galabiyya bi wist* has a waist.

Further south, the dress styles are influenced by ethnic factors. All wear a *sharb*, a square scarf folded into a triangle with the ends knotted behind and then tied on top of the forehead. Over the *sharb*, the northern Delta women wear a long flowing *tarha*, whereas the women from Middle Upper Egypt may also wear a *shal*, wrapped around their head and shoulders, usually black. Delta women might also add the *shal* in the winter.[28] However, there were special styles within these two categories. The dresses of Bahaira were colored, had a square neckline, an empire waist, lines of piping that contrasted with the dress color, tucks, a ruffle at the hem, and might be decorated with mirrors or lanterns. The dress of Sharqiyya was black with a trailing hem and often was decorated with *shababik*, a lattice-like pattern with openings showing the skin. The dresses of Gharbiyya and Minufiyya are also particular in style,[29] as are those of Sohag and points south. The *tilly* (or *talle*) fabrics

Six. Al-Raqs al-Sha'bi wa al-Musiqa al-Sha'biyya 135

Galabiyya bi wist on the right and *galabiyya bi sufra* on the left. Sketch by Elizabeth Rodenbeck, in Andrea Rugh, *Reveal and Conceal: Dress in Contemporary Egypt*, Syracuse: Syracuse University Press, 1986, p. 20 (courtesy Max Rodenbeck).

(known as "assiut" outside of Egypt, but also as *talle* in Syria) were made on Shandawil island in Sohag, and a project in the 1990s revived them (for sale, not wearing). It is interesting to observe how closely folkloric troupes represented these costume details.

Mahmoud Reda created a dance of the *fallahin* from his imagination, rather than from an observed dance. He defined their dress simply as a *gargar*, a long, full dress, typically in bright colors with a ruffled hem, and had them balancing a *ballas*, a water pot, with men competing for their attention. To dance with the *gargar*, or the full *galabiyya,* required some training and skill, as the skirts had to be held so as to show and not disguise the dancer's female figure or movements. The skirt might be held up in front or far out to the side to emphasize a step with hip-raised pose. This had been staged for a female soloist (Farida Fahmy), a male soloist (Mahmoud Reda), and a group of male dancers. The male dancers throw the pots through the air and catch them while dancing. Different recreations of this style outside of Egypt may involve only female dancers. As we will see in Chapter Seven, the trope of the *fallaha* is not necessarily romantic but can be comedic, and the ritual of breaking of the *ballas* can mean the end of a relationship.

Siwi *Dances*

Siwa is an oasis in the western desert inhabited by Amazigh people, who have their own language, costumes, and traditions, but have to some degree assimilated into Egypt's culture. The choreography of Mahmoud Reda's Siwan dance, which is faithfully recreated outside of Egypt by Nesma and al-Andalus company in Spain, showcases certain signature movements and employs the Moiseyev tradition's theatricality and athletic quality. The music has Siwi themes, rather than being purely, or even mostly, Siwan. The signature male movements involve holding of the arms stiffly out in front of the body and dancing with the posterior somewhat sticking out, jumps, and turned jumps. The women, dressed in the typical black long shirt with orange and white embroidery, also do

Siwa puppet representing Siwi dress (author's collection).

a series of jumps moving backwards, while extending their arms in a push to the front position. They also do a side *chassé* movement (one foot "chases" the other in a slide) with their feet while holding their hands limp and hanging down from the wrist in a "dead dog" position in front. A female soloist dressed in an *'amis* (long shirt) of a white background *chassé*s between the female chorus.

Zar

The *zar* is a ceremony conducted to contact an evil or a troublesome spirit, a *jinn*, or *'ifrit/a*[30] who may be causing distress or illness. The spirit must be appeased with certain behavior, clothing, gifts, or sacrifices and dancing to special music. The source of the problem may be an *'amaliyya*, or act of black magic (*sihr*) or sorcery set in motion by an enemy, a neighbor, or a relative.[31] The *zar* cults appeared in Egypt in the nineteenth century led by Sudanese *shaykhat*. Popular history attributes it back to ancient times or at least before the Prophet Muhammad and to Ethiopia. The *zar* is practiced quite widely across North Africa, in the Horn of Africa, and in the Gulf. It used to be held in public settings and during Egyptian *mawalid*, but it is now is convened only in private settings, in part because the Islamists and salafis disapprove of these practices, calling them heterodox.

Whereas the *zar* is a continuing ritual, since once possessed initially, an individual will be chronically revisited by a spirit, people also resort to ceremonies of exorcism practiced by *shaykhs*. They also try to identify the possessing spirits and whether they had arrived through *'amaliyat*. The exorcisms are not accepted by religious conservatives, but the *zar* is considered far worse.[32]

Certain musicians who specialize in music for the *zar* are hired, and attendees dance to the music in a *hadhra* (the same word that is used for the Sufi ritual). Depending on which spirit is diagnosed as "riding" the afflicted, different songs will be selected and played.[33] Prominent in the music is the use of the *sagat*; a good *sagat* player could count on being hired for such events. The band-leader wears a belt (*mangur*) hung with goats' hooves, which rattle loudly. Women used to wear a particular cap, belt, and pendant at the *zar*. A *shaykha* (also called *kudia* by the Sudanese) trains as a *zar* leader and diagnostician. She interns with experienced leaders. When finally recognized as being sufficiently proficient, such *shaykhat* are often over forty years old.

The leader of the *zar* diagnoses the person afflicted or who has called for the *zar*, naming the *jinn* who has afflicted or disturbed the person, and that *jinn* is referred to as a master, *sayyid* (and the plural, *asyad*). *Zar* amulets depict a lot about those spirits commonly identified and what they require: the Sa'idiyya (a woman from Sa'id), requires the possessed to wear a *galabiyya* and balance a *ballas* (water jug) on her head as she dances. Abu Damfa is a Sa'idi, and his possessed one must dance with a *nabut* while wearing a dark *galabiyya*. Yawra Bey, an aristocrat, possesses attractive women who must offer good food, beer, and whiskey. Each amulet is inscribed with the Ayat al-Kursi (the Throne Verse), Surah 2:255 Qur'an for protection.[34] Now that fewer people participate in the *zars*, these may be found for sale in the suqs of Cairo.

The dancing in the *zar* is curative and provides a psychological release. However, this is not a one-time permanent cure. A person who has previously been contacted by a spirit will need to deal with it again. The *asyad* will actually expect a woman to stay in contact with them, so these women will attend weekly *hadhrat*. The connection with the spirit allows women to adopt forbidden behavior, possibly smoking cigarettes or drinking, dressing up, wearing perfume, or avoiding her husband if that is the spirit's preference. The afflicted woman is called *ma'zura* (the one excused for her behavior).[35]

The Abu al-Ghait, a clan also known for their performance of *tannura* dancing (mentioned briefly in Chapter Four), are known for one type of *zar* and its music, and the other types of *zars* are Sa'idi and Sudanese. The *jinn* are believed to observe the ceremony, which is also called a *farah* (party). First the room to be used is thoroughly

Zar ceremony Hagga Anhar (age about 70) leading a *hadhra* with her daughter Karima in pink at her home in Darb al-Ahmar. The woman in green is a client (courtesy Nicolaas H. Biegman from his *Egypt: Moulids, Saints, Sufis*, London: Kegan Paul International, 1990, p. 167).

infused with the smoke of incense. The patient is treated and dressed as an *'arusa* (bride), and an altar of a high stool with a tray bears food items and the bride's jewelry.[36] A blood sacrifice may be made in a bowl on that altar; perhaps a chicken will be killed.

Zar *in Performance*

Zar music is being performed for tourists and others by a group called Mazaher at the Egyptian Center for Cultural Arts weekly, led by three women with other, male musicians since 2018 through the time of writing. This is billed as a cultural experience rather than a ritual. *Zars* are convened regularly outside of Cairo in Luxor, Aswan, and other areas of Upper Egypt.[37]

Certain dancers have included *zar* music as a climactic segment of their performances with its torso movements and hair swirling. Nadia Gamal (1935–1992), born Maria Carydias, trained as a dancer in Egypt but came to be primarily regarded as a Lebanese dancer after she moved there. Gamal added a *zar* segment in her Oriental show in 1969, mainly for its dramatic effect. The *ayyub* rhythm may be called *zar*; the name refers to the Biblical figure of Job. It is also played in Sufi music. When I was dancing in my teens, we learned to include certain movements into the *ayyub* sections of songs that were intended for *raqs sharqi*, including head rolls and torso movements that originally derived from the *zar*. However, only certain viewers were cognizant of their origin.

The Syrian dancers and sisters Eghra (born Nihad 'Ala'addin) and Fitna moved to Egypt from Damascus in 1958 and danced as *raqs sharqi* performers, and Eghra also became a "bikini" actress. They appear in the 1967 film *'Ariyat bila Khataya* (Naked Without Sin), in which they include similar movements to the *iqa' ayyub* in a dance sequence.[38] That film also featured the Syrian singer Fahed Ballan.

Mahmoud Reda did not stage a *zar* and suggested it was not "beautiful." He stated: "As an artist, I don't like bad things. I try to look for the beautiful. I ignore the dirt and look for the flowers."[39] Perhaps he felt it is too raw and visually and spiritually disturbing. Yet it was filmed by a number of ethnographers including Egypt's former prima ballerina Magda Saleh for her dissertation on Egyptian folklore.

Shu Shu Amin (described in Chapter Two) hired real *zar* musicians to include a *zar* segment in her show. She came out of retirement and taught this in 2010, thus bringing the idea of a tableau with references to the *zar* to a new generation of dancers.

Mona al-Sa'id (see Chapter Three) included a segment in her cabaret show alluding to the *zar* in one of her shows with the authentic type of music. Numerous non–Egyptian dancers have used the *zar* as a group piece, but the question remains as to whether it is proper to stage a "trance dance"/ritual. Since trance dances are shown in cultural festivals in Morocco (by *shikhat*) and as an enactment in Cairo, then dancers have reasoned they might also perform them. Ibrahim Farrah, who thought very highly of Gamal (who used the *zar*), created a dance piece called Bayt al-Zar, a highly theatricalized piece which owes far more to modern dance than typical *zar* movement.[40]

The expressionist Iraqi dancer Assala Ibrahim incorporated the *zar* into a dance about the tribulations of May Ziadeh (1886–1941), a Lebanese-Palestinian poet and essayist important in the *nahda*, or revival of Arabic literature, whose relative tried to commit her to a psychiatric hospital.[41]

Dhikr *and* Tannura

As explained in Chapter Four, Sufism is an important and ubiquitous expression of religion in Egypt. Estimates vary as to the size of Sufi brotherhoods or *tariqat*, with the official estimate at fifteen percent of the population in 2017; others claim it is twenty percent or that as many as a third of Egyptian men are Sufis. The Sufi *dhikr*, the performance of which is called the *hadhra* or *layla* in Egypt, is the ceremony of the remembrance of Allah. It may be performed at the *mawalid*, festivals that honor the holy men and women, the *awliya'*, who were great Sufis. The chants performed in the *dhikr* vary from simple repetitions to complex *anashid* (hymn-like poetic songs) offered by a professional *munshid* to the music of a band. The movements of the *muhibbin*, devotees, are not thought of as dance but are ritualized, involving swaying, sometimes in a figure-eight of the torso, and moving of the head and upper body and arms.[42] While the *dhikr* itself was not theatricalized, some of its movements have found its way into the performance of *aghani mulid* as discussed in Chapter Four.

The government also has supported the performance of *tannura* dancers, who spin during a simulation of a *dhikr* performance, with their wide and brightly colored skirts (*tannura*) controlled by strings. The *tannura* are said to date back to Fatimid times, when the Fatimid rulers brought their eastern traditions of spinning with them (if the Isma'ili *da'wa* [the proselytizing movement of this esoteric branch of Shi'ism] had such a tradition or not, this is what is said in Egypt). The *tannura* were mainly performed by clan members, who taught the dance father to son or uncle to nephew, but also by some folkloric dancers. The dance has been performed as a tourist attraction at the al-Ghuri palace of traditional culture by the Tannoura Egyptian Heritage Folklore Group since 1988.[43] The group includes musicians who play the *rabab, nai, sagat, tabla, tabl* drum, and *mizmar*. The *tannura* dance is also one of the acts performed by Hassan Saber's troupe at Felfela Village in Giza,[44] and it is performed on the floating Nile boat-nightclubs.

The *tannura* dance had been exported by certain male dancers prior to this time to Europe and North America. It is also performed at resorts in Egypt, and in the Gulf, in Dubai for instance.

Hagalla

The Hagalla dance is found in the far northwestern coast of Egypt where tribes from Libya had settled about two hundred and fifty years ago. The largest tribe is the Awlad 'Ali who acknowledge their Bedouin identity and call the people of the Nile Valley "Egyptians," as compared to themselves. The longer poetry and songs of their men have been collected for a century, but the Awlad 'Ali are also famous for the *ghinnawa*, short poems composed by women.[45]

Mahmoud Reda visited the area of Marsa Matruh to see this dance performed. Many members of these tribes were forcibly settled by the government decades ago, and they claim the dance is also performed in Libya. It was theatricalized by Reda and the Qawmiyya Ensemble, as well as the regional dance group, the Matruh Folklore Ensemble, and also by *raqs sharqi* dancers. Reda was explicit about his aim to make folkloric dance fulfill a narrative role, to tell stories, and thus avoid the tedium of traditional movements which might continue at length. So, in this dance, his version has a dialogue of sorts between the lead female dancer and male dancers.

Hagalla means to skip or jump. The dance was supposed to represent a coming-of-age ceremony of a young female dancer, but it evolved over time and was performed by a female professional dancer who is referred to *al-hagalla*. The music for the dance has three parts, referred to either as the *shitaywa*, the *ghinaywa*, and the *magruda*, or in a different version, the *samir*, the *dahiyya*, and the *reeda* (*rīda*). The dance used to be performed at weddings before any national folklore groups existed in Egypt. Men clap in groups; they are the *kaffafin* (those who clap). The female dancer, *al-hagalla*, approaches them and dances for them, lifting her feet

Farida Fahmy in *hagalla* style dress with Mahmoud Reda and iconic national scenes in Egypt. Postcard circa 1974 (author's collection and courtesy www.faridafahmy.com).

while doing a three-quarter shimmy. She might hold a stick and hand it to a male, sit down and remove her bracelets, and he might then give her bracelets. Mahmoud Reda enhanced and added to traditional steps with acrobatic feats for the men and turns and group choreography for women to a song composed by 'Ali Isma'il. The women's costume of that area included a peplum skirt over a dress with a fitted waist and boots. As her skirt is not so long as to cover her boots, the boots emphasize her footwork while moving forward, and the peplum skirt accentuates the shimmying she does as she moves.

Although not a Cairene nor an urban style, many dancers have learned and performed *hagalla,* including the Firqat Qawmiyya, which presented it with a full stage of dancers, followed by male dancers showing off their dancing talents to the lead *hagalla* dancer, Denise Enan (b. 1944, who left Egypt for Canada in 1975) in a filmed version.[46] *Raqs sharqi* stars 'Azza Sharif and Nagwa Fu'ad incorporated the *hagalla* into certain of their routines. A *hagalla* dress for a night club show would be made of net, tightly fitted in the waist, with a peplum skirt also in net, and paillettes to emphasize the movement. This contrasts with the larger skirt in use for the folkloric versions.

Sinai Peninsula

The inhabitants of the Sinai Peninsula are also Bedouin and share with the northeastern tribes some antipathy to the Egyptians of the Nile Valley (heightened with almost two decades of low-grade or more intense war fought in the northern Sinai). The Bedouin of the Sinai have survived primarily from tourism, and its expansion in the southern Sinai has meant the staging of dance and musical performances for tourists and the performance of Bedouin culture, as in the coffee ceremony. Some dances not native to the Sinai, like those of the *tannura* dancers, are also performed to entertain tourists, and some intrepid dance students have tried to learn dance from particular groups like the large tribe, the Mzaina, (who did not teach dance decades ago, but are willing to explore a new market).

Like the Awlad 'Ali, the Sinai Bedouin celebrate marriages with dance and music. This includes male clappers and singers and the dance called the *dahiyya*. The national dance companies and the regional company at Isma'iliyya have included this dance in their repertoire, changing it for the stage. While some define it as a male dance, women—not professional dancers—danced in weddings, wearing a highly sequined long veil which also covers their faces, as the men perform their own movements and music.

Serena Ramzy (of Brazil) and Hossam Ramzy choreographed and have taught Bedouin dance; their recording includes the *hagalla* along with the songs of the distant Sinai tribes.[47]

Nubian Dance and Music

Nubia, the home of the Noba people, was divided between Egypt and the Sudan when the latter separated from Egypt in 1956. After the High Dam at Aswan was constructed, many Nubians were forcibly resettled or left as Lake Nasser was created. They fought to obtain some political representation and only did so recently.[48]

Nubian music is sung and played on a pentatonic scale, in comparison with Arabic music that uses the *ajnas* of the *maqamat* as the melodic structure. Nubian music and dance are mainly consumed by Nubians, with Egyptians ignoring this trend; for example it is rare to hear Nubian music on the radio unless performed by an artist supported by the Egyptian government like Mohammad Mounir.

Musical and cultural specialist Hytham M. Hammer informed me that Nubian singers who had recorded in Ratahana (Nubian and simplified Arabic) were Yassan Arrouda, Dahab Khalil, Ahmad Badry, Fanghary, and Husain Alala—so called after a song "Ya Nass La La." Others sang in Arabic: Ahmadun, Sayyid Idris, Wad al-Naqhy, Hassan Ghanim, and Sayyid Donga (actually Sayyid Muhammad Badr), Jamal Zaidan, and Sayyid Jabr. The Wadi Halfa region was famous for the styles called "Asmar Alluna" and "Abyad Alluna" known in the 1930s and 1940s.

In northern Nubia, the singing style is called Kalakia. Before 1964, Nubian songs were rendered in Arabic. Muhammad Wardi introduced a new style called "*aghani al-tahjir*" (the songs of forced migration). Then other modern Nubian singers sang in Arabic like Abdallah Bata, Hamou Bata, Hassan al-Saghir, Fikri Kashif, and Sayyid Jabr in the 1970s and 1980s.

An even earlier dislocation of Nubians from 1902 produced songs that "described Nubia like Oubash and 'Sandalliya' a sailor of a small boat who can't moor it anywhere as he has no land." Some rhythmic styles were "*al-hampbe, al-jaboudi, al-naqlut*, and *al-ter.* Dance song styles included *Komban kash, shir ri*, and *fig gi*. Other styles which are Arabic mixed with Nubian are *aghani al-sira, aghani ad-daluka*, and *aghani al-dulib*."[49]

Dances may be performed in a line or circle formations and performed in long, trailing gowns (these are shortened somewhat for stage performances) and long headdresses. 'Aida Nur, whose mother is Nubian, has taught a Fadikka-style dance in which women dancers wear the *thob* (also the national dress of the Sudan), which is a length of cloth tied around the waist and draped over the shoulder and head. Some signature movements include chest circles, chest pushes, and a "pigeon" movement, pushing out and retracting the neck like a pigeon. The most common traveling step is a shuffle where the dancer steps on the right foot on count one, and pushes off the left ball of the foot on the "and" count. Sometimes women hold or balance woven food trays (*shewer*) on their heads.[50]

The Fadikka people perform a famous dance:

> called *ar-ragid* (pronounced *arageed*)—from the verb *ra-ga-da* which means in Arabic dancing with the feet beating the ground.[51] Only elderly people are allowed to dance this dance, performed by a row of standing men and women (Note: Unlike Sudan and Egypt, Nubia had dances performed by both genders together which were very common[52]), combining hands while moving forward, then backwards in a reenactment of the movement of the River Nile's waves. The lyrics are in the Fadija language. The men dress in their white *galabib* and the women dance wearing a unique, long, flimsy blue-black dress called *al-jarjar* (here, the letter *jim* is pronounced as 'j' unlike the 'g' heard in Cairo) heavily adorned with gold. A Nubian dance troupe by this name performs in Cairo.[53] Another form of this dance is circular, using the arms held up as a way to mimic the turning of the waterwheel. Another gesture that mimics nature is called *al-tabshir* with which one greets guests raising the arms held up together, whilst the dancers shake palms to imitate palm fronds, this was how Muslims greeted their Prophet.[54]

Other dances are: *grishad* (Arabic, sometimes rendered *nagrishad*, or *nagrashod*, a circular dance with downward-pointing claps), *komban kash/kumba gash/kounbun kash* (Arabic; an amorous light dance performed in rows of 10–12), *ham bee*, a dance of three to seven nomadic men who perform without any singing or instruments, and *kom bak/ollin,* a fast dance to clapping by women.

Another dance in Nubia is called *al-wastaniyya* and is performed by women forming a half-circle while clasping their hands and walking half a step forward, then backwards using the right foot followed by the left one, shaking to the sides and pushing out their chests as a lady jumps into the dance in a very powerful way. Men stay in another half-circle holding *daff*s on the opposing side and usually sing a song called *belajah*, famous among the Fadikka people, as well as the Kunuz, who sing it with a little alteration in its original lyrics.

Famous in Nubia is the *tanbura,* an instrument found from Dongola up to Wadi Halfa. It is also called *al-kisir*, or *simsimiyya* in Egypt. People believe the *tanbura* can ward off evil spirits, and its sound is called *kri* or *krir* (roaring of lions). It can vary from a very small size to a large one.[55] There are songs of the *tar,* also of many sizes. The *sfarah* is a cylindrical bamboo flute which is now made from metal; also played are the *rabab,* a single string bowed instrument, the *riqq,* a tambourine; and the '*ud,* the plucked lute.

There are twenty-three documented rhythms in Nubian music. Performances vary from spoken-word poetry readings to public recitals in which Nubian musicians introduce a song to their audience in a *zajal* method called *masaliyya* (from *mathaliyya*); they tell jokes and make fun of various topics to warm up the audience, and then the singer loudly belts out the song's lyrics.[56]

Early pioneers of Nubian music were Muhammad 'Osman al-Nei, who modified and played the *tanbur* in the middle to late nineteenth century. 'Abdullah Kabarbar was a singer, tanburist, and magician well known in Egypt in the 1930s. 'Abd al-Wahid 'Abd al-Wahhab was considered a master singer along with Hassan 'Osman Jazuli (b. 1936) from Qortah, Markaz Nasr, Aswan, who is called Qetharat (Lyre) of Nubia, and Sadqi Ahmad Salim (b. 1936); Ahmad Munib (b. 1924) in Aswan was the mentor of Mohammed Munir. Mohamed Hamam was born in Ramlat Bulaq in Cairo and imprisoned in the 1960s. 'Abd al-Razzaq Rashid (b. 1934) in Amberkab, who settled in Alexandria, was an *'ud* player who formed the first Nubian band. Hassan al-Saghir, of Alexandria, who died in 2018, was considered a master singer, referred to as Karawan al-Nuba (the Nubian nightingale). And there are many more: "Musa Hassan Khalil, 'Abdullah Kati, Jabr 'Awwad, Mahmud 'abd al-Rahim, Hamdi Shalali, 'Ala' Nu'man, Muhammad Faruq, and Sha'ban Awwad."[57]

Hamza 'Ala' al-Din's (1929–2006) Nubian music was recognized internationally as a result of his performing, teaching, and recording efforts in the United States. As a child he acted in one of Asmahan's films, playing the part of a Nubian child servant.[58] He was born in Toshka and studied music in Rome, Cairo University, Ibrahim Shafiq's Institute of Music and the Higher Institute of Middle Eastern Music. He collected recordings in the field. Rock, folk and classical musicians like the Grateful Dead, and the Kronos Quartet collaborated with him. He relocated to the United States where he taught music.

Mohammad Munir became known through his Nubian songs, one of the genres he performs. He was admired and written about at length by Daniel Gilman as a pop (*shababiyya*) singer. One reason for Gilman's admiration, based on that of his interlocutors, was that Munir was "socially conscious" and his lyrics had some depth; Munir's music was considered the "*musiqa al-tarab* of the *shababiyya*."[59]

There are other traditional forms such as the funeral songs of the Kunuz, which women sing. The lyrics are based on syncopated, poetic lines called *manaha,* which literally mean "wailing"; "yowling," or *ghina al-'adid*, which mention the benevolent nature of the deceased. Other tribes with special funeral songs are the al-'Ababid, who use *al-nuqqara,* a hung skin-drum with a hole in its skin beaten with small sticks.

Nubian Dance and Raqs Sharqi

While Nubian dances are distinct from *raqs sharqi*, certain *sharqi* stars like Lucy at her club Parisiana have featured them.[60] 'Aida Nur has taught Nubian dance as folkloric dance. In pop music videos flavored by her identity, singer/actress Gawaher (Nubian from northern Sudan) includes Nubian along with *raqs sharqi* movements in a flash mob dance in her 2013 "'Ala Kurnish."[61] Her 2015 song "Haylouh," continues a *sha'bi*-Egyptian-Nubian and multicultural theme with dancing which is not specifically Nubian.[62]

Suez Region

The *simsimiyya* (a different version than used by Nubians as it has many [12–24] strings and is tuned so that the *maqamat* can be played) is in use in the Suez Canal region (and also in Yemen, Saudi Arabia, and I found it during my research in the Sinai Peninsula). Weekly gatherings for music and dance were held in Suez, where the *simsimiyya* was introduced in 1938. Mohamed Shabana, an ethnomusicologist, said these included themes from the *hadhra* (Sufi rituals), *muwashshahat*, workers' songs, music of the *'awalim*, and other local music. In the 1950s, bands began to use nationalist lyrics reflecting the hostilities with the British, then against Israel. In 1967, Israel destroyed many homes in Suez, and Captain Ghazali (Muhammad Mahmud Ghazali), a leader of the resistance, formed the Awlad al-Ardh *simsimiyya* band, which incorporated politicized lyrics about the resistance movement. The band played on a blanket on the ground, and with spoons, tin cans, glasses and a wash basin to accompany the *simsimiyya*.[63] The al-Tanbura band of Port Said formed in 1989.[64] Its more specialized songs, called *damma* or *simsimiyya*, begin with an introduction on the *simsimiyya*, whereas the *jawab damma* begin with an unmetered *mawwal* known as the *istihlat*.[65]

Dancing of this area included Charleston-like steps, hip movements, jumps and leaps, clapping (*kaff*), the playing of spoons while dancing, and clothing of the fishermen or rowers (*bombutiyya*, bumboat captains), who gave their name to a specific dance.[66]

Alexandria

Folkloric dances created in order to evoke Alexandra featured sailors, or men dressed in full baggy *sirwal*, and vests and hats to protect from the sun. The men might carry knives or suggest they that they are by making fists with the thumbs extended. The female dancer(s) usually appears in a fitted dress extending to the knee, with a ruffle or short sleeves meant to suggest going to beach. This was meant to be a modest-style beach dress, although when used as a dance interlude in *raqs sharqi* shows, it may be very tight and short rather than modest. The dancers may use the *malayya laff* (also used in the portrayal of *sha'bi* urban women and discussed in Chapter Three) because this black outer wrap was used by women in most of Egypt's cities or large towns, in Alexandria as well as Cairo.

Alexandria is Egypt's second most important city but has been neglected in many respects in comparison to the capital. It has developed a special sense of identity, perhaps comparable to Chicagoans, or those of other second cities.[67] A large number of the dancers listed in Chapters One through Three hailed from Alexandria, as do many musicians and singers. The city used to regularly host large numbers of summering Cairenes, who in recent decades have flocked instead to 'Ain al-Sukhna or further west along the North Coast for their vacations. They were replaced by other vacationers from the Delta and Upper Egypt, which caused Alexandrians to seasonally complain of the *fallahin* thronging their beaches.[68]

Some seventy years after these dances were first staged, it is impossible to know how faithfully they reflected local dances. Certain signature movements signal authenticity while others derive from Mahmoud Reda's own preferred styles of movement. For instance, Reda utilized a particular run with a hop traveling forward through space that appears his own, whereas a movement signified as Alexandrine is seen in a circle dance that the men perform while lifting the right knee and leg, jumping and tapping it front and then side again, a movement somewhat similar to the *dabka* of the Levant, as in as regional dance company's performance which is shown on Egyptian television.[69]

Do Egyptians from locales outside the capital mind being stereotyped through dance and music? It seemed to me that it might irritate young Alexandrines to be identified with a knife-wielding sailor or a young college-bound Sa'idi to be seen as a horse-trainer. A friend has reminded me that no instructor can speak in Sa'idi, Sharqawi, or Sinawi dialect if teaching in a university in Egypt, as their students would complain.[70] On many occasions, I heard Cairenes mocking the speech of some friends from Bahaira.

The given wisdom is that the mission of the Reda Troupe and the Qawmiyya was to resuscitate and make local dances respectable by reshaping them onstage. This was supposed to unite many strands of local identity into a complex Egyptian one. I am not certain that is actually the case, but that effort was more successful than *raqs sharqi*'s struggle with its tawdry image and poor standing in the minds of Egyptians.

Folkloric dance references may enliven *raqs sharqi*, or they may simply provide a greater cultural understanding to dancers; hence they are included in international belly dance festivals, though not always garnering as much interest as modern *sharqi* choreographies.

These many forms of popular dance and music in Egypt are important to a more complete picture of Egypt's heritage. Let us now consider dance used as a foil for sarcasm and a dancer who is an anti-heroine. It would be not be realistic to overlook the comedic or slanderous side of dance's social meaning in Egypt.

Seven

Bad, Bad *Baladi*

Sama al-Masry[1] and Dance as Sarcasm

"Badness"—transgressiveness—is a core aspect of Egyptian culture as expressed through music, language or images, nationalist or revolutionary messages, and references to sex, drugs, corruption, or violence. Certainly "badness" is part of *sha'bi* music in the sense of swagger, self-parody, and self-imaging. So too, it is part of *mahragan* and *mulid* lyrics. "Badness" may even be part of *raqs sharqi* as we have seen in naughty or provocative *dall'a*. This is true despite the rather innocent and virtuous image of Egyptians in *raqs sha'bi*, as we saw in the previous chapter.

Should a dancer be funny? An object of fun or sarcasm? Can a dancer use sarcasm to challenge? Egyptians are known for their sense of humor, jokes, and use of satire, and a joker is *ibn nukta* (son of a joke), so Egyptians are called *ibn nukta* (son of a joke) in Egypt and within the Arab world.

Satire is more than mere punning or ridicule as it attempts to change, challenge, or alter some truth.[2] Egyptian humor and political satire apparently date back to the ancients. The Arabs who invaded Egypt had developed *hija'*, satirical poetry used to denigrate enemies.[3] There are examples of Egyptians satirizing the Ottomans, who were their overlords and collected taxes from them.[4] Egyptians have ever since continuously satirized their governments, each other, and the outside world in jokes, stories, cartoons, verse, plays, films, and songs. When I first moved to Cairo, I had perilously little money and rode the public bus, a crowded and miserable way to travel, if I could not walk or come up with taxi fare. On the bus, the *komsari* (fare collector) moved around collecting money and punching and issuing tickets. To entertain the passengers, he told joke after joke, many of them with sexual innuendos; others were political.

Comedian Mahmud Shokoko (1912–1985) included political and social critique in his monologues and musical sketches in the 1940s, including a famous one, "Hashish." Isma'il Yasin appeared in numerous films that included his comedic monologues. He starred in eighty-one movies in which he was often a quixotic and semi-tragic fool with a funny appearance and large mouth. He appeared several times as a *raqs sharqi* dancer and imitated Samia Gamal in one film.

A trio of comedians, George Sidhom, Samir Ghanim, and ad-Daif Ahmad, has appeared in theaters, films, and on television since the 1960s. They presented the first of the "Fawazir Ramadan" (Ramadan Riddles), a very popular television program which was aired an hour after sunset. Since then, comedic musical sketches have generally declined.[5] However political satire has remained part of theater and moved onto social media. It was quite important during and following the 25th of January 2011 revolution and the further "coupvolution," a portmanteau to describe the events after July 3, 2013, when President Morsi was ordered to be arrested by then–Defense Minister 'Abd al-Fattah al-Sisi.

Let us contrast funny women who provide comedic entertainment and the beautiful, serene, or playful dancer. Are they so sharply distinguished, if we remember the historic connections between comedy and musical and dancing entertainment? These persisted from the nineteenth into the twentieth century in the *salat* and clubs with male and female comedians, with men impersonating women as dancers as well as in theatrical programs. This included dancers and actresses such as Zinat Sidqi (1912 or 1913–1978) who danced and performed what we call "stand-up" comedy in monologues at weddings prior to acting with Nagib al-Rihani and playing film roles as a maid, a spinster, and a landlord with great comedic skills.[6] She made faces, crossed her eyes, and was not considered beautiful. Yet she was able to quite faithfully portray the attractions of *raqs sharqi* within a *mulid* in the film *Sahibat al-'Azima* in 1956. She played that scene "straight," aware of and manipulating the wave of attraction from her male audience.

Sanu'a (described in Chapter Two) introduced the political cartoon to Egypt in 1877, and then Abdullah Nadim did.[7] Dancers have appeared in cartoons about Egypt since the early twentieth century, chosen either as an object of sarcasm or to represent Egypt herself. Egypt's image changed—she often appeared as an elite woman with a gauzy *yashmak* across her face or Egypt-Hanim. Or she might be a feisty *fallaha*, a baby, or a *raqs sharqi* dancer, and then she morphed into La Nouvelle Femme (the New Woman, a symbol of modernization).[8] The earliest cartoon I have seen depicting Egypt as a dancer, "The Dance" drawn by Mustafa Affandi Khulusi, depicts couples ballroom dancing, a relatively novel, shocking, and popular activity, challenging Oriental mores (to not touch strange women) and contrasting with *raqs al-baladi*, which does not involve closed ballroom positions. In the cartoon, Gabriele D'Annunzio, a decadent soldier, womanizer, and musician of the World War I era who offered the Yugoslavian city of Fiume to Italy (Italy turned him down, but he conquered the city and ruled it as a dictator with anarchic ideas for about two years), is dancing with a dancer labeled as the city of Fiume; General Gouraud of France is partnered with Syria, dressed in a costume bra, a strip skirt, and pantaloons. The British soldier is soliciting Egypt to dance with him. She is partially wrapped in her *malayya laff* and demurring. Britain invites her: "Come dance my dearest Egypt" and Egypt refuses with: "Not on your life."[9] So dance is related to conquest and submission, and Western and Oriental ways are contrasted.

Caricatures are a visual form of a joke, usually with a specific social and political message. For instance, in 1923 a great deal of arguing took place over the creation of the Constitution. In one cartoon, Egypt is depicted as a grossly overweight dancer from whom the Constitution's authors have withdrawn their support, and she is left to battle a "fever from the Constitution."[10]

In Egyptian jokes that mention dancers or musicians, their compromised social

→← الطائف المصورة في ٨ ديسمبر سنة ١٩١٩ →←

[Cartoon with Arabic speech/labels: دانونزيو مع فيوم ، جورو مع سوريا ، تعالى نرقص يا عزيزى مصر]

هذه الصورة مكاتبة رمزية من نوع الكاريكاتور الاوربي انفردت اللطائف المصورة بافتباسه في الصحافة العربية ولاقى استحسان حضرات القراء
وارتياحهم والصورة هنا تمثل احتلال دنونزيو لمدينة فيوم ورضوخها لهوسيرها معه على النغم الذي يطلبه وقبول سوريا ان ترقص دورها مع جورو
عن طيبة خاطر (ولو لم يجمع رأي سائر السوريين على ذلك) وتفور مصر من الرقص واعتذارها. والصورة اقترحها حضرة الشاب الاديب مصطفى افندي الحكيم
فعهزنا الى مصورنا ايهاب افندى خلوصى ان
يرسمها فجاءت غاية فى الاتقان وهى تعبر عن الحالة
الحاضرة ورمز الباب بطريقة مكاتبة لا بأس بها

"The Dance," drawn by Mustafa Affandi Khulusi, in *al-Lata'if al-Musawarra*, 1919. This shows the city of Fiume's submission to D'Annunzio as Fiume dances to his tune and Syria dancing with Gen. Gouroud ... when the British general asks Egypt to dance, she refuses ... "Not on your life." Tonia Rifaey, "An Illustration of the Transitional Period in Egypt During, 1919–1924," Master's thesis. American University in Cairo, 1997, p. 24 (courtesy Tonia Rifaey).

position is assumed. Dancers' relationship to money is mocked, as is their manipulation of men. *Raqs sharqi* dancers have often featured as puppets, with puppeteers drawing movements from contemporary dancers and using songs like "Shik Shak Shok" by Hassan Abu al-Si'ud[11] or instrumental sections from Umm Kulthum's songs.[12] A belly dancer was a stock character in these dramas, and she remains so in the *Lailat al-Kabira* which parades all the characters who live in the *ahya sha'biyya* in a *zaffa* on their way to the *mulid* as described in Chapter Four.

The shamefulness of dancing is the other side of the dancer's ubiquitous presence in society. Fifi 'Abdu has played a dancer or retired dancer numerous times in her acting career, sometimes to good comedic effect. For instance, in the early 1990s, she starred in *Hazzimni ya Baba* (*Tie the dancing belt on me, o father!*)—the play's title was considered funny, even ridiculous, because no father was supposed to want his daughter to engage in the promiscuous activity of dancing.[13]

The puppet character (who looks like a Muppet) Abla Fahita, a respectable widow famous for her sarcastic and witty repartee, has appeared ever since 2010 on "Abla Fahita Live from the Duplex" on the *CBC* channel. She presents satire but also commentary on life in Egypt. She has a daughter, Carcoura (Caro), and a son, Boudi. Over the years, she has presented dance and music because they are a quintessential aspect of Egyptian life, and Abla Fahita knows how to stay on top of what's hot. Dina has appeared on her show several times, masked in one episode and giving "dance lessons" to the sounds of a crying baby and car horns with the accompaniment of percussion.¹⁴ The rules disallowing *raqs sharqi* on television were not invoked, because Dina is Dina, and she wore a high-necked dress revealing no skin. Abla Fahita hosted Alla Kushnir and Mustafa Haggag after their hit song "Ya Mna'na'."¹⁵ Abla Fahita herself surprised female host Wafa' Kilani by "dancing" after asking, "Do you have good music?" She moves a bit to Sawarikh's *mahragan* hit "La."¹⁶

The cartoon caption reads: "Egypt: [Hussein] Rushdi [Pasha] is allegedly sick, [Ahmad] Hishmat [Pasha], (who served as minister of foreign affairs) has been abandoned by the government. Therefore both have abandoned me and left me to treat this fever from the constitution which is going to kill me." From "The Constitution between the Committee Head and Its Deputy," *Kashkul*, 86, January 7, 1923. In Rifaey, "An Illustration of the Transitional Period in Egypt During, 1919–1924," Master's thesis. Cairo: American University in Cairo, 1997, p. 204 (courtesy Tonia Rifaey).

Leaping forward to the revolutionary and post-revolutionary period in Egypt, we find that many Egyptians were quite startled by the swift—eighteen days—demise of Hosni Mubarak's presidency after thirty years. Egyptians had been forbidden to hold demonstrations since the 1960s, yet this rule against public protests changed in 2004 when violence against the Kifaya (Enough) movement's protests brought an international reaction against Mubarak's government. Demonstrations were held frequently through 2010 by the supporters of Mohammad El Baradei and those protesting the murder of Khalid Sa'id by police in Alexandria in June 2010.¹⁷ Few if any of the reform-minded Egyptians opposed to the regime had really expected the success of staging mass demonstrations starting on Police Day— January 25—in 2011. This turned out to be an illusive revolution because the military, who had supported Nasser, Sadat and Mubarak, then assumed governmental power as the Supreme Council of the Armed Forces. Violence broke out during the revolution, and in subsequent protests, many sexual and physical attacks against female protesters occurred.

Although many Egyptian women participated in the 2011 revolution and then in the Tamarrod (Protest) movement which collected signatures on a petition asking President Mohammed Morsi to step down in 2013, there was no social revolution for women accompanying the political shift. Despite statutory discrimination under civil and religious laws and women's concern about violence against them, the majority of Egypt's women were not challenging gender roles per se but rather hoped to ameliorate their situation. Therefore, "badness" even long before the Revolution could mean challenging restrictions against women.

Women's presence in public in demonstrations—like their public actions over the last century—is often construed as a violation of expected gender codes. In entertainment videos for several decades, actresses and dancers have also violated these codes (according to increasingly conservative Egyptians, whether Islamist or pro-government) through their voices, bodies, and movements. Others disagree that gender codes are "violated"—public entertainment has long held the two-fold purpose of entrancing the audience through music or dance genres and some degree of sexual innuendo or titillation. Salafists and conservatives, however, long argued that women's display of their bodies is illicit, constituting *tabarruj*, and even more so in live or video entertainment to music.

Egypt has acquired in its civil laws the notion of a stable public order which regulates women's bodies and behavior and is maintained through patriarchy and the enforcement of criminal punishments against lewd behavior, abortion, the obvious presence of prostitution, and so on. Many comments have been made already in this volume concerning the close association of prostitution and dance, efforts to restrict women's movements in public, and rules intended to limit dancers' interactions with their audiences. Criminal punishments against women who misuse their own bodies are primarily borrowed from the Napoleonic code, although the pre-existing corpus of *shari'a* and Ottoman laws also regulate women and their bodies and prevent them from living alone, having children as single mothers, as well as protecting them from certain abuses.

Especially with the proliferation of visual materials online and the refinement of cellular phone technology, music videos or short clips considered salacious may be freely exchanged. Not a year passes without some scandal and arrest of a female artist or actress in which the visual material is deemed an offense or effort to corrupt public values and dangerous to youth (indeed lately there has been an organized campaign to go after women who are less well-known but who have followings on social media). This leads to accusations that dancers and actresses may push the envelope to get more attention in their careers. In 2015, Reda al-Fouly was arrested for a music video that went viral called "Sibb Idi" (Hands Off).[18] In the same year, dancers Shakira and Bardis were jailed for "inciting debauchery" in their music video. Pop singer Shyma Ahmad was arrested in November 2017 and sentenced to two years in prison for a music video "'Indi Zuruf" (I have issues). In that video, Ahmad appears first in a bra saying she not ashamed and "has issues," applies lipstick, then licks an apple on a stick and peanut butter off of a piece of bread as a crowd of appreciative young men, some of them in hard hats, watch her. She sucks on a banana and eats a bite of a taco.[19] After her release of the song "Inta 'Arif Leh" (You Know Why), the singer Ruby was widely criticized for being provocative, and she appeared as a belly dancer in this video. Films or videos can be removed from circulation (censored) for violating officials' ideas of decency, as can books or book covers.

Artists are not always the culprits, and liberals do not always support those who "go too far." In 2011, a young woman, Aliaa Magda Elmahdy, posted a nude photo of herself on her Blogspot page, received 2 million hits and fled to Sweden. She thereafter joined in certain protests by the activist group FEMEN, including one in which she menstruated on an ISIS flag. Elmahdy was widely denounced as an attention seeker when the incident first broke, and reactions hardened against her when she declared herself an atheist.

In fact, there is as little sympathy for dancers who are viewed as exploiting their own bodies as for mavericks like Elmahdy because Egyptians of all ages usually accept certain standards (arguably double standards) of control for the common good[20] and avoid nudity and affronts to public decency. So it was when the Russian dancer Johara, Ekatarina Andreeva, was sentenced to a year in jail for "inciting debauchery" because authorities claimed she performed without the required shorts under her white lace costume and that her costume was not standard, or according to regulations.

It seems that conservative attitudes toward dancing have narrowed even with respect to non-professionals. In 2018, colleagues and administrators of Dr. Mona Prince, a professor of literature at Suez University, got her fired for posting a photo in a bathing suit and a video of herself dancing on her personal Facebook page. The Ministry of Higher Education had so far indicated in her case that personal freedom is allowed but not if it compromises a "good reputation."[21] Apparently universities have not moved beyond the moral dilemma of the characters in the film *Khalli Ballak min Zuzu*, (1972). That film, starring Su'ad Husni, Husain Fahmy, and Tahia Kariuka, told the story of a professor who falls for a student who is secretly a dancer and the daughter of a dancer from a Muhammad 'Ali Street family. Her cousin reveals her secret to the professor, and all her peers who are shocked. A happy ending is achievable only because she gives up dancing and returns to her studies. If dancing was and is always disrespectable, one wonders how it was acceptable for Farida Fahmy to teach in a university while a graduate student,[22] or how she remains a beloved national symbol? It is much easier then, to accept the controversial image of a dancer than to challenge it.

With the January 25, 2011, revolution, musical artists introduced aural violations into Egypt's music. From that time many revolutionary tropes impacting popular music swept across the Middle East. One could hear presentations of revolutionary themes by singers and rappers like Ramy Essam, or Tunisian El Général in Egypt, Libya, Syria and even in countries where no revolution took place—as in Saudi Arabia, with the ironic lyrics of "No Woman, No Drive" or in the West Bank.[23] After the January revolution, Ramy Essam continued writing political messages to condemn the SCAF and to call on President Mohammed Morsi to resign.

Egypt had a lengthy tradition of politicized songs to which the young revolutionaries alluded by reviving Sayyid Darwish's song "Aho Dah Illi Sar" (That's What Happened). This song was written to memorialize the 1919 uprising against the British. Hip-hop, rap, rock, and Arabic music, and even local genres like the *simsimiyya* repertoire of the *suhbagiyya* (musicians) of Port Said preserved in the music of El Tanbura,[24] provided edgy settings of rebellious lyrics. *Mahraganat*, first attributed to DJ Figo (Vigo) (see Chapter Five), talk about ordinary Egyptians' lives and travails. While not necessarily political, they also celebrates badness, as in the group Tamanya fi-l-Miyya's (8%) "Ana Aslan Gamid," ("I'm Also Tough"—*gamid* also means sexy). Yet, these lyrics are not accompanied by the embrace of sexual freedom nor any general acceptance of women who perform or dance for a living.

In this context of the Arab Spring and all the insecurities in Egypt, Sama al-Masry, an actress and dancer, became a counterrevolutionary satirist. She drew on the transgressiveness of sexual and political humor to further her career and opinions. Although she is educated and possesses certain social and political connections, she utilizes the ambiguous image of a dancer to ridicule her targets via the medium of privately-produced satirical videos.

Baladi *Badness*

Al-Masry cultivated a *baladi* badness in a combination of two predominantly male genres: *sha'bi* (or *baladi*) performance and comedic satire. Evelyn Early explains that *baladi* is "a rich cultural concept based on a series of traditional-modern (*baladi-afrangi*) oppositions, which contrast *baladi* people (who are resourceful, authentic, religious and honorable) with *afrangi* [foreign] people (who are gullible, superficial, nonreligious and pampered)."[25] Al-Masry's *baladi* badness might be expected to, and does indeed offend, members of the middle class or elite circles of urban, educated Egyptians. Yet, many were amused by and applauded her performances due to their political content and identified with the subversiveness of her references to *baladi* versus elite, Egyptian versus foreigner, religious hypocrites versus national patriots. It is obvious to many Egyptians that al-Masry wields vulgarity to emphasize Egyptian identity and goals and to draw red lines that should not be crossed.

Being strong, or strongly sexy, is "bad," admired, and problematic. A woman who has these qualities and who stands up for herself is *gada'a* or a "real guy." If she is simultaneously gorgeous then she is "*gamda*" (the feminine of *gamid*, tough and "majorly" sexy). These were not the most long-lived or emphasized qualities of the relatively few female performers who attained political power, notably the singer Umm Kulthum. Umm Kulthum's love life, for instance, was rarely questioned after her rise to fame due to her masterful technique and dominance over her field.[26]

Sama al-Masry, on the other hand, embodies a new version of a tradition of aggressive hyper-femininity. Female aggression featured for decades in Egyptian films in which women respond to violence, actively and in kind, in roles played by actresses like Najla Fathy and Nadia al-Gindi,[27] who has played the roles of many dancers, since she can dance, and spies. Al-Masry also draws on slapstick comedy as employed by the comedians 'Adil Imam, or Muhammad Sa'd playing the character Lembi in *al-Lembi*, as well as the hyper-sexualized performance style of singers like Nancy Ajram, Ruby, Haifa Wahbe, and dancers such as Dina, Camelia, and Safinaz, who like Fifi 'Abdu and Nagwa Fu'ad before them, are "super dancers."

Al-Masry herself is not a top dancer, and she's not dependent on hotel or boat bookings. She is well aware of the sexual aspect of visual appeal and the tumultuous reputation of dancers and can project "super-sexy." This trend of sexiness developed in many performance videos by female "pop" (*shababiyya*) stars about twenty to twenty-five years ago and drew the ire of Egypt's conservatives and the Ministry of Information.[28]

Free but Not Immoral: Sama as Hurriyya

Sama Al-Masry was born Samia Attia Hadaqa (her name is also given as Samia Ahmad Attia 'Abd al-Rahman) on February 8, 1978, in Hihya, Sharqiyya. She worked as a news presenter and appeared in three films. One of these, *'Ala Wahda wa al-Nuss*[29] (2011),[30] which she wrote and in which she starred, brought her to the Egyptian media's attention. It depicts the gendered and sexual exploitation of a dancer named Hurriyya (translating to freedom) who is a "bad girl," a young woman or adolescent forced to go reside in a rehabilitative program. As she travels to this facility, her taxi driver harasses her verbally and gets into an accident, wrecking his cab.

She is not supposed to dance in the facility, but she soon does. Then, she is hired by a sleazy journalist. Convinced that she will obtain an important scoop, she attracts the attention of a master criminal of Haram Street in Giza, where many night clubs were located. Her journalist employer produces an *'urfi* marriage contract showing she has married this criminal, Akram, for 100,000 L.E. Her "husband" demands his money and enacts his right to confine her to *bayt al-ta'a*. *Bayt al-ta'a*, literally meaning house of obedience, allowed a husband to force his wife to return to the conjugal home if she tried to leave or went to work without his permission. He could confine her to a room within her flat or home and not permit her to leave. If she refused the terms of *bayt al-ta'a*, he could have her declared *nashaz* (wayward), allowing him to divorce her without paying the deferred *mahr*. While this was regulated somewhat in 1967 and 1985, a husband could still threaten his wife with a forcible return to the home, and she would have to assent to divorce without compensation. The idea of enforced obedience through confinement to the home continued on because society supported the idea that women should be supported by men but owe them obedience and believed *bayt al-ta'a* to be part of *shari'a*.[31] It continued on as an accepted practice in *shari'a* courts in Gaza and in Saudi Arabia.

Through this blackmail, Hurriyya is forced against her will to enter her husband's world of alcohol and sin, to drink and give in to being used as a prostitute—a grim portrait of the entertainment and sex trafficking industry. In a popular segment of the film, Hurriyya performs the rhythm for which the film is named—*wahda wa al-nuss*.[32] Later, she has gotten drunk and gives a dream-like lampoon of a dance performance in "Do[q] (Hit, or Play)" complete with hiccups.[33] Understanding Hurriyya as a character is important because she provides instant recognition for some of Sama al-Masry's subsequent video ventures, much as Farid al-Atrash was identified with Wahid (the lonely and then love-struck hero of several of his films) and 'Adil Imam with his Minister of Youth and "dad" (Ya Bob) character. Hurriyya as a *bint al-balad,* forcibly corrupted (like Egypt itself), danced to the bacchanalian song "Yakhty Kamila" delivered by a beguiling Ahmad 'Adawiyya[34]–like singer. The camera tracks her high-heeled feet wearing *khulkhal* (tinkly anklets) entering as the singer calls, suggestively punning on her name, "*warrini al-huriyya*" (Show me the freedom!). She is wrapped in a *malayya laff,* the traditional lower-class outer wrap, with a fishnet *burqa* covering her face until both are discarded as she dances in a ruffled short dress, typical of that genre and its seductiveness.[35]

Bint al-Balad

Characterizations of the *bint al-balad*, the quintessential lower-class Egyptian girl,[36] appear repeatedly in Egyptian cinema as discussed in Chapter Three, in literature, and in songs. Tahia Kariuka often played a strong *bint al-balad* character, a dancer, and also a *mu'allima* (master of her trade), notably in *al-Futuwwa* ("The Thug," dir. Salah Abu Seif, 1957). The *bint al-balad*'s dance with *malayya laff* in its Alexandrian form, by Farida Fahmy of the Mahmoud Reda dance troupe, or the *malayya laff* Cairene style as performed by Nadia Hamdi and Sahra Saeeda (see Chapter Three), strikes familiar tropes for Egyptian viewers. Sama's take is turbo-charged by her sexual teasing, with its play on freedom and captivity. Eventually, in the film, Huriyya escapes after setting in motion a sting on Akram and his journalist clients.

'Ala Wahda wa al-Nuss was harshly criticized and censored prior to release because it offended al-Azhar University, the religious establishment, and the Egyptian journalists' syndicate (as it lampooned the journalist who first entraps the character of Hurriyya). Al-Masry defended the film in a television interview[37] in which the sympathetic interviewer nevertheless suggests that Sama must have known the film had gone too far. Journalist Gamal 'Abd al-Rahim claimed that the film gives an incorrect picture of "respectable" journalists.

Sama retorted that women's exploitation has been featured in numerous other works, which were received with less approbation, such as *The Yacoubian Building* (dir. Marwan Hamed, 2006, an "art" film). She asks provocatively: "Wasn't this a question about the freedom to address social issues?" Sama realized that the freedom of expression demanded by many revolutionary youth and intellectuals and which was a part of the discourse of the moment was not being extended to her.

Sama has insisted on her right to portray uncomfortable truths about sexual exploitation, unlike some other Egyptian entertainers who depict themselves as being tricked into compromising roles. Nicole Saba, for instance, played a Danish sex-bomb who wished to import free love from Denmark to Egypt in *al-Tajruba al-Danmarkiyya* (The Danish Experience) starring 'Adil Imam. It contrasts the initially conservative views of Imam, playing a governmental minister, with Saba, playing a free-spirited Danish woman who lectures about sexuality and free love, and Imam's four sons and a large number of other Egyptian men who go mad for Saba. Saba later claimed that she regretted participating in the film because it was too frank and made her image too sexy.[38] Lebanese-Egyptian star, Haifa Wahbe, in the film *Halawat al-Ruh*, (Sweetness of the Spirit), suspended in April 2014, evades some responsibility by affecting unconsciousness of her disturbing performance. This film likewise depicts a vortex of corruption as the dancer seduces, yet remains sympathetic. We see similar shots of the dancer's feet, as in Sama's film, *Wahda wa Nuss*, treading across a drink-laden table.[39]

Sama al-Masry. From her Facebook page, 2019.

Being coquettish and flirtatious is a trademark of the *bint al-balad* of Egyptian popular culture, whether in speech, gestures, walk, or interactions, but it does not compromise her sexual reputation. Choosing to assume the role of a populist archetype and a dancer, on the other hand, is a form of "badness" that deliberately crafts an "us and them" (Egypt versus the world) narrative in al-Masry's videos. Some have criticized Sama's dancing by saying she merely poses[40] instead of dancing, perhaps out of irritation with her ability to grab headlines. Nor was she at first a beguiling singer; her early vocal efforts are kittenish and slightly off-key, although her voice improves in later videos. None of this diminishes her impact as a social satirist.

Yet, she has not been credited as a satirist as was Bassam Youssef, the star of the comedic satirical show 2011–2014 "Barnamag," which became the first live audience show in Egypt. Youssef was a cardiac surgeon by profession but was dissatisfied with the conditions of medical practice in Egypt and had been preparing to emigrate. Then the revolution broke out, and he treated wounded protesters in Tahrir Square. Youssef collaborated with Tarek al-Kazzaz in creating a satirical comedy program that mounted five-minute segments to his YouTube channel. It was called "B+" for Youssef's blood-type and as a pun. He was able to express the anger of many Egyptians because the events of the revolution and its aftermath were not covered with great honesty by the mainstream channels. ONTV offered to let him create and host "al-Barnamag" (literally means "the program"), and he continued his social commentary, hosting many Egyptian public figures who were able to speak freely about events. Youssef admired Jon Stewart and mentioned him in many interviews. Stewart then invited Youssef on his *Daily Show* in 2012. "Al-Barnamag" was well-researched and attained great ratings, and Youssef intended to spare no subject from his satire but ran into trouble with the government.

After "al-Barnamag" ran several episodes in its second season, Youssef was interrogated and jailed. Both Sama al-Masry and Bassam Youssef were opposed to the government of Mohammad Morsi, who became president on June 30, 2012. This occurred after the Muslim Brotherhood created the Freedom and Justice Party. Other parties with religious agendas were also created (as was explained in Chapter Four concerning parties with a Sufi or *salafi* base) since the rules that had been operating under Mubarak intended to maintain his own stranglehold on power had dissolved. In "al-Barnamag"'s Episode 12, Part 2, Youssef plays clips of Morsi showing his finger pointing and lightening bursts of static. Later he makes fun of a comment which Morsi had delivered in his strongly accented English while he was visiting Germany that "gas and alcohol don't mix." Youssef delivers each of the words marked with italics in heavily accented English:

> No he's correct. Gas and alcohol *don't mix*. Like English and Arabic *don't mix*. Like religion and politics *don't mix*. The *drunk* doesn't do the *driving*. The *liar* goes to the *fire* and sometimes becomes president. Not necessarily in Egypt, somewhere else I mean.[41]

Although he added "not necessarily in Egypt," it was obvious that he meant *in* Egypt and was accusing the Islamist president of lying and hypocrisy. He also mocked Morsi by wearing a gigantic hat to court, just as Morsi had when receiving an honorary doctoral degree in Pakistan.[42]

Unlike Youssef, Sama al-Masry was not as recognized for her satire because (a) she is a woman, (b) worse, she is a woman who is perceived as a dancer, (c) her humor is mostly inaccessible to an international audience, and (d) she did not achieve Youssef's level of success. He began broadcasting from his laundry room but moved to channels widely available in the Arab world. Also, whereas Youssef continued on in his critique of the ridiculous and unfair actions of government in Egypt under acting president Adly Mansour and would have carried on under President al-Sisi had he not been threatened (by the police) into fleeing, leaving in 2014, al-Masry took the side of the government, protesting those who were in her view, supporting the prior Morsi regime or criticizing al-Sisi.

Many Egyptians agreed with her views and were infuriated by the U.K. and U.S. media's stance on the Muslim Brotherhood and President Morsi—that is, that as a democratically elected president he should not have been overthrown. In their view, the protests of thousands upon thousands of Egyptians on July 30, 2013, signified popular support and not a mere military coup, although more evidence appeared over time that the military had manipulated the situation. Her kitsch lampooning of American tone-deafness was approved and imitated. Nevertheless, some other Egyptians, especially those abroad or supportive of the Islamists or liberals or of freedom of protest, reviled her as an "*askariyya*" (an Egyptian Army supporter).

Meanwhile, critics of Youssef labeled him an *'aragoz* (the name of the traditional shadow puppet)—a person whose views could be dismissed. Youssef said he was "proud to be one. Yet he wondered if he was just an *'aragoz*, why were they afraid of him?"[43]

Raqs Sharqi

Raqs sharqi is, as we've demonstrated, is despised and appreciated, popular yet performers "repented" from it for some decades, and is a quintessential symbol of Egypt. So much so that Bassam Youssef begins his own memoir of his experiences with comedy in Egypt by saying "not all of us ride camels and are married to belly dancers."[44] And he countered the Islamists' claims that the Egyptian protesters were leaving evidence of their immorality in Tahrir Square by quipping, "So far they have drugs, coal for water pipes, condoms and money. All they need is a couple of belly dancers and five men from the Gulf to open a nightclub."[45] If even the liberal Bassam Youssef so disparages the *raqs sharqi* dancer, why would Sama al-Masry choose her as a symbol of Egyptian identity? Because a dancer is the symbol with which Sama can best mock her targets.

As explained earlier, hundreds of the once vibrant nightclubs hosting *raqs sharqi* closed, live *raqs sharqi* was removed from television, and numerous dancers gave up their jobs and adopted Islamic dress.[46] To appear even on a family-friendly show like "Abla Fahita from the Duplex," a dancer must wear a *baladi* dress, completely covering her body, and not a *badla*, (the bra and abdomen-revealing sequined or beaded belt, and skirt, or beaded skirt); otherwise there was a risk the censors would cut them. A dancer's social position in Egypt is complex. At the lowest end of the profession, the ordinary wedding dancer can wear a scandalously short skirt[47] or other types of revealing *badla* and is considered by any outside the musical or entertainment professions to be close to a prostitute. However, many such dancers marry and lead fairly strict, religiously observant lives off stage. Their task is to perform; doing so with their bodies causes some to gossip, but the profession is "a trade like any other," as Karin van Nieuwkerk put it,[48] with its own rules of comportment.

Yet, dancing of *raqs al-baladi* in Egyptian Arabic, in its unpaid, unprofessional form is ubiquitous. Men dance at shop-openings, weddings, in street parties, and on the Nile taxis (which play music). Women delighted in dancing to celebrate President 'Abd al-Fattah al-Sisi's electoral victory in late May of 2014. All are examples of non-professional dancing. Although a professional dancer can live respectably, on her own terms, and support her family, she will be criticized by many Egyptians because those socially or religiously conservative have and continue to consider belly dance, indeed all dance, to be scandalous. Karin van Nieuwkerk showed that dancers' primary reason for performing is the economic support of their families. Some were married, while others were single heads of households.[49] An additional problem (or advantage) of dance is its identification with being *baladi*.[50]

Farida Fahmy and Magda Saleh, forging careers in folkloric dance and ballet respectively, and both contributing to dance ethnology, were both unusual figures for their time, and both had the support of their prominent Egyptian fathers (who had both married non–Egyptians, Fahmy's mother being English and Saleh's mother being Scottish) and their social circle.

During the salafization of Egypt, critics of dance, music, pictorial art, and film grew. Shaykh Sha'rawi called on female entertainers to "repent" and give up their careers. President Morsi appointed a Minister of Culture who threatened to ban ballet and Islamize the arts, as Iran has done. Artists protested this Minister of Culture. Had President Morsi remained in power, it is likely that *raqs sharqi* and other forms of dance would have been further restricted.

Do Oriental dancers have agency? Is that why Sama al-Masry chooses the guise of a dancer? She appears often in folk garb (probably concerned with the above-mentioned censorship), and only sometimes in a *raqs sharqi* costume. First, to respond to those who claim that Oriental dance has no aesthetics, I would respond that given the review of dance history presented in Chapter One and Two, dancers are creative and innovate in Arabic dance within a set format and expectations.[51] Super dancers (the most highly paid and well-known) have power based on the wealth they acquire from performing, and less-powerful dancers also obtain agency to the extent that they control their own earnings. Super dancers also have a certain degree of artistic integrity, and Sama takes that to the next degree in inserting satire. Less economically successful dancers are clearly exploited, as is illustrated in the 2011 documentary *At Night They Dance (Fi al-layl yarqusna)* about a family of wedding dancers. The matriarch of that family certainly exerts some control over the careers of her daughters, and in relation to the men who hire them, but the dancers themselves find that their profession impinges on their romantic relationships and keeps them in a legally tenuous position vis-à-vis the state. Still, al-Masry perceived that a dancer has agency as to mock, and as spokesperson for *"baladi"* thinking, with its sharp thinking and quick retorts.

Al-Masry and the Salafist

Sama al-Masry became even more intriguing to the public as they learned another fact about her: she had been secretly married to a Salafist leader, MP Anwar al-Balkimy, who was forced to resign from the Nur Party after claiming to be the victim of an assassination /carjacking attempt. He claimed this in order to explain his absence from the Majlis al-Sha'b, Egypt's parliament. In fact, he was in the hospital for cosmetic surgery to alter his nose.[52] Al-Balkimy accused Sama of revealing his (nose and marital) secrets, as she filed for divorce on the grounds that he was married to another woman with children. He had not informed her of his status, which is a common practice of Egyptian men and another issue that feminists have tried to reform legally. Al-Balkimy denied he had been married to Sama and filed charges against her for damaging his reputation.[53] The Nur Party suspended his membership and eventually al-Balkimy apologized to his party (not to Sama) and resigned.[54] Sama went to the parliament's building and smashed a clay pot there, a ritual folk action symbolizing the end of a relationship. She then took the entire incident and spoofed the salafis in a video, as if their political duplicity mirrored al-Balkimy's own.

Discovering a Metier: "Bad" Videos

Sama al-Masry moved beyond her divorce by creating a series of low-budget satirical videos which mocked the Muslim Brotherhood, President Morsi, President Obama, and more. She strongly backed the transitional government announced by then-Defense Minister Abd al-Fatah al-Sisi in July of 2013. She attacked many political critics of the military and Defense Minister (and later President) al-Sisi. Eventually she hosted her own television show.

Sama's first video effort was "Act Thuggish"—in which she accuses the Muslim Brotherhood and freedom and Justice party of acting like *baltagiyya* or thugs who have beaten people and molested women since the large protests of the 2011 revolution. She sings "*Baltagi inta, inta wa huwwa*" (you are a thug, you and him!) The video mocks President Morsi's Renaissance project (his initial promise to fix the economy, lower the prices of gas and bread, and clean up garbage and traffic within one hundred days) and lampoons Muslim Brotherhood leaders like 'Issam al-'Arian and Khairat al-Shatir. The video starts with the chants from the Friday of Accountability when Egyptians demonstrated against the Muslim Brotherhood in October of 2012. Here, Sama dances with two cleavers, lampooning the Muslim Brotherhood's emblem on its flag, which is two swords crossed over the Qur'an. She also demonstrates that she does not fear the *baltagiyya* (who were then viciously attacking women and protesters) and wields two mangoes, at breast-level to mock Morsi's lackluster boast that he had successfully lowered the price of mangoes.[55]

Twitter users made a hashtag of Sama's name in Arabic—and each of her videos spread on social media. "Ibn al-Amrikaniyya" (son of the American woman) made fun of the Freedom and Justice Party's preferred candidate, Hazim Salah Abu Isma'il, who wasn't allowed to run for president in 2012 because Abu Ismai'l's mother had American nationality. Addressing "Hazimuna" (our Hazim), she adopts the persona of a *fallaha*, yelling at him to not lie. She reclines on the ground, revealing her long cotton underwear and makes faces, similar to Zinat Sidqi's. She peppers the song with charges of corruption, eschatological references, and drops the names of politicians right and left.[56] The video delighted the opposition to the Muslim Brotherhood and salafis, but infuriated these groups and clerics.

The salafis angrily quoted the shocking words of her song on television and her behavior.[57] They were even more incensed by her next video and issued a death threat to al-Masry. In this video titled "Ahaay" or "Sama al-Masry Tirqus bi al-Niqab wa Tighanni li-Morsy 'Ahay'" ("Sama al-Masry Dances in the *niqab* and sings 'ahay' to Morsi"), three figures appear: a dancer flanked by women dressed in the *hijab* and *niqab*. All three are played by al-Masry, which raised the wrath of Islamists who argued that a "hooker" (they called Sama, a fornicator, one who practices *zina*') "should not wear *hijab*."[58] According to their centuries-old reasoning, women who reject covering their hair or also their face are the same as ancient whores, who proclaimed their availability by not veiling. Al-Masry depicts the Islamists as sheep blindly following the Muslim Brotherhood's General Guidance Council, imitates their *hashish* smoking (intoxication by any means is a form of hypocrisy), notes their corruption, and in the last frame, lifts off her *burqa* to reveal her face.[59] No other dancer or singer, indeed not many unveiled women, would normally dare mock Egypt's *muhagibat* and *munaqibat* in public, for all that unveiled women have castigated them for creating a public norm in which it is impossible for the unveiled to function without censure or sexual harassment.

In June 2013 after Tamarrod activists presented 22 million signatures calling for an end to the Morsi government and incited a huge public protest in favor of a political transition, a nerve-wracking showdown between General 'Abd al-Fattah al-Sisi and President Morsi began, and violence broke out. Muslim Brotherhood supporters attacked Christians, their churches and businesses, and police and government supporters in Egypt. The *Al Jazeera* channel was accused of supporting the Muslim Brotherhood and airing its leader's calls for violence. Sama al-Masry responded with a video berating the *Al Jazeera* channel. To the tune of the song "'Ala Rimsh al-'Ayyun,"[60] she sings lyrics which refer to the channel, "*khanzira*" (pork, to rhyme with Jazeera) as she washes the dirty underwear of the Muslim Brotherhood in a laundry tub in the style of an Egyptian housewife and sings that "the army of Egypt is inside (my) heart." She also impersonates and simultaneously taunts *Al Jazeera*'s patroness, Shaykha Moza of Qatar, turning and calling her "*khanzira*" too, and the darling of Obama and Israel.[61]

Sama subsequently attacked President Obama for insisting that Morsi had been democratically elected and that he and the Muslim Brotherhood should be reinstated. This attack video builds on a longstanding populist nationalism, also apparent in singer Sha'ban al-Rahim's work, when he sang that he "hated Israel" (Egypt's enemy and America's friend). Sama expressed the anti–Americanism and growing anti–Islamism reflected in the overthrowing of Morsi and eventual banning of the Muslim Brotherhood. In this regard she was a trendsetter and not merely a fad follower; after all, she had long mocked Morsi when others were silent. Sha'bula later came out with versions of his own song sarcastically mocking Obama, Qatar, and Erdogan.[62]

The music of Sama's anti–Obama video includes the melody of a song made popular by the hit singer, Ahmed al-'Adawiyya in the 1970s "Salamitha Umm Hassan" ("God Bless Hassan's Mother," [discussed in Chapter Five] as Sama dances in a *baladi* dress and in a white *galabiyya* twirling a bamboo cane in the Sa'idi, or Upper Egyptian style).[63] Sama rudely spoofs the original title to obscenely curse Obama's father and mother: "*Ya Obama, abuk wa ummak!*" she sings. The expression means: "Obama, fuck your father and your mother" (although the verb is implied but not stated). She then refers to a conspiracy theory about America's pro–Morsi, anti–Sisi stance on Egypt with American threats to suspend aid to Egypt. She accuses Obama of joining forces with "the terrorists," calling them "all the disgusting guys." The same accusations were repeatedly made against Obama by many anti–Muslim Republican Party supporters during the Trump campaign.

At 3:36 in the video, Sama switches from Arabic to heavily accented English in which she curses Obama for his friendship with Israel, Turkey, and Qatar. She continues:

"[To hell with] your father and your mother / Your Israel, your Turkey, and your Qatar / All of you, Go to hell! / Listen, Obama: We are Egyptian / We are civilization! / *Are you listen, Obama?*"

At the end of the video, we see the image of then–Defense Minister al-Sisi declaring, "Egypt is the mother of civilization," and English subtitles appear reading, "When Egypt talking, should be America shut up." The video went viral when it was released in June of 2013. It channeled some of the Egyptian rage at the American and other Western media's insistence that it was unfair for Morsi and the Muslim Brotherhood to be ousted. It was also a means of responding to Washington's postponement of the military aid package to Egypt. Certainly, Sama influenced or reflected the views of other Egyptians, who three years hence supported Donald Trump's candidacy for U.S. president and continued circulating the anti–Obama accusations.

The last stanza of the video at least, if not the entire video, probably inspired Mona al-Behairy. Al-Behairy appeared in a video as an unnamed "*muhagiba* in green"; she lectures the U.S. president: "You are listen, Obama? We are Egyptian [sic] woman. Shut Up Your Mouse, Obama! Sisi yes, Morsi no!" in March of 2014.[64] Her video went viral on social media.

This effort was meant to reach English-speakers, most of whom were simply appalled by Bahairy's linguistic failure, whereas Egyptians thought it hysterically funny. Sama, offstage or on, is by no means as inarticulate as Mona. Mona al-Behairy, possibly emboldened by Sama al-Masry, also reviles U.S. foreign policy in Egypt.

Sama also staged a "good riddance" performance when U.S. Ambassador Anne Patterson departed Egypt. Like many Egyptians, Sama al-Masry was incensed (but not surprised) by the Wikileak revelations of Patterson's meetings with the Muslim Brotherhood. She paraded outside of the U.S. Embassy in Cairo to celebrate with her followers, and a marching band in a full-fledged raucous *baladi* performance was filmed on television.[65] She dressed a sheep in an American flag and launched into her *baladi* insults (like *hija'* or the Dozens ["signifying" verse in U.S. African-American communities]) calling Patterson *'aryana* (naked) and *kahyana* (cheap). She set fire to an American flag and then smashed a huge clay pot, which in Egypt's symbolic language means that a relationship has ended (as with her former husband) and "don't come back."[66]

In the "Ughniyat Rab'a" video ("Song of Rab'a" [al-'Adawiyya] the site where Morsi's supporters carried on a huge demonstration which ended in bloodshed as the army killed a huge number of protesters in August of 2013), Sama mocked those who were demonstrating against Egypt's new transitional government by donning the white shroud they wore as a costume. She also appears in red mini-skirt and a white fur stole, smoking a cigarette (in mockery of liberals) while holding a protest sign about the Freedom and Justice party.[67] Another video mocks the leftist allies of the Muslim Brotherhood, the 6th of April party.[68] Her video "al-Motahadis al-'Askary," on the other hand, was a light-hearted love ballad to the military.

In 2013, Sama launched her own television show "Ayu Bah" on the *Falul* channel on NourSat. One of her first targets was the politician Mohammad El Baradei. The show was also designed to counter the Muslim Brotherhood's new *Rab'a* channel. Her show was ridiculed by those who were condemning the new government as being a throwback to Mubarak. Sama saw it as a vehicle for further revelations. She targeted El Baradei both because he had mounted protests against the Mubarak government in the years leading up to the revolution and because he had dissented with the transitional government over ending the Muslim Brotherhood's *Rab'a* and Nahda protests and resigned from the government. Here she castigates him for his role in the politics of the revolution.[69] By the time this segment was made, audiotapes had been aired on Egyptian television revealing that Baradei had communicated directly with someone in the United States following January 25, 2011, in recorded conversations which sound as if he is reporting back to his handlers.

In the spring of 2014, Sama al-Masry put out the video "Bassam, ya Bomba!" mocking comedian Bassam Youssef because of his attacks on then-presidential candidate al-Sisi. Once again, she draws on *sha'bi* heritage with the melody of the 1970s song "as-Sah ad-Dah Ambu." Bassam is everything that Sama is not: debonair, sophisticated, and popular with foreigners. The refrain of her lyrics to Bassam are: "The Americans love you, and the Brits draw near you—go on *NBC*, on *CBC*..."[70] (meaning, appear on foreign media channels rather than Egyptian ones). She dances lightly in her tight jeans next to a home-made bomb, the type that was exploding and being defused throughout 2013–2014 after being planted by Morsi's supporters. She calls Bassam "*ya bomba*" because she felt his satire gave shelter to those who had criticized the new government, whether the Islamists who were engaging in acts of sabotage or those trying merely to protest along with other political groups.

Sama al-Masry then attacked Mortada Mansour, the head of the Zamalak sports club, because he had decided, briefly, to run for president against 'Abd al-Fattah al-Sisi, Sama's hero. She sings "Ya Mortada, Ya Mortada" to the tune of the Arabo-Turkish song, "Ya Mustafa," vamping in a long gown and then dressed in a Zamalak football team t-shirt and playing with a soccer ball.[71] The lyrics are suggestive and insulting, referring to Mansour's consumption of alcohol and womanizing. Mortada had been previously accused along with his son and nephew of attacking and killing demonstrators in Cairo in the Battle of the Camel in February of 2011.[72] He and his co-defendants were not convicted. Mortada was furious with al-Masry (and remains her foe) and vowed to have her television show pulled. Soon after Sama's video spoofed him, the Ministry of the Interior filed charges against her show involving the licensing requirements of satellite television. Al-Masry was arrested on April 20, 2014, and detained, although the *Falul* channel possessed a license issued by Ras Al Khaima Media Centre in the United Arab Emirates. Mortada Mansour's hired thugs broke into the courtroom and threatened her. She argued that she had supported al-Sisi and the government, although no one had asked her to do so, and the least it could do was to provide security in the courtroom. She was fined LE 20,000 (about $2,900), and her unlicensed equipment was seized. Among the charges brought by the prosecution was that her show challenged public morals.

By Ramadan of 2014, however, she was back to the celebrity circuit and photographed at the *MIPTV iftar* dinner event. She was criticized by some who called her "stupid" and compared her to Oka and Ortega, populist stars of *mahragan*. At the same time, she was praised by those strongly opposed to the Muslim Brotherhood, the extremists, and the April 6 movement, which was allied with the Muslim Brotherhood in its opposition to Defense Minister al-Sisi's actions in June and to the new protest law.

In early 2014, Sama announced her intent to run for a seat in parliament representing Azbakiyya.[73] Whether to further humiliate Islamists, as she has said was her goal,[74] or to influence policy beyond satire[75] and form a new party, she almost missed the filing date. She began her campaign with a video, which infuriated her critics. A judge then ruled that she was not allowed to run due to her being "unrespectable."

It is not unbelievable that a dancer could serve as a representative in a government body. Other entertainers, such as the actor 'Adil Imam, the actor Samir Sabry, and the singer Umm Kulthum, have wielded strong influence in the country. Pithy humor in Egypt, which calls for goodness through mocking "badness," is also a long-standing tradition in political cartoons, jokes, and stories. Sama al-Masry, lacking the wealth and power of Mortada Mansour and the platform of Tawfiq Okasha (a television anchor, channel owner, and former MP who had opposed the revolution), nonetheless showed a way for a transgressive woman to influence politics without becoming an "honorary male."

Mortada could force Sama off her channel but not out of her entertainment niche. She returned to public attention in autumn of 2014 when a movie poster for Apple Charcoal, in which she was cast, appeared showing a woman's legs clad in black hose and in black high heeled shoes, with some sort of bottle (champagne) held along one leg, and with smoke from a *shisha* wafting upwards. The *shisha* is set smaller than scale, so it appears the legs are about to walk over it.[76] This set off complaints about the ad's impropriety, although the photo was probably photo-shopped from an ad for an Oriental Lounge in Berlin, the original of which was printed in *Cairo Scene*.[77]

In 2014, Sama made a music video titled "Ahmad al-Shibshib Dha'" (Ahmad, Find My Sandal) which is referred to in Chapter Two. The original *sha'bi* song by Hamasa begins with the word *aha* (*Aha al-Shibshib Dha'*), which is considered obscene, since it is supposedly resembles the sound made by a woman having sex. This video expresses mild *sha'bi* feminism; she mocks an immature man who does nothing but lift weights. She can't get a rise out him as she washes her thong underwear, no matter how outrageous her demeanor. Predictably, the video elicited very angry comments by viewers and also heightened al-Masry's popularity.

In 2018, she was again the target of a lawsuit filed by Tariq Mahmud for offending the religious sentiments of Egyptians after she had announced her intention to host a religious show during Ramadan. In the release video for "Barnamag Sama al-Masry," she wore a loosely wrapped *hijab* and told her followers not to judge her until they saw the show.[78]

Sama continued to raise eyebrows. In April of 2020, she was sued by television host Reham Saeed for libel and slander and detained for debauchery and immorality for the publishing of certain photos on her social media account, although she argued she was not the one who published them.[79]

Through her videos and adopted public persona, al-Masry taps into a long tradition of Egyptian popular satire. Like other populist performers, she uses specifically Egyptian art forms (dance and music), archetypes (the *bint al-balad*), tradition (regional costumes, the smashing of clay pots), and language to arouse populist sentiments around her political messages. What makes her works transgressive, however, is that she also mobilizes her sexuality towards that end and that she does so within the lively, male-dominated realm of Egyptian politics. Al-Masry's performances do not ensure a revival of *raqs sharqi* or even its survival given Islamization's continuing inroads. While she describes herself as a moral *bint al-balad* dancing to make a point, she never meant to foreground or "save" belly dance. Rather, her message has consistently been that Egypt should be true to itself and its *mulid/carnival*[80]/ self-mocking spirit, rejecting Islamism and American dominance when necessary.

Next, we should consider the ways in which professionalized dance in Egypt has connected it to the outside world through a *raqs sharqi* industry, and how it in turn has been affected by an influx of foreign dancers and their interests.

Eight

Globalization of Egyptian Dance

Egyptian dance, arguably a major national product and industry as well as a controversial and comedic symbol, as discussed in the previous chapter, has had an impact far beyond *umm al-dunya* (Egypt's epithet, "mother of the world," or civilization). *Raqs sharqi* fascinated international audiences and dancers, just as the tango, flamenco, and Polynesian dance genres have attracted international audiences and practitioners beyond Argentina, Spain, Tahiti, Hawaii, Samoa, and New Zealand.

The outside world has also infiltrated and reshaped dance and music in Egypt. Globalization of Egyptian dance forms was as complex as the evolution of *raqs sharqi* itself, beginning with the travelers who sought to create reputations for themselves with their spicy memoirs and who sparked an Egyptomania in Europe following Napoléon's incursion into Egypt.

The French first used the term *danse du ventre* as an alternative title for Jean-Léon Gérôme's 1863 painting, *La danse de l'almée*, which was exhibited at Paris's annual art exhibition the Salon in 1864. The fact that the Orientalist painters and Gérôme (whose prior work included neo–Grécque and historical subjects) used inaccurate costuming and Western models did not deter viewers who were fascinated by the suggestion of abdominal and hip movements. From this term came the translation, "belly dance" in English.[1] By this time, the *salat* or *café chantants* described in Chapters One and Two were the performance spaces of *'awalim* in Egypt. It was in this era that in Egypt, as van Nieuwkerk put it, their image suffered a "drastic transformation" from "learned women to fallen women."[2]

In the West, Middle Eastern women's images were already eroticized and troubled by clouded cultural readings. The main features of dance in Egypt, as observed by travelers, contrasted strongly with European dance, which relied on many elaborate leg and foot articulations and a rather still and upwardly held posture. They thought torso and hip movements in *raqs sharqi* to be erotic and depicted it accordingly. The later appellation of *danse du ventre* was applied even though the movements did not much involve the belly. The French were both attracted to and repelled by Gérôme's erotic imagery. Hawthorn points out that most of the French public would not at that time have been familiar with the actual movements of this dance form, but "from the earliest periods of its use, the phrase *danse du*

Jean-Léon Gérôme (French, 1824–1904), *The Dance of the Almeh*, 1863, oil on wood, 19¾ × 32 inches (50.2 × 81.3 cm) (courtesy The Dayton Art Institute, Gift of Mr. Robert Badenhop, 1951).

ventre was inextricably entangled with notions of sexual libertinism and moral lassitude."[3]

Non-MENA (Middle East and North Africa) dancers staged performances of the *danse du ventre* in France, and they were preferred to real *'awalim* who were introduced to the Folies-Bergère to great hisses from the audience. (It is startling that a century later, dancers of non-*ghawazi* background who offered fake *ghawazi* dances were preferred to the real *ghawazi* when the Musicians of the Nile toured Europe, the group directed by Alain Weber, featuring Matqal Qinawi Matqal, Shamandi Tawfiq Matqal, and Muhammed Murad Majali.) "Real" *ghawazi* weren't preferred as they weren't as young or svelte as belly dancers dressed as *ghawazi*. Yet these European comments are also dubious after one views a young woman of *ghawazi* background practicing with the male musicians who has a nicely athletic body, if not as thin as a runway model.[4]

In May 1889, the *Exposition Universelle* in Paris offered an exhibit called the *Rue de Caire* (a Cairo street), which provided a staging of the *danse du ventre* of the *'alma* 'Aicha. This was so popular that numerous Paris entertainment establishments—cabaret and *café chantants*—began offering this form of dance in 1889, mostly by local performers who developed their own versions of the dance.[5]

In 1893, Sol Bloom included belly dance at the pavilions of the Columbia World's Exposition in Chicago. The performers in his Algerian Village were the same group that had danced in the Paris Exposition. Bloom remarked:

> It is regrettable … or if anyone should choose to disagree, it is at least a fact that more people remember the reputation of the *danse du ventre*, than the dance itself. This is very understandable. When the public learned that the literal translation was "belly dance," they delightedly concluded that it must be salacious and immoral. I had a gold mine.[6]

The idea that dancers were immoral came from the earlier travelers' descriptions of erotic encounters with dancers and because the dancers appearing in the exhibitions were unconstrained by corsets, and their movements, especially the shimmy, were considered extremely indecent. In addition to "fake Oriental dancers," there were real ones, for instance Fatima and Raja who appeared respectively in films made by Thomas Edison's Kinetoscope Company in 1893 and 1897 and at Coney Island and Huber's Museum.[7] Raja danced while holding a chair in her teeth, a feat that would continue to be performed by Sunbati *ghawazi* dancers into the 1970s at Sahara City in Cairo.

Meanwhile, Europeans continued to visit the *salat* and dance halls in Egypt, among them members of the military as well as travelers. While the reputation of the *'awalim* had suffered, the dance itself was not regarded as "outlandish" as in the West. That is, the pelvic and torso movements were not in and of themselves perceived as wild or horrifying (as to Europeans), but a normal part of the local movement vocabulary. What garnered social approbation in Egypt was entertainers' association with or alleged prostitution and also that *fath* was permitted, as explained in Chapters One and Two.

Travel became more available to larger numbers of Europeans from the later nineteenth century. *Thomas Cook's Handbook*'s (1897) general information on Egypt notes that weddings were occasions for music and dance, and that

> here are many public performers, wandering comedians, who act a rude farce; male and female musicians; female singers, or Almeh; reciters of romances; the public female dancers, or Ghawizee [sic] whose improper performances are, as a matter of fact, under Government prohibition; jugglers, serpent-charmers, fortune-tellers, and magicians, whose skill seems, indeed, very remarkable. All these assist in breaking the monotony of Eastern life.[8]

The guide mentions the opera house and *café chantants* in the Azbakiyya district and music halls in Alexandria, and that Kenah (Qena) was noted for its dates and dancing girls.[9] Europeans were free to arrange their preferred itineraries, which emphasized visits to the ancient sites as has tourism to Egypt up to the present.

Perceptions of dance in Egypt and the rest of the Middle East was shaped largely by writing, art, postal cards, and in fantasies about the region included in cinema, illustrations and themes for music for player pianos, comic books, bodice rippers, and advertisements for tobacco, oranges, dates, condoms, and other products associated with the Middle East.[10] That is, the imagery of the Middle East was developed externally, internally, and as a feature of colonial conquest. Dancers were the female foil to turbaned Muslims and Arab sheikhs and only vaguely historicized. Dancers, producers, and directors in Egypt could not very well reverse the way that Westernizers perceived MENA dance (nor did they try to), nor the manner in which Hollywood used dance over the following decades to contextualize films about Arabs and the Middle East. It was instead as if there were parallel universes where this music and dance were situated.

Globalization is a term that appeared in 1930 as: "the act or process of globalizing: the state of being globalized especially: the development of an increasingly integrated global economy marked especially by free trade, free flow of capital, and the tapping of cheaper foreign labor markets."[11] This economically-oriented definition does not preclude its application to cultural products.

Globalization is not a unidirectional process, although it is regulated by the relative balance of dominant and subordinate cultures and economies. Currently, it is popular to say that changes in dance and in music are an aspect of globalization, rather than an outcome of globalization—"working on," destroying, or transforming expressive culture. Egypt has long been open to the outside world and yet experienced decline, stultification, and struggles as a result of reverse industrialization, dependency, internalized colonialism, and other processes. A debate about Egyptian identity has been ongoing since the nationalist movement of the twentieth century, even before it, and so it is natural that dance and music trends would reflect that.

Globalization has changed urban spaces, tourism, and housing in Egypt, contributing to a less "local" and a more cosmopolitan or "global" atmosphere.[12] Visible in desirable housing complexes, large hotels, and museums are certain symbols of Egypt's location and history; for instance, homeowners or hotel architects might incorporate some Pharaonic or Nubian features or nods to Islamic Cairo.

Beyond caricaturizing Egypt—a practice done by Egyptians as well as outsiders— the outside world exercised strong influences over time. Consumer tastes have altered leisure practices, with upscale coffee shops[13] standing in for the traditional male-patronized *qahwat baladi* (coffee houses) for the middle class and elites. Imports and imported ideas have radically transformed the availability of food items (from European vegetables like asparagus to premeasured fresh food cooking kits) and clothing. The advent of satellite TV, MP3 files, and YouTube indelibly altered entertainment in Egypt and what represented Egypt globally.

Over the course of the late nineteenth and early twentieth centuries, the format of the Egyptian dancer's shows changed, as did the music to which they performed from the 1880s to the 1940s. Recordings hint at the popularity of certain dance songs, and these are used in historical recreations of the early era (in particular "Raqs al-Hawanim" originally entitled "Raqs al-'Awalim"). One problem is reconstructing what was actually performed compared to extant recordings. It was already mentioned that Sami al-Shawwa, the violinist, recorded pieces suitable for dance and which we know were used for dance. His was the small ensemble, the *takht* with an *'ud*, *qanun* and percussion (*riqq*). The *tempi* are slower than music of later decades, and one recording of "Raqsat 'Arus al-Nil" (Dance of the Bride of the Nile), includes Badi'a Masabni on *sagat* (finger cymbals).[14] Al-Shawwa, a Syrian described in Chapter Two, was important on the musical scene, playing for both Muhammad 'abd al-Wahhab and Umm Kulthum until the mid–1930s. Incidentally, music somewhat similar in some respects to al-Shawwa's style was featured by Muhammad al-Bakkar, an actor and singer who immigrated to America, and in his performances and recordings there with Eddie (the Sheik) Kochak and violinist Haqqi Obadia.[15] The *raqs sharqi* style developed there was far from exclusively Egyptian, as audiences, musicians, and dancers were more often from other Arab countries, Turks, Armenians, and Greeks or Americans.

In Egypt as well, *raqs sharqi* and variety shows blended Egyptian and non–

Egyptian dance movements, yet the non–Egyptian references were grounded by music or movements recognizably "Egyptian." Influential dancer and producer Badi'a Masabni was naturally impacted by her early life in the Levant and South America, but also by what she saw and sensed and competed with in Egypt, and by incorporating elements of novelty into her stage shows, as well as hiring dancers of different nationalities. Heather Ward has documented some examples of Turkish, Algerian, Tunisian, Iraqi, and other "foreign" dances such as *dabka* on public programs in Cairo from 1918 to 1933.[16]

Variety was obtained as well within an all-Egyptian program. The summer program at al-Khidawiyya Garden in Assiut was typical (from some unspecified year in the 1930s). It featured: "the virtuoso" Muhammad Salama; "delighting the audiences with dialogues and monologues," the Rushdi sisters (Ratiba and Ensaf, sisters of Fatima, and they also performed with the al-Rihani troupe); actor al-Qal'awi; the female impersonator, Muhammad 'Aql; *raqs sharqi* by Jeanette, Samira, Mary, Su'ad, 'Aziza, Badi'a, Na'ima, Zainab, Fardous (probably Shalaby); the orchestra conducted by Ustaz Muhammad al-Dibs; and an instrumental *takht*, conducted by Farid al-Sunbati.[17] We can deduce that the elite enjoyed getting out of Cairo to Assiut where presumably they had country houses. Though unclear from the program, the *raqs sharqi* was probably performed as *tableaux* with soloists and not nine separate dances. This program featured some of the same performers as at Badi'a's club that year. By 1938, programs remained similar and might typically also include a play.

Some movements—or entire numbers—were added from other dance styles. For instance, dance crazes from outside of Egypt were reflected in specially choreographed songs to the samba, or a version of it, which gave Tahia her new second name—the *kariuka* (Carioca). These were not attempts to faithfully render Latin dances, but rather set them within a particular musical framework featuring a larger orchestra—the *firqa*—than had appeared in the smaller *takht* of traditional acoustic Arab instruments. By 1917, some performances of ensembles included piano, and other Western instruments might also be played. Presenting a varied program and publicizing it well was a factor in the competition between the many *salat*. When the police came through to issue penalties for the presentation of *raqs sharqi* in the 1930s (when this was banned and enforced), clever club-owners like Badi'a Masabni could schedule dance "numbers" with foreign titles and costumes suggesting foreign origin onstage and avoid being fined.

I am not arguing, as have some Western dance historians, that the dance form is so hybrid that it lacks any claim to Egyptianness. The *ghawazi* and *'awalim* styled movements as discussed in Chapter One were seen less frequently as *raqs sharqi* developed, or integrated and altered these movements. Some dancers have claimed a connection with these traditions (Lucy and Dandash), while others like Ni'mat Mukhtar disavowed ties with *'awalim*.

Still *raqs sharqi* was perceived as a national dance. An argument about hybridity is more useful to those constructing a history of the art form in its diaspora, or justifying their own participation in it. While I witnessed a certain period of history of that diaspora, which remains largely unwritten, I did not want to distract in this work from a focus on Egypt, a few allusions to the dance's travels in this chapter notwithstanding.

Dance music was important to composers, performers, and audiences in dedicated dance numbers, plays, and also in cinema which began in the 1930s. It could include vocals, or not, thereby providing an introduction to or a break for the vocalists. Certain songs were extremely popular in the 1940s, but not necessarily a decade or two later. In the 1940s and 1950s, during which Cairo was the third most important center for cinema-making in the world, the silver screen conveyed dancing and dance music to the rest of the Arab world. Arab tourism to Cairo for leisure existed from the 1920s through the 1940s, but increased in volume in the 1960s—such tourists could see live dancing if they wished. With the outbreak of the civil war in Lebanon in 1975, tourism shifted decidedly to Cairo until the end of the decade.

Dancers featured in multiple films, which cemented their reputations, but many still continued appearing in nightclubs. Others also performed in the traditional *mawalid* and weddings in this era. As was earlier stated, dancers in films might be portrayed by actresses who danced adequately, rather than actual dancers. Film directors were concerned with the visual effect of dancing scenes more than the totality of a dance show, which would have been far too lengthy to include.

Egyptian *raqs sharqi* has strongly impacted *raqs sharqi* or *raqs 'arabi* in neighboring countries. While there is no space to fully explore this topic, Egyptian Oriental styling was important in Lebanon and remained so when the civil war eventually ended, though the performing scene had radically constricted. Many Egyptian dance stars and actresses performed in Lebanon, and also in Jordan and Syria, and vice versa, when possible. Nadia Gamal (1937–1990), who was mentioned earlier in connection with her *zar* segment (see Chapter Six), is sometimes credited with the development of a Lebanese *raqs sharqi* style. Her Greek father and Italian mother had a cabaret act at Casino Opera. In her mother's act, Nadia performed folk dance and gave her first *raqs sharqi* show when she was age fourteen. She appeared in films from the 1950s through the early 1970s and was the first *raqs sharqi* performer at the Ba'lbak International Festival in 1968. American dancer and teacher Ibrahim Farrah twice brought her to New York to teach. She performed sometimes with *sagat*, or *'asaya* and sometimes used the *zar* in her show. Andrea Deagon explained how powerful archetypes of the possessed bride or the dancing slave invoked by Gamal in her *raqs sharqi* could be understood by her audience, despite *raqs sharqi*'s normally plot-free performances.[18]

Nadia Gamal taught other dancers in Lebanon, notably the Iraqi-born Samara, popular in the 1980s and 1990s, and influenced Amani (Angel Nabil Ayub, b. 1970), who remains popular today. Lebanese musicians continued to allude to Egyptian [style] dance music in the 1990s and 2000s, by which they mean showy, percussion-driven formats originating in Egypt. However, performances retained a local character with references to Lebanese rural music that Lebanese call *baladi* (*musiqa sha'biyya*), including that with *tabl baladi* and the use of *'asaya*, which differ in repertoire and other aspects from the bands and dancing of the Sa'id.

Costuming and Appearances

The shifting beauty standards of each time period affected performing dancers and their images on contemporaneous film or video. Dancers with short, curly, or highly coiffed hair were popular in the 1940s and 1950s, for example, the dancer Zinat Olwi. In the 1960s, when "mod" fashions were introduced, dancers sported longer, bigger hair, falls or wigs, and the newly available false eyelashes. In the 1980s, very curly hair or permanent waves were used to create a "natural" hair look, also rather big in size. From 2010–2020, a universally adopted fashion look of very long straight hair (Egyptian hair is not always or even typically straight) achieved through extensions, and large or enhanced bosoms and bottoms, trimmer figures and regular facial features, and Botoxed lips and faces were considered desirable.

Costumes have also undergone serious transformations, from nearly transparent skirts and heavily sequined *badlat* to skirts made of strips (referred to in the West as car-wash style) and then layers, to straight, tight skirts using less fabric and seemingly "naked" costume styles, using flesh-toned netting in cut-outs. Each iteration was adopted by foreign dancers outside of Egypt as well as Egyptian dancers. Some modifications were imposed by Egypt's officials, like the wearing of net or a body stocking, *shabaka*, with the *badla* to cover the abdomen, unless the dancer is wearing a type of dress which already covers the midriff and now, shorts (*short*) worn under the costume that should not be beige in color. The morality police, *mosanifat*, may visit without warning. Foreign dancers began to wear the shorts as well, asserting that they were more modest, although there are no morality police outside of Egypt, and the total effect of the costume is far from modest.

Extremely well-made and heavily beaded costumes were made by Madame Abla Ibrahim (d. 2006), and her atelier continues. Madame Noussa, Mustafa Afifi, Yasser, Amira El Kattan, and a large number of others make costumes for local and foreign dancers. They compete with foreign costume makers or distributors outside of Egypt. Current styles now involve less elaborate beading, yet may be very dramatic and expensive.

As earlier mentioned, Dina Tal'at was criticized for outrageous and non-traditional costumes (such as a *badla* belt with leggings, dancing in a short skirt, and in pantaloons over shorts, or barely-there coverage of Lycra) but these were promptly copied by other costume makers. (The main basis of the criticism of her from Egyptians is not her costuming; it is that she is educated and from a wealthy family, and she wasn't performing out of financial need.) In Dina's stage review, she might appear in a different costume for each song, with her band filling in while she changed, a visual effect that emphasized the originality and importance of costuming. As she wrote, "I do not want an ordinary costume. I do not want to be like all the other dancers."[19]

Even for dancers who never have and never will achieve superstar status, high expectations remain concerning their appearances. For instance, it is preferred by some that they should be very young or look as young as teenagers, although it is illegal to have a license for dancing under a certain age. Dancers of low-income backgrounds who perform in *sha'bi* neighborhoods pay make-up artists to fix them up just prior to their show, buy wigs and costumes, and negotiate deposits for parties in advance. Much of this book, unfortunately, gives a picture of the relatively few dancers on whom there is more data—who have been the study of any serious articles or who have appeared in cinema. Of the vaster majority of Egyptian dancers, some are treated as outcasts, often rejected as marriage partners, unless within their own families.[20]

Dance Music

As explained earlier in this book, Arabic music changed immensely from what Egyptians called *al-qadim* to *al-gadid*. Western musical themes were borrowed and introduced by different composers, not through entire songs, but in segments of the song. Muhammad 'abd al-Wahhab and Farid al-Atrash were well-known for their linear and flowing ability in their compositions. 'Abd al-Wahhab introduced a waltz in one song, borrowed from Russian composers, and wrote a rock and roll rhythm in to his 1957 song for 'Abd al-Halim Hafiz, "Ya 'Albi Ya Khali." Not only borrowing, but expanding on folk themes or melodic possibilities which he explored through new types of instrumentation and experimentation with the *maqam*, he was an innovator, yet sang very traditionally.

Whereas some music for dance was specially composed for particular dancers and their shows or films, in other cases, the bands would play a popular song, then an instrumentalist would improvise and bridge to a new song played by the entire *firqa*, then another improvisation provided another break in tempo and feeling, and then a new song led into a drum solo and finale.

The audio cassette culture was described in Chapter Five, and that Egypt's radio stations would not play *sha'bi* music like that of Ahmad 'Adawiyya. Yet, his songs became so popular that eventually bands might perform them in a dancer's show. And they might continue referring to them years beyond their initial popularity. With the advent of CDs and DVDs, satellite channels and the digital and YouTube era, music spread more easily.

New compositions of *majence*s, or dance cameo/openers, continued. These are now mixed electronically and not exactly "composed" by a lead instrumentalist as in the past. One important advent was dancers or musicians from outside Egypt who wanted to record in Egypt with an ensemble larger than possible in their own home setting and who promoted these recordings on their own, outside of Egypt. This has occurred mostly since the 1980s. Another was externally-generated globalizing and Egyptian musicians trying to quickly satisfy or guide those who arrange the recordings.

Globalization Outside In and Inside Out

In the staging of *fulklur* shows, the effects of the Soviet folk music and dance spectacles and the addition of certain balletic and Western theatrical movements were unmistakable and not a cause for objections. Nasser's government was advised by a large number of personnel from the USSR and others of its satellite nations. Many young Egyptians studied in Soviet universities or military academies, including Hosni Mubarak. Nasser's Third Worldism had been admired there, and he became an ally of the Soviet Union when the United States opposed him. The Soviet Union was celebrating its heritage and staging dances in such ensembles such as Igor Moiseyev's dance company. Likewise, Mahmoud Reda and the Firqat Qawmiyya were influenced by the "folk-driven" intent of staging indigenous culture. Additionally, Reda was affected by his gymnastic background (he was on Egypt's Olympic team), his experiences in an Argentinian dance company which he joined in 1954, attendance of dance classes while in Paris,[21] and admiration of Fred Astaire's style. Balletic influence is clear in his duet with Farida (Melda) Fahmy (playing Tika Tika) in Abd al-Halim Hafiz' film *Fata Ahlami* (1957). Within Reda's choreographies, certain movements were performed *en relevée* (on a raised heel and balanced on the ball of the foot), and this carried over to certain of his and other dancers' styles in *raqs sharqi*. But other movements were mainly done on a flat foot, which were a *raqs baladi* style.

Another aspect of *raqs sha'bi*, at least outside the national dance ensembles, is that the musicians of Upper Egypt sometimes had more foreign exposure than the dancers. Yet, later on, dancers who could teach outside Egypt had more exposure than such musicians. The *ghawazi* dancers who were included in the European-arranged tours of "authentic" music of the Nile did not please the audiences, and instead, as was previously mentioned, non-*ghawazi* dancers were chosen who would dance in their style. In yet another paradox, their dance style, now limited to the one surviving bint Mazin (Khairiyya) and a few other families of *ghawazi*, was preserved in a eclectic and bastardized fashion first by the Salimpours, (Jamila and Suhaila, mother and daughter) and secondly by the Tribal Dance phenomenon which arose in the United States in the 1990s, and others influenced by them.

Khairiyya lacks her own teaching space (though she sometimes teaches in Egypt at festivals or for visitors) and said she never had the resources nor found "girls she could trust" to train and charge with carrying on her legacy. Also, there is no one left in her family to do so, as they are now educated (and prefer not to dance).[22] So unfortunately, it is only dancers of a non-*ghawazi* background who may have learned these dances through *al-fulklur al-sha'biyya*, or who emulate it, who will carry it on. Dancers in the clubs, hotels, and boat shows are uninterested in heritage if it is subtle or unmarketable.

As *al-musiqa al-sha'biyya* performers and certain *sha'bi* and *mahragan* artists toured, a sort of "globalization from below" occurred in which they were portrayed and then saw themselves as "marginalized," "gypsies" (for *al-musiqa al-Sa'idiyya*), and "revolutionary" (for *mahragan*). This process is described by musicologist Martin Stokes in reference to the expansion and transformation of *rai* music which expressed great creativity—"an advent that had little to do with American cultural hegemony or the dominance of the six majors." (These six major recording companies were Time-Warner, Thorn-EMI, Bertelsmann, Sony, PolyGram, and Matsushita.) He also explains that creativity in a "native form" of world music is not expected, nor is attribution (for example, naming the composer of a *sama'i* or a song which is expected by an audience of Arabic music, but may not appear on a Western program).[23]

Things came almost full circle in the 1990s, when a very large (but disputed) number of women and musicians from the former Soviet bloc came to Egypt and began performing. Eastern bloc-born musicians often played for the national orchestras at the Cairo Opera complex and different musical ensembles. This occurred as there was a severe drop in the number of dancers of Arab or Egyptian background because of the increasing preference by women to wear the *hijab* and cease working as entertainers. Many ambitious dancers of Russian, Ukrainian, Slovenian, and other backgrounds often arrived with some training in dance, like ballet, and "good" (thinner or more svelte) bodies. With their desirable light skin and foreign features, they were promised work in *raqs sharqi* by Egyptian managers and hoteliers. Also, Brazilian, Argentinian, American, Spanish, and dancers from other countries arrived. Egyptian dancers felt the sting of these competitors and complained that their poor Arabic meant they did not understand the lyrics, instead merely focusing on movement; also, they were overly athletic and overly sexual. Some claim that as many as 20,000 dancers from the former Soviet countries appeared in the Gulf countries, Egypt, the resort hotels in the Sinai, and other Middle Eastern countries.[24] I think there might have been about a quarter of that number, perhaps less.

There were also many dancers from all world regions. Each of these regions and additional nations in Asia host their own annual workshops and festivals in *raqs sharqi* or related Arabic dance forms. Several of these areas provide very important examples of *raqs sharqi*'s development[25] beyond Egyptian influence and synthesis not least because Egyptian musicians were relatively rare, and musicians were of other Arab nationalities, or non–Arabs, and because some of those teaching dance lacked in-depth exposure.

From my own history, I recall certain Egyptian dancers in the U.S.—in San Francisco, Los Angeles, and New York among a larger pool of dancers of various Middle Eastern origins scattered throughout the U.S. (Detroit, Denver, Chicago, Houston, Boston), some of whom who had actually lived in the Middle East. Teachers of American background were probably far more influential than these performing dancers (especially after clubs with live music dried up), in that they connected with other Americans whom they inducted into the dancing field. There were a few Egyptian dancers, in New York, several in the Los Angeles area, Fatma 'Akif in San Francisco, and Jodette in Sacramento. But one could not identify *raqs sharqi* in America as being Egyptian—unless it was performed by an Egyptian—until a newer Egyptian format was introduced in the mid–1970s. Thereafter, many dancers made a pilgrimage to Egypt, some traveling every few years.

Also, a huge gulf between Eastern and Western perceptions of dancers emerged as career opportunities expanded for Western women in the U.S. Possibly some aspect of this is due to the sexual revolution of the 1960s, which caused greater acceptance of entertainers in general. To perform irregularly and teach dance as a second income appealed to many outside Egypt. In Egypt, a few teachers offered *raqs sharqi* training in gyms beginning in the 1990s, and Samia Allouba's gym and fitness centers continued offering master classes in *raqs sharqi* into 2020. A few customers complained about Allouba's advertisement in 2020, showing a dancer's body in a *badla*. Also, when students see dance solely as a form of exercise, they may not be as motivated as those who planned to perform.

The competition for international students and clients within Egypt at the end of the 1990s and early 2000s became fiercer. Dance students would travel to Egypt to festivals to study with known dancers and teachers of international backgrounds, vying with Egyptians for spots in international festivals held all year long. These became more popular after about 2000 when the Ahlan wa Sahlan festival, which had 170 attendees that year, was established by Raqia Hassan.[26] There was a festival run by Muhammad Shebika's Nile Group. Other festivals were scheduled regularly in all countries of Europe, in Latin America, and elsewhere.

In that year—2000—it was estimated that there were 450 schools or teachers of *raqs sharqi*, or belly dance, worldwide.[27] These differed from the process of learning and performing dance in Egypt, since in the students' and teachers' cultures of origin, women were not penalized for dancing. Students were taught that the dance was a form of feminine self-discovery, yet their teachers' knowledge of Egyptian culture, dance, or music could be extremely limited or quite detailed, depending on their background. At that time, there was a stronger market for what had become known as Tribal belly dance—which is not necessarily related to its Egyptian origins and would dispute said origins—throughout the U.S. (far larger than in 2020).

We don't know what the accurate number of dancers or students of *raqs sharqi* is in 2021, nor how regularly they train or perform. In the U.S. fewer venues exist, despite the rise of hookah lounges both in Europe and the U.S., partially due to bans on public smoking. The international coronavirus pandemic interrupted all performance venues, festivals, and workshops from March of 2020, but many students continue to train online.

Some like Ika, an Indonesian dancer who performs and teaches in Bali, proclaim that the best teachers are no longer Egyptian, but "Ukrainians, Argentineans and Russians" and that "Egypt is only good for theory now" because belly dance has "opened to modernization."[28] I thoroughly disagree with that opinion, but there are many who agree with her; that is because the current styling of *raqs sharqi* is evolving quickly away from its antecedents, and dancers neither respect the origins or history of this dance, nor understand the importance of seeing it as an Egyptian dance, rather than a world sport. As such, they are disinterested in the related Egyptian musical and other dance genres.

Foreign dancers had been traveling to work in Egypt with some regularity since the 1970s, but owners claimed that they needed to hire dancers with ability. Sometimes this was true, and at the same time, it appeared that owners were in fact interested in attractive dancers who would bring in more high-spending customers. The broader field of *raqs sharqi* split between a decreasing number of regularly performing dancers, and a teaching field that experienced some decline but held steady in certain areas. This means that the many international schools continue to have some bearing on *raqs sharqi* tourism—for festivals, costumes, or the credibility of having visited Egypt.

Dina Tal'at, whose career was promoted and grew since the 1990s, and some other famous dancers led a movement to pressure the government to stop issuing licenses to foreign dancers in 2003.[29] The plan to ban foreign dancers was announced in August 2003 and then Nawal al-Naggar, in the Ministry of Labor, claimed that the dance is firstly Egyptian and secondly "not hard"—difficult to perform.[30] Foreigners were also banned from being tour guides or customs collectors. Several dancers filed lawsuits or appealed to their governments. Raqia Hassan (perhaps due to the numbers of foreign students she was teaching) and Nagwa Fu'ad opposed the ban. What became apparent was that no one agreed on the numbers of foreign dancers in Egypt or how many of these were Russophones and truly *raqs sharqi* performers or "club dancers." No-one agreed on precisely how much less foreign dancers were paid than Egyptian, but they were (and are today) paid less. It was reported after the ban took place that while top dancers continued to book events, the venues trying to hire middle-level dancers had difficulty filling slots, and also that dancers were expected perform for "as little as LE 800 (L. 80)."[31] (In the early 1980s, wages were as low as LE 40 or as high as LE 200, but the value of the pound was higher, thus approximately the same value as $120–$600.)

Some voiced their opinion (including some Egyptians) that foreign dancers aided dance tourism, costumers and teachers, and that since many Muslim women had left entertainment, there was a need for foreign dancers.[32] The authorities relented in 2004. However, it was reported that authorities only issue 100 licenses (to Egyptians) per year. Foreign dancers nevertheless must comply with many regulations, obtaining a license, getting an HIV test (all foreign workers must), working in one primary location, and not working until all of the paperwork is in place. Foreign dancers are subject to discrimination on the basis of age (because they cannot work informally), race/color, and looks, and may be pressured by their managers or other men who seek to take advantage of them.

Overall, considering the dance festivals, the teaching and costuming market, and the availability of employment, the situation has meant that foreign dancers had a role in prolonging *raqs sharqi* to its benefit and its detriment. Although Egyptians and others complain about the negative impact of foreign dancers on the scene and dance styles, without foreign dance students, there would be few Egyptian ones. And Egyptian audiences clamor for certain of the foreign performers, some of whom were discussed in Chapter Three, because of their naughty and provocative use of *dall'a* (coquettishness), or that they don't bother with *dall'a*, but are overtly sexual, or so perceived.

Additional reasons that leading Egyptian dancers may have felt not threatened, but concerned, by dancers who were paid less and expected to interact with customers onstage and off in a manner forbidden by industry regulations, is really brought home in recent research about dancers in Cairo. Through selected in-depth interviews, Christine Sahin introduces some Egyptian performers who are respected by others, married, and do not share the stage with back-up or chorus folkloric dancers, relying instead on their individual capabilities in their shows. They permit no disrespect by audience members. Both those she describes, Camelia and Randa, have connections with teaching and performing in the West; their careers extend beyond Egypt. In contrast, Farah, a dancer seen as foreign, breaks rules of interacting with the audience, though playfully, and indicating that her status is "different," she must act "stupid" (*'abita*) to get what she wants (continued employment and good tips). Some drunken Gulf Arabs clearly had the impression they can do whatever they want in her show. It is not surprising that Farah was perceived by some Egyptians (including the female bathroom attendant) as an overtly sexy, crass performer, and that she defends her own hard-nose tactics to the interviewer.[33] However, Sahin regards and describes her as skilled and well-rehearsed in comparison to Amina (an Egyptian), who was less in control of her space, her movements (dancing with legs too far apart), her male dancers, her interactions with the audience, and even her tips, which she handed over to her manager, who was not only sleazy (pinching her behind) but rude in the way he spoke about and treated her.[34] Although Amina is disrespected by her audience and manager according to Sahin, following a *malayya laff Iskandarani* set with her *funun sha'biyya* (folklore dancers as a chorus), she then performed an amazingly sensitive *baladi* progression which drew the attention of the audience in all the right ways, signaling their appreciation for the subtlety and relaxed dancing, completely synchronizing with her musicians. This led into a percussion solo, and Sahin revises her opinion of Amina's show and her skills, including her extended shimmy performed while bent over, thus exhibiting her prominent derrière,[35] as she is able to transport her audience to an unexpected place. As became clear gradually in Sahin's review of Cairene performance spaces, other Egyptian dancers were also marginalized, or less powerful, or more mediated through male or misogynist ideas and practices in these dance spaces; thus, the repute or degree of agency of dancers, is not only a matter of national origin.

Rendering judgments (especially coming from outside of a culture), juggling perceptions of skill, presumed social class, cabaret versus a five-star background, the economics of the performance, or who is foreign and who is not, is quite difficult when combinations of all these factors along with current standards and practices determine the perception of dancers.

Sahin repeatedly emphasizes that the Egyptian stars she interviewed, Camelia and Randa as well as Dina (not interviewed), believed they were *shamla*. By this Sahin (who brought along a hired translator/male protector) did not mean they were simultaneously musicians, singers and dancers, the definition given earlier in this book, but they were "enough"—such compelling performers that they did not need the addition of *funun sha'biyya* (folklore dancers as a chorus) to hold the audience's attention. They upheld a solo female performing tradition, whereas Farah and other foreign and Egyptian dancers (like Amina) continued a different tradition of *tableaux* involving male as well as female energy as a means of filling their fairly lengthy entertainment slot.[36]

One of the regulations is that dancers must hire Egyptian musicians. Historically, there were many Arab and non–Egyptian musicians, as we saw in Chapters One and Two. The size of Egyptian orchestras cannot be replicated in the United States or Europe at this time; for instance, Dina's orchestra has at least seventeen members. In 1994, Nagwa Fu'ad had over fifty musicians. Many performances I saw had twenty-five or more musicians; a performance with Fifi 'Abdu in Alexandra had about fifty people onstage with at least forty musicians. In most restaurant or club situations outside of Egypt, much smaller bands play or recorded music is used.

Current or historic films and YouTube clips of performances have never displayed all of the best dancers or best dancing. In an effort to spread potentially embarrassing footage, it seems that more foreign dancers are filmed (on cell phones). It is common that people are sharing footage of only some ten to fifteen native Egyptian dancers regularly, and obviously there are many more. This, together with limitations on music, makes it difficult to study the breadth and variety of dance movements.

Relationships

From the outset of the *sala* era through the development of Egyptian theater and cinema and the Golden Era of hotel shows and nightclubs, relationships between dancers, musicians, and actors have been very important to the entertainers' survival or success. Certain families were composed of multiple entertainers—siblings, spouses, children, parents and even grandparents. Exposure, training and encouragement aided their pursuit of entertainment. It was quite common for dancers or musicians to flee disapproving parents to pursue their art, even among contemporary dancers, like Randa Kamel. Despite society's strongly negative views, they did so.[37] Others' families understood society's approbation but were able to support their relatives' right to pursue their talents, or it was a matter of financial need or opportunity. For a time, the spirit of the old entertainment guilds carried on, and they did to some extent, in training, evaluating, and aiding certain performers who required peer allies as well as patrons.

As mentioned earlier in the book, performers might consider it shameful to perform behind a dancer, but they did so to earn income, particularly after the Egyptian wedding circuits dried up for bands with dancers. Families were not any more likely to permit daughters to sing or play an instrument than to dance, unless these women had received professional training. In the folkloric sphere and in the state-funded ensemble such as that employed by the Balloon theater, women musicians received a steady, though small, income. The licensing regulations separated the genres quite thoroughly for dancers, but less so for musicians. Throughout, dancing *raqs sharqi* or folklore is still a profession in Egypt as is the performance of Arabic music, whereas outside of Egypt, it is either a hobby, a sideline, or requires that nearly all performers have a second job.

If we examine the marriage or romantic partners of various performers, a web of relationships appears: Aziz 'Id's marriage with Fatima Rushdi, Badi'a Masabni with Nagib Rihani, Samia Gamal hoping to marry Farid al-Atrash, Tahia Kariuka marrying Rushdie Abaza and later Fayiz Halawa, singer Laila Murad, the sister of composer Munir Murad, marrying Anwar Wagdy, the actor. Asmahan had a brief marriage with director Ahmad Badrkhan and then with actor, radio, and film director Ahmad Salem (he had also married Tahia Kariuka, and Asmahan's friend Amina Barudi), Nagwa Fu'ad's marriage to Ahmad Fu'ad Hassan, and many other unions.

Fatima Rushdi's sisters, Ensaf and Ratiba, danced and acted with Sayyid

Darwish, then in the Rihani and the 'Ali Kassar troupes. They opened a club in Cairo in 1929, danced together in their own and other clubs, as earlier mentioned in Assiut, and opened a club on Alfi Bey street in 1935. The nieces of the *'alima*, Bamba Kashar, Fathiyya, Ratiba and Mufida Ahmad, were all singers and owned a *sala*.[38] Beba 'Izz-Din was the sister of Shu Shu Amin, who married singer Muhammad 'abd al-Muttalib. Asmahan and Farid al-Atrash were brother and sister; their mother 'Alia al-Mundhir had been a musician/singer of much lesser fame. Fatma and Na'ima 'Akif were sisters and the granddaughters of Miriam al-Masriyya and the nieces of Ibrahim 'Akif, the choreographer.

The Jamal twins, actually sisters, Laila (Bertha, b. 1930, known as Lys) and Lamia (Helena, b. 1932, known as Lyn), daughters of a Jewish violinist from Czernowitz and a Jewish mother who sang, grew up in Egypt and learned *raqs sharqi* there. The sisters performed at the Helmieh Palace and also toured in Singapore, India, China, Japan, the Philippines, Vietnam, and elsewhere in Asia. While in India, they were warned that they were being charged with espionage in Egypt in 1957. At this time, Nasser's government was seizing the property of many Egyptians of Jewish, Italian, British, Maltese, and Greek origins. So, they traveled to the United States, where they worked for some years including with Eddie "the Sheik" Kojak, before marrying and merely teaching dance.[39]

Dunia Samir Ghanim (singer) is the daughter of actor/comedian Samir Youssef Ghanim. Actress Sherine Reda, the daughter of Mahmoud Reda, married the singer 'Amr Diab, earlier in her career. Dina Tal'at (dancer) was married to the late director, Samih al-Bagoury. It would be impossible to list all the relationships between entertainers, which are generally known to the Egyptian public. Couples met while working on movie sets or at musical events, and it was somewhat more acceptable for a male to marry a woman in entertainment. They could understand the pressures of their industry and the need for publicity. Traditionally, the male would then forbid his wife to work, but in the twentieth century, more and more women continued on in the field until the Islamization movement convinced many to quit.

From Relationships to Performance Formats

In Egypt as well as abroad, family relationships had secondary effects on the type of music composed for dancers and the format of shows. For instance, Nagwa Fu'ad's fame allowed her to innovate her show format, adding dance choruses, multiple songs, and costume changes. She added dance sequences in a *sha'bi* or *fallahi* style but which remained glamorous. She has remarked on how freeing and extraordinary it was for her to realize that people loved her dances, and that she was onstage sometimes for three hours.[40] She also borrowed from older music, incorporating special choreography, wigs, and costumes to add to the effect. She essentially built on the revue model of Badi'a Masabni and other club-owners of her era, making her own original format. Simultaneously, she used very special dance music that had many different segments set to different rhythms. Other dancers copied both the style her music and the practice of having a chorus of *funun sha'biyya* (as with Farah above) and incorporating a "*baladi* set" following the section performed in *raqs sharqi* costume. Depending on the dancer, the *sharqi* and *baladi* sets could be blended genres; there is no purity required of elements in either style.

Ultimately, one needs *wasta*, clout, whether via family members or other associates, in most occupations in Egypt and the Middle East. This may be a determining factor in the length, brevity, or success of a career.

Relationships and Styles Abroad

The persistence of families of musicians and dancers, and sometimes guild behavior, is very much a part of the history of Arabic music in the diaspora. Partially, because the music scene was vibrant in Egypt, fewer musicians migrated to the United States from Egypt than from other countries, though some did. Turkish-style persisted in Chicago and New York for some time, and other areas exhibited the influence of particular dancers rather than "national styles." Oddly or not, Egyptian dance music played a strong role in the musical careers of many Arab musical families; at least three Palestinian families come to mind. Fadil Shahin and his brothers, from Bethlehem, migrated to San Francisco where he sang and played beginning about 1962, first at the Bagdad Supper Club with his brother Walid. Then he opened the Casbah club with his brother (who later moved to Kuwait) and operated it. The Casbah was also on Broadway Street in San Francisco, two doors from the Bagdad. Shahin's nephews Nader and Basheer continue playing music in their own club, Marrakech, and in Shahin's subsequent club, El Morocco, and sometimes for other restaurants featuring Arabic music. These clubs and others allowed many musicians, singers, and dancers to survive in a performance atmosphere. Brothers Georges, Elias, and Antoine Lammam were born to a Palestinian father who opened a nightclub in Dubai and a Greek mother who sang. They moved to California where they played Egyptian classical, pop, and dance music in addition to Arabic music more broadly. '*Ud* and violin virtuoso Simon Shaheen, and his brothers, Najib and William (his sisters sang), owe their musical background to their father Hekmat Shaheen, who taught an orchestra and led a large chorus in Tarshiha, Palestine (Israel, inside the Green line). The Shaheen brothers also played for years for dancers in the New York area, although building their teaching and performing reputations in Arabic "classical" ("*tarab*") music and mostly excluding dance music from that endeavor, except when collaborating with dancer Cassandra of Minneapolis.

The Darwish brothers, Ghazi (percussionist) and Muhammad 'Ali (keyboard and accordion), and their nephew 'Ali (percussionist), hailed from Lebanon but performed Egyptian dance music for years in Detroit and then in southern California. Also in Los Angeles, cousins Maroun Saba and Maurice Saba (both '*ud*ists from Nazareth) worked for years with dancers. These are but a few examples of many to illustrate that music could be a family business, and that Egyptian music was specifically learned and performed by immigrant musicians as both dance and listening music.

While the above-mentioned Palestinian and Lebanese musicians integrated Egyptian dance music along with other Arab musical styles, some dancers went into

Dancers performing with *sham'adans*; Laura, Mirit, and Valentina, in "From the Sala to the Stage" show, Al-Masri Restaurant, 2018, with Amina Goodyear (courtesy Amina Goodyear).

the business of recording and producing music for other dancers. These reflected the centrality and excitement of Egyptian music for *raqs sharqi*. They used briefer and thus more practical song lengths than those used live in Egypt for solo or group performances and in teaching.[41] For instance, the Spanish dancer Nesma, who worked for five years in Cairo in the 1990s, recorded the CD *Memories of Cairo* in 1998, and subsequent CDs for this purpose. Yasmine of Cairo, Leila Farid, Samasem (Swedish), Outi (Finnish), Katya (Russian), Horacio (Columbian), Beata (German), and Judy Reda also produced recordings in Egypt but for sale elsewhere.

Raqs sharqi in the United States had never been exclusively influenced by Egyptian dance, rather various other immigrant groups composed the audiences and provided most musicians and club-owners until the mid–1970s. While some Egyptians migrated to the United States in the late 1950s and 1960s, particularly after 1969, the majority of these were Copts. In fact, the majority of Egyptian-Americans are Christians, with Muslims being a minority. *Raqs sharqi* in the southern American hemisphere has been impacted more so by the interest in other communities including Lebanese in Brazil and Syrians in Argentina. Syrians going back four generations had migrated to Salta, in northern Argentina, where children and adults enthusiastically attended a traveling workshop in *raqs sharqi* in 2001,[42] and Argentina remains on the Oriental dance workshop map thanks to teachers throughout the country.

Although there were a few Egyptian-American musicians already settled in Los Angeles and the New York area, in the mid–1970s, the tours of a particular group of Egyptian musicians who moved from Egypt to Florida to Los Angeles and San Francisco and then to London to work with Mona al-Sa'id impacted the style and interests of local dancers. A few who stayed, Yusuf Mustafa and drummer Reda Darwish, found the nightclubs couldn't support large ensembles, so they had to work in smaller bands (and often work outside of music). As the advent of their introduction of new Egyptian dance music and a new format coincided with dancers' organization of festivals for promotion, a "modern Egyptian style" bearing some semblance to that in Egypt became very popular for ten years and perhaps longer. It was overtaken and perhaps superseded by the era of second-wave Tribal Dance style in the 1990s and has now been overtaken by yet a new style, featuring high-energy Russo-pseudo-Egyptian athleticism.

"Classic Tarab" Music, Teaching, and Special Genres

Dance music was previously both increasingly and less separated from vocal music than it is today. Whereas singers stood next to dancers, singing for them in films of the 1940s and 1950s, the actual practice in evening entertainment shifted in the Golden Age from the earlier programs combining comedy, dance, theater, and a singer, to a dance show followed by a more famous dancer who warmed up for an important or well-known singer, and so forth through the evening. The long-running comedic and partially improvised play *Madrasat al-Mushaghabin*, which established actor 'Adil Imam's career, had dancing and musical scenes embedded, as did other plays, but any dancing was for comedic effect and not a highlighted performance. As a variety and vaudeville feeling continued in such reviews as those of Samir Sabry and his troupe in other settings, fans of music, dance, theater, or comedy might be distinct.

Although Nagwa Fu'ad performed as a warm-up dancer at 'Abd al-Halim Hafiz' concerts, their shows were completely separate. Dancers did not perform with Umm Kulthum or precede her in concert. It is disputed which dancer first used Umm Kulthum's music to dance to (Suhair Zaki or Tahia Kariuka). As a matter of musical etiquette, dancers did not typically use her songs in their shows; it was considered to be music too heavy and emotional to dance to. Only in special circumstances did one see a dancer onstage with a singer in the past, although I have given many examples of this in *mulid* and *sha'bi* music, and it occurs during the *baladi* section of a dancer's show. It is somewhat a signifier of nostalgia for a previous era. Foreign dancers today in Egypt explain that they are often directed to perform with the *mutrib* (male singer) and "pretend flirt" with him onstage but never with the *mutribat* (female singers).

Other exciting music for dancers was composed by Muhammad 'abd al-Wahhab, Ahmad Fu'ad Hassan, and also by Baligh Hamdi (1932–1993). His songs were made famous by many singers including his wife, Warda al-Jaza'iriyya (a Lebanese-Algerian singer who first came to Egypt in 1960 and returned there in 1962 for the rest of her career), as concert or nightclub showstoppers and recorded. He also married other entertainers and wrote songs for many others, which became used as dance tunes. Those composed for Warda began to be played for dancers only in the following decade (except in the diaspora, where musicians were expected to play more recent hits). Hamdi's compositions were ideal for the previous long format dance shows which prevailed in Egypt because they had different musical and rhythmic sections with contrasting dynamics.

When the songs of 'Abd al-Halim Hafiz, composed by Baligh Hamdi, Muhammad Mugi, and Munir Murad, were first adapted for dance shows by musicians outside of Egypt, these were considered pop songs rather than "*tarab* music." To satisfy aficionados of *tarab*, other compositions (called "heavy stuff,") and older music and songs written for Umm Kulthum might be played (without a dancer) late in the evening.

Three famous singers died in the early-to-mid 1970s. First, in 1974, was Farid al-Atrash (of Syrian origin) who had moved to Lebanon, and among his more three hundred songs, were those played for *raqs sharqi*. Umm Kulthum passed away in 1975, and four million Egyptians crowded the streets to mourn her. Her death was followed by 'Abd al-Halim Hafiz's demise in 1977. By that time, much popular music in Egypt had introduced electrified instruments as described in Chapter Five and began to rely heavily on keyboard, changing the music's aural quality as it became ever more globalized, although retaining some traditional features of Arabic music as in the songs of Kat-Kut al-Amir. 'Adawiyya's appearances with Fifi 'Abdu and other top dancers also signified a change in music, resulting eventually in *al-gil*. Longer dance show routines with few or no vocals were recorded and emulated, such as "Princess of Cairo" (for Nagwa Fu'ad) and "Sahara City" named for the nightclub.

Dancers besides Suhair Zaki and Tahia Kariuka began to use Umm Kulthum's songs for dance performances, whether on their own initiative or because musicians were able to play them. Perhaps because musicians outside Egypt were not as familiar with all other dance music, we began to hear the initially odd term "*tarab*" dancing based on the idea that certain music is inherently "*tarab* music" rather than the Egyptian or Arab concept that any music, well-played or well-sung and appealing, may possess *tarab*.

Today, however: "*Tarab* has become misused for anything that is old—such as 'Abd al-Halim, who used to be a pop singer and now is considered *tarab*."[43] In Egypt, it became accepted in the 1990s for a *raqs sharqi* dancer to perform to a portion of a song composed for Umm Kulthum or another classic in a portion of her lengthy show. Despite a wave of nostalgia and somewhat more enthusiasm for evocations of the Golden Age, an attitude that the female professional performer of *raqs sharqi* or *raqs baladi* is déclassé and embarrassing still prevailed in Egypt of the 1990s, as it continues today among upper and middle class Egyptians (and Arab-Americans). For as Noha Roushdy put it, "The public dancing of amateurs appears to be slowly undermining the need for professional entertainment."[44]

In one respect this is a positive, in that Egyptians are enjoying their own music and dancing to it. But from the other side, it is too bad that the unique skills of professional dancers are so embarrassing to Egyptians who have, in some cases, newly discovered a fondness for their own country's popular music and dance.

What dancers now consider "*tarab* music" or "classical *tarab*" for *raqs sharqi* is largely conceived and disseminated outside of Egypt (however foreign dancers request these songs in Egypt, and they are rerecorded there) and can merely mean "classic" songs that are mostly devoid of a *baladi* or *shaʻbi* feeling. These include (often only sections of the following songs, and listed by the singer who made them popular, unless the composer did so): "Ahwak," ('Abd al-Halim Hafiz), "Alf Laila wa Laila" (Umm Kulthum), "Amal Hayati" (Umm Kulthum), "Ana Fi-Intizarak" (Umm Kulthum), " al-Atlal" (Umm Kulthum), "Baʻid ʻAnnak" (Umm Kulthum), "Bint al-Balad," ('Abd al-Wahhab), "Bitwannis Bik," (Warda), "Fi Yum wa Laila," (Warda), "Gana al-Hawa," ('Abd al-Halim Hafiz), "Habbina" (Farid al-Atrash, which is between a folk and *tarab* feel), "Haramt Ahabbak" (Warda, an example of a pop song identified as *tarab* due to the performer), "Hubb Aih" (Umm Kulthum), "Inta ʻUmri" (Umm Kulthum), "Ismaʻuni" (Warda), "Lissa Fakkir" (Umm Kulthum), "Mawʻud" (Abd al-Halim Hafiz), "Qariʼat al-Finjan" ('Abd al-Halim Hafiz), "Sawah" ('Abd al-Halim Hafiz), "Sirat al-Hubb" (Umm Kulthum), "Ya Zalamni" (Umm Kulthum), "Wahashtuni," (Warda), "Wi Darit al-Ayam" (Umm Kulthum), "Zay al-Hawa" ('Abd al-Halim Hafiz), "Zaina" (Muhammad ʻabd al-Wahhab), and maybe oddly, as from a different era, "Zidini ʻAshqan" (Kadhim as-Sahir), and other non–Egyptian singers' songs. They might also include instrumental-only dance pieces like "Mashal" and the other dance pieces by Muhammad ʻabd al-Wahhab such as '"Aziza," "al-Hubb al-Awwil," "Inta al-Balad," "Khatwat Habibi," or "Lailat Hubb" (originally a vocal piece for Umm Kulthum, typically, the *muqadimma* [the introduction] alone is played for a dancer). For some reason, pieces like "Hawwil Taftakarny" ('Abd al-Halim Hafiz) and "Nebtidi min al-Hikaya" ('Abd al-Halim Hafiz) used to be widely played for dancers, but fewer know and request these now "classic" songs today. It is also true that what super-star dancers teach in international workshops tends to influence dancers' song selections or may revive popularity in an older song.

In contrast to the above list, the song from the banned film "Halawat al-Ruh" of the same name is still perhaps the most popular song in any spontaneous dancing in Egypt, such as at weddings and Ahmad al-Shiba's "Ah Ya Laʻbt ya Zahr" or *mahragan* hits such as "Elʻab Yalla."

Musical and stylistic confusions are exaggerated in the interplay between the international *raqs sharqi* scene and the international Arabic music scene in which some musicians promoted Arabic music within world music as a classical genre, unworthy of pollution by dance. Notwithstanding, dance shows were an important gateway to musical performances. The confusion reflects a situation in which most dance and music topics are created by dance educators rather than full-time performers (of whom there are fewer) as part of the international festival workshop and competition scene.

In the 1980s, dancers outside of Egypt used many recordings which were reissues or covers of well-known songs set to exciting percussion tracks. These were produced for dancers from the early 1980s through 2010 (a huge period to cover) and were not always by Egyptians. Some of these were by Setrak Serkassian (Lebanese), Hamouda ʻAli (Egyptian in the U.S.), Khamis Henkish (in Egypt to Mokhtar Saʻid), Hossam Ramzy (Egyptian, but worked internationally), Dr. Samy Farag (Egyptian based in the U.S.), and Susu Pampanin (American, though two of her albums are recorded in

Egypt). These contrast with the music presented inside of Egypt in the same time period, but they in some ways are better suited to teaching or performing due to the briefer length of songs. The large percussion sections, which animate dance music in Egypt, are not usually possible to find outside it. Also, the song selections differ. For instance, at the outset of the 1980s in Egypt, I was assigned to dance (due to my vocalist) certain songs which he had recorded, and it was unthinkable to my band leader for me to use some of the pop or *sha'bi* songs that I might have preferred in the five-star hotel venues. To signal that we should add a folkloric coda, he might launch into an imitation of singer Wadi al-Safi. Others have related similar experiences regarding the distaste for *sha'bi* in a similar time frame.[45]

Since these years, teaching of dance has often become more important than performance. Teachers, including Egyptians, generally prepare and present choreographies rather than improvisation, which is traditional to the *raqs sharqi* format. This is because they have a background in learning and teaching choreography, as for instance former members of dance troupes like 'Aida Nur and Raqia Hassan.

It is also an outcome of foreigners being the primary audience and market for workshops. Foreigners usually have no idea how to improvise because they do not perform regularly to live music and require choreographies, which they memorize, perform, and then reproduce. In contrast, many Egyptian performers often are more comfortable teaching without explanation and detailed breakdowns of movements, in the method dancers refer to as "follow the bouncing butt." Quite a large number of teachers are very effective in any case, including Mohamed Shahin, Mo Geddawi, Momo Kadous, Randa Kamel, Yousry Sharif, Tito, Dandash, Raqia Hassan, and 'Aida Nur. It has been observed that some instructors chose music that was somewhat more Western sounding, thinking that their workshop participants would be better able to deal with it.

Another innovation was the reclassification of the special overture song that came to be known as a *majence*. Overture songs were employed by Nagwa Fu'ad but also many other dancers in the Golden Era, in which the dancer paraded and turned around the performance space, greeting her public and establishing a mood of excitement for her show. It could begin with an instrumental salute, then a *taqasim*, and then a song to a very rapid rhythm, followed by others, and at that time, might be as long as a half hour. During an Oriental introduction, Randa Kamel explained that the audience sized her up and could comment on her body, hair, or costume. Candace Bordelon explains that the dancers she interviewed told her they make use of this part of their show to gather information about the crowd, their social location, and their preferences. The dancer Tamr-henna said she evaluates the audience as she dances to see if they prefer Umm Kulthum or 'Amr Diab,[46] in other words, how to orient her show.

The new overture songs fit well into the practice of dancing brief performances at festivals and competitions. Whereas earlier, the themes in the introduction hinted at the different parts of the show, and they were further elaborated later on. In this new format, there is no chance to further elaborate; what you hear is what you get. The term *majence* (*magence*) had not been employed in Egypt in the 1970s or 1980s; it entered the parlance of dancers, dance students, and musicians in the mid–1990s.

According to one person, it was a mistaken version of a balletic term.⁴⁷ However, a more accepted explanation is that it came from the French word *émergence* (emerging).

There is reciprocity in the dance's evolution. Foreign dancers who are part of the scene in Egypt influence the Egyptian dancers, just as Egyptian dancers and their environment influence these foreign dancers. Managers have learned that teaching and workshops are also lucrative. Foreign dancers learn about the type of music that appeals to their audiences, whether light songs, Sa'idi songs, or "classic" songs such as those by Umm Kulthum. Egyptian dancers, and foreign dancers with extensive dancing experience with Egyptian musicians, explained dancing with feeling and how they or other dancers interpreted sadness or happiness when interviewed by Bordelon. For example, Randa, who often executes movements with great strength, demonstrated a movement which showed a shock moving into her body and another in which the energy moved out of her hip. Shareen El Safi wrote about Mona al-Sa'id's use of lip-synching and trembling hands to "Lissa Fakkir" in a 1994 performance.⁴⁸

Randa Kamel, performing at the Nile Maxim, Cairo 2009 (Judith Scheepstra, Wikimedia Commons).

The problem is that inexperienced dancers and those who are not so skilled or have trouble relating to the music perform steps that are traditional to the dance but have no idea how or why these steps evolved because they copy other dancers. Thus, they perform these steps without context and are criticized for being "without emotion" or robotic. These may be dancers hired at a lower level of pay and expertise, or perhaps they are paid at a higher rate based on their appearance. This criticism also pertains to the chorus dancers in various clubs who combine semi-burlesque costumes with *raqs sharqi* sets, as for example the foreign dancers who were the warm-up

Randa Kamel teaching a dance workshop attended by many Eastern European women, 2019 (photograph by Laura Boushnak).

act at Lucy's club, the Parisiana, early in 2000. Using Western or Russophone (in Egypt) dancers in skimpy costumes who are not particularly skilled in *raqs sharqi* is not restricted to Egypt. I've visited clubs from Beirut, Lebanon, to Casablanca, Morocco, where such dancers are very popular and thought to attract customers.

Yet, certain Egyptian dancers with their own individual style take note of the popularity of foreign dancers with better dancing skills and adopt their more frenetic pace and the trend of robotic isolations into their own shows. Genres are confused; for example the hair dance movements which originated on the Arabian Peninsula, Gulf region and Iraq, have been moved into *raqs sharqi* performances by dancers with beautiful long hair like Oksana or Alla Kushnir. Nagwa Fu'ad criticized newer dancers who sport tattoos and what she called "ugly movements," while Dina spoke of those who are too sexual, using movements from striptease.[49] In these same filmed interviews, both Dina and Nagwa noted that in their own careers, they were innovative and creative onstage; Dina said, "My life's greatest moments were on stage."[50] The difference—to these two—is what degree of innovation can occur without changing the essential character of the dance. These dancers (Nagwa and Dina) innovate because they acquired sufficient knowledge of the dance to break certain rules. Many will regard these statements as being relative, perhaps hypocritical, and that it may be impossible for other dancers without a top-level reputation to avoid the hyper-sexuality which is preferred by managers and audiences at present.

A few teachers and dancers have shifted from their previous emphasis on "arabesque style"—to understand this, one might visualize dance movements that Mahmoud Reda choreographed to *muwashshahat*—and instead have begun to teach dancing to *sha'bi* music, choosing older *sha'bi* songs or "tradition," in a manner that was unfashionable several decades ago. This is so as to carve out new territory in teaching, and not so much an issue in performance.

It has even become popular to teach *mahragan* style dancing (it was not, when I first began writing this book, and I offered among the first *mahragan* workshops outside of Europe) but to *raqs sharqi* movements. These changes make it quite difficult to pin down which is *raqs sharqi* or *mahragan* in Egyptian style and which is Russian or "festival fusion." After all, it is also normal for a dance form to undergo transformations or be influenced by adjacent dance forms if it does not transform much over time. For instance, with the longevity and relative staticity of ballet, modern dance emerged as a challenge.

I should also mention a different gender dimension to Egyptian dance as a national and international phenomenon. Top dancers pay and therefore control their musicians in Egypt. In other words, a woman is providing income to a group of male musicians. Whereas women were *shamla* (complete performers) in the past, playing music and singing as well as dancing, this situation is much less common today. Less well-known dancers who charge less may be hired separately from the band and negotiate their own fee (or this may be the case at weddings as compared to regular venues). More often, their manager charges a fee, and they receive some part of that and are required to turn over their tips to the manager, having little ability to negotiate any other sort of economic arrangement.

A few musicians have gone outside the normal performing venues, and alongside some male dancers, present themselves as teachers of dance and music to benefit from the additional income and notoriety. While there have been male choreographers (and female) for some time, often a second career for folkloric dancers, it is fascinating that some women prefer males as teachers. All over the world, women are socialized into patriarchy and an acceptance of male authority, not only in Egypt, so this is also the case in the related fields of dance and music. What strikes one, however, with reference to *raqs sharqi*, is that the men teaching, usually, have more limited performance opportunities than women. Admittedly, these have expanded with the use of social media and videos, but still, how many men have the experience of their female counterparts of performing nightly solo shows to live audiences? That may or may not affect their coaching ability or the differences in the appearance of movements on male versus female bodies.

The gender dynamic is further altered when a large proportion of dancers are unpaid but musicians still earn a fee as occurs outside of Egypt. (This has happened as owners found they could obtain free, or nearly free dancers, and because many dancers are hobbyists; even working dancers feel they must appear in free showcases to promote their work.) Dance was an occupational area historically open to women in Egypt, yet the relatively recent male dominance in the fields of music and entertainment management presents some challenges to women's control over their livelihood or artistic choices. The preferences of male managers (for younger and cheaper dancers) are remarked on, as are abuses of these relationships.

Dance performance as a source of income became very insecure after the January 25, 2011, revolution, with dancers reporting that about half their income disappeared. The huge fall in tourism has not yet fully recovered, and some dancers have relocated entirely. Some shows in hotels ceased for a time before resuming, and some venues reopened with a DJ format, a smaller stage area, and continued the bias to hiring foreign dancers. The "boat shows," which offered entertainment on the Nile, were attended by a mixed audience of Egyptians and non–Egyptians. The insecurity of the dance scene under President Morsi, with the government's implicit threat to censor dance or send it underground, has been replaced with a sense that such commercial entertainment is permitted. Yet, economic uncertainty has continued under President Sisi's government, which means that the music and dance industries are reliant to some degree on tourism. Dance shows were in session as I prepared this book, with the largest regular event being Dina's regular weekly show at the Semiramis hotel. Then, the coronavirus epidemic hit the industry hard in the spring of 2020.

Foreign and local dancers are vulnerable to mistreatment and look for situations in which they will not be abused or harassed. In the spring of 2019, a certain manager was soliciting dancers via social media, promising them hotel stays and contracts, as he attacked one dancer and built up the reputation of another client. Needless to say, when he did not meet the terms of an arriving dancer, others warned her of his unreliability and volatility. Such abuses are supposed, theoretically, to be controlled by the guiding regulations of the industry, but in fact, there is room for abuse.

Another dynamic that has taken place over several decades has been the gradual replacement of female dancers with male ones at weddings and private parties and the dance professional with the audience of amateurs (dancing to a DJ who has replaced musicians, a disaster for the latter[51]). Also, certain *raqs sharqi* performers remain solo dancers while others have added *funun sha'biyya* to enrich their performances. As we related in Chapter One, a gender shift had occurred in the nineteenth century in Egypt when the *khawal* and *gink* dancers continued performing although female dancers were exiled to Upper Egypt. The broader history of Arabic dance and music would include that of effeminate males who sang, played instruments, and were comedians and matchmakers called *mukhannathun*, first in Medina[52] and on into the Abbasid era. But dancing males need not be transvestites or emulating women; the *gink*s were not, and Egyptian men have their own dances, as explained in Chapter Six in rural dances. Men may also dance *raqs baladi*. It is when they present *raqs sharqi* as professionals that there is substantial criticism.

In the 1980s and 1990s, the *sahwa Islamiyya*, or Islamic revival, hit Egypt hard, influencing many women to adopt the *hijab*, and many female entertainers gave up performing in front of men, or altogether. The traditional *zaffa* at weddings, at least those held indoors, typically in hotels but sometimes in hired halls, had included an Oriental dancer, but it had become popular as far back as the 1960s to hire a *firqat zaffa*, a group of male dancers to process, followed by young women and then a *raqs sharqi* performer (referred to as the *'alima*, or *raqqasa*). Carolee Kent and Marjorie Franken pointed out that if the female dancer did not appear, this was understood as a cost-saving measure as male dancers performed for a much lower fee.[53] However by the 1990s, upper-middle class, even some middle class or lower class, weddings eschewed the female *raqs sharqi* performer because it was thought that the increasingly religious guests might be offended by women dancers as compared to the *firqat zaffa*. This situation provided an employment opportunity for folkloric dancers at "*halal*" weddings.

At a wedding where dancer Dina Tal'at performed, singer Sa'd al-Soghayar was also hired, and he brought with him a group of male dancers. They performed *raqs baladi* as a group and choreographies while playing frame drums but in regular clothing rather than folkloric costumes and in a very masculine style.

Beginning in the 1990s up to the time of writing, at weddings and parties, it also became popular to hire DJs. These DJs are active in encouraging the audience to dance.

With the September 23, 2013, criminalization of the Muslim Brotherhood, many women continue to wear *hijab*, yet the tide seems to have turned with regard to women "repenting" and forswearing acting, dancing, or singing, and a few actresses began reappearing on television and in films without their *hijab*s. Although conservatives ensure that live Oriental dance remains banned from official Egyptian television channels (with very few exceptions), it is obvious that there remains interest in *raqs sharqi*. Three private channels featuring many *raqs sharqi* performances including *El Tet* were closed in 2013 when Morsi was president. In early 2014, a program called "al-Raqisa" aired by *Al-Qahira wa-al-Nas* introduced a contestant format with Dina as a judge,[54] along the lines of "Arab Idol" or "Voice Arabia," but uniquely including dancers of many nationalities. It was quite fascinating to witness Dina's swift judgments as to the potential of the contestants recorded with a green check (approval) or a red X (dismissal). Although the program was controversial and immediately attacked by opponents of dance and music, and thus censored, it illustrated the distinctions between excellent and more mediocre *raqs sharqi*.

Professional dancing remains very much in demand as evening entertainment, at the five star hotels, the tour boats, and clubs on Haram Street, at weddings, and in the newer nightclubs. It must be mentioned that women wearing *hijab* are not permitted in nightclubs or in most upscale establishments with entertainment (and not even at many resort venues with entertainment). No one knows the exact proportion of women wearing *hijab*, but some believe it is up to 90 percent. The policy is discriminatory, but it is also a way of both protecting venues against the criticism of conservatives and declaring it a space where men may drink and enjoy themselves.[55] Today, at weddings, there may be a female dancer or not, possibly with her back-up folkloric dancers, or instead of them, a group of men who play percussion and dance and who circulate and perform to liven up the festivities.

That *raqs sharqi* is seen by Egyptians themselves as a symbol of flirtation and worth including in bridal lingerie is illustrated in a 2019 photograph of a clothing store, on page 192.

An interesting argument made during the 2003–4 ban on foreign dancers denied that *raqs sharqi* is an exclusively Egyptian dance; this was a part of Nour and Caroline Evanoff's legal appeal backed by the Association of Foreign Artists. They view *raqs*

Cairo store "Half for Allah, Half for Abdullah" displaying fashions for *muhagibat* (covered women) and also *raqs sharqi* outfits (photograph by Yasmin Amin).

sharqi as a transcultural product. On the other hand, many of us believe it expresses Egyptian identity, culture, and history. There has been discussion of recognizing *raqs baladi* as an intangible cultural heritage practice according to UNESCO's definitions and listings. Unfortunately, those writing about this effort have taken Buonaventura and others' narrative, which claims that *raqs baladi* is a product of the Dom people transplanted to Egypt.[56] Also, those who more recently argued that *raqs sharqi* is a transcultural phenomenon do not understand that the dance predates the 1920s and overemphasize its hybridity.[57]

Noha Roushdy has insisted that Egyptian dance is *raqs baladi*, that it has survived because the quality of being *baladi* is prized, and that the distinctions between versions of *raqs sha'bi* or between *raqs sharqi* and *raqs baladi* (dance performed by non-professionals) are somewhat meaningless to Egyptians and only meaningful to outsiders.[58] By that I believe that what is meant is that dance is completely rejected by some. And obviously the regional distinctions in the forms of *raqs sha'bi* were not meaningless to those who collected them, such as Mahmoud Reda, Magda Saleh, and Nelly Mazloum. In the end, Roushdy's argument helps explain how dance has survived despite the antipathy of Islamists to dance in general, and the suspect status of dancers.

Thus, we have witnessed a strangely circular movement from present to past and back again within Egyptian dance in the midst of similarly circular argumentation about dance and its globalization. Even as Western dance forms or Latin dance forms were more popular earlier in time and now young people prefer to dance *baladi* at their gatherings, the professional dance seen is both Egyptian-centered and transformed by other influences. It is only natural that dance will evolve over time, and that the distinctions which once had special meaning may not hold over the course of decades.

It has been my aim in this chapter and throughout this book to explain those aspects of Egypt's dance forms connecting across time and space and how they globalize, and are globalized, yet remain Egyptian. Let us hope that dance and dance music will remain important aspects of Egyptian entertainment, enjoyment, and the country's gift to the world.

Glossary

Certain figures are mostly known mostly by their last name (i.e. Saʿd al-Zaghlul) whereas others, including nearly all female performers and certain male performers, are known by their first name only, or by a stage name of two names. For the reader's convenience, they are listed here as if the second name was their last name. In the case of Zuba al-Klubtiyya or Shafiqa al-Qibtiyya, that second name is an identifier, not a family name. A stage name was taken to boost one's career and because entertainment was considered shameful. In Egypt, men and women are often known by their first name and their father's name rather than a "last" or family name, though official documents may list the latter. Arabic names beginning with the definite article are conventionally alphabetized by ignoring the definite article. Thus, for example, al-Zaghlul is alphabetized under Z. However, when the Al stands for the family of, as in Al Qasemi, then it is alphabetized under A, and when the author's name appears in English sources as El Baradei, it is under E.

Abaza, Rushdy (1926–1980) an actor who appeared in more than a hundred films from 1948 to his death. Among the women he married were Tahia Kariuka, Samia Gamal and Sabah (the singer).

ʿAbbas Hilmi or referred to as **ʿAbbas I** (1812–1854), a grandson of Muhammad ʿAli Pasha, wali of Egypt and the Sudan. He built a palace in a new suburb ʿAbbasiyya, and encouraged members of Egypt's royal family to live there.

ʿAbbas II, or **Abbas Hilmy II** (1874–1944), the great great grandson of Muhammad ʿAli Pasha. He ruled Egypt from 1892 to 1914, when the British removed him in favor of Husain Kamel.

ʿAbd al-Muttalib, Muhammad (1910–1980). A singer who influenced **Ahmad al-ʿAdawiyya**. He sang in a *tarab* style, but with popular styling, contributing to what became *shaʿbi* music. Married to Shu Shu ʿIzz al-Din, and also to Nabawiyya Mustafa.

ʿAbd al-Wahhab, Muhammad (1902–1991). Born in Bab al-Shaʿriyya, Cairo. ʿ*Ud*ist, and prolific composer of 1,820 songs; he also sang and appeared in seven films. He was promoted by poet **Ahmad Shawqi**. ʿAbd al-Wahhab first wrote traditional melodies but later incorporated some Western and non–Arabic elements into his compositions, modernizing Arabic music. At first a rival of **Umm Kulthum**'s, she sang his composition "Inta ʿUmri" in 1964.

ʿAbdu, Fifi. Dancer/actress, born ʿAtiyat ʿAbd al-Fattah Ibrahim, April 26, 1953, in Cairo (however some sources say in a village outside of Cairo). She danced at the Arizona and al-Lail clubs and major hotels in 1970s. Was one of the top three dancers (with Lucy and Dina) when she retired from dance in 2004 and continued on primarily as an actress. She dances at private events, in videos on Instagram, and teaches dance. A dynamic performer, she has been identified with *bint al-balad* because of her *shisha* tableau and roles played in films and on television.

Abla Fahita. A puppet character portraying an Egyptian widow famous for her sarcasm and wit. She has been the star of "Abla Fahita Live from the Duplex" on the *CBC* channel since 2010. She has a daughter Carcoura (Caro) and a son, Boudi.

Glossary

Abu al-Ghait. A clan known for their *tannura* dancing. Also entertained at zars.

Abu Si'ud, Hassan. Long-time accordion player for Ahmad al-'**Adawiyya**.

Abu Zayd al-Hilali. Hero of an epic poem, or *sira*. Born black to white parents. A hero who led his tribe, the Bani Hilal.

Abu Zuluf. A style of *mawwal* with specific lyrics which date back to Abbasid Iraq and performed in Lebanon for centuries. Also performed in Syria and Iraq. In *lahja* (dialect) *al-furutiyya* of Baghdad, *jaysh al-zuluf* means a hubbub, complete chaos (similar to **mulid bidun shaykh** in Egyptian dialect), the *fusha* word *dhalfa'* means a beautiful woman with a straight nose; and *zulf* may have meant the [curly] sidelock of hair as Jews in Iraq were forced to wear and is associated with the color green. Popularized by Wadi' al-Safi, Samira Tawfiq and others, the eastern (*shami*) style *mawawil* were performed in Egypt by singers like Farid al-Atrash, Asmahan (and her mother 'Alia), and Nur al-Huda, and they differ from Egyptian *mawawil* in some respects.

Adab. Good manners. Also refers to literature, or *belle lettres* in *fusha*.

al-'Adawiyya, Ahmad (b. 1945). Grew up in a *sha'bi* area near Ma'adi, south of Cairo. He worked as a waiter as he began singing in weddings and parties. The massive popularity of his songs since 1971 continued until he was found comatose in a hotel in 1990, reportedly the victim of a jealous Kuwaiti husband. He recovered partially and began singing again some years ago.

Adhan. The call to prayer, chanted five times a day.

al-'Adil, Nazla. An *'alima* of Muhammad 'Ali street. Appeared in *Qasr al-Shuq* (1966) and a German documentary *Die Königin der Mohammed-Ali-Strasse* (Queen of Muhammad 'Ali Street) c. 1991, in which she does the splits (**al-fashkha**) while playing finger cymbals. She may be over 80 years old (in that film). She married Sayyid al-Birri, an *'ud* player who was the brother of **Zuba al-Klubtiyya**'s husband.

Afandi (*Effendi* in Turkish). Honorary title for an educated Egyptian given to men and women prior to World War I. As a group, they are *afandiyya*. After World War I, the term referred solely to men. Even today, a polite manner of answering the telephone in Egypt is "Afandim?"

Afrangi. Used to describe non-traditional lifestyles and values of modern, middle class (or higher), more secular, less loyal people. Literally means the Franks or French (foreigners).

Afranza Hanim. A dancer from Turkey who was a headliner for Badi'a's sala when she first added dance in 1927. She performed both *raqs sharqi* and "Turkish dance."

Aghani, pl. (*ughniya*, s.). Songs.

Aghani al-tahjir. Means the songs of forced migration. A new style of Nubian song introduced by Muhammad Wardi after the Egyptian government displaced the Nubian population in Egypt.

Ahl al-Bayt. The family of the Prophet Muhammad, including his daughter Zainab (her tomb being in Cairo), his nephew 'Ali, his grandson Husain, great-granddaughter Nafisa, and other descendants.

Ahmad, Fathiyya (1898–1975). Began her singing career about 1910. She was in **Nagib al-Rihani** and Amin Sidki's theater companies. She then focused on singing in the tradition of the *'awalim* and the **wasla** (a song cycle). She had an audience in Syria and Palestine, as well as Egypt. After Umm Kulthum's first successful season, Fathiyya went on tour to Syria, but she returned with a recording contract to Odeon and sang for six years at Sala Badi'a, frequently advertised as a "Turkish-style" singer.

Ahya sha'biyya. Literally means popular neighborhoods or quarters. Areas where the *awlad al-balad* live such as Sayyida Zainab, Bulaq, al-Ghuriyya, al-Khalifa, al-Muski, Khan al-Khalili, Old Cairo, al-Ghuriyya, Bab al-Sha'riyya.

'Akif, Fatma (c. 1926–200?). Born in Tanta. The eldest of three sisters. Performed as a child in her family's 'Akif circus as an acrobat and **ghawazi** dances with her sisters in her mother Gamila's *teatro*. Possibly from the Sunbati *ghawazi*. Her grandmother was Miriam al-Masriyya, a circus acrobat and dancer, and her uncle was Ibrahim 'Akif, the choreographer. She left Egypt in 1946, worked in Europe, then South America and arrived in the U.S. in 1966. She and her husband Isma'il (known as Gilli Gilli, she was his 17th wife) performed at the Bagdad Supper Club in San Francisco, where she danced and he drummed, managed, did magic tricks and "barked" (brought in customers, as in **barrada**).

'Akif, Na'ima (1928–1966). Born in Tanta, performed in her mother's *teatro*, and her family's 'Akif Circus from ages 4–14, including as a trapeze artist. Her dance style was consequently dramatic and acrobatic. She formed her own troupe with a clown, and then performed with Badi'a Masbani, dancing and singing, and then at the Kit-Kat and other clubs. She married Husain Fawzy, director and screenwriter. Her film career began in the late 1940s, and she made 14 musicals with her husband. She portrayed the *ghaziya* Tamr Hinna in the 1957 film of that name.

'Ala 50 Cent ('Ala al-Din Abdel-Rahman). *Mahragan* artist from Salam City. He partnered with Sadat and then in 2008 with 'Amr Haha.

Almaz (1860–1897). An *'alima* born as Sakina in Alexandria to a Lebanese family. She attracted the attention of Khedive Isma'il and was married to 'Abduh al-Hamuli, the singer.

Amin, Shu Shu. Began dancing in the 1970s in Cairo through the 1980s. She performed with Hassan Si'ud in Japan for a year and frequently danced in London. Famous for a shimmy all the way to the floor and a shimmy with abdominal accents. She brought *zar* performers into her show and danced to *zar*.

'Amir, Aytin. Born Samar Ahmad Abd al-Ghaffar (1990) in Alexandria. The sister of actress Wafaa 'Amir. She has appeared in about a dozen films and television series.

al-Amir, Kat-Kut (1945–2012). Born Hanafi Muhammad Rizq in the Rod al-Farag neighborhood of Cairo. He began his career as a *tabbal* (a drummer) and became a *sha'bi* singer in the 1970s, best known for his song "al-Ghazal al-Darb al-Ahmar" (the beautiful girl of the Darb al-Ahmar neighborhood). He married 'Azza Sharif.

'Amma. The common people, the masses, includes the rural citizens, as well as the urban poor and working classes.

'Ammiyya. Egyptian colloquial Arabic. Certain letters and words are pronounced differently than in classical Arabic (and hence some differences between my transliterations and others). Some words in *'ammiyya* (*aih* or *ayy*? = what?) do not exist in classical Arabic; grammar and syntax are simpler than in *fusha*, classical Arabic.

'Amr Haha or **DJ 'Amr Haha**. One of the founders of *mahragan*. Was working as a PC repairman and heard DJ Figo's "Salaam City Festival." Initially competed with Figo, then joined him with his computer skills.

Amraz. He flirted. *Amaruzat*, flirtations in *sim al-fannanin*, or the entertainer's argot. The derivation of the word is probably French.

Anashid, pl. (*inshad*, s.). Usually referred to as *inshad dini* in Egypt. Religious hymns.

al-'Aqqad, Muhammad (1850–1931) Was considered the most gifted qanun player of his era, accompanying top singers like 'Abduh al-Hamuli.

Arabian Knightz. Egyptian rap group which formed in 2005. Includes Karim 'Adel. To counter the "corrupt" music industry, the group founded "The Arab League" to include other Arab rappers, and filmmakers, graffiti artists, etc. Their song "Not Your Prisoner" was performed in 2011.

[Q]Aragoz (From Qaragoz; the letter *qaf* is not pronounced). This was a character in a shadow puppet theater throughout the Ottoman era, but now the word refers to the puppet show itself. It can be used in a demeaning or mocking way to mean a clown-like figure, someone not to be taken seriously, as in *huwwa 'aragoz* (he's just a clown).

Arghul. Double reed pipe—one is a melody pipe, and one is a drone. Played in rural music now but also in some settings in cities.

'Arusa al-Mulid. Literally means "bride of the **mulid**." Sugar doll made at the mulid for children. The real bride of the mulid is the mosque of the shrine where the mulid is held. Mahmoud Reda choreographed a dance of the 'Arusa al-Mulid. **Tahia Kariuka** performed an extensive set of dances with a chorus all dressed in *'arusa al-mulid* costumes in the film *'Arusa al-Mulid*.

Ashwayyat. Slum areas of informally and illegally constructed housing in Cairo and Alexandria.

'Askariyya. Female supporter of Egypt's armed forces.

Asmahan (1917–1944). Born Amal al-Atrash to a Syrian-Lebanese Druze family. She emigrated to Egypt as a child. Dawud Husni, the composer, gave her the stage name Asmahan. She performed at Mary Mansur's *sala* and later at Badi'a's *sala*. She starred in two films before dying in an automobile accident. Her voice and musicality were so admired that she was said to rival Umm Kulthum. One musicologist considered her among the seven greatest Arabic musicians.

al-Asmar, Hassan (1959–2011). Moved from Qena to the 'Abbasiyya district of Cairo. Was considered the second singer of *sha'bi* after 'Adawiyya. Appeared in films and became known for songs like "Kitab Hayati," "Mawwal 'Umri," and others.

al-Atrash, Farid (c. 1915–1974). Born in Suwayda, Syria, he immigrated to Egypt with his mother and siblings. He played in the **takht,** accompanying his sister Asmahan at Sala Mary Mansur as early as 1931 and was recommended by Riyadh al-Sunbati to the radio, where he was hired as an 'ud player and singer. He was a composer of more than 500 songs, starred in 31 films, and was called Prince of the 'Ud for his instrumental virtuosity and **taqasim**. His songs feature in some of the dance repertoire of the mid–twentieth century and he co-starred in nine films with dancer Samia Gamal.

'Awalim (pl. of *'alima*, sometimes rendered *'alma*). Women who sang, danced, played instruments, composed music, and recited poetry or drama until the twentieth century. They performed in private homes for women and men (separately). The term also applied to women who merely danced at weddings and *mawalid* but who were not as artistically accomplished.

Awlad al-balad. Literally means children of the town but refers to urban lower class. **Ibn al-balad** is the male, and **bint al-balad** is the female.

Awlad al-kar. Literally means children of the occupation or trade of entertainment and refers to the families of entertainers from the Muhammad 'Ali street area. Can also refer to prostitution.

Awliya', pl. (*wali*, m., *waliyya*, f.). Saints. Holy men and women who are celebrated in the traditional **mawalid** (mulids).

'Awra. Means those parts of the male or female body that must be covered. The exact definition may vary according to different schools of Islamic thought. For a male this means between his navel and his knees while in public or praying. For a woman it is the same area of the body in front of other women (though possibly not non–Muslim women) but all her body except face and hands is *'awra* in front of a non-**mahram** male or when praying. This explains why some believe the sight of women dancers' bodies is sinful. Some conservative scholars claimed that women's voices were *'awra*.

Azbakiyya Gardens (sometimes spelled Ezbekiyya). Opened in 1872, built on the area of Birqat Azbakiyya. It was an octagonal park where **salat** (music halls) and kiosks opened and offered entertainment, including variety shows such as the El Dorado in 1886 and Sala Santi. Close to Azbakiyya was a red light district.

'Azuzah. Soda, pop, carbonated drinks.

Badawiyya. A *ghaziya* in Upper Egypt (post-ban) who danced her sword dance for Europeans who were brought to the opening of the Suez Canal in 1869, and then went down the Nile to see her performances.

Badla. Literally means a suit, or outfit. Two-piece costume for *raqs sharqi* covering the chest and the hips over a (usually) ankle-length skirt, or a bra with the hip portion of the skirt decorated. Some theorize that the *badla* was imported from Europe, where neo-Grecque or Cambodian style metallic bra tops were used in costuming in the 1920s or 1930s. Other theorize that the tightly-fitted vest of Egyptian dancers transitioned into the bra-style top, and that dancers stopped wearing material or leotard-like garments covering the midriff (although regulations were imposed to require chiffon, net, or body stockings to cover the same area at different times).

Bakhur. Incense. Burned at the *mulid* for the *dhkir* and before the *zar*.

Balloon (Theater). On Corniche al-Nil in the Agouza neighborhood, this is a national theater which presents folkloric dance shows, plays, and more. The Reda Troupe and the Firqat Qawmiyya, as well as the Lyric Operetta Musical Theater, performed here. It retains a musical ensemble with male and female instrumentalists and singers who receive a steady salary. Quite a number of musicians from traditional Muhammad 'Ali street families are employed here along with others.

Baladi. Means "of the country" but includes urban lower-class traditions with rural ones. Can be used to mean "authentic"; may be used either in a derogatory or proud manner.

Baladi progression. A Western term for a section of an Oriental dance; some Egyptian musicians will understand what is meant, others won't. Originally played on a **rabab** or a **mizmar** and with percussion. Begins with a **taqsim** by an instrumentalist, more recently, an accordion, or **org** without percussion, and then percussion is added. It may progress to a drum (*tabla*) solo.

Baltagi. Thug or bully of the neighborhood who (unlike the *futuwwa*) uses his strength for bad purposes. *Baltagiyya* (gangs of thugs) plagued the clubs in the 1930s and were active during and since Egypt's revolution.

Ban of 1834. Muhammad 'Ali Pasha banned dancers who performed in public and prostitutes from Cairo. The aim was to diminish foreigners' interaction with local women, either over concerns for health and public order or because the *'ulama* (religious clerics) pressured the ruler to do so. Some describe it as the ban to Upper Egypt. Dancers lost their audiences even though foreigners traveled to see them. In general, this situation impoverished these women and curtailed the careers of *'awalim* and *ghawazi*; men and boys dancing in public supplanted them. Some dancers and prostitutes returned to Cairo in the 1860s; others had never left.

Banat Mazin. A family of *ghawazi* dancers, five sisters, the daughters of Yusuf Mazin of Luxor and from the Nawwar tribe. Two have died, two married, and Khairiyya, the youngest, was still performing and teaching in 2019.

Bango. Dried cannabis, usually from the Sinai area. Poor man's *hashish*.

Baraka. Blessedness and charisma. A transmittable blessing from the saint (*wali*) to the believer. Given to those who pray to him/her or from the *shaykh* or *qutb* or through the *inshad*. People seek *baraka* by attending the *mulid*. People may wear a medallion inscribed with a Quranic verse which gives *baraka*.

Barrada. A *sim* term; to act so as to encourage tips or attract an audience. Entertainers might tip each other if the audience wasn't generous. Women stood in front of entertainment stores in costumes with castanets (or **sagat**) to attract customers or just danced in front of the store.

Ba[q]shish (pronounced ba'sheesh). To pay a tip, or a bribe, or extra money.

Bayt al-Ta'a. Literally means "house of obedience." This was a legal punishment for a disobedient wife, whereby her husband confined her to a room within her home and did not allow her to go out in public. If she fled *bayt al-ta'a*, she could be declared *nashaz* (wayward) and divorced without the payment of her deferred **mahr**.

Be'ah (some pronounce it *bee'ah*). 1. Generally, and outside of Egypt, this means environment. 2. In Egyptian slang it means very low class, as in *al-fustan da be'ah 'awi* (that dress is cheap and terrible-looking).

Bey (from the Turkish *bek*). An honorary title for prominent, landowning men.

Bint al-balad. Lower-class, urban Cairene-born woman with her own honorable code of behavior, modest and upright, slaps or yells at any man who bothers her. The name means "daughter of the country." She expresses *baladi* (traditional) values whereas *bint al-zawat* expresses *afrangi* (modern/foreign) mores. Considers herself an authentic Egyptian. Wore the **malayya laff** before the *hijab* became popular. Her male counterpart is **ibn al-balad**. She may be illiterate or not; some feel that once educated, she is no longer of this class. She distinguishes herself from the *fallaha*, whom she considers to be stupid and naïve, whereas she sees herself as alert, inquiring, and able to navigate the city. She has been depicted on stage and in cinema as wearing *malayya laff*, washing laundry in a large container, sitting on the floor rather than on sofas, and using her hands to eat instead of cutlery.

Bint al-suq. A *bint al-balad* who works as a merchant or in the *suq* (marketplace). However, like all *banat al-balad*, she must care for her husband, cook for him, and dress nicely for him.

Bint al-zawat. Elite or aristocratic (at least before 1952) woman or girl. Considered by *bint al-balad* to be snooty, lazy (doesn't do housework), uses Western utensils and wears Western style clothing, is remote and not neighborly.

Burqa. Face veil worn by Bedouin women and other Egyptian women in previous eras.

Buza. 1. A lower-class or *baladi* bar. 2. *Buza*, a beer-like malt drink made from barley is consumed in a *buza*.

Café chantant. In France's Belle Epoque (roughly 1871–1914), this was an outdoor café where singers and musicians entertained the patrons. The term overlapped with *sala* or *casino* and was used by Europeans and some Egyptians for music clubs by the 1880s.

Cartes de visite. Small postcards depicting dancers and scenes, mainly produced for foreigners' use and popular since the 1860s.

Casino. First meant a music hall or nightclub with outside and inside seating, and only later included gambling.

Chipsy, Islam (al-Islam Sa'id). A very talented keyboardist, active in the electronic music scene since 2013. He plays in a more experimental electronic style and with the group EEK.

Concubines. Slaves who had sexual relations with their master, who also had to support them. The harems in Egypt included legal wives and concubines. (Slaves trained in entertainment in the medieval Mamluk and Ottoman era harems might belong to their mistresses, not their masters—and so were not concubines.)

Copts. Previously estimated at ten to fifteen percent of Egypt's population and now less due to flight from Egypt. The largest Christian sect in Egypt is Coptic Orthodox, and there is a smaller Coptic Catholic church. Christians have their own *mawalid*. Many Christians may also follow Muslim saints.

Daff. A frame drum that may range in size, with a head made of goat or deer skin, or today, plastic. It has been important to Sufi music.

Dahiyya. A dance of the Sinai Bedouin.

Dalal. Coquettishness, pampering.

Dall'a. Spoil, pamper, a flirtatious manner of interacting with the opposite sex. It is an attitude, a style of speech, walking, dancing, and interacting, and could apply to a cute child as well as a woman. Might also be used with *mudalal/mudalala*, like a pampered child.

Dallala. Women who peddled goods or foodstuffs to the segregated upper (and middle) class women in harems.

Daminat al-maghani. In medieval Egypt, this woman was responsible for collecting taxes from performers who were paid (not slaves attached to the court or wealthy owners). These singers performed at weddings, but also at funerals, as *dhikr* chanters and other events. The *damina* also bought, trained, and sold entertainers (who were slaves).

Dandash. Dancer from Alexandria where her parents were a singing duo. She began dancing at age seven. Dandash's family traveled to perform outside of Alexandria, to Mansoura and Sonbat, where she saw Sunbati *ghawazi*. These and *'awalim* influenced her style. She says she idolized Suhair Zaki. After she moved to Cairo, she became a dance star.

Danse du ventre. A French term used first as an alternative title for Jean-Léon Gérôme's 1863 painting *La danse de l'almée*, which was exhibited at Paris' annual art exhibition, the Salon, in 1864. The term was employed to mean *raqs sharqi* and was translated into English as belly dance.

Darb al-Ahmar. A *sha'bi* area of Cairo between Gamaliyya and Sayyida Zainab.

Darwish, s. (*darawish*, pl.). Dervish. A follower of a Sufi order (**tariqa**) who may live a devoted, often poor lifestyle. May also refer to all brethren in a Sufi order and many of these were merchants, artisans, and today, professionals. An ascetic Sufi was also known as a *faqir*. During the British rule over Egypt, they used snakes (as in India) cut themselves with razors, or performed other feats in public (**dosat**) or at *mawalid* to earn their subsistence.

Darwish (al-Bahr), Sayyid (1892–1923). An Egyptian singer and composer, born in Kom al-Dikka, Alexandria. Trained in **tajwid** and as a *munshid* (singer of religious songs) but also worked as a bricklayer. He went to Syria with the 'Attala Brothers troupe and returned to sing in salat and cafes. Then he worked with and composed for Nagib al-Rihani and 'Ali al-Kassar's troupes. Many melodies he wrote became standards and were nationalist, including Egypt's national anthem, "Biladi Biladi," and "Salma, ya Salama." He also composed *muwashshahat* and *adwar*, many operettas, and more than 200 songs.

Dawr, s. (*adwar*, pl.). A composed vocal form that was popular from the end of the nineteenth century to the 1930s and was part of the *wasla* musical cycle. It may start with a *dulab*, followed by *ahaat*. A famous *dawr* is Muhammad 'abd al-Wahhab's "Ahibb ashufak kull yom."

Dawsha. Loud noise, intolerable racket.

Dhikr (pronounced as *zikr* in Egypt). Sufi ceremony of remembrance of Allah. Includes poetry, singing, or simple repetitive chants of "Allah" or another of God's names, or "*huwwa*" (he) and movement. The participants are *dhakkira* led by an imam and guided by a *mustaftih*, who indicates changes in the meter or tempo.

Diesel. Mahragan artist, Mohamed Saber.

Dinshaway. 1. An Egyptian village. 2. An incident in 1906 in this Egyptian village where British soldiers went to shoot pigeons for sport. As villagers raised the pigeons, they attacked the soldiers. One shot and wounded the wife of an **imam**. While villagers further attacked, two soldiers fled, and one died of heat stroke. When a villager found him, the soldiers accused him of murder and killed him. A group of judges handed down harsh sentences including hanging and life terms in prison in a brief and cursory trial. This heightened Egyptian nationalist and anti-British sentiment, which only increased during World War I.

Dosa (*dawsa* in classical Arabic). A feat such as skewering one's cheek or balancing on knives. Before such feats were outlawed, the *shaykh* would ride a horse over the prostrate bodies of believers.

Drowning of 400 Women (referred to as *ghawazi* or prostitutes). Women who allegedly infected the French with venereal disease, or in some accounts, spread the plague. They were killed, then their bodies sewn in sacks and thrown in the Nile.

EEK. Mahragan band including Islam Chipsy on keyboard, drummer Khaled Mando, Islam Ta'Ta' and Mahmoud Refat, second drummer and manager.

Fahmy, Farida (b. 1940). Born as Melda Hassan Fahmy to an Egyptian father and an English mother. After performing with Mahmoud Reda in 1957 in the Soviet Union, they decided to form the Reda Troupe with his brother 'Ali Reda. The troupe had twelve dancers and twelve musicians, and she danced the lead female roles. She married 'Ali Reda and retired from the troupe in 1983, then obtained her master's degree in dance ethnology at UCLA and continued to teach workshops.

Fahmy, Hikmat (1907–1974). Worked in 'Ali al-Kassar's theater, was a featured dancer at al-Sala al-Masriyya, Casino Badi'a, and later at the Kit-Kat club. Charged and imprisoned for spying on British officers for the Germans; through her involvement with John (Johann) Eppler, a half-German, half-Egyptian spy, he obtained information from the men she seduced. She supposedly danced for Hitler and Mussolini. Both she and Anwar Sadat went to jail for this crime. At the end of her life she found refuge in the church.

Fallah, m. (*fallahin*, pl.). Peasant or resident of Egypt's countryside. The same term is used for those who cultivate the land in eastern Arab dialects.

Fallaha, f. Peasant woman; woman from rural Egypt. Works in the fields but cannot be caught alone with a man, or sit in the all-male evening circle of drinking tea and talking. Wanted as many children as possible to help with work. Never wore the face veil of urban Egypt, but covers her hair with a *tarha* and wears a conservative long *galabiyya* (dress).

Fallahi. 1. Literally means: of the peasant, or people of rural Egypt. 2. A rhythm.

Fann. Art. Refers to music, art, dance, and theater. **Fannana** (f.) **fannan** (m.) An artist or performer; used for musicians, singers, visual artists actors, and dancers as it is more respectable than *raqisa/raqqasa*.

Fantasia. An evening of entertainment.

Farah, s. (*afrah*, pl.). Wedding party. Or the joyful party of any celebration such as a *sabu'* (the seventh day after a baby's birth) or a *mulid*.

Fashkha. The splits. Performed by *'awalim* or Muhammad 'Ali Street style dancers in their shows, and also while dancing with the **sham'adan**.

Fath. After performances, dancers or singers sat and drank alcohol with customers and received a portion of the sale. Their low wages were supplemented by this activity. The Egyptian government forbade it briefly in 1933 in establishments catering to locals, not foreigners, but owners served in tea cups. Sitting and drinking with customers was forbidden again in 1951, and more effectively banned under Sadat. However, it continued in some establishments.

Fatiha. The opening verse of the Qur'an. Recited at the beginning of any ceremony, at betrothals and weddings, when a tree or plant is planted, during the five times daily prayers, when in danger, at death, and during the *dhikr*.

Fawzy, Imtithal. A dancer/actor and club owner. She was killed by thugs employed by Fu'ad al-Shamy. Her story was memorialized in a 1972 film directed by Hassan al-Imam.

Fida'iyin. Resistance fighters in the Suez Canal area. The same word is used for Palestinian fighters against Israel.

Figo or **DJ Figo** (Vigo, Ahmed Farid). A "father," or founder of *mahragan* from Madinat Salam, he debuted with 'Ala' 50 Cent in 2007 with the single "Mahragan Al Salam" made for a wedding, which was a big hit. He released his single "Ana, Baba Yallah" in 2011.

Firqa. A musical ensemble larger than the traditional *takht*. By 1917, some performances included piano, and other Western instruments might be included.

al-Firqa al-Qawmiyya lil-Funun al-Sha'biyya. The National Folkloric Dance Troupe of Egypt (est. 1960).

Firqat Reda. The Mahmoud Reda Troupe established in 1959 by Mahmoud Reda, 'Ali Reda, and Farida Fahmy and her family.

Firqat zaffa. A folkloric dancing group which performs in the procession of a wedding party. The group might have male and female dancers, but increasingly Egyptians preferred all-male groups.

Fituwwat (*futuwwa*). The strong male youth or men of the neighborhood. They would protect the *zaffat al-gihaz* of the women and female performers. The word refers to a code of chivalry possessed by brotherhoods of fighters, guilds, and *darawish* (dervishes).

Fu'ad, Nagwa (b. 1943). Born 'Awatif Muhammad 'Ajami, in Alexandria to a Palestinian mother from Nablus and an Egyptian father. Her mother died, and her father remarried. They returned to Nablus but were expelled and she and her stepmother fled to al-'Arish. She began dancing at Sahara City and the Auberge des Pyramids nightclub. She married Ahmad Fu'ad Hassan who encouraged her to train in the Nelly Mazloum dance school and in the Qawmiyya (National) ensemble. She became better known through a film *Shari'a al-Hubb,* with the singer, 'Abd al-Halim Hafiz, and appeared in over 100 films. She danced in many five-star hotels since the 1970s.

Fu'ad, Nelly. Born in Alexandria and took her Armenian grandmother's name as a stage name. She joined an *'awalim* troupe at age 13, trained by Sinaya. She filled in for Suhair Zaki in a stage production and that led her to Cairo. Had a long career in the 1970s and 1980s, dancing in five-star hotels and in films. She performed in Farid al-Atrash's nightclub in Lebanon for a year.

Fulklur (Borrowed from folklore). Means musical or dance traditions from rural Egypt. Also, *musiqa sha'biyya*.

Funun sha'biyya. Literally means folkloric arts. Folk artists would be *fannanin* or *fannanat sha'biyya*, but in Cairene colloquial may refer to a group or chorus of male folkloric dancers who perform in certain numbers with a *raqs sharqi* artist, backing her up, and augmenting the size and impact of her show.

Fursa l-hadd. Luck from someone, meaning that someone will help you. 50 Cent said "*ma fish fursa l-hadd*" (no one will help you) here in Egypt,

Fusha (pronounced fus-ha). Classical Arabic. A literary language spoken by those with religious training or for official speeches and used in theater and films, where colloquial Arabic began to replace it in Egypt due to a popular movement. In Egyptian theater, dialogue in *fusha* was satirized by adding the letter "*qaf*," where it should not be.

Gada'. A tough guy; also, brave, courageous, won't take any abuse. May be said of a tough guy of the neighborhood who smokes (and possibly drinks or gambles) but is good-hearted and watches out for others. Said by women performers of themselves or each other in the masculine, or as a descriptive, *bint gada'a*.

al-Gadid. The "new" twentieth century musical style, as opposed to **al-[q]adim**, the Arab-Ottoman forms more popular in the nineteenth century. This term is now mostly defunct, but was used to describe earlier Arabic classical music.

Galabiyya. Long dress worn by women and men in rural areas, especially. *Galabiya bi sufra* is a granny-style gown with a yoke from the Northern Delta; the *galabiya bi wist* has a waist and is seen from Beni Suef to Assiut. The first style may also be called *gargar* by Egyptians (and *jarjar* by the Nubians).

Gamal, Nadia (1937–1990). Born Maria Carydias in Alexandria to a Greek father and Italian mother. Her mother performed a cabaret act at Casino Opera in which Nadia did folk dance. Her first *raqs sharqi* show came about when she was age 14. She appeared in films from the '50s through the early 1970s and was the first *raqs sharqi* performer at the Ba'lbak International

Festival in 1968. American dancer and teacher Ibrahim Farrah brought her to New York to teach.

Gamal, Samia (1924–1994). Born Zainab Ibrahim Mahfuz in Wana al-Qiss in Bani Suwaif and moved to Cairo near Khan Khalili. She joined Badi'a's troupe as a chorus dancer and studied with choreographer Isaac Dickson who worked with Casino Opera. She also studied some ballet and Western and Latin dance forms, developed her own dance style, and co-starred in a series of films with Farid al-Atrash. She appeared in 50 movies from the '40s to the '60s. She danced into the early '70s, quit and returned to dance in the '80s at the urging of actor Samir Sabry.

El Gezawe. Mahragan artist of electronic music. His music has no lyrics.

Ghajar. 1. A general term for Gypsy. 2. A specific type of Gypsy. The other groups in Egypt are Halab, Jamasa, Tatar, Maslub, Ghawazi (possibly pseudo-*ghajar*), Su'ayda, Shahaniyya; Nabil Hanna classifies them as Nawwar, Halab, and Ghajar; the others are subgroups of each. The Halab are often either blacksmiths or poets.

Ghandi (Nasser Ghandi). *Mahragan* artist who sang with the Shubaik Lobaik band. Sang the song "There Ain't No Such Thing as a Real Friend."

Ghanim, Dunia Samir (b. 1985). Actress/singer, daughter of actor Samir Yusif Ghanim. Known for being able to imitate other singers. She mostly sings Arab pop but can sing *sha'bi*.

Ghawazi, pl. (*ghaziya*, s.). Clans of Upper Egypt who danced and performed in public when Cairo performers were banned from holding public festivals in the nineteenth century. Also, performers from the Delta area. Some believe they are originally gypsies (*ghajar* or *nawwar*). Their style is unique, related to *raqs sharqi* and yet distinct from it.

al-Ghuz. The Turks. Although rulers of Egypt, they exploited the native Egyptians and were mocked as being cruel, (*akhir khidmat al-ghuz 'a'la*—working for the Turks will only lead to being beaten) dirty, only a little better than the feared Bedouin (*Gur al-ghuz wala' 'adl al-'arab* meant oppression of the Turks is better than the justice of the Arabs). This denigrating term came from the imposition of a foreign group on the native born and a sharp social division between them.

al-Gil (pronounced *al-geel*, from *al-jil*). Term for the new Egyptian popular music, which succeeded the first wave of *sha'bi*. Synonym for *shababiyya*, or youth music. Hakim and 'Amr Diab were considered part of *al-gil*, but the former is a *sha'bi* singer; the latter is not.

Gink. Comes from the word *jank*, which was a harp. A *jankiyya*, a medieval term for a dancer/musician and one who taught dance by the 1830s had come to mean a boy or male dancer. (In Turkey the term for a female dancer was a similar sounding word—*Çengi*.) These were often (not always) from minorities and danced sometimes in athletic and non–Egyptian styles (Turkish, Greek, Albanian) but also as transvestites in *raqs baladi*. Ginks and **khawalat** continued to dance in public coffee houses after the 1834 ban.

Glissando (Ital.). Sliding from one note to another. Used in Arabic and Egyptian music as an ornament.

Habit, m. (*habta*, f.). Vulgar, of low-class, devoid of meaning and sensitivity.

Hadhra (pronounced as *hadra*). Main event at the *mulid*. There's a short opening ceremony, a *dhikr* performed as a group, and a closing ceremony. There may also be speeches. The *hadhra* is also the term for a *zar* ceremony.

Hadith, s. (*ahadith*, pl.). A text of the words, actions, or habits of the Prophet Muhammad, preceded by a chain (*isnad*) of transmitters. These were collected in 8th and 9th centuries and give information about matters not mentioned in the Qur'an. They are a source of jurisprudence (*fiqh*).

Hafiz, 'Abd al-Halim (1929–1977). Born 'Abd al-Halim Shabana in al-Hilwat in Sharqiyya province. Known as *al-'andalib al-asmar*, the dark-skinned nightingale. He studied at the Higher Music Institute and appeared in films as a romantic singing lead from 1955 onwards. He was identified with the age of Nasserism and sang compositions by Muhammad Mugi, Muhammad 'abd al-Wahhab, Baligh Hamdi, and many others. At first, he was criticized for being a "crooner" and then years later, considered a classic singer.

Hagalla. A dance of the Bedouin of northwestern Egypt. The word means to skip or jump and refers to the female dancer who performs along with men who dance and clap. The dance was at one time a coming-of-age ceremony of a young female dancer but it came to be performed by a female professional dancer.

Hakim ('Abd al-Hakim 'Abd al-Samid Kamil, b. 1962). from Maghagha, Minya, a *sha'bi* singing star who moved to Cairo in his 20s. In 1989 he met producer Hamid al-Sha'iri and signed with Sonar Lmtd/Slam. His first album was *Nazra* (1992), and he came out with *'Ala Wadh'ak* in 2017. Hakim has appeared internationally and collaborated with Western artists.

Hal, s. (*ahwal*, pl.). A state of consciousness (*wa'y*) achieved through belief (either Sufism or more conservative beliefs). The Sufi aims to ascend into new states of consciousness, the final one being an ecstatic merging of the self with Allah or the death of individual ego.

Halal. That which is allowed for Muslims in Islamic jurisprudence as opposed to that which is forbidden, or frowned upon.

Hamdi, Baligh (1931–1993). Trained in law, and music and singing. Became a prolific composer. Among his hits were "Hubb Aih" and "Fat al-Mi'ad," sung by Umm Kulthum; "Tkhunuh," "Sawah," and "Zayy al-Hawa" sung by 'Abd al-Halim Hafiz; "'Ayunak Sud" and "Mali wa ana mali" sung by Warda. He was married to the singers Warda and Sabah.

al-Hamdi, Nadia. Born 'A'isha 'Ali Muhammad Mahmoud. From a Muhammad 'Ali Street family (great-niece of Najia Iskandarani) she danced at weddings and parties since the early '70s, performing with the sham'adan in an *'awalim* style. She adopted *hijab* and stopped performing.

Hamida, 'Ali. Singer of Bedouin origin from Marsa Matruh. Sang "*Lawlaki*" a big hit, which touched off ***al-gil*** music—we see this simply as a new stage of electronic sha'bified pop.

Hamuda, 'Abd al-Basit. Born in Abu Qir, Alexandria, in 1960. Active since the 1980s. A *sha'bi* singer who performed "Ana Mish 'Arafni" in the film *al-Farah* and many other hits.

'al-Hamuli, Abduh. (c. 1841–1901) Born in Tanta, he sang at the 'Uthman Agha café. He formed his own band which included Muhammad al-'Aqqad (*qanun*) and Ahmad al-Laythi (*'ud*). Khedive Isma'il sponsored him and brought him to Istanbul. His beautiful voice combined Egyptian and Turkish elements. He became famous and married the *'alima* Almaz.

Hanim. Turkish term for a lady. It is attached to the first name as a form of respectful address, i.e., Munira Hanim, or as for the dancer Kuchuk Hanim.

Hantur. Horse-drawn carriage, mostly serving tourists in Cairo, Alexandria, Luxor, and Aswan.

Haqiqa. The esoteric Truth; the aim of the Sufi. At the center of *haqiqa* is the invisible *ma'rifa*.

Harafish. Rabble or riff-raff. Those in menial jobs, the unemployed, and the homeless. Sub-proletariat.

Hara. An alley or a small street in a traditional urban neighborhood in Egypt. **Harat al-'awalim** was the alley of the *'awalim* in the Muhammad 'Ali street area.

Haram. That which is forbidden for Muslims in Islamic jurisprudence. The opposite is *halal* (allowed). There are actually five possible rulings by jurists: *fard* or *wajib* (required), *mandub* or *mustahabb* (recommended), *mubah* (neutral), *makruh* (reprehensible), and *haram* (forbidden). Many contemporary **salafi** Muslims consider dancing (women's) and music to be *haram* (with the exception of certain religious music and *tajwid*, Qur'anic recitation, which is not considered to be music at all). 2. A sacred area in and around a mosque.

Harem. An institution guarding the segregated female members of a family in the Ottoman era and Egypt under British dominion. It encompassed a man's wives, concubines, children, unmarried female relatives, slaves or servants, possibly eunuchs among them. These women are known as the *harim* (pronounced *hareem*) of the man. It wasn't polite for men to refer to them, nor to look upwards to where they might be listening or watching from the **haremlek**. The institution began before Islam in other Near Eastern societies, and was observed by the Abbasid era by the upper classes.

Haremlek. The areas in an Ottoman-era or Ottoman-Arab home, villa, or palace reserved for the women. Interior or upstairs (in a multi-story) rooms.

Hasabullah band. A brass band in the style of Muhammad Hasabullah's original ensemble on Muhammad 'Ali Street.

Hasabullah, Muhammad. A clarinetist in the military band of Khedive Abbas Hilmy taught by

Italians, who started a band on Muhammad 'Ali Street. He and this band style transformed essentially Western (and Turkish) music into an Egyptian musical style.

al-Hashim, Huwaida. Lebanese dancer. Performed on LBC in the late 1980s. Has not performed since the late 1990s.

Hashishin. Smokers of hashish. One who is addicted or chronically smokes is a *hashshash*. Young Egyptians also smoke *bango* (marijuana).

Hass. To feel, sense, with the preposition *bi*, as in *hass bi* (something), to have emotion for something or feel something. *Ihsas* means emotions or feelings. The *hassas* is the leading tone, the note immediately below the tonic in a *jins* (3 to 6 notes of a *maqam*).

Haya'. Sexual modesty which women are supposed to exhibit in Egypt. *Raqs sharqi*'s and *raqs baladi*'s use of the body is at odds with this value.

Hayatim (1950–2018). Born Suhair Hassan in Alexandria. Dancer/actress, described as a complete "*femme fatale.*" She began dancing in Alexandria, then moved to Cairo where she appeared in her first film in 1972, *Lailat Hubb Akhira*, and thereafter in many others. Married Muhammad Khairy, and a football player, Mahmoud El Khawaga.

Haysa. A loud and raucous time; fun and joyful; a DJ with **mahraganat** or *mulid* songs brings *haysa*.

Henkish, Sayyid. Accordion player, son of al-Rayyis Henkish. Brother to Ramadan, Rida, and Khamis (now deceased), percussionists. Interviewed by Karin van Nieuwkerk (also his family members are her respondents) for two books: one on female dancers and singers and the other on Henkish himself and masculinity. Also interviewed by other researchers.

Hetarai. A type of prostitute in ancient Greece and Hellenic Egypt. Scholars thought they were more elite than another type of prostitute; they might be free women or slaves and provide companionship, conversation, and entertainment as well as sex, hence similar to the **qiyan**.

al-Higazi, Salama (1852–1917). Raised in Alexandria. A trained *munshid* (singer of *anashid*, Sufi religious songs) who formed a *takht* for secular music in the 1880s and became known as a *mutrib*. In 1885, he joined the al-Qurdahi-Husayn troupe as an actor; he then formed his own troupe in 1888, teaming up with actress Labiba Manoli and singer, Milya Dayan, Mariam Sumat, and the 'Ukasha brothers and toured outside of Egypt.

Hija'. Satirical poetry or "invective poetry" used to denigrate enemies, which developed in the Jahiliyya (the historic period predating Islam).

Hijab. Scarf or head-wrap covering the hair and neck, as part of Islamic dress, *ziyy Islami* adopted by the Association of Muslim Sisters affiliated with the Muslim Brotherhood in the 1930s and 1940s and more widely by many Egyptians since the end of the 1970s.

Hilmy, Safiya. Actor and dancer who performed with Badi'a Masabni. Danced in *Gharam al-Shuyukh* in 1946. She became the owner of the Arcadia nightclub.

Hishik bishik. Means something carnival-like, related to low-class dancing, with a connotation of being trashy. A **shami** term used (a) specifically in Beirut for performances that highlighted the golden era of entertainment in Egypt and (b) as part of a discussion in Egypt about the fetishizing of *hishik bishik*, or watered-down, inauthentic dance.

Hubb. Love. Profound and romantic in the lyrics of Egyptian songs. In the context of the *mulid*, it is spiritual, not profane love. Love is the message and purpose of Sufism or opening the heart, learning and knowing through love and not through intellectualism or institutions.

Husain (also transliterated as Husayn). The son of Imam 'Ali and grandson of the Prophet Muhammad. His head is buried in Cairo. The mosque where the tomb is located and the area surrounding it is called al-Husaini.

al-Husaini (al-Hussaini), **Mahmud**. Egyptian *sha'bi* and *mulid* singer. Known for "al-'Abd wal-shaitan," "Sigara bunni," "Bikam ya farah," "Yom al-hisab," "Ya Ibn Adam." Appeared in the 2009 film *al-Farah*, then disappeared for a time, and was reportedly jailed in 2018 for three months for beating his wife.

Husni, Dawud (1870–1937). Studied the *'ud* with Muhammad Sha'ban. Famous for *adwar*, compositions for singers and many *taqatiq* for the dancers Qamar and Lila and composed the first Egyptian opera, *Samson and Delila*.

Husni, Su'ad (1943–2001). Actress who appeared in 83 films and known as the Cinderella of the Screen. Her death in London was considered suspicious.

Hysa and **Halabesa** (pronounced Heesa and Halabeesa). Mahragan artists. Perform as a duo and also with Ahmad al-Souissi.

Ibn 'Arabi (d. 1240 CE). A great Muslim scholar, philosopher, and Sufi whose poetry is used by many Sufi orders.

Ibn al-Balad. A [true] son of the country [Egypt]. A lower-class Cairene-born man, who is moral and has a *baladi* identity. Typically lived in certain areas of Cairo (*al-ahya al-sha'biyya*). Other social groups view the *awlad al-balad* (pl.) differently. With the 1952 revolution, to be a "son of the country" was a source of pride, and as the government took the property of the aristocrats, then the name for this group, *ibn al-zawat*, became more shameful. There has been some residual resentment against *awlad al-balad* from the upper classes and the *afandi* class (the children of craftsmen, merchants, and fellahin who were educated to become civil servants and who emulated Western tastes) who rejected the tastes of *awlad al-balad*.

'Id, 'Aziz (1884–1942). Playwright, actor, director, who established a theater of dedicated to vaudeville comedy in 1907, the al-Juq al-Kumidi al-'Arabi (the Arabic Comedy Troupe). He encouraged many performers who went on to join the theatrical companies of **Munira al-Mahdiyya**, **'Ali al-Kassar**, **Salama al-Higazi** and **Nagib al-Rihani**. He wrote very controversial plays after World War I began, but the censors were less harsh on theater than print. He mentored **Fatima Rushdi** (the Sarah Bernhardt of Egypt) and then converted to Islam to marry her, and they formed their own theatrical troupe.

'Ifrit, m. (*'ifrita*, f., *'afarit*, pl.). These are a type of *jinn*. Might be a spirit attracted to the blood of a murder victim who seeks to avenge him. The ancient Egyptians believed in spirit/life forces and their ability to possess humans.

Iftar. Breakfast. Refers as well to the meal breaking the day's fast during **Ramadan** which is also an occasion for dining together.

Imam. A prayer leader for Muslims. May be appointed or simply the most knowledgeable of the group praying.

Imam, 'Adil (b. 1940). An extremely popular stage, film and television actor active since the early 1960s. He has often played roles which concern political issues.

Infitah. Economic open-door policies issued by President Sadat, allowing for more private and foreign investment, but which widened the income gap. Those profiting from these policies were called *infitahiyun*.

Intifadha. An uprising or revolt. Literally means shaking off.

Inshad dini, s. (*anashid*, pl.). Hymn or devotional song performed at the *dhikr* (zikr) or Sufi ceremony of remembrance of God, or at a *mulid*, or in other gatherings. Written by, or attributed to great Sufis.

Iqa', s. (*iqa'at*, pl.). Meter or rhythm. Each meter can be notated as two sounds, a *dum* (sustained) and a *tak* (sharp) and a rest *iss* (no tone is played on it). Upon this skeleton, the percussionist elaborates. Time signatures occur from 2/8 up to 32/4 and differ based on genre and region. Among them are Ayyub 2/4, Malfuf 2/4, Fallahi 2/4, Wahda Saghira 2/4, Sama'i Darij 3/4, Maqsum 4/4, Wahda wa-Nuss 4/4, Rumba 4/4, Hacha 4/4, Yuruk Sama'i 6/8, Dawr Hindi 7/8, Masmudi Kabir 8/4, Bambi 8/4, Jurjina 10/8, Sama'i Thaqil 10/8, Fakhit 20/4, and Sittatu 'Ashar Masri 32/4.

'Irfan. Mysticism as studied by Muslim scholars.

'Izz al-Din, Beba (1910–1951). Began her career in Beirut. A dancer and rival of Badi'a Masabni. She bought Badi'a's club on Imad al-Din street from Badi'a's nephew Antoine (who was Beba's lover) in 1936, and she refused entry to Badi'a. Owned Teatro Beba in 1939 when Badi'a had her Casino Opera next door. She bought Badi'a's club in 1950 but was killed in an automobile accident just a few months later. Sister of Shu Shu 'Izz al-Din, actress/dancer who married **Muhammad 'abd al-Muttalib**.

Jahiliyya. The period before Islam, considered a time of barbarism.

Jamal Twins. Actually sisters, Laila (Bertha Alpert 1930–2016, known as Lyz) and Lamia (Helena Alpert 1932–1992 known as Lyn), daughters of an Jewish violinist from Czernowitz and his singing wife, also European, who grew up in Egypt, learned *raqs sharqi*, and performed at the Helmieh Palace. They traveled to Singapore, India, China, Japan, the Philippines, and Vietnam and danced with snakes, appeared in films, and then moved to the U.S. in 1957.

al-Jaza'iriyya, Warda (1939–2012). Born Warda Fatouki in Puteaux, France, to an Algerian father and a Lebanese mother. She started singing as a child and worked in Lebanon when her family was forced to leave France. She first sang in Egypt in 1960, moving there again in 1962, where she married composer Baligh Hamdi and recorded many hit songs, some of which are now part of the *raqs sharqi* so-called "*tarab*" genre.

Jinn. Supernatural beings who are neither innately good nor evil. The bad spectrum of *jinn* are the **shayatin**, (devils) who are demon-like.

Jumhuriyya al-Funun. The first Western-style theatre erected by Napoléon in Cairo across from Azbakiyya pond, where plays were performed in French for his soldiers. Destroyed in the 1799 uprising. Rebuilt as Masrah al-Jumhuriyya by General Minou.

Kafafin (pronounced *kafafeen*). A (usually) male chorus of clappers, important in different forms of *al-musiqa sha'biyya*.

Kamanja. Bowed, long-necked string instrument. The name referred to the Persian, Kurdish, and Armenian instrument. In Egypt, a somewhat similar instrument was the *rabab* (called *djoze* in Iraq), with a limited range of about an octave. The violin has replaced the *rabab* (and the *kamanja*) in Arabic music, although it is still used in *musiqa sha'biyya*. Thus, the violin is called *kamanja*, or *kaman* for short, and a *kamanjati* is a violin player. For Arabic music, the violin strings are typically tuned G, D, G, D and played with slides, trills, and double stops.

Kamil, Mustafa (1874–1908). An Egyptian lawyer, journalist, and nationalist who petitioned the French to pressure the British to leave Egypt in 1895. He founded the paper *al-Liwa* in 1900, in which he expressed his nationalism and covered independence movements elsewhere in the world.

Kanto, s. (*kantolar*, pl.). Term refers both to singing on stage in an improvisational (*tuluat*) theatrical performance which included *cifteteli* and the songs written for this purpose from the 1870s in Istanbul. Nearly all the *kantocular* were non–Muslims (Greek or Armenian).

Kar. Trade or work. Refers to entertainment, dancing, the playing of or making of musical instruments, and also prostitution.

Karamat, pl. (*karama*, s.). refers to *karamat al-awliya'*. Supernatural miracles performed by a saint during his/her lifetime or after death, predictions of the future, or interpretations of secrets of the hearts.

Kariuka, Tahia (Tahiyya) (often rendered Carioca) (1915–1999). Born Badawiyya Muhammad Karim al-Nirani in Isma'iliyya to an older father who died; she then lived with her brother who "tortured her" and shaved her head. She moved to Cairo to dance and worked with Su'ad Mohasan at her club, then Badi'a Masabni hired her in 1933. She began performing as a solo dancer and learned a version of the samba called the "*kariuka*" (thereafter changing her name from Tahia Muhammad to Kariuka). She began appearing in movies in the early '40s. She married 14 times, including an American army officer and Mustafa Kamal Sidqi, an Egyptian army officer. In 1962, she formed a theater troupe with her husband of that time, Fayiz Halawa.

Kashar, Bamba (c. 1860–c. 1930). Her father was a famous Qur'an reader and her mother was the granddaughter of a Mamluk Sultan. Her niece was Fathiyya Ahmad. In 1874 when her mother remarried, she and her siblings left and settled next door to the Turkish *'alima*, Salem, who helped train her. Bamba Kashar sang *muwashhahat* and became well known as a singer and dancer until the end of 1920s. After leaving Salem's troupe, she started her own troupe and created an annual festival called Zar Concerts featuring a Hasaballah band and beautiful girls singing. She married eight times and several films were made about her.

al-Kassar, 'Ali (1887–1957). Born 'Ali Khalil Salem. Had a theatrical troupe, which was a rival of Nagib al-Rihani's. He became famous for his character Osman 'abd al-Basit, al-Barbari al-Wahid fi Misr (the Only Nubian of Egypt), whom he played in blackface.

Katb al-kitab. Following marital engagement, a couple sign a contract. They don't cohabit until the *farah* (wedding party) and consummation of the marriage. This could happen the same day or be separated by years.

Kawala. End-blown cane flute with six holes. Was typically used in traditional *mulid* music. It is shorter than the *nai* and lacks a hole in the back. Often played in *mada'ih* and *mada'ih an-nabi*. Was originally used by shepherds to guide their flocks.

Khadiwi. (or *khadawi* in Egypt) The Khedive, or viceroy, and ruler of Egypt under the Ottoman empire. Used unofficially for Muhammad 'Ali Pasha and officially for his descendants from 1867 to 1914.

Khafif. Light-hearted and humorous.

Khalifa. Caliph. 1. The civil and religious leader of Muslims, regarded as the successor of the Prophet Muhammad. 2. Head of a local branch of a Sufi order.

Khashana, or **khushniyin** (both are plurals). People from outside the groups (*awlad al-kar*) who were traditionally part of the entertainment trade. Newcomers to entertainment.

Khassa. The elites and the ruling class in the past. Some of the professionals, military, and merchants allied with them.

Khawaga, m. (*khawagiyya*, f.). Pronounced "khawagayya" in Egyptian urban Arabic. The word was an honorific coming from Persian but now refers to a foreigner, a non–Egyptian, usually a European. Their Arabic was mocked in Egypt's vaudeville and in films by the way they confused the male and female genders in verbal constructions, and pronouncing the "ha" as "kha." The term *agnabi/agnabiyya* also means a foreigner, but who is not necessarily a European.

Khawal, s. (*khawalat*, pl.). 1. Men or boys who dressed like women and danced in the style of the *ghawazi*. They continued performing in public after the ban of 1834 and were parodied in Egyptian films and plays into the twentieth century. 2. In Egyptian slang, the word means a homosexual, the passive partner.

Khidma. Literally means service. At a *mulid*, it is the service of free food or drinks in a tent or area of the festival.

Khil (pronounced *kheel*). Dance of the specially trained dancing horses. Also dance performed by women pretending to be these horses. There is additionally a dance of two human dancers inside a horse costume, led by a male dancer with a stick.

Khul'. A female-initiated divorce in which the wife must return gifts given to her in the marriage and return the portion of the **mahr** she has received.

Khulkhal. Traditional silver anklets worn in Egypt with dangling pieces which jingle when the foot hits the ground.

Khutuba. Second stage of engagement when rings are exchanged and gold jewelry is given to the woman. Often a party is held.

Kit. Tips, in a nightclub where they used to be pooled, but now are given over to the management. *Takyit* is when customers throw the money over the performer. The dancer or singer may acknowledge the *takyit* over the microphone with the **tahayya**, saying, "Thank you to our brothers from x" (Kuwait, for example).

al-Klubtiyya, Zuba. Famed Muhammed 'Ali Street dancer who supposedly first danced with the *sham'adan* (candelabra). Her name derived either from the glass lamp or *klob* (globe) she balanced, or because her family sold this style of lighting known as *klubatiyya*. She was part of an *'awalim* group who found and then adopted Lucy's mother when she got lost as a child. Her first husband was Najib al-Salahdar (a pianist), her second husband was *qanun* player, Ahmad 'Ali, and her third husband was 'Abd al-Mun'im al-Biri, an accordion player (a brother of Nazla al-'Adil's husband).

Köçekler, pl. (*Köçek*, s.). Young (beardless) men who danced while dressed as women; judged on their dancing skill and proficiency in playing the *çarpare* (a kind of castanet) and were popular in the harem culture from the 17th through the 19th century even more so than female belly dancers. There were at least 600 of them in Istanbul in 1805, and they danced to music known as the *köçekçe*. They were subject to a ban in 1857 and had become less popular by the turn of the century.

Kohl. An ancient cosmetic made of stibnite used as eyeliner and mascara in Egypt by elite women since about 3100 BC. It may also be used to make designs on the face, the chin, and the bridge of the nose, a custom thought to have originated on the Arabian peninsula.

Komsari. Fare collector on a public bus in Egypt.

Kuchuk Hanim (active 1850–1870). A *ghaziya* in Isna in Upper Egypt mentioned in both Gustave Flaubert's (who claimed she was from Damascus) and George William Curtis's travel accounts. Her name literally means "little woman" in Turkish; her true name is unknown.

La'ibiyya, f. (*la'ib*, m.). Very flirtatious, which is extremely negative when said of a woman. *Al-mar'a di, la'ibiyya, dayman bitgarri wara ar-rigala* (this woman is a huge flirt; she's always running after men). However, when applied to men, it means he's lazy, or frivolous; he likes to play but not to work.

Laila al-Kabira. 1. The climactic final "great" night of the *mulid*. 2. The name of a puppet theater operetta about the great night by Salah Jahin (1930–1986) with music by Sayyid Makkawi, first performed in the '60s because the puppet theater (*aragoz*) was performed at the *mawalid*. It has been variously recorded and many Egyptians know parts of it by heart. Also, the name of a film written by Ahmad Abdalla and directed by Sameh Abdelaziz (2015).

Al-Laithy, Hamada. A *sha'bi* singing star, cousin of Mahmud al-Laithy.

al-Laithy, Mahmud (Mahmoud El-Leithy) (b. 1979). A *sha'bi* singing star who began performing the new "*mulid*" songs with his (2005) song "Qasadt Babak" (I Reached Your Door) in the musical style of Skaykh 'Arabi Farhan al-Balbisi and Shaykh Yasin al-Tuhami on the *al-'Asfurayn* album. Al-Laithy's second album *Ya Rabb* (O Lord) included the song "Al-Anbiya'" (The Prophets) and his third album *Kan Fih Walad* came out in 2008.

Lazima, s. (*lawazim*, pl.). A filler or response (*gawab*) by one instrument, or the ensemble to the phrase or "call" played by the lead instrument or vocalist. Instruments may be silent for the "call" section and play only the *lawazim*, or play the full line and emphasize the *lawazim*.

Lucy (Sa'd). Born En'am Sa'd Muhammad 'Abd al-Wahhab c. 1960 in Cairo. Dancer/actress who grew up in Cairo's Old City near Muhammad 'Ali street. Owner/proprietor of the nightclub Parisiana. Her mother was adopted by Zuba al-Klubtiyya. She is still performing.

Lun, s. (*alwan*, pl.). Color.

Madad. Assistance. Chanted in a traditional *mulid*, as in "Madad, ya Badawi!" (Assist me, O Sayyid Badawi) and also found in the new *mulid*.

Mada'ih nabawi. Eulogies sung for the Prophet Muhammad. *Mada'ih* are sung for all the holy men and women, used interchangeably with *inshad*.

Madfa'giyya (The Gunners or Artillery Men). A *mahragan* group produced by Ahmad Refaat.

Madinat al-Salam (Salam City). A *sha'bi* area in Cairo constructed to house those displaced from the earthquake in 1992.

Maganin (*magnun*, m.s.). Madmen. Certain insane people were regarded as holy. They were supported by shopkeepers in Egypt in the medieval period. They may wander in and around the *mulid*. Because the *mulid* is a place of equality, everyone from elites to beggars and madmen are welcome.

al-Mahdiyya, Munira (1884 [another date given is 1895]–1965). Born Zakiyya Husain Mansur in Zagazig or Alexandria. She sang in the cabarets of Azbakiyya and recorded as early as 1906. She joined the theater of Salama al-Higazi and sang the role written for him, dressed as a man. She became a leading singer and had her own theatrical/dance/musical company for 10 years, which often performed nationalistic songs as well as directly supporting nationalists, leading to the saying "*hawa al-hurriyya fi masrah Munira al-Mahdiyya.*"

Mahfouz, Naguib (1911–2006). Author of 34 novels and more than 350 short stories and film scenarios who won the Nobel Prize for Literature in 1988. He grew up in the Gamaliyya and 'Abbasiyya areas of Cairo and became a civil servant. His Cairo Trilogy (*Palace Walk*, 1956, *Palace of Desire*, 1957, and *Sugar Street*, 1957) tells the story of a Cairene family from 1917 to 1952. His *Children of Our Alley* (*Children of Gebalawi* in English) was censored by al-Azhar.

Mahmal. Also known as *hawdig* or *tabut*. A frame of palm leaves or sticks over which a cover (*kiswa*) is placed—usually a new one to replace the previous covering the saint's tomb, carried on a camel in the *zaffa*. Children are lifted up to touch the *kiswa* to obtain *baraka*. A camel is led in a procession which circumambulates the tomb; this is called the *dora*.

Mahmal al-sharif. The processional palanquin or carriage bearing the covering for the Ka'ba which was sent yearly from Egypt for the *hajj*, the annual pilgrimage to Mecca from the thirteenth century until 1926.

Mahr. A bride price, required in an Islamic marriage, and it must be specified in writing. Usually, a half or a part is paid to the bride upon the marriage, and the other part is deferred and paid if the husband divorces the wife, or if he dies.

Mahragan (Literally means festival). A form of music played at parties held outside in the streets that developed in Egypt in the decade before the January 2011 revolution. Also called electro-*sha'bi*. Does not utilize a wide range of traditional instruments and is played on the electrified keyboard with the *tabla*, trap drums, or prerecorded rhythm. It has daring lyrics. Some *mahragan* artists are Sadat, Figo, Islam Chipsy, Oka and Ortega, Hysa, Halabesa, and Ahmad al-Souissi.

Mahraganat. The songs of *mahragan*. (Also the plural of *mahragan* as a festival.) Some in the belly dance industry, and also some Egyptians, don't differentiate and may call the genre *mahraganat*.

Mahram. A male relative of a Muslim woman either by blood or through marriage whom she is not permitted to marry. She need not cover to the same degree in front of them as to non-*mahram* males.

Majence or ***megence***. A term used since the late 1990s for an opening musical number for a *raqs sharqi* set, but from then on, also used separately by a festival dance performer or in competitions. Its derivation is either from *èmergence* (Fr. emergence, emerging) or perhaps the term *manèges*. Dancers used to travel swiftly and turn around their performance space in the opening musical piece, which contained musical motifs to be played at length later.

Makwagi. A man who irons clothes. In recent decades, he or helpers pick them up and deliver to clients. The traditional method was with a foot iron, pushing a hot piece of metal with the foot. Also used are hand-held, steam, and electric irons. Women rarely do this job.

Malayya laff (*Laff* means to wrap). A black outer wrap worn by urban women, draped over the head and held under one arm. Once the elite women adopted Western-style dress, it was a marker of the urban lower class. In the early 1980s, women of different social backgrounds began to wear "Islamic dress" including the *hijab*, and only certain women continued wearing the *malayya laff*.

Mandara. A sitting room used for entertaining visitors in the harem; as these included males unrelated to the family, the women of the family did not enter. In a grand home, it might have a sunken fountain and an area for a *takht* to sit and play music. After the harem system ended, the *mandara* transitioned to the *salon*, or formal living room.

Mandil. A headscarf that predates the *hijab*. A thin *mandil* decorated with pom poms might be worn in folkloric dances or by the *ghawazi*.

Maqam. 1. Place of the saint's burial; tomb built for the saint, as the word means place in general. 2. Musical mode, the melodic structure of Arabic music. Some of these are considered "families" that begin with a shared *jins*, or note fragment—such as those in the 'Ajam, Bayati, Hijaz, Kurd, Nahawand, Nikriz, Rast, and Sikah families. Others are unique like Jaharkah, Lami, Sikah baladi, and Saba.

Marbutin. Men who were fans of the *'awalim* or *qiyan* (earlier), attended their performances, and patronized them. So-called because they were "tied" to them in affection.

Marwa (b. 1974). Lebanese singer. Also played accordion. Banned from singing in Egypt in 2007 for her "demoralizing" effect on young men. She covered Laila Nazmi's song, "Mashrabsh ash-shai," which shocked some as she filmed her video in a bar and with her flirtatious style.

Masabni, Badi'a (1894–1974). Born in Damascus as Wadi'a Masabni. She joined George Abaid's theater group in Egypt and then married Naguib al-Rihani. She first opened Sala Badi'a Masabni (formerly the Sendex) on 'Imad al-Din Street in 1926; dance was first offered in '27/28. In 1938, she renovated the Majestic Theater and opened it as Casino and Cabaret Badi'a; in 1940 she moved to Ibrahim Pasha Square, also known as Opera Square, so that was known as Casino Opera. She performed and taught dance and hired choreographers, making *raqs sharqi* more famous with the accompaniment of large orchestras and the use of the veil, sequined costumes, and staging. After touring Europe, she sold her club to Beba in 1950 and left for Lebanon.

Masaliyya (from *mathaliyya*). A Nubian method of performing *zajal*, in which the singer makes jokes and jests about various topics and then dramatically presents song lyrics.

Mashrabiyya (also known as *shanashil* in Iraq and *rushan* in Saudi Arabia). Wooden lattice-work screen which covered the windows externally, or the internal balconies of a building, to allow women to see out but protect them from view. At one time, a bride would ride in a *mashrabiyya* carriage in a *zaffa*.

al-Masriyya, Naʿima (1894–1976). Born Zainab Muhammad Idris Sallam, the daughter of a merchant of Moroccan origin and his (second) wife from Assiut. Raised in Cairo, she had a child at age fifteen and became a singer after a divorce, when her neighbor, an *ʿalima*, al-Shamiyya, heard her singing. She performed with two other women from her neighborhood at weddings and trained in Aleppo from 1911 to 1914. As she became better known, she sang in *salat* in provincial areas of Egypt, then moved to Rod al-Farag, and then to the theater district. She bought the Alhambra theater in 1927 and was the manager and lead singer. She married five times, then her daughter married a conservative man who forbade Naʿima from singing, and she was essentially forgotten as a performer.

al-Masry, Sama (b. 1978). Actress/dancer. She wrote and starred in *ʿAla Wahda wa Nuss*, a film about a dancer. She used dance in satirical videos targeting the Egyptian government when headed by Morsi, the Muslim Brotherhood, Mortada Mansour, the American ambassador, and others.

Matariyya. A poorer area of Greater Cairo, north of Masr al-Gadida. Contains the Virgin's Tree, a site for pilgrims.

Matwa, s. (*matawi*, pl.). Small knives used by men and sometimes during *mahragan* dancing.

Mawlidiyya. People of the *mulid*s, who travel from one to another, setting up in advance to provide services.

Mawwal, s. (*mawawil*, pl.). Vocal improvisation by a singer either to a few words (*ya layl, ya ʿayn* [oh night, oh eye]) or a short poem. Was an essential part of *al-musiqa al-shaʿbiyya*, *shaʿbi* music, and also "the old" classical Arabic music, *al-[q]adim*.

Mazag. Mood, but also a habit, or craving. People are in *mazag* when they are happy, enjoying music, or intoxication (drugs). *Mazag mulid* = feeling of mulid. *Mazag tarab* = mood of *tarab*. Musicians who play with *mazag* are praised above those who play "straight"—just as written.

Mazhar. In Egypt, the *mazhar* is a large frame drum (larger than the **riqq**) without cymbals. The term may also refer to a *daff* in Egypt and Syria. A *mazhargi* is a frame drum or tambourine player.

Mazziqa. Music, in Egyptian dialect.

al-Mihna. The (entertainment) trade.

Mirmah. Horse riding shows offered at mulids in Upper Egypt such as Abu al-Haggag. The horses and horsemanship of their riders are shown off in the late afternoon.

Missy Maira. Female rapper from Alexandria, recording since 2008.

Mizmar (or **muzmar** in Egyptian Arabic, which refers to the instrument and the player), **baladi** (*mazamir*, pl.). A reeded horn-like instrument which is played using a circular breathing technique. In the Eastern Arab countries this is known as the *zurna*. There are four sizes used in Egypt, each with a different tone. It used to be made of apricot wood but now is often made of beech or metal. In a *mizmar wa tabl baladi* ensemble, there are typically three *mizmar* players and two drummers.

Monolog (*munuluj* in non-Egyptian Arabic). 1. A song with an irregular structure, that began to appear in the twentieth century, by composer Muhammad Qasabji (1892–1966) and singer, Umm Kulthum. 2. A monologist was an actor/comedian who performed alone or with a dancer, or as a warm-up for music or dance.

Mosanifat. Morality police who may fine dancers or establishments.

Muʿallima. Head or chief, experienced woman who works, possibly in a "male" job, as a butcher, coffeehouse keeper, or hashish merchant. If in charge of a group of dancers, she was called an *usta*.

Mughanni, m. (*mughanniyya*, f.). A singer.

Mughanni al-habit. A vulgar singer, meaning of singer of vulgar songs, or songs in poor taste. Said of *shaʿbi* singers.

Muhabbazin (pronounced *muhabbazeen*). Male actors who put on comedic skits in the 1830s. The *mihabbazatiya* troupes included music and dance; the boys and men played any women's roles. Sometimes the group was named after the leader, who might be the father of a family, so, Awlad Tariq were Tariq's group.

Muhammad ʿAli Pasha. Khedive and ruler of Egypt from 1805 to 1848, a Mamluk from Albania.

He defeated the Egyptian Mamluks and ruled on behalf of the Ottomans, while acting like an independent ruler and establishing his own dynasty. He banished female dancers to Upper Egypt in 1834, began an industrialization of Egypt, and used enforced peasant labor to build roads and infrastructure.

Muhammad 'Ali Street (*Shari'a* Muhammad 'Ali). This street, named for Muhammad 'Ali Pasha, Khedive of Egypt, was constructed between 1872 and 1874. It extends from 'Ataba Square up to the Rifa'i Mosque, the Mosque of Sultan Hassan and the Citadel. Was called *shari'a al-fann* because musicians, dancers, circus performers, actors, musical instrument makers, and costume makers lived and had shops here.

Muhibb. Literally, one who loves. One who may practice Sufism but who may not be attached to any particular *tariqa*.

Muhtarama. Respectable, adjective applied to a female.

Mukhaddarat. Drugs. Hashish has been used for centuries in Egypt, first reported in the eleventh century. Napoléon initially banned hashish but rescinded his ban, and it remained a widespread (mainly male) habit. Increased use of imported cocaine and heroin began in World War I, and restrictive laws were adopted in 1925; still there was an intravenous heroin problem from 1925 to 1930. Perhaps 70,000 men between 24 and 40 were addicted. Sayyid Darwish is said to have died from cocaine use. Hashish remained popular after the 1952 revolution. The association between tough drug lords and the entertainment business is shown in some popular films; also, the CSF (central security forces) have been involved. Drug addiction has increased since the '70s, markedly in the last decade. Even the government admits to a 10 percent addiction rate (which is probably higher). Other drugs of choice are *bango* (marijuana), tramadol, cocaine, and MDMA. Campaigns against drug use have featured footballer Mohammed Salah and actor/singer Mohamed Ramadan.

Mukhannath, s. (*mukhannathun*, pl.). Effeminate and transvestite males in pre–Islamic and early Islamic society. They associated with women, acting as marriage brokers and messengers, and often sang, played music, and apparently danced. They were condemned in various *ahadith* (stories that are a source of Islamic jurisprudence) but often tolerated because they were not sexually interested in women.

Mukhtar, Ni'mat (1932–1989). Born in Alexandria. Her mother may have been and certainly had *'awalim* friends. Her mother fled her father, and after their flat was destroyed by a bomb, they lived with singer Umm Zaytun who taught Ni'mat to sing. Ni'mat performed monologues and imitated singers with Nabiwiyya Salim (who was said to "raise her") and her dance troupe, then transitioned to dance. She joined Na'ima 'Abdu's dance troupe, performed with Farid al-Atrash, 'Abd al-Halim Hafiz and others. She was said to be a favorite dancer of Umm Kulthum and performed for President Nasser. She also performed Bedouin style dances and quit dancing in the 1970s.

Mulahhan. Composer.

Mulid. 1. Celebration of the Friends of God's (*awliya'*, saints) birthdays, including that of the Prophet Muhammad. With the exception of the Prophet, the festivals are held on the day commemorating their death. Mulid is a *farah*—an expression of joy, like a wedding. 2. Can also refer to a traffic jam, or a day or a situation spent in chaos. 3. Also now a sub-genre of *sha'bi* music, in which *anashid* references were "made cool."

Mulid Abu Khatzaira. Jewish *mulid* held in January in Damanhur. Egyptian Muslims are not usually permitted to attend for security reasons. Most visitors are foreigners.

Mulid al-'Adhra'. The Coptic Mulid of the Virgin Mary held in August at her monastery in Durunka near Assiut.

Mulid al-Kahana al-Thalatha (Mulid of the Third Priest). Held in the Siwa oasis and in the Siwi (a Berber) language in Egypt's Western Desert.

Mulid an-Nabi. The celebration of the Prophet Muhammad's birth in 570 CE. Celebrated first in Mecca, it is celebrated all over the Islamic world (except under *salafis* who dislike the mulids, so it is not celebrated in Saudi Arabia).

Mulid Sayyid Husain. *Sayyid* is a holy man, *sayyidna* means our holy man; some just say "Sidna Husain," the martyred grandson of the Prophet Mohammed whose head is buried in a mosque

Glossary

devoted to him near the Khan Khalili and facing the al-Azhar University. Usually held in the last week of November.

Mulid Sayyid al-Rifaʻi. Founder of the Rifaʻiyya Sufi order. Held at Citadel Square in Cairo outside his tomb and the mosque named for him each September.

Mulid Sayyida Fatima al-Nabawiyya. She was the daughter of Sayyid (Imam) al-Husain, the grandson of the prophet. She was born in Madina and became a great scholar and transmitter of *ahadith*. Her *mulid* is held in the Darb al-Ahmar district of Cairo.

Mulid Sayyida Nafisa. Nafisa was the great-granddaughter of the Prophet.

Mulid Sidi Gabr. Held in the district of Alexandria named after him, which has the main railroad station. One of five *mawalid* held in Alexandria in consecutive weeks.

Munshid, s. (*munshidin*, pl., pronounced munshideen). One who chants or sings the *inshad*.

Murad, Laila (1918–1995). Born Lillian Zaki Murad Mordechai. She began her singing career at age nine at Salat Badiʻa, trained by her father who was singer and cantor Zaki Murad (1880–1946) and the composer Dawud Husni. Besides Husni, Muhammad ʻabd al-Wahhab composed for her, and she made many successful films. Later she was accused (falsely) of being a spy for or sending money to Israel. Sister of composer Munir Murad.

Murid. Follower of a Sufi *shaykh*.

Murshid. A religious guide or teacher in Sufism. A *shaykh*.

Musiqa. Music in *fusha*, classical Arabic.

Mustafa, Nabawiyya. Dancer popular in the late 1940s and 1950s with excellent fluid hip-work and the deep backbends and floorwork of an earlier *ʻalima* style. She appeared in *Sirr Abi* (1946), *Sahibat al-ʻImara* (1948), *Ana [q]Albi Dalili* (1947), and other films, and with Muhammad ʻAbd al-Muttalib in *Wana Mali*.

Mutayyib, m. (*mutayyiba*, f.). An intermediary who arranged events for musicians and singers and collected money for entertainers so as not to render the relations between patrons and entertainers crass or impolite. Communicated the wishes of the audience to the entertainers. Very loudly praised the singers and dancers. Usually male (but not always).

Mutrib, m. (*mutriba*, f.). A singer. The term means s/he is capable of inspiring *tarab* and is an extraordinary singer, not simply an ordinary *fannan/a* (artist/performer).

Muwashshah, s. (*muwashshahat*, pl.). A complex vocal form based (allegedly) on poems from Andalusia (Muslim-ruled Spain), however they are mainly composed in Syria and Egypt and date back only one or two centuries. The *iqaʻat* used may be in 5/4, 7/4, 7/8, 10/8, 11/8, 13/8, 17/8. The *mutrib* sings and a chorus or back-up singers respond. As the *mutrib* repeats verses, s/he may improvise, adding different ornaments or modulations to other *maqamat*; this practice is called *tafrid* in musical terminology. It can last a minute or up to longer than ten minutes and may occur in other types of songs.

Nabatchi. The master of ceremonies who collects tips and compliments those who give them. A past tradition, which continues at *shaʻbi* celebrations including the *lailat al-fannanin*, which are parties to raise money for the entertainers.

Nafs. The lower part of the self, the ego (as opposed to the spirit, **ruh**). The Sufi or any good Muslim seeks to free him/herself from the *nafs*.

Nagma. Star—in the sky—or of music, dance, or cinema. *Nugum* (pl).

Nai. Reed flute used in many forms of Egyptian music but is important in *mulid* and *shaʻbi* music, and *al-musiqa al-shaʻbiyya*.

Nasib. Fate, or destiny.

Nazmi, Laila. A singer from Alexandria. Graduate of the High Institute of Music in 1968. She collected popular songs for her dissertation on Egyptian folk music in the early '70s, then she released an album (her career was in the late '60s and 1970s). Her songs portray the small-town girl, or *bint al-balad*, and Egyptian national identity and were part of a Lebanese theatrical production on Egyptian music, *Hishik Bishik* in 2015.

Nimra. Act, "number," performance. The *nimar* system referred to dancers who arrive at a club, give their performance, and then move on to their next booking.

Niqab. Modern version of the face veil. Worn by *munaqabat*, women who cover their faces as well as their hair, entire bodies, and often wear gloves and sunglasses.

Nubia. Homeland of the Noba people who have their own languages and music, which was in southern Egypt extending down into Sudan. When the High Dam at Aswan was constructed, the Nubians were forcibly resettled and may live today in the Sudan, Egypt, or abroad.

Nuqta, s. (*Nuqut*, pl.; *tan'it* means tip-giving). A monetary gift made at a wedding or to a performer or at a **mulid**. The attendees of a *mulid* give tips before leaving; the donor may ask for blessings (intercession of the saint) on himself and his family or some specific wish. The *shaykh* distributes the money to those left, especially *munshidin*. Also refers to tips given to dancing horses and their rider. Tips, at a performance or wedding, could be collected in a tambourine, in a scarf placed on the bride's lap, or (as coins) pasted on the dancer's face, and later, garlands of paper money on the dancer's neck, or throwing money on her, or put in in the costume, or in her hand. Tips, **takyit**, are sometimes thrown by the maître d' or waiters and people who are acting for the management to encourage others to tip. Then these are collected into boxes during the shows. In clubs, tips are now taken by the house (the club) or a dancer's manager (and given to the house), defeating the purpose of augmenting entertainers' salaries. In five-star hotels, individual dancers and their bands may have negotiated their portion of the tips.

Nur al-Huda (a forename, not a first and last name) (1924–1998). Born Alexandra Nicholas Badran in Mersin, Turkey. Actor Yusuf Wahbi met her while he toured Lebanon and offered her a contract in Egypt, where she first appeared in *al-Jawhara* in 1943. She starred in 30 films and sang over 100 songs, including with Muhammad 'abd al-Wahhab, Riyadh al-Sunbati, and Muhammad al-Qasabji. She co-starred in several films with Farid al-Atrash. She returned to Lebanon in 1983.

Oka (Muhammad Salah, b. 1991) and **Ortega** (Ahmed Mustafa). DJ *mahragan* artists who became very successful circa 2013. They performed together with (Shehata) Karika in 8%, making such hits as "Ana Aslan Gamid" and "El'ab Yalla."

Olwi, Zinat (1930–1988). Born in Alexandria, she escaped her abusive family at age sixteen, running away to Cairo, where she had a relative who was also a runaway dancer. Badi'a Masabni hired her. Known as Zurah as a dancer, she was said to be skilled with the *'asaya,* and like other Masabni dancers, played *sagat*. One of her better-known performances was in the 1955 film *Ayyam wa Layali*, directed by Henri Barakat. She tried to form a dancers' union, was unsuccessful, and retired first in 1965 and then in 1968.

al-Opera. Refers to Dar al-Obera al-Masriyya, the Cairo Opera House as part of the National Culture Center in Zamalek, which has theaters, the most used being the Main Hall and the Small Hall, which feature the Cairo Opera Company, the Cairo Symphony, the national orchestra of Arabic music, the Cairo Ballet, various choirs, and concerts with guest artists and guest companies, a music library, a gallery and museum of modern art. It is state funded.

Org. Musical electronic keyboard, (from organ). Replaced by the Oriental Keyboard at the end of the twentieth century, a quarter-tone enabled synthesizer which can replicate the sound of traditional Arab instruments like the violin, *qanun*, or others like the saxophone. Many include a rhythm generator so the player can use pre-recorded rhythms from Arabic percussion instruments.

Pasha (pronounced *basha* [*bashawat*, pl.] from Turkish). A title given to prominent landlords and officials in politics, it could be conferred by the ruler (the Khedive, or later, the King) for those who donated or offered public services. Not restricted to Egypt, used in Iraq, for instance.

Polygyny. Polygamy, a more commonly heard term, refers to multiple spouses. Muslims may marry up to four wives. Egyptians began to prefer monogamy in the twentieth century, but a significant number of men still marry more than one wife.

Qahwa (*ahwa* in colloquial Egyptian). A coffee house or café serving coffee and tea patronized by men. Coffee, introduced at the start of the sixteenth century, became very popular, and entertainers performed or gave samples of their craft at cafes even before the formation of a newer entertainment districts in the nineteenth century. May be called *nadi* (sing.), *cafitiria* (implies women and men), and *borsa* (on the seashore).

Qanun. A plucked zither. Used to be played on the lap, and now in Egypt, on a trestle-like stand. The *qanunji* quickly raises or lowers the mandals to change the pitch of a string. Possibly originated in ancient Greece. It was an essential instrument in a **takht**.

Qasida, s. (*qasa'id*, pl.). 1. A form of strophic poetry in classical Arabic 2. A composed (or improvised) form of music in which a singer sings such a poem accompanied by an ensemble.

al-Qibtiyya, Shafiqa (Shafiqa, the Copt, c. 1851–1926). Dancer who studied with the *'alima* Shuq. Her family disowned her when she began dancing at the *mawalid*. She later performed at the Alf Laila, was (also) said to have started the *sham'adan* (candelabra) dance, and to be among the last of the *'awalim*. One of her admirers bought champagne for the horses which pulled her carriage to drink, and she was showered with gold when she danced.

Qirayat Fatiha. A first-stage informal engagement in which the Fatiha, the first verse of the Qur'an, is recited.

Qiyan, pl. (*qayna*, s.). Singing slave girls; they also were musicians and composers of Arab and other ethnicities in the medieval period. Besides their owners, they had fans who attended their concerts, their *marbutin* (tied to them in attraction). A different term than *al-jawari* (slave girls, which may also mean concubines).

Qutb, s. (*aqtab*, pl.). A very holy *wali* or chief of a Sufi order is called the Qutb. His true identity is not known to the world; he is a modest person. The Qutb refers to the axis of the earth (around which the dervish turns). The four Qutbs referred to the founders of four great Sufi orders (*turuq*): 'Abd al-Qadir al-Jilani, Ahmad al-Badawi, Ibrahim ad-Disuqi, and Ahmad al-Rifa'i. The chief Qutb was referred to as al-Mutawali. Bab Zuwayla, a gate of Old Cairo, was also called al-Mutwalli because the place of the Qutb was behind the huge wooden door.

Rabab (or *rababa*, or *djoze* in Iraq). A bowed, usually spiked fiddle, played for the *sira* Bani Hilal (epic poetry). Still played in Upper Egypt and by the Bedouin but has been replaced in Arab classical and popular music by the violin (*kamanja*).

Ragid (pronounced *rageed*). Dance of the Fadikka Nubian people, performed to the *daff* while singing in response to a main singer.

Raki. A strong liqueur made from grapes and anise. Similar to *'araq*, or Egyptian *zbib*, made from raisins. Flaubert refers to it, perhaps meaning the latter.

Ramadan. Holy month in which Muslims fast in the daytime hours, a religious requirement for all healthy adults.

Raqs. Dance. *Raqisa* (f.) A dancer. May be defined by the dance form. *Raqisat balleh* would be a ballet dancer. **Raqqasa** (*ra'asa*) similarly means dancer, but is often used in a pejorative or negative manner to indicate someone who shows her body, hence a dancer may be called *fannana* (artist).

Raqs 'asaya. Dancing with a stick or a cane. It is identified with the Sa'id, and certain movements are traditional to Sa'idi style music and rhythms. One type of stick used is called *nabut* (pronounced *naboot*).

Raqs al-'awalim. Dance of the *'awalim*. The original name for the early twentieth century dance composition based on a traditional song and known subsequently as "Raqs al-Hawanim" (Ladies Dance) as played by violinist Sami Shawwa. Also used by other dancers in the Golden Era.

Raqs baladi. Egyptian style dancing. It can be "folk-dancing" or dancing in *raqs sharqi* style, but not as a soloist; for example, non-professionals dancing at a wedding or professionals dancing onstage in a *baladi* dress or other non-*raqs sharqi* costuming.

Reda, Mahmoud (1930–2020). His father was an author and chief librarian at Cairo University. He was a gymnast and a dancer while his brother 'Ali was a ballroom dancer and a filmmaker. In 1959, he, his brother, and dancer Farida Fahmy offered the first performance of the Reda folkloric troupe—six male and six female dancers and twelve musicians. He traveled through Egypt to research local dances and then restaged them. Reda succeeded in legitimizing folkloric dance as beautiful and tasteful performances that could be enjoyed by families and gained support from the Egyptian state. By the mid-1970s, the troupe had one hundred and fifty members. He taught internationally and retired in 1990.

Revolution. Rap collective in Alexandria including Czar, Rock, teMraz, etc. They opposed Mubarak and then the SCAF and the military in their signature song "Kazeboon" (liars).

al-Rihani, Nagib (1889–1949). Egyptian actor, recognized as the father of comedy. Formed his own theatrical group, adapted several French plays for the stage and film, and many Arabic

plays. He invented the character of Kish Kish Bey, a rich village headman squandering his fortune on women in Cairo. Was married to Badi'a al-Masabni.
Riqq (*ri'* in Egyptian Arabic). A small frame drum with cymbals in a wooden frame. Fish skin was a traditional head, now replaced by Mylar. The *riqq* was normally the only percussion instrument in a traditional *takht*.
Rod al-Farag. An area of Cairo featuring entertainment which was separate from (and to the north of) Azbakiyya.
Ruh. The soul. The animated breath of life. Believed to leave the body during sleep and upon death.
Rushdi, Fatima, Ensaf and **Ratiba**. Fatima (1908–1996) was born in Alexandria and was the best known of the three sisters. An actress, she was called the Bernhardt of Egypt as she played many of Sarah Bernhardt's roles. She married 'Aziz 'Id, acted in films, and directed a film in 1933, which she allegedly destroyed. Ensaf and Ratiba danced and acted with Sayed Darwish, then in the Rihani and the 'Ali Kassar troupes. They opened a club in Cairo in 1929, danced together in their club in Assiut in 1930, and opened a club on Alfi Bey street in 1935.
Rushdi, Muhammad (1928–2005). Singer who influenced Ahmad al-'Adawiyya.
Sabah (1927–1914). Born Jeanette Gergis al-Feghalli. Lebanese singer considered a music diva and affectionately called "Sabuha" and "Shahrura" by Lebanese. She recorded 50 albums, releasing more than 3,000 songs, and appeared in 98 films. She included the Lebanese style *mawwal* (vocal improvisation) and folk melodies in her songs. She continued performing until 2009, and married seven times.
Sabahiyya. A procession in the morning, which may conclude a *mulid*.
Sabry, Nahid (b. 1925). Born in Tanta. She moved with her sister to Cairo, studied with Nelly Mazloum, and was a leading dancer in the 1960s and '70s. In *Yom bila Ghad* (https://vimeo.com/160186070).
Sabu'a. A celebration and ritual held the seventh day after a baby's birth for Muslims and Copts in Egypt. The baby is placed in a *ghurbal* (used to be made of leather, but today it is commercially made and decorated), a sieve to let any bad spirits disappear. A *qollah*, or jug with candleholders attached, is decorated for a girl, and an *ibrit* is decorated for a boy. Candles are lit, a phrase is sung to advise the infant to obey the parents, and coins are dropped into a bowl of soaking beans.
Sadat (Sadat Muhammad Ahmad 'Abd al-'Aziz). From Madinat al-Salam, began making *mahraganat* with 'Ala' 50 Cent. In 2011, he sang "The People and the Government" about the revolution, and sang in Beirut and Europe. He opened a YouTube channel, Sadat al-3alamy.
Safinaz. Sofinar Grigoryan (b. 1983 in Armenia). Dancer in Egypt who has also appeared in films since 2013 with video clips on the channel *Dalaa*. She was sentenced in 2015 for wearing a costume made to look like the Egyptian flag, but the sentence was overturned. Famous for her chest pops, doing the splits, and her lively exchanges with the audience during her show.
Safiya (or Sophia). Cairo-bred *ghaziya* who went to Isna, in Upper Egypt. Her dance career was approximately from 1830 to 1850. By the 1840s, only she and one other dancer were there, according to Combes (1846) (not very likely true). She was supposedly discovered by 'Abbas, Muhammad 'Ali's grandson and became his mistress, but she was banned anyway to Upper Egypt along with other dancers. She was relatively well-to-do and married and retired by 1851.
Sagat. Brass finger cymbals from 1½ to 2 inches in diameter worn on the thumb and third finger of each hand. The *sagat* accent or fill in beats of other percussion instruments. Played since antiquity but in their current form, from the nineteenth century through the 1960s, by dancers skilled in their use. By the 1970s, some dancers no longer played them, instead including a professional *sagat* or **toura** (larger *sagat*) player in their bands. They are important for *zar* music.
Sahib kursi. Literally, owner of a chair. A professional musician of Muhammad 'Ali street was said to have his own *kursi* (chair) in the musician's café, meaning he was known for his talent.
Sahwa Islamiyya. A term for the Islamic revival movement recognized from the 1970s in Egypt and about 1979 elsewhere, but which had its origins in earlier conservative Muslim groups. Its members called for heightened religiosity, less mixing of males and females, and bans on music and dance, and clashed violently with Egypt's security and military forces on occasion.
Sa'id. Sa'id Misr is Upper Egypt, from the Cataracts of the Nile above Aswan to al-Ayait. Cairenes

characterize Saʻidis, who speak in a different accent, Saʻidi Arabic, as tough, stubborn, unsophisticated, and tough fighters. Saʻidis characterize Cairene women as decadent and men as effeminate.

al-Saʻid, Mona (b. 1954). Was born Mona Ibrahim Wafaʻ in the Suez Canal zone. Her parents are Bedouin from the Sinai oasis of Musa. When the family was evacuated during the 1967 war from the Canal Zone, she came to Cairo. At 12, she was seen dancing in a disco, and Anwar Amar, the owner of Sahara City, and the singer Laila Murad told her she should dance. She danced for two months at Sahara City and then fled her father's wrath. She danced for five years at Casino Lebanon in Beirut, then the Cairo Méridien for a year, then in London, where she bought the Omar Khayyam club. Known for her calm composure, graceful arms, and height.

Sala, s. (*salat*, pl.). Italian word adopted in Egypt to mean a space used as a nightclub or music hall. The word is not exclusive to entertainment; *salat hadid* means an ordinary, or *baladi* weight-lifting studio/gym.

Sala Badiʻa. Also known as Casino Badiʻa. Run by the singer/dancer Badiʻa Masabni. Actually, her club had many different locations over the years.

Sala Masriyya. Also known as Salat Mary Mansur, was on ʻImad al-Din street, and owned by Mary Mansur. Where Asmahan debuted as a singer with Farid al-Atrash and Hikmat Fahmy performed.

Salafiyya. 1. A movement of Islamic reform mostly in Egypt since the nineteenth century. 2. The contemporary movement of piety and purity developing mainly in Arabia and gaining adherents since the 1930s. An adherent of 2. is a *salafi*. *Salafis* abjure music and dance and detest the Sufis, calling their practices *shirk* (polytheism) or *bidʻa* (illicit innovation).

Salamlek. Reception room, dining room, and halls in an Ottoman-era or Ottoman-Arab home, villa, or palace, which were open to guests (male) unrelated to the family. Music might be performed in this space, as women listened from upper galleries protected from view with *mashrabiyyat* (turned wood screens).

Saltana. A condition or state of feeling ecstasy while playing or hearing music deriving from its *tarab*. The musician is able to deeply concentrate on his improvisation or playing; "gets deeper into it." The non-musician listener is swept into *mazag* and so intoxicated with feeling that he experiences *saltana*.

Samaʻ. Sufi session in which celebrants seek ecstasy (to achieve a state of *saltana*, or feel *tarab*) through movement or music; they experience oneness with God through the act of listening to this music or through the meditative process of turning (spinning).

Samaʻi, s. (*samaʻiat*, pl.). An Ottoman or Arabo-Ottoman style composition structured in four *khanat*, each followed by playing the *taslim* (refrain). The fourth *khana* is usually in a new rhythm, 3/8, 6/8, or 7/8. The *samaʻiat* are both a foundation for teaching the *maqamat* and their exposition and are still performed and composed today.

Sammiʻah (pl.). Aficionados of Arabic music. The *sammiʻ* or *sammiʻa* knows and loves Arabic music, knows quite a lot of repertoire and what level of music is being played. They seek *tarab* and "feel they have a right to respond personally and loudly to the performer … their input … causes him to excel."[1]

Sanuʻa, Yaʻqub (James) (1839–1912). Satirical journalist, playwright (called the father of Egyptian theater), nationalist, and polyglot. Born in Cairo to a Jewish family; his father worked for Prince Yakan, grandson of Muhammad ʻAli Pasha. At 13, he recited a poem for the prince who sent him to Italy to be educated. On his return, he tutored the prince's children, and in 1877, he started *Abu Naddara Zarqa*, a satirical journal, the first to feature cartoons and using Egyptian Arabic. His journal mocked the sale of Egypt to foreign bidders, the rulers, censorship, and lionized the rebellion of Ahmad al-ʻUrabi.

Sarhan, Fatma. Singer known as the Queen of Baladi. Singer of songs from rural Egypt and also some *shaʻbi* songs. Accompanied dancers Nagwa Fuʻad and Dina.

Sarsagi, s. (**sarsagiyya**, pl.). A fan of *mahragan*. Implies a low-income but also a male sartorial style; wearing of bright clothes, gelled, hair and long nails. It deliberately rhymes with *sabrsagi*, meaning someone so poor that he would pick up cigarette butts from the ground and smoke them.

al-Sawarikh. *Mahragan* duo of MCs Dok Dok and Funky who sang "La'" December 2017.[2]

Sayyid, m. (*sayyida*, f.). A holy man or woman. *Sayyidna* means our holy man; some just say Sidna Husayn or Sittna Zainab. *Asyad* refer to the spirits who possess or trouble humans and desire the **zar**.

Sayyid Ahmad al-Badawi. A much-loved religious scholar and saint born in Fes, Morocco, and who died in 1239 in Tanta, Egypt, where his *mulid* is held. It attracts up to three million pilgrims.

Sayyid Ibrahim ad-Disuqi. His mulid is held in Disuq.

Sayyidna Zainab. The granddaughter of the Prophet Muhammad, the daughter of Fatima and ʿAli. Her mulid is held in September in Cairo. An entire neighborhood is named after her shrine. She also has a tomb in Damascus, a pilgrimage site for an enormous number of Iranians (the same pertains to Husain).

Shabaka. Body stocking currently required (along with *short* [spandex shorts]) of a dancer in Egypt.

Shaʿbi. 1. Means of the people (meaning the masses or ordinary people, the **shaʿb**, as opposed to the **khassa**, or elites). 2. Refers to the musical genre that came out of folk music and which was popularized by Ahmad al-ʿAdawiyya and others.

Shaʿbiyya. Folk. Refers to the rural areas, as in *al-musiqa al-shaʿbiyya*.

Shabka. The gifts of jewelry given by a man to his bride. Usually gold and negotiated in advance. For the middle class this would be a heavy gold necklace and earrings and a fancy ring of 21-karat gold. If the couple break off the engagement, the gold is given back. If a girl gives in and has premarital sex, she is not offered the *shabka*, and probably not the *mahr* (or it is lowered substantially). Also refers to the *khutuba* or engagement.

Shafaʿa. Intercession. The Saints or *ahl al-Bayt* (descendants of the Prophet Muhammad) are asked to intercede for the believer to safeguard him, grant him access to heaven, or sometimes in a specific request; to heal the sick, or solve a problem. *Shafaʾa* is a goal of the *mulid* attendee.

Shahatin. Beggars. Not simply homeless people, but those who make a living by begging. Beggars are organized in guilds and may take part in or be aggressive at the *mawalid*. Because the *mulid* is a place of equality, everyone is welcome. Also, the giving of alms to the poor is important on religious holidays including ʿAshura, the 10th of the month of Muharram, which marks the killing of Sayyid Husain and is the date of his *mulid*.

al-Shaʿiri, Hamid. Libyan-Egyptian musician, composer, and producer. Was said to be the leading figure in *al-gil*. Arab pop in the 1980s. His song, "Lawlaki" sung by ʿAli Hamida was a huge hit, and he produced 17 albums between 1983 and 2006.

Shaitan. A devil. There are believed to be many under the arch-devil Iblis, who is similar to Satan in Christianity.

Shakwa. A complaint in Egyptian folk (rural) and *shaʿbi* poetry about the cruelty of fate and harsh conditions encountered.

Sham al-Nassim. Means "inhale the breeze." Spring holiday coming the day after Coptic Easter. Dates back to 2,700 BC. In the Coptic language, it was *Tshom Ni Tshom*, meaning garden meadows. Eggs are decorated, and families celebrate outside in picnics, with eggs, onion, and a salty fish called *fasikh*.

Shamʿadan. Candelabra balanced on the head during an Egyptian **zaffa**, wedding procession, or during a dance performance. It is believed to date back to the nineteenth century. *Sagat* are played with the *shamʿadan* (and as many modern dancers do not know how to play *sagat*, this is proof of an earlier origin) and floor work performed while balancing it. It was traditional to include the splits and other "tricks."

Shami. Refers generally to the Arab East or the Levant, or in the Arab East, specifically to Damascus.

Shamla. Complete. 1. A woman entertainer who knows how to both sing and dance, or play an instrument and sing and dance. 2. Sahin (2018) heard this term more recently used about a female entertainer who is masterful enough to perform solo without a backup folkloric chorus of dancers. However, one of these performers also sings, so Sahin's interlocutors may have meant the original meaning, and she interpreted it in this context.

Shams al-Din, Huda (1925–2002). Discovered by Niazi Mustafa and performed at Badiʿa's Casino.

In *Khulud* (1948), she portrays an *'alima* with a group of *'awalim* as supporting dancers (https://vimeo.com/182938606).

Sharaf. Honor; refers to the code of honor for men, who must protect the good name of their family and restrict their daughters, wives, and mothers.

Sharb. A square scarf folded into a triangle with the ends knotted behind and then tied on top of the forehead.

Shari'a. Islamic law. Its main sources are the Qur'an, the *hadith*, *ijma'* (consensus of the *'ulama*), and *qiyas* (analogy). Early jurists used their own opinion (*ra'y*), and *ijtihad* was used by some Sunni and many Shi'a scholars, and there are some other secondary principles used. Muslims must observe the *shari'a*.

Shari'a Haram (some simply say Haram). Pyramids Road, which was constructed by Khedive Isma'il to convey tourists to visit the pyramids. Many nightclubs were built there as the area expanded to incorporate prior villages.

al-Sharif, Ahmad (1916–1969). He started out playing for Sufi *dhikr* ceremonies and was later a singer and *'ud*ist for Badi'a Masabni and appeared in films.

Sharif, 'Azza (1947–2019). Began dancing at age eighteen in Cairo, then in Lebanon, England, and Germany, and then returned to the Mena House, and continued back and forth to Beirut prior to the Lebanese civil war. She appeared in twenty-one films including *Khalli Balak min Zuzu* and *Nibtidi mnain al-Hikaya*, was very close to her percussionist, and married Kat-Kut al-Amir (https://www.youtube.com/watch?v=hwv_NCnKqzU).

Sharif, Nahid (1942–1981). Born as Samiha Zaki al-Nial. Made her debut in 1958, married director Husain Hilmy al-Mohandis, and then, actor Kamal al-Shinnawi. She moved to Lebanon, began making films there in 1973, and remarried. She appears here in *al-Azwag al-Shayatin* (1976) (https://thecarovan.com/2016/01/22/nahed-sherif-1977-%D9%86%D8%A7%D9%87%D8%AF-%D8%B4%D8%B1%D9%8A%D9%81/).

Sharit, s. (pronounced shareet) (*sharayit*, pl.). Audio cassette.

al-Shawwa, Sami, Syrian born in Cairo; his father performed with 'Abduh al-Hamuli. He became known as a child prodigy on the violin in Aleppo, Syria, and then returned to Cairo where he played for leading singers, recorded and taught music using European notation with Mansour 'Awad. He was involved in the planning of the 1932 Arabic Music conference.

Shawqi, Ahmad (1868–1932) was called the Prince of Poets. His protégé was Muhammad 'abd al-Wahhab.

Shehata Karika. *Mahragan* artist Ahmad Shehata Karika who has performed with Oka and Ortega.

Sherihan (b. 1964). Sherihan Ahmad 'Abd al-Fattah al-Shalakani is an actress, singer, and dancer who performed in numerous films and television series, often portraying a dancer. Half-sister of guitarist 'Omar Khurshid (1945–1981).

Shewer. Woven food trays which incorporate designs in different colors. These are balanced on the head by women in certain Nubian dances. This style of basketry dates back to ancient times.

Shirk. Polytheism. Believing in more than one God. The *salafiyya* who oppose Sufis accuse them of *shirk* for showing devotion to figures other than Allah or for deviant practices which are "innovations" not observed by the Prophet Muhammad.

Shisha. Water pipe. Referred to as hookah in the U.S. and as *arghileh* in eastern Arab countries.

Shokoko. Mahmud (May 1, 1912, or 1913 in Darb al-Ahmar–1985). Born Mahmud Shokoko Isma'il Ibrahim Musa. An actor who always played the lower-class man, artist, and monologist, known for his puppet character of Aragozsho.

Sidi (or **Sayyid**) **Abu al-Haggag**. Came from Iraq, and his *mulid* is held in Luxor, Egypt.

Sidq. Sincerity. Arabic music fans praise and desire to hear this quality in a great singer, that she/he sounds as if they absolutely believe the lyrics they sing, and also that they are really improvising (in the improvisational section).

Sidqi, Zinat (1912 or 1913–1978). Born Zainab Muhammad S'ad in Alexandria, some sources say to a Jewish mother. She began performing as a belly dancer and monologue artist at weddings and tried to join a theatrical troupe in Alexandria but had to run away to Syria due to her family's opposition. On returning, she worked with Badi'a Masabni. She then joined Nagib al-Rihani's troupe and the troupes of Yusuf Wahbi, Fatima Rushdi, and then Isma'il Yasin, performing in numerous plays and films with him. Often cast as a maid, or a single woman, and occasionally in quite different roles, she was a master of farce and dry humor. Completely neglected and forgotten as an older person, she had to sell her own furniture.

Sihr. Magic.

Silsila. The designated succession of Sufi *shuyukh* or Qutb to Qutb, over time. Their special wisdom and esoteric knowledge pass from one to the other.

Sim. Similar to the argot or language known elsewhere in the Middle East and North Africa as *sin* (or *lisan al-ghuraba*), once the language of the Banu Sasan who were beggars and entertainers. Van Nieuwkerk describes this as an argot, cant, or crypolect, whereas Richardson says it is a sociolect comprised of some different linguistic influences. The *sim al-'awalim* or *sim al-fannanin* is used by Egypt's entertainers but known only to those who grew up as *awlad al-kar*, performing in the popular circuit. Some words are inversions, as *rafah* for *farah*; some words came from Italian—*biano* means "shut up"; or other sources. It is not the only secret language in Egypt; those working with tourists, gold and silversmiths, and homosexuals have their own. It is interesting to compare to the *sin* in which, for example, words for wine, copulation, good, bad, or a desirable youth have Greek, Persian, Akkadian, Aramaic or Arabic roots.[3]

Simsimiyya. A plucked instrument (a type of lyre or harp, or it may be made from an oil can with a wooden neck). Also called *tanbura*, played on Egypt's Red Sea coast and in the Sinai. A different version is made and played in the Nubian towns of Upper Egypt and Aswan.

Sira. Epic poem, documenting someone's or a group's life. Sirat Banu Hilal, or *al-sirat al-hilaliya*, is an oral poem about the journeys of the Banu Hilal tribe.

Siwa. An oasis in the Western desert inhabited by Amazigh people who have their own language, music, costumes, and traditions.

al-Soghayar, Sa'd (b. 1970). A *sha'bi* singer whose first hit song was "Esh .. Foq." He appeared in *Lakhmat Ra's* (Mixed-up Head) in 2006, produced by Mohammad El Sobky (who has produced other films with *mulid* songs), and had a hit song from this film, and recorded many other *sha'bi* and *mulid* hits since.

Sowan. Brightly colored tents used at the *mulid*. These were appliqued in the past; now the material is merely printed.

al-Souissi, Ahmad. *Mahragan* singer who can sing in *sha'bi* and *mulid* styles and improvise. Performs with Hysa and Halabesa in "Hitta Minni" (2015).

Su'al wa gawab. Call and response. A general feature of Arabic and Egyptian music where one instrument or voice issues the "call" and other instruments or a chorus give a "response."

Sufism (*Tasawwuf*). Mysticism within Islam. The inward direction of Islam. Those who follow the Sufi path. Most are Sunni Muslims in Egypt, but in the broader Islamic world, some Sufis are Shi'a Muslims. Not a distinct sect, but a methodology of religion in which one turns one's heart explicitly to Allah and hopes to directly experience Him. This trend developed early in Islamic history and became organized in different orders or brotherhoods (see *Tariqa*).

Suhbagiyya. Musicians of the Port Said area.

Tabarruj. Illicit display. Refers to women who show their bodies whether dancers or ordinary women who did not adopt Islamic dress (by those who preferred *hijab*).

Tabl baladi. A large drum with a head on each side, played with a thick stick on one side and with a twig (or a thinner stick) on the other side. Popular in Upper Egypt, also in rural (and today also in urban) Lebanon.

Tabla (referred to as *darbekke* in Levantine dialects and *darbuka*, or *dumbek* in Western countries). A goblet shaped drum. Used to be made from clay with a fish or goat skin head and now often made from aluminum with a Mylar head.

Tableaux. Scenes in dramatic or musical dance shows which may depict a historical or imaginary event. Literally means "paintings."

Tafrid. When a lead singer improvises vocally, often repeating verses or phrases that were already part of a song, but takes it in whatever direction s/he wishes, adding different ornaments or modulating to other *maqamat*, and returning to the main *maqam*. Shows his/her creativity and mastery.

Taha, Muhammad. Singer performing from 1955 to 1965 who influenced *sha'bi* singer Ahmad al-'Adawiyya.

Taharosh jinsi (sometimes merely *taharosh*). Sexual harassment in public, whether physical or verbal. Referred to in some *mahraganat*.

Tahayya (Cairene pronunciation of **tahiyya**). Literally, greetings. Given in response to tips given to dancers or singers, and usually mentioning the tippers' nationalities or names, if known.

Tahmila. An instrumental piece with a repeated chorus or *taslim* with phrases that are partly composed and partly improvised. Usually played by a small *takht* in which musicians take turns playing and adding their own improvisations.

Tahtib. Its original name was *fann al-nazaha wa al-tahtib* (art of being honest and chivalrous and [with the] stick) Traditional stick dancing was performed in the Pharaonic period by men as a martial art. It is now taught as both a martial art and for performance with music from the Sa'id. The aim is to hit the head or a body part, but not the arm or shoulder. There is a Nubian version. The stick held is called *'asa, 'asaya,* and *nabut* (pronounced *naboot*). The form developed in France from Egypt; "modern *tahtib*" allows women to practice as well as men.

Taj. Means a crown. Designed by the Banat Mazin *ghawazi*. A turban-like headdress/headband, beaded and jeweled, to keep the hair back.

Takht. A small musical ensemble including vocalists. This was named for the small raised stage on which they performed. It might have included the *'ud, qanun, riqq, nai* and *kamanja* and vocalist.

Talaq. Divorce initiated by the male. Commonly translated as repudiation. The man is supposed to undergo two waiting periods before the third and final pronouncement of *talaq* and reconciliation should be attempted. It was relatively easy for a man to divorce in Egypt and rather difficult for women to do so prior to legal reforms in the twentieth century.

Tal'at Sayyid Muhammad, Dina (most commonly referred to simply as **Dina**) (b. 1964 in Rome). Dancer and actress. Holds a master's degree in philosophy from 'Ain Shams University. She began dancing in the Mahmoud Reda Troupe in the '70s and began performing *raqs sharqi* in the 1980s, becoming a major star in the '90s. She wrote an autobiography, *Hurriyati fi-al-raqs* (2011), which also appeared in French as *Ma liberté de danser*.

Tamarrod (rebellion) **movement.** Started by five activists who collected signatures from 2012 to the end of June 2013, showing opposition to President Morsi and asking for early elections. Fueled the June 30, 2013, protests which ended with a coup d'etat against Morsi.

Tanbura. A Nubian plucked instrument found from Dongola up to Wadi Halfa. It is also called *al-kisir*, or *simsimiyya*, and is made in different sizes and styles. The sound it makes is called *kri*, or *krir* (roaring of lions).

Tannura. 1. A skirt. 2. The whirling male dancers who performed at *mawalid* and now perform a staged version at the al-Ghouri palace, or at other shows for the public, and in new *mulid* songs and videos.

Taqsim, s. (*taqasim* pl.). Instrumental improvisation in Arabic music. Improvisation in each *maqam* has certain conventions of starting and ending phrases and directional movement through the *ajnas*, although with individual styling, imagination and ornamentation.

Taqtuqa (*taqatiq*, pl., pronounced *'ta'ati'* in Cairene). A short composed song that became more popular after the turn of the century.

Tarab. Ecstasy that is created by great emotion-based music (or poetry and the *dhikr*) and the musicality, improvisation, and elaboration in it. People also refer to *lun tarab* (literally the color of tarab) being present in music, and in foreign languages, and now increasingly in Arabic, "*tarab* music" (generally referring to older classical repertoire).

Tarbush. Felt, brimless hat known as the fez and related to the North African *chachia*. Ottoman Sultan Mahmud II ordered citizens to wear the *tarbush* in 1829 in place of the wrapped turban. With a tassel in Egypt, it became a symbol of the educated class, the *afandiyya* in Egypt, and was worn by those in the government and the military until 1956. It is worn to signify an earlier historical period in films, theater, or musical *tableaux*.

Tarha. A long hair and headcover worn over a *sharb*, or *mandil*, a shorter scarf by rural women. It trails behind the head and is usually black.

Tariqa, s. (*turuq*, pl.). A Sufi order or brotherhood such as the Khalwatiyya, Ahmadiyya, or Shadhiliyya, the three largest orders in Egypt. The word *tariqa* also means road or path and refers to the Sufi's progress along the path to God (Allah). There are at least 120 different Sufi orders. A *murid* follows a shaikh for guidance; similarly his brotherhood supports his aim for self-development.

Tashkil. Variation. A specialization done while dancing to *mulid* music or *mahragan* in pairs or alone. Like a dance "number," it combines some elements of hip-hop moves and steps while holding large knives or small knives (*matawi*), or movements from the *tahtib* (stick/cane) or *raqs 'asaya* (stick/cane). Secondary meaning refers to caricatures or cartoons.

Tashnib. A word from the entertainers' secret language. A way of behaving which shames or almost forces the viewer to tip the performer; also, if the band leader tells the dancer to go out for tips.

Taslim. A refrain in a song or a musical composition or repeated chorus.

Tattooing. Used to be offered to Christians at Christian mulids by Muslims—usually of a snake, a name and address, a cross, St. George, Christ on the Cross, or the hero Abu Zayd.

Thawra. Revolution. Most recently, January 25, 2011, in Egypt. *Thuwwar* are revolutionaries, those who supported the revolution.

Toura. Larger **sagat** (cymbals), approximately 10 cm in diameter. If used, they are usually played by a band member today.

Turath. Cultural heritage. Pertaining to music, oral poetry, dance, and customs.

'Ud (or *oud*). Means wood. A pear-shaped, short-necked, fretless lute which is either the ancestor of the European lute or developed simultaneously with it. It usually has five sets of double strings and a single bass string. Was essential to Arabic music in the music of the *takht*. Farid al-Atrash, Muhammad al-Qasabji, and George Michel were known for their virtuosity on the *'ud*.

Ughniyya. Song format introduced by composers in the 1930s–1940s, which was considered Egyptian and modern; the "long song." It had an instrumental introduction; the singer might begin with very light accompaniment, and then it moved into sections of different meters with full accompaniment. There might be one or more *taqasim* in the song and a vocal improvisation.

Ughniyya habta. Vulgar song.

'Ulama. Muslim scholars or clerics. They usually study with an *'alim* (enlightened one) of a particular subject and obtain a *shahada* (certificate of completion of study, or mastery of a particular topic) from him. *Fuqaha* may be heard as a synonym for those who are masters of *fiqh* (jurisprudence), but not all scholars are qualified as *fuqaha*.

'Umda. Village headman.

Umm al-Dunya. Refers to Egypt as the mother of the world or mother of all countries. So-called by medieval scholar Ibn Khaldun in his *Muqadimma*.

Umm Kulthum (not a first and second name, but a mononym) (1904 [est.]–1975). born Fatima Ibrahim al-Baltagy. Referred to as Kawkab al-Sharq (Planet of the East), al-Sitt (the lady), and Souma (a shortened version of her name) She began singing as a child at weddings and mulids dressed as a boy (her brother's idea of preserving the family honor). She moved to Cairo in 1923 and was in demand as a singer by the late 1920s. She starred in the first of six films in 1936 (*Widad*). From 1937 she regularly offered a concert on the first Thursday night of the month in the summer, and these were broadcasted throughout the Arab world. She eventually became the head of the musicians' syndicate and sang many patriotic songs as well as romantic and poetic ones and raised money for Egypt after its defeat in the June '67 (Six Day) war.

Umma. The "nation" or community of all Muslims.

'Urf. Customary and/or tribal law predating *shari'a*, although it is a one of the defining criteria in *fiqh*. It is possibly better to speak of customary laws, in the plural, since it is not a unitary or codified entity.

'Urfi marriage. *Zawaj 'urfi* is a more informal type of marriage than *zawaj nikah*. Often done secretly, as it was considered shameful, and women did not obtain all the rights that they do in *zawaj nikah*. It is unacceptable to parents, but young people contract it because they can't afford the costs of marriage.

Usta. The female leader and experienced performer of a troupe of *'awalim* who performed for women's celebrations, mainly weddings. They traveled veiled on a cart to their work.

Venyara. Earlier name for the *sham'adan*, or candelabrum, which was balanced on the forehead by Shafiqa al-Qibtiyya, and later on the head of dancers, but without the metal cap crafted later on.

Voutsaki, Katy (or Kety) (1927–1980). A dancer appearing in a number of Egyptian films from the 1940s to 1965. She was from Alexandria, born to an Egyptian mother and a Greek father. She appeared as well in two Greek films after moving to Greece.

Wahda wa al-nuss. An *iqa'* or meter. Is also a form of *maqsum*, a 4/4 beat.

Wali, s. (*awliya'* pl.). A Friend of Allah. One who knows Allah's secrets. The tombs of these saints are the focus of the *mawalid*. Often mosques are constructed over these tombs, as is the mosque of Husain.

Wasa'a. District of Cairo including the fish market, brothels, coffee houses, and entertainment halls (*salat*). Shari'a Clot Bey, where Shafiqa al-Qibtiyya, the singer/dancer first worked, was in the Wasa'a (which Europeans called, the Fishmarket). The "Battle of Wazzir" took place here April 2, 1915, involving some 2,500 Australian and New Zealander soldiers, many of whom were drunk and burned brothels and attacked firefighters.

Wasla, s. (*waslat*, pl.). A suite of pieces usually in the same *maqam*. These pieces may be linked by *taqsim* played by different instruments. It might end with a *dawr* or *qudud* or a *taqtuqa*.

Weza. A *mahragan* artist from Matariyya. Part of the original 8% with Oka and Ortega.

Wlad al-sis. Name for *mahragan* fans (*sarsagiyya*), which implies they are foppish, obsessed with their self-image, narcissistic, and constantly online.

Yashmak. The face veil worn by elite women in the late Ottoman era.

Yasin, Isma'il (1912–1972). Actor/comedian born in Suez. He worked while still a child as a barker, singing outside a shop, as a valet, and traveled to Lebanon before returning to Egypt. Playwright/journalist/lyricist Abu al-Sa'ud al-Ebiary "discovered" Yasin, and he joined Badi'a Masabni's troupe and later, 'Ali al-Kassar's troupe. He starred in 81 movies in which he was often a quixotic fool, with a funny appearance and a large mouth. He appeared several times as a *raqs sharqi* dancer and imitated Samia Gamal in one film. He died in poverty.

Youssef, Bassam (b. 1974). Egyptian surgeon, comedian, and television host. He created the very successful television and online program "Al-Barnamag" (2011–2014) before fleeing Egypt for the United States. Called the Egyptian Jon Stewart.

al-Yusuf, Ruz (1898–1958). Born Fatima in Lebanon, she moved to Egypt and became a vaudeville actress. She was in 'Aziz 'Id's and 'Ukasha's troupes, and she played music. She had no formal education, so 'Id hired a *shaykh* to teach her to read and write. She became quite famous in one of Aziz 'Id's plays (in which she wore a bathing suit) and in other roles. She moved into journalism and established a magazine named for her, *Ruz al-Yusuf* in 1925, followed by *Ruz al-Taba'i* covering entertainment and politics.

Zaffa, s. (*zaffat*, pl.). A procession, often for a wedding, or a *mulid*. A *zaffat al-gihaz* is the wedding procession of the furniture and trousseau bought for a bride, which was accompanied by a *hasabullah* band.

Zaffat al-Mulid. The *zaffa* is a procession through the street held for weddings and mulids. It used to and may still involve riding on horses in Upper Egypt.

al-Zaghlul, Sa'd (1857–1927). Nationalist leader of the Wafd Party who argued for greater independence from Britain and was exiled by the British, which led to the revolution of 1919. He became prime minister in 1924. After the assassination of Sir Lee Stack, the Sirdar of the Sudan, in November 1924, Britain imposed an indemnity on Egypt, and Zaghlul resigned. Al-Zaghlul was reportedly a fan of Munira al-Mahdiyya. Songs were written for him while he was exiled, which referred to him indirectly as Egyptians were forbidden from any direct mention.

Zajjal, s. (*azjal*, pl.). Traditional, colloquial, short rhyming couplets which were composed extemporaneously at weddings or other festivities. They also comprise the lyrics of popular music. *Zajjalun* are the creators/composers of this popular poetry. This tradition exists in the Levant as well as Egypt. In the late nineteenth century, *zajjalun* started to write brief songs in colloquial

Zaki, Suhair. Born 1945 in Mansura. Began her dancing career in Alexandria, later appearing on television and in over 100 films. She danced for many heads of state and was greatly admired by Anwar al-Sadat. Some have stated that she and Nagwa Fu'ad were rivals, but Nagwa has stated this was not really true and that they had good relations. Married Muhammad 'Amara and retired in 1992.

Zambalak. (or zambalek) A spring. Someone who dances in a fast and springy style, or a piece that requires fast dancing. There is a similar term in Turkish Romani style dance.

Zar. A ceremony held to identify or contact an evil or a troublesome spirit, a *jinn*, who may be causing distress or illness. A *shaykha* or *kudia* (Sudanese) presides as special music is played, and the participants dance. The spirit usually requires clothing, certain types of gifts, food, and sacrifices.

Zawaj. Marriage. *Zawaj nikah* is the more accepted form of marriage. Actual consummation of the marriage may be celebrated long after the engagement, because the man isn't able to immediately pay the *mahr* and the *shabka* and provide a flat for the couple to live in and other demands. The *bint al-balad* is advised to choose in marriage "he who desires you, not who you desire."

Zina'. A capital sin. Fornication or adultery. Sex outside of marriage.

Ziyara, s. (*ziyarat*, pl.). Literally means a journey or a visit. Pilgrims undertake a *ziyara* to a specific tomb or shrine of a saint. People also make a *ziyara* to the graves of their family members.

Zuluf. See *Abu Zuluf*.

Expressions/Amthal

Akhtob l-bintak wa matakhtobsh l-ibnak. Betroth your daughter, but not your son. Meaning: it's fine for parents to speak about their daughters and offer them as brides to those trustworthy. Used when a proposal comes from the bride's family, because men customarily propose.

Ana basha, inta basha, meen yasu' al-humar? I'm a pasha, you're a pasha, who will drive the donkeys? Too many specialists.

Biyihki [q]issit Abu Zayd. He's telling the epic story of Abu Zayd al-Hilali. Meaning: he will drone on and on.

Dall'a ragil wala dall'a hita. Literally, the shadow of a man is better than the shadow of a wall. Meaning: it's better to have a man than none. Said when a woman is about to marry a man who isn't wonderful.

ad-Dinya zayy al-ghaziya, al-ra'isa tur'us li-kull wahid shwayya. Life is like a *ghaziya*; the dancer dances just briefly for each.

Hawa al-Hurriyya fi Masrah Munira al-Mahdiyya. There is love of freedom in the theater of Munira Mahdiyya.

Hishik bishik. A cabaret-style performance (or *raqs sharqi*), or something which is thought to be obscene or licentious. (Fayed, 2015). *Qanat hishik bishik* would mean trashy music channels. Calling a girl *hishik bishik* is like calling her a slut.

Hiyya fannana, mish ra'asa bass. She's an artist, not just a dancer. Said of a more skillful dancer.

Hizzi ya wizz. Literally, "Shake it, oh you goose." Meaning: shake your hips.

Ibn ra'asa. (or **ibn ghaziya**). This is an insult. Son of a dancer. Shows that the profession is not or is no longer esteemed.

Kayyif musiqa. (pronounced *moo-see-qa*) A music connoisseur. Like **sammi'a.**

Khiffat al-damm. Light hearted, good personality, funny, as in *dammuh khafif* (he is light-hearted) as opposed to *ta'il* (heavy). Said of Egyptians in comparison to some other nationalities.

Ma fish dukhkhan min ghair nar. No smoke without fire. Can be said of someone who needs to practice music or dance more or of someone who is beginning to improve. Or said of dancers who were suspected (or actually did) engage in prostitution as well as entertaining. Or of a couple suspected of carrying on together.

Ma kansh fih karama, ma kansh fi hadd mishi. If there were no miracles, no one would bother.

Masr umm al-dunya. Egypt is the mother of the world, the source of civilization. *Umm al-dunya* can be used as the epithet for Egypt.

al-Mulid, mulid. The mulid is rocking, is a real mulid.

Mulid bidun shaykh. Total chaos and disorganization. Said of something like a *mulid* without a *shaykh* to lead it. Was used to refer to Midan Tahrir in central Cairo during the January 2011 Revolution.

Mulid wa sahbu ghayyib. Means the same as above. Here is a mulid but its saint (lit. the owner) is absent, and no one is in charge. Line of the lyrics in "Zahma ya dunya zahma" as sung by 'Adawiyya.

Tamut ar-ra'asa wa wastaha biyil'ab. Literally, the dancer dies and her waist is still moving. Meaning: old habits die hard.

Til'a bil-mulid bila hummus. Leaving the mulid without the chickpeas. Meaning: losing a good opportunity, failing to make a profit.

Ur'us lil-'ird fi dawlitu. When the monkey reigns (is a ruler), dance before him.

Wikala ghayr bawwab. A gate without a doorman. Means that dancing and music is a profession with no gatekeepers—something anyone can start doing. Used by older performers of the Muhammad 'Ali street background to complain about the outsiders who brought down the standards of the profession.

Yimut az-zummar, wa-sawab'uh bitil'ab. The horn player dies, but his fingers keep playing. Old habits die hard.

al-Zawaj nisf al-din. Marriage is half of religion. Attributed to the Prophet Muhammad. Said in Egypt, Sudan and throughout the Muslim world.

[iz]Zayyik, ya nagma? Not a proverb, but a typical greeting to a dancer as she arrives to dance for the evening. "How are you, star?"

Zayy himar al-ghaziya, yisma'a at-tabla yihizz wasatih. Like the donkey of the dancer, when it hears the drum, it shakes its middle. A habit has become second nature. Said of (or to) pretty woman or girl in Egypt.

Zayy al-'amar, 'aishta, 'asal, hilwa, gamila, laziza, moza. If said to you by an unknown man, this is rude—unless you are the dancer!

Chapter Notes

Introduction and Notes on Music and Transliteration

1. Sherifa Zuhur, ed., *Colors of Enchantment: Theater, Dance, Music and the Visual Arts of the Middle East* (Cairo: American University in Cairo Press, 2001); Sherifa Zuhur, ed. *Images of Enchantment: Visual and Performing Arts of the Middle East* (Cairo: American University in Cairo Press, 1998).
2. Guernica. "This is Also My World." *Guernica*, March 3, 2014.
3. (Albany, New York: State University of New York Press, 1992). Reprinted 1996.
4. 'Ali Jihad Racy, "Musical Attitudes and Spoken Language in Pre-Civil War Beirut." In Sherifa Zuhur, ed., *Colors of Enchantment: Theater, Dance, Music and the Visual Arts of the Middle East* (Cairo: American University in Cairo Press, 2001) 336–351.
5. I list a few here for those less familiar with Arabic music: Ali Jihad Racy, "Musical Aesthetics in Present-Day Cairo," *Ethnomusicology* 26/3, 1982, pp. 391–406; Ali Jihad Racy, *Making Music in the Arab World: The Culture and Artistry of Tarab*. (Cambridge: Cambridge University Press, 2003), Habib Hassan Touma, *Music of the Arabs*. Trans. Laurie Schwarts (Portland: Amadeus Press, 1996); Dwight Reynolds, *Heroic Poets, Poetic Heroes: The Ethnography of Performance in an Arabic Oral Epic Tradition* (Ithaca and London: Cornell University Press, 1995); Scott Marcus, *Music in Egypt: Experiencing Music, Expressing Culture* (New York: Oxford University Press, 2006); Christian Poché, *Musiques du monde arabe: écoute et découverte* (Paris: Institut du Monde Arabe, 1994) with CD; Frédéric Lagrange, Mohsen Sawa and Mustapha Saeed, *Youssef Al-Manyalawy, Singer of the Arabic Renaissance, His Artworks and Era* (Beirut: Dar Al-Saqi, 2011); Virginia Danielson's book on Umm Kulthum is a biography and social history, not a musical analysis of the *maqamat* in her songs: Virginia Danielson, *The Voice of Egypt: Umm Kulthum, Arabic Song and Egyptian Society in the Twentieth Century* (Chicago: University of Chicago Press, 1997); Johnny Farraj and Sami Abu Shumays, *Inside Arabic Music: Arabic Maqam, Performance and Theory in the Twentieth Century* (New York: Oxford University Press, 2019); Salwa El Shawan, "Traditional Arabic Music Ensembles in Egypt since 1967: The Continuity of Tradition within a Contemporary Framework." *Ethnomusicology*, 28: (1984) 271–288; Salwa El Shawan, "The Socio-Political Context of Musika al-'Arabiyyah in Cairo, Egypt: Policies, Patronage, Institutions and Musical Change" (1922–77) *Asian Music*. 12 (1980) pp. 86–128.
6. Daniel J. Gilman, *Cairo Pop: Youth Music in Contemporary Egypt* (Minneapolis: University of Minnesota Press, 2014).
7. Jefferson, NC: McFarland, 2018.
8. Wendy Buonaventura, *Serpent of the Nile: Women and Dance in the Arab World* (New York: Interlink Books, 1998) 149 and as discussed by Heather D. Ward, *Egyptian Belly Dance in Transition*, 10.
9. Valeria Loiacono and Julia M. Fallon, "Intangible Cultural Heritage Beyond Borders: Egyptian Bellydance (Raqs Sharqi) as a Form of Transcultural Heritage," *Journal of Intercultural Studies*, 39: 3 (2018) 286.
10. Omar D. Foda, "The Pyramid and the Crown: The Egyptian Beer Industry from 1897 to 1963," *International Journal of Middle East Studies*, 46: 1 (February 2014).
11. Hanan Hassan Hammad, "Mechanizing People, Localizing Modernity: Industrialization and Social Transformation in Modern Egypt: Mahalla al-Kubra 1910–1958," Ph.D. dissertation, University of Texas at Austin (2009) 261.
12. Ziad Fahmy, *Ordinary Egyptians: Creating the Modern Nation through Popular Culture* (Stanford, CA: Stanford University Press, 2011).
13. Frédéric Lagrange, "Women in the Singing Business: Women in Songs," *History Compass* 7/1 (2009), 226–250.
14. Mostly true of the argument made by Maira Sunaina, "Belly Dancing, Arab-Face, Orientalist Feminism and U.S. Empire," *American Quarterly* (June 2008) Vol. 6, Issue 2, pp. 317–345.
15. However, in Egyptian colloquial Arabic, *al-mazziqa*.

Chapter One

1. Ali Jihad Racy, "Record Industry and Egyptian Traditional Music: 1904–1932," *Ethnomusicology*, 20: 1 (January 1976) 23–48.
2. A rare sample of a *ghaziya* dancing in this film

to an old song (that did not originally accompany this footage) "Hilwa ya balha ya ma[q]amaha," composed and sung by Ahmad al-Sharif. Published on November 3, 2016. This song is traditionally sung for weddings. https://www.youtube.com/watch?v= S3ugoJvHUr0&feature=youtube. Ahmad al-Sharif (1916–1969) started out playing for Sufi *dhikr* ceremonies and was later a singer and *'ud*ist for Badi'a Masabni and appeared in films. The song speaks of the endocarp of the date *([q]umu'u)* which keeps it perfect and intact, until it is deseeded and eaten, an analogy to the beauty of the virgin who has saved her family's reputation. Communication by Hytham M. Hammer.

3. In the world's fairs of the late nineteenth and early twentieth century, a dance style closer to Egyptian *ghawazi* (not *'awalim*) style was displayed as well as dancers performing in an Algerian style. They used handkerchiefs, as in the Algéroise, a dance of Algiers.

4. Farida Fahmy, "The Founding of the Reda Troupe: An Historical Overview." *FaridaFahmy.com*, 2008. http://www.faridafahmy.com/history.html Reda briefly notes his distaste for the *ghawazi* in an interview: "Mahmoud Reda" interviewed by Shira, *Shira.Dotnet*. July 31, 2006. http://www.shira.net/about/reda-interview12-other.htm. Yet, I personally learned two choreographies which included certain movements later cut or altered from an original Reda Troupe member, Faruq Mustafa, which others (including one of my anonymous reviewers) identified as too vulgar i.e., placing the *nabut* (*naboot*) on the stomach of each of two dancers and then traveling around in a circle.

5. Edward Lane, *Manners and Customs of the Modern Egyptians* (1836) (New York: Cosimo Classics, 2005) 361.

6. Since I likewise see the great dancers of the first half of the twentieth century as heirs to the *'awalim* (and dancers of lower classes still used the term), this took me aback. John Rodenbeck, "'Awalim' or The Persistence of Error," in Jill Edwards, ed. *Historians in Cairo: Essays in Honor of George Scanlon*. (Cairo: American University in Cairo Press) 107. I suppose it was made to suggest that Said was not really an expert on Egypt, as were certain Orientalists, such as Lane. Still Said has great insight into the "messiness" and uncaptured achievements of Kariuka's life. Said's piece in question appeared in my own edited volume and earlier, in the media. Edward Said, "Farewell to Tahia" in Sherifa Zuhur, ed., *Colors of Enchantment: Theater, Dance, Music and Visual Arts of the Middle East*. (Cairo: American University in Cairo Press, 2001) 228–232.

7. Lane, *Manners and Customs*, 362.

8. He visited Egypt again after the work was published in 1836 and expanded the work.

9. Billie Melman, *Women's Orients: English Women in the Middle East, 1718–1918* (Ann Arbor: University of Michigan Press, 1992) 73–74.

10. Lane, 1973, 350–351.

11. Marjorie A. Franken, "From the Streets to the Stage: The Evolution of Professional Female Dance in Colonial Cairo," in Paul Tiyambe Zeleza and Cassandra Rachel Veney, eds., *Leisure in Urban Africa* (Trenton, NJ and Asmara, Eritrea: Africa World Press, 2003) 88.

12. The term "gypsy" is currently rejected by the Roma. However, other groups do not necessarily use their tribal designation as their label (for example, the *gitanos* of Spain). Although we believe Egypt's *ghawazi* are Dom as in Palestine, Lebanon, or Syria, they use the term "*ghajar*" and other sub-tribal names. The marketing of Upper Egyptian musicians and dancers as '*ghajar*' or "Gypsy" has continued on in the world music scene regardless of its accuracy.

13. Karin van Nieuwkerk, "*A Trade Like Any Other": Female Singers and Dancers in Egypt* (Austin: University of Texas Press, 1995) 26.

14. Sarah Graham-Browne, *Images of Women: The Portrayal of Women in Photography of the Middle East 1860–1950* (New York: Columbia University Press, 1988) 312–314.

15. Graham-Browne, *ibid.*, 175.

16. van Nieuwkerk, "*A Trade Like Any Other*"; and Karin van Nieuwkerk "Changing Images and Shifting Identities of Female Performers in Egypt" in Sherifa Zuhur, *Images of Enchantment: Visual and Performing Arts of the Middle East* (Cairo: American University in Cairo Press, 1998).

17. Accepted without question by Khaled Fahmy who is highly conversant with the terminology used through the nineteenth century, "Prostitution in Egypt in the Nineteenth Century," in Eugene Rogan, ed., *Outside In: On the Margins of the Middle East* (London: I.B. Tauris, 2001).

18. Confusion over their precise history is conveyed by Edwina Nearing "Sirat al-Ghawazi Part 1" (1976) reprinted on GildedSerpent.com http://www.gildedserpent.com/articles25/edwinaghawazich1.htm.

19. Frédéric Lagrange, "Women in the Singing Business: Women in Songs," *History Compass*. 7/1 (2009) 226–250, http://mapage.noos.fr/fredlag/FL-Women-History%20Compass.pdf last accessed December 13, 2018.

20. Here they were comparing two of al-Mahdiyya's recordings of "Asmar malak ruḥi," one from 1905/6 and the other from 1923. Frédéric Lagrange hosted by Mustafa Said. "Munira al-Mahdiyya 3" on "Min Al Tarikh," *AMAR, Foundation for Arab Music Archiving and Research*, August 27, 2015 http://www.amar-foundation.org/126-munira-al-mahdiyya-3/ They also discuss '*alima* characteristics of her singing in a previous episode (2).

21. Charles Douin, *Histoire du règne du Khédive Ismail*. (Rome: Istituto Poligrafico dello Stato/Société Royale de Géographie d'Egypte/IFAO, 1933–1961), 114.

22. Joyce Tyldesley, *Daughters of Isis: Women of Ancient Egypt*. (London: Penguin Books, 1994) 173–174.

23. Emma Brunner-Traut, *Der Tanz im alten Ägypten. Traut Nach bildichen und inschriftlichen Zeugnissen*. (Glückstadt, Germany: J.J. Augustin, 1938) p. 44–5.

24. Joyce Tyldesley, *Daughters of Isis*, 126.
25. Tyldesley, *Daughters*, 127; and "All female dinner band," (after Davies, N. de G, 1963) *Private Tombs at Thebes: Scenes from Private Tombs*. Vol. 4. Oxford: Oxford University Press, Plate 6. (hand drawing copied from that source).
26. *Ibid.*, 128.
27. Patricia Spencer "Dance in Ancient Egypt," *Near Eastern Archaeology*. 66 3 (September 2003) 111-21.
28. Joshua J. Marks, "Festivals in Ancient Egypt," *Ancient History Encyclopedia*. (Last modified March 17, 2017) https://www.ancient.eu/article/1032/.
29. Marks, "Festivals."
30. Irena Lexová, "Costumes of the Ancient Egyptian Women and Men Dancers," *Ancient Egyptian Dancers*, K. Haltmar, trans. (Mineola, New York: Dover Publications 2000) (originally published Prague: Oriental Institute, 1935) 10; Gayle Kassing "Dances of Ancient Egypt," *History of Dance: An Interactive Arts Approach, Human Kinetics*. (2007) p. 46.
31. Lexová, "Costumes," 11. She indicates they aren't shown accompanied to music here, but accompany themselves.
32. Sarah B. Pomeroy, *Women in Hellenistic Egypt from Alexander to Cleopatra* (Detroit: Wayne State Press, 1990 originally published in 1984), 60.
33. *Ibid.*, 142-143.
34. Habib Hassan Touma, *Music of the Arabs*. Trans. Laurie Schwarts (Portland: Amadeus Press, 1996) 2.
35. *Ibid.*, 2-3.
36. *Ibid.*, 4-7.
37. The use of the *maqamat* is well described for classical Arabic music as a theoretical system in Johnny Farraj and Sami Abu Shumays, *Inside Arabic Music: Arabic Maqam, Performance and Theory in the Twentieth Century*. (New York: Oxford University Press, 2019); for the medieval period see: Henry George Farmer, *A History of Arabian Music to the XIII Century*. (London: Luzac and Co. 1929). As I was revising this chapter, I was taking a *maqam* course with Sami Abu Shumays, which is once again emphasizing the high regard for these forms of music.
38. Huda Lutfi, "Manners and Customs of Fourteenth Century Cairene Women: Female Anarchy versus Male Shar'i Order in Prescriptive Texts," in Nikki Keddie and Beth Baron, eds. *Women in Middle Eastern History* (New Haven: Yale University Press, 1993) 101-102.
39. Leila Ahmed, *Women and Gender in Islam: Historical Roots of a Modern Debate* (New Haven and London: Yale University Press, 1992) 116, 119.
40. Ahmad 'Abd ar-Raziq, *La femme au temps des mamlouks en Égypte* (Cairo: Institut français d'archéologie orientale du Caire, 1973) 68.
41. Leila Ahmed, *Women and Gender in Islam*, 119.
42. J.C. Burget, "Love, Lust and Longing: Eroticism in Early Islam as Reflected in Literary Sources" in Afaf Lutfi al-Sayyid Marsot, ed. *Society and the Sexes in Medieval Islam*. Sixth Giorgio Levi Della Vida Biennial Conference (Malibu, CA: Undena Publications, 1979) 103-104.
43. Margot Badran, *Feminists, Islam and Nation: Gender and the Making of Modern Egypt* (Princeton: Princeton University Press, 1994) 89.
44. This word was also in use in rural Upper Egypt in the late 1920s for the receiving or reception room, somewhat similar to the *mudhafa* of rural Syria. Winifred S. Blackman, *The Fellahin of Upper Egypt* (Cairo: American University in Cairo Press, 2000) (originally published by George G. Harrap and Co. Ltd. 1927), Glossary.
45. Gabriel Baer, *Egyptian Guilds in Modern Times* (Jerusalem: Israel Oriental Society, 1964) 32, 33, 43.
46. Sophie Lane-Poole, *An Englishwoman in Egypt: Letters from Cairo written during a residence there in 1845-46*. Second Series (London. Charles Knight and Co. 1846). 96 in Kathleen W. Fraser, "Public and Private Entertainment at a Royal Egyptian Wedding: 1845." *Best of Habibi*, Vol. 19, No. 1 (February 2002) http://thebestofhabibi.com/vol-19-no-1-feb-2002/royal-egyptian-wedding/.
47. Fraser, "Public and Private."
48. Heather D. Ward, *Egyptian Belly Dance in Transition: The Raqs Sharqi Revolution* (Jefferson, NC: McFarland, 2018) 96.
49. *Descriptions de l'Égypte, ou Recueil des observations et des recherches qui ont été faites en Égypte pendant l'expédition de l'armée française. Publié par les ordres de Sa Majesté l'empereur Napoléon le Grand*. (Paris: Imprimerie impériale, [1809-1828]). From 1812, 109; and see Fraser, *Before They Were Belly Dancers: European Accounts of Female Entertainers in Egypt, 1760-1870*. (Jefferson, NC: McFarland, 2015) 67.
50. Guillaume Villoteau, "*De l'état actuel de l'art musical en Égypte, ou Rélation historique et descriptive des Recherches et Observations faites sur la musique en ce pays.*" In *Descriptions de l'Égypte*, État Moderne, Vol. 1 (1809), 694-697.
51. Kathleen W. Fraser, *Before They Were Belly Dancers*, 229.
52. Saad El-Khadem, *al-Raqs al-sha'bi*. (Cairo: Egyptian General Book Organization, 1972) 60-68.
53. Fraser, *Before They Were Belly Dancers*, 232.
54. Nidhal Mamduh, "Ta'araf 'ala asbab nafi Muhammad 'Ali ghawazi Sunbat ila Sa'id." *Dostor.org* (June 7, 2017). https://www.dostor.org/1384264?fbclid=IwAR15o2q5DgCoG9L6-cNX-_5lGNyGCyBLY76rm3dZ0OJXEjZ1Z51QsNWChYs.
55. Najwa Adra, "Belly Dance: An Urban Folk Dance Genre," In Anthony Shay and Barbara Sellers-Young, eds., *Belly Dance: Orientalism, and Transnationalism and Harem Fantasy*. (Costa Mesa: Mazda, 2005), 44; and cited in Ward, *Egyptian Belly Dance in Transition*, 109.
56. Gustave Flaubert, *Flaubert in Egypt. A Sensibility on Tour*. Francis Steegmuller, Trans. and ed. (New York: Penguin, 1972) 118.
57. *Ibid.*, 116.
58. *Ibid.*, 115-119.

59. These were not exclusively in this field, by any means; an *iltizam* could be set up over crop-producing land (hence the translation of 'tax-farm') or other kinds of properties.

60. 'Abd al-Rahman Al-Jabarti, *Napoleon in Egypt: Al Jabarti's Chronicle of the French Occupation*. Trans. Shmuel Moreh. Introduction by Robert Tignor (Princeton: Markus Weiner, 2004) 26.

61. *Ibid.*, 27.

62. *Ibid.*, 28–29.

63. A copy of which was fortuitously held at the University of California, Los Angeles at UCLA where I was a graduate student.

64. Jeffrey Charles Burke, "The Role of the 'Ulama During the French Rule of Egypt 1798–1801." Master's thesis. McGill University (1992).

65. Niqula El-Turk, *Histoire de l'expédition française en Egypte, publiée et traduite par M. Desgranges aîné* (Paris: Imprimerie Royale, 1839) 65, 76.

66. El-Turk, *Histoire de l'expédition française en Egypte*, 173, 204.

67. 'Abd al-Rahman al-Jabarti's History of Egypt. *'Aja'ib al-Athar fi 'l-Tarajim wa 'l-Akhbar*, edited by Thomas Philipp and Moshe Perlmann (Stuttgart: Franz Steiner Verlag, Stuttgart, 1994) vol. 3, 252; and discussed in Evgeniya Prusskaya, "Arab Chronicles as A Source for Studying Bonaparte's Expedition to Egypt," *Napoléonica. La Revue*, 3: no. 24 (2015) 48–60.

68. *Ibid.*, 253.

69. Khaled Fahmy, "Prostitution in Egypt in the Nineteenth Century," in Eugene Rogan, ed., *Outside In: On the Margins of the Middle East*. (London: I.B. Tauris, 2001) 77–103. 79; Judith Tucker, *Women in Nineteenth Century Egypt*. (Cambridge UK and New York: Cambridge University Press 1985) 150. Prostitution remained legal but with different rules for women of various nationalities until 1949.

70. Juan Cole wrote that the French "periodically made war on the prostitutes" in a vain effort to prevent "the plague." *Napoleon's Egypt: Invading the Middle East*. (New York: Palgrave Macmillan 2007) 235, and he describes the plagues' ravages (235–23), but not this mass drowning.

71. Suggesting the women drowned were prostitutes, but not *ghawazi* is Ivor, "Did Napoleon Really Behead 400 Ghawazee?," n.d. http://www.shira.net/about/400ghawazee.htm; Kathleen Fraser rejects the story as being myth, at some length (disputing even Galland's account because he does not mention the number of four hundred were killed, or that they were beheaded). Fraser, *Before They Were Belly Dancers*, 151–157. Ultimately, she also sketches a framework in which great anxiety over female dancers' behavior is expressed in the policies of the following period, when they were banned from Cairo.

72. "All the public women caught in relationships with the French were put into sacks and thrown into the water." A. Galland, *Tableau de l'Égypte pendant le séjour de l'armée française*. (Au depot de Code civil officiel, libraire de la Palais du Tribunal, 1804, Tome 1) 171–172; André Raymond, *Égyptiens et Français au Caire 1798–1801* (Cairo: Institut Francais d'Archéologie Orientale 1998) 303; Hanan Hammad and Francesca Biancani, "Prostitution in Cairo," in Magaly Rodríguez García, Lex Heerma van Voss, Elise van Nederveen Meerkerk eds., *Selling Sex in the City: A Global History of Prostitution 1600s–2000s*. (Leiden: Brill, 2017) 240.

73. Leila Ahmed "Feminism and Feminist Movements in the Middle East," in Azizah Hibri, *Women and Islam* (Oxford: Pergamon Press, 1982) 154.

74. Mona Mikhail, "Revisiting the Theater in Egypt: An Overview," in Sherifa Zuhur, ed. *Colors of Enchantment: Theater, Dance, Music and the Visual Arts of the Middle East*. (Cairo: American University in Cairo, 2001) 17.

75. His tribe, the Banu Hilal, left Yemen for the Hijaz, fought in the early wars of the Muslims, and then moved to Egypt, where the ruler urged them to conquer Tunisia. Abu Zayd, a great fighter, was a black baby born to white parents. He subsequently almost killed his father in battle. A different version of the story explains that his mother became infertile after bearing a daughter, and fed couscous to the birds to ask one to intercede with Allah to give her a child. A crow first landed on the food, and then her son was born black, but with white features. Caroline Stone, "The Great Migration of the Bani Hilal," *Aramco World*. (November/December 2016). https://www.aramcoworld.com/Articles/November-2016/The-Great-Migration-of-the-Bani-Hilal.

76. Stone, "The Great Migration of the Bani Hilal."

77. Some dancers were able to avoid its effects by appeal or by paying bribes according to Fraser, *Before They Were Belly Dancers*, 162.

78. Khaled Fahmy, *All the Pasha's Men: Mehmed Ali, His Army and the Making of Modern Egypt* (Cairo: American University in Cairo Press, 2002, 2nd edit. 2010) 230, 231.

79. Fahmy, *All the Pasha's Men*, 221–229. Clot Bey wrote about his efforts in *Risala min mashurat al-sihha ila hukama' al-jihadiyya* (A treatise from the Health Council to the physicians of the army. [Cairo: 1835]).

80. Khaled Fahmy, "Women, Medicine and Power in Nineteenth Century Egypt" in Lila Abu-Lughod, ed. *Remaking Women: Feminism and Modernity in the Middle East* (Princeton: Princeton University Press, 1998) 35–72.

81. Fahmy, *All the Pasha's Men*, 230.

82. Nidhal Mamduh, "Ta'araf 'alay asbab nafi Muhammad 'Ali Pasha" (here refers to Widad as being Sunbati *ghawazi* from the tribe which conquered Egypt from Gaza). This might explain why locals in Sonbat claim that this group had relocated from Upper Egypt.

83. Fraser, *Before They Were Belly Dancers*, 247.

84. Stavros Stavrou Karayanni, *Dancing Fear and Desire: Race, Sexuality, and Imperial Politics in Middle Eastern Dance* (Waterloo: Wilfrid Laurier University Press, 2004) 85–87.

85. Gerard de Nerval, *The Women of Cairo: Scenes of Life in the Orient* (London: Routledge, 1929) in Karayanni, *Dancing Fear and Desire*, 91.

86. For two centuries their counterparts in Istanbul, the *köçekler,* were very popular. These were young men dressed as women; they were subject to a ban in 1857.

87. Combes (1846) 220 as cited in Fraser, *Before They Were Belly Dancers,* 128.

88. Liat Kozma, "Wandering About as She Pleases: Prostitutes, Adolescent Girls and Female Slaves in Cairo's Public Space 1850–1882," *Hawwa, Journal of Women in the Middle East and the Islamic World,* 10 (2012) 23.

89. Photo from Akram al-Rayyes.

90. Fahmy, *Ordinary Egyptia*ns, 89.

91. *Ibid*, 95–96.

92. Judith Tucker, *Women in Nineteenth Century Egypt* (Cambridge: Cambridge University Press, 1985) 144–145.

93. Liat Kozma, "Wandering About as She Pleases," 18, 19.

94. *Ibid.*, 23.

95. This uprising was led by and named after Colonel Ahmed 'Urabi. It aimed to depose the Khedive Tawfiq Pasha and curtail British and French influence over Egypt.

96. Ziad Fahmy, *Ordinary Egyptians: Creating the Modern Nation through Popular Culture* (Stanford: Stanford University Press, 2011) 50–51.

97. Fahmy, *Ordinary Egyptians,* 42, 43.

98. Omar D. Foda, "The Pyramid and the Crown: The Egyptian Beer Industry from 1897 to 1963." *International Journal of Middle East Studies,* 46: 1 (February 2014) 146.

99. *Ibid.*, 144.

100. *Ibid.*

101. Muhammad al-Muwaylihi, *Hadith 'Isa ibn Hisham* translated as *A Period of Time,* trans. Roger M.A. Allen (Reading, U.K.: Middle East Centre, 1992) 329.

102. Adam Mestyan, "Power and Music in Cairo: Azbakiyya," *Urban History* Vol. 40, Issue 4, 2013, 687.

103. *Ibid.*, 687–688.

104. A *dawr* (plural *adwar*) is a musical vocal genre sung through the 1920s which could be sung in classical or colloquial Arabic and was often ornamented with *ahat*—singing on the syllable "ah" as a sigh. *Adwar* from this now "classical" period are still performed in concerts of "heritage" music or at the International Festival of Arabic Music.

105. Amira Noshokaty, "Cairo Cafes: A Century of Music and Coffee." *Al-Ahram Online,* May 29, 2014.

106. "Shafiqa al-Qibtiyya: al-raqasah allati shribt khuyulha shampanya," *al-Kawakib,* January, 1955 (available at al-Bostah.com April 7, 2012) http://www.bostah.com/%D8%B4%D9%81%D9%8A%D9%82%D8%A9-%D8%A7%D9%84%D9%82%D8%A8%D8%B7%D9%8A%D8%A9-%D8%A7%D9%84%D8%B1%D8%A7%D9%82%D8%B5%D8%A9-%D8%A7%D9%84%D8%AA%D9%8A--%D8%B4%D8%B1%D8%A8%D8%AA-%D8%AE%D9%8A%D9%88%D9%84%D9%87%D8%A7-%D8%A7%D9%84%D8%B4%D9%85%D8 8%A8%D8%A7%D9%86%D9%8A%D8%A7.html To those who consider *al-Kawakib* or el-Nemr to be insufficiently academic sources, it is the practice in history to draw on reasonable information in print media and from those knowledgeable in the field where scholarly books or articles are unavailable or do not cover the topic in question.

107. Heather D. Ward, "Desperately Seeking Shafiqa: The Search for Shafiqa al-Qibtiyya." *Gilded Serpent.* http://www.gildedserpent.com/cms/2013/10/03/nisaa-desperately-seeking-shafiqa/#axzz54mUJvqdK.

108. Fraser, citing Edward William Lane, *An Account of the Manners and Customs of the Modern Egyptians.* (The Hague and New York: East-West Publications, [1895] 1978) 423–424 in *Before They Were Belly Dancers,* 113.

109. *Ibid.*, 424 in Fraser, *Before,* 113–114.

110. Huda Shaarawi, *Harem Years: The Memoirs of an Egyptian Feminist.* Trans. M. Badran (New York: Feminist Press, 1987) 57.

111. Fraser, *Before,* 114.

112. Fraser, *Before,* 61.

113. Documented by Karin van Nieuwkerk who found the list of terms which Kahle collected in 1926–1927. I heard some of these in use in the early 1980s, mostly by *awlad al-kar* (those who grew up in the entertainment profession) and a few other entertainers. In fact, one told a joke at my expense, and upon hearing responses in *sim,* I insisted on knowing what these unfamiliar words meant. *Sim al-sagha* (referred to as *sin* in areas outside Egypt) is used by silver and gold sellers, money changers, drug dealers, but the entertainers' slang or *argot* is used by musicians, dancers, the [Q]*aragoz* and there is a variant used by homosexuals. It was influenced by gypsies (writes van Nieuwkerk, but more precisely it seems to come from the Banu Sasan) and has some Italian words in it as well, and inversions: *furti* meaning hurry up, *saluti* to say good bye, *biano,* slow or shut up; *rafah* or *bilbil* means *farah* (party); instead of *badla* one says *labda; rahamiya* for *haramiyya, amraz/amaruz* means to flirt, or express interest in; *tashnib* as discussed above, a way of behaving which forces the person to tip the performer or if the band leader tells the dancer to go out for tips; *taknish* is stealing the tips by hiding them in the costume; *ammeh* means to stop (as in "Stop talking, be silent!"). Van Nieuwkerk, "Secret Communication and Marginality. The Case of Egyptian Entertainers" *Sharqiyat* 10:1 (1998) 27–41 and *"A Trade Like Any Other": Female Dancers and Singers in Egypt* (Austin: University of Texas Press, 1995) 97–101. Entertainers elsewhere in the Middle East also used a secret language linked to their profession, and allege that its origins are 'gypsy,' i.e., tribal. Kristina Richardson, "Tracing a Gypsy Mixed Language through Medieval and Early Modern Arabic and Persian Literature," *Der Islam,* vol. 94, no. 1 (2017) 115–157.

114. Frédéric Lagrange, "Women in the Singing Business," 228.

115. Ratiba al-Hifni, *al-Sultana Munira al-*

Mahdiyya: *Wa al-ghina' fi Misr qablaha wa fi zamaniha* (Cairo: Dar al-Shuruq, 1968) 86–87. There is also a 2001 edition.

116. Sherifa Zuhur, ed. *Colors of Enchantment*, 1.

117. Ali Jihad Racy, *Making Music in the Arab World: The Culture and Artistry of Tarab* (Cambridge: Cambridge University Press, 2003) 4.

118. Ali C. Gedik, *Made in Turkey: Studies in Popular Music* (London: Routledge, 2018.)

Chapter Two

1. Faruq Yusuf Iskandar, "Bamba Kashar" as translated by Priscilla Adum. *Al-Qahira*. No date or issue number is given and the website provided is no longer active. In English at Shira.net, http://www.shira.net/about/bamba-kashar-alkahira.htm. Also see Faruq Yusuf Iskandar, "Faruq Iskandar yiktib Bamba Kashar usturat al-raqs al-sharqi," *Misr al-Mahrusa*, January 31, 2012 http://www.misrelmahrosa.gov.eg/NewsD.aspx?id=1406. Another description says that she studied at al-Azhar, sang *anashid,* and was descended from a Seljuk ruler. Because her father was blind, she accompanied him to many gatherings and weddings and loved singing and dancing even more. This material seems lifted from a written source, but is unidentified. "Bamba Kashar's Rise." At *Pharounic*, the website of Sameh El Dessouki, http://www.sameh-pharaounic.com/en/shkola/istoriya-egipetskogo-tantsa/bamba-kasar-s-rise.php.

2. Iskandar, "Bamba Kashar."

3. Heather D. Ward, *Egyptian Belly Dance in Transition: The Raqs Sharqi Revolution* (Jefferson, NC: McFarland, 2018) 56–57.

4. Ward, *Egyptian Belly Dance in Transition*, 58.

5. *Al-Zuhur*, November 1913, 359–360. No author is listed, but this is presumably "Al-Raqs al-misri."

6. Francesca Biancani, *Sex Work in Colonial Egypt: Women, Modernity and the Global Economy* (London and New York: I.B. Tauris, 2018) 77–80.

7. Margot Badran, *Feminists, Islam and Nation: Gender and the Making of Modern Egypt* (Princeton: Princeton University Press, 1994) 189.

8. Alissa Douer, *Egypt—The Lost Homeland: Exodus from Egypt, 1947–1967: The History of the Jews in Egypt, 1540 BCE to 1967 CE*. Translated by Karin Hanta-Davis. (Berlin: Logos Verlag Berlin, 2015) 80.

9. Yunan Labib Rizk, "Al-Ahram, A Diwan of Contemporary Life, 252," *Al-Ahram Weekly Online* Issue 396, September 24–30, 1998. http://weekly.ahram.org.eg/Archive/1998/396/chrncls.htm.

10. Nabila Ramdani, "Women in the 1919 Egyptian Revolution: From Feminist Awakening to Nationalist Political Activism," *Journal of International Women's Studies*, Vol. 14. Issue 2 (March 2013) 46–47.

11. Afaf Lutfi al-Sayyid Marsot, "The Revolutionary Gentlewomen in Egypt," in Lois Beck and Nikki Keddie, *Women in the Muslim World* (Cambridge: Harvard University Press, 1978) 261–276.

12. It is not absolutely certain where she was born. She was raised by her older sister, as they had lost their parents. Ratiba al-Hifni wrote that she was born in the village of Mahdiyya which is in Sharqiyya governorate. Fakhri Haghani states that she was born in "Mahdiyya" Syria in "The New Woman of the Interwar Period: Performance, Identity and Performative Act of Everyday Life in Egypt and Iran." *Al-Ra'ida*. Issue 122–123 (Summer-Fall 2008) 38. This is either a misunderstanding of al-Hifni or a mistake.

13. Frédéric Lagrange, "Munira al-Mahdiyya (1)"Min al-Tarikh," Arab Music Archiving and Research Foundation (AMAR) in collaboration with the Sharjah Art Foundation http://sharjahart.org/sharjah-art-foundation/web-radio/rawdat-al-bababel/muniira-al-mahdiyya-1.

14. Walid Badran, "Sex, Drugs, and Alcohol: A History of Drugs in Egyptian Songs." *Raseef*. 22, January 2, 2017. https://raseef22.com/en/2017/02/01/sex-drugs-alcohol-history-debauchery-egyptian-songs/.

15. Ziad Fahmy, *Ordinary Egyptians: Creating the Modern Nation through Popular Culture* (Stanford: Stanford University Press, 2011) 113.

16. "Munira al-Mahdiyya," Arab Music Archiving and Research Foundation (AMAR) http://www.amar-foundation.org/munira-al-mahdiyya/.

17. Mustafa Said and Frédéric Lagrange define and discuss vocal style through examples throughout 4 episodes on Munira, "Min al-Tarikh," "Munira al-Mahdiyya" 1–4, AMAR Foundation.

18. Mustafa Said with Frédéric Lagrange in "Min al-Tarikh," "Munira al-Mahdiyya 2," August 20, 2015, Amar Foundation, http://www.amar-foundation.org/125-munira-al-mahdiyya-2/.

19. Virginia Danielson, "Artists and Entrepreneurs: Female Singers in Cairo in the 1920s," in Nikki Keddie and Beth Baron, eds., *Women in Middle Eastern History: Shifting Boundaries in Sex and Gend*er (New Haven: Yale University Press, 1991) 296.

20. Fahmy, *Ordinary Egyptians*, 113–114.

21. Negar Azimi, "A Life Reconstructed: A Lost Musical Legacy Finds Its Voice in Cairo. *Bidoun* (Fall 2004) https://www.bidoun.org/articles/a-life-reconstructed.

22. Fahmy, *Ordinary Egyptians*, 123.

23. "This Afternoon," *al-Afkar* (February 23, 1917) cited by Fahmy, *Ordinary Egyptian*s, 123.

24. Biancani, *Sex Work in Colonial Egypt*, 119.

25. Ziad Fahmy, *Ordinary Egyptians*, 159.

26. Ibid., 160–166.

27. Badi'a al-Masabni, Bi qalam Nazik Basila. *Mudhakirrat Badi'a al-Masabni* (Beirut: Maktabat al-Hayat, 1960) 278.

28. Layla Rostom, "Interview of Badia Masabni," *Nugum 'ala al-Ardh*, 1966. https://www.youtube.com/watch?v=8yBO4TELvqQ Available in English on Shira.net http://www.shira.net/about/badia-interview-1966.htm.

29. For a detailed look at al-Kassar's insights and portrayal of nationalism and discrimination, see Eve Trout-Powell, "Burnt-Cork Nationalism: Race and

Identity in the Theater of Ali al-Kassar," in Sherifa Zuhur, ed., *Colors of Enchantment: Theater, Dance, Music and the Visual Arts of the Middle East* (Cairo: American University in Cairo Press, 2001) 13–26.

30. Fahmy, *Ordinary Egyptians*, 130.

31. Layla Rostum, "Interview of Badi'a Masabni." *Nugum 'ala al-Ardh*, (1966) https://www.youtube.com/watch?v=8yBO4TELvqQ Available in English on Shira.net as "Badia Masabni in 1966 Television Interview," http://www.shira.net/about/Badi'-a-interview-1966.htm and per costuming, see the section subtitled in English "Badia Sings."

32. Ibid., in the section "Family."

33. Ibid., regarding her situation in Lebanon late in her life, "More Thoughts on Marriage."

34. Ward, *Egyptian Belly Dance in Transition* 58–62, and 63–64.

35. Her grandfather's circus was well known. Her grandmother was Miriam al-Masriyya and her uncle was Ibrahim 'Akif, the choreographer. Fatma (c. 1926–c. 2007) and her husband Isma'il (known as Gilli Gilli) did an act in the '60s and '70s at the Bagdad Supper Club in San Francisco, where she danced and he drummed, managed, did magic tricks, and "barked" (brought in customers). She balanced on water glasses, balanced a goblet and a *sham'adan* on her head, did the splits, and her parrot was part of this theatrical act; she talked to it as she balanced it on her cane. Her day job was a hotel maid. Information from Amina Goodyear, and from my own interactions with Fatma as we both worked with Fatma. Fatma was more formally interviewed by Katherine Zirbel in an effort to trace "Banat Mariam," the female relatives of Fatma's grandmother and reveal how thoroughly separated she was from her family in Egypt. Katherine Elizabeth Zirbel, "Musical Discursions: Spectacle, Experience and Political Economy." Ph.D. dissertation, University of Michigan (1999) 342–349.

36. "Casino Badia's Dance Troupe." Available at http://www.shira.net/about/Badi'a-group-and-stage-names.htm.

37. Randa Ali, "Feyrouz, Child Prodigy Forever," *Mada Masr*, February 6, 2016. https://madamasr.com/en/2016/02/06/feature/culture/feyrouz-child-prodigy-forever/.

38. Walter Armbrust, *Mass Culture and Modernism in Egypt* (New York: Cambridge University Press, 1996) 73–75.

39. Deborah Hunter, "Playing for Peace: Meeting with Nabil Azzam." *Habibi*, Vol. 15, No. 3 (Summer 1996) archived at *The Best of Habibi* http://thebestofhabibi.com/vol-15-no-3-summer-1996/nabil-azzam/ also see Nabil Salim Azzam, "Muhammad 'Abd al-Wahhab in Modern Egyptian Music." Ph.D. dissertation, University of California, Los Angeles, 1990.

40. Amira Noshokaty, "'Toha' Chanteuse of Egypt and Levant." *Ahram Online,* December 5, 2014.

41. Sherifa Zuhur, *Asmahan's Secrets: Woman, War and Song* (Austin, Texas: Center for Middle Eastern Studies, UT/University of Texas Press, 2000 and London: Al-Saqi Publications, 2001).

42. Sherifa Zuhur, "Musical Stardom and Male Romance: Farid al-Atrash," in S. Zuhur, ed., *Colors of Enchantment: Visual and Performing Arts of the Middle East* (Cairo: American University in Cairo Press, 2001).

43. Layla Rostum, "Badi'a Masabni." https://www.youtube.com/watch?v=8yBO4TELvqQ Available in English on Shira.net http://www.shira.net/about/Badi'a-interview-1966.htm.

44. Rostum, "Badi'a Masabni."

45. Omar D. Foda, "The Pyramid and the Crown: The Egyptian Beer Industry from 1897 to 1963." *International Journal of Middle East Studies.* 46: 1 (February 2014) 146.

46. Foda, "The Pyramid and the Crown," 152.

47. Foda, "The Pyramid and the Crown," 151, based here on van Nieuwkerk, *A Trade Like Any Other,* 43–35.

48. Lagrange, "Women in the Singing Business," 228.

49. In contemporary parlance, this means any female singer, but originally it meant a talented and dedicated vocalist who was capable of repertoire beyond the *taqtuqa*.

50. Ibid., 229–245.

51. "Yousef al-Sharif Discusses Zouba al-Klobtiyya," From *Al-Masri al-Youm*, May 2, 2009 Available at: http://www.shira.net/about/zouba-el-klobatiyya.htm.

52. Rostum, *"Badi'a Masabni,"* See the section "Western Influences" in the translation.

53. Salwa El-Shawan Castelo-Branco, "Radio and Musical Life in Egypt," *Revista de Musicología* Vol. 16, No. 3, Del XV Congreso de la Sociedad Internacional de Musicología: Culturas Musicales Del Mediterráneo y sus Ramificaciones: Vol. 3 (1993)1232–1234.

54. Sherifa Zuhur, "Les divas sur grand écran," in *Divas arabes—D'Oum Kalthoum à Dalida*, Paris: Editions Skira/Institut du monde arabe, 2021.

55. Barry Iverson, "Van Leo: Master of Lights and Shadows." *Photorientalist*. n.d. Abridged from *The Life of Cairo Master Photographer Van Leo.* http://www.photorientalist.org/exhibitions/van-leo-master-lights-shadows/article/.

56. Nabawiya Mustafa in *Nargis* (1948) https://vimeo.com/134365475?fbclid=IwAR1G1dOHl-dYeEcduFVo4iiQVIjxK0W808lviumzPPK9sjEAIdpkKaLJOgw.

57. Nabawiya Mustafa in *Ibn al-Falah* (1948) https://vimeo.com/239928366.

58. Shareen El Safi, "An Uncommon Woman: Nagwa Fouad, Queen of Oriental Dance," *Best of Habibi*. Vol. 18, No. 3 (March 2001). http://thebestofhabibi.com/vol-18-no-3-march-2001/nagwa-fouad/ I personally performed with Nagwa Fu'ad at a number of private parties with Samir Sabry in 1980–81, and saw her regular hotel shows in those years, observing her extremely hard work on stage.

59. Souheir Sami, "Nagwa Fouad: Hours of Glory," *Al-Ahram Weekly* Issue 390. August 13–19, 1998. http://weekly.ahram.org.eg/Archive/1998/390/people.htm.

60. The party then moved to the Auberge Nightclub. It was attended by Suhair Zaki, Zizi Mustafa, Muhammad al-'Izabi, Su'ad Husni, Sherihan ('Omar Khurshid's sister), and many other stars of Egypt's music and cinema scene. Courtesy of Hytham M. Hammer who knew 'Omar Khurshid and his family.

61. I was able to see her performances over a range of years, in 1973, worked with her in 1980-'81, 1988, and finally in the early 1990s. I also saw Suhair's, 'Azza's, and many other dancers' performances including one of Samia Gamal's. I enlisted male friends to take me, or persuaded girlfriends to come with me performances since I could not attend alone; they were relatively patient with my comments analyzing movements and interactions in the show.

62. Safa Azeb, "Nagwa Fu'ad to Majalla," *Majalla*, August 16, 2019. https://eng.majalla.com/node/75141/nagwa-fouad-to-majalla-i-did-not-know-who-henry-kissinger-was-when-he-proposed-to-me.if.

63. Paul Schemm and Sebastian Abbot, "Cairo's Nightclubs Relics of Bygone Era." *SF Gate* (from Associated Press). December 14, 2008. https://www.sfgate.com/news/article/Cairo-s-nightclubs-relics-of-bygone-era-3258319.php.

64. Foda, "The Pyramid and the Crown." In researching the life of the singer, Asmahan, Amal al-Atrash, I learned that she, her brother Farid al-Atrash, and numerous other entertainers drank alcohol, but the advent of Islamism began to discourage greater numbers of Egyptians from drinking. Others do not drink simply being more conservative Muslims (although not Islamist).

65. Daniel Williams, "Making a Comeback: Male Belly Dancers in Egypt," *New York Times*, Jan 2, 2008.

66. Stavros Stavrou Karayanni, "Tito Seif: The Moment of Eternal Shimmy." *Gilded Serpent*, n.d. but circa 2008. http://www.gildedserpent.com/art44/stavrostito.htm.

67. Others based outside of Egypt are excluded here like Mohamed El Hosseny, although Khaled Mahmoud moved to London.

68. From an interview of Amie Sultan, March 5, 2017 quoted in Christine M. Sahin, "Core Connections: A Contemporary Cairo Raqs Sharqi Ethnography." Ph.D. dissertation. University of California, Riverside, 2018, 93.

69. Mariam Nader, dir. "*Fi Baladi*." (There is Balady) 2019.

Chapter Three

1. Judith Butler, *Gender Trouble: Feminism and the Subversion of Identity* (London: Routledge,1990) 7.

2. Sherifa Zuhur, *Revealing Reveiling: Islamist Gender Ideology in Contemporary Egypt* (Albany, New York: State University of New York Press, 1992.) Reprinted 1996.

3. Because sex is considered a vital part of marriage and a woman could obtain a divorce if her husband denied her sex, people may speak rather openly about sex. This contrasts with the Victorian prudishness about sex, which affected marriage in the West until quite some decades later.

4. Their numbers have increased, but landlords and neighbors are still suspicious of single women.

5. Karin Van Nieuwkerk, *Manhood Is Not Easy: Egyptian Masculinities through the Life of Sayyid Henkish* (Cairo: American University in Cairo Press, 2019), 96, 97–98, 100, 114.

6. Women who support, or partially support, themselves are far from uncommon, yet mainstream thinking about gender roles marginalizes them. Not exclusive to Egypt, this idea was addressed quite thoroughly by Dutch anthropologist Willy Jansen in *Women without Men: Gender and Marginality in An Algerian Town* (Leiden: E.J. Brill, 1987). She describes the stigma attached to wage earning and women who must make their own living and are widowed, divorced, orphaned, or whose male family members are absent, and specifically the occupations of bathhouse personnel, washers of the dead, healers, sorcerers, prostitutes and courtesans, those who assist in births, custodians, industrial workers, politicians, and professionals.

7. Coptic Orthodox couples also have a betrothal ceremony. They give each other rings which have their partner's name engraved on it. In some areas of Egypt, the church has required Coptic women intending to marry to undergo virginity tests.

8. Samuli Schielke, *Egypt in the Future Tense: Hope, Frustration and Ambivalence before and after 2011* (Bloomington: Indiana University Press, 2015) 41.

9. *Ibid.*, 90.

10. Sherifa Zuhur, "Mixed Impact of Feminist Struggles in Egypt during the 1990s," *Middle East Review of International Affairs Journal*, Vol.5, No.1 (March 2001).

11. All of this information and the social groups' perceptions of each other is described in great detail in Sausan El Messiri, *Ibn al-Balad: A Concept of Egyptian Identity* (Leiden: Brill, 1978).

12. Karin Van Nieuwkerk, *Manhood is Not Easy*, 76.

13. She recorded two albums. The first was *Fulklur Sha'bi*, Sono Cairo, 7017043, 1970; the second was *Sahra ma'a ahdath al-mutriba Laila Nazmi*, Sono Cairo 87–77037, 1977, and twenty-one singles.

14. Laila Nazmi's "Ma Ashrabsh Shay," https://www.youtube.com/watch?v=Tf_JJqK2Y1U or here in "al-Bey al-Bandari," https://youtu.be/RMOXTeEcJYE.

15. Samia Nasser, "Iraqi Ra'qisah's Life in America." *Gilded Serpent.com*, May 20, 2011 http://www.gildedserpent.com/cms/2011/05/20/samia-nasser-iraqi-dancer/.

16. "Najwa Fouad 1974 Fuad Najwa," *TheClassicCarovan*, https://vimeo.com/187521454.

17. Marwa's version of "Ma Ashrabsh Shay" https://www.youtube.com/watch?v=ZKzxsLysHak.

18. Scroll in *Lailat Hinna* to about :27, "Katy" *TheCaroVan*. From *TheClassicCarovan*. https://thecarovan.com/category/katy-1927-1980/.

19. "Hayatim Egyptian Belly Dancer Dancemeacademy." Posted on April 11, 2011. https://www.youtube.com/watch?v=G7Gkc7LAm2s&feature=youtu.be.

20. They appear on the stage at the wedding scene after the general greetings to the wedding attendees are delivered at 25:28. *Al-Darb al-Ahmar*, Dir. 'Abd al-Fatah Madbouli (1980) https://www.youtube.com/watch?v=-DVypbpQbNM.

21. "Tatiana Eshta, Ghazal al-Darb al-Ahmar Improvisation." 2013. https://www.youtube.com/watch?v=rSDsMmqUngM.

22. "Lylia Bourbia, Ya Ghazal al-Darb al-Ahmar." Eilat Festival, 2019 https://www.youtube.com/watch?v=AVyQCwF50ow.

23. "1 Place Shaabi Ya Ghazal al-Darb al-Ahmar, Cairo Mirage" 2018 https://www.youtube.com/watch?v=S3G8PiIT2es.

24. "Fallahat Baladna" in the film, *al-Qahira fi al-layl* as sung by Karim Mahmud. https://www.youtube.com/watch?v=TtaVBh15nMU.

25. Here in 1976 in the film *The Beauty and the Scoundrel* https://www.youtube.com/watch?v=ZyXPeUuUSss And here to "Agadan Alkak," https://www.youtube.com/watch?v=hP47dllH3Qg.

26. Note Nelly's smooth yet complicated style here: "Nelly Fouad." https://vimeo.com/104373596 (from the Shwaya Balady series); also an example of *dall'a* here: "Nelly Egyptian Belly Dancer ¼" (recorded from television) https://www.youtube.com/watch?v=DIUtpdPPj9M.

27. "Badia Masabni, 1934 performing at the Casino Badia," Presented to Gilded Serpent by Jalilah via al-Hamy Hassan. https://www.youtube.com/watch?v=26V9iOEw1co&t=4s.

28. Her glamorous costume is car-wash sequin strips showing her legs in lamé wedge heels, and yet she has a veil on her head, which she removes leaving a circular headpiece. https://vimeo.com/103208800.

29. "Sah al-Num" (1975) https://vimeo.com/129307082 This was removed from the site when I last checked. Unfortunately, this occurs with frequency on websites and YouTube.

30. Morocco, "Nadia Hamdi Giving Joy to the Heart and Eyes," *Habibi*, Vol. 15, No. 2 (Spring 1996) available at Casbahdance.org https://www.casbahdance.org/giving-joy-to-the-heart-and-eyes/.

31. "Nadia Hamdi in America" 1995. Provided by Aswan Dancers and Amina Goodyear to Gilded Serpent. https://www.youtube.com/watch?v=p5ZRxcb9uuI.

32. "Nadia in America." 1995. As recorded by Amina Goodyear.

33. Private video from performance following a workshop: "Cairo in San Francisco. Sahra and Members of the Sahra Show on Tour from Egypt. "Baha'i Center, San Francisco, May 4, 1996.

34. "Dandash" Published in 2008. https://www.youtube.com/watch?v=fHQzjW7u7VA.

35. "Howaida al-Hashem." (as transliterated on this site) Published August 8, 2011. (https://www.youtube.com/watch?v=mdvPip7csNs&fbclid=-IwAR3-d2z_fjmyng4eVD0Sb_AMjSuk6l1fWTQ20HW0kEqaKCXpjT3vNm_rnR0.

36. "Howaida Hachem." Recorded from television and published in 2015. https://www.dailymotion.com/video/x301hsu?fbclid=IwAR0w_VNprPMjXaAjWu9Nuhl8oD2H7BBW5ro0cw3FDirZaxCD1bgGXO53Rb4.

37. Mustafa Marie, "ET (Egypt Today) Commemorates Birth Anniversary of Samia Gamal." *Egypt Today*, March 5, 2019 https://www.egypttoday.com/Article/4/66678/ET-commemorates-birth-anniversary-of-Samia-Gamal.

38. "Samia Gamal, Egyptian Belly Dancer" Published October 28, 2006. https://www.youtube.com/watch?v=DJNHfmETiVk.

39. Fouad Muawad, "Samia Gamal, a Dancer Who Believes the Middle Ground is Best," *Kawakib*, 1968, republished at *Akadimia al-Funun*, 2010 http://egyptartsacademy.kenanaonline.com/topics/58701/posts/149210 and translated by Priscilla Adum on Shira.Dotnet http://www.shira.net/about/samia-gamal-1968-interview-kawakeb.htm.

40. "Shoo Shoo Amin." Clip from film published by Serpentine.org, October 9, 2009. https://www.youtube.com/watch?v=aEHzDX_GLF8.

41. Fifi 'Abdu to "Ya Ma'allima" with a *malaya laff* in "Fifi 'Abdo, Cane, Melaya" https://www.youtube.com/watch?v=h5TB9p8m5dU&feature=youtu.be.

42. "Azza Sherif at Paradis, Pyramids Street, Cairo '83" Footage from Morocco from 1983. Published January 30, 2010. https://www.youtube.com/watch?v=hwv_NCnKqzU.

43. "Azza Sherif" Part 1, published September 16, 2008. https://www.youtube.com/watch?v=WWB7CzuLsw4.

44. *Cairo Unveiled*, Part I, National Geographic Explorer, dir. Karen Goodman and Kirk Simon, https://www.youtube.com/watch?v=V950x1OhpoI.

45. *Cairo Unveiled*, Part II, National Geographic Explorer https://www.youtube.com/watch?v=kp52dgmvhEo.

46. "Egyptian Bellydancer Lucy, Nubian and Drum Solo, Pariziana, 2008." The first part is to the song "So ya so, habibi habba so," popularized by Mohamed Munir in 2001. https://www.youtube.com/watch?v=tTDHRcFkZZw.

47. "Tadmir Kazinu wa malha layla al-fannana Lucy" *Storm.com* February 10, 2011 available at web.archive.org. https://web.archive.org/web/20110308003938/http://www.urstorm.com/vb/t15692.html.

48. Many of the first group of "new style" Egyptian musicians who performed in Florida, then in Los Angeles and San Francisco, subsequently traveled to London to work with her at Omar Khayyam. As well, this clip includes Reda Darwish on bongos. https://www.youtube.com/watch?v=R1dqyznoX2A.

49. "Egyptian Belly Dancer Mona El Said—Tabla Solo in London, 1970s," Prince Kayammar Oriental Dance published June 21, 2015. https://www.youtube.com/watch?v=JuF_A5qA16g.

50. Shareen El Safi, "Mona El Said: Moving in

Mysterious Ways," *Habibi*, Vol. 15, No. 1 (Winter 1996). http://thebestofhabibi.com/vol-15-no-1-winter-1996/mona-el-said/.

51. Mona Saʻid. "Mona Black Gold Baladi Taksim." https://www.youtube.com/watch?v=gtPuZ2dsgho&feature=youtu.be&fbclid=IwAR3J2qK-L_5nYrPrYgCU19FBr8vhHpoY6mDdtDToE3MuGZOtu-BNk38uqrE.

52. Shown here at the Marriott in a Madame Abla costume with an opening by Wahba Hassan in 1988. "Aida Nour at Marriott '88." Published February 18, 2009. https://www.youtube.com/watch?v=ooyhBfk1WNA.

53. ʻAmir was born Samar Ahmad ʻAbd al-Ghaffar, in 1990 in Alexandria, and is the sister of actress Wafaʼ ʻAmir. She has appeared in about a dozen films and television series.

54. "Suq al-Banat," https://www.youtube.com/watch?v=sgLEwFWee0E This is labeled Mahmud al-Hussaini, but it is Laithy's song.

55. Here watch for her facial expressions as well as the pops and shimmies. "Ahla raqs maʻa Sofinar (Sofinaz)," Published October 15, 2018. https://www.youtube.com/watch?v=kbYM3vrNlX4.

56. "Belly Dancer Dina from Early Career on Film," published April 26, 2011. https://www.youtube.com/watch?v=kSUeC2UdSv4&fbclid=-IwAR0t7e-z03oboLz-8jV6D6Zb9rUq_kewuglvOvbSioEDZqn7OpcYR0Nfpg8.

57. "Fifi ʻAbdou, Cane and Malayya." Circa, 1973. Published August 10, 2009. https://www.youtube.com/watch?v=h5TB9p8m5dU&feature=youtu.be.

58. "Gu Lounge," Posted by Hassan Elkholaky on Instagram, March 22, 2019. https://www.instagram.com/p/BvVRmdxHktg/?fbclid=IwAR0DHYHNPeRR7VUL1cGqrvb0CfRRU3BIyhhglgvmG9Dsup911vpXWxfVfS0.

59. Sahin contrasts Camelia's show and personal statements (47) with her observations of Randa Kamel's (155) and with Farah Nasri (157, 171–173) who even jiggles her breasts on men's heads, pulled up women and men from the audience to dance, and subverted efforts by male audience members to hold her. Christine M. Sahin, "Core Connections: A Contemporary Cairo Raqs Sharqi Ethnography," Ph.D. dissertation, University of California, Riverside, 2018.

60. "Raqs al-ughniya nar Dominique Hourani "al-Wad Hadoʼa." Published November 29, 2015. https://www.youtube.com/watch?v=3ifJunoYmT0&feature=youtu.be.

61. Scene from *al-Azwag al-Shayateen* (1977) https://thecarovan.com/2016/01/22/nahed-sherif-1977-%D9%86%D8%A7%D9%87%D8%AF-%D8%B4%D8%B1%D9%8A%D9%81/.

62. "Sahar Hamdi, 1992" Dancing to "Si Abdo." Scene from *al-Mushaghibun fi-Nuwayba*, 1992. TheClassicCaroVan. Published 2015. https://vimeo.com/110043920.

63. "Sama al-Masry, "Ahmad al-shibshib, dhaʼ." Arabic Music TV. Published December 27, 2017. https://www.youtube.com/watch?v=URtGMKjp40U.

64. Dareen, "Darren" [sic] 2015. https://www.youtube.com/watch?feature=youtu.be&v=jaf-k6oynK8&fbclid=IwAR0G4ywgf3h0HeVgawuj3dFEknLiDMpD8ZV57gg-FVwb9yjqw65UbChMxOI&app=desktop.

65. Dareen, 2016. The videographers have not listed her name: https://www.youtube.com/watch?v=hQXdNh5qDYU&feature=share&fbclid=-IwAR2d1sF_f7TVhzAG6ctE9oWCaT2aYSjCEX1cy7WoY2mO6BZKKUk-DU1qyGE.

66. Sabah, "Ya Dalaa Dallaa," (Farid al-Atrash) Voice of Lebanon—VL 2180, 1973. This song was used for dancers around the world, following its release well into the 1990s, but not in the musical *raqs sharqi* compositions coming from Egypt.

67. She asked for people to dance *dabka* at her funeral, and they did. https://www.youtube.com/watch?v=dz5U_q2t0Mo.

68. In the Lebanese accent, ʻ*kel*' is for *kull* (all).

69. Sherine Bou Saʻd, Youssef Hassan, wa Leen al-Hayak, "Ya Dallʻa" marhala al-muwajih, *MBC* "The Voice Kids," published February 20, 2016. https://www.youtube.com/watch?v=-rjJT-1cZok.

70. Johnny Farraj and Sami Abu Shumays, *Inside Arabic Music: Arabic Maqam, Performance and Theory in the Twentieth Century* (New York: Oxford University Press, 2019) 380.

71. Amina Goodyear uses the term "*dallʻa*" to refer to songs which include a male-female interaction through lyrics designed for a male singer and female singer or chorus, but useful as this is to communicate the feeling to American dancers, I believe the repertoire of *dallʻa* is broader.

72. "Ahmed Adaweia, Ya Zaid fe al-halawa" Karakashangy, published April 13, 2014 https://www.youtube.com/watch?v=fSmObFWQD74&feature=youtu.be The song appears on the same audio cassette *Adawiyya 77* as "Mit ful wa ʻashara" (on side 1).

73. Thomas Burkhalter, Kay Dickinson, and Benjamin J. Harbert, eds. *The Arab Avant-Garde: Music, Politics, Modernity* (Wesleyan: 2013). http://www.magisterseniusu.com/uploads/1/8/0/0/1800340/_music_culture__thomas_burkhalter_kay_dickinson_benjamin_j._harbert-the_arab_avant-garde__music_politics_modernity-wesleyan__2013_.pdf.

74. Personal interview with Nidaa Abou Mrad, Beirut, 2003.

75. Randa Jarrar, "Why I Can't Stand White Belly Dancers." *Salon.com*. March 5, 2014. https://www.salon.com/2014/03/04/why_i_cant_stand_white_belly_dancers/.

76. To "*amaruz*" pertains to smiling, looking or talking to customers, and earning more money by pleasing them. As customers may try to arrange rendezvous, the performers use their secret language to describe these interactions and may not admit they are ongoing. Karin van Nieuwerk, "*A Trade Like Any Other*": *Female Singers and Dancers in Egypt* (Austin: University of Texas Press, 1995) 98–99.

Chapter Four

1. This chapter was developed from "*Mulid*: Regenerating Spiritual and Popular Legitimacy in Egyptian Music and Dance and the Sister Genres of *Sha'bi* and *Mahragan*." Presented at the World Congress for Middle East Studies, Seville, Spain, July 19, 2018. Appears in *Pakistan Journal of Historical Studies*, Vol. 4, Nos 1–2 (Summer–Winter 2019) 35–54. I also presented "Mulid and Mahragan: Invoking Spirituality and Popular Authenticity in Egyptian Music and Dance, at the Association for the Study of the Middle East and Africa, September 15, 2018.

2. Harvard Divinity School. "Sufism in Egypt." Religious Literary Project. FAQ. n.d. https://rlp.hds.harvard.edu/faq/sufism-egypt.

3. Kristin Deasy, "The Sufi's Choice: Egypt's Political Wild Card," *World Affairs*, Vol. 175, No. 3 (September/October 2012) 45–52.

4. *Shafa'a* means intercession. Sherifa Zuhur, "Intercession in Middle Eastern Society" in Maryanne Cline Horowitz, ed. *New Dictionary of the History of Ideas*. 6 vols. New York: Charles Scribner and Sons, 2005.

5. Sarah El Masry, "Sufi Islam in Egypt," *Daily News Egypt*, October 21, 2012. https://ww.dailynewssegypt.com/2012/10/21/sufi-islam-in-egypt/.

6. Described at length by Michael Frishkopf, "Tarab ('enchantment') in the Mystic Sufi Chant of Egypt," in Sherifa Zuhur ed. *Colors of Enchantment: Theater, Dance, Music, and the Visual Arts of the Middle East* (Cairo: The American University in Cairo Press, 200) pp. 233–269.

7. (Syracuse: Syracuse University Press, 2012).

8. During the most crowded night of the *mulid*, the *laila al-kabira*, a *dhikr* is held all night. In the *mulid* of Sayyid al-Badawi held after the cotton harvest, a morning procession is led by the order's *khalifa* (Caliph) riding a horse. The *mulid* was completed by the time of *juma'a* (Friday noon) prayer.

9. This relates to a *hadith* Qudsi (the direct words of Allah) about Allah: "I was a Hidden treasure and I loved to be known and so I created the creation," and which is cited in numerous descriptions of the *mawalid*.

10. Anna Madoeuf, "Mulids of Cairo: Sufi Guilds, Popular Celebrations and the 'Roller-Coaster Landscape' of the Resignified City," in Diane Singerman and Paul Amar, eds. *Cairo Cosmopolitan: Politics, Culture and Urban Space in the New Globalized Middle East* (Cairo: American University in Cairo Press, 2006) 72.

11. Somewhat similar to the Moroccan *fantasias* but usually moving through a town.

12. Schielke, "Perils," 57.

13. Asef Bayat, *Life as Politics: How Ordinary People Change the Middle East* (Stanford, CA: Stanford University Press, 2010) 131.

14. Baher Ibrahim, "Salafi Intolerance Threatens Sufis," *Guardian*, May 10, 2010. https://www.theguardian.com/commentisfree/belief/2010/may/10/islam-sufi-salafi-egypt-religion.

15. Samuli Schielke, *Egypt in the Future Tense: Hope, Frustration and Ambivalence before and after 2011* (Bloomington: Indiana University Press, 2015) 129–139.

16. The Muslim Brotherhood, usually referred to as the *Ikhwan* in Arabic, was banned in the 1940s and was made illegal once again following an assassination attempt on Gamal abd al-Nasser in 1954.

17. Jennifer Peterson, "Remixing Songs, Remaking MULIDS: The Merging Spaces of Dance Music and Saint Festivals in Egypt," in Samuli Schielke and G. Stauthe, eds. Dimensions of Locality, Muslim Saints, Their Place and Space. *Yearbook of the Sociology of Islam,* 8, Bielefeld, Transcript Verlag (2008) 75; Also see *Electro Chaabi*. Directed by Hind Meddeb. 2013.

18. Maria Golia, *Cairo: City of Sand* (London: Reaktion Books, 2004) 169–170.

19. Ali Jihad Racy, *Making Music in the Arab World: The Culture and Artistry of Tarab* (Cambridge: Cambridge University Press, 2003), 121.

20. *Tarab* was explained in Chapter One as being both a process and esteemed quality in Arabic music and the repertoire similar to that in Egypt and the Arab East before World War I. However as will be explained in Chapter Eight, it may now be used to refer to music composed as late as the 1970s, though previously it often meant music composed and played prior to the 1940s.

21. Frishkopf, "'Tarab.'"

22. Nicolaas H. Biegman, *Egypt: Moulids, Saints, Sufis* (London: Kegan Paul International, 1990) 165.

23. Biegman, *Egypt*, illustration 95.

24. Or *khushniyin*, as described by Sayyid Henkish, "merchants or others from outside the trade who weren't obliged to give tips," (84) or who used to "sell fruit" and who began organizing parties and weddings (107) Karin van Nieuwkerk, *Manhood is Not Easy: Egyptian Masculinities through the Life of Sayyid Henkish* (Cairo: American University in Cairo Press, 2019) 84, 107.

25. Karin van Nieuwkerk, "Secret Communication and Marginality. The Case of Egyptian Entertainers," *Sharqiyat* 10:1 (1998) 27–41.

26. Sayed Mahmoud, "Into the World of Moulid: Director Sameh Abdelaziz on His New Film El-Leila El-Kebira," *Al-Ahram Online*, November 19 2015. http://english.ahram.org.eg/NewsContent/5/32/169043/Arts--Culture/Film/-Into-the-world-of-Moulid-Director-Sameh-Abdelaziz.aspx.

27. Ziad Elmarsafy, *Sufism in the Contemporary Arabic Novel* (Edinburgh: Edinburgh University Press, 2012) 14.

28. Directed by Samir Seif and written by Mohammed Galal and Abdel Qawi starring 'Adil Imam, Youssra and Amina Rizk. *Al Mouled* DSRIP Published July 10, 2013. https://www.youtube.com/watch?v=ZgqPnAa7eFs&list=PLvYo2Onecc8UScAP5dxgSrsX2ik3hU27m.

29. The Lebanese singer, Wadi' al-Safi sang this on film, addressing/flirting with the daughter of singing star Sabah, and also the Oriental dancer

who performs throughout the clip. https://www.youtube.com/watch?v=H4nN5P1O48M.

30. Hamada al-Laithy and Russian Armenian *raqs sharqi* star Safinaz (Sofinar Grigoryan) in "Film Qashshah 'Ala Rimsh 'Ayyun," Hamada Laithy, New Century Production, published May 5, 2014. https://www.youtube.com/watch?v=RD3A7obUh74.

31. Patrick A. Desplat and Dorothea A. Schulz, eds. *Prayer in the City: The Making of Muslim Sacred Places and Urban Life* (Bielefeld, Germany: Transcript, Verlag, 2012).

32. See for example, Jonathan Pieslak, "Al Qaida Culture and Anashid," in Pieslak, *Radicalism and Music: An Introduction to the Music Cultures of al-Qa'ida, Racist Skinheads, Christian-Affiliated Radicals and Eco-Animal Rights Militants* (Middletown, CT: Wesleyan University Press, 2015) 14–44.

33. "From Mosque to Marquee." Mo4 Network, https://www.youtube.com/watch?v=Hd4zxdwr_X0 and see: "Na'alna al-fann dah min al-masagid-lil-masrah: Hiwar ma' al-firqat al-hadhra lil-inshad." *Elfasla.com*, (at Go Daddy last accessed June 12, 2018, http://elfasla.com/ArtsAndCulture/interview-with-al-hadraa-band.

34. Peterson, "Remixing Songs, Remaking Mulids," 75.

35. As James Grippo had described for the *sha'bi* star, Ahmad 'Adawiyya, see "What's Not on Egyptian Television and Radio: Locating the 'Popular' in Egyptian Shaabi," in Michael Frishkopf, ed. *Music and Media in the Arab World* (Cairo: American University in Cairo Press, 2010) 143. This might be true only for some singers of modern romantic singers, but is not often the case for those singing Western styles with Arabic lyrics.

36. Jennifer Peterson, "Sampling Folklore: The Repopularization of Sufi Inshad in Egyptian Dance Music," *Arab Media and Society*. January 27, 2008. https://www.arabmediasociety.com/sampling-folklore-the-re-popularization-of-sufi-inshad-in-egyptian-dance-music/.

37. Male singers of *mulid* have popularized it, but there are strong female *sha'bi* singers like Fatme Sarhan (her style is often classified as *baladi* and *Sa'idi*). She begins with a traditional format of a *sha'bi mawwal* here and sings for the super dancer Dina. "Dina and Fatma Serhan," Published May 15, 2009. https://www.youtube.com/watch?v=FRaNHnurW-s.

38. Karin van Nieuwkerk, "Female Entertainers in Egypt: Drinking and Gender Roles," in Demitra Gefou-Madianou, ed. *Alcohol, Gender and Culture* (London and London: Routledge, 1992).

39. Katherine Elizabeth Zirbel, "Musical Discursions: Spectacle, Experience and Political Economy." Ph.D. dissertation, University of Michigan, 1999, 156.

40. Karin van Nieuwkerk, "Changing Images and Shifting Identities of Female Performers in Egypt," in Sherifa Zuhur, *Images of Enchantment: Visual and Performing Arts of the Middle East* (Cairo: American University in Cairo Press, 1998).

41. Zirbel, "Musical Discursions," 158.

42. Peterson explains that due to being banned, the tape on which "al-Mulid" was included became a best seller, commanding a higher price on the black market. It was banned because a *shaykh* objected to a certain phrase, and the song was re-produced without it. Jennifer Peterson, "Playing with Spirituality: The Adoption of Mulid Motifs in Egyptian Dance Music," *Contemporary Islam*. 2: No. 3 (2008) 281.

43. Peterson, "Playing with Spirituality," The lyrics follow.

44. Peterson, "Sampling Folklore."

45. al-Laithy, "Inti Dinya." https://www.youtube.com/watch?v=XmZBcrWKCI4.

46. Koen Van Eynde, "Mohamed 'el-Limby' Saad and the Popularization of a Masculine Code." *Networking Knowledge*: Journal of the MeCCSA Postgraduate Network, Vol. 4, No. 1 (2011); Imam Hamam, "Disarticulating Arab Popular Culture: The Case of Egyptian Comedies" in Tarik Sabry, ed. *Arab Cultural Studies: Mapping the Field* (London: I.B. Tauris, 2012).

47. José Sánchez Garcia, "De las celebraciones para los santos a la mulid dance music: Utopía y juventud en Egipto," *Trans*. 14 (2010). https://www.sibetrans.com/trans/article/24/de-las-celebraciones-para-los-santos-a-la-mulid-dance-music-utop-a-y-juventud-en-egipto.

48. Personal interview with Fahed Ballan, Suwayda, Syria, September 1993.

49. "Ughniya Flus, Mahmud al-Laithy min Film Kabareh," El Sobky Production, Published November 24, 2012. https://www.youtube.com/watch?v=KsxT4stvcpE.

50. The Arabian Knightz is an Egyptian hip-hop trio of Rush (Karim 'Adil), Sphinx (Hisham Abed), and E-Money (Ehab 'Adil). "Arabian Knightz—Al Donia Mouled Mahmoud ElLeithy" Production ClubWreckers, published August 20, 2012. https://www.youtube.com/watch?v=eNFl0wy7BRU.

51. Directed by Sameh Abdelaziz. "Mahmoud El-Leithy, Mulid Sidna al-Husayn," Film *al-Laila al-Kabira*, El Sobky Production, published June 19, 2016, https://www.youtube.com/watch?v=PeJW15m7mqY&feature=youtu.be.

52. The filmed version of "Sai'di ya Ra's" was posted at: https://www.youtube.com/watch?v=Gc1Lo7gTuCU (last accessed June 2018). The recording company had blocked the film from YouTube. An audio-only version is available here: "Mahmud il Lithy, Saedy" Published September 11, 2018, https://www.youtube.com/watch?v=DmtcC39oaAU.

53. Peterson, "Playing with Spirituality" also cited in Garcia, "De las celebraciones para los santos."

54. Peterson "Remixing Songs," 127; Presented as history and choreography, Sherifa Zuhur, "Mulid Moods and Moves," San Francisco, October 28–29, 2017; see also Sherifa Zuhur, "Mulid and Mahragan: Invoking Spirituality and Popular Authenticity in Egyptian Music and Dance, Presented to the Association for the Study of the Middle East and North Africa, September 15, 2018, 9.

55. The lyrics describe injustice:

Kan fi-d-dunya fituwwat
There were thugs on earth
Biyu'ulu: "ihna ahsan nas"
who said they were the best people
Sabahum ramadun, ya khuya
They became ashes, my brother
Widahwisuh 'alayhum in-nas
People stepped on them

Listen to the words of our Lord the beloved
That he said to all people
Eternal heaven is entered by people
Who contain their anger and forgive people

56. https://www.youtube.com/watch?v=Yt5P60-J6EQ.
57. Peterson, "Sampling Folklore."
58. Amira El-Azhary Sonbol, *The New Mamluks: Egyptian Society and Modern Feudalism* (Syracuse: Syracuse University Press, 2000) xxix.
59. Sonbol, *The New Mamluks*, xxii.
60. Ziad Fahmy, *Ordinary Egyptians: Creating the Modern Nation through Popular Culture* (Stanford: Stanford University Press, 2011) 120.
61. Peterson, "Sampling Folklore."
62. Peterson, to her credit, cites Ali Jihad Racy on this point; Racy, "Musical Aesthetics in Present-Day Cairo." *Ethnomusicology* 26/3 (1982), 391.
63. The lyrics continue:

I was helping all people and love good for them
I became humiliated and many people betrayed me

(Refrain) What if the dice has been rolled and conditions changes
I may take the first step to become millionaire
I would go to the first one I asked him for what I needed
He disappointed me and made me feel the need
I'll do the right thing and help him in time of distress
I'll assist him in ordeals and will be patient
and I will be patient

Life was neglected and I never keep a cent
Life was neglected and I never keep a cent

Whatever I wished, it lost
What's my fault to be sorrowful for weeks
I got tired of moving constantly and not finding a stable place
I lived a naive life and did not get anything from life
and who will take anything
All of us will leave and die

(Refrain repeats)

64. "Ughniya Hakim Halawat Ruh—kamila—min film "Halawat Ruh"—Haifa Wahbe." El Sobky Productions. Published April 13, 2014. https://www.youtube.com/watch?v=Hd4zxdwr_X0.
65. With 227,817,737 hits and this is not the only version mounted: "Ahmad Shiba Ah law la'bat zahr—wa al-raqisa Alla Kushnir," El Sobky Productions. Published January 27, 2016. https://www.youtube.com/watch?v=0I9-NJZ8Vxk&feature=youtu.be.
66. Miriam Elba, "It's Crowded and There is No Mercy!" Khabar Keslan. *DISORIENT*. Issue 1 (August 28, 2017).
67. Was available at https://www.youtube.com/watch?v=cdVqmpn91kU in July 2018 and has been removed.
68. Peterson, "Sampling Folklore."
69. The intervening lyrics are:

They asked me what happened to me. I smoked a brown cigarette
(Chorus: brown, brown).
I felt my head splitting. I'm sitting in the street and falling (dazed)
(Chorus: falling. Falling), And the laundry hung out to dry was dripping on me.
And the street was in back of me and in front of me (repeats)
And the words were on the tip of my tongue.
I started to speak but my words were messed up. (Chorus: Messed up)
Oh uncle, light it up! O sir, light it up!
Ku ka ku ka ku ka (Chorus: Ku ka) (repeats this section)
Go, go, go, go, go, go (4 times) Light it up, uncle (music).
I smoked another cigarette and I forgot my name for a second (repeats).
And I asked (Chorus: I asked) I asked (Chorus: I asked)
I asked where is the door of our home? They told me this isn't yours. (repeat)
They kicked me out, and made me go out. (twice)
They kicked me out and told me to go, I wish they hadn't made me smoke (twice)
It dazed me and made me tired (twice)
Oh uncle light it up! Oh sir light it up.
Ku ka ku ka ku ka (Chorus: Ku ka) Go, go, go, go, go
Wala *yaba* (light it up dad!)
This story's finished. Don't bring it up again.
Leave me to live my life and that's enough of this story (twice)
Mush hashrab! I won't smoke (Chorus: Aha)
I won't smoke (Chorus: Aha)
I won't smoke anything brown. I'll know it when I see it again.
Oh uncle light it up. O sir, this is too much. Ku ka ku ka ku ka.

https://www.youtube.com/watch?v=MsdDdhAxQxs
70. "*Hashrab hashish*," Luka Blue. http://beehy.pe/luka-blue-hashrab-hashish-egypt/.
71. Requisite modesty and observation of segregation of the sexes in Egypt differs from puritanism.
72. https://www.youtube.com/watch?v=mhs3y8b2IGk&feature=youtu.be.
73. A key feature of all *sha'bi* forms.
74. As interviewed by Peterson in Imbaba (an area of Cairo) 25 April 2007 when he was 28 years old.
75. Mahmud al-Lithy, "Inta ya inta," ElWadyMusicRecords. Published May 21, 2013. https://www.youtube.com/watch?v=M7OspTogDM0.
76. The lyrics have been sung quite differently by the romantic pop singers Adam, Kadhim al-Sahir and Ghada al-Rajab, and by as-Sahir and al-Rajab together here: "Kadhim al-Sahir wa Ghada al-Rajab, 'Ib'ad 'anni ya ibn al-nas." Alaa Alaa, Published December 7, 2013. https://www.youtube.com/watch?v=Kbo4wWph3MI.
77. "Ughniya "Ib'ad 'anni," Hassan al-Radad, Mahmud al-Laithy, Amy Samir, Aytin 'Amir, Mayy Salim. El Sobky Production, Published March 19, 2015. https://www.youtube.com/watch?v=JvslJkOzxv0.

Chapter Five

1. As this book concerns Egypt, I limit the discussion to Egyptian *sha'bi*; there are Algerian, Iraqi, Tunisian, Libyan, Moroccan, and other national variants of *sha'bi* music, generally referring as well to music and dance of the common people, rural or urban.

2. A friend, the late pianist and music critic Selim Sednaoui, frequently reviewed or wrote about music in *Ahram Hebdomodaire* (in French). See Selim Sednaoui, "Western Classical Music in Umm Kulthum's Country," in Sherifa Zuhur, ed. *Images of Enchantment, Images of Enchantment: Visual and Performing Arts of the Middle East* (Cairo: American University in Cairo Press, 1998) 123–134.

3. Oka and Ortega, "Lissah hanghani: mahragan "Hatti bosa ya bit" ghina' Oka wa Ortega wa Shahta Karika," published May 16, 2013. https://www.youtube.com/watch?v=xsGQaT6RhxQ.

4. 'Abd al-'Aziz Mahmud sings a more classically-tinged ballad which yet invokes the traditional girl, "Ya Labsa Tarha" (O you who wear the long scarf), as many dancers perform with *sham'adan* on their heads in this scene from *Khulud*, 1948, starring Fatin Hamama. The dancer without a *sham'adan* is Huda Shams al-Din. Notice that the costumes aim to represent those worn around or before the turn of the century with the ribbon skirt and vest. https://vimeo.com/channels/882356/108696972.

5. "Ah min gamal 'ayyun." https://www.youtube.com/watch?v=Fv0AvBKOHk0.

6. James R. Grippo, "What's Not on Egyptian Television and Radio: Locating the 'Popular' in Egyptian Shaabi," in Michael Frishkopf, ed. *Music and Media in the Arab World* (Cairo: American University in Cairo Press, 2010) 147–148.

7. Sayed Mahmoud, "Singing in the Shadow." *Al-Ahram Weekly Online*, 16–22 October, 2008. http://weekly.ahram.org.eg/Archive/2008/918/sc2.htm.

8. Dwight Reynolds, "Interplay of Genres in Oral Epic Performance: Differentially Marked Discourse in a Northern Egyptian Tradition," in Joseph Harris, ed., *The Ballad and Oral Literature* (Cambridge, MA and London: Harvard University Press, 1991) 294–296.

9. Elham Abdel Wahhab al-Mufti, "Shakwa in Arab Poetry during the Abbasid Period." Ph.D. thesis, School of African and Oriental Studies, University of London. 1990.

10. The Conservatory educates musicians in Western and Arabic musical forms. The Higher Institute of Arabic Music was established earlier in 1929 and now includes two musical ensembles. Certain colleges and universities such as Helwan University and American University in Cairo now offer Arabic and Western musical training, but in my earlier years of study and teaching at the AUC, Arabic music was not offered in the Department of Performing and Visual Arts. Indeed, then-Provost Earl Sullivan found it very comical and inappropriate that I and another faculty member, Dr. Suad Joseph, suggested bringing in Prof. A.J. Racy in for a lecture/master class when he visited Cairo.

11. Walter Armbrust, *Mass Culture and Modernism in Egypt* (New York: Cambridge University Press, 1996) 180–181, 185, 196.

12. 'Abd al-Halim Hafiz (1929–1977), described in Chapter Two, was greatly attractive to many Egyptian and Arab women once he attained fame. He sang in a romantic and (at the time) modern style, with lyrics that were sometimes closer in musical feeling to popular folk songs, whereas other elements of his singing suited the long-form song.

13. Youssef Rakha, "Hoarseness: a Legend of Contemporary Cairo," *The White Review* (June 2014). http://www.thewhitereview.org/feature/hoarseness-a-legend-of-contemporary-cairo/.

14. This was a high point of my fieldwork back in 1973, when I tried recording music on an audio recorder in my purse and quickly writing my notes each night. My companion, a Turkish man, was foreign, yet understood Arabic and a fan of Arabic music. The excitement of the audience was palpable.

15. Sayed Mahmoud, "Singing in the Shadow."

16. Sayyid described how with a weakened wedding party market he went to "play with a *nimra*" (playing for dancers who stop in and perform their set, and then leave for another club), but then when another accordionist retired, he was asked to play for the national ensemble Firqat al-Qawmiyya lil-Funun al-Sha'biyya. Karin van Nieuwkerk, *Manhood is Not Easy: Egyptian Masculinities through the Life of Sayyid Henkish* (Cairo: American University in Cairo Press, 2019) 121, 124, 126–129.

17. "Haqiqat ihsa Ahmad 'Adawiyya bi sabab amira Kuwaitiyya." https://www.youtube.com/watch?v=TpNgQNZJncU&feature=youtu.be. Perhaps the sadness in "Bint al-Amir" is due this scenario. "Bint al-Amir," Ahmad 'Adawiyya https://www.youtube.com/watch?v=sGF6n90bQhc&feature=youtu.be.

18. *Wa kulli haga, ba'ayna gharbi/ ma fish malayya, wala sharbi/ wa kull yum moda i-gdida/ hatta al-kalam maba'ash a-'arabi/ a-'arabi, ... nasyin 'a-adatna wa taqalidna.* Sha'bula's song "Ahl al-Tarab" also hilariously criticizes new trends: https://www.youtube.com/watch?v=dV2dHTPRjdU (accessed September 10, 2018).

19. "Wa'fat Nasyat Zaman," Mekky Productions (2017) https://www.youtube.com/watch?v=DjLpLaGPANM (accessed September 10, 2018).

20. Walter Armbrust, *Mass Culture and Modernism in Egypt*, 178–180.

21. Nivin Wihish, "Hakim: From Mohammed Ali Street to Radio City Music Hall," *Al-Ahram Weekly Online* 10–15 October 2002, http://weekly.ahram.org.eg/Archive/2002/607/profile.htm.

22. Ibid.

23. van Nieuwkerk, *Manhood is Not Easy*, 121, 123. I performed at weddings held in five-star hotels, mostly before the decline of the wedding party scene in the musicians' perspective, and at that time, these almost never featured *sha'bi* music, although some musicians in the bands played *sha'bi* music.

24. Carolee Kent and Marjorie Franken, "A Procession through Time: The *Zaffat al-'Arusa* in Three Views," in Sherifa Zuhur, ed., *Images of Enchantment: Visual and Performing Arts of the Middle East* (Cairo: American University in Cairo Press, 1998) 74, 75, 79.

25. Katherine Elizabeth Zirbel, "Musical Discursions: Spectacle, Experience and Political Economy," Ph.D. dissertation, University of Michigan, 1999, 196.

26. Zirbel, "Musical Discursions," 236.

27. *Ibid.*, 237–9.

28. *Ibid.*, 237.

29. Communication in interviews from Cairo, 2020.

30. "Missy Maira Talking about Her Life and Rap in Egypt," 2012 https://www.youtube.com/watch?v=8hWGvW3eyfY or on SoundCloud: https://soundcloud.com/missy-maira-princess/missymaira-talking-about-her-life-rap-in-egypt?in=shahd-shrief-elhify/sets/ntdeutushzbo.

31. "Egypt's First Veiled Rapper," 2013. https://www.youtube.com/watch?v=MZsZaQ5gXMw. Also see "Mayam Mahmud" *Arabs Got Talent* 2013, https://www.youtube.com/watch?v=L1MrA3435Ik.

32. "Liqa' ma'a Basma Galal, al-awwil bint DJ fi Masr, 'ala qanat al-Wasl." Published January 27, 2019. https://www.youtube.com/watch?v=pGO6I1141_o.

33. Ahmad Makky "Naighy al-Mustahil," lyrics by Ashraf Soliman, 2017. https://www.youtube.com/watch?v=51FPig-8QfY.

34. "al-'Inab." https://www.youtube.com/watch?v=RvC9Ldf0SCQ.

35. *Electro Chaabi.*

36. Adel Abdel Ghafar, "Youth Unemployment in Egypt: A Ticking Time Bomb." Markaz. Brookings. July 28, 2016. https://www.brookings.edu/blog/markaz/2016/07/29/youth-unemployment-in-egypt-a-ticking-time-bomb/.

37. "Egypt Completes Demolition of 75% of Maspero Triangle Slums." *Egypt Today.* August 14, 2018.

38. The various paths young men (and a few young women) adopt and their frustrations are examined in Samuli Schielke, *Egypt in the Future Tense: Hope, Frustration and Ambivalence before and after 2011* (Bloomington: Indiana University Press, 2015).

39. As Sadat said when interviewed for Hanan Fayad, "Mahraganat: Egyptian Ghetto Meets Western Electronic," *Egypt Today*, October 9, 2018. https://www.egypttoday.com/Article/4/58662/Mahraganat-Egyptian-ghetto-meets-Western-electronic.

40. El Gezawe, "Dupstep Mahragan," August 2018. https://www.youtube.com/watch?v=r3mUJD4k7LM&feature=share (accessed September 10, 2018).

41. As in "*Aha al-shibshib dha'a,*" roughly, "Fuck, I lost my slipper." http://www.twistmedia.info/save/video/SXhUtIMwX9A/A7a%20El%20Shebsheb%20Daa3%20Youtube.html (accessed September 18, 2018) The song was further satirized by the dancer/actor Sama al-Masry in a 2017 video "*Ahmad al-shibshib dha'a*" (Ahmad, I lost my slipper) See https://www.youtube.com/watch?v=URtGMKjp40U (accessed September 13, 2018) see Chapter Seven.

42. Peter Holslin, "Six Explosive Tracks that Define Mahraganat, Egypt's Wildly Popular Street Music," *Thump / Vice.com* (March 29, 2017). https://thump.vice.com/en_us/article/ezwqke/explosive-mahraganat-egypt (Accessed August 10). Some experimentation with *mahragan* took place as in this collaboration with *nai* solo and trap drums in *Barra Sura* (Outside the Picture) with keyboardist Islam Chipsy at the El Geneina Theater, 2012 https://www.youtube.com/watch?v=wV21eNqOTDg (accessed September 11, 2018).

43. *Saltana* is the feeling of ecstasy resulting from playing or hearing music (but which is not necessarily that defined as '*tarab* music'). The musician/singer concentrates and elaborates so beautifully in the *maqam* (mode), or sings so sensitively, that the listener is swept into *mazag*, and, intoxicated with feeling, experiences *saltana*.

44. As James Grippo had described for Ahmad 'Adawiyya, see "What's Not on Egyptian Television and Radio," 143.

45. Ali Abdel Mohsen, "A Q & A with Leading Mahraganat Singer Sadat," *Egypt Independent* April 13, 2013, http://www.egyptindependent.com/qa-leading-mahraganat-singer-sadat/.

46. Wegz, "21" (Wahda wa 'Ishrin). https://www.youtube.com/watch?v=WwB5w-Rt88k.

47. Sultan Sooud Al Qassemi, "New Arab Hip Hop: Between Love and Rebellion," *Raseef22,* June 16, 2020. https://raseef22.net/article/1078683-new-arab-hip-hop-between-love-and-rebellion?fbclid=IwAR2l1DKzVzZbfmOStdeCMh6-0J56tuP6AgO0utObw5_Os-c6vYgSs4P7A0Y.

48. Ferida Jawad, "Guest Bloggers Around the World: Mahraganat—Musical Revolution in Egypt." Afropop. *PRI.org* June 12, 2014. https://www.pri.org/stories/2014-06-12/guest-bloggers-around-world-mahraganat-musical-revolution-egypt.

49. *Ibid.*

50. Meaning "children of the profession." They claimed to regulate their relatives' behaviors. Guilds had controlled standards of performance, ethics, prices and taxes.

51. Ali Gamal, "The Music Craze with a Dark Side Splitting Opinion in Egypt," *BBC Arabic.* (January 13 2016) https://www.bbc.com/news/world-middle-east-35135699 (accessed August 10, 2018).

52. Ted Swedenburg draws here on Jawad and Bechaouia's descriptions of *mahraganat* fans: Ferida Jawad, "Mahraganat" and see Tarek Adam Benchouia, "Festivals: The Culture and Politics of Mahraganat Music in Egypt" Master's thesis, University of Texas, Austin, 2015 25–27; see Swedenburg, "From Sayed Darwish to MC Sadat: Sonic Cartographies of the Egyptian Uprising," in Valerie J. Hoffman, ed. *Making the New Middle East: Politics, Culture and Human Rights* (Syracuse: Syracuse University Press, 2019) 434–435.

53. Benchouia, "Festivals," 25.

54. *Ibid.*, 26–27.

55. Yousif Nur, "A Radical Century: Mahmoud Refat of 100 Copies Cairo Interviewed." *The Quietus.* December 17, 2014.

56. This verse puns off of the ubiquitous protest chant of the January 11, 2011, revolution *"ash-sha'b yurid isqat an-nizam"* (the people want the end of the regime).

57. DJ Haha and DJ Vigo's song "The People Demand Five Pounds Credit," cited in Ted Swedenberg, "Egypt's Music of Protest From Sayyid Darwish to DJ Haha." *Middle East Report* 265, Vol. 42 (Winter 2012).

58. "DJ Zo'la's Funeral Takes Place in Cairo." *Ahram Online.* 29 January 2015. http://english.ahram.org.eg/NewsContent/5/32/251886/Arts--Culture/Film/Art-Alert-Documentary-on-electrodance-phenomenon-t.aspx.

59. Mohsen, "A Q & A with Leading Mahraganat Singer Sadat." While Sadat is self-conscious of the broader meaning of "political," here, populism and nationalism do not necessarily imply support for the revolutionaries of 2011; some of the *sha'b* supported Mubarak and now support Sisi.

60. The 2012 song "I Just Wish For a President" by 'Amr Haha, Sadat, Figo and 'Ala' 50. https://www.youtube.com/watch?v=BumLRk_ji2k (accessed August 16, 2018).

61. Golia, "Egypt's Mahragan."

62. *"Ahla raqs 'ala mahragan al-makanah Oka wa Ortega,"* (The best dance at the heavy [machine] *mahragan* of Oka and Ortega). 2013. Unidentified dancer. https://www.youtube.com/watch?v=CFB0Y02yE7w.

63. Marwan Menawy, "Egypt Fights a Losing Battle Against Drugs," *Arab News.* February 26, 2018 https://www.arabnews.com/node/1254306/middle-east.

64. "Egyptian Star Mohamed Ramadan Releases New Music Video 'Bum Bum,'" *Ahram Online,* January 1, 2020. http://english.ahram.org.eg/NewsContent/5/33/358752/Arts--Culture/Music/Egyptian-star-Mohamed-Ramadan-releases-new-music-v.aspx.

65. Yara Sameh, "Musicians' Syndicate Bans Mohamed Ramadan, Others from Singing," *Sada El Balad* February 17, 2020. https://see.news/musicians-syndicate-bans-mohamed-ramadan-others-from-singing/ See also Sarah Ramadan, "Legalizing Mahraganat: Recognition vs. Identity Erasure," *AFTE Freedom of Thought and Expression Law Firm,* June 20, 2020. https://afteegypt.org/en/afte_releases/2020/06/20/19282-afteegypt.html.

66. Hysa, Halabesa and Souessi, *"Mahragan Hitta Minni,"* Produced in 2015. https://www.youtube.com/watch?v=RnhKBJzWBaA&list=PLFJ_U7Bp J4h3fDfc6prmXcfff948EzupC&index=9 (accessed June 14, 2019).

67. al-Sawarikh (Dok Dok and Funky) *"La'"* December 2017, https://www.youtube.com/watch?v=xf9s_h8S2XM (accessed July 31, 2018).

68. At 8:08 in this clip from *Electro Chaabi.* Directed by Hind Meddeb. 2013. https://www.youtube.com/watch?v=NHdy8b3dukQ.

69. *Mahragan: The Story of Egypt's Street Dance.* Dir. by Noah Chasek-McFoy (2015). https://vimeo.com/106879244 (trailer) (accessed July 1, 2018).

70. "Street Shaabi Dance Improvisation by Kareem Gad." https://www.youtube.com/watch?v=MHxuV_cPxOc (accessed September 13, 2018).

71. "Mahragan Aywa aywa Shahta Karika, Weza, Ortega, Oka, 8%," Adams4Productions. Published April 24, 2012. https://www.youtube.com/watch?v=zLtyGjBMFHY.

72. "Ahla raqs 'ala al-mahragan al-makana Oka wa Ortega." 2013. https://www.youtube.com/watch?v=CFB0Y02yE7w.

73. Online discussion on Ramadan's "Bum Bum." June 16, 2020.

74. Asef Bayat, *Life as Politics: How Ordinary People Change the Middle East* (Stanford, CA: Stanford University Press, 2010) 14–15.

Chapter Six

1. Farida (Melda) Fahmy, "The Creative Development of Mahmoud Reda, A Contemporary Egyptian Choreographer," Master's thesis. Los Angeles: University of California at Los Angeles, 1987, 24.

2. Anthony Shay, *Choreographic Politics: State Folk Dance Companies, Representation and Power* (Middleton, CT: Wesleyan University Press, 2002) 142–162.

3. Magda Ahmed Abdel Ghaffar Saleh, "A Documentation of the Ethnic Dance Traditions of the Arab Republic of Egypt," Ph.D. dissertation, New York University, 1979.

4. "Magda Saleh Discusses Being Egypt's Iconic Prima Ballerina as She Prepares for From the Horse's Mouth's: A Footnote in Ballet History." *The Dance Enthusiast,* March 13, 2018. https://www.dance-enthusiast.com/features/the-dance-enthusiast-asks/view/Magda-Saleh-Prima-Ballerina-Egypt-Horses-Mouth-Footnote-Ballet-History.

5. Communication from Khaled Sefarat, June 9, 2020.

6. *Music of the Ghawazee.* Recorded at Thebes in 1973 by Aisha Ali, performed by various artists. Araf DA-700. Phonodisc (2 e. 12 in. 33 1/3 rpa.) « Discs Araf; 30Sep73: N11607. N11608.

7. This usage is found in Syria and also in Egypt, see the information from Nawaz Jabri to Edwina Nearing, "Sirat al-Ghawazi" Part 9, 1977 http://www.gildedserpent.com/enearing/edwinaghawazich9.htm. There appears a reference to 32 *ghawazi* coins and a piece of jewelry stolen by a young Misr Spinning and Weaving Company worker from his grandmother (found in court records) saving to fund his male friend/companion's wedding, in Hanan Hammad, *Industrial Sexuality: Gender, Urbanization and Social Transformation in Egypt* (Austin: University of Texas Press, 2016) 170.

8. A feature of the Egyptian dialect of Arabic is that certain consonants can elide to others (and sometimes there is an inversion of consonant order

called metathesis). Therefore, some pronounce Sunbat as Sumbat, whereas in written Arabic it contains the letter 'nun' not 'mim.' An example of metathesis is the use of *guz* and *guzi* (my husband) in Egypt for *zawji* (my husband, from *zawj*, a pair).

9. This village was divided between peasants and Bedouin from the Dirn tribe on the other side of Alexandria. Napoléon dispatched General Verdier to fight the Dirn there after the French had put down a rebellion in Mansura. Juan Cole, *Napoleon's Egypt: Invading the Middle East* (New York: Palgrave Macmillan, 2007) 144. Curiously, the *ghawazi* may have come there from Upper Egypt.

10. Aurel d'Agostino recorded this after visiting the Banat Mazin with Sahra Saeeda, "And Raja Danced," https://www.ancientartstudios.com/and-raja-danced/?v=7516fd43adaa.

11. Whereas in Aleppo, Syria, or Lebanon, the term *nawwar* is vague and very pejorative, referring to the Dom people and their nomadism rather than to a specific tribe, in Egypt the term is used as if it is the name of a tribe by the *ghawazi* and also the singer/poets and musicians of Upper Egypt, who call themselves "gypsy" when touring in Europe.

12. *Music of the Ghawazee.*

13. Giovanni Canova, "Notizie sui Nawar e sugli altri gruppi Zingari presenti in Egitto," La Bisaccia dello Sheikh, Quaderni del Seminorio di Iranistica, Uralo-Altaistica e Causasologia dell' Universita' Degli Studi di Venezia, 19: May 29, 1981, 71–84.

14. Katherine Elizabeth Zirbel, "Musical Discursions: Spectacle, Experience and Political Economy," Ph.D. dissertation, University of Michigan, 1999, 72–78.

15. Edwina Nearing, "Sirat al-Ghawazi," 1985, Part 7 (from 1976) available here: http://www.gildedserpent.com/enearing/edwinaghawazich7.htm.

16. "Song of the Banat Mazin," Nearing "Sirat" Part 8.

17. Su'ad, Tukha and Ferial dancing in the film *al-Zawaj al-Thaniya* (1967). https://vimeo.com/109361887 All the sisters appeared in *Ana al-Duktur* in 1968. https://www.youtube.com/watch?v=tPkPFQURY_8.

18. Edwina Nearing, "Ghawazi on the Edge of Extinction," *Habibi*, Vol. 12, No. 2 (1993) http://thebestofhabibi.com/2-vol-12-no-2-spring-1993/ghawazi/.

19. "Letter from Khairiyya Mazin. The Last of the Ghawazi," 2011 to Edwina Nearing. http://www.aswandancers.org/ghawazee-history.

20. Mahmoud Reda in an interview with Shira, July 31, 2006. http://www.shira.net/about/reda-interview12-other.htm.

21. "Letter from Khairiyya Mazin," 2011.

22. Hanan Hassan Hammad, "Mechanizing People, Localizing Modernity: Industrialization and Social Transformation in Modern Egypt: Mahalla al-Kubra 1910–1958," Ph.D. dissertation. University of Texas at Austin, 2009, 160.

23. Nile Cultural Channel, Episode June 18, 2017, which discussed the history of the form and states it is a sport, not an art form. *Qanat al-Nil Thaqafiyya*, https://www.youtube.com/watch?v=ry0MMnnrOys&feature=youtu.be&fbclid=IwAR1PSJifH5Ew3PJfjHqD0bOBv1DI3LSBBIGLjOwsbs3YdRePNsMxpkrT1g4.

24. Adel Paul Boulad, "Naissance de Modern Tahtib." n.d. circa 2014. http://www.tahtib.com/media%7Carticles%7CNaissance%20de%20Modern%20Tahtib.

25. "Horse Dancing at Mulid Abu al-Qomsan," 2017. https://www.youtube.com/watch?v=ogt5JIc7TnI The band plays a patriotic song at first, then Sa'idi music.

26. "Dancing Horses of the Nile Delta." AP Archive, February 18, 2017. https://www.youtube.com/watch?v=rrAZ7oQtQvM.

27. "Teenager Makes Horse Dance in Egypt." *Voice of America*, 2018. https://www.facebook.com/voiceofamerica/videos/10155914841133074/?v=10155914841133074.

28. Andrea Rugh, *Reveal and Conceal: Dress in Contemporary Egypt* (Syracuse: Syracuse University Press 1986) 18–24.

29. Rugh, *Conceal*, 27–31.

30. Widely believed and discussed in Winifred S. Blackman, *The Fellahin of Upper Egypt* (Cairo: American University in Cairo Press, 2000, originally published by George G. Harrap and Co. Ltd. 1927) 227–239 and elsewhere in her work.

31. Zirbel, "Musical Discursions," 246.

32. Zirbel "Musical Discursions," 245–247.

33. As collected on Awlad Abou El Gheit, *Zar: Trance Music for Women* CD, B000A0ED12 2005, and explained by Yasmin Henkish, *Trance Dancing with the Jinn: The Ancient Art of Contacting Spirits through Ecstatic Dance* (Woodbury, Minnesota: Llewellyn Publications, 2016).

34. Karel Innemée and Yasmine El Dorghamy, "Meet the Masters of the Underworld," *Rawi*, Issue 5 (2013). https://rawi-magazine.com/articles/zaramulets/.

35. Henkish, *Trance Dancing* 268.

36. 'Adel al-'Alimi, *al-Zar wa Masrah al-Tukus* (Cairo: 1993) 136.

37. Nada Deyaa', "Study Reveals Zar Ritual Still Heavily Performed in Egypt." *Daily News Egypt*, June 12, 2018. https://ww.dailynewssegypt.com/2018/06/12/study-reveals-zar-rituals-still-heavily-performed-in-upper-egypt/.

38. "'Ariyat bila Khatiya," *The Classic Caro-Van*. https://www.facebook.com/thecarovan.bellydancevideos/videos/1915998465166935/?comment_id=2398220010389372&notif_id=1560105216113494&notif_t=group_comment_reply.

39. "At the time he was creating dances, Reda didn't really think about why he didn't feel moved to include it in the repertoire. Now, looking back on his career, he begins to analyze the choices he made." In "Origins of Other Reda Troupe Dances. Part 12. Other Dance Notes." Interview with Shira, July 31, 2006. http://www.shira.net/about/reda-interview12-other.htm.

40. Reissued as *The Zar Dance* (DVD) New York: Costodio Productions with Ibrahim Farrah, Bahijah

and Valerie Camille (2007 from 1981); and *American Arabesque* (DVD with Ibrahim Farrah, Bahijah and Valerie Camille) produced by John Costodio, 1981 is about the making of Bayt al-Zar.

41. Iraqi dancer Assala Ibrahim. 2012. https://www.youtube.com/watch?v=rPYsSaUd1iM.

42. *Dhikr*, filmed of the Rifa'i order https://www.youtube.com/watch?v=rgxFf1vI4sM.

43. Mona L. Russell, *Egypt* (Santa Barbara, Denver and Oxford, UK: ABC-Clio, 2013) 339. I saw the group in the first year of their residence at the Ghuri, where the artist Salah Enani was their director from 1988-1996.

44. "Cairo Insider Show at Hassan Saber Show." Filmed by Allegra Pena, January 27, 2013. https://www.youtube.com/watch?v=nO1jYxb469E.

45. Lila Abu Lughod. *Veiled Sentiments: Honor and Poetry in a Bedouin Society* (Berkeley: University of California Press, 1986, 2016).

46. The CaroVan. The lead dancer is Denise Enan. https://thecarovan.com/tag/hagalla/.

47. Hossam Ramzy, Bedouin Tribal Dance, KDX1604, EUCD2047, 2007; Serena Ramzy, Bedouin Tribal Dance: Gypsies of the Nile, DVD, EUDV0012, 743037001250, 2007.

48. Sherifa Zuhur, "Claiming Space for Minorities in Egypt after the Arab Spring" in Moha Ennaji, ed. *Multiculturalism and Democracy in North Africa: Aftermath of the Arab Spring* (London: Routledge, 2014) 254–255.

49. Communication from Hytham M. Hammer.

50. I enjoyed learning and performing certain Nubian-style dances re-choreographed (from years earlier choreography) by Amina Goodyear in 2018–2019 and then learning Nubian musical pieces for violin for an Aswat Ensemble concert in spring 2019.

51. Hammer wrote that he believes *ragada* is the word from which "ragtime" dance derives. Others claim it comes from a syncopated rhythm produced by the right hand (which may not preclude his assertion).

52. As in this dance featuring one woman and four women presented on television, from Daniella's channel, posted 2015, performance likely earlier. https://www.youtube.com/watch?v=ALsd5CcyHKQ.

53. "In a Corner of Cairo This Nubian Group Creates the Sound of Home," *Middle East Eye*, March 17, 2019. https://www.middleeasteye.net/discover/corner-cairo-nubian-group-creates-sound-home Here is the Aragid group performing at Makan in Cairo in 2016 https://www.youtube.com/watch?v=4rwXG_RlwDs.

54. Communication from Hytham M. Hammer.

55. It can also vary in terms of the shape of the base; some have a neck made of goat horn, whereas the '*simsimiyya*' version is made with multiple 'necks' extending to tunable pegs.

56. Hammer says this is "in a manner which is something that's really, uniquely Nubian." I have accompanied a Sudanese singer, Salma al-Assal, who performs something very similar to this format (with Arabic lyrics).

57. Communications from Hytham M. Hammer. I included these detailed descriptions after repeatedly expressing my wish that Hammer should write a book with his detailed knowledge of Arab, Nubian, and Sudanese music. He refused. Also, his style of transliteration differs from mine.

58. According to B., his name isn't in the film credits because his family thought it shameful that he appeared in that role. Communication from B., January, 2020. I am here following the normal procedure of social scientists in protecting the identity of certain interlocutors.

59. Daniel J. Gilman, *Cairo Pop: Youth Music in Contemporary Egypt* (Minneapolis: University of Minnesota Press, 2014) 135, 136–137.

60. Lucy here first in a Nubian interlude and then an "African" inspired drum solo at the Parisiana, 2008. https://www.youtube.com/watch?v=tTDHRcFkZZw.

61. "'Ala Kurnish," https://www.youtube.com/watch?v=osIn9v_9k_I.

62. "Haylouh," https://www.youtube.com/watch?v=QSIhZGV9ms0.

63. Tuija Rinne, "Sing, O Simsimiya." Translated from Finnish "Laula simsimiyya," *Ishtar* (January 2005) available at El Hosseny Dance, http://www.elhossenydance.com/layali_simsimiyya.html.

64. *Ibid.*

65. Martin Stokes, "Review of *La Simsimiyya du Port Saide*. Ensemble al-Tanbura, dir. par Zakariya Ibrahim." CD with liner notes by Christian Poché. Institut du Monde Arabe, 1999. https://www.umbc.edu/MA/index/number7/stokes/simsi.htm.

66. *Ibid.*

67. 'Amro Ali, "Understanding The Agency of a Second City: The Case of Alexandria." Presented to the World Congress of Middle East Studies, Seville, Spain, July 18, 2018.

68. 'Amro Ali, "Alexandria's Anti-Fellah Problem," *The Alexandria Files*, July 1, 2017. https://amroali.com/the-alexandria-files/.

69. From Daniella of Cairo's channel https://www.youtube.com/watch?v=e1gdJ_C2YCc.

70. Communication from Khalid Sefarat, June 9, 2020.

Chapter Seven

1. This chapter is largely based on Sherifa Zuhur, "Bad Bad Baladi: Sama al-Masry Cheerleader of Egypt's June 30, 2013 Transition," in Sherifa Zuhur and Marlyn Tadros, *Egypt's Conflicting Interests since 2011: Political, Business, Religious, Social and Popular Culture* (Lewiston NY and Lampeter, Wales: The Edwin Mellen Press, 2017) 149–178 with permission from the publisher and my co-author.

2. Marlyn Tadros, in Sherifa Zuhur and Marlyn Tadros, *Egypt's Conflicting Interests since 2011*, 41. While Tadros wrote about Egypt's satire in social media, and I wrote about Sama al-Masry, these two satirical methodologies had a lot in common.

3. *Ibid.*, 39.

4. Adel Hamouda, *Al-nukta al-siyasa fi misr: Kayfa yashkar al-masriyun min hukumahum* (Sphinx for Publishing and Distribution, 1990) 114.

5. Yahya Sakr, "Egyptian Troupe Revives Art of Musical Sketches," *Al Monitor*, July 13, 2017. The article actually focuses on Muhammad 'Ali Hashem and the Masr al-Qadima troupe formed in 2004.

6. Ashraf Gharib, "Remembering Zeinat Sidki: The Most Famous Spinster in Egyptian Cinema." *AhramOnline*, March 2, 2018. http://english.ahram.org.eg/NewsContent/5/32/291981/Arts--Culture/Film/Remembering-Zeinat-Sedki-The-most-famous-spinster-.aspx ; Lara Ahmed, "5 Reasons Zeinat Sedki Still Shines: Remembering Egypt's Queen of Comedy," *Women of Egypt Mag*, May 4, 2019 https://womenofegyptmag.com/2019/05/04/5-reasons-zeinat-sedki-still-shines-remembering-egypts-queen-of-comedy/.

7. Tonia Rifaey, "An Illustration of the Transitional Period in Egypt During 1919–1924: Political Cartoons in Egypt's Revolutionary History," Master's thesis. Arabic Studies, American University in Cairo, 1997, 10–11, 22.

8. Tonia Rifaey and Sherifa Zuhur, "Visualizing Identity: Gender and Nation in Egyptian Cartoons," In Sherifa Zuhur, ed., "Visualizing Identity: Gender and Nation in Egyptian Cartoons," in Sherifa Zuhur, ed. *Colors of Enchantment: Theater, Dance, Music, and the Visual Arts of the Middle East* (Cairo: The American University in Cairo Press, 2001).

9. "The Dance" *al-Lata'if al-Musawarra*, 1919 in Rifaey "An Illustration," 24.

10. "The Constitution between the Committee Head and Its Deputy," *Kashkul*, 1923 in Rifaey, "An Illustration," 204 and this cartoon is discussed on 165–166.

11.
Shik shak shok, Shik shak shok, Shik shak shok
Nassik ya habibi ar-rap war-rock
My darling, I'm going to make you forget about rap and rock (repeats)
Wi ta'la nar'us baladi
Come, let us dance baladi
Halawa
How beautiful!
Da l-baladi ya nur 'aini
This baladi is the light of my eyes (section repeats)
Bil-albi bi-shok
In the heart it pierces
Shik shak shok…

12. "Egyptian Puppet Belly Dancing," 2009 https://www.youtube.com/watch?v=GZcG2A5lTG0; Ahmad Na'im with Zizi, "Egyptian Arts," *CCTN Africa*, 2014. https://www.youtube.com/watch?v=Ko3um3v3VCo.

13. Andrew Hammond, *Pop Culture Arab World! Media Arts and Lifestyle* (Santa Barbara, CA, Oxford: ABC-Clio, 2005) 188.

14. "Abla Fahita Live min al-Duplex, al-halqa al-ula al-kamila raqisa Dina," 2018 https://www.youtube.com/watch?v=UQzunsFtqqY&t=2099s.

15. "Abla Fahita Live min al-Duplex," Season 3, mounted April 5, 2017. https://www.youtube.com/watch?v=GdaUaDNiG0Y.

16. "Abla Fahita tafaji' Wafa' al-Kilani bi-waslat raqs," *Takharif*, published December 10, 2018. https://www.youtube.com/watch?v=ztCs0Y_NeLA.

17. Issandr El Amrani, "The Murder of Khaled Said." *The Arabist*, June 14, 2010. https://arabist.net/blog/2010/6/14/the-murder-of-khaled-said.html.

18. Associated Press, "Egyptian Woman Arrested Over Racy Music Video," *New York Daily News*. May 25, 2015. https://www.nydailynews.com/news/world/watch-egyptian-woman-arrested-racy-music-video-article-1.2234970.

19. Mohammed Tawfiq and Naira Oberoi, "Egyptian Singer Sentenced to Prison for Video 'Inciting Debauchery.'" *CNN.com*, December 14, 2017. https://www.cnn.com/2017/12/13/middleeast/egypt-singer-shyma-ahmed-prison-intl/index.html.

20. In the sense intended by the Napoleonic Code, but also in accordance with the Islamic legal principle of *maslaha* (literally meaning "public interest").

21. "Egypt Professor Ousted of [sic] Her Position at Suez University," *Egypt Today*, June 5, 2018. https://www.egypttoday.com/Article/1/51584/Professor-Mona-Prince-ousted-of-her-position-at-Suez-University.

22. Fewer in the United States, as compared to Egypt, consider dancing to be detrimental to a professional or academic reputation, at least not for those studying dance or dance ethnology. A differing response would be that folkloric dancing is more respectable than *raqs sharqi*, but that would be debated by many Egyptians.

23. For reference see the Facebook group, "Songs of the New Arab Revolutions" a project initiated by Michael Frishkopf and which included songs collected by myself and many others. Accessed December 25, 2016, accessed November 16, 2016, https://www.facebook.com/groups/songsnar/?ref=bookmarks; also *France24*'s multimedia documentary, *The Songs of Tahrir Square: Music at the Heart of the Revolution*, http://musictahrir.france24.com/index-en.html summarized by Torie Rose De Ghette, "The Rhythms of Egypt's Revolutionaries," *Jadaliyya*, March 4 2012, accessed November 2, 2016, http://www.jadaliyya.com/pages/index/4545/the-rhythms-of-egypts-revolutionaries

24. Ted Swedenburg, "Egypt's Music of Protest from Sayyid Darwish to DJ Haha," *Middle East Report*, Middle East Research and Information Project, 42 (Winter 2012). Accessed November 14, 2016, http://www.merip.org/mer/mer265/egypts-music-protest.

25. Evelyn Early, *Baladi Women of Cairo: Playing with an Egg and a Stone* (Boulder: Colorado, Lynne Rienner, 1993) 51; also see: "The term '*baladi*' (of the land, i.e., country, homeland) once distinguished Egyptians from occupiers of other nationalities, the French and British, or the Mamluks and Turks," Early, *Ibid.*, 54. However, *baladi* is not necessarily a complimentary term—a dress in startling bright colors might garner the comment "*baladi [q]*

awi!" (really loud! i.e., tasteless). In fact, the upper classes or would-be-elites might scoff at the *bint al-balad* or *fallaha*, who are both *baladi*. *Baladi* was not replaced in all senses by the adjective *sha'bi*.

26. Virginia Danielson, *The Voice of Egypt: Umm Kulthum, Arabic Song and Egyptian Society in the Twentieth Century*, (Chicago: University of Chicago Press, 1997).

27. Sherifa Zuhur, "Victims or Actors: Centering Women in Egyptian Commercial Film," in Sherifa Zuhur, ed., *Images of Enchantment: Visual and Performing Arts of the Middle East* (Cairo: American University in Cairo Press, 1998) 211–228.

28. This resulted in the Egyptian parliament's censure of the singer, Nancy Ajram, and the music syndicate's censure of Ruby, and subsequent censorship of entertainers. Sherifa Zuhur, "Singing a New Song: Arab Muslim Women and Entertainment" in Fereshte Nouraie-Simon, ed., *On Shifting Ground: Muslim Women in the Global Era*. (New York: Feminist Press, 2005) 108.

29. *Wahda wa al-nuss* (one and a half) is one of the typical Egyptian rhythms played for *raqs sharqi*.

30. *'Ala Wahda wa al-Nuss* (2012) in two parts. Part One. Media HD https://www.dailymotion.com/video/x3sx1qv The song from the film appears here, accessed June 5, 2020 here: https://www.youtube.com/watch?v=tBHUOQvl5cE.

31. Nemat Guenena and Nadia Wassef, *Unfulfilled Promises: Women's Rights in Egypt*. (Cairo: Population Council, 1999) 22–23.

32. This *baladi* dance segment is at the end of part 1 and the start of *'Ala Wahda wa al-Nuss* part 2 Media HD https://www.dailymotion.com/video/x3sxae6.

33. At minute 20:38 in part 2 accessed May 22, 2017. https://www.dailymotion.com/video/x3sxae6.

34. Ahmad 'Adawiyya was described in Chapter Four. The idea that 'Adawiyya was "vulgar" (or "lowbrow") as in Walter Armbrust, "Popular Culture and the Decline of the Middle Class," *Journal of the International Institute*. 3 (Summer, 1996) is both a classist statement and a political one reflecting the idea that performers' products should be difficult, respectable, and artistic, and not simply fun peppered with social comment.

35. The sleeveless, ruffled short dress is either a style of sun dress or beach dress meant to reference Alexandria (See Chapter Five) or *sha'bi* neighborhoods in the capital (See Chapter Three). The singer's rather overt comments to Hurriyya are in one sense atypical as they cross a line, but at the same time are meant to evoke *dall'a* in *sha'bi* songs. The dance is at minute 26:13 of "Wahda" (as previously divided in two parts).

36. Sawan El-Messiri compared *bint al-balad* (more clever, modern, and witty, *fahlawiyya*) to a *fallaha* (rural or peasant woman) (90) and to an upper-class woman, *bint al-zawat* (more remote, spoiled, Europeanized) (91) and for the *bint al-balad*'s views on flirting, husbands etc. *Ibn Al-Balad: A Concept of Egyptian Identity* (The Hague: Brill, 1978) 91–97.

37. "Liqa' Sama al-Masry fi On TV," March 23, 2012 accessed May 22, 2017, https://www.youtube.com/watch?v=f39FF16qrtw.

38. The film caused a temporary breakup in her marriage with Yousif Khal. "Nicole Saba Regrets Acting with Adel Imam," *AlBawaba* January 1, 2012, accessed December 25, 2016, http://www.albawaba.com/entertainment/nicole-saba-regrets-acting-adel-imam-407339.

39. "Ughniyat Halawat al-Ruh, kamila, min film Halawat al-Ruh, Haifa Wahbe," Hakim, singing with Haifa Wahbe, dancing (playing Ruh) in the song "Halawat al-Ruh" in the film of the same name, directed by Samih 'Abd al-'Aziz, 2014, accessed December 25, 2016, https://www.youtube.com/watch?v=Hd4zxdwr_X0.

40. Personal communication from C. as part of a discussion about Sama al-Masry by professional and amateur dancers, May 20, 2014.

41. "Al-Barnamag," "*Almania rayih, jayy*." 12, part 2. https://www.youtube.com/watch?v=NLqWsXN3LX4.

42. Marlyn Tadros, "What's So Funny? Political Satire in Revolutionary Times," in Sherifa Zuhur and Marlyn Tadros, *Egypt's Conflicting Interests since 2011*, 62–63. I'm indebted to Marlyn's explanations of Bassam Youssef and Abla Fahita, and satire more generally, and also those provided by Afaf Lutfi al-Sayyid (Marsot).

43. *Ibid.*, 63.

44. Preface, Bassam Youssef, *Revolution for Dummies: Laughing through the Arab Spring* (New York: Dey Street Books, 2017).

45. David Kirkpatrick and Mayy El Sheikh, "For Liberals in Egypt, A Champion Who Quips," *New York Times* December 30, 2012. https://www.nytimes.com/2012/12/31/world/middleeast/bassem-youssef-a-champion-for-egypts-liberals.html.

46. Karin van Nieuwkerk, "On Religion, Gender, and Performing: Female Performers and Repentance in Egypt," in Tullia Magrini, ed., *Music and Gender: Perspectives from the Mediterranean* (Chicago: University of Chicago Press, 2003) 267–286.

47. The Egyptian state regulates dance costumes, but this control does not extend necessarily to venues for private parties, nor is it enforced in all hotel or other venues. Midriffs are supposed to be covered by net or material. Styles of skirts showing a great deal of leg were once banned but periodically return.

48. As in her book's title, van Nieuwkerk, '*A Trade Like Any Other*.'

49. Karin van Nieuwkerk, '*A Trade Like Any Other': Female Singers and Dancers in Egypt* (Austin: University of Texas Press, 1995).

50. Noha Roushdy deals with the history and perception of belly dance (identified as *raqs al-baladi*) over time. Noha Roushdy, "Baladi as Performance: Gender and Dance in Modern Egypt." *Surfacing* Vol. 3 (August 2010). She asserts the professional form "was" fully Cairene (although mentioning the *ghajar* [gypsy] or *ghawazi* contributions) in the Muhammad 'Ali street guild legacy, and then

overtaken by "migrants"—meaning non-Cairenes—and now by "Western" dancers (mostly Russophone women).

51. In this dance form's aesthetics, lifting of the legs and kicking in the air are not generally considered to be beautiful or necessary (except in folkloric dance by men), although certain dancers like Randa Kamel have included kicks, and one leg is lifted slightly in a certain segment of a *baladi* progression.

52. "Hips Don't Lie: Egypt [sic] Belly Dancer Seeks to Shake Rising Islamists." *Al Arabiya*, November 12, 2013 accessed November 15, 2016, http://english.alarabiya.net/articles/2012/11/14/249595.html.

53. MENA, "Nose Job MP Files Complaint Against Belly Dancer Who Says She's His Wife," *Egypt Independent,* March 26, 2012.

54. Mohammed Khawly, "Nose Job Scandal Topples Egyptian Salafi MP." *Al-Akhbar English* March 6, 2012, accessed December 25, 2016, http://english.al-akhbar.com/node/4876.

55. *Al Arabiya,* "Hips Don't Lie."

56. "Ibn al-Amrikaniyya Sama al-Masry," [Son of the American Woman, Sama al-Masry] Accessed December 25, 2016, https://www.youtube.com/watch?v=R06-OifqT7k.

57. "Yadhak shaykh yatlu kamilat ughniyat Sama al-Masry 'ala qanat al-hafidh," January 17, 2013 accessed December 25, 2016, https://www.youtube.com/watch?v=0DB62LlkuCs.

58. "Sama al-Masry ba'd al-fidiu al-akhir laha: Wasalatni makalamat tahdid nust 'ala "Haya waslat al-hijab wa al-niqab, ya fagira." *ElCinema.com* June 20, 2013 accessed December 16, 2016, http://www.elcinema.com/news/nw678932489/.

59. "Fadhiha ... Sama al-Mursi turqus bi-niqab wa-tghanni li-Mursi." June 17, 2013 accessed December 16, 2016, https://www.youtube.com/watch?v=3gu4YbTmho4.

60. Made famous by Lebanese singer Wadi' al-Safi, and more recently reissued by Hamada al-Laithy in a video with dancer Safinaz.

61. "Sama al-Masry Ta'adh Shaikha Moza wa al-Jazira." August 25, 2013 accessed December 25, 2016, https://www.youtube.com/watch?v=JZ9vw-mp2aQ.

62. "Terrorism "Obama-Style," Video from Egyptian Singer Shaaban abdel Rahim," February 23, 2013 accessed October 31, 2016, https://www.youtube.com/watch?v=lTXidqs2Ofc Then he produced the same song with different words lampooning Erdogan ("Ishrab, ya Erdogan! (Drink up, oh Erdogan!) "Al-fanan Sha'ban 'Abd al-Rahim 'an Erdogan," October 14, 2014, accessed December 16, 2016. https://www.youtube.com/watch?v=AZWrNJggVCY&list=RDAZWrNJggVCY.

63. "Sama al-Masri tafshakh Obama wa tasbah al-abb wa-l-umm." July 20, 2013, accessed December 16, 2016, https://www.youtube.com/watch?v=WL_mEYP8N-A.

64. "Shut Up Your Mouse Obama." March 4, 2014 accessed December 25, 2016, www.youtube.com/watch?v=qeBTyhN2Bu4.

65. "Sama al-Masry takassar ziran wara' al-sifara al-Amrikiyya," *al-Masry al-Yum*, Sept. 2, 2013, https://www.youtube.com/watch?v=A-cVC9G34y4 and embedded in Katelynn Fossett, "The Belly Dancer and the Brotherhood: Meet the Exotic Performer Trying to Take Down Egypt's Islamists," *Foreign Policy*, January 30, 2014. https://foreignpolicy.com/2014/01/30/the-belly-dancer-and-the-brotherhood-meet-the-exotic-performer-trying-to-take-down-egypts-islamists/.

66. Ibid.

67. "Sama al-Masry ughniyat Rabi'a," "Ayuh Bah," March 13, 2014, accessed December 16, 2016, https://www.youtube.com/watch?v=-tzizWG3lqM.

68. "Sama al-Masry ughniyat 6 April," March 6, 2014, accessed December 26, 2016, https://www.youtube.com/watch?v=MZCtn2e13rU.

69. "Ya Baradei Sama al-Masry" April 6, 2014, accessed December 26, 2016, https://www.youtube.com/watch?v=Ng—ncygT6o.

70. "Bassam Bomba Sama al-Masry," April 6, 2014, accessed December 26, 2016, https://www.youtube.com/watch?v=bp749VV1pFw.

71. "Ya Mortada Sama al-Masry," April 23, 2014, accessed December 26, 2016, https://www.youtube.com/watch?v=oyE0lF5XANs.

72. Al-Masry al-Youm, "Defendants Accuse Mansour of 'Manipulation' in Battle of the Camel Trial," *Egypt Independent*, May 12, 2012. http://www.egyptindependent.com//news/defendents-accuse-mortada-mansour-manipulating-others-accused-battle-camel-trial.

73. Hugo Gerling, "L'incroyable combat de Sama El Masry, la danseuse du ventre égyptienne qui se bat contre les islamistes." *Gentside*, February 12, 2014. http://222.gentside.com (art59112).

74. Lora Moftah, "Egyptian Belly Dancer Takes a Shot at Islamists," *Blouin News Blogs*, January, 30 2014 accessed May 22, 2017 http://blogs.blouinnews.com/blouinbeatworld/tag/sama-el-masry/.

75. "5 Questions for a Parliamentary Candidate Sama al-Masry," *Mada Masr*, September 24, 2015, accessed December 26, 2016, http://www.madamasr.com/en/2015/09/24/news/u/5-questions-for-a-parliamentary-candidate-sama-al-masry/.

76. "Egypt Abuzz over Racy Poster of anti-Obama Belly Dancer" *Jerusalem Post*. November 6, 2014, https://www.jpost.com/not-just-news/egypt-abuzz-over-racy-movie-poster-featuring-anti-obama-belly-dancer-380996; "Sexual Movie Poster of Egyptian Belly Dancer Sparks Anger," *Al Arabiya*, November 6, 2014. https://english.alarabiya.net/en/life-style/entertainment/2014/11/06/-Sexual-movie-poster-of-Egyptian-belly-dancer-sparks-controversy.

77. "Too Sexy or Too Disgusting? Egyptian Film Poster Fuels Anger," *Cairo Scene*, June 11, 2014, accessed December 26, 2016, http://www.cairoscene.com/ArtsAndCulture/Too-Sexy-or-Too-Disgusting-Egyptian-Film-Poster.

78. "Bromo (promo) barnamag Sama al-Masry

fi Ramadan," released on her Facebook page. https://www.facebook.com/watch/?ref=external&v=1698970670224488.

79. Farah Tawfeek, "Egypt's Public Prosecution Arrests Belly Dancer Sama al-Masry,0333 *Egypt Independent,* April 26, 2020 https://egyptindependent.com/aegyptian-public-prosecution-arrests-belly-dancer-sama-al-masryegyptian-public-prosecution-detains-belly-dancer-sama-al-masry/.

80. As alluded to by Samia Mehrez and Sahar Karaitim, "Mulid al-Tahrir: Semiotics of a Revolution" in Samia Mehrez, ed., *Translating Egypt's Revolution: The Language of Tahrir* (Cairo: American University in Cairo Press, 2012) 30; and as commented on by Elizabeth Bishop in her review of the book for the *Review of Middle East Studies* (Winter 2015).

Chapter Eight

1. Ainsley Hawthorn, "Middle Eastern Dance and What We Call It." *Dance Research,* 37: 1, 2019. https://www.euppublishing.com/doi/full/10.3366/drs.2019.0250.

2. Karin van Nieuwkerk, "Changing Images and Shifting Identities of Female Performers in Egypt, in Sherifa Zuhur, ed., *Images of Enchantment: Visual and Performing Arts of the Middle East* (Cairo: American University in Cairo Press, 1998) 22.

3. Hawthorn, "Middle Eastern Dance."

4. A non-*ghawazi* (*raqs sharqi*) dancer hired for the Musiciens du Nil's show in Europe communicated to me that the organizers did not want the *ghawazi* dancers, but others stated that they simply did not show up or weren't granted visas.

5. van Nieuwkerk, *Ibid.*

6. Sol Bloom, *The Autobiography of Sol Bloom* (New York: Putnam's Sons, 1946) 135, cited by Rebecca Stone, "Reverse Imagery: Middle Eastern Themes in Hollywood," in Sherifa Zuhur, ed., *Images of Enchantment: Visual and Performing Arts of the Middle East* (Cairo: American University in Cairo Press, 1998) 250.

7. Stone, "Reverse Imagery," 251.

8. Thomas Cook, Ltd., *Cook's Tourists' Handbook for Egypt, the Nile, and the Desert* (London: T. Cook & Son, 1897) 45.

9. *Ibid.*, 191.

10. As shown in "Seducing America: Selling the Middle Eastern Mystique." Curated by Jonathan Friedlander. Exhibition, Powell Library, University of California, Los Angeles, 2005 and Judith Gabriel, "Seducing America: Selling the Middle Eastern Mystique." *Al-Jadid,* 2005 available at: http://dunyati.blogspot.com/2007/05/seducing-america-selling-middle-eastern.html.

11. Merriam-Webster.

12. Petra Kuppinger, "Globalization and Exterritoriality in Metropolitan Cairo," *Geographical Review.* Vol. 95, No. 3, New Geographies of the Middle East (Jul., 2005), 348–372.

13. Anouk de Koning, "Café Latte and Caesar Salad: Cosmopolitan Belonging in Cairo's Coffee Shops," in Diane Singerman and Paul Amar, eds., *Cairo Cosmopolitan: Politics, Culture and Urban Space in the New Globalized Middle East* (Cairo: American University in Cairo Press, 2006), 221–234.

14. "Raqsat 'Arus al-Nil," featuring Sami al-Shawwa. https://www.youtube.com/watch?v=mml3e7711a0&fbclid=IwAR1QXMJQWdzRAf1RfWWuTPSJ5Z2_ehU6b2Zz1mb_N4udHntvUl6jrMKptQ.

15. Eddie Soubhi Ibn Farjallah Kochakji was a Syrian-American from Brooklyn who played Arabic drum and together with Iraqi violinist, Haqqi Obadiah, developed a style he called Ameraba, mainly performing with belly dancers. Also see Anne Rasmussen, "The Music of Arab Americans: Performance Contexts and Musical Transformation," *Pacific Review of Ethnomusicology,* Vol. 5 (1989) 25.

16. Heather Ward, *Egyptian Belly Dance in Transition: The Raqs Sharqi Revolution* (Jefferson, NC: McFarland, 2018) 93.

17. Advertisement for "Firqa Ratiba wa Ensaf Rushdie," from the 1930s on Shira.net http://www.shira.net/about/ads-flyers/1930s-rushdie-sisters.htm. The year is unclear. It may be before the sisters opened their own club in Cairo in 1935 or after. The ad itself is here: http://www.shira.net/photos/articlephotos/egyptian/ads-flyers/1930s-rushdie-sisters-detail.jpg.

18. Andrea Deagon, "Dancing the Eternal Image: Visual and Narrative Archetypes," *Habibi,* Vol. 14, No. 1 (Winter 1995) "http://thebestofhabibi.com/vol-14-no-1-winter-1995/archetypes/.

19. Dina Talaat avec Claude Guibal, *Ma liberté de danser: La derniere danseuse d'Égypte* (Neuilly-sur-Seine: Michel Lafon, 2011) 74.

20. "At Night, They Dance," (*La nuit, elles dansent*). Directed by Isabelle Lavigne and Stéphane Thibault (2011).

21. Farida (Melda) Fahmy, "The Creative Development of Mahmoud Reda, A Contemporary Egyptian Choreographer." Master's thesis, University of California, Los Angeles (1987) 17.

22. Interview and recordings of Khairiyya bint Mazin, put onto Facebook (Live) by Saad Hassan, June 10, 2020. https://www.facebook.com/samrah.masoud/posts/2972662222840583. https://www.facebook.com/samrah.masoud/posts/2972729262833879. https://www.facebook.com/saad.hassan.902604/videos/3289425237757229/.

23. Martin Stokes, "Creativity, Globalization and Music." *Volume! La revue de musique populaires.* Vol. 10, No. 2 (2014) 17. https://journals.openedition.org/volume/4561.

24. The figure seems too high but was communicated by veteran dancer Asmahan Jonsin.

25. As in Anne Vermeyden, "Hybridization and Uneven Exchange: The Popularization of Belly Dance in Toronto, Canada (1950–1990), Ph.D. dissertation, University of Guelph (2017).

26. Latifa, "Raqia Hassan's Dance Festival, Ahlan wa Sahlan 2000," *Gilded Serpent,* n.d. http://www.

gildedserpent.com/articles13/raqiareviewlatifa.htm.

27. L.L. Wynn, *Pyramids and Nightclubs: A Travel Ethnography of Arab and Western Imaginations of Egypt: From King Tut to a Colony of Atlantis, Sex Orgies, Urban Legends about a Marauding Prince, and Blonde Belly Dancers* (Austin: University of Texas Press, 2007) 218.

28. Eric Buvelot, "Ika, the Great Businesswoman of Belly Dance." *Indonesia Expat*, January 16, 2020, https://indonesiaexpat.biz/featured/ika-the-great-businesswoman-of-belly-dance/.

29. Hannah Allam, "Foreigners Preserve Cairo as a Belly Dance Capital" *McClatchy*, February 15, 2010. https://www.mcclatchydc.com/news/nation-world/world/article24573610.html. Also, information from prominent dancers from that year.

30. Paul Garwood "Egypt Bans Foreign Belly Dancers." *Associated Press*, November 10, 2003.

31. Janet Johnstone and G.J. Tassie, "Egyptian *Baladi* Dances—A Contested Tradition" in F.A. Hassan, F.A., G.J. Tassie, A. De Trafford, L.S. Owens and J. van Wetering, *Managing Egypt's Cultural Heritage: Proceedings of the First Egyptian Cultural Heritage Organisation Conference on Egyptian Cultural Heritage Management* (London: Golden House and ECHO Publications, 2009) 113.

32. Information gathered in Egypt (2003–2005) and subsequently during the writing of this book (2016–2019); this topic is also covered by Caitlin McDonald, "Belly Dance and Globalization: Constructing Gender in Egypt and on the Global Stage." Ph.D. Thesis, Arab and Islamic Studies, University of Exeter (January 1, 2010) 67–70.

33. Christine Sahin, "Core Connections: A Contemporary Cairo Raqs Sharqi Ethnography." Ph.D. dissertation. University of California, Riverside, 2018. Many comparisons are made between dancers, first suggesting different treatment and self-conceptions of two Egyptians, and the "foreign" dancer, ethnically, but not experientially an Arab, 47–173.

34. Sahin, "Core Connections," 224–238.

35. *Ibid.*, 241–244.

36. *Ibid.*, 47–173.

37. Dina Tal'at has stated that if she been prevented from dancing, she would have run away to pursue it, saying, "We [Egyptian dancers] used to do so." And that stigma continued for some; Randa Kamel explained that her father, who disapproved of her dancing, beat her. Declan Walsh. "Foreign Belly Dancers: Egyptians Shake Their Heads (and Hips)." *New York Times*, July 8, 2018.

38. "Munira al-Mahdiyya," Amar Foundation for Arab Music Archiving and Research. http://www.amar-foundation.org/munira-al-mahdiyya/.

39. Gil Weissblei, "The Egyptian Belly Dancers with A Secret Jewish Identity," *The Librarians*, September 27, 2018. https://blog.nli.org.il/en/jamal_sisters/; also, Ofer Aderet, "The Secret Jewish Identity of the Jamal Twins, Egyptian Belly-dancing Stars," *Haaretz*, July 14, 2018. (Aderet's article may be the original, and the *Jerusalem Post* also published on them).

40. *Fi Baladi*, Mariam Nader, dir. 2019.

41. Using recorded music lessened work for musicians, meaning there were fewer musicians working outside of Egypt as full-time hires. Consequently, more played part-time and turned to teaching to supplement their work. The same circumstances did not prevail within Egypt, although overall, the music industry was impacted by fewer nightclubs, though weddings provided good income (except during Ramadan).

42. Tamalyn Dallal, "An Explosion in Salta: "La Danza Arabe" in the Hinterlands of South America," *The Best of Habibi*, Vol. 18, No. 3 (March 2001). http://thebestofhabibi.com/vol-18-no-3-march-2001/salta/.

43. Communication from Amina Goodyear, June 22, 2019.

44. Noha Roushdy, "What is Baladi about Raqs al-Baladi? On the Survival of Belly Dance in Egypt," in Caitlin McDonald and Barbara Sellers-Young, eds., *Belly Dance Around the World: New Communities, Performance and Identity* (Jefferson, NC: McFarland, 2013) 22.

45. Communications from Sahra (Carolee Kent) and Brenda Bell.

46. Candace Bordelon, "'Finding the Feeling': Oriental Dance, *Musiqa al-Gadida* and *Tarab*," in Caitlin McDonald and Barbara Sellers-Young, eds., *Belly Dance Around the World*, 35.

47. According to Farida Fahmy, as relayed by Keti Sherif, an Egyptian dance teacher while teaching in a workshop mistakenly substituted the term '*majence*' for *manèges* which supposedly is a balletic term, apparently describing a series of turns and traveling steps in the opening. "Where the Term Megance Comes From." Shira.dotnet. n.d. http://www.shira.net/music/.htm#Etymology.

48. Bordelon, "'Finding the Feeling,'" 41.

49. *Fi Baladi*. Mariam Nader, dir. 2019.

50. *Ibid.*

51. Karin van Nieuwkerk, "Popularizing Islam or Islamizing Popular Music: New Developments in Egypt's Wedding Scene." *Contemporary Islam*, Vol. 6, No. 3 (2012) 243.

52. Everett K. Rowson, "The Effeminates of Early Medina," *Journal of the American Oriental Society*, Vol. 111, No. 4 (Oct.-Dec.1991) 671–693.

53. Carolee Kent and Marjorie Franken, "A Procession through Time: The Zaffat al-'Arusa in Three Views," in Sherifa Zuhur, ed., *Images of Enchantment: Visual and Performing Arts of the Middle East* (Cairo: The American University in Cairo Press, 1998) 74.

54. al-Qahira wa al-Nas. al-Halqa al-'ula min barnamag al-Raqisah, "Ikhtabarat al-raqisah fi kull 'anha al-'alam," January 9, 2014. https://www.youtube.com/watch?v=y7GD1BSyddo.

55. Kate Roberts, "Cairo Clubs Don't Forget to Take Off Your 'Hat.'" *Egyptian Streets*, February 8, 2019.

56. Janet Johnstone and G.J. Tassie, "Egyptian *Baladi* Dances—A Contested Tradition." In F.A. Hassan, G.J. Tassie, A. De Trafford, L.S. Owens, and

J. van Wetering, eds. *Managing Egypt's Cultural Heritage: Proceedings of the First Egyptian Cultural Heritage Organisation Conference on Egyptian Cultural Heritage Management* (London: Golden House and ECHO Publications, 2009).

57. Valeria Loiacono and Julia M. Fallon, "Intangible Cultural Heritage Beyond Borders: Egyptian Bellydance (Raqs Sharqi) as a Form of Transcultural Heritage." *Journal of Intercultural Studies*. 39: 3 (2018) pp. 286–304.

58. Noha Roushdy, "What is Baladi about Raqs al-Baladi?

Glossary

1. Johnny Farraj and Sami Abu Shumays, *Inside Arabic Music: Arabic Maqam, Performance and Theory in the Twentieth Century* (New York: Oxford University Press, 2019) 8 and this has been communicated similarly to me by A.J. Racy.

2. "'La'" al-Sawarikh," 100CopiesMusic, published December 21, 2017 https://www.youtube.com/watch?v=xf9s_h8S2XM.

3. Karin van Nieuwkerk, "Secret Communication and Marginality. The Case of Egyptian Entertainers." *Sharqiyat*. 10:1 (1998), 27–41; Kristina Richardson, "Tracing a Gypsy Mixed Language through Medieval and Early Modern Arabic and Persian Literature." *Der Islam*, vol. 94, no. 1 (2017) 115–157.

Bibliography

Alphabetization as in the Glossary.

Abadir, Rami. "Talking to Phil Battiekh: A Swiss DJ Who Plays Mahraganat." *MadaMasr.com* June 6, 2017. https://madamasr.com/en/2017/06/06/feature/culture/talking-to-phil-battiekh-a-swiss-dj-who-plays-mahraganat/.

'Abd al-Rahim, Sha'ban. "Ahl al-tarab. " Mazika wa al-afrah al-Wady. Published November 28, 2014. https://www.youtube.com/watch?v=dV2dHTPRjdU.

'Abd al-Rahim, Sha'ban. "al-Tramadol." ElWady Music Records. Published February 18, 2013. https://www.youtube.com/watch?v=pvFUTvflmAo.

Abd ar-Raziq, Ahmad. *La femme au temps des mamlouks en Égypte*. Cairo: Institut français d'archéologie orientale du Caire, 1973.

Abdel Ghafar, Adel. "Youth Unemployment in Egypt: A Ticking Time Bomb." *Markaz*. Brookings. July 28, 2016. https://www.brookings.edu/blog/markaz/2016/07/29/youth-unemployment-in-egypt-a-ticking-time-bomb/.

Abdel Mohsen, Ali. "A Q & A with Leading Mahraganat Singer Sadat." *Egypt Independent*. April 13, 2013. http://www.egyptindependent.com/qa-leading-mahraganat-singer-sadat/ (accessed August 20, 2018).

Abdullah, Yaser. "The Singing Waist: Oriental Dance as a Translation of Music. Ma'azef.com 05/06/2016. https://ma3azef.com/the-singing-waist/.

"Abla Fahita Live min al-Duplex, al-halqa al-ula al-kamila raqasa Dina." 2018 https://www.youtube.com/watch?v=UQzunsFtqqY&t=2099s.

"Abla Fahita Live min al-Duplex," Season 3. Mounted April 5, 2017. https://www.youtube.com/watch?v=GdaUaDNiG0Y.

"Abla Fahita tafaji' Wafa' al-Kilani bi-waslat raqs." *Takharif*, published December 10, 2018. https://www.youtube.com/watch?v=ztCs0Y_NeLA.

Abu Lughod. Lila. *Veiled Sentiments: Honor and Poetry in a Bedouin Society*. Berkeley: University of California Press, 1986, reissued 2016.

Aderet, Ofer. "The Secret Jewish Identity of the Jamal Twins, Egyptian Belly-dancing Stars." *Haaretz*. July 14, 2018.

Adra, Najwa. "Belly Dance: An Urban Folk Dance Genre." In Anthony Shay and Barbara Sellers-Young, eds. *Belly Dance: Orientalism, and Transnationalism and Harem Fantasy*. Costa Mesa: Mazda, 2005.

"*Aha al-shibshib dha*'." (Fuck, I lost my slipper.) http://www.twistmedia.info/save/video/SXhUtIMwX9A/A7a%20El%20Shebsheb%20Daa3%20Youtube.html.

"Ahmed Naeem (Na'im) with Zizi." "Egyptian Arts." *CCTN Africa* 2014. https://www.youtube.com/watch?v=Ko3um3v3VCo.

Ahmed, Lara. "5 Reasons Zeinat Sedki Still Shines: Remembering Egypt's Queen of Comedy." *Women of Egypt Mag*. May 4, 2019. https://womenofegyptmag.com/2019/05/04/5-reasons-zeinat-sedki-still-shines-remembering-egypts-queen-of-comedy/.

Ahmed, Leila. "Feminism and Feminist Movements in the Middle East." In Azizah Hibri, ed., *Women and Islam*. Oxford: Pergamon Press, 1982.

Ahmed, Leila. *Women and Gender in Islam: Historical Roots of a Modern Debate*, New Haven and London: Yale University Press, 1992.

Al Arabiya. "Hips Don't Lie: Egypt [sic] Belly Dancer Seeks to Shake Rising Islamists." *Al Arabiya*. November 12, 2013 accessed November 15, 2016, http://english.alarabiya.net/articles/2012/11/14/249595.html.

Al-Darb al-Ahmar. Directed by 'Abd al-Fatah Madbouly. 1980. https://www.youtube.com/watch?v=-DVypbpQbNM.

al-Laila al-Kabira. Poetry, Salah Jahin (Mohammed Salah el-Din Helmi Bahgat) Music, Sayyid Makkawy. Directed by Salah El-Sakka. Puppets Nagi Shaker, 1959. The filmed version of the operetta is on Vimeo: https://vimeo.com/50891213.

Al Qassemi, Sultan Sooud. "New Arab Hip Hop: Between Love and Rebellion." *Raseef22*. June 16, 2020. https://raseef22.net/article/1078683-new-arab-hip-hop-between-love-and-rebellion?fbclid=IwAR2l1DKzVzZbfmOStdeCMh6-0J56tuP6AgO0utObw5_Os-c6vYgSs4P7A0Y.

'Ali, 'Amro. "Alexandria's Anti-Fellah Problem." *The Alexandria Files*. July 1, 2017. https://amroali.com/the-alexandria-files/.

'Ali, 'Amro. "Understanding the Agency of a Second City: The Case of Alexandria." Conference paper presented to the World Congress of Middle East Studies, Seville, Spain, July 18, 2018.

Ali, Randa. "Feyrouz, Child Prodigy Forever." *Mada Masr*. February 6, 2016. https://madamasr.com/en/2016/02/06/feature/culture/feyrouz-child-prodigy-forever/.

Allam, Hannah. "Foreigners Preserve Cairo as a Belly Dance Capital." *McClatchy*. February 15, 2010. https://www.mcclatchydc.com/news/nation-world/world/article24573610.html.

Arabian Knightz. Rush (Karim 'Adil), Sphinx (Hesham Abed), and E-Money (Ehab 'Adil) and featuring Mahmoud El-Leithy. "Al Donia Mooled." 2012. https://www.youtube.com/watch?v=eNFl0wy7BRU.

Armbrust, Walter. *Mass Culture and Modernism in Egypt*. New York: Cambridge University Press, 1996.

Armbrust, Walter. "Popular Culture and the Decline of the Middle Class." *Journal of the International Institute*. 3, Summer, 1996.

Ashraf, Bara. "Thawra bila raqs ... thawra la tastahiq." *al-Araby.co.uk* November 20, 2014. https://www.alaraby.co.uk/supplements/2014/11/19/%D8%AB%D9%88%D8%B1%D8%A9-%D8%A8%D9%84%D8%A7-%D8%B1%D9%82%D8%B5-%D8%AB%D9%88%D8%B1%D8%A9-%D9%84%D8%A7-%D8%AA%D8%B3%D8%AA%D8%AD%D9%82.

Associated Press. "Egyptian Woman Arrested Over Racy Music Video." *New York Daily News*. May 25, 2015. https://www.nydailynews.com/news/world/watch-egyptian-woman-arrested-racy-music-video-article-1.2234970.

At Night, They Dance. (*La nuit, elles dansent*) Directed by Isabelle Lavigne and Stéphane Thibault, 2011.

Azeb, Safa. "Nagwa Fu'ad to Majalla," *Majalla*. August 16, 2019. https://eng.majalla.com/node/75141/nagwa-fouad-to-majalla-i-did-not-know-who-henry-kissinger-was-when-he-proposed-to-me-if.

Azimi, Negar. "A Life Reconstructed: A Lost Musical Legacy Finds Its Voice in Cairo. *Bidoun*. Fall 2004. https://www.bidoun.org/articles/a-life-reconstructed.

Azzam, Nabil Azzam. "Muhammad 'Abd al-Wahhab in Modern Egyptian Music." Ph.D. dissertation. University of California, Los Angeles, 1990.

Badran, Margot. *Feminists, Islam and Nation: Gender and the Making of Modern Egypt*. Princeton: Princeton University Press, 1994.

Badran, Walid. "Sex, Drugs, and Alcohol: A History of Drugs in Egyptian Songs." *Raseef*. 22, January 2, 2017.

Baer, Gabriel. *Egyptian Guilds in Modern Times*. Jerusalem: Israel Oriental Society, 1964.

Baron, Beth. *Egypt as a Woman: Nationalism, Gender and Politics*. Berkeley: University of California Press, 2005.

Bayat, Asef. *Life as Politics: How Ordinary People Change the Middle East*. Stanford, CA: Stanford University Press, 2010.

BBC News. "Egypt's Controversial New Music Craze Mahragan." January 12, 2016. https://www.bbc.com/news/av/world-middle-east-35284443/egypt-s-controversial-new-music-craze-mahragan.

Benchouia, Tarek Adam. "Festivals: The Culture and Politics of Mahraganat Music in Egypt." Master's thesis. University of Texas, Austin, 2015.

Biancani, Francesca. *Sex Work in Colonial Egypt: Women, Modernity and the Global Economy*. London and New York: I.B. Tauris, 2018.

Biegman, Nicolaas H. *Egypt: Moulids, Saints, Sufis*. London: Kegan Paul International, 1990.

Blackman, Winifred S. *The Fellahin of Upper Egypt*. Cairo: American University in Cairo Press, 2000 (originally published by George G. Harrap and Co. Ltd. 1927).

Bloom, Sol. *The Autobiography of Sol Bloom*. New York: Putnam's Sons, 1946.

Boraie, Sherif, ed. With essays by Mustafa Darwish, Rafik el-Sabban, Yasser Alwan. *The Golden Years of Egyptian Film: Cinema Cairo 1936–1967. Al-Sanawat al-dhahabiyya fi al-sinima al-misriyya: Sinima Cairo*. Cairo: Zeitouna; Cairo: American University in Cairo Press, 2008.

Bordelon, Candace. "'Finding the Feeling': Oriental Dance, *Musiqa al-Gadida* and *Tarab*." In McDonald, Caitlin McDonald and Barbara Sellers-Young, eds. *Belly Dance Around the World: New Communities, Performance and Identity*. Jefferson, NC: McFarland, 2013.

Boulad, Adel Paul. "Naissance de Modern Tahtib." n.d. circa 2014. http://www.tahtib.com/media%7Carticles%7CNaissance%20de%20Modern%20Tahtib.

Brunner-Traut, Emma. *Der Tanz im alten Ägypten. Traut Nach bildichen und inschriftlichen Zeugnissen*. Glückstadt, Germany: J.J. Augustin, 1938.

Burget, J. C. "Love, Lust and Longing: Eroticism in Early Islam as Reflected in Literary Sources." In Afaf Lutfi al-Sayyid Marsot, ed., *Society and the Sexes in Medieval Islam*. Sixth Giorgio Levi Della Vida Biennial Conference. Malibu, CA: Undena Publications, 1979.

Bulaq. Directed by Wael Alaa. *Nowness*. 2017. https://www.nowness.com/story/bulaq-wael-alaa?utm_source=FB&utm_medium=SM&utm_campaign=FB31%2F12%2F17.

Buonaventura, Wendy. *Serpent of the Nile: Women and Dance in the Arab World*. New York: Interlink Books, 1998.

Burke, Jeffrey Charles. "The Role of the 'Ulama During the French Rule of Egypt 1798–1801." Master's thesis. McGill University, 1992.

Burkhalter, Thomas, Dickinson, Kay, and Harbert, Benjamin J., eds. *The Arab Avant-Garde: Music, Politics, Modernity*. Middleton, CT: Wesleyan University Press, 2013.

Butler, Judith. *Gender Trouble: Feminism and the Subversion of Identity*. London: Routledge, 1990.

Buvelot, Eric. "Ika, the Great Businesswoman of Belly Dance." *Indonesia Expat*, January 16, 2020, https://indonesiaexpat.biz/

featured/ika-the-great-businesswoman-of-bellydance/.
Cairo Unveiled, Part I. National Geographic Explorer, dir. Karen Goodman and Kirk Simon, https://www.youtube.com/watch?v=V950x1OhpoI; Part II, https://www.youtube.com/watch?v=kp52dgmvhEo.
Canova, Giovanni. "Notizie sui Nawar e sugli altri gruppi Zingari presenti in Egitto." *La bisaccia dello sheikh*, Quaderni del Seminorio di Iranistica, Uralo-Altaistica e Causasologia dell' Universita' Degli Studi di Venezia, 19: May 29, 1981, 71–84.
"Casino Badia's Dance Troupe." *Shira.Net.* http://www.shira.net/about/badia-group-and-stage-names.htm.
Castelo-Branco, Salwa El-Shawan. "Radio and Musical Life in Egypt." *Revista de Musicología* Vol. 16, No. 3, Del XV Congreso de la Sociedad Internacional de Musicología: Culturas Musicales Del Mediterráneo y sus Ramificaciones. Vol. 3 1993, pp. 1229–1239.
Cifuentes, Horacio. "Tahia Carioca and Samia Gamal: Reflections from the Stars of the Forties." *Habibi.* 13, No. 3 Summer 1994. http://thebestofhabibi.com/vol-13-no-3-summer-1994/tahia-carioca-and-samia-gamal/.
Clot Bey. *Risala min mashurat al-sihha ila hukama al-jihadiyya.* (A treatise from the Health Council to the physicians of the army). Cairo: 1835.
Clynton Jace. "Cairo Something New." *The Fader.* October 16, 2012. http://www.thefader.com/2012/10/16/cairo-something-new.
Cole, Juan. *Napoleon's Egypt: Invading the Middle East.* New York: Palgrave Macmillan, 2007.
Cuellar-Moreno, Maria. "Flamenco Dance. Characteristics, Resources and Reflections on Its Evolution." *Cogent Arts and Humanities.* Vol. 3, Issue 1, 2016.
Cugusi, Laura. "Shariʿ Mohamed Ali: The Surviving Legend of a Cairene Street." http://www.egyptindependent.com/shari-mohamed-ali-surviving-legend-cairene-street/. May 30, 2010.
Dallal, Tamalyn. "An Explosion in Salta: 'La Danza Arabe' in the Hinterlands of South America." *The Best of Habibi.* Vol. 18, No. 3, March 2001. http://thebestofhabibi.com/vol-18-no-3-march-2001/salta/.
Danielson, Virginia. "Artists and Entrepreneurs: Female Singers in Cairo in the 1920s." In Nikki Keddie and Beth Baron, eds. *Women in Middle Eastern History: Shifting Boundaries in Sex and Gender.* New Haven: Yale University Press, 1991.
Danielson, Virginia. *The Voice of Egypt: Umm Kulthum, Arabic Song and Egyptian Society in the Twentieth Century.* Chicago: University of Chicago Press, 1997.
Deagon, Andrea. "Dancing the Eternal Image: Visual and Narrative Archetypes." *Habibi.* Vol. 14, No. 1, Winter 1995.
Deasy, Kristin. "The Sufi's Choice: Egypt's Political Wild Card." *World Affairs.* Vol. 175, No. 3, September/October 2012.

Descriptions de l'Égypte: ou Recueil des observations et des recherches qui ont été faites en Égypte pendant l'expédition de l'armée française. Publié par les ordres de Sa Majesté l'empereur Napoléon le Grand. Paris: Imprimerie impériale, 1809–1828.
Desplat, Patrick A., and Schulz, Dorothea A., eds. *Prayer in the City: The Making of Muslim Sacred Places and Urban Life.* Bielefeld, Germany: Transcript, Verlag, 2012.
Deyaa', Nada. "Study Reveals Zar Ritual Still Heavily Performed in Egypt." *Daily News Egypt.* June 12, 2018. https://ww.dailynewssegypt.com/2018/06/12/study-reveals-zar-rituals-still-heavily-performed-in-upper-egypt/.
DJ Sadat. "Dracula." 2018. https://www.youtube.com/watch?v=AkT-09J6Y-E.
"DJ Zo'la's Funeral Takes Place in Cairo." *Ahram Online.* 29 January 2015. http://english.ahram.org.eg/NewsContent/5/32/251886/Arts—Culture/Film/Art-Alert-Documentary-on-electrodance-phenomenon-t.aspx.
Doran, John. "The Playlist: Middle Eastern and North African—EEK & Islam Chipsy, Souad Abdullah and More." *The Guardian.* October 15, 2014. https://www.theguardian.com/music/musicblog/2014/oct/15/playlist-world-eek-islam-chipsy-souad-abdullah-maurice-louca-faycal-azizi.
Doran, John. "The Revolutionary Party Islam Chipsy of EEK Interviewed." *Quietus.* February 17, 2014. http://thequietus.com/articles/14507-islam-chipsy-eek-interview.
Douer, Alissa. *Egypt: The Lost Homeland, Exodus from Egypt 1947-1967: The History of the Jews in Egypt, 1540 BCE to 1967 CE.* Translated by Karin Hanta-Davis. Berlin: Logos Verlag Berlin, 2015.
Dougherty, Roberta L. "Badiʿa Masabni, Artiste and Modernist: The Egyptian Print Media's Carnival of National Identity." In Walter Armbrust, ed., *Mass Mediations: New Approaches to Popular Culture in the Middle East and Beyond.* Berkeley: University of California Press, 2000, 243–268.
Douin, Charles. *Histoire du règne du Khédive Ismail.* Rome: Istituto Poligrafico dello Stato/Société Royale de Géographie d'Egypte/IFAO, 1933–1961.
Duff Gordon, Lucy. *Letters from Egypt.* London: 1997.
Early, Evelyn. *Baladi Women of Cairo: Playing with an Egg and a Stone.* Boulder, Colo, Lynne Rienner, 1993.
"Egypt: Mahraganat Artists Challenge Limits." *FreeMuse.* February 23, 2016. https://freemuse.org/news/egypt-mahraganat-artists-challenge-limits/.
"Egypt Professor Ousted of [sic] Her Position at Suez University." *Egypt Today.* June 5, 2018. https://www.egypttoday.com/Article/1/51584/Professor-Mona-Prince-ousted-of-her-position-at-Suez-University.
"Egyptian Puppet Belly Dancing," 2009. https://www.youtube.com/watch?v=GZcG2A5lTG0.
"Egyptian Star Mohamed Ramadan Releases New Music Video 'Bum Bum.'" *Ahram Online.* January 1, 2020. http://english.ahram.org.eg/NewsCon

tent/5/33/358752/Arts—Culture/Music/Egyptian-star-Mohamed-Ramadan-releases-new-music-v.aspx.

El Amrani, Issandr. "The Murder of Khaled Said." *The Arabist*. June 14, 2010. https://arabist.net/blog/2010/6/14/the-murder-of-khaled-said.html.

El-Khadem, Saad. *al-Raqs al-sha'abi*. Cairo: Egyptian General Book Organization, 1972.

El Masry, Sarah. "Sufi Islam in Egypt." *Daily News Egypt*. October 21, 2012. https://ww.dailynewsegypt.com/2012/10/21/sufi-islam-in-egypt/.

El Messiri, Sawsan. *Ibn Al-Balad: A Concept of Egyptian Identity*. The Hague: Brill, 1978.

El-Turk, Niqula. *Histoire de l'expédition française en Egypte, publiée et traduite par M. Desgranges aîné*. Paris: Imprimerie Royale, 1839.

Elba, Miriam. "It's Crowded and There is No Mercy!" Khabar Keslan. DISORIENT. Issue 1, August 28, 2017.

Electro Chaabi. Directed by Hind Meddeb. 2013.

Elmarsafy, Ziad. *Sufism in the Contemporary Arabic Novel*. Edinburgh: Edinburgh University Press, 2012.

ElNabawy, Maha. "Band of the Week: Islam Chipsy." *Mada Masr*. April 1, 2014.

ElNabawy, Maha. "Band of the Week: Sadat and Alaa Fifty." *MadaMasr.com*. November 25, 2013. https://madamasr.com/en/2013/11/25/feature/culture/band-of-the-week-sadat-and-alaa-fifty/.

El Shawan, Salwa. "The Socio-Political Context of Musika al-'Arabiyyah in Cairo Egypt: Policies, Patronage, Institutions and Musical Change (1922–77). *Asian Music*. 12, 1980, pp. 86–128.

El Shawan, Salwa. "Traditional Arabic Music Ensembles in Egypt since 1967: The Continuity of Tradition within a Contemporary Framework." *Ethnomusicology*. 28: 1984, 271–288.

"*Fadhiha ... Sama al-Mursi turqus bi-niqab wa-tghanni li-Mursi*." June 17, 2013 accessed December 16, 2016. https://www.youtube.com/watch?v=3gu4YbTmho4.

Fahmy, Farida (Melda). "The Creative Development of Mahmoud Reda, A Contemporary Egyptian Choreographer." Master's thesis. Los Angeles: University of California at Los Angeles, 1987.

Fahmy, Farida. "The Founding of the Reda Troupe: An Historical Overview." *FaridaFahmy.com*, 2008. http://www.faridafahmy.com/history.html.

Fahmy, Khaled. *All the Pasha's Men: Mehmed Ali, His Army and the Making of Modern Egypt*. Cairo: American University in Cairo Press, 2002. 2nd edit. 2010.

Fahmy, Khaled. "Prostitution in Egypt in the Nineteenth Century." In Eugene Rogan, ed. *Outside In: On the Margins of the Middle East*. London: I.B. Tauris, 2001.

Fahmy, Khaled. "Women, Medicine and Power in Nineteenth Century Egypt." In Lila Abu-Lughod, ed., *Remaking Women: Feminism and Modernity in the Middle East*. Princeton: Princeton University Press, 1998.

Fahmy, Ziad. *Ordinary Egyptians: Creating the Modern Nation through Popular Culture*. Stanford, CA: Stanford University Press, 2011.

Farmer, Henry George. *A History of Arabian Music to the XIII Century*. London: Luzac and Co., 1929.

Farraj, Johnny, and Abu Shumays, Sami. *Inside Arabic Music: Arabic Maqam, Performance and Theory in the Twentieth Century*. New York: Oxford University Press, 2019.

Fayad, Hanan. "Mahraganat: Egyptian Ghetto Meets Western Electronic." *Egypt Today*. October 9, 2018. https://www.egypttoday.com/Article/4/58662/Mahraganat-Egyptian-ghetto-meets-Western-electronic.

Fi Baladi. Directed by Mariam Nader, 2019. (Features Dina Tal'at and Nagwa Fu'ad speaking about dancing). This version is subtitled in Spanish. https://www.youtube.com/watch?v=7Vr—KMBU3c.

Flaubert, Gustave. *Flaubert in Egypt. A Sensibility on Tour*. Francis Steegmuller, Trans. and ed. New York: Penguin, 1972.

Foda, Omar D. "The Pyramid and the Crown: The Egyptian Beer Industry from 1897 to 1963." *International Journal of Middle East Studies*. 46: 1, February 2014.

Fossett, Katelynn. "The Belly Dancer and the Brotherhood: Meet the Exotic Performer Trying to Take Down Egypt's Islamists." *Foreign Policy*. January 30, 2014. https://foreignpolicy.com/2014/01/30/the-belly-dancer-and-the-brotherhood-meet-the-exotic-performer-trying-to-take-down-egypts-islamists/.

France24. *The Songs of Tahrir Square: Music at the Heart of the Revolution*. Hussein Emara and Priscilla Lafitte. Web documentary, nd. http://musictahrir.france24.com/index-en.html.

Franken, Marjorie A. "From the Streets to the Stage: The Evolution of Professional Female Dance in Colonial Cairo." In Paul Tiyambe Zeleza and Cassandra Rachel Veney, eds. *Leisure in Urban Africa*. Trenton, NJ and Asmara, Eritrea: Africa World Press, 2003.

Franken, Marjorie A. *Daughter of Egypt: Farida Fahmy and the Reda Troupe*. Glendale, CA: Armenian Reference Books, 2001.

Fraser, Kathleen W. *Before They Were Belly Dancers: European Accounts of Female Entertainers in Egypt, 1760–1870*. Jefferson, NC: McFarland, 2015.

Fraser, Kathleen W. "Public and Private Entertainment at a Royal Egyptian Wedding: 1845." *Best of Habibi*. Vol. 19, No. 1, February 2002. http://thebestofhabibi.com/vol-19-no-1-feb-2002/royal-egyptian-wedding/.

Frishkopf, Michael. "Inshad Dini and Aghani Diniyya in Twentieth Century Egypt: A Review of Styles, Genres, and Available Recordings." Middle East Studies Association Bulletin. Vol. 34, No. 2, Winter 2000, pp. 167–183.

Frishkopf, Michael. "Introduction: Music and Media in the Arab World and *Music and Media in the Arab World* as Music and Media in the Arab World: A Metadiscourse." In Michael Frishkopf, ed. *Music and Media in the Arab World*. Cairo: American University in Cairo Press, 2010.

Frishkopf, Michael. "Tarab ('enchantment') in the Mystic Sufi Chant of Egypt." In Sherifa Zuhur, ed., *Colors of Enchantment: Theater, Dance, Music, and the Visual Arts of the Middle East*. Cairo: The American University in Cairo Press, 2001, pp. 233–269.

"From Mosque to Marquee." Mo4 Network, https://www.youtube.com/watch?v=Hd4zxdwr_X0.

Gabriel, Judith. "Seducing America: Selling the Middle Eastern Mystique." *Al-Jadid*, 2005 available at: http://dunyati.blogspot.com/2007/05/seducing-america-selling-middle-eastern.html.

Galland, A. *Tableau de l'Égypte pendant le séjour de l'armée française*. Au depot de Code civil officiel, libraire de la Palais du Tribunal, 1804, Tome 1.

Gallup. "Egypt: The Arithmetic of the Revolution." Gallup. n.d. https://news.gallup.com/poll/157043/egypt-arithmetic-revolution.aspx.

Gamal, Ali. "The Music Craze with a Dark Side Splitting Opinion in Egypt." *BBC Arabic*. January 13, 2016. https://www.bbc.com/news/world-middle-east-35135699.

Garcia, José Sánchez. "De las celebraciones para los santos a la mulid dance music: Utopía y juventud en Egipto," *Trans*. 2010. https://www.sibetrans.com/trans/article/24/de-las-celebraciones-para-los-santos-a-la-mulid-dance-music-utop-a-y-juventud-en-egipto.

Garwood, Paul. "Egypt Bans Foreign Belly Dancers." *Associated Press*. November 10, 2003.

Gedik, Ali C. *Made in Turkey: Studies in Popular Music*. London: Routledge, 2018.

Gerling, Hugh. "L'incroyable combat de Sama El Masry, la danseuse du ventre égyptienne qui se bat contre les islamistes." *Gentside*. February 12, 2014. http://222.gentside.com (art59112).

Gharib, Ashraf. "A Little Bit of Belly-Dancing and a Lot of Acting." *Ahram Online*. October 4, 2017.

Gharib, Ashraf. "Remembering Zeinat Sidki: The Most Famous Spinster in Egyptian Cinema." *AhramOnline*. March 2, 2018. http://english.ahram.org.eg/NewsContent/5/32/291981/Arts—Culture/Film/Remembering-Zeinat-Sedki-The-most-famous-spinster-.aspx.

De Ghette, Torie Rose. "The Rhythms of Egypt's Revolutionaries." *Jadaliyya*. March 4, 2012.

Gilman, Daniel. J. *Cairo Pop: Youth Music in Contemporary Egypt*. Minneapolis: University of Minnesota Press, 2014.

Golia, Maria. *Cairo: City of Sand*. London: Reaktion Books, 2004.

Golia, Maria. "Egypt's Mahragan Music of the Masses." *Middle East Institute*. July 7, 2015. http://www.mei.edu/content/at/egypt%E2%80%99s-mahragan-music-masses.

Golia, Maria, and Ilona Regulski, eds. *Asyut: Guardian City*. London: The British Museum, 2018.

Graham-Browne, Sarah. *Images of Women: The Portrayal of Women in Photography of the Middle East 1860–1950*. New York: Columbia University Press, 1988.

Grippo, James R. "What's Not on Egyptian Television and Radio: Locating the 'Popular' in Egyptian Shaabi." In Michael Frishkopf, ed., *Music and Media in the Arab World*. Cairo: American University in Cairo Press, 2010.

Guenena, Nemat, and Wassef, Nadia. *Unfulfilled Promises: Women's Rights in Egypt*. Cairo: Population Council, 1999.

Haghani, Fakhri. "The New Woman of the Interwar Period: Performance, Identity and Performative Act of Everyday Life in Egypt and Iran." *Al-Ra'ida*. Issue 122–123. Summer-Fall 2008.

Haha, 'Amr, Sadat, Figo and 'Ala' 50 Cent. "I Just Wish For a President." 2012. https://www.youtube.com/watch?v=BumLRk_ji2k.

Hamam, Imam. "Disarticulating Arab Popular Culture: The Case of Egyptian Comedies." In Tarik Sabry, ed. *Arab Cultural Studies: Mapping the Field*. London: I.B. Tauris, 2012.

Hammad, Hanan. *Industrial Sexuality: Gender, Urbanization and Social Transformation in Egypt*. Austin: University of Texas Press, 2016.

Hammad, Hanan. "Regulating Sexuality: The Colonial-National Struggle over Prostitution after the British Invasion of Egypt." In Marilyn Booth and Anthony Gorman, eds., *The Long 1890s in Egypt: Colonial Quiescence, Subterranean Resistance*. Edinburgh, AU: Edinburgh University Press, 2014, 195–221.

Hammad, Hanan Hassan. "Mechanizing People, Localizing Modernity: Industrialization and Social Transformation in Modern Egypt: Mahalla al-Kubra 1910–1958." Ph.D. dissertation. University of Texas at Austin, 2009.

Hammad, Hanan, and Biancani, Francesca. "Prostitution in Cairo." In Magaly Rodríguez García, Lex Heerma van Voss, Elise van Nederveen Meerkerk, eds. *Selling Sex in the City: A Global History of Prostitution 1600s–2000s*. Leiden: Brill, 2017.

Hammond, Andrew. *Pop Culture Arab World!: Media, Arts and Lifestyle*. Oxford: ABC Clio, 2005.

Hamouda, Adel. *Al-nukta al-siyasa fi misr: Kayfa yashkar al-masriyun min hukumahum*. Sphinx for Publishing and Distribution, 1990.

Hanna, Nabil Subhi. *Ghajar of Sett Guiranha: A Study of a Gypsy Community in Egypt*. 1982. Vol. 5, Monograph One, *The Cairo Papers*. The American University in Cairo, June 1982.

al-Haqqi, Yahya. *Qindil Umm Hashim* (The Lamp of Umm Hashim: The Saints Lamp), 1944. Available as *The Lamp of Umm Hashim and Other Stories*. Translated by Denys Johnson Davies. Cairo: The American University Press in Cairo, 2006.

Hassan, Abdalla F. *Media, Revolution and Politics in Egypt: The Story of an Uprising*. London: IB Taurus, 2015.

Hassan, Yasmine, and El Kashoty, Aly. "Ahmed Mekky: Street Smarts." *Egypt Today*. January 22, 2018. http://www.egypttoday.com/Article/15/40755/Ahmed-Mekky-Street-Smarts.

Hawthorn, Ainsley. "Middle Eastern Dance and What We Call It." *Dance Research*. 37: 1, 2019. https://www.euppublishing.com/doi/full/10.3366/drs.2019.025.

Henkish, Yasmin. *Trance Dancing with the Jinn: The*

Ancient Art of Contacting Spirits through Ecstatic Dance. Woodbury, Minnesota: Llewellyn Publications, 2016.

Henni-Chebra, Djamila and Poché, Christian, and et al. *Les danses du monde arabe ou l'héritage des almées.* Paris/Montréal: L'Harmattan, 1996.

al-Hifni, (El Hefni) Ratiba. *al-Sultana Munira al-Mahdiyya: Wa al-ghina' fi Misr qablaha wa fi zamaniha.* Cairo: Dar al-Shuruq, 1968 and 2001.

Hoffman, Valerie J. *Sufism, Mystics, and Saints in Modern Egypt.* Columbia: University of South Carolina Press, 1995.

Holslin, Peter. "Six Explosive Tracks that Define Mahraganat, Egypt's Wildly Popular Street Music." *Thump Vice.com,* March 29, 2017. https://thump.vice.com/en_us/article/ezwqke/explosive-mahraganat-egypt.

Hubbard, Ben. "Out of Egypt's Chaos, Musical Rebellion." *New York Times.* May 11, 2013. https://www.nytimes.com/2013/05/12/world/middleeast/egypts-chaos-stirs-musical-revolution.html.

Hunter, Deborah. "Playing for Peace: Meeting with Nabil Azzam." *Habibi.* Vol. 15, No. 3, Summer 1996 archived at *The Best of Habibi* http://thebestofhabibi.com/vol-15-no-3-summer-1996/nabil-azzam/.

al-Husaini, Mahmoud. "Inta Dinya Dhikr." https://www.youtube.com/watch?v=XmZBcrWKCI4.

Ibrahim, Baher. "Salafi Intolerance Threatens Sufis." *Guardian.* May 10, 2010. https://www.theguardian.com/commentisfree/belief/2010/may/10/islam-sufi-salafi-egypt-religion.

"In A Corner of Cairo This Nubian Group Creates the Sound of Home." *Middle East Eye.* March 17, 2019. https://www.middleeasteye.net/discover/corner-cairo-nubian-group-creates-sound-home.

Innemée, Karel, and El Dorghamy, Yasmine. "Meet the Masters of the Underworld," *Rawi,* Issue 5, 2013. https://rawi-magazine.com/articles/zaramulets/.

"Interview with Islam Chipsy & EEK (Egypt)." *World Skip the Beat.* (Parker Mah) nd. https://www.mixcloud.com/worldskipthebeat/interview-with-islam-chipsy-eek-egypt/.

Iskandar, Faruq Yusuf. "Bamba Kashar" as translated by Priscilla Adum. *Al-Qahira.* nd. In English at Shira.net. http://www.shira.net/about/bamba-kashar-alkahira.htm.

Iskandar, Faruq. "Faruq Iskandar yiktib Bamba Kashar usturat al-raqs al-sharqi," *Misr al-Mahrusa,* January 31, 2012. http://www.misrelmahrosa.com.eg/NewsD.aspx?id=1406.

Islam Chipsy with EEK. "Islam Chipsy (EEK) aux Trans Musicales" December 2014. https://www.youtube.com/watch?v=tZgT5swCGIo.

Ivor. "Did Napoleon Really Behead 400 Ghawazee?" *Shira.Net.* nd. http://www.shira.net/about/400ghawazee.htm.

al-Jabarti, 'Abd al-Rahman. *'Abd al-Rahman al-Jabarti's History of Egypt. 'Aja'ib al-Athar fi 'l-Tarajim wa 'l-Akhbar.* Thomas Philipp and Moshe Perlmann, eds. Stuttgart: Franz Steiner Verlag, Stuttgart, 1994.

al-Jabarti, 'Abd al-Rahman. *Napoleon in Egypt: Al Jabarti's Chronicle of the French Occupation.* Trans. Shmuel Moreh. Introduction by Robert Tignor. Princeton: Markus Weiner, 2004.

Jace, Clynton. "Cairo Something New." *The Fader.* October 16, 2012. http://www.thefader.com/2012/10/16/cairo-something-new.

Jansen, Willy. *Women without Men: Gender and Marginality in An Algerian Town.* Leiden: E.J. Brill, 1987.

Jarrar, Randa. "Why I Can't Stand White Belly Dancers." *Salon.com.* March 5, 2014. https://www.salon.com/2014/03/04/why_i_cant_stand_white_belly_dancers/.

Jawad, Ferida. "Guest Bloggers Around the World: Mahraganat—Musical Revolution in Egypt." *Afropop. PRI.org.* June 12, 2014. https://www.pri.org/stories/2014-06-12/guest-bloggers-around-world-mahraganat-musical-revolution-egypt.

Johnstone, Janet, and G.J. Tassie. "Egyptian *Baladi* Dances—A Contested Tradition." In F.A. Hassan, G.J. Tassie, A. De Trafford, L.S. Owens, and J. van Wetering, eds. *Managing Egypt's Cultural Heritage: Proceedings of the First Egyptian Cultural Heritage Organisation Conference on Egyptian Cultural Heritage Management.* London: Golden House and ECHO Publications, 2009.

Karayanni, Stavros Stavrou. "Tito Seif: The Moment of Eternal Shimmy." *Gilded Serpent,* n.d. however, photos and references are made to 2008. http://www.gildedserpent.com/art44/stavrostito.htm.

Karayanni, Stavros Stavrou. *Dancing Fear and Desire: Race, Sexuality, and Imperial Politics in Middle Eastern Dance.* Waterloo: Wilfrid Laurier University Press, 2004.

Karkar. Directed by 'Ali Ragab, 2007.

Kassing, Gayle. "Dances of Ancient Egypt." *History of Dance: An Interactive Arts Approach. Human Kinetics, 2007.*

Kent, Carolee, and Marjorie Franken. "A Procession through Time: The *Zaffat al-'Arusa* in Three Views." In Sherifa Zuhur, ed., *Images of Enchantment: Visual and Performing Arts of the Middle East.* Cairo: American University in Cairo Press, 1998, 71–80.

Khairiyya bint Mazin, recorded interview and performance, uploaded on Facebook (Live) by Saad Hassan, June 10, 2020. Several segments, the third includes extended playing by the *baladi mizmar* band. https://www.facebook.com/samrah.masoud/posts/2972662222840583, https://www.facebook.com/samrah.masoud/posts/2972729262833879, https://www.facebook.com/saad.hassan.902604/videos/3289425237757229/.

Khawly, Mohammed. "Nose Job Scandal Topples Egyptian Salafi MP." *Al-Akhbar English.* March 6, 2012, accessed December 25, 2016. http://english.al-akhbar.com/node/4876.

Al-Kilani, Muhammad Sayyid. *Fi rubu' al-Azbakiyyah: Dirasa adabiyya tarikhiyya ijtama'iyya.* Cairo: Dar al-Firjani, 1985.

Kirkpatrick, David, and El Sheikh, Mayy. "For Liberals in Egypt, A Champion Who Quips." *New*

York Times. December 30, 2012. https://www.nytimes.com/2012/12/31/world/middleeast/bassem-youssef-a-champion-for-egypts-liberals.html.

De Koning, Anouk. "Café Latte and Caesar Salad: Cosmopolitan Belonging in Cairo's Coffee Shops." In Singerman, Diane Singerman and Paul Amar, eds. *Cairo Cosmopolitan: Politics, Culture and Urban Space in the New Globalized Middle East.* Cairo: American University in Cairo Press, 2006, 221–234.

Kozma, Liat. "Wandering About as She Pleases: Prostitutes, Adolescent Girls and Female Slaves in Cairo's Public Space 1850–1882." Hawwa, Journal of Women in the Middle East and the Islamic World. 10, 2012, 18–36.

Kuppinger, Petra. "Globalization and Exterritoriality in Metropolitan Cairo," *Geographical Review*. Vol. 95, No. 3. New Geographies of the Middle East. July 2005, 348–372.

Lagrange, Frédéric. "Munira al-Mahdiyya 3," hosted by Mustafa Said. On "Min Al Tarikh." *AMAR, Foundation for Arab Music Archiving and Research*. August 27, 2015. http://www.amar-foundation.org/126-munira-al-mahdiyya-3/.

Lagrange, Frédéric. "Women in the Singing Business: Women in Songs," History Compass 7/1, 2009, 226–250. http://mapage.noos.fr/fredlag/FL-Women-History%20Compass.pdf, last accessed May 31, 2019.

Lane, Edward. *Manners and Customs of the Modern Egyptians*. (1836) New York: Cosimo Classics, 2005.

Lane-Poole, Sophie. *An Englishwoman in Egypt: Letters from Cairo written during a residence there in 1845–46*. Second Series, London: Charles Knight and Co. 1846. Also published as *The Englishwoman in Egypt: Letters from Cairo Written During a Residence There in 1842/3/4 with E.W. Lane Esq., Author of "The Modern Egyptians" By His Sister*. (1844).

Latifa. "Raqia Hassan's Dance Festival, Ahlan wa Sahlan 2000," *Gilded Serpent*, n.d. http://www.gildedserpent.com/articles13/raqiareviewlatifa.htm.

Lepp, Haley. "Saʿad Zaghlul's Gramophone: The Effects of Popular Music on the Egyptian Nation." *Intersect*. Vol. 6, No. 3, 2015.

"Letter from Khairiyya Mazin. The Last of the Ghawazi," 2011 to Edwina Nearing. Aswan Dancers. http://www.aswandancers.org/ghawazee-history.

Lexová, Irena, "Costumes of the Ancient Egyptian Women and Men Dancers." *Ancient Egyptian Dancers*. Translated by Haltmar, K. Mineola, NY: Dover Publications, 2000 (originally published Prague: Oriental Institute, 1935).

"Liqaʾ maʿa Basma Galal, al-awwil bint DJ fi Masr, ʿala qanat al-Wasl." Published January 27, 2019. https://www.youtube.com/watch?v=pGO6I1141_o.

"Liqaʾ Sama al-Masry fi ONTV," March 23, 2012, accessed May 22, 2017. https://www.youtube.com/watch?v=f39FF16qrtw (now removed).

Loiacono, Valeria, and Fallon, Julia M. "Intangible Cultural Heritage Beyond Borders: Egyptian Bellydance (Raqs Sharqi) as a Form of Transcultural Heritage." *Journal of Intercultural Studies*. 39: 3, 2018, pp. 286–304.

"Lorna (Gow) at Saqarra Hafla." September 12, 2009. https://www.youtube.com/watch?v=rRatPMg6Pjk.

Lueg, Maren. "Ecstasy and Trance in Tarab Performance." *Middle Eastern Music and Dance*, December 2007. Course Notes Department of Music Course: Performance Theory, December 2007. http://arabicmusicband.com/articles/tarab.

Lutfi, Huda. "Manners and Customs of Fourteenth Century Cairene Women: Female Anarchy versus Male Sharʿi Order in Prescriptive Texts." In Nikki Keddie and Beth Baron, eds. *Women in Middle Eastern History*. New Haven: Yale University Press, 1993.

Madoeuf, Anna. "Mulids of Cairo: Sufi Guilds, Popular Celebrations and the 'Roller-Coaster Landscape' of the Resignified City." In Diane Singerman and Paul Amar, eds. *Cairo Cosmopolitan: Politics, Culture and Urban Space in the New Globalized Middle East*. Cairo: American University in Cairo Press, 2006, pp. 465–487. https://halshs.archives-ouvertes.fr/halshs-01023614/document.

Mahfouz, Naguib. *Karnak Café*. (The original title is *Karnak*) Trans. Roger Allen. New York: Anchor Books, 1974.

Mahmoud, Sayed. "Into the World of Moulid: Director Sameh Abdelaziz on His New Film El-Leila El-Kebira." *Al-Ahram Online*. November 19, 2015. http://english.ahram.org.eg/NewsContent/5/32/169043/Arts—Culture/Film/-Into-the-world-of-Moulid-Director-Sameh-Abdelaziz.aspx.

Mahmoud, Sayed. "Singing in the Shadow." *Al-Ahram Weekly Online*. October 16–22, 2008. http://weekly.ahram.org.eg/Archive/2008/918/sc2.htm.

Mahmud, ʿAbd al-ʿAziz. "Ya Labsa Tarha." Scene from *Khulud*, 1948. https://vimeo.com/channels/882356/108696972.

"Mahragan: Music as Revolution." *14Km.org*, November 29, 2015. http://14km.org/2015/11/mahragan-music-as-revolution/?lang=en.

Mahragan: The Story of Egypt's Street Dance. Noah Chasek-McFoy, dir. 2015. https://vimeo.com/106879244 (trailer).

Mahraganat: Cairo's Music Revolution. A Report by Khalid Koutit. April 12, 2014. https://www.dw.com/en/mahraganat-cairos-music-revolution/a-17563477.

Mamduh, Nidhal "Taʿaraf ʿala asbab nafi Muhammad ʿAli ghawazi Sunbat ila Saʿid." *Dostor.org*, June 7, 2017. https://www.dostor.org/1384264?fbclid=IwAR15o2q5DgCoG9L6-cNX-_5lGNyGCyBLY76rm3dZ0OJXEjZ1Z51QsNWChYs.

Marcus, Scott. *Music in Egypt: Experiencing Music, Expressing Culture*. New York: Oxford University Press, 2006.

Marie, Mustafa. "ET (Egypt Today) Commemorates Birth Anniversary of Samia Gamal." *Egypt Today*. March 5, 2019. https://www.egypttoday.

com/Article/4/66678/ET-commemorates-birth-anniversary-of-Samia-Gamal.

Marks, Joshua J. "Festivals in Ancient Egypt." *Ancient History Encyclopedia*. (Last modified March 17, 2017) https://www.ancient.eu/article/1032/.

al-Masabni, Badi'a. Bi qalam Nazik Basila. *Mudhakirrat Badi'a al-Masabni*. Beirut: Maktabat al-Hayat, 1960. This publication was first serialized in 1939.

al-Masry, Sama. "Ibn al-Amrikaniyya Sama al-Masry," ["Son of the American Woman" Sama al-Masry] Accessed December 25, 2016 but now made private, https://www.youtube.com/watch?v=R06-OifqT7k.

McDonald, Caitlin. "Belly Dance and Glocalisation: Constructing Gender in Egypt and on the Global Stage." Ph.D. thesis. Arab and Islamic Studies, University of Exeter, January 1, 2010.

McDonald Caitlin. *Global Moves: Belly Dance as An Extra/Ordinary Space to Explore Social Paradigms in Egypt and Around the World*. Zarafa/LeanPub, 2012.

McDonald, Caitlin, and Sellers-Young, Barbara, eds. *Belly Dance Around the World: New Communities, Performance and Identity*. Jefferson, NC: McFarland, 2013.

Mehrez, Samia, ed. *Translating Egypt's Revolution: The Language of Tahrir*. Cairo: American University in Cairo Press, 2012.

Melman, Billie. *Women's Orients: English Women in the Middle East, 1718–1918*. Ann Arbor: University of Michigan Press, 1992.

MENA. "Nose Job MP Files Complaint Against Belly Dancer Who Says She's His Wife." *Egypt Independent*. March 26, 2012.

Menawy, Marwan. "Egypt Fights a Losing Battle Against Drugs." *Arab News*. February 26, 2018. https://www.arabnews.com/node/1254306/middle-east.

Mestyan, Adam. "Power and Music in Cairo: Azbakiyya." *Urban History*. Vol. 40, Issue 4, 2013, 681–704.

Metwaly, Ali. "Warda: The Algerian Rose's Legacy Will Live On." *AhramOnline*. May 19, 2012.

Mikhail, Mona. "Revisiting the Theater in Egypt: An Overview." In Sherifa Zuhur, ed., *Colors of Enchantment: Theater, Dance, Music and the Visual Arts of the Middle East*. Cairo: American University in Cairo, 2001.

Mohsen, Ali Abdel. "A Q & A with Leading Mahraganat Singer Sadat." *Egypt Independent*. April 13, 2013. http://www.egyptindependent.com/qa-leading-mahraganat-singer-sadat/.

Morayef, Soraya. "We Are the Eight Percent: Inside Egypt's Underground Shaabi Music Scene." *Jadaliyya*. May 29, 2012. https://www.jadaliyya.com/Details/26088.

Mostyn, Trevor. "Warda Jazairiya—Obituary." *Guardian*. May 29, 2012.

"Al-Mouled." Directed by Samir Seif and written by Muhammad Galal 'abd al-Qawi starring 'Adil Imam, Yusra and Amina Rizq. 1989. https://www.youtube.com/watch?v=ZgqPnAa7eFs&list=PLvYo2Onecc8UScAP5dxgSrsX2ik3hU27m.

Muawad, Fouad. "Samia Gamal, A Dancer Who Believes the Middle Ground Is Best." *Kawakib*. 1968, republished at Akadimia al-Funun, 2010. http://egyptartsacademy.kenanaonline.com/topics/58701/posts/149210.

al-Mufti, Elham Abdel Wahhab. "Shakwa in Arab Poetry during the Abbasid Period." Ph.D. thesis. School of African and Oriental Studies, University of London, 1990.

"Munira al-Mahdiyya," (brief sketch) and recordings with Mustafa Said and Frédéric Lagrange on "Min al-Tarikh." "Munira al-Mahdiyya" 1–4 Amar Foundation for Arab Music Archiving and Research. http://www.amar-foundation.org/munira-al-mahdiyya/.

Music of the Ghawazee. Recorded at Thebes in 1973 by Aisha Ali, performed by various artists. Araf DA-700. Phonodisc (2 e. 12 in. 33 1/3 rpa.) « Discs Araf; 30 Sep 73: N11607. N11608.

al-Muwaylihi, Muhammad. *Hadith 'Isa ibn Hisham*. Translated as *A Period of Time* by Roger M.A. Allen. Reading, UK: Middle East Centre, 1992.

Nabaweya Mustafa in "Ibn al-Falah." 1948. https://vimeo.com/239928366.

Nabaweya Mustafa in "Nargis." 1948. https://vimeo.com/134365475?fbclid=IwAR1G1dOHl-dYeEcduFVo4iiQVIjxK0W808lviumzPPK9sjEAIdpkKaLJOgw.

"Nagwa Fouad Baladi" c. early 1980s https://www.youtube.com/watch?v=g9-palv_E2M&feature=youtu.be&fbclid=IwAR0q5k2-sUhHLKrnL_MbMihGIRVQ9rvcxtYkQl3tFfVZCxhdO_pkhJeOleY.

"Nagwa (Fouad) Haggalah." https://www.youtube.com/watch?v=QKgVSPDXmCY&feature=youtu.be&fbclid=IwAR336aSVdX85ziEfkrfCMRrHtL5PcB2RQA248jFg3Ceh178c1_UDQM0ISjo.

"Na[q]alna al-fann dah min al-masagid lil-masrah: Hiwar ma'a al-firqat al-Hadhra lil-inshad." *Elfasla.com*. June 12, 2018. http://elfasla.com/ArtsAndCulture/interview-with-al-hadraa-band. This site is inactive, but al-Hadhra has a Facebook page. The interview appears here in translation: https://scenenoise.com/Features/from-mosque-to-marquee-a-conversation-with-sufi-collective-al-hadra.

Nasser, Samia. "Iraqi Ra'qisah's Life in America." *Gilded Serpent.com*. May 20, 2011. http://www.gildedserpent.com/cms/2011/05/20/samia-nasser-iraqi-dancer/.

Nassib, Sélim. Translated by Alison Anderson. New York: Europa Editions, 2006.

Nazmi, Laila. *Fulklur Sha'bi*. Sono Cairo, 7017043, 1970.

Nazmi, Laila. *Sahra ma'a ahdath al-mutriba Laila Nazmi*. Sono Cairo 87–77037, 1977.

Nearing, Edwina. "Ghawazi on the Edge of Extinction." *Habibi*. Vol. 12, No. 2, 1993. http://thebestofhabibi.com/2-vol-12-no-2-spring-1993/ghawazi/.

Nearing, Edwina. "Sirat al-Ghawazi" Part 1, 1976, reprinted on GildedSerpent.com. http://www.gildedserpent.com/articles25/edwinaghawazich1.htm.

Nearing, Edwina. "Sirat al-Ghawazi." Part 7. http://www.gildedserpent.com/enearing/edwinaghawazich7.htm.

Nearing, Edwina. "Sirat al-Ghawazi." Part 8. http://www.gildedserpent.com/enearing/edwinaghawazich8.htm.

de Nerval, Gerard. *The Women of Cairo: Scenes of Life in the Orient*. London: Routledge, 1929.

"Nicole Saba Regrets Acting with Adel Imam." *Al Bawaba*. January 1, 2012, accessed December 25, 2016. http://www.albawaba.com/entertainment/nicole-saba-regrets-acting-adel-imam-407339.

Noshokaty, Amira. "Cairo Cafes: A Century of Music and Coffee." *Al-Ahram Online*, May 29, 2014.

Noshokaty, Amira. "'Toha' Chanteuse of Egypt and Levant." *Ahram Online*. December 5, 2014.

Nur, Yousif. "A Radical Century: Mahmoud Refat of 100 Copies Cairo Interviewed." *The Quietus*. December 17, 2014.

Oka and Ortega. "Lissah hanghani: mahragan "Hatti bosah ya bit" ghina' Oka wa Ortega wa Shahta Karika." Published May 16, 2013. https://www.youtube.com/watch?v=xsGQaT6RhxQ.

Peterson, Jennifer. "Going to the Mulid: Street-smart Spirituality in Egypt." In Samuli Schielke and Liza Debevec, eds. *Ordinary Lives and Grand Schemes: An Anthropology of Everyday Religion*. Oxford and New York: Bergahn, 2012.

Peterson, Jennifer. "Playing with Spirituality: The Adoption of Mulid Motifs in Egyptian Dance Music." *Contemporary Islam*. 2: No. 3, 2008, 271–295.

Peterson, Jennifer. "Remixing Songs, Remaking MULIDS: The Merging Spaces of Dance Music and Saint Festivals in Egypt." In Samuli Schielke and G. Stauthe, eds. *Dimensions of Locality, Muslim Saints, Their Place and Space*. Yearbook of the Sociology of Islam, 8. Bielefeld: Transcript Verlag, 2008, pp. 67–88.

Peterson, Jennifer. "Sampling Folklore: The Repopularization of Sufi Inshad in Egyptian Dance Music." *Arab Media and Society*. January 27, 2008.

Pieslak, Jonathan. "Al Qaida Culture and Anashid." In Pieslak, Jonathan. *Radicalism and Music: An Introduction to the Music Cultures of al-Qa'ida, Racist Skinheads, Christian-Affiliated Radicals and Eco-Animal Rights Militants*. Middletown, CT: Wesleyan University Press, 2015.

Poché, Christian. *Musiques du monde arabe: écoute et découverte*. Paris: Institut du Monde Arabe, 1994.

Pomeroy, Sarah B. *Women in Hellenistic Egypt from Alexander to Cleopatra*. Detroit: Wayne State Press, 1990. Originally published in 1984.

Prusskaya, Evgeniya. "Arab Chronicles as A Source for Studying Bonaparte's Expedition to Egypt." *Napoléonica. La Revue*, 3: no. 24, 2015, 48–60.

Puig, Nicholas. "Egypt's Pop-Music Clashes and the 'World-Crossing' Destinies of Muhammad Ali Street Musicians." 2004. IRD. Also in Diane Singerman and Paul Amar, eds. *Cairo Cosmopolitan: Politics, Culture and Urban Space in the New Globalized Middle East*. Cairo: American University in Cairo Press, 2006, pp. 513–538.

Racy, Ali Jihad. *Making Music in the Arab World: The Culture and Artistry of Tarab*. Cambridge: Cambridge University Press, 2003.

Racy, 'Ali Jihad. "Musical Aesthetics in Present-Day Cairo." *Ethnomusicology*. 26/3, 1982, 391–406.

Racy, 'Ali Jihad. "Musical Attitudes and Spoken Language in Pre-Civil War Beirut." In Sherifa Zuhur, ed., *Colors of Enchantment: Theater, Dance, Music and the Visual Arts of the Middle East*. Cairo: American University in Cairo Press, 2001, 336–351.

Racy, 'Ali Jihad. "Record Industry and Egyptian Traditional Music: 1904–1932," Ethnomusicology. 20: 1, January 1976, 23–48.

Rakha, Youssef. "Hoarseness: A Legend of Contemporary Cairo." *The White Review*. June 2014. http://www.thewhitereview.org/feature/hoarseness-a-legend-of-contemporary-cairo/.

Ramadan, 'Abd al-'Azim. *Tatawwur al-haraka al-wataniyya fi Misr sanah 1918 ila sanah 1936*. 1983.

Ramadan, Sarah. "Legalizing Mahraganat: Recognition vs. Identity Erasure." *AFTE Freedom of Thought and Expression Law Firm*, June 20, 2020. https://afteegypt.org/en/afte_releases/2020/06/20/19282-afteegypt.html.

Ramdani, Nabila. "Women in the 1919 Egyptian Revolution: From Feminist Awakening to Nationalist Political Activism." *Journal of International Women's Studies*, Vol. 14. Issue 2, March 2013.

"al-Raqisa." Al-Qahira wa al-Nas. "al-Halqa al-ula min barnamag al-Raqisa. Ikhtabarat al-raqisa fi kull anha' al-'alam." January 9, 2014. https://www.youtube.com/watch?v=y7GD1BSyddo.

"Raqs Masri Fifi 'Abdu," circa 1973, upload date January 26, 2010, accessed December 26, 2016. https://www.youtube.com/watch?v=mmnqEeeWh60.

"Raqsat al-Hagallah." Nagwa Fu'ad and Fatima Sarhan. https://www.youtube.com/watch?v=KXSCN4ISeC0&feature=youtu.be&fbclid=-IwAR2ytUhSqqxw-FQi8JVW2fBbJ_DN7BOjdEaygW6dsjmSipSjDQt9ZpPzsVY.

Rasmussen, Anne. "The Music of Arab Americans: Performance Contexts and Musical Transformation." *Pacific Review of Ethnomusicology*. Vol. 5, 1989, 13–32.

Raymond, André. *Égyptiens et Français au Caire 1798–1801*. Cairo: Institut Francais d'Archéologie Orientale 1998.

Reda, Mahmoud. As interviewed by Shira. *Shira. Dotnet*. July 31, 2006. http://www.shira.net/about/reda-interview12-other.htm.

Reynolds, Dwight. *Heroic Poets, Poetic Heroes: The Ethnography of Performance in an Arabic Oral Epic Tradition*. Ithaca, NY: Cornell University Press, 1995.

Richardson, Kristina. "Tracing a Gypsy Mixed Language through Medieval and Early Modern Arabic and Persian Literature." *Der Islam*. vol. 94, no. 1, 2017, 115–157.

Rifaey, Tonia. "An Illustration of the Transitional

Period in Egypt During 1919–1924: Political Cartoons in Egypt's Revolutionary History." Master's thesis. Arabic Studies, American University in Cairo, 1997.

Rifaey, Tonia, and Sherifa Zuhur. "Visualizing Identity: Gender and Nation in Egyptian Cartoons." In Sherifa Zuhur, ed., *Colors of Enchantment: Theater, Dance, Music, and the Visual Arts of the Middle East*. Cairo: American University in Cairo Press, 2001.

Rinne, Tuija. "Sing, O Simsimiya." Translated from Finnish. "Laula simsimiyya." *Ishtar*. January 2005; available at *El Hosseny Dance*, http://www.elhossenydance.com/layali_simsimiyya.html.

Rizk, Yunan Labib. "Al-Ahram, A Diwan of Contemporary Life, 252." *Al-Ahram Weekly Online* Issue 396, September 24–30, 1998. http://weekly.ahram.org.eg/Archive/1998/396/chrncls.htm.

Roberts, Kate. "Cairo Clubs: Don't Forget to Take Off Your 'Hat.'" *Egyptian Streets*, February 8, 019.

Rodenbeck, John. "'Awalim' or The Persistence of Error." In Jill Edwards, ed., *Historians in Cairo: Essays in Honor of George Scanlon*. Cairo: American University in Cairo Press.

Rostum, Layla. "Interview of Badia Masabni." *Nugum 'ala al-Ardh*, 1966. https://www.youtube.com/watch?v=8yBO4TELvqQ Available in English on Shira.net http://www.shira.net/about/badia-interview-1966.htm.

Roushdy, Noha. "Baladi as Performance: Gender and Dance in Modern Egypt." *Surfacing*. Vol. 3, August 2010.

Roushdy, Noha. "What is Baladi about Raqs al-Baladi?: The Survival of Belly Dance in Egypt." In McDonald, Caitlin and Sellers-Young, Barbara, eds. *Belly Dance Around the World: New Communities, Performance and Identity*. Jefferson, NC: McFarland, 2013.

Rowson, Everett K. "The Effeminates of Early Medina." *Journal of the American Oriental Society*. Vol. 111, No. 4, Oct.-Dec. 1991, 671–693.

Rugh, Andrea. *Reveal and Conceal: Dress in Contemporary Egypt*. Syracuse: Syracuse University Press, 1986.

Russell, Mona L. *Egypt*. Santa Barbara, CA: ABC-Clio, 2013.

Ryzova, Lucy. "The Battle of Muhammad Mahmud Street: Teargas, Hair Gel and Tramadol." *Jadaliyya*. November 28, 2011.

Sabah. "Ya Dalaa Dallaa," (Composed by Farid al-Atrash) Voice of Lebanon—VL 2180, 1973.

El-Safi, Shereen. "Interview with Raqia Hassan: The Mother of Invention." *The Best of Habibi*. Vol. 14, No. 1, Winter 1995. http://thebestofhabibi.com/vol-14-no-1-winter-1995/raqia-hassan/.

El-Safi, Shereen. "Mona El Said: Moving in Mysterious Ways." *The Best of Habibi*. Vol. 15, No. 1, Winter 1996. http://thebestofhabibi.com/vol-15-no-1-winter-1996/mona-el-said/.

El-Safi, Shereen. "An Uncommon Woman: Nagwa Fouad Queen of Oriental Dance." *Best of Habibi*. Vol. 18, No. 3, March 2001. http://thebestof habibi.com/vol-18-no-3-march-2001/nagwa-fouad/.

Safinaz (Sofinar Grigoryan) in "'Ala Rimsh al-'Ayyun," with singer Hamada al-Laithy. https://www.youtube.com/watch?v=RD3A7obUh74.

Sahin, Christine M. "Core Connections: A Contemporary Cairo Raqs Sharqi Ethnography." Ph.D. dissertation. University of California, Riverside, 2018.

Saiah-Baudis, Ysabel. *Oum Kalsoum Forever*. Paris: Orient Éditions, 2012.

Said, Edward. "Farewell to Tahia." In Sherifa Zuhur, ed. *Colors of Enchantment: Theater, Dance, Music and Visual Arts of the Middle East*. Cairo: American University in Cairo Press, 2001.

Saʿid, Mona. "Mona Black Gold Baladi Taksim." https://www.youtube.com/watch?v=gtPuZ2dsg ho&feature=youtu.be&fbclid=IwAR3J2qK-L_5n YrPrYgCU19FBr8vhHpoY6mDdtDToE3MuGZ Otu-BNk38uqrE.

Sakr, Yahya. "Egyptian Troupe Revives Art of Musical Sketches." *Al Monitor*. July 13, 2017.

Saleh, Magda Ahmed Abdel Ghaffar. "A Documentation of the Ethnic Dance Traditions of the Arab Republic of Egypt." Ph.D. dissertation. New York University, 1979.

"Sama al-Masry Baʿad al-Akhir Laha: Wasalatni Maʿakamalat Tahdid Nust 'ala 'Haya Waslat al-Hijab.'" *ElCinema.com*. June 20, 2013, accessed December 16, 2016, http://www.elcinema.com/news/nw678932489/.

"Sama al-Masry taʿadh Shaykha Moza wa al-Jazira." August 25, 2013, accessed December 25, 2016. https://www.youtube.com/watch?v=JZ9vw-mp2aQ.

Sameh, Yara. "Musicians' Syndicate Bans Mohamed Ramadan, Others from Singing." *Sada El Balad*. February 17, 2020. https://see.news/musicians-syndicate-bans-mohamed-ramadan-others-from-singing/.

Sami, Souheir. "Nagwa Fouad: Hours of Glory." *Al-Ahram Weekly*. Issue 390. August 13–19, 1998. http://weekly.ahram.org.eg/Archive/1998/390/people.htm.

Sampson, John. "The Ghagar of Egypt: A Chapter in the History of Gypsy Migration," *Journal of the Gypsy Lore Society*. 3rd series, Vol. VII, no. 2, 1928.

Sarhan, Fatima. "Fatme Serhan with Dina." https://www.youtube.com/watch?v=FRaNHnurW-s.

Sarhan, Fatima, with Dina. "'Ala Wardi kulli dall'a." 1994. https://www.youtube.com/watch?v= Ky2BJiTLS-A&feature=youtu.be&fbclid=-IwAR2VfcH89lvTt4qMYb-veJzwxcApX_ PQfXttH6J2ewi7RBlqlnF7flDph8s.

al-Sawarikh (Dok Dok and Funky) "*La.*" December 2017. https://www.youtube.com/watch?v=xf9s_ h8S2XM (accessed July 31, 2018).

al-Sayyid Marsot, Afaf Lufi. "The Revolutionary Gentlewomen in Egypt." In Lois Beck and Nikki Keddie, eds. *Women in the Muslim World*. Cambridge: Harvard University Press, 1978.

Schemm, Paul, and Abbot, Sebastian. "Cairo's Nightclubs Relics of Bygone Era." *SF Gate* (from

Associated Press). December 14, 2008. https://www.sfgate.com/news/article/Cairo-s-night clubs-relics-of-bygone-era-3258319.php.

Schielke, Samuli. *Egypt in the Future Tense: Hope, Frustration and Ambivalence Before and After 2011*. Bloomington: Indiana University Press, 2015.

Schielke, Samuli. *Perils of Joy: Contesting Mulid Festivals in Contemporary Egypt*. Syracuse: Syracuse University Press, 2012.

Sednaoui, Selim. "Western Classical Music in Umm Kulthum's Country." In Sherifa Zuhur, ed. *Images of Enchantment, Images of Enchantment: Visual and Performing Arts of the Middle East*. Cairo: American University in Cairo Press, 1998, pp. 123–134.

Shaarawi, Huda. *Harem Years: The Memoirs of an Egyptian Feminist*. Trans. Margot Badran. New York: Feminist Press, 1987.

"Shafiqa al-Qibtiyya: al-Raqasa allati sharrabt khuyulha shampanya," *al-Kawakib*, January 1955 (available at al-Bostah.com April 7, 2012) http://www.bostah.com/%D8%B4%D9%81%D9%8A%D9%82%D8%A9-%D8%A7%D9%84%D9%82%D8%A8%D8%B7%D9%8A%D9%A9-%D8%A7%D9%84%D8%B1%D8%A7%D9%82%D8%B5%D8%A9-%D8%A7%D9%84%D8%AA%D9%8A-%D8%B4%D8%B1%D8%A8%D8%AA-%D8%AE%D9%8A%D9%88%D9%84%D9%87%D8%A7-%D8%A7%D9%84%D8%B4%D9%85%D8%A8%D8%A7%D9%86%D9%8A%D8%A7.html.

Shannon, Jonathan H. *Among the Jasmine Trees: Music and Modernity in Contemporary Syria*. Middletown, CT: Wesleyan University, 2006.

Shannon, Jonathan H. *Performing al-Andalus: Music and Nostalgia across the Mediterranean*. Bloomington: Indiana University Press, 2015.

al-Sharif, Ahmad. "Halwa ya balha ya ma[q]amaha." Composed and sung by Ahmad al-Sharif. Published on November 3, 2016. https://www.youtube.com/watch?v=S3ugoJvHUr0&feature=youtu.be.

Shay, Anthony. *Choreographic Politics: State Folk Dance Companies, Representation and Power*. Middleton, CT: Wesleyan University Press, 2002.

Shenker, Jack. *The Egyptians: A Radical History of Egypt's Unfinished Revolution*. New York: The New Press, 2016.

Sonbol, Amira El-Azhary. *The New Mamluks: Egyptian Society and Modern Feudalism*. Syracuse: Syracuse University Press, 2000.

Spencer, Patricia. "Dance in Ancient Egypt." *Near Eastern Archaeology*. 66, 3, September 2003.

Stokes, Martin. "Creativity, Globalization and Music." *Volume! La revue de musique populaires*. Vol. 10, No. 2, 2014, 30–45. https://journals.openedition.org/volume/4561.

Stokes, Martin. Review of *La Simsimiyya du Port Saide*. Ensemble al-Tanbura, directed by Zakariya Ibrahim. CD with liner notes by Christian Poché. Institut du Monde Arabe, 1999. https://www.umbc.edu/MA/index/number7/stokes/simsi.htm.

Stone, Caroline. "The Great Migration of the Bani Hilal." *Aramco World*. November/December 2016. https://www.aramcoworld.com/Articles/November-2016/The-Great-Migration-of-the-Bani-Hilal.

Stone, Rebecca. "Reverse Imagery: Middle Eastern Themes in Hollywood." In Sherifa Zuhur, ed., *Images of Enchantment: Visual and Performing Arts of the Middle East*. Cairo: American University in Cairo Press, 1998, pp. 247–263.

"Street Shaabi Dance Improvisation by Kareem Gad." https://www.youtube.com/watch?v=MHxuV_cPxOc (accessed September 13, 2018).

Sunaina, Maira. "Belly Dancing, Arab-Face, Orientalist Feminism and U.S. Empire." *American Quarterly*. June 2008, Vol. 6, Issue 2, pp. 317–345.

Swedenberg, Ted. "Egypt's Music of Protest from Sayyid Darwish to DJ Haha," *MERIP* (Middle East Research and Information Project) 42, Winter 2012, accessed November 14, 2016. http://www.merip.org/mer/mer265/egypts-music-protest.

Swedenburg, Ted. "From Sayed Darwish to MC Sadat: Sonic Cartographies of the Egyptian Uprising." In Valerie J. Hoffman, ed. *Making the New Middle East: Politics, Culture and Human Rights*. Syracuse: Syracuse University Press, 2019, pp. 394–454.

"Tadmir kazinu wa malha layli al-fannana Lucy" *Storm.com*. February 10, 2011, available at web.archive.org. https://web.archive.org/web/20110308003938/http://www.urstorm.com/vb/t15692.html.

Talaat, Dina avec Claude Guibal. *Ma liberté de danser: La derniere danseuse d'Égypte*. Neuilly-sur-Seine: Michel Lafon, 2011.

Tawfeek, Farah. "Egypt's Public Prosecution Arrests Belly Dancer Sama al-Masry." *Egypt Independent*. April 26, 2020. https://egyptindependent.com/aegyptian-public-prosecution-arrests-belly-dancer-sama-al-masryegyptian-public-prosecution-detains-belly-dancer-sama-al-masry/.

Tawfiq, Mohammed, and Oberoi, Naira. "Egyptian Singer Sentenced to Prison for Video 'Inciting Debauchery.'" *CNN.com*. December 14, 2017. https://www.cnn.com/2017/12/13/middleeast/egypt-singer-shyma-ahmed-prison-intl/index.html.

"Teenager Makes Horse Dance in Egypt." *Voice of America*, 2018. https://www.facebook.com/voiceofamerica/videos/10155914841133074/?v=10155914841133074.

"Terrorism 'Obama-Style'" Video from Egyptian Singer Shaaban abdel Rahim," February 23, 2013, accessed October 31, 2016. https://www.youtube.com/watch?v=lTXidqs2Ofc.

"This Afternoon." *al-Afkar*. February 23, 1917.

Thomas Cook, Ltd. *Cook's Tourists' Handbook for Egypt, the Nile, and the Desert*. London: T. Cook & Son, 1897.

"Tito, Egyptian Male Egyptian Raks Sharki" [sic] filmed by Tariq Sultan. Giza, July 2005. https://www.youtube.com/watch?v=6autbeh_tUk.

"Too Sexy or Too Disgusting? Egyptian Film Poster Fuels Anger." *Cairo Scene*, June 11, 2014, accessed December 26, 2016. http://www.cairoscene.com/ArtsAndCulture/Too-Sexy-or-Too-Disgusting-Egyptian-Film-Poster.

Touma, Habib Hassan. *Music of the Arabs*. Trans. Laurie Schwarts. Portland, OR: Amadeus Press, 1996.

Trout-Powell, Eve. "Burnt-Cork Nationalism: Race and Identity in the Theater of Ali al-Kassar." In Sherifa Zuhur, ed. *Colors of Enchantment: Theater, Dance, Music and the Visual Arts of the Middle East*. Cairo: American University in Cairo Press, 2001.

Tucker, Judith. *Women in Nineteenth Century Egypt*. New York: Cambridge University Press 1985.

Tyldesley, Joyce. *Daughters of Isis: Women of Ancient Egypt*. London: Penguin Books, 1994.

Van Eynde, Koen. "Mohamed "el-Limby" Saad and the Popularization of a Masculine Code." *Networking Knowledge*. Journal of the MeCCSA Postgraduate Network. Vol. 4, No. 1, 2011.

van Nieuwkerk, Karin. "Changing Images and Shifting Identities of Female Performers in Egypt." In Sherifa Zuhur, ed., *Images of Enchantment: Visual and Performing Arts of the Middle East*. Cairo: American University in Cairo Press, 1998.

van Nieuwkerk, Karin. "Female Entertainers in Egypt: Drinking and Gender Roles." In Demitra Gefou-Madianou, ed. *Alcohol, Gender and Culture*. London: Routledge, 1992.

van Nieuwkerk, Karin. *Manhood Is Not Easy: Egyptian Masculinities through the Life of Sayyid Henkish*. New York: American University in Cairo Press, 2019.

van Nieuwkerk, Karin. "On Religion, Gender, and Performing: Female Performers and Repentance in Egypt." In Tullia Magrini, ed. *Music and Gender: Perspectives from the Mediterranean*. Chicago: University of Chicago Press, 2003, pp. 267–286.

van Nieuwkerk, Karin. "Popularizing Islam or Islamizing Popular Music: New Developments in Egypt's Wedding Scene." *Contemporary Islam*. Vol. 6, No. 3, 2012.

van Nieuwkerk, Karin. "Secret Communication and Marginality. The Case of Egyptian Entertainers." *Sharqiyat*. 10:1, 1998, 27–41.

van Nieuwkerk, Karin. *"A Trade Like Any Other": Female Singers and Dancers in Egypt*. Austin: University of Texas Press, 1995.

Varga Dinicu, Morocco C. "Nadia Hamdi Giving Joy to the Heart and Eyes." *Habibi*, Vol. 15, No. 2 (Spring 1996). Available at Casbahdance.org, https://www.casbahdance.org/giving-joy-to-the-heart-and-eyes/.

Varga Dinicu, Morocco C. *You Asked Aunt Rocky: Answers and Advice about Raqs Sharqi & Raqs Shaabi*. Virginia Beach, VA: Hypatia-Rose Press, 2013.

Vermeyden, Anne. "Hybridization and Uneven Exchange: The Popularization of Belly Dance in Toronto, Canada (1950–1990)." Ph.D. dissertation, University of Guelph, 2017.

Vermeyden, Anne. "The Reda Folkloric Dance Troupe and State Support during the Nasser Period." *Dance Research Journal*. Vol. 48, Issue 3, December 2017.

Wahda wa al-Nuss starring and written by Sama al-Masry, 2012. In two parts Media HD Part 1: https://www.dailymotion.com/video/x3sx1qv, Part 2: https://www.dailymotion.com/video/x3sxae6.

Walsh, Declan. "Foreign Belly Dancers: Egyptians Shake Their Heads (and Hips)." *New York Times*. July 8, 2018.

Ward, Heather D. "Desperately Seeking Shafiqa: The Search for Shafiqa al-Qibtiyya." *Gilded Serpent*. http://www.gildedserpent.com/cms/2013/10/03/nisaa-desperately-seeking-shafiqa/#axzz54mUJvqdK.

Ward, Heather D. *Egyptian Belly Dance in Transition: The Raqs Sharqi Revolution*. Jefferson, NC: McFarland, 2018.

Ward. Heather D. "The Search for El Dorado." *Gilded Serpent*. http://www.gildedserpent.com/cms/2013/03/13/nisaa-el-dorado-cairo/#axzz54mUJvqdK.

Wegz. "21," (Wahda wa 'Ishrin). https://www.youtube.com/watch?v=WwB5w-Rt88k.

Weiss, Ellen. "Egyptian Hip Hop: Expressions from the Underground." *Cairo Papers in Social Science*. Vol. 34, No. 1, 2016.

Weissblei, Gil. "The Egyptian Belly Dancers with A Secret Jewish Identity." *The Librarians*. September 27, 2018. https://blog.nli.org.il/en/jamal_sisters/.

Wihish, Niveen. "Hakim: From Mohammed Ali Street to Radio City Music Hall." *Al-Ahram Weekly Online*. 10–15 October 2002. http://weekly.ahram.org.eg/Archive/2002/607/profile.htm.

Williams, Daniel. "Making a Comeback: Male Belly Dancers in Egypt." *New York Times*, Jan 2, 2008.

"*Yadhak shaykh yatlu kamilat ughniyat Sama al-Masry 'ala qanat al-hafidh*," January 17, 2013, accessed December 25, 2016, https://www.youtube.com/watch?v=0DB62LlkuCs.

Young, William C. "Women's Performance in Ritual Context: Weddings among the Rashayda of Sudan." In Sherifa Zuhur, ed. *Images of Enchantment, Images of Enchantment: Visual and Performing Arts of the Middle East*. New York and Cairo: American University in Cairo Press, 1998.

"Yousef al-Sharif Discusses Zouba al-Klobtiyya." From *Al-Masri al-Youm*, May 2, 2009. Available at http://www.shira.net/about/zouba-el-klobatiyya.htm.

Youssef, Bassam. *Revolution for Dummies: Laughing through the Arab Spring*. New York: Dey Street Books, 2017.

Zahara, Isis. "The Contemporary Dance Scene—Interview with Mohamed Shahin." *Oriental Limelight*. April 20, 2012. http://orientallimelight.blogspot.com/2012/04/contemporary-dance-scene-in-egypt.html.

Zar: Trance Music for Women. Music by Awlad Abou El Gheit. Notes by Yasmin Henkish. Audio CD, B000A0ED12, 2005.

The Zar Dance (DVD). (1981). New York: Costodio

Productions with Ibrahim Farrah, Bahijah and Valerie Camille. 2007.

Zirbel, Katherine Elizabeth. "Musical Discursions: Spectacle, Experience and Political Economy." Ph.D. dissertation, University of Michigan, 1999.

Al-Zuhur. Editor, Antun al-Jumayyil. 1910–1913.

Zuhur, Sherifa. *Asmahan's Secrets: Woman, War and Song*. Austin: Center for Middle Eastern Studies, University of Texas Press, 2000; and London: Al-Saqi Publications, 2001.

Zuhur, Sherifa. "Claiming Space for Minorities in Egypt after the Arab Spring." In Moha Ennaji, ed. *Multiculturalism and Democracy in North Africa: Aftermath of the Arab Spring*. London: Routledge, 2014.

Zuhur, Sherifa. *Colors of Enchantment: Visual and Performing Arts of the Middle East*. Contributing editor, Sherifa Zuhur. Cairo: American University in Cairo Press, 2003.

Zuhur, Sherifa. *Egypt: Security, Political, and Islamist Challenges*. Carlisle: Strategic Studies Institute. U.S. Army War College, 2007.

Zuhur, Sherifa, ed. *Images of Enchantment: Visual and Performing Arts of the Middle East*. Cairo: American University in Cairo Press, 1998. Reprinted 2000.

Zuhur, Sherifa. "Intercession in Middle Eastern Society." In Maryanne Cline Horowitz, ed. *New Dictionary of the History of Ideas*. 6 vols. New York: Charles Scribner and Sons, 2005.

Zuhur, Sherifa. "Les divas sur grand écran." In *Divas arabes—D'Oum Kalthoum à Dalida*. Paris: Editions Skira/Institut du monde arabe, 2021.

Zuhur, Sherifa. "Mixed Impact of Feminist Struggles in Egypt during the 1990s." *Middle East Review of International Affairs Journal*. Vol 5, No. 1, March 2001.

Zuhur, Sherifa. Personal interview with Fahed Ballan, in the musicians' syndicate, Suwayda, Syria, September 1993.

Zuhur, Sherifa. Personal interview with Nidaa Abou Mrad. Beirut, Lebanon, August 2003.

Zuhur, Sherifa. *Revealing Reveiling: Islamist Gender Ideology in Contemporary Egypt*. Albany: State University of New York Press, 1992. Reprinted 1996.

Zuhur, Sherifa. "Singing a New Song: Arab Muslim Women and Entertainment." In Fereshte Nouraie-Simon, ed., *On Shifting Ground: Muslim Women in the Global Era*. New York: Feminist Press, 2005.

Zuhur, Sherifa, and Marlyn Tadros. *Egypt's Conflicting Interests since 2011: Political, Business, Religious, Social and Popular Culture*. Lewiston, NY and Lampeter, Wales: The Edwin Mellen Press, 2017.

Index

Numbers in *bold italics* indicate pages with illustrations

'Abaza, Rushdi (actor) 73, 179
'Abbas I 26, 216
'Abbas II 33, 205
Abbasid era 18, 110, 190, 196
'Abbasiyya 28, 113, 209
'Abd al-Basit, 'Usman (al-Barbari al-Wahid fi Misr) (character of 'Ali al-Kassar) 39
'Abd al-Hayy, Salah (singer) 33
'Abd al-Muttalib, Muhammad (singer) 52, 110, 180, 195, 206
'Abd al-Rahim, Sha'ban (singer) 92, 96, 107, 113, 161, 240n18
'Abd al-Wahhab 'Abd al-Wahid (singer) 144
'Abd al-Wahhab, Muhammad (composer, singer) 4, 42, 48, 49, 55, 57, 101, 107, 111, 129, 169, 173, 185, 195, 200, 203, 213, 214, 233n39
'Abd al-Wahhab, Shirin (singer) 58
"al-'Abd wal-Shaitan" 96
'Abdu, Fifi (dancer) 56, 71, 74, 77, 96, 112, 115, 149, 154, 178, 184, 195
'Abdu, Na'ima (dancer) 42
Abi Foqq al-Shagara 49
al-Abiad, George (actor, troupe leader) 34, 40
Abou Mrad, Nidaa (violinist) 83
Abu Dira' (singer) 110
Abu al-Ghait clan 100, 137
Abu Isma'il, Hazim Salah (politician) 160
Abu Naddara Zarqa (journal) 34, 217
Abu Seif, Salah (film director) 46, 155
Abu Shumays, Sami (musician, music scholar) 3, 227n5, 229n37
Abu Si'ud, Hassan (musician) 74, 149, 196, 197
accordion 9, 42, 58, 110, 115, 181, 196, 198, 205, 208, 210, 240n16
acrobats 11, 41, 196, 197
"Act Thuggish" 160
actors 1, 11, 24, 31, 34, 36, 37, 38, 39, 40, 42, 43, 44, 48, 49, 55, 71, 73, 91, 111, 116, 117, 123, 144, 147–148, 153, 164, 170, 179, 180, 183, 196, 200, 203, 205, 206, 207, 210, 211, 215–216, 219, 220, 223

adab 96, 196
'Adawiyya, Ahmad (singer) 56, 57, 82, 92, 106, 110, 111–113, *112*, 115, 116, 123, 161, 173, 184, 195, 196, 198, 216, 218, 221, 225 236n72 246n34
adhan 18, 196
al-'Adil, Nazla (dancer) 52, 72, 196, 208
Adra, Najwa (anthropologist) 21
afandi (*afandiyya*) 28, 97, 196, 206, 221
'afarit 36, 37, 64, 206
Afifi, Mustafa (costumer) 172
afrangi 68, 153, 196, 199
agency 6, 77, 101, 124, 159, 178
aghani: mulid 6, 9, 59, 61, 75, 85, 88, 94–100, 101, 103, 104, 106, 107, 108, 109, 124, 140, 209, 212; of revolution 6, 39, 108, 117, 119, 121, 122, 152, 153, 174, 215; *sha'bi,* 3, 6, 9, 56, 57, 58, 68, 69, 70, 79, 82, 84, 85, 90, 91, 92, 93, 94, 95, 96, 98, 99, 103–104, 106–108, 109–115, 116, 117, 120, 124, 128, 129, 130, 161, 173, 185, 191; *al-tahjir* 142, 196
"Ah Ya La'bt Ya Zahr" 97–98, 239n63
Ahibbak ya Hassan 32
ahl al-bayt 196, 218
Ahmad, al-Daif (actor, comedian) 147
Ahmad, Fathiyya (singer) 15, 33, 36, 43–44, 48, 180, 196, 205, 207
Ahmad, Shyma (singer) 151–152
Ahmad, Zakariyya (composer) 48
"Aho Dah Illi Sar" 153
ahya sha'biyya 57, 67, 94, 104, 113, 118 196 149, 196, 200, 211, 206, 209; *see also sha'bi* neighborhoods
'Aida 52
"Aih al-Hikaya" 107, 114
ajnas 18, 142, 205, 210, 221; *see also maqamat*
Ajram, Nancy (singer) 58, 96, 144, 246n28
'Akif, Fatma (dancer) 41, 127, 175, 180, 196, 233n35
'Akif, Ibrahim (dancer,

choreographer) 61, 180, 196, 233n35
'Akif, Na'ima (dancer) 32, 41, 49, 180, 197
'Ala' 50 Cent (singer) 94, 107, 122, 197, 216
'Ala Wahda wa al-Nuss (film) 144–155, 156, 211
Alala, Husain (singer) 142
alcohol 5, 17, 22, 28, 33, 35, 39, 46, 61, 94, 98, 122, 137, 154, 157, 163, 201, 234n64
Alexandria 6, 9, 15, 28, 29, 30, 35, 29, 40, 53, 54, 56, 59, 60, 68, 69, 70, 71, 72, 75, 77, 98, 114, 116, 117, 126, 127, 144, 145–146, 150, 168, 197, 200, 202, 204, 205, 209, 211, 212, 213, 214, 215, 216, 219, 220, 223, 224
Alf Laila wa Laila (*sala*) 29, 37, 215
Ali, Aisha (dancer, dance researcher) 126, 128, 130
'Ali, Hamouda (drummer) 185
'Ali, Sami (singer) 107, 117
al-Allati, Hassan (musician, poet) 28
Allouba, Samia (fitness centers operator) 175–176
Almaz (*'alima*) 15, 29, 195, 197
Almaz wa 'Abduh al-Hamuli 29
'amaliyya 137
Amani (Lebanese dancer) 60, 171
Amar, Anwar (clubowner) 57
al-'Amary, Safia (actress) 49
Amazigh 104, 136, 220
American University in Cairo 2, 9, 51, 131
'Amir, Aytin (actress) 75, 197
Amir, 'Aziza (actress, producer, screenwriter) 48
al-Amir, Kat-Kut (drummer, singer) 56, 58, 69, 70, 74, 113, 115, 184, 197, 210
'amma 67, 85, 96, 97, 103, 197
'ammiyya 9, 10, 11, 28, 30, 39, 34, 104, 197, 202, 211, 214, 223, 242–243n8
'Amr Haha or DJ 'Amr Haha (singer/performer) 107, 122, 197
amraz 197, 231n113, 236n76
amthal 3, 224–225; *see also* proverbs

265

Index

Ana 'Albi Dalili 52
"Ana Aslan Gamid" 153
"Ana Bakrah Isra'il" 107, 113
"Ana Mish 'Arafni" 98
"Ana Nifsi 'Ayyiz Ra'is" 108, 122
anashid 30, 86, 88, 90, 91, 92, 97, 104, 106, 139, 197, 205, 206, 212
"al-Anbiya'" 94
ancient Egyptian dance 21, 15–16, *16*, 64
Angham (singer) 58
Anhar, Hagga (*shaykha*) **138**
Anisat Sayidat 69, 77
al-'Aqqad, Muhammad (musician) 29, 204
Arab heritage *see turath*
Arab Spring 8, 61, 86, 88, 108, 121, 122, 148, 153, 245*n*23
Arabian Knightz (rap group) 105, 108, 197
Arabic: colloquial *see 'ammiyya*; poetry
'aragoz (*qaragoz*) 11, 24, 90, 149, 158, 197, 209, 219
arghul 110, 197
al-'Arian, 'Issam (politician) 160
'Ariyat bila Khataya 139
Arizona (club) 74
Armbrust, Walter (anthropologist) 111
'arusa al-mulid 90, 197
al-'Arusa al-Mulid (film) 90, 197
'asharat al-tabl 128
ashwayyat 90, 118, 119, 197
al-'Askari, Anwar (singer) 110
'askariyya 157, 197
Asmahan (singer) 2, 42, 44, 46, *46*, 47, 48, 49, 50, 144, 179, 180, 196, 197, 198, 205, 217
al-Asmar, Hassan (singer) 58, 107, 113, 198
Assiut 134, 170, 180, 202, 211, 212, 216; fabric (*tull talli* or *talli*) *132*, 133, *134*, 135
Aswan 106, 138, 142, 144, 204, 214, 216, 220
al-Aswani, 'Alaa (writer) 60
asyad 137, 218
'Atallah brothers (Salim and Amin; theatrical troupe) 34, 39
al-Atrash, Farid (singer, composer) 2, 39, 44, *45*, 46, *46*, 48, 49, 50, 53, 56, 58, 71, 73, 106, 111, 155, 179, 180, 196, 198, 203, 212, 214, 217, 222; compositions 79, 173, 184, 185; and *Intisar al-Shabab* 44, *46*
'awalim 11, 12–15, 19, 20, 21, *23*, 25, 27, 29–30, 32, 33, 35, 36, 37, 47, 56, 85, 93, 112, 127, 166, 168, 198, 202, 204, 208, 210, 212, 215, 223, 228*n*6; language about 20, 112; music for 145, 169, 215; style of dancing 12 52, 59, 62, 71, 115, 127, 130, 168, 170, 200, 201, 204, 219; style of singing 9, 15, 35, 36, 196
Awlad 'Ali 140, 142

awlad al-balad 67, 68, 87, 94, 103–104, 113, 196, 198, 206
awlad al-kar 49, 57, 121, 198, 208, 220
awliya' 16, 86, 87, 139, 198, 207, 212, 223
'awra 19, 198
al-'Awwada, Bamba 15
"Aywa, Aywa" 123
Ayyam wa Layali 214
Azbakiyya 22, 27, 28, 29, 32, 33, 35, 39, 49, 90, 164, 168, 209, 216; Gardens 27, 198; pond 24, 27, 207
al-Azhar 22, 86, 87, 155, 209, 213
"'Aziza" (song) 42, 185
al-Azwag al-Shayateen 7
Azzam, Nabil 42

"B+" 156–157
Bab al-Hadid 49
"Bab al-Haya" 99–100, 109
Badawiyya (dancer) 26, 198
al-Badawiyya (*tariqa*) 86
badla 40, 41, *43*, *45*, *50*, 59, 62, 72, *76*, 109, *150*, 158, 159, 172, 176, *187*, *192*, 198
Badrkhan, Ahmad (director) 45, 179
badrona 33
Bahaira 133, 134, 146
Bahlawat 128
Baidaphon Records 35, 36, 42, 219
al-Bakkar, Muhammad (actor, singer) 169
al-Bakri, Shaykh Abu Khalil (Naqib al-Ashraf, grand shaykh of Sufi orders) 24
al-Bakri, Zainab bint Abu Khalil (mentee of Napoléon) 24
Bal Anat 130
baladi 11, 57, 72, 74, 93, 103, 116, 153, 158, 159, 162, 185, 198, 199, 243*n*25; *'aish* 90; *awadi* 115; baladization 68; bar 199; coffee houses 5, 27, 169; gym 217; identity 68, 70, 74, 116, 153, 158, 159, 192, 199, 206; insults 162; Lebanese 171; *lun* 9; neighborhood 72; progression (or *taqsim*) 58, 75, 115, 116, 178, 198; Queen of 52, 58, 116, 217; *raqs* 4, 7, 57, 69, 84, 100, 101, 115, 121, 123, 124, 125, 149, 174, 184, 190, 191, 192, 193, 203, 205, 215, 247*n*51; set 78, 115, 181, 183; and social divisions 67, 68 245–246*n*25; store 93; *tet* 115, 116; thinking 67
baladi dress 58, 62, 67, 69, 109, 129, 134, *134*, 158, 161, 215; *see also galabiyya; malayya laff*
al-Balbaissi, Hassan (dancer) 21, 26
al-Balbisi, Shaykh 'Arabi Farhan (*munshid*) 94, 107, 209
al-Balkimy, Anwar (politician) 159, 160

Ballan, Fahed (singer) 95, 139
ballas 115, 135, 137
baltagiyya 47, 61, 93, 94, 160, 199
ban of dancers: 'Adawiyya 57, 113; *dhikr* 87; in 1834 20, 21, 25–26, 199; in 1894 33; foreign dancers in 2003–4, 177; *mahragan* 122–123, 124; in 1990s 129; on television (live) 59, 150, 158
Banat Mazin (*ghawazi*, dancers) 60, 127, 128, 129, 130, 131, 199, 221
bango 94, 199, 204, 212
"al-Bango" (song) 99, 113, 133, 122
al-Banna, 'Abd al-Latif (singer) 33
baqshish 30, 65, 78, 199; *see also nuqut*
El Baradei, Mohammad (diplomat, politician) 150, 163
baraka 86, 87, 89, 199, 209
Barakat, Henri Antoun (film director) 45
Bardees (dancer) 60
"al-Barnamag" 7, 156, 157, 223
barrada 30, 196, 199; *see also nuqut; tashnib*
bars 27, 28, 41, 46, 60, 61
basha/bashawat see *pasha*
"Bassam Ya Bomba" 163
Bast (cat goddess, or Bastet) 16
Bata, Abdullah (singer) 142
Bata, Hamou (singer) 142
Batshan, Hamdi (singer) 107, 114
Bayat, Asef (sociologist) 124
bayt al-ta'a 154
Bazaeva, Oxana (dancer) 60
Beata (Zadou) and Horacio (Cifuentes) (dancers) 182
Bedouin 6, 17, 18, 57, 67, 75, 106, 107, 114, 128, 140, 141, 142, 204, 212, 215, 217; dances of/about 78, 142, 200, 203–204
bee dance 21
beer 5, 16, 17, 28, 30, 46, 61, 137
al-Behairy, Mona 162
belly dance 14, 56, 64, 70, 96, 130, 132, 146, 149, 152, 158, 165, 166, 167, 176, 200, 208, 210, 219; *see also danse du ventre; raqs baladi; raqs sharqi*
Biancani, Francesca (historian) 33
Biegman, Nicolaas H. (diplomat, author) 89, 138
bint al-balad 53, 58, 67, 68, 71, 113, 133, 156, 198, 199, 224, 245–246*n*25, 246*n*36; Farida Fahmy as 53, 155; Fifi 'Abdu as 56, 74, 195; Hayatim as 69, 70; Laila Nazmi as 68, 213; Nadia Hamdi as 72, 155; Sahra Saeeda as 72, 155; Sama al-Masry as 68, 79, 155, 156, 165; songs about 185; and Tahia Kariuka 71, 155; *see also awlad al-balad*
"Bint al-Giran" 123
bint Mazin, Khairiyya (dancer) 60, 127, *127*, 128, *129*, 130, 131, 174, 199

Index

bint al-suq 67, 199
bint al-zawwat 67, 68–69, 199, 246n36
Black Saturday 40, 52
Bloom, Sol (entertainment impresario, politician) 167
Blue, Luka (singer) 99
bombutiyya 145
Bordelon, Candace (dancer, dance scholar) 186, 187
Borhamiyya (Borhaniyya) Disuqiyya (*tariqa*) 86
Boulad, Adel (*tahtib* specialist and coach) 131
Bourbia, Lylia (dancer) 70
bread riots 57, 106, 114
British occupation 28, 34, 36, 39, 52, 88, 97, 109, 148, 153, 200, 201, 204, 207, 223; in the Canal Zone 40, 52, 145
brothels 22, 27, 33, 94, 223
"Bum Bum" 109, 122, 124
Buonaventura, Wendy (dancer, writer) 4, 192
Burckhardt, Johann Ludwig (John Lewis) (traveler, writer) 12, 13
burqa 155, 161, 199
Butler, Judith (gender theorist) 64
buza 5, 17, 39, 199

café chantant 166, 167, 168, 199; *see also* casino; *sala*
Cairene culture: historic 6, 12, 13, 19, 24, 25, 26, 27, 28, 29, 32, 39, 51, 67, 75, 93–94, 110, 180, 199, 204, 206; more recent 57, 58, 60, 65, 68, 88, 90, 93, 113, 114, 118–119, 124, 131, 147, 171, 175, 177, **192**
Cairene dialect 88, 143, 202, 221; *see also 'ammiyya*
Cairo 1, 2, 5, 6, 12, 13, 22, 23, 24, 25, 26, 27, 28, 29, 32, 34, 35, 39, 42, 48, 53, 54, 56, 57, 59, 60, 63, 67, 70, 71, 72, 73, 74, 75, 78, 106, 113, 114, 118, 119, 127, 130, 131, 132, 133, 137, 138, 139, 144, 145, 163, 167, 168, 169, 170, 182, 197
Cairo Liberation Front (European band) 108
Cairo Opera House *see* Opera House
Cairo 30 49
Cairo Trilogy 49, 209
Cairo University 144, 215
Cairophone 42
Camelia (dancer) 60, 154, 177, 178
Capitulations 33
Carioca, Tahia *see* Kariuka, Tahia
cartoons 7, 34, 147, 148, **149**, **150**, 164, 217, 222
casino 11, 110, 199, 200; Alhambra 37; Badi'a 40, 49, 53, 201, 210, 217, 218; Lebanon 57, 75, 217; Opera 4, 5, 40, 73, 107, 171, 202, 203, 206, 210
Cassandra (dancer, choreographer) 181

"Catcall but Don't Grope" 122
censorship 8, 34, 43, 71, 117, 122, 159, 217, 246n38; *see also* ban of dancers
chobi 78
cinema 1, 6, 29, 32, 33, 35, 36, 37, 38, 39, 40, 41, 42, 43, 44, 45, 46, 47, 48, 49, 50, 52, 53, 54, 55, 56, 58, 59, 60, 62, 63, 68, 69, 70, 71, 73, 74, 78, 79, 91, 93, 95, 96, 97, 98, 100, 101, 107, 111, 113, 117, 126, 128, 133, 139, 147, 148, 152, 153, 154, 155, 156, 168, 171, 173, 174, 179, 195, 196, 197, 199, 201, 202, 203, 204, 205, 206, 207, 208, 209, 210, 211, 212, 213, 214, 216, 219, 220, 222, 223, 224
circus 32, 41, 196, 197, 212
clerics *see 'ulama*
Clot (Bey), Antoine Barthelemy (physician) 25, 30; Clot Bey area 27
coffee cup dance 21
coffee houses 5, 27, 28, 30, 39, 169, 203, 223
Cole, Juan (historian) 24, 230n70, 243n9
Combes, Edmond (traveler, writer) 26, 216, 231n87
comedians 7, 11, 27, 49, 111, 147, 148, 154, 163, 168, 180, 190, 223; *see also* monolog
Coptic 17, 21, 22, 29, 39, 64, 104, 106, 182, 200, 215, 216, 218, 234n7; *mulid* 212
Crystal Nile 61
cultural heritage *see turath*

daff 55, 116, 143, 200, 211, 215
dahiyya 140, 142, 200
Dahlena (dancer) 56
dall'a 6, 62, 63–64, 65, 68–70, 70–76, 77–79, 83, 84, 147, 200; in songs 70, 81–82; *see also* flirtation; "Ya Dall'a, Ya Dall'a"
daminat al-maghani 19, 200
dance costume 15, 17, 30, 40, 41, 45, 59, 60, 61, 62, 70, 72, 75, 77, 78, 79, 135, 172–173, 187, 188, 191, 198, 212, 214; for Alexandria 246n35; ancient Egyptian **16**, 17; for *'arusa al-mulid* 197; of *'awalim* **23**, **167**; for Badi'a Masabni 40; Badi'a's *sala* 170, 210; in Cairo nightclubs in 1940s **51**; in caricature (1923) **150**; for Dina 76, 77, 172; for *fallahin* 135; for Farida Fahmy **132**, **133**, **134**, **141**; for Firqat al-Qawmiyya **54**; for *ghawazi* 127, 129; for Hagalla 141; for Johara 152; for Khairiyya bint Mazin 127, **127**, **129**; for *khil* 132, 208; as lingerie **192**; of Nagwa Fu'ad **55**, 78, 180; of Qena 25; for Randa Kamel **187**; for Safinaz 91, 216; Sa'idi 132–133, **132**, **134**, 135; for Sama al-Masry 159, 162; for Samia Gamal **50**;

for *sha'bi* 79; Siwi 136; for Suhair Zaki **70**; for Tahia Kariuka **43**, **45**; for *tannura* **89**, 100; Western inspired by Egyptian 130; after World War One (circa 1919) **149**; *see also badla; baladi* dress
The Dance of the Almeh 166, **167**
Dandash (dancer) 59, 60, 71, 72, 127, 170, 200
D'Annunzio, Gabriele (poet, soldier) 148
danse du ventre 39, 166, 167, 200; *see also* belly dance; *raqs sharqi*
darawish 88, 200, 202
al-Darb al-Ahmar 69, 113, 138, 197, 200, 213, 219
Dareen (dancer) 79, 236n64, 236n65
Darwish, 'Ali (drummer) 181
Darwish, Ghazi (drummer) and Muhammad 'Ali (keyboardist) 181
Darwish, Reda (drummer) 183, 235n48
Darwish (al-Bahr), Sayyid (singer, composer) 37, 39, 109, 153, 212, 219
Dauzats, Adrien (painter) 30
dawr 29, 200, 223, 231n104
Dayan, Milya (Milia) (singer, actress) 31, 205
Deagon, Andrea (dancer, classical scholar) 171
Delta (Nile) 12, 20, 26, 71, 110, 131, 132, 133, 134, 146, 202, 203
Descriptions de l'Égypte 23, **23**
dhikr 18, 19, 85, 87, 88, 90, 95, 97, 99, 100, 101, 139, 140, 200, 201, 203, 206, 219, 221
Diab, 'Amr (singer) 58, 97, 180, 186, 203
Dickson, Isaac (choreographer) 42, 43, 73, 203
Diesel (singer) 200
al-Din, Hamza 'Ala' (musician) 144, 244n58
Dinshaway incident 34, 201
dirges 18, 19, 144
Dom 11, 192, 228n12, 243n11
Domari 11
Donga, Sayyid (singer) 142
El Dorado 27, 35, 198
dosat 88, 200
drowning of 400 women (*ghawazi*) 23–24, 201, 230n70, 230n71
drugs 35, 49, 88, 94, 98, 99, 117, 122, 147, 158, 211, 212; *see also mukhaddarat*
Dubois (published as Dubois-Aymé), Jean Marie Jospeh Aymé (engineer, *savant* with Napoléon) 20
Dukhul al-Hammam Mish Zayy Khuruguh 38
"al-Dunia Mulid" 95, 108

Early, Evelyn (anthropologist) 153, 245n25

Index

Al-Ebiary, Abu Saʻud (playwright, lyricist, screewriter) 223
economic issues 6, 32, 40, 52, 57, 65, 68, 94, 98, 106, 110, 112, 117, 118, 119, 122, 124, 158, 159, 168–169, 189, 190, 206, 217, 223; in songs 97–98, 99–100
economic liberalization *see infitah*
EEK (band) 120, 201
Egypt Dances 126
Egyptian (colloquial) dialect *see ʻammiyya*
Electro Chaabi 108, 123
electronic music 3, 9, 42, 83, 93, 109, 110, 114, 118, 120, 173, 200, 203, 204, 214
elites 2, 11, 13, 19, 20, 24, 27, 28, 33–34, 35, 46, 48, 49, 50, 52, 62, 67–68, 73, 90, 92, 93, 97, 99, 103, 109, 110, 112, 119, 121, 122, 125, 148, 153, 169, 170, 199, 206, 208, 218, 223; *see also ibn/bint zawwat; khassa*
ElMahdy, Aalia Magda (atheist, Internet activist) 152
Enan, Denise (dancer) 141, 244n46
Enani, Salah (artist) 90
engagement, marital 65, 66, 207, 208, 215, 218, 224; as betrothal 201, 234n7
Eshta, Tatiana (dancer) 70
Essam, Ramy (singer) 152

Fadikka 143, 215
Fadil, Sherifa (actress, clubowner, singer) 36, *38*, 47, 55, 112
Fahita, Abla (puppet character) 78, 149–150, 158, 195–196
Fahmy, Farida (dancer) 2, 53, 60, 72, 125, 126, *132*, *133*, *134*, 135, *141*, 152, 155, 158–159, 174, 201, 202, 215
Fahmy, Hikmat (actress, dancer) 41, 42, 201
Fahmy, Husain (actor) 32, 152
Fahmy, Khaled (historian) 25, 228n17
Fahmy, Ziad (historian) 5, 28, 97
Fairuz (child actress) 42
fallahin 26, 67, 68, 97, 133, 134, 135, 146, 199, 201, 212, 246n36; dance of 53, 96, 131, 132, 133, 135; dress of 77, 134–135, *135*; Farida Fahmy as 53; Nabawiyya Mustafa as 52; Nahid Sabry as 70; Sama al-Masry as 68, 160; songs of/about 68, 70; *see also raqs ʻasaya; tahtib*
fannana 201, 202, 215, 224; *see also raqqasa*
farah (afrah, pl.) 6, 7, 86, 87, 91, 95, 129, 132, 137, 201
al-Farah 95, 98, 107, 204, 205
Farid, Leila (dancer) 60, 182
Farrah, Ibrahim (dancer) 139, 171, 203

al-farraj 89
Farraj, Johnny (musician, music scholar) 3
Fata Ahlami 174
fath 17, 33, 39, 46, 47, 168, 201
al-Fatiha (Qurʾanic verse) 201, 215
Fathy, Najla (actress) 153
Fatima and Raja (dancers) 168
"Fawazir Ramadan" (television series) 147
Fawzy, Imtithal (dancer, actress, club owner) 41, 46, 47, 201
Felfela Village 132, 140
femininity 65, 67, 75, 121, 124, 153, 176; *see also dallʻa*
fertility 16, 64, 66
Figo/DJ Figo (singer, songwriter) 107, 108, 120, 122, 153, 197, 202, 210
finger cymbals *see sagat*
firqa 82, 170, 173, 202: *zaffa* 115, 190, 191, 202; *see also* orchestra
Firqat Qawmiyya al-Funun al-Shaʻbiyya 3–4, 12, 54, 125, 133, 140, 141, 146, 174, 198, 202
Firqat Reda *see* Reda Troupe
Flaubert, Gustave (traveler, writer) 12, 21, 26, 208, 215
flirtation 6, 56, 63–64, 65, 66, 67, 68–71, 72, 75, 78–79, 82 83, 156, 183, 191, 197, 200, 209, 210; *see also dallʻa*
"Flus" (song) 95
Foda, Omar (historian) 5, 28, 61
foreign dancers 4, 5, 7, 8, 20, 53, 57, 59, 60, 61, 62, 63, 79, 109, 116, 126, 165, 170, 172, 175, 176, 177, 178, 179, 183, 185, 186, 187, 188, 190, 191
foreigners (in Cairo or Egypt) 12, 22, 23, 24, 28, 29, 33, 34, 35, 39, 40, 41, 52, 61, 88, 107, 109, 126, 145, 148, 153, 163, 177, 186, 196, 199, 201, 207, 208, 212
France 21, 22, 23–24, 106, 131, 148, 167, 196, 199, 201, 207, 215, 221, 243n9; language of 29, 34, 39, 40, 59, 166, 187, 197, 200, 207, 221; school 39
Franken, Marjorie (anthropologist) 190–191
Fraser, Kathleen (dance historian) 20, 230n71
Freedom and Justice (political party) 157, 160, 162
Friday of Accountability 160
Frishkopf, Michael (ethnomusicologist) 88, 237n6
Fuʾad, Nagwa (dancer) 50, 52, 53, 54–55, *54*, *55*, 56, 57, 58, 59, 62, 69, 72, 77–78, 96, 115, 116, 125, 141, 154, 177, 178, 179, 180, 183, 184, 186, 188, 202, 217, 224
Fuʾad, Nelly (dancer) 26, 56, 60, 71, 113, 202
fulklur 2–3, 53, *54*, 61, 71, 75, 77, *89*, 90, 101, 109, 125, 126–130, 131–133, *132*, *134*, 135–136, 137,

138–139, 140–141, *141*, 142–146, 155, 159–160, 161, 162, 164, 174, 178, 179, 180, 190, 191, 196, 197, 202; goal of 146; *see also* Balloon (Theater); Firqat Qawmiyya al-Funun al-Sha'biyya; Firqat Reda; *funun shaʻbiyya*; El Tanbura; al-Tannoura Egyptian Heritage Folklore Group
funerals 16, 19, 144, 200
funun shaʻbiyya 2, 3, 12, 115, 125, 133, 140, 141, 146, 174, 178, 180, 190, 198, 202; *see also musiqa; shaʻbiyya*
fusha 9, 10, 28, 30, 58, 104, 196, 197, 201, 202, 213, 215
futuwwa 199, 202
al-Futuwwa 155

gadaʻa 67, 153, 202
al-gadid (musiqa) 107, 114, 173, 184, 202
galabiyya 58, 67, 69, 109, 111, 118, 121, 134, *134*, 135, *135*, 137, 161, 201, 202; *see also gargar; jarjar*
galabiyya bi sufra 134, *135*, 202
galabiyya bi wist 134, *135*, 202
Galal, DJ Basma (rapper/DJ) 117
Galal, Shafiq (singer) 110
Galland, Antoine (traveler, translator) 230n70, 230n72
Gamal, Nadia (dancer) 50, 138, 171, 202
Gamal, Samia (dancer) 40, 42, 43, 44, 45, 46, 49, 50, *50*, 59, 71, 72, 73, *73*, 74, 147, 179, 198, 223
gamda 235, 294
gargar (jarjar) 67, 134, 135, 143, 202
Gaspard de Chabrol, Gilbert Joseph (prefect, traveler) 21
Gatlif, Tony (film-maker) 128
Gawaher (actress, singer) 144
Geddawi, Mo (dancer) 61, 186
gender 5, 13, 14, 15, 16, 17, 19, 20, 21, 23, 24, 25, 26, 27, 33, 40, 47, 49, 50, 58, 59, 61, 62, 63–64, 65, 66, 78, 87, 93, 94, 118, 119, 125, 143, 151, 152, 154, 159, 173, 179, 189, 190, 207, 208, 209, 210, 212, 222–223, 224, 225; in the *dahiyya* 140, 142; in the *hagalla* 140–141; in *mahragan* 121, 122–124; in *mulid* 75; in *raqs al-ʻasayya* 131; in *shaʻbi* 115–116; in Siwi dances 136; in *taqasim baladi* 115–116; in the *zar* 137
El Général (Tunisian rapper) 152
al-Geretly, Hassan (theater and dance director) 131
Gérôme, Jean-Léon (painter, sculptor) 166, *167*, 200
El Gezawe (Mohamed al-Gazawe, musician) 203, 241n40
ghajar 11, 127–128, 203, 228n12
ghalaba 98
Ghandi (Nasser Ghandi, singer) 203

Index

Ghanim, Donia Samir (actress, singer) 99, 109, 116, 180
Ghanim, Hassan (singer) 142
Ghanim, Samir Yusuf (actor, comedian) 116, 147, 180, 203
al-Gharbiyya 89, 127, 133, 134
ghawazi 11, 12, 13, 14, 19, 20, 22, 23, **25**, 26, 41, 52, 59, 62, 71, 72, 85, 88, 127-131, 167, 168, 170, 174, 196, 199, 200, 201, 203, 208, 210, 221, 228n3, 228n12, 230n71, 243n9; *see also* Aisha Ali; Banat Mazin; Nearing, Edwina
Ghazali, Muhammad Mahmud (Captain) (resistance leader) 145
al-ghina' al-mutqan 18
al-ghuz 203
gihaz 66, 202, 223
al-gil 114, 184, 203, 204, 218; *see also shababiyya*
Gilman, Daniel (anthropologist) 3, 144
al-Gindi, Nadia (actress) 41, 49, 153
gink 11, 26, 190, 203
globalization 3, 7, **51**, 103, 166, 168-169, 173-177, 178, 181-183, 184, 185, 186-188, 189, 190, 191-193
Golden Age (of Egyptian entertainment) 49, 56, 58, 62, 71, 82, 111, 130, 183, 184
Goodyear, Amina (dancer, teacher) vi, 72, **182**, 204, 236n71
Gouraud, Henri (general) 148
Graham-Brown, Sarah (author, scholar) 13
Graves-Brown, Carolyn (Egyptologist) 16
guilds 19, 20, 21-22, 67, 179, 202, 218
gymnastic movements 15, 17, 38, 53, 126, 174

"Habba Fo' Habba Taht" 107, 112
Habib al-'Umr 45
hadhra (*hadra*, coll. Egyptian) 88, 137-138, **138**, 139, 145, 203; al-Hadhra Collective 92; *see also farah*; *laila*
hadith 203, 212, 213, 219, 237n9
Hafiz, 'Abd al-Halim (singer) 32, 49, 54-55, **55**, 58, 106, 110, 111, 112, 173, 174, 183, 185, 202, 203, 204, 212, 240n12
hagalla 74, 78, 140-141, **141**, 142, 203-204
Haggag, Mustafa (singer) 150
hajj 19, 209
Hakim (singer) 3, 58, 92, 98, 107, 108, 114, 203, 204
al-Hakim, Tawfiq (writer) 30
hal 204
Halab 128, 203
halal 191, 204
Halawat al-Ruh 98, 108, 156, 185
Hamam, Mohammed (singer) 144

Hamama, Fatin (actress) 240n4
Hamdi, Baligh (composer, singer) 55, 80, 183, 184, 203, 204, 207
Hamdi, Nadia (dancer) 56, 71, 77, 155
Hamdi, Sahar (dancer) 78, 117
Hamida, 'Ali (singer) 107, 114, 204, 218
Hammer, Hytham M. (music specialist) 54, 55, 142, 228n2
Hamuda, 'Abd al-Basit (singer) 95, 98, 99, 100, 107, 109, 117, 204
al-Hamuli, 'Abduh (singer) 15, 28-29, 35, 195, 197, 219
Hamza al-Din (singer, musician) 144, 204
hanim 204: Egypt- 148
Hanim, Afranza (dancer) 41, 196
Hanim, Jeshm Affat (princess) 27
Hanim, Kuchuk (dancer) 21, 26, 204, 208
hantur 123, 204
Haqqi, Yahya (writer) 90
haqiqa 204
hara 32, 49, 67, 90, 204; *harat al-'awalim* 204
harafish 109, 204
haram 88, 204
Haram Street *see* Shari'a Haram
harem 19, 20, 30, 200, 204, 208, 210
haremlek 13, 204
Harvey Pasha, Colonel George Samuel Abercrombie (police commandant in Alexandria, later, in Cairo) 39
Hasabullah, Muhammad (musician, bandleader) 32, 205
hasabullah band 32, 55, 104, 162, 205, 223
al-Hashim, Huwaida (dancer) 71, 72, 204
hashish 67, 94, 99, 122, 147, 161, 199, 204, 211, 212
hass 205
Hassan, Ahmad Fu'ad (composer, musician) 54, 57
Hassan, Raqia (dancer) 59, 60, 176, 177, 186
Hathor (goddess) 16
Hawthorn, Ainsley (cultural historian) 166
haya' 22, 23, 96, 101, 205; *see also* modesty
Hayatim (dancer) 56, 69, 70, 205
haysa 205
Hazzimni ya Baba 149
Hegazy, Sarah (activist) 124
Henkish, Khamis (drummer) 185, 205
Henkish, Sayyid (accordionist) 13, 65, 68, 185, 205
henna 17
Herodotus (historian) 16
al-Higazi, Shaykh Salama (singer, actor) 30, 34, 36, 205, 206, 209
hijab 49, 59, 67, 72, 77, 93, 96, 101, 114, 116, 117, 118, 134, 160, 161, 164, 175, 190, 191, 199, 204, 205, 210, 220
al-Hilali, Abu Zayd (tribal leader) 24, 196, 222, 224, 230n75
Hilmy, Safiya (actress, singer, clubowner) 46, 205
"Hilwa ya balha ya maqamaha" 228n2
Hindiyya (dancer) 117
hishik bishik 69, 205, 224; show 69, 213
"Hitta Minni" 108, 121, 123, 220
Hoda, al-Hagga (*'alima*) 29
honor, code of (family) 5, 35, 37, 46, 65, 67, 128, 199, 219, 222; *see also sharaf*
horses, dancing 88, 104, 131, 132, 208, 214; dancers emulating 132, 208
hospitality 6, 17, 18, 19-20, 30, 115, 143, 210, 217; *see also* weddings
Hourani, Dominique (actress) 78
hubb 66, 79-80, 80-82, 205
"al-Hubb Kulluh" 80-82
Husain ibn 'Ali (grandson of the Prophet Muhammad) 196, 205, 213, 218
al-Husaini, Mahmud (singer) 95, 96, 98, 107, 122, 205
Husni, Dawud (musician, composer) 29, 197, 205, 213
Husni, Su'ad (actress, singer) 32, 49, 55, 152, 234n60
Hysa and Halabesa (singers) 108, 123, 206, 210, 220

Iblis 98, 218
"Ibn al-Amrikaniyya" 160
Ibn al-'Arabi (mystic, poet, philosopher) 88, 206
ibn al-balad 67, 68, 79, 94, 198, 199, 206; *see also baladi*; *sha'b*
Ibn al-Fallah 52
Ibn al-Hajj (al-Abdari) (scholar, writer) 19
ibn al-nas 68
ibn al-zawat 68, 206; *see also* elites; *khassa*
Ibrahim, Assala (dancer) 139
Ibrahim, Madame Abla (costumer) 172
'Id, 'Aziz (actor) 36, 37, 38, 179, 216, 223
Idris, Sayyid (singer) 142
Iftar 74, 163, 206
ihsas 18, 30, 31, 55, 205
iltizam 22
Imad al-Din Street 40, 206, 210, 217
imam 22, 48, 200, 201, 206
Imam, 'Adil (actor) 49, 78, 91, 111, 154, 155, 156 164, 183, 206, 237n28, 246n38
al-Imam, Hassan (director) 47, 50, 201
Imbaba 92, 118
improvisation: dance, 186; musical 9, 13, 19, 36, 39, 58, 92,

93, 96, 104, 112, 173, 207, 211, 216, 217, 219, 221, 222 (*see also mawwal; taqasim*); theatrical 31, 183 (*see also kanto*)
Imtithal 47, 208
"al-'Inab" 117
infitah 57, 68, 110, 206
inshad 30, 86, 88, 90, 91, 92, 94, 97, 104, 106, 139, 197, 199, 205, 206, 209, 212, 213
Institut d'Égypte 52
"Inta Inta" 101
"Inti Dinya Dhikr" 95
intifadha 101, 102, 124, 206
Intisar al-Shabab 44, **46**
iqa' 18, 48, 98, 99, 104, 120, 138, 139, 143, 144, 154, 186, 201, 206, 214, 215, 217, 246*n*29
'irfan 206
Iskandariyya *see* Alexandria
Islam 2, 4, 7, 8, 17, 18, 19, 22, 37, 64, 65, 85, 86, 91, 94, 106, 108, 116, 198, 204, 209, 212, 217, 219, 220
Islam Chipsy (musician) 120, 124, 201, 210
Islamists 1, 2, 8, 57, 61, 65, 88, 103, 107, 108, 114, 126, 129, 137, 151, 157, 158, 160, 161, 163, 164, 165, 192; *see also* salafists
Islamization 7, 53, 59, 93, 128, 165, 180; see also *sahwa islamiyya*
Isma'il, 'Ali (musician, composer) 141
Isma'il, Khedive 15, 24, 26–27, 29, 195, 197, 219
Isma'iliyya 42, 52; Square 27
al-'Izabi, Muhammad (singer) 55, 110, 234*n*60
'Izz al-Din, Beba (dancer and clubowner) 40, 46, 180, 206

al-Jabarti, 'Abd al-Rahman (historian) 22–23, 65
Jabr, Sayyid (singer) 142
Jahiliyya 15–17, 18, 110, 205, 206
Jahin, Salah (cartoonist, poet, lyricist, playwright) 90, 209
Jamal Twins, Lyz/Laila and Lyn/Lamia (dancers) 180, 206
Jarada of 'Ad (*qayna*, singer) 18
jarjar 143, 202
Jarrar, Randa (writer) 83
al-Jasusa Hikmat Fahmy 41
jawab damma 145
al-Jaza'iriyya, Laila (dancer) 50
al-Jaza'iriyya, Warda (singer) 29, 69, 183, 184, 185, 204, 207
Jazuli, Hassan 'Osman (singer) 144
jinn 18, 64, 111, 136, 137, 143, 206, 207
Johara (dancer) 60, 109, 152
jokes 7, 28, 144, 147, 148, 164, 210
Jollois, Jean-Baptiste Prosper (engineer) 20
Jomard, Edmé François (cartographer, scholar) 21

Jukov, Alexei (dancer, ballet director) 53
Jumhuriyya al-Funun 24, 207
al-Juq al-Kumidi al-'Arabi 37, 206

Kabarbar, 'Abdullah (singer, musician, magician) 144
Kabareh 95, 107
Kadous, Momo (dancer) 186
kaffafin 140, 142, 143, 145, 207
Kalakia 142
kamanja 69, 207, 215, 221
Kamel, Randa (dancer) 60, 70, 177, 178, 179, 186, 187, **187, 188**
Kamil, Ahmad Shafiq (poet) 80
Kamil, Mustafa (journalist, lawyer) 34, 207
Kamil, Pasha (statesman) 20
kantolar 31, 207
kar 207; *awlad al-* 57, 121, 198, 208, 220
karamat 86, 207, 225
Karika, Shehata (singer) 108, 121, 123, 214, 219
Karim, Mahmoud (dancer) 61
kariuka (dance) 43, 170
Kariuka, Tahia (dancer, actress) 12, 32, 42–43, **43, 44, 45**, 49, 50, 52, 59, 71, 72, 73, 74, 79, 90, 107, 152, 155, 170, 179, 183, 184, 197, 207
Kariuka-Halawa troupe 43
Karkar 95; DJ Karkar 94
Karnak 16
Kashar, Bamba (singer, dancer) 29, 32, 33, 35, 36, 49, 180, 207, 232*n*1
al-Kassar, 'Ali (actor) 34, 37, 39, 40, 41, 200, 201, 206, 207, 223, 232–233*n*29
El Kattan, Amira (of Pharaonics, costumer) 172
Kawakib (dancer) 60
kawala 86, 207
Kent, Carolee (Sahra Saeeda, dancer, dance ethnologist) 72, 155, 190
keyboard 9, 42, 91, 94, 98, 106, 110, 114, 115, 120, 181, 184, 200, 201, 210, 214, 198, 214
Khadhra wa-l-Sindibad al-Qibli 52
khafif 68, 208, 224
Khairi, Badi'a (lyricist) 39
Khairi, Susi (dancer) 50
Khala'at al-Nisa' 38
khalifa 208, 237*n*8; neighborhood of Khalifa, 196
Khalil, Khalil (dancer) 61
Khalil, Mohammed (dancer, choreographer) 54
Khalli Balak min Zuzu 32, 49, 56, 74, 152, 219
Khamsa Bab 49
al-Khamsa Gnaih (Guinea) 47
khashana 90, 208, 237*n*24
khassa 67, 96, 97, 103, 208, 218; *see also bint/ibn al-zawwat*; elites

al-Khatib, Magda (actress, producer) 49
khawagat 49, 57, 61, 208; *see also afrangi*; foreigners
khawal (khawalat) 11, 26, 190, 203, 208
khidma 208
khil 88, 104, 131, 132, 208
"Khudi (or Hati) Bosa Ya Bit" 108
khulkhal 72, 155, 208
Khulud 219 240*n*4
Khulusi, Mustafa Affandi (artist) 148, 149
Khurshid, 'Omar (musician) 55, 110, 219, 234*n*60
khutuba 66, 207, 208, 218
Kifaya (political movement) 150
kirdan 133, **134**
Kish Kish Bey (character) 39, 216
kit see tips and *takyit*
Kit-Kat Club 41, 197, 201
al-Klubtiyya, Zuba (dancer) 29, 47, 57, 74, 195, 196, 208, 209
köçekler 208, 231*n*86
Kochak, Eddie (the 'Sheik') (musician) 169, 180, 248*n*15
kohl 17, 26, 64, 208
komsari 147, 208
Die Königin der Mohammed-Ali-Strasse 196
Kozma, Liat (historian) 26, 27
Kuchuk Hanim (dancer, musician) 21, 26, 204, 208
"Kulluh 'ala Kulluh" 107, 111
al-Kumthariyya, Asma (singer) 15
Kunuz 143, 144
Kushnir, Alla (dancer) 60, 71, 78, 98, 150, 188

"La'" 109, 123
Lagrange, Frédéric (music scholar) 3, 5, 14, 15, 36, 37, 47
Lahn Hubbi 50
al-Lail (club) 47, 56, 74, 107, 112, 195
laila 48, 88, 139
Laila, Bint al-Rif 71
laila al-kabira 237*n*8; as puppet show or film, *al-Laila al-Kabira* 90, 96, 108, 149
lailat al-fannanin 213
Lailat Hinna 69
Lailat Hubb Akhira 69
Lailat al-Nuqta 64
al-Laithy, Ahmad (musician) 29
al-Laithy, Hamada (singer) 91, 92, 238*n*30, 209
al-Laithy, Mahmud (singer) 58, 75, 92–93, 94, 95, 96, 97, 100, 101, 107, 108, 209
Lakhmat Ra's (film) 94, 220
"Lakhmat Ra's" (song) 94, 220
Lammam, Antoine (musician) 181
Lammam, Elias (musician) 181
Lammam, Georges (musician) 181
Lane, Edward (traveler, writer) 12–13, 24, 30

Index

Lane Poole, Sophia (traveler, writer) 13, 20
Latcho Drom 128
al-Lawandiyya, Sayyida (*'alima*) 30, 35
Layali Lan Ta'ud 56
al-Laythi, Ahmad (musician) 29
lazima (lawazim) 8, 19, 115, 209
Lebanon 7, 23, 38, 40, 41, 49, 50, 56, 57, 71, 73, 74, 75, 78, 83, 96, 125, 131, 171, 181, 184, 188, 196, 202, 207, 210, 214, 217, 219, 220, 223
al-Lembi (film) 154
Lembi (*sha'bi* anti-hero) 95
licensing (and registering of channels, entertainers, prostitutes, *tariqat*) 7, 23, 27, 28, 33, 60, 61, 86, 115, 119, 126, 163, 172, 177, 179
love 9, 16, 18, 21, 35, 49, 66, 87, 90, 94, 96, 153, 205, 212; free 155–156; in songs 79–82, 104, 162, 168; *see also hubb*
Love Dance 20–21
luck (or lack of luck) 32, 64, 66, 90, 97, 117, 202; *see also nasib; shakwa*
lun 9, 115, 209
Lutfi, Nadia (actress) 49
Luxor 14, 21, 126, 127, 128, 138, 199, 204, 219

Ma'adi 111, 113, 196
macho 65, 69, 94, 202; *see also gad'a*
madad 87, 89, 91, 209
mada'ih 92, 104, 207; *nabawi* 207, 209
Ma'darsh **45**
Madfa'giyya (*mahragan* group) 119, 209
Madi, Zuzu (actress) 46
Madinat al-Salam 118, 197, 209, 216
Madrasat al-Mushaghabin 183
maganin 209
Magdy, Abir (equestrian) 132
magence see *majence*
Maghraby, Maya (dancer) 60
Mahalla al-Kubra 5, 20, 131
al-Mahallawiyya, Bahiya (singer) 115
Mahasan, Su'ad (dancer, clubowner) 42, 46, 71
Mahdi clan 89, 100
al-Mahdiyya, Munira (singer) 9, 14–15, 30, 33, 35–36, 37, 38, 48, 206, 209, 223, 228n20
Mahfouz, Naguib (writer) 49, 112, 209
mahmal 19, 209; *al-sharif* 209
Mahmoud, Khalid (dancer) 209
Mahmoud, Mayam (rapper) 116
Mahmoud al-Suhagy, Sabri (specialist and founder of *tahtib* center) 131
Mahmud, 'Abd al-'Aziz (singer) 110, 240n4

Mahmud, Karim (singer) 54, 70, 235n24
mahr 66, 118, 154, 199, 208, 209
mahragan 5, 6, 9, 59, 61, 83, 85, 91, 92, 93, 94, 98, 101, 102, 103, 106, 107–109, 115, 116, 118, 119, 120–124, 147, 150, 153, 164, 174, 185, 189, 197, 200, 201, 202, 203, 205, 206, 209, 210, 211, 214, 216, 217, 218, 219, 220, 221, 222, 223
mahraganat see *mahragan*
mahram 198, 210
Maira, Missy (rapper) 116
majence 173, 186, 210
Makawi, Sayyid (singer, musician, composer) 90
Makki, Ahmad (rapper) 109, 113, 117
makwagi 113, 210
malayya laff 67, 72, 74, 77, **77**, 145, 148, **149**, 155, 178, 199, 210
male dancers 20, 21, 26, 45, 60, 61, **89**, 100, 132, 134, 135, 137, 140, 141, 178, 186, 189, 190, 191, 202, 203, 208, 215, 221; *see also firqat zaffa; funun sha'biyya; gink; khawal*
al-Maligi, Mahmud (actor) 40
Mamluks 19, 20, 22, 24, 32, 90, 200, 207, 211, 212
manaha 144
mandara 20, 210
mandil 129, 210, 222
mangur 137
Manoli, Labiba (actress) 31, 205
Mansour, 'Adly (interim president) 122
Mansour, Mortada (lawyer, politician) 163, 164, 211
Mansur, Mary (actress, clubowner) 41
maqam (musical) 3, 5, 8, 9, 18, 30, 80, 83, 92, 104, 120, 142, 145, 173, 205, 210, 213, 217, 221, 223; *see also ajnas*
marbutin 19, 210
Marre, Jeremy (film-maker of music documentaries) 128
marriage 5, 14, 37, 39, 47, 49, 50, 64, 65, 66, 71, 93, 118, 119, 125, 142, 173, 179, 207, 208, 209, 210, 212, 214, 225, 234n3; '*urfi* 154, 222–223
Marwa (singer, musician) 69, 210
Masabni, Badi'a (dancer, singer, club-owner/producer) 39, 40–41, 42, 43, 44, 45, 46, 47, 48, 53, 71, 73, 106, 169, 170, 179, 180, 196, 197, 201, 203, 205, 206, 207, 210, 213, 214, 216, 217, 218, 219, 220, 223
masaliyya 144, 210
mashrabiyya 13, 210, 217
Maspero massacre 108
Masr al-Gadida 211
El Masri, Shakira (dancer) 60
al-Masriyya, Na'ima (singer, nightclub owner) 37, 46, 204, 211

al-Masry, Sama (actress, dancer) 6, 7, 68, 79, 108, 112, 153–156, 157, 159–165; and Anne Patterson 162; and Bassam Youssef, 163; Hazim Salah Abu Isma'il 160; and *Al Jazeera* 161; mocking liberal allies of the Muslim Brotherhood 162; and Mohamed Morsi 160, 161; and Mohammad El Baradei, 163; and Mortada Mansour 163; and Muslim Brotherhood 160, 161, 162; and Obama 161–162
masses see *'amma*
Matariyya 94, 122, 211, 223
matwa 100, 123, 145, 211
mawkib 87
mawlidiyya see *mulidiyyin*
mawwal 9, 13, 36, 44, 58, 79, 80, 92, 93, 96, 98, 99, 104, 110, 113, 120, 145, 196, 211, 216, 238n37; *see also* improvisation, musical
mazag 62, 88, 92, 95, 112, 211, 217, 241n43
Mazaher (musical ensemble) 138
mazhar 211
Mazhar, Shaykh 86
Mazin, Su'ad 129
Mazloum-Calvo, Nelly (dancer, choreographer) 53, 54, 70, 133, 192, 202, 216
ma'zura 137
media: print 5, 14, 24, 28, 33, 34, 38, 94, 119, 154, 157, 162, 164, 217, 223, 224; social 56, 109, 124, 148, 158, 160, 162, 189, 190
Memories of Cairo 182
Mesbah, Farid (dancer) 61
Michel, George (musician) 222
al-mihna 211
al-milla 42
Minutoli, Wolfradine von Watzdorf (traveler, writer) 30
Minya 92, 111, 114, 204
mirmah 87, 211
mizmar baladi 72, 96, **127**, 128, 131, 140, 211; see also *zummarin*
modesty, female 21, 22, 23, 65, 96, 101, 239n71; *see also haya'*
Mohammed, Amina (dancer, screenwriter, film director, producer) 49
Moiseyev, Igor (choreographer) 174; style of 136
Monolog 24, 147, 148, 170, 211, 212, 219; as song form 211; *see also* comedians
monologue see *monolog*
Morocco (Carolina Varga Dinicu, dancer) 72, 204
Morocco (nation) 23, 59, 88, 125, 139, 188, 218
Morsi, Mohamed (ousted president of Egypt) 68, 108, 122, 148, 151, 152, 157, 159, 160, 161, 162, 163, 190, 191, 211, 221
mosanifat 172, 211
Moseley, Sydney (journalist) 33

Index

"al-Motahadis al-'Askary" 162
al-Mouled 91
Mu'allaqat 18
Mubarak, Hosni (president) 8, 61, 86, 107, 108, 121, 150, 157, 163, 174, 215
mughanni 211
muhabbazin 24, 211
Muhammad, Huriyya (dancer) 42
Muhammad 'Ali Pasha (Khedive) 13, 20, 24, 25, 26, 34, 199, 208, 211–212
Muhammad 'Ali street 20, 29, 32, 33, 47, 57, 71, 74, 90, 92, 114, 152, 196, 198, 201, 205, 209, 212, 216, 225; *see also* Shari'a Muhammad 'Ali
Muhandis, Fu'ad (comedic actor) 49
muhibb 87, 88, 139
muhtarama 68, 212
mukhaddarat 35, 49, 67, 70, 88, 93, 94, 99, 113, 122, 161, 199, 212; *see also* drugs
mukhannath 190, 212
Mukhtar, Ni'mat (dancer, monologist, singer) 170, 212
mulahhan 212
mulid 5, 6, 7, 9, 32, 59, 61, 75, 85, 86–87, 88–89, 90–102, 103, 104, 107, 108, 110, 111, 117, 120, 122, 124, 132, 140, 147, 148, 149, 165, 183, 196, 197, 198, 199, 201, 203, 205, 206, 207, 208, 209, 211, 212, 213, 214, 216, 218, 219, 220, 222, 223, 225, 237n8; *kharbana* 98, 122; tape 238n42
Mulid Abu Khatzeira 212
Mulid Abu Qomsan 132
Mulid al-'Adhra' 212
Mulid al-Kahana al-Thalatha 212
Mulid al-Nabi 86, 212
Mulid Sayyid Ahmad al-Badawi 89
Mulid Sayyid Husain 212
Mulid Sayyid al-Rifa'i 213
Mulid Sayyida Fatima al-Nabawiyya 92, 213
Mulid Sayyida Nafisa 213
Mulid Sayyida Sakina 92
Mulid Sayyida Zainab 87
Mulid Sidi Gabr 213
mulidiyyin 87, 211
munaqibat 161
al-Mundhir, 'Alia (Amira 'Alia) (singer, musician) 44, 180, 196
Munib, Ahmad (singer) 144
Munib, Mary (actress) 69
Munir, Mohammad (singer) 112, 144
munshid 30, 39, 86, 88, 139, 200, 205, 213, 214
al-Muqaddam, Muhammad (singer) 29, 195
Murad, Laila (singer) 48, 49, 57, 75, 179, 205, 213, 217
Murad, Munir (composer) 179, 184, 213

Murad, Zaki (cantor, singer) 205, 213
murid 213, 222
al-Mushaghibun fi Nuwaiba 72
Musiciens du Nil (musical ensemble) 128
al-musiqa al-sha'biyya 3, 9, 58, 68, 88, 92, 96, 97, 104, 110, 124, 125, 128, 129, 131, 132, 137, 138, 140, 141, 142–144, 145, 171, 174, 197, 202, 207, 211, 213, 217, 218, 220
Muslim Brotherhood (Ikhwan al-Muslimin) 8, 86, 88, 103, 108, 122, 157, 160, 161, 162, 163, 164, 191, 205, 211, 237n16
Mustafa, Faruq (dancer) 61, 228n4
Mustafa, Nabawiyya (dancer, actress) 52, 195, 213
Mustafa, Zizi (dancer, actress) 55, 56
Mut (goddess) 16
Mutasharida 41
mutayyib/a 30, 213
mutrib/a 36, 47, 117, 183, 213; style 35, 36
muwashshahat 145, 189, 213
al-Muwayhili, Muhammad (writer) 28
Mzaina 142

al-na'asi 128
nabatchi 30, 213
nabut 131
Nadim, Abdallah (writer, activist) 28, 148
nafs 213
Nagi, Karim (musician, dancer) 60
Nagib, Sulaiman (actor, politician, writer) 43
nagma 213, 226
nagrishad 143
nai 99, 111, 140, 207, 213
Nany (dancer) 17
Napoléon (Bonaparte) 13, 20, 21, 22, 23, 24, 65, 166, 243n9; legal code of 151, 245n20
"al-Nar" 96
Nargis 52
nasib 213
Nasri, Farah (dancer) 60, 177–178, 180
al-Nasser, Gamal Abd (president) 10, 52, 52, 68, 103, 106, 111, 119, 174, 195, 212
Nasser, Lake 142
Nasser, Samia (dancer) 69
Nasserism 10, 53, 55, 103, 111, 203
nawwar 128, 199, 203, 243n11
Nazmi, Laila (singer) 68, 69, 77, 78, 210, 213
Nearing, Edwina (dance researcher) 14, 72, 128, 129, 130
al-Nemr, Esmat (music enthusiast, writer) 29
Nerval, Gérard de (Labrunie) (traveler, writer) 26
Nesma (dancer) 136, 182

Nibtidi Mnain al-Hikaya 56
nightclubs 2, 17, 28, 35, 39, 40, 41, 50, 57, 58, 60, 61, 63, 93, 94, 106, 107, 110, 115, 116, 140, 158, 171, 179, 183, 191, 219; *see also* sala
Nile (river) 22, 23, 24, 26, 64, 143, 174, 198, 201, 216; cruising (tourist) boat-nightclubs 60, 61, 78, 140, 187, 190; taxis 158
Nile Maxim 60, 61, 78
Nile Pharaoh 61
nimra 213 240n16
niqab 160, 161, 213
al-nizzawi 128–129
North Coast 6, 126, 146
Noussa, Madame (costumer) 172
La Nouvelle Femme 148
Nubia 106, 142–145
Nubians 6, 27, 39, 67, 74, 104, 106, 131, 142–145, 196, 214: architecture 169; dress 202; *grishad* or *nagrishad* 143; language 17; *masaliyya* 210; *ragid* 215; *simsimiyya* 143, 145, 153, 220, 221; songs of migration 196; *tanbura* 104, 143, 221; *al-wastaniyya* 143
al-nuqqara 144
nuqut 78, 88, 132, 214; *see also* *baqshish*; *takyit*; *tashnib*; tipping
Nur, 'Aida (dancer) 60, 75, 125, 143, 144, 186
Nur al-Huda (singer) 44, 49, 196, 214
Nuzhat al-Nufus 35

Obadia, Haqqi (musician) 169
Obama, Barack (president) 160, 161, 162
Ocean 14 97
Odeon Records 30, 35, 44, 196
Oka and Ortega (singers) 108 109, 120, 121, 122, 123, 164, 210, 214, 219, 223
Okasha, Tawfiq (television presenter) 164
Olwi, Zinat (actress, dancer) 172, 214
Omar Khayyam (nightclub) 47, 57, 75, 217 238n48
Open Door policy *see infitah*
opera 34, 43, 58, 195, 205; (Cairo) Opera House and complex 27, 29, 43, 52, 53, 56, 58, 168, 175, 195, 214; Square 27, 40, 210
orchestra 8, 20, 27, 41, 50, 83, 112, 113, 125, 170, 175, 178, 181, 210, 214; Diamond 54; *see also firqa*; *takht*
org 9, 110, 198, 214; *see also* keyboard
Oriental dance 3, 12, 29, 53, 88, 109, 130, 131, 159, 168, 182, 190, 191, 198; *see also* belly dance; *danse du ventre*; *raqs sharqi*
Orientalism/Orientalist(s) 4, 5, 12, 13, 15, 20, 21, 22, 24, 26, 30, 73, 78, 82, 130, 168

Index

Othman, Mustafa (puppet master/ *aragoz* actor) 90
oud see *'ud*
Outi (dancer) 182

Palestine 2, 44, 181, 196
Pampanin, Susu (drummer) vi, 185
Parisiana 47, 57, 61, 74, 144, 188, 209
pasha 214, 224
Patterson, Anne (ambassador) 162
payment of dancers 13, 19, 30, 32, 45, 47, 177, 187, 189, 201, 213; see also *takyit*
peasants 26, 52, 53, 67, 73, 97, 201, 212 243n9, 246n36; see also *fellahin*
Peterson, Jennifer (researcher, writer) 92, 96, 97
pigeon movement 143
pilgrimage 19, 175, 209, 218, 224; see also *hajj*; *ziyara*
pimp 27, 49, 99
Pimp Pasha 27
police 26, 27, 33, 39, 40, 49, 52, 61, 88, 96, 97, 107, 108, 117, 150, 157, 161, 170, 172, 211
polygyny 47, 214
Pomeroy, Sarah (classics and women's studies scholar) 17
poverty 32, 40, 49, 52, 87, 97, 98, 103, 106, 117, 118, 124, 223
Prince, Mona (writer, professor) 152
Prince, Ramadan (I and II) (singers) 58
Prisse d'Avennes, Émile (archaeologist) 21
Prophet Muhammad 86, 87, 137, 196, 203, 205, 208, 212, 218, 219, 225; intercession of 97; metaphor for 96; mulid for 86, 212; songs for 209
prostitution 5, 12, 14, 17, 21, 22, 23, 24, 25, 26, 27, 28, 33, 47, 49, 78, 88, 94, 130, 151, 154, 158, 168, 198, 199, 201, 205, 207, 224
proverbs 3, 224–225; see also *amthal*
puppets 11, 24, 90, **136**, 149, 158, 195–196, 197, 209, 219
Pyramids Road see Shari'a Haram

qahwa 169, 214; see also coffee houses
"Qamar al-Arba'tashar" 55
Qamar and Lila (dancers) 205
qanun 14, 29, 35, 169, 195, 208, 214, 219, 221
al-Qasabji, Muhammad (composer, musician) 48, 211, 214, 222
"Qasadt Babak" 94, 96, 107, 239n55
al-Qashqash 91
qasida 9, 30, 36, 110, 215

Qasr al-Shuq 196
Qattawi Bey, Yusuf (businessman) 28
Qena 25, 113, 129, 168, 198
al-Qibtiyya, Shafiqa (dancer) 29–30, 33, 46, 49, 195, 215, 223
Qitar al-Layl 50
qiyan pl. (*qayna*, sing.) 18, 19, 205, 210, 215
qudud 9, 223
Qur'an 18, 66, 137, 160, 201, 203, 215, 219; reciter 18, 32, 203, 207
al-Qurdahi-Husain troupe 31, 205
qutb (*aqtab* pl.) 100, 199, 215, 220

Ra (sun god) 16
Rabab 41
rabab 21, 24, 86, 88, 104, 120, 128, 130, 140, 143, 198, 207, 215
Racy, 'Ali Jihad (ethnomusicologist) 2, 3, 88
ragid 143, 215
Ramadan 74, 113, 163, 206
Ramadan, Muhammad (actor, singer) 109, 122, 123, 124
Ramazen, Boris (dancer, *fulklur* director) 53
Rami, Ahmad (poet, lyricist) 48
Ramzi, Suhair (actress) 69
Ramzy, Hossam (drummer) 57, 142, 185
Ramzy, Serena (dancer) 142
raqisa 215
"al-Raqisa" (television show) 191
raqqasa 215, 224, 225; see also *fannana*
raqs 'arabi 171, 215
raqs 'asaya 21, 72, 79, 100, 131, 132, 133, 171, 215
"Raqs al-'Awalim" (song) 169, 215
raqs baladi 4, 7, 11, 84, 100, 101, 121, 123, 124, 125, 174, 184, 190, 191, 192, 203
"Raqs al-Hawanim" (song) see "Raqs al-'Awalim"
raqs al-jihayni 128
raqs al-khil/al-khil 104, 132
raqs sha'bi 5, 6, 75, 84, 112, 115, 116, 125–130, 131–134, 135–136, 140–146, 147, 166, 168, 173, 174, 191
raqs sharqi 3, 4, 5, 6, 7, 11, 12, 34, 39, 40, 41, 42, 50, 52, 53, 55, 57, 58, 59, 60, 61, 62, 63, 69, 71, 74, 75, 78, 101, 104, 109, 112, 115, 121, 123, 124, 125, 127, 130, 131, 133, 139, 140, 141, 144, 145, 146, 147, 148, 149, 150, 158, 159, 166, 169, 170, 171, 174, 175, 176, 177, 180, 181–189, 190, 191, 196, 198, 200, 202, 203, 206, 207, 210, 215, 221, 223, 224; see also belly dance; *danse du ventre*; Oriental dance
raqs al-takht 128
recording(s) 3, 11, 14, 30, 32, 35, 36, 55, 79, 93, 94, 114, 126, 128, 144, 169, 173, 182, 185
Reda, Mahmoud (dancer, choreographer) 12, 53, 61, 90,
133, 135, 136, 139, 140, 141, ***141***, 155, 174, 180, 189, 192, 197, 201
Reda, Mustafa (director of the Arab Music Institute) 48
Reda, Shirine (actress) 180
Reda Troupe 2, 10, 59, 60, 72, 75, 90, 109, 125, 130, 132, ***132***, 133, ***134***, 135, 136, 189, 202, 221
Refaat, Mahmoud (producer, musician) 122
refrain see *taslim*
revolution 1, 5, 122, 152, 174, 175, 222; of 1919 5, 33, 35, 97, 152, 223; of 1952 52, 106, 206, 212; of January 25, 2011 6, 8, 39, 61, 75, 86, 88, 108, 114, 116, 117, 118, 119, 121, 122, 148, 150, 152, 156, 160, 163, 164, 190, 199, 210, 216, 222, 225
Revolution (rap collective) 215
Reynolds, Dwight (ethnomusicologist) 3, 110
Richardson, Kristina (historian) 220, 231n113
Rifaey, Tonia (migration and development specialist) 149, 150
al-Rifa'iyya *tariqa* 86
al-Rihani, Naguib (actor) 34, 39, 40, 148, 179, 210, 215–216; theatrical troupe of 37, 38, 39, 40, 48, 170, 180, 196, 200, 206, 207, 216, 220
riqq 64, 115, 116, 143, 169, 211, 216, 221
Rod al-Farag 33
Rodenbeck, Elizabeth (artist, scholar, conservationist) 77, 135
Rodenbeck, John (scholar, professor, actor) 12, 228n6
The Romany Trail: Gypsy Music into Africa (Vol. 1) 128
Rotana 58
Roushdy, Noha (writer) 184, 192
Ruby (singer) 58, 96, 152, 154, 246n28
Rue de Caire 167
Rugh, Andrea (anthropologist) vi, 77, 134, 135
ruh 213, 216; "Halawat al-" 98, 108, 185
rumors 26, 54, 56, 61, 68, 113
Rushdi, Ensaf (actress, clubowner dancer) 170, 172, 179, 216
Rushdi, Fatima (actress, clubowner, dancer) 37, 170, 172, 179, 206, 216, 220
Rushdi, Husain (politician) 36
Rushdi, Muhammad (singer) 110, 216
Rushdi, Ratiba (actress, clubowner, dancer) 170, 172, 179, 216
Russian 60, 70, 152, 173, 182; Russophone influence 60, 70, 175, 176, 189
Rustum, Hind (actress, dancer) 49

Ruz al-Taba'i 38
Ruz al-Yusuf 37, 38, 223

Saba, Nicole (actress) 96, 155–156
Sabah (singer) 79, 204, 216
sabahiyya 216, 237n8
Saber, Hassan Hassaan (dancer, historian) 132, 140
Sabry, Samir (actor, singer) 43, 73, 164, 183, 203
sabu'a 19, 64, 216
Sa'd, Lucy (dancer) 47, 57, 60, 61, 71, 74–75, 96, 127, 144, 170, 188, 195, 208, 209
Sa'd, Muhammad (actor) 95, 154
Sadat (singer, Sadat Muhammad Ahmad 'Abd al-'Aziz) 107, 108, 119, 120, 122, 197, 210, 216
Sadat, Anwar (president) 56, 57, 103, 106, 107, 112, 113, 114, 150, 201, 206, 224
al-Safi, Wadi' (singer) 196
Safinaz (Sofinar Grigoryan, dancer) 60, 75, 77, 91, 154, 216
"Safini Marra" 54
Safiya (dancer) 26, 216
El Safy, Shareen (dancer, author) 187
sagat 12, 14, 17, 30, 40, 64, 72, 128, 129, 137, 140, 169, 171, 199, 214, 216, 218, 222; *see also toura*
Al-Saghir, Hassan (singer) 142
"as-Sah ad-Dah Ambu" 106, 111, 163
Sah al-Nom 71
Sahara City (club) 57, 75, 127, 168, 202, 217; (song) 184
sahib kursi 216
Sahibat al-'Azima 148
Sahibat al-'Imara 52
Sahin, Christine (dance scholar) 61, 78, 177, 178, 218
sahwa Islamiyya 2, 53, 61, 190, 216; *see also* Islamization
al-Sa'id 21, 25, 26, 52, 96, 106, 110, 113, 126, 129, 131–133, 142, 146, 168, 204, 216–217, 221; bands 104, 131, 171, 187; dialect 10, 146, 217; songs 96, 104, 108, 115, 126, 131, 187; women's dress of 133, 134; in *zars* 137, 138; *see also* Upper Egypt
Said, Edward (writer, critic) 17, 71, 228n6
Sa'id, Khalid (victim of Egyptian police) 150
al-Sa'id, Mona (dancer) 47, 57, 60, 71, 74, 75, 139, 183, 187, 217
Sa'idi dance 12, 14, 96, 100, 116, 126, 131–133, 171, 215, 221; *see also ghawazi; khil; tahtib*
"Sa'idi Ya Ra's" 96
St. John, James Augustus (author, traveler) 21
saints' day celebrations *see mulid*
Sakina (*'alima*) 15; *see also* Almaz
Sakna (*'alima*) 15
sala 4, 11, 15, 27, 28, 32, 33, 35, 36, 39, 40, 41, 42, 43, 44, 45, 47, 48, 50, 62, 71, 148, 166, 168, 170, 179, 180, 182, 196, 197, 198, 199, 200, 201, 210, 211, 213, 217, 223; *see also cafés chantants; casino*
Sala Badi'a 40, 42, 44, 45, 48, 71, 196, 210, 217; *see also* Casino Badi'a; Casino Opera
Sala Masriyya 44, 198, 217
Sala Santi 27, 198
salafists 6, 85, 86, 87, 88, 96, 101, 137, 151, 157, 159, 160, 204, 212, 217, 219
"Salamitha Umm Hassan" 111, 161
salamlek 13, 217
Saleh, Magda (ballerina, dance researcher) 64, 126, 139, 158, 192
Salem (*'alima*) 32, 207
Salem, Ahmad (actor) 179
Salimpour, Jamila (dancer) 26, 130, 174
Salimpour, Suhaila (dancer) 174
saltana 92, 112, 120, 217, 241n43
sama' 217
"Sama al-Masri Tafshakh Obama wa Tasbah al-Abb wa-l-Umm" 161–162
"Sama al-Masry Tirqus bi al-Niqab wa Tighanni li-Morsy 'Ahay'" 160–161
sama'i 217
Samara (dancer) 171
Samara, Sahar (dancer) 60
Samasem (dancer) 182
sammi'ah 217
Samson and Delila 205
Sánchez García, José (social anthropologist) 95
Sanu'a, Ya'qub (James) (journalist, playwright) 34, 148, 217
Sarhan, Fatma (singer) 58, 93, 116, 217
sarsagiyya 121, 217, 223
satire 7, 28, 34, 68, 79, 85, 147–149, 153, 154, 156, 157, 159, 160, 161–163, 164, 165, 202, 205
savants (with Napoléon) 20, 22, 24
al-Sawarikh (musical duo) 123, 150, 218
Sawt al-Qahira 42
Sawt al-Tarab 92–92
sayyid 137, 213
al-Sayyid (Marsot), Afaf Lutfi (historian) 2, 24
Sayyid Ahmad al-Badawi (holy man) 89, 215, 218; Sufi order of 86
Sayyid Ibrahim al-Disuqi (holy man) 218
Sayyida Zaynab (holy woman) 87, 89; district 118, 196, 200
"Sayyidna Husain" 96
Schielke, Samuli (anthropologist) 66, 86, 87
seduction 6, 26, 63, 65, 69, 71, 147, 156, 201; *see also dall'a*; flirtation
Seif, Tito (dancer) 60, 61, 186

Sekhmet (goddess) 16
Serkassian, Setrak (percussionist) 185
shababiyya 3, 58, 95, 107, 114, 119, 144, 154, 203; *see also al-gil*
shabaka 172, 218
Sha'ban, 'Isam (singer) 96
Sha'ban, Professor (also known as Shaykh) (singer, musician) 29, 195
Shabana, Mohamed (ethnomusicologist) 145
sha'bi 6, 88, 90, 95, 115, 118, 119, 124, 212, 218; and cinema 117; costume 79; dance 4, 5, 6, 58, 61, 70, 75, 84, 101, 115–116, 125, 126, 132, 145, 147, 174, 180, 189; *lun* 9, 95, 99, 185; music 3, 6, 9, 57, 58, 59, 68, 70, 82, 83, 85, 88, 90, 91, 92, 94, 95, 96, 98, 103–104, 106, 109–114, 116, 120, 147, 153, 163, 164, 183, 185, 186, 195, 197, 198, 203, 204, 205, 209, 211, 212, 217, 220; neighborhoods 57, 67, 74, 118, 149, 172, 173, 196, 200, 206, 209; *see also baladi; fulklur*
sha'biyya see *al-musiqa al-sha'biyya; fulklur*
shabka 118, 208, 218, 224
al-Shadhiliyya *tariqa* 86
Shadia (actress) 49, 69
shafa'a 87, 89, 214, 218
Shafiqa al-Qibtiyya 49
shahatin 28, 209, 220
Shaheen, Hikmat (musician) 181
Shaheen, Najib (musician) 181
Shaheen, Simon (musician) 2, 181
Shaheen, William (musician) 181
Shahin, Basheer (musician) 181
Shahin, Fadil (musician) 181
Shahin, Mohamed (dancer) 42, 60, 186
Shahin, Nadir (musician) 181
Sha'iri, Hamid (composer, producer, singer) 107, 114, 204, 218
Shaitan 96, 218
Shaker, Hani (singer, actor, composer) 123
Shakosh, Hassan (singer) 123
shakwa 99, 110, 112, 120, 218; *see also sira* Bani Hilal
shal 134
Shalabi, Mena (actress) 56
Sham al-Nassim 64, 218
sham'adan 14, 29, 47, 72, 127, 182, **182**, 201, 204, 208, 215, 218, 223, 233n35, 240n4
shame: and entertainment 46, 49, 57, 79, 96, 109, 117, 123, 149, 151, 158, 164, 167, 168, 179, 195, 198, 222, 244n58
shami 4, 80, 196, 205, 218
al-Shami, Fu'ad (thug) 47
shamla 19, 35, 178, 189, 218
Shams al-Din, Huda (dancer, actress) 41, 218–219

Shanuda, Hani (musician, composer) 111
sharaf 8, 87, 122, 418, 425; *see also* honor, code of
Sha'rawi, Huda (activist) 30
Sha'rawi, Shaykh Muhammad Metwelli 159
sharb 134, 219
shari'a 38, 151, 154, 219, 222
shari'a al-fann 32, 212
Shari'a Haram 32, 57, 60, 61, 106, 107, 114, 154, 191, 219
Shari'a al-Hubb 32, 54, 55, 202
Shari'a Muhammad 'Ali *see* Muhammad 'Ali street
al-Sharif, 'Azza (dancer) 56, 60, 71, 74, 113, 141, 197, 219
al-Sharif, Nahid (actor, dancer) 69, 78, 219
al-Sharif, Nur (actor) 69
Sharif, Yousry (dancer) 186
sharit 57, 93, 94, 105, 106, 109, 219
Sharqiyya 35, 54, 68, 133, 134, 154, 203
al-Shatir (Shater), Khairat (politician) 160
Shawqi, Ahmad (poet, lyricist) 42, 48, 195
Shawqi, Ahmad (singer) 117
Shawqi, Farid (actor) **38**
al-Shawwa, Sami (musician) 35, 169, 215, 219
Shehata Karika (Ahmad) (singer) 108, 121, 123, 214, 219
Sherihan (actress, dancer, singer) 55, 219
shewer 143, 219
Shiba, Ahmad (singer) 97, 98, 108, 185
"Shik, Shak, Shok" 149, 245n11
al-Shinnawi, Kamal (actor) 69
shirk 87, 217, 219
shisha 56, 74, 112, 158, 164, 195, 219
Shokoko, Mahmoud (actor, comedian) 147, 219
"Shokolata" 117
shu'ara 4, 24, 99, 110, 203
Shuq (Shawq) ('*alima*) 29, 215
"Shut Up Your Mouse, Obama" 162, 247
Sidhom, George (comedian) 147
Sidi (or Sayyid) Abu al-Haggag (holy man) 219
Sidqi, Mustafa Kamil (military officer) 43
Sidqi, Zainab (actress) **44**
Sidqi, Zinat (comedic actress, dancer) 40, 148, 160, 219–220
"Sigara Bunni" 98, 107, 122, 205, 239n69
sihr 137, 220
silsila 220
Sirr Abi 52
al-Sisi, Abd al-Fattah (president) 108, 109, 122, 148, 157, 158, 160, 161, 162, 163, 164, 190, 242n59
sim: *al-'awalim* or *al-fannanin* 20,

30, 90, 197, 220, 222, 231n113; *al-sagha* 231n113
simsimiyya 104, 143, 145, 153, 220, 221, 244n55
Sinai 1, 57, 75, 106, 141–142, 145, 175, 199, 217, 220; dances of 6, 78, 126, 142, 200
singers, religious *see* munshid
sira Bani Hilal 24, 110, 196, 215, 220, 224, 230n75
Siwa 6, 136, 212, 220; costume of **136**; dances of 126, 136
slaves 16, 17, 18, 19, 20, 171, 200, 204, 205, 215
al-Sobky, Gamal (singer) 96, 98, 107
El Sobky, Mohammad (producer) 220
social class 6, 12, 37, 48, 67, 68, 112, 118, 119, 178
al-Soghayar, Sa'd (singer) 58, 94, 107, 117, 191, 220
Sohag 134, 135
al-Souissi, Ahmad (singer) 93, 108, 120, 123, 206, 210, 220
Stokes, Martin (musicologist) 174
storytellers 11, 20
su'al wa gawab 8, 19, 115, 220; *see also lazima*
Sudanese 27, 33, 39, 86, 104, 133, 134, 137, 142, 214, 223, 224
Suez 52, 57, 75, 201, 217, 223; dances 145; music 145
Suez Canal: 26, 27, 106, 198; Company 27
Suez War 106
Sufism 85, 86, 87, 102, 139, 204, 205, 212, 213, 220; *see also ariqa*; *dhikr*; *haqiqa*; *mulid*; *qutb*
sufur 47
suhbagiyya 153, 220
Sultan 49
Sultan, Amie (dancer) 60, 61
Sultan, Tarik (dancer) 61
Sultana al-Tarab 36, **38**
Sumat, Mariam (actress) 31, 34, 105
Sunbati, Riyadh (musician, composer) 44, 48, 198, 214
Supreme Council of Sufi Orders 86
Supreme Council of the Armed Forces 86, 101
Surur, Samir (musician) 110
syndicate, musicians' 48, 58, 107, 109, 110, 115, 121, 122, 123, 124, 222
Syria 4, 23, 25, 35, 39, 40, 44, 49, 71, 78, 83, 95, 106, 108, 125, 135, 139, 148, 149, 152, 169, 171, 182, 184, 196, 197, 198, 200, 211, 213, 219, 220

tabarruj 151, 220
tabbal 56, 57, 69, 72, 128, 183, 197
tabl baladi 72, 128, 140, 171, 211, 220
tabla 21, 56, 58, 115, 116, 130, 140, 198, 210, 220, 225

tableaux 56, 68, 71, 74, 139, 170, 178, 195, 220, 221
tafrid 8, 19, 220–221, 223
Taha, Muhammad (singer) 110, 221
taharosh jinsi 114, 116, 122, 161, 221
tahayya 30, 208, 221
tahmila 221
tahtib (dance/martial art) 88, 96, 100, 109, 123, 128, 131, 134, **134**, 221, 222
taj 129, 221
al-Tajruba al-Danmarkiyya 155–156
tajwid 18, 204; *see also* Qur'an reciter
Takfir wa al-Higra 57
takht 14, 27, 30, 35, 44, 48, 86, 113, 169, 170, 198, 202, 205, 210, 214, 216, 219, 221, 222; *al raqs al-* 128
takyit 65, 75, 208, 214; *see also* tips
talaq 66, 221
Tal'at, Dina (dancer) 58, 59, 60, 62, 68, 74, 75–77, **76**, 96, 101, 116, 117, 150, 154, 172, 176, 178, 180, 188, 190, 191, 195, 217, 221
Tamarrod (movement) 108, 151, 161, 221
Tamr Hinna 41, 197
tanbura 17, 104, 143, 220, 221
El Tanbura (musical group) 153
al-Tannoura Egyptian Heritage Folklore Group 140
tannura 64, 88, 89, **89**, 95, 100, 101, 137, 140, 142, 221
Tanta 29, 70, 89, 127, 195, 196, 197, 216, 218
taqasim 9, 19, 44, 58, 69, 75, 92, 104, 112, 115, 116, 173, 186, 198, 221, 222, 223
taqtuqa 14, 30, 36, 47, 80, 97, 109, 205, 221, 223
tarab 18, 30–31, 42, 92, 96, 99, 101, 104, 110, 111, 112, 144, 184, 194, 213, 217, 221; *mazag* 211; musical genre of 5, 9, 30–31, 83, 91, 104, 181, 184–185, 207
tarbush 37, **182**, 221
tarha 67, 134, **135**, 201, 222
tariqa 85, 86, 87, 95, 139, 200, 212, 222
tashkil 100, 101, 123, 222
tashnib 30, 78, 222, 231n113; *see also barrada*
taslim 69, 78, 80, 82, 98, 120, 122, 123, 163, 217, 221, 222, 239n63
tattoos 87, 188, 222
Tawfiq, Khedive 231n95
Tawfiq, Samira (singer) 196
Tekh festival 16
television 6, 56, 57, 58, 59, 72, 74, 90, 91, 93, 111, 113, 117, 119, 121, 123, 124, 131, 146, 147, 150, 155, 158, 160, 162, 163, 164, 191, 195, 197, 219, 223, 224
thawra 222; *see also* revolution
thob 143

thugs 47, 61, 160, 163, 201, 239n55; see also *baltagiyya*
tips 30, 65, 78, 88, 100, 115, 132, 178, 189, 199, 208, 213, 214, 221, 222; *see also baqshish; takyit; tashnib*
Tita Wong 49
tob see baladi dress
toura 216, 222
Tucker, Judith (historian) 25, 27
al-Tuhami, Shaykh Yasin (*munshid*) 94, 107, 209
tull talli see Assiut; fabric
al-Tunsi, Bayram (lyricist) 48
turath 6, 91, 92, 96, 101, 103, 222
El-Turk, Niqula (historian) 22
Turkey 20, 100, 103, 104, 125, 162, 169, 170, 181, 196, 203, 214
Turks 19, 20, 24, 29, 32, 41, 72, 103, 169, 203
"21" 120

'ud 14, 29, 42, 44, 110, 111, 143, 144, 169, 181, 195, 196, 205, 219, 221, 222
ughniya 196, 222; *habta* 111, 112, 211, 222
"Ughniyat Rab'a" 162, 247n67
'Ukasha, Tharwat (government minister) 103, 126
'Ukasha brothers (theater troupe) 38, 205, 223
'ulama 22, 25, 199, 219, 222
'umda 39, 222
al-'Umda al-'Abit 38
umm al-dunya 166, 222, 225
Umm Kulthum (singer) 15, 26, 42, 48, 49, 55, 56, 58, 67, 80, 101, 106, 113, 149, 153, 164, 169, 183, 184, 185, 186, 187, 195, 196, 197, 204, 205, 211, 212, 222
umma 222
Ummayad 18
Upper Egypt 9, 12, 14, 25, 26, 52, 100, 110, 123, 127, 128, 129, 130, 131, 134, 138, 146, 161, 174, 190, 198, 199, 203, 208, 211, 212, 215, 216–217, 220, 223; *see also* al-Sa'id
'urf 222
'urfi marriage 154, 222–223
usta 29, 211, 223
Usta Hassan 46

Van Leo (Levon Boyodjian, photographer) 51, 52, 73, 133

van Nieuwkerk, Karin (anthropologist) 13, 65, 68, 158, 166, 205, 220
vaudeville 5, 34, 37, 38, 39, 41, 183, 206, 208, 223
veiling *see hijab; niqab; yashmak*
venyara 29, 127, 223; *see also sham'adan*
Villoteau, Guillaume André (musicologist) 21
virginity 26, 65, 66, 234n7, 228n2
Voutsaki, Katy (dancer) 69, 223
vulgarity 22, 60, 111, 112, 114, 126, 130, 153, 203, 211, 222

"Wa'fat Nasyat Zaman" 109, 113–114
Wafd (party) 35, 223
Wagdy, Anwar (actor) 42, 171, 179
Wagh al-Birka 27
Wahbe, Haifa (actress) 58, 96, 98, 108, 154, 156
Wahbi, Yusuf (actor) 40, 49, 214, 220
Wadi Halfa 142
al-Wahsh dakhil al-Insan 69
wali see awliya'
Wana Mali 52
Ward, Heather (historian) 4, 5, 20, 30, 33, 170
Wardi, Muhammad (singer) 142
Wasa'a 27, 223
wasla 44, 196, 200, 223
Weber, Alain (musicologist) 128, 167
weddings 4, 6, 15, 19, 20, 26, 45, 47, 48, 62, 66, 71, 72, 83, 84, 90, 92, 93, 94, 95, 100, 107, 110, 111, 112, 115, 116, 117, 118, 119, 121, 123, 124, 129, 131, 140, 142, 148, 158, 159, 168, 171, 179, 189, 190, 191, 196, 198, 200, 201, 202, 204, 207, 211, 212, 214, 215, 218, 219, 222, 223; in films 70, 91; *see also* marriage
Weza (*mahragan* artist) 119, 123, 223
Widad 48, 222
wlad al-sis 121, 223
women and Egypt's legal system 27–28, 151–152, 154
women without men 65, 204, 234n4, 234n6

World War I 5, 30, 33, 34, 37, 38, 148, 196, 201, 206, 212
World War II 41, 42, 201

"Ya Bint al-Sultan" 111, 116
"Ya Dall'a, Ya Dall'a" 79–80
"Ya Ghazal Darb al-Ahmar" 70, 113, 197, 235n21, 235n22, 235n23
"Ya Mortada, Ya Mortada" 163
"Ya Obama, Abuk wa Ummak" 161–162
Ya Sitti Ma Timshish Kida 'Iryana 38
The Yacoubian Building 155
Yahia al-Wafd 43, 71
yashmak 30, 148, 223
Yasin, Isma'il (actor, comedian) 40, 147, 220, 223
Yasmin 42
Yasmine of Cairo (dancer) 182
Yasser (costumer) 172
Youssef, Bassam (comedian) 7, 156, 157, 158, 163, 223
al-Yusuf, Ruz (actress, singer, journalist) 37, 38, 223

zaffat 33, 66, 87, 90, 114, 190, 191, 209, 210, 223; *firqat* 115, 191, 191, 202; *al-mulid* 89, 149, 223
al-Zaghlul, Sa'd (politician) 35, 36, 223
"Zahma, Ya Dunia, Zahma" 106, 111, 225
zajjal 28, 38, 97, 104, 223
zajjalun 28, 223
Zaki, Ahmad (actor 117
Zaki, Suhair 55, 56, 59, 70, 71, 72, 115, 183, 184, 200, 202
zambalak 52, 224
Zanqat al-Sittat 101
zar 6, 64, 87, 88, 90, 97, 104, 136–138, **138**, 139, 171, 197, 198, 203, 216, 218, 224; amulets for 137; *arusa* 138
zawaj 65, 222, 223, 224; *see also* marriage and weddings
"al-Zayid fi-l-Halawa" 82
Zenah **25**
zills/zil *see sagat*
zina' 160, 224
ziyara 224
Zo'la, DJ 122
Al-Zughby, Sami (hotelier) 54
al-Zuhur (journal) 33
zummarin 128; *see also mizmar*

www.ingramcontent.com/pod-product-compliance
Lightning Source LLC
Chambersburg PA
CBHW080801300426
44114CB00020B/2794